Texts from the Pyramid Age

Society of Biblical Literature

Writings from the Ancient World

Number 16
Texts from the Pyramid Age
by Nigel C. Strudwick
Edited by Ronald J. Leprohon

Texts from the Pyramid Age

by
Nigel C. Strudwick

Edited by
Ronald J. Leprohon

Society of Biblical Literature
Atlanta

TEXTS FROM THE PYRAMID AGE

The Semitica transliteration font used in this work is available from Linguist Software (www.linguist software.com), 425-775-1130.

Library of Congress Cataloging-in-Publication Data

Strudwick, Nigel.
Texts from the pyramid age / by Nigel C. Strudwick.
p. cm. — (Writings from the ancient world ; no. 16)
Includes bibliographical references and index.
English translation of Egyptian texts from the Old Kingdom.
ISBN-13: 978-1-58983-138-4 (paper binding : alk. paper)
ISBN-10: 1-58983-138-1 (paper binding : alk. paper)
1. Egypt—History—Old Kingdom, ca. 2686-ca. 2181 B.C.—Sources.
2. Inscriptions, Egyptian—Translations into English. I. Title. II. Series.
DT85.S74 2005
932—dc22

2005016945

13 12 11 10 09 08 07 06 05 5 4 3 2 1
Printed in the United States of America on acid-free, recycled paper conforming to ANSI/NISO Z39.48-1992 (R1997) and ISO 9706:1994 standards for paper permanence.

To the memory of

William J. Murnane
(1945–2001)

Peter J. Strudwick
(1926–2003)

and
Audrey Strudwick
(1926–2004)

Contents

List of Figures xi

List of Texts xiii

Series Editor's Foreword xxv

Preface xxvii

Chronological Table xxix

Map of Egypt xxxiii

Abbreviations xxxv

I. Introduction 1
- 1. Preliminary Remarks 1
  - 1.1 Range of Material Presented 1
  - 1.2 Selection and Presentation Criteria 2
- 2. Previous Work on Old Kingdom Texts 4
  - 2.1 Collections and Translations of Large Bodies of Old Kingdom Material 4
  - 2.2 Translations of Egyptian Literature in English incorporating Some Old Kingdom Texts 5
  - 2.3 The Study of Old Kingdom Texts 6
- 3. Historical Matters 7
  - 3.1 Outline 7
  - 3.2 Dating Events in the Old Kingdom 10
    - 3.2.1 Methods of Dating Years 10
    - 3.2.2 *Sed* Festivals 12
    - 3.2.3 The Different Seasons 13
  - 3.3 Royal Names 14
  - 3.4 Dating Private Monuments 16
- 4. Literary and Linguistic Aspects of Old Kingdom Texts 17

4.1 The Importance of Context 17
4.2 Are the Texts Herein "Literature"? 19
4.3 Are the Texts in Verse or Prose? 19
4.4 Old Kingdom Egyptian and Its Characteristics 20
4.4.1 Phonetics 21
4.4.2 Writing 22
4.4.3 Grammar 23
4.5 Scripts 24
5. Particular Points of Translation 24
5.1 Grammar 25
5.1.1 Second Tenses 25
5.1.2 The Infinitive 26
5.2 Titles 26
5.2.1 Honorific Titles 26
5.2.2 Administrative Titles 28
5.2.3 Priestly Titles 28
5.2.4 "King's Son" or "King's Daughter" 29
5.3 Other Issues 30
5.3.1 *imakhu* 30
5.3.2 *hem* 31
5.3.3 The Offering Formula 31
5.3.4 Egyptian Nomes 32
5.3.5 Pyramid Names 33
6. Principal Types of Text Translated in This Volume 33
6.1 Historiographic Texts 34
6.2 Temple Texts 35
6.3 Inscriptions Set Up by or on Behalf of Kings 36
6.3.1 Rock Inscriptions 36
6.3.2 Royal Decrees 37
6.4 State Administrative Texts 39
6.5 Texts from the Tombs of Officials 40
6.5.1 Standard Formulaic Inscriptions in Tombs 40
6.5.2 More Unusual Types of Text in Tombs, Other Than Biographies 41
6.5.3 Private (Auto)biographical/Commemorative Texts from Tombs 42
6.5.4 Captions 47
6.5.5 Miscellaneous Texts from Tombs 48
6.6 Private Legal Texts 48
6.7 Private Administrative Texts 50

6.8 Texts of Women 50
6.9 Graffiti 51
6.10 Expedition Inscriptions 53
6.11 Builders' or Quarry Marks 54
6.12 Letters 55
7 A Final Word 57
8 Conventions 57

II. Annals and Lists of Kings 65

III. Texts from Temples 81

IV. Royal Decrees 97

V. Objects Bearing Royal Names 129

VI. Rock Inscriptions of Kings and Expedition Leaders 133

VII. Quarry and Constructional Marks and Phyle Texts 153

VIII. Graffiti 161

IX. State Administrative Texts 165

X. Letters 175

XI. Private Legal Texts 185

XII. A Selection of Offering Formulae and Titles 209

XIII. Appeals to the Living and Warnings to Evildoers and the Uninitiated 217

XIV. Commemorative and Dedicatory Texts 239

XV. Texts relating to Payment of Workmen and Tomb Acquisition 251

XVI. Biographical Texts from the Memphite Region 261

XVII. Biographical Texts from the Provinces 327

XVIII. Texts of Women 379

XIX. Captions to Tomb Scenes 401

XX. Miscellaneous Texts from Tombs and Objects in Tombs 423

XXI. Addendum 437

List of Sources 443

Bibliography 465

Glossary 503

Indexes 511
- Names of Kings 511
- Names of Persons (excluding Kings) 511
- Sites of Origin 514
- Objects in Museums 515

Cross-reference List of Tomb Text Types 519

Concordance of Texts in *Urkunden I* 521

List of Figures

1. Map of Egypt xxxiii
2. The Development of the Old Kingdom Biography over Time 46
3. Layout of Decree of Neferirkare (No. 17) 99
4. Drawing of Decree of Neferirkare (No. 17) 100
5. Flake of Limestone from the Step Pyramid (No. 78) 153
6. Lintel of Nyankhpepy (No. 143) 227
7. Slab Stela of Nefretiabet (No. 327) 430

List of Texts

II. Annals and Lists of Kings

1 The Palermo Stone and Associated Fragments 65
2 Three Annalistic Vessel Inscriptions from Elephantine 74
3 Annals on the Sarcophagus of Ankhesenpepy from South Saqqara 75
4 A Writing Board from Giza 78
5 A List of Kings in the Tomb of Sekhemkare at Giza 78
6 Royal Names from the Tomb of Netjerpunesut at Giza 78

III. Texts from Temples

7 Reliefs of Netjerykhet Djoser 81
8 From the Temples of Sneferu at Dahshur 82
9 Block from the Mortuary Temple of Userkaf at Saqqara, Reused at Lisht 83
10 Texts from the Temple of Sahure at Abusir 83
11 Festival Offerings Calendar for the Sun Temple of Niuserre at Abu Gurob 86
12 Blocks from the Causeway of the Pyramid of Unas at Saqqara 91
13 Texts of Pepy I and Teti from Tell Basta 92
14 A Sed Festival Monument of Pepy II 93
15 Building Inscriptions from Temples 94

IV. Royal Decrees

16 Decree of Shepseskaf from the Pyramid Temple of Menkaure at Giza 97
17 Decree of Neferirkare from Abydos 98
18 Two Decrees from the Abusir Papyri of Neferefre 101

19 Decree of Teti from Abydos 102
20 Decree of Pepy I from Dahshur 103
21 Decree of Pepy I from Koptos (Koptos A) 105
22 Decree of Pepy II from Abydos 106
23 Decree of Pepy II from the Valley Temple of Menkaure at Giza 106
24 Decree of Pepy II from Koptos (Koptos B) 107
25 Decree of Pepy II from Koptos (Koptos C) 109
26 Decree of Pepy II from Koptos (Koptos D) 112
27 Decree of Pepy II (?) from Koptos (Koptos G) 114
28 Decree of Pepy II from Dakhla Oasis 115
29 Decree of a Successor of Pepy II from Saqqara 115
30 Decree of Horus Kha ... from Koptos (Koptos H) 116
31 Decree of (probably) Neferkauhor from Koptos (Koptos I) 117
32 Decree of Neferkauhor from Koptos (Koptos J) 118
33 Decree of Neferkauhor from Koptos (Koptos K) 119
34 Decree of Neferkauhor from Koptos (Koptos L) 120
35 Decree of Neferkauhor from Koptos (Koptos M) 121
36 Decree of Neferkauhor from Koptos (Koptos N) 121
37 Decree of Neferkauhor from Koptos (Koptos O) 122
38 Decrees of Neferkauhor from Koptos (Koptos P and Q) 122
39 Decree of Horus Demedjibtawy from Koptos (Koptos R) 123
40 Lists of Offerings for Cults from Koptos 124

V. Objects Bearing Royal Names

41 Statue of Netjerykhet from Saqqara 129
42 Offering Stand of Khafre 129
43 Vessels of Djedkare Izezi 129
44 Sistrum of Teti 130
45 Objects of Pepy I 130
46 Objects of Merenre 131
47 Vessels of Pepy II 132

VI. Rock Inscriptions of Kings and Expedition Leaders

48 Inscription of Unas at Elephantine 133
49 Naos of Pepy I from Elephantine 133

50 Inscription of Merenre to the South of the First Cataract 133
51 Inscription of Merenre near Philae 134
52 Inscriptions of Merenre and Pepy II on Elephantine 134
53 Inscription of Pepy II at Elephantine 134
54 Inscription of Netjerykhet in Wadi Maghara 135
55 Inscription of Sneferu in Wadi Maghara 135
56 Inscription of Khufu in Wadi Maghara 135
57 Inscriptions of Sahure in Sinai 135
58 Inscription of Niuserre in Wadi Maghara 136
59 Inscription of Menkauhor in Wadi Maghara 136
60 Inscriptions of Djedkare in Wadi Maghara 137
61 Inscriptions of Pepy I in Wadi Maghara 138
62 Inscriptions of Pepy II in Wadi Maghara 139
63 Inscription of Ity 140
64 Inscriptions of Pepy I 140
65 Expedition Inscription of Djaty 143
66 Expedition Inscription of Shemai 143
67 Expedition Inscriptions relating to Tjautyiqer 143
68 Inscriptions of Tjetji 144
69 Inscription of Khufu 145
70 Inscriptions of Teti 145
71 Inscriptions of Pepy I 146
72 Inscription of Merenre 147
73 Inscriptions of Pepy II 147
74 Graffito in the Wadi Dungash in the Eastern Desert 149
75 Graffito in the Bir Mueilha (Wadi Umm Hoda) in the Eastern Desert 149
76 Two Inscriptions from Khor el-Aquiba 149
77 Inscriptions at Tomas 150

VII. Quarry and Constructional Marks and Phyle Texts

78 Construction of a Curve at the Step Pyramid at Saqqara 153
79 Dates from the Pyramid of Meidum 153
80 Dates from the Red Pyramid of Dahshur 154
81 Giza Pyramid Crew Names 154
82 Crew Name from the Unfinished Pyramid at Zawiyet el-Aryan 155
83 Crew Names and Other Related Texts from Abusir 155

84 Quarry Marks from Private Tombs at Giza 156
85 Phyle Texts from the Sun Temple of Userkaf at Abusir 158
86 Brief Texts of Phyles Which Appear in the Decoration of Tomb Chapels 158

VIII. Graffiti

87 A Graffito on the Pyramid of Pepy II at South Saqqara 161
88 A Selection of Graffiti from el-Kab 161
89 A Graffito from Hindallab 163

IX. State Administrative Texts

90 Selections from the Abusir Papyri from the Neferirkare Temple 165
91 List from the Abusir Papyri from the Neferefre Temple 172

X. Letters

92 Letters in the Abusir Papyri from the Neferirkare Temple 175
93 A Sixth Dynasty Letter, Probably from Saqqara 176
94 A Protest to the Vizier from Saqqara 177
95 Part of a Letter regarding Work on a Pyramid, Probably from Saqqara 178
96 The "Crimes of Sabni," from Elephantine 178
97 A Letter about Complaints over Farming 179
98 Fragments of Letters from the Elephantine Archive 180
99 Letters from the Oasis of Dakhla 180
100 Letter from Izezi in the Tomb of Reshepses at Saqqara 181
101 Two Letters to the Dead 182

XI. Private Legal Texts

102 House Purchases from the Gebelein Papyri 185
103 A Dispute over an Inheritance from Elephantine 186
104 Legal Text from the Tomb of Akhethotep Hemi/Nebkauhor at Saqqara 187
105 Inscription above a Shaft in the Tomb of Idu Seneni at el-Qasr wa es-Sayed 188

106 Block Bearing a Legal Text of (possibly) Kaiemnefret 189
107 Provision of a Doorway by Khenemti in the Tomb of Iarti at South Saqqara 191
108 Decrees Setting Up the Estates of Metjen from His Tomb at Saqqara 192
109 Agreement with Soul Priests from the Tomb of Nyankhkhnum and Khnumhotep at Saqqara 194
110 Texts of Nykaiankh from Tehna 195
111 Record of the Disposal of the Estates of Nykaure in His Tomb at Giza 200
112 Disposition of the Funerary Estate of Penmeru in His Tomb at Giza 200
113 Part of the Dispositions of Pepi, Possibly from Giza 201
114 Instructions for the Funerary Priests of Sennuankh from Saqqara 201
115 Instructions for the Cult of Tjenti and His Family from Giza 202
116 Wepemnefret Grants His Son Rights to Use Parts of His Tomb at Giza 203
117 From the False Door of Yotefnen from Giza 203
118 Fragment of a Document relating to a Mortuary Estate from Saqqara 204
119 Purchase of a Plot of Land for a Tomb from Saqqara 204
120 A Legal Fragment Found Reused at Lisht 204
121 Sale of a House, Found at Giza 205

XII. A Selection of Offering Formulae and Titles

122 From the Tomb of Kaiemsenu at Saqqara 209
123 From the Tomb of Kaipure at Saqqara 209
124 Formulae from the False Door of Mereri at Saqqara 210
125 Formulae in the Tomb of the Physician Nyankhre at Giza 211
126 Formulae from the False Door of Ptahhotep II in His Tomb at Saqqara 212
127 Formulae on the Sarcophagus of Sedjefaptah Called Fefi from Giza 213
128 From the Tomb of Sekhemka at Saqqara 214
129 Formulae of Sneferunefer II from Saqqara 214
130 Formulae from the False Door of Tepemankh at Saqqara 215

XIII. Appeals to the Living and Warnings to Evildoers and the Uninitiated

131 Texts of Ankhi Called Intji from His Tomb at Saqqara 217
132 Texts from the Tomb of Ankhwedja Itji at Giza 218
133 Lintel in the Tomb of Herymeru at Saqqara 219
134 Offering Table of Ishetmaa from Saqqara 220
135 Text of Khenu from Saqqara 221
136 Texts from the Tomb of Khui at Saqqara 221
137 Text of Khuit, Perhaps from Saqqara 222
138 Architrave of Mehi from Saqqara 223
139 Inscriptions over the Entrance to the Tomb of Mereri at Saqqara 224
140 Text of Meru Called Bebi from Saqqara 225
141 Lintel of Nedjemib from Saqqara 225
142 Texts from the Tomb of Nenki from Saqqara 226
143 Texts at the Entrance to the Tomb of Nyankhpepy at Saqqara 227
144 Texts on the Pillars of the Tomb of Nyhetepptah at Giza 229
145 Inscriptions at the Entrance to the Tomb of Nykauizezi at Saqqara 231
146 Text of Pehenwikai from Saqqara 232
147 Inscription on Blocks of Reherytep Iti from Saqqara 232
148 Texts on False Door of Sekhentyuka and Nyankhsheret from Giza 233
149 Texts from the Tomb of Tjetu at Giza 234
150 Inscription in the Tombs of Tjy and Mereruka at Saqqara 235
151 Stela of Nipepy from Abydos 237

XIV. Commemorative and Dedicatory Texts

152 From the Tomb of Ankhires and Medunefer at Giza 239
153 Text on a Statue of Ankhirptah, Perhaps from Saqqara 239
154 Text on Offering Basin of Hebi from Giza 240
155 Texts from the False Door of Inikaf at Giza 240
156 Text from the Tomb of Inpuhotep at Giza 240
157 Text over the Entrance Doorway of the Tomb of Iy at Giza 241

158 Texts on a Wooden Door Panel from the Family Tomb of Kaiemhezet at Saqqara 241
159 Texts from the Tomb of Kaiemrehu at Saqqara 242
160 Commemoration of the Scribe Seni in the Tomb of Kaihap at Hawawish 243
161 Dedication on a Relief Panel from the Tomb of Kaihersetef at Saqqara 243
162 From the Texts on the False Door Niche of Kainefer from Dahshur 243
163 Text at the Entrance to the Tomb of Khufuhotep at Giza 244
164 Text of Medunefer from His Tomb at Giza 244
165 Commemoration of Workmen in the Tomb of Nebemakhet at Giza 244
166 Offering Basin of Nefer 245
167 Text of Neferseshemptah from Saqqara 245
168 Text of Nyankhsokar, Perhaps from Giza 245
169 Text from the False Door of Nykauptah from Saqqara 246
170 Inscription of Pepysoneb in the Tomb of His Father Memi at Hawawish 246
171 Texts of Sehetepu from His Chapel at Saqqara 246
172 Libation Basin of Shedy from Saqqara 247
173 Texts in the Tomb of Tepemankh II at Saqqara 248
174 Text at the Entrance to the Tomb of Tjenti at Giza 249
175 Dedication on a Jamb from the Tomb of Tjetji at Giza 249
176 From a Stela of Tjezi at Giza 249
177 Text of Ty from Hawawish 250
178 Text from the Tomb of an Unknown Person 250

XV. Texts relating to Payment of Workmen and Tomb Acquisition

179 From the Tomb of Abdu at Giza 251
180 Text of Akhetmehu from His Tomb at Giza 252
181 Statue Inscription of Memi from Giza 253
182 Text of Meni, Probably from Giza 253
183 From the Tomb of Merankhef at Giza 253
184 Inscriptions of Merkhufu from Giza 254
185 Texts from the False Door of Nefer at Giza 255

186 Inscriptions of Nymaatre from His Tomb at Giza 255
187 Text on the False Door of Nysuredi from Giza 256
188 Inscriptions of Remenuka from His Tomb at Giza 257
189 Architrave of Tetiseneb Called Iri from Saqqara 257
190 Inscription of Zeftjwa in Berlin 258
191 Scenes of Visiting the Tomb from Giza 259
192 A Nameless Tomb from the Teti Pyramid Cemetery at Saqqara 260
193 Texts from a Monument of an Unknown Man in the British Museum 260

XVI. Biographical Texts from the Memphite Region

194 Text from the Tomb of Akhethotep at Saqqara 261
195 Text from the Tomb of Akhethotep Hemi/Nebkauhor at Saqqara 261
196 False Door Inscriptions of Ankhkhufu from Giza 262
197 Text of Ankhmahor from Saqqara 264
198 Texts of Ankhmeryremeryptah Called Nekhebu from Giza 265
199 Text of Bia from Saqqara 269
200 Text of Debehen from Giza 271
201 Inscription on the False Door of Geref from Saqqara 272
202 Texts from the Tomb of Hetepherakhet at Saqqara 273
203 Pillar Text from the Tomb of Hetepherenptah 274
204 From the Left Jamb of the False Door of Hetepu at Saqqara 274
205 Inscriptions of Hezi from Saqqara 275
206 Facade Text from the Tomb of Idu at Giza 277
207 Text of Ipi from Saqqara 279
208 Lintel from the Tomb of Iyenhor at Saqqara 280
209 Inscription of Izi from Saqqara 281
210 Texts from the Tomb of Kaiaper at South Abusir 281
211 Texts from the Tomb of Kaiaper at Saqqara 282
212 Inscriptions of Kaiemtjennet from His Tomb at Saqqara 282
213 Texts from the Facade of the Mastaba of Kaigemni at Saqqara 285
214 Part of a Lintel of Kaihap Tjeti 287
215 Texts from the Tomb of Kaikherptah at Giza 288
216 Texts from the Tomb of Khentika at Saqqara 288

217 Text of Khenu from Saqqara 291
218 Text of (another) Khenu from Saqqara 292
219 Inscriptions of Khuiwer from Giza 293
220 Architraves from the Tomb of Mehu at Saqqara 294
221 Text of Mersuankh from His Tomb at Giza 296
222 Texts of Metjetji, Probably from Saqqara 297
223 Texts from the Tomb of Neferseshemptah at Saqqara 299
224 Texts from the Tomb of Neferseshemre at Saqqara 300
225 Inscriptions of Nyankhsekhmet from Saqqara 302
226 False Door of Ptahshepses from Saqqara 303
227 Inscription of Rewer from Giza 305
228 Inscriptions of Sabu Ibebi from Saqqara 306
229 Inscriptions of Sabu Tjeti from Saqqara 309
230 Inscriptions from the Tomb of Sankhuptah Called Nyhetepptah at Saqqara 309
231 Inscriptions of Sekhemankhptah from Giza 310
232 Texts from the Mastaba of Senedjemib Inti at Giza 311
233 Texts from the False Door of Seshemu at Giza 316
234 Inscriptions of Seshemnefer IV and His Son Ptahhotep from Giza 317
235 Inscriptions of Washptah from Saqqara 318
236 A Fragment of a Biography from West of the Step Pyramid at Saqqara 320
237 Anonymous Biographical Fragment of the Reign of Teti from Saqqara 321
238 Block Found near the Pyramid of Teti at Saqqara 321
239 Block from Giza 322
240 Text of an Unnamed Person from Giza 322

XVII. Biographical Texts from the Provinces

241 Texts on the Facade of the Tomb of Harkhuf at Qubbet el-Hawa 328
242 Inscriptions of Pepynakht Called Heqaib from His Tomb at Qubbet el-Hawa 333
243 Inscriptions on the Facade of the Tomb of Sabni and Mekhu I at Qubbet el-Hawa 335
244 From the Tomb of Another Sabni at Qubbet el-Hawa 339
245 Text of Khnumhotep in the Tomb of Khui at Qubbet el-Hawa 340

246 Inscriptions of Izi from Edfu 340
247 Inscriptions of Meryrenefer Qar from Edfu 342
248 Stela of Hekenu, Perhaps from Moalla 345
249 Text from the Tomb of Shemai at Kom el-Koffar 345
250 Inscriptions of Idu I from Dendera 347
251 Inscriptions of Idu II from Dendera 348
252 Texts on the Facade of the Tomb of Idu Seneni at el-Qasr wa es-Sayed 348
253 Slab of Djadjay from el-Qasr wa es-Sayed 349
254 From the Tomb of Idu Menza from el-Qasr wa es-Sayed 350
255 Architrave of Per-shenay from Abydos 351
256 Inscription of Weni from Abydos 352
257 Inscription of Djau from Abydos 357
258 Ideal Biography from the Tomb of an Unknown Person at Abydos 358
259 Stela from Tomb 253 at Sheikh Farag 359
260 Text of Bawy from Hawawish 359
261 Fragments of the Biography of Iy Mery at Hawawish 360
262 Text of Nehutdesher at Hawawish 361
263 Text of Qereri at Hawawish 361
264 Inscription from the Tomb of Mery I at Hagarsa 361
265 Inscription of Mery II at Hagarsa 362
266 Texts from the Tomb of Ibi at Deir el-Gebrawi 363
267 Inscription of Djau at Deir el-Gebrawi 365
268 Fragment from the Tomb of Nebib at Deir el-Gebrawi 366
269 Text of Henqu from Deir el-Gebrawi 366
270 Inscription of Pepyankhheryib at Meir 368
271 Inscriptions of Inti at Deshasha 371
272 On the Architrave of Khnumnedjem from Busiris 373
273 Stela from the Chapel of Khentyka at Balat 374
274 Stela from the Chapel of Khentykawpepy at Balat 375

XVIII. Texts of Women

275 Text relating to Meretites I from Giza 379
276 Texts from the Mastaba of Meresankh III at Giza 379
277 Texts in the Mastaba of Khamerernebty II at Giza 381
278 Inscriptions relating to the "Khentkawes Problem" 381

279 From the Tomb of Nebet, Wife of Unas, at Saqqara 383
280 From the Pyramid of Iput, Wife of Teti and Mother of Pepy I, at Saqqara 383
281 Texts of Two Queens of Pepy I Named Ankhesenpepy from Saqqara 384
282 Inscriptions of Queens of Pepy II from the Area of His Pyramid Complex at Saqqara 385
283 Inscriptions of Hemetre Called Hemi from Her Tomb at Saqqara 386
284 A Text of Iabtet from Giza 387
285 Texts of Inti from Her Tomb at Saqqara 387
286 From the Saqqara False Door of Merut Called Zeshzeshet 388
287 Formulae of Nensedjerkai from Her Tomb at Giza 389
288 Dedicatory Text of Djenwen 390
289 False Door of Hemire, Perhaps from Busiris 391
290 Inscribed Slab of Henutsen from Saqqara 392
291 Inscriptions of Hetepheres from Giza 392
292 Inscriptions of Hetepheres Called Khenut from Giza 393
293 From the Stela of Iret, Said to Come from Akhmim 394
294 False Door of Khenit from Giza 394
295 Stela of Nebet and Khui from Abydos 395
296 False Door of Nedjetempet from Saqqara 396
297 Inscriptions of Neferesres from Giza 397
298 Texts of Nubhotep from Saqqara 397
299 Inscriptions of Rudjzas from Giza 398
300 Texts of Shepset and Nykauhathor from Giza 398

XIX. Captions to Tomb Scenes

301 Musical Scenes in the Tomb of Akhethotep Hemi/Nebkauhor at Saqqara 401
302 From the Tomb of Ankhmahor at Saqqara 402
303 From the Tomb of Ibi at Deir el-Gebrawi 403
304 From the Tomb of Kaiemnefret at Saqqara 404
305 Caption to Butchers on the Architrave of Khnumnedjem from Busiris 404
306 From the Tomb of Mehu at Saqqara 404
307 From the Tomb of Merib at Giza 407
308 From the Tomb of Mery II at Hagarsa 407

309 From the Tomb of Nyankhkhnum and Khnumhotep at Saqqara 407
310 Fishing and Fowling Scenes in the Tomb of Nyankhpepy Kem at Meir 410
311 Musical Scenes in the Tomb of Pepyankhheryib at Meir 411
312 Offering Bearers in the Tomb of Persen at Saqqara 411
313 From the Tomb of Qar at Giza 412
314 From the Tomb of Sekhemankhptah at Saqqara 414
315 From the Tomb of Sekhemkare at Giza 415
316 Bringing Cattle out of the Marshes in the Tomb of Tjy at Saqqara 416
317 Boat Texts from Tombs 416
318 Carrying Chair Scenes 417
319 Some Funerary Domains 418
320 Scenes of Pulling Papyrus 419

XX. Miscellaneous Texts from Tombs and Objects in Tombs

321 Titles of Nesutnefer from His Tomb at Giza 423
322 Sarcophagus Lid Texts 423
323 Titles on the Sarcophagus of Weta from Giza 425
324 Inscription of Abutyu from Giza 425
325 Hieratic Texts on Pots from Qubbet el-Hawa 426
326 Texts on the Sarcophagus of Minkhaf from Giza 427
327 Short Offering and Linen List of Nefretiabet from Giza 430
328 Long Offering List from the Chapel of Ankhmeryre at Saqqara 432
329 Linen Lists on a Wooden Box from Gebelein 433
330 List of Linen on a Box from the Tomb of Nefer and Kahay at Saqqara 434
331 Inscriptions on Pieces of Linen from Abusir 435

XXI. Addendum

332 Warning to Visitors from the Tomb of Peteti at Giza 437
333 Warning and Biographical Texts of Merefnebef from Saqqara 438

Series Editor's Foreword

Writings from the Ancient World is designed to provide up-to-date, readable English translations of writings recovered from the ancient Near East.

The series is intended to serve the interests of general readers, students, and educators who wish to explore the ancient Near Eastern roots of Western civilization, or compare these earliest written expressions of human thought and activity with writings from other parts of the world. It should also be useful to scholars in the humanities or social sciences who need clear, reliable translations of ancient Near Eastern materials for comparative purposes. Specialists in particular areas of the ancient Near East who need access to texts in the scripts and languages of other areas will also find these translations helpful. Given the wide range of materials translated in the series, different volumes will appeal to different interests. But these translations make available to all readers of English the world's earliest traditions as well as valuable sources of information on daily life, history, religion, etc. in the preclassical world.

The translators of the various volumes in this series are specialists in the particular languages and have based their work on the original sources and the most recent research. In their translations they attempt to convey as much as possible of the original texts in a fluent, current English. In the introductions, notes, glossaries, maps, and chronological tables, they aim to provide the essential information for an appreciation of these ancient documents.

The ancient Near East reached from Egypt to Iran and, for the purposes of our volumes, ranged in time from the invention of writing (by 3000 B.C.E.) to the conquests of Alexander the Great (ca. 330 B.C.E.). The cultures represented within these limits include especially Egyptian, Sumerian, Babylonian, Assyrian, Hittite, Ugaritic, Aramean, Phoenician, and Israelite. It is hoped that Writings from the Ancient World will eventually produce translations from most of the many different genres attested in these cultures: letters (official and private), myths, diplomatic documents, hymns, law collections, monumental inscriptions, tales, and administrative records, to mention but a few.

Significant funding was made available by the Society of Biblical Literature for the preparation of this volume. In addition, those involved in preparing this volume have received financial and clerical assistance from their respective institutions. Were it not for these expressions of confidence in our work, the arduous tasks of preparation, translation, editing, and publication could not have been accomplished or even undertaken.

It is the hope of all who have worked with the Writings from the Ancient World series that our translations will open up new horizons and deepen the humanity of all who read these volumes.

Theodore J. Lewis
The Johns Hopkins University

Preface

The original idea for writing this book came from the late William J. Murnane in August 1994. He was not to know it, but the idea of translating *Urkunden* I had been with me since the days of postgraduate research, although I never thought I would have the opportunity to fulfill it. Bill Murnane also offered to be editor for the volume. After making the initial proposal, the opportunity to begin the serious collecting of texts did not present itself until I was in Heidelberg in 1996–1997 on a fellowship from the Alexander von Humboldt-Stiftung. On a visit to the United States in 1998 I was able to visit Simon Parker, then editor of the *Writings from the Ancient World* series, and discuss the project, and also to discuss matters with Bill in Memphis. From this point, work on the translations began to pick up speed, and I was going to be in a good position to consider individual texts and the shape of the volume with Bill when I was to be in Memphis with the British Museum exhibit *Eternal Egypt* in the summer of 2001.

But this was not to be. Bill Murnane had to enter hospital in November 2000 for emergency heart surgery, and he never made it through, passing away on November 17th. This was a enormous shock to all who knew him. Simon Parker and the Society of Biblical Literature moved quickly to find me a new editor, and I was fortunate that Ronald J. Leprohon acceded to the request. To my great relief, the project did not lose momentum with Bill's passing, and progress has been steady from that point on.

It is always pleasurable to thank people in connection with this work. Edward Brovarski and Karl Seyfried both permitted me to see and use copies of texts on which they were working in advance of publication. Rita Freed, Christiane Ziegler, and Peter Manuelian have permitted me to reproduce drawings of the decree of Neferirkare in the Museum of Fine Arts, Boston, and the slab stela of Nefretiabet in the Louvre. Society of Biblical

Literature series editors Simon Parker and Ted J. Lewis have offered continual support in my determination to see this project through to completion, and the involvement with practical and technical matters at the Society of Biblical Literature of Frank Ames, Leigh Andersen, and Bob Buller has been essential to the successful production of this volume. Others who have been helpful in many different ways include James P. Allen, Antonio Loprieno, Peter Manuelian, and Richard Parkinson. And, as always, I must thank Helen Strudwick for her continual help and support, and for reading parts of the text.

I must also thank in general terms all participants in the conference "Old Kingdom Art and Archaeology," which took place in Prague in May and June 2004. I was able to attend this around the time this manuscript was submitted and gained many interesting insights and references which I have tried to incorporate into the final text. I hope no one will feel aggrieved if I fail to acknowledge properly their ideas, and we all look forward to the publication.

I will be forever grateful to Bill Murnane, both for setting this book in motion and supporting me through the first few unproductive years. How I regret he was unable to see its completion! A colossal debt I owe Ron Leprohon. He has read the manuscript and checked every text and spotted a vast number of oversights and foolish errors on my part. His comments have been very penetrating, and they have made me review many fundamental aspects of these texts, resulting in changes in the text or a formal justification of why I did what I did. My appreciation to him is of the deepest, for he has had to combine this work with his teaching and to the detriment of his own research. I have of course to say that I am fully responsible for the errors that remain.

The writing of this book has been marred by the passing of three persons. I believe I have outlined my debt to Bill Murnane already, but what I owe my parents is so important and yet much more difficult to put in words. They supported me en route to Egyptology, often wondering whether I was doing the right thing but never saying it and always being there when needed. Both my mother and father followed my faltering progress always positively and took delight in regaling others with the latest thing Helen and I had done in Egypt or elsewhere. I had hoped that Bill, Peter, and Audrey would see this book published, but the next best thing I can do is to dedicate it to them and hope that in some small way it is worthy of their memory.

Chronological Table

This table is based on von Beckerath 1997, as simplified in Schulz and Seidl 1998: 528. All dates prior to 664 B.C. *and, especially for the Old Kingdom, are approximate; see chapter I, §3 for comments on problems of chronology and dating. The table only lists kings of the third to eighth dynasties, with their cartouche, Horus, and pyramid names; for their other names, see von Beckerath 1999.*

Predynastic period

Naqada I	3700–3300
Naqada II	3300–3200
Naqada III	3200–3032

Early Dynastic period

Dynasties 1–2 **3032–2707**

Old Kingdom

Dynasty 3	**2707–2639**		
Horus name		*Possible cartouche name*	*Pyramid name*
Zanakht	2707–2690	Nebka	
Netjerikhet	2690–2670	Djoser	
Sekhemkhet	2670–2663	Djoserteti	
Khaba			
Qaihedjet	2663–2639	Huni	

Dynasty 4	**2639–2504**		
Cartouche names		*Horus name*	*Pyramid name*
Sneferu	2639–2604	Nebmaat	(two pyramids) Sneferu appears
Khufu	2604–2581	Medjedju	The horizon of Khufu
Djedefre	2581–2572	Kheper	Djedefre is a shining star
Khafre	2572–2546	Userib	Khafre is great
(possible ephemeral king)	2546–2539		

Menkaure	2539–2511	Kakhet	Divine is Menkaure
Shepseskaf	2511–2506	Shepseskhet	The cool place of Shepseskaf
(possible ephemeral king)	2506–2504		
Dynasty 5	**2504–2347**		
Cartouche names		*Horus name*	*Pyramid name*
Userkaf	2504–2496	Irmaat	Pure of places is Userkaf
Sahure	2496–2483	Nebkhau	The appearance of the *ba* of Sahure
Neferirkare Kakai	2483–2463	Userkhau	The *ba* of Neferirkare
Shepseskare ?[a]	2463–2456	Sekhemkhau	
Neferefre Izi	2456–2445	Neferkhau	Divine are the *ba*s of Neferefre
Niuserre Ini	2445–2414	Setibtawy	The places of Niuserre endure
Menkauhor Ikauhor	2414–2405	Menkhau	The places of Ikauhor are divine
Djedkare Izezi	2405–2367	Djedkhau	Djedkare is perfect
Unas	2367–2347	Wadjtawy	The places of Unas are perfect
Dynasty 6	**2347–2216**		
Cartouche names		*Horus name*	*Pyramid name*
Teti	2347–2337	Sehetepibtawy	The places of Teti are stable
Userkare ? Ity ?	2337–2335		The bas of Ity ?
Pepy I Neferzahor/ Meryre	2335–2285	Merytawy	Pepy is enduring and perfect
Merenre I Nemtyemzaf	2285–2279	Ankhkhau	The appearance of the perfection of Merenre
Pepy II Neferkare I[b]	2279–2219	Netjerkhau	Neferkare is enduring and living
Merenre II Nemtyemzaf	2219–2218		
Netjerkare Saptah ("Nitocris")[c]	2218–2216		

a. It is uncertain whether Izi belongs to Shepseskare or Neferefre; see Verner 2000 for the possibility that the order of these kings may be reversed.

b. As there is only one other reference to the other two kings named Neferkare in this book, the mention of "Neferkare" without a number refers to Pepy II.

c. See Ryholt 2000 for the revision of this name and comments on other kings of the end of the Old Kingdom.

Dynasties 7–8	**2216–2170**	
Cartouche names[d]	*Horus name*	*Pyramid name*
Netjerkare		
Menkare		
Neferkare II		
Neferkare III Nebi		Stable of life is Neferkare
Djedkare Shemai		
Neferkare Khendu		
Merenhor		
Neferkamin		
Nykare		
Neferkare Tereru		
Neferkahor		
Neferkare Pepysoneb		
Neferkamin Anu		
Qakare Ibi*		(unknown)
Neferkaure		
Neferkauhor Khuwyhapi*	Netjerybau	
Neferirkare		
Wadjkare†	Demedjibtawy	

First Intermediate Period

Dynasty 9–10	**2170–2020**
Dynasty 11	**2119–1976**

Middle Kingdom

Dynasty 11 (continued)	
Dynasty 12	**1976–1794/3**
Dynasty 13	**1794/3–1648**
Dynasty 14	**?–1648**
Dynasty 15	**1648–1539**
Dynasty 16	**(parallel to 15th dynasty)**
Dynasty 17	**1645–1550**

New Kingdom

Dynasty 18	**1550–1292**
Dynasty 19	**1292–1186/5**
Dynasty 20	**1186–1070/69**

d. All but the last are taken directly from the Abydos list without comment; only those marked * are certainly known from monuments. † is added as a Koptos Decree of his is in this book, although his position is uncertain. Further names are perhaps known, see von Beckerath 1999.

Third Intermediate Period	
Dynasty 21	**1070/69–946/5**
Dynasty 22 and 23	**946/5–714**
Dynasty 24	**740–714**
Dynasty 25	**?–664**
Late Period	
Dynasty 25 (continued)	
Dynasty 26	**664–525**
Dynasty 27 (Persian)	**525–401**
Dynasty 28	**404/1–399**
Dynasty 29	**399–380**
Dynasty 30	**380–342**
Second Persian period	**342–332**
Greek Rulers	**332–306**
Roman Period	**30 BC–AD 330**
Byzantine Period	**330–642**
Islamic Period	**642–present**

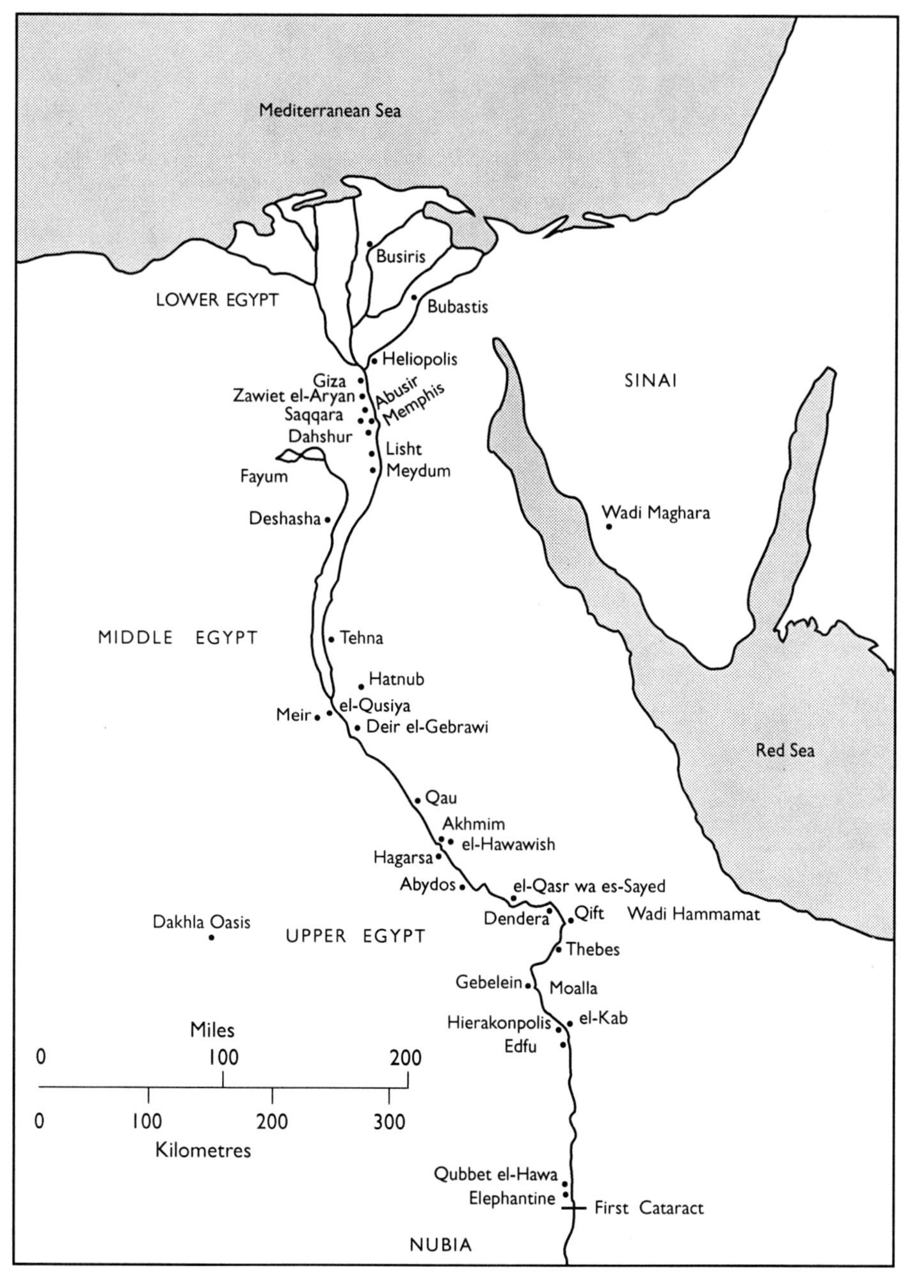

Fig. 1: Map of Egypt. The locations of the major sites from which texts translated in this book come are indicated.

Abbreviations

Ä&L — *Ägypten und Levante. Zeitschrift für ägyptische Archäologie und deren Nachbargebiete.* Vienna.

ÄA — Ägyptologische Abhandlungen. Wiesbaden: Harrassowitz.

ÄAT — Ägypten und Altes Testament. Studien zu Geschichte, Kultur und Religion Ägyptens und des Alten Testaments. Wiesbaden: Harrassowitz.

ADAIK — Abhandlungen des Deutschen Archäologischen Instituts Abteilung Kairo. Mainz: von Zabern/Berlin: Achet Verlag.

ÄF — Ägyptologische Forschungen. Glückstadt: J. J. Augustin.

APAW — Abhandlungen der Preußischen Akademie der Wissenschaften.

ASAE — *Annales du Service des antiquités d'Egypte.* Cairo.

ASE — Archaeological Survey of Egypt. London: Egypt Exploration Fund/Society.

AV — Archäologische Veröffentlichungen. Deutsches Archäologisches Institut Abteilung Kairo. Mainz: von Zabern.

BdE — Bibliothèque d'étude. Cairo: IFAO.

BeiträgeBf — Beiträge zur ägyptischen Bauforschung und Altertumskunde.

BIFAO — *Bulletin de l'Institut français d'Archéologie orientale.* Cairo: IFAO.

BM — British Museum, London.

BMFA — *Bulletin of the Museum of Fine Arts.* Boston: Museum of Fine Arts.

BSAE — British School of Archaeology in Egypt.

BSEG — *Bulletin de la Société d'Égyptologie de Genève.* Geneva.

CG — Cairo, Egyptian Museum, Catalogue Général.

DE — *Discussions in Egyptology.* Oxford.

EEF — Egypt Exploration Fund, Memoirs. London: Egypt Exploration Fund.

ERA — Egypt Research Account. London: BSAE.

FIFAO — Fouilles de l'Institut français d'Archéologie orientale. Cairo: IFAO.

GM *Göttinger Miszellen. Beiträge zur ägyptologischen Diskussion.* Göttingen.

HÄB Hildesheimer Ägyptologische Beiträge. Hildesheim: Gerstenberg Verlag.

IFAO Institut français d'archéologie orientale.

JARCE *Journal of the American Research Center in Egypt.* Cambridge, Mass./Boston/Princeton, N.J./New York.

JE Cairo, Egyptian Museum, Journal d'entrée.

JEA *Journal of Egyptian Archaeology.* London: Egypt Exploration Fund/Society.

JESHO *Journal of the Economic and Social History of the Orient.* Leiden.

JNES *Journal of Near Eastern Studies.* Chicago: University of Chicago Press.

JSSEA *Journal of the Society of the Study of Egyptian Antiquities.* Toronto.

LÄ Helck and Otto 1972–92.

LD Lepsius 1849–59.

LD Text Lepsius 1897–1913.

LD Erg. Lepsius 1913.

LG Lepsius numbers for tombs at Giza.

LS Lepsius numbers for tombs at Saqqara.

MÄS Münchner ägyptologische Studien. Berlin: Bruno Hessling; Munich/Berlin: Deutscher Kunstverlag.

MDAIK *Mitteilungen des Deutschen Archäologischen Instituts Abteilung Kairo.* Mainz: von Zabern.

MFA Museum of Fine Arts, Boston.

MIFAO Mémoires publiés par les membres de l'IFAO. Cairo: IFAO.

MIO *Mitteilungen des Instituts für Orientforschung.* Berlin.

MMA Metropolitan Museum of Art, New York.

MMJ *Metropolitan Museum Journal.* New York: Metropolitan Museum of Art.

NAWG Nachrichten der Akademie der Wissenschaften in Göttingen.

OBO Orbis Biblicus et Orientalis. Freiburg: Universitätsverlag/ Göttingen: Vandenhoeck & Ruprecht.

OLA Orientalia Lovaniensia Analecta. Leuven: Peeters.

PM III^2 Porter and Moss 1974–81.

PMMA Publications of the Metropolitan Museum of Art, New York, Egyptian Expedition.

PSBA *Proceedings of the Society of Biblical Archaeology.* London.

PT	Pyramid Texts, section number following Sethe 1908–22.
RAPH	Recherches d'archéologie, de philologie et d'histoire. Cairo: IFAO.
RdE	*Revue d'Égyptologie*. Cairo/Paris.
SAGA	Studien zur Archäologie und Geschichte Altägyptens. Heidelberg: Heidelberger Orientverlag.
SAK	*Studien zur altägyptischen Kultur*. Hamburg: Buske.
SAOC	Studies in Ancient Oriental Civilizations. Chicago: University of Chicago Press.
SAWW	Sitzungsberichte/Akademie der Wissenschaften in Wien: philos.-hist. Kl., Vienna.
SDAIK	Sonderschriften des Deutschen Archäologischen Instituts Abteilung Kairo. Mainz: von Zabern.
UGAÄ	Untersuchungen zur Geschichte und Altertumskunde Ägyptens. Leipzig: Hinrichs.
Urk I	Sethe 1933 (second edition of Sethe 1903).
Wb	Erman and Grapow 1926–53.
WVDOG	Wissenschaftliche Veröffentlichungen der Deutschen Orient-Gesellschaft. Leipzig: Hinrichs.
ZÄS	*Zeitschrift für ägyptische Sprache und Altertumskunde*. Leipzig/Berlin.

I

Introduction

Preliminary Remarks

The Old Kingdom is the earliest major historical period of ancient Egypt to leave behind a considerable body of continuous writing. From the late Predynastic and Early Dynastic periods many names, titles, labels, and otherwise enigmatic writings have come down to us, but nothing which could be termed continuous texts which lend themselves to presentation in a volume of translations such as this. Records must have existed which were used for the later Palermo Stone, and there are some simple formulae which may look forward to the biographical texts of the Old Kingdom.

It is normal to begin the Old Kingdom with the third dynasty (ca. 2707–2639 B.C.). In tombs, names and titles still predominate at that time, but parallel to the development of the first large-scale stone architecture in the reign of Netjerikhet Djoser short texts of religious import begin to appear, which are significant in that they set the basic pattern for the next three thousand years. With the rise of the fourth dynasty, an expansion of the scale of tomb inscriptions is seen; the existence of (as yet unpublished) administrative papyri is known. Tomb inscriptions gradually increase in complexity throughout the Old Kingdom, and in the later fifth dynasty the longest continuous texts from the age appear, the "Pyramid Texts," religious texts so called because they are written on the walls of the burial chambers of pyramids, although it is plausible that they existed much earlier in oral forms. The earliest "wisdom" or "instructional" texts have also been dated by some to this period.

1.1 Range of Material Presented

The aim of this volume is to provide translations, as far as possible, of examples of all major categories of text from the Old Kingdom with the exception of the Pyramid and wisdom texts. The Pyramid Texts have been intensively studied in their own right and are so fundamentally different in spirit from the texts treated here that they belong in a separate volume on Egyptian religious texts, or indeed one on their own. Three "wisdom" or "instructional" compositions have been ascribed to the Old Kingdom: these texts would have us believe that they were the teachings of the important officials or "sages" Djedefhor, Ptahhotep, and Kaigemni.[1] However, analysis of these texts is providing mounting evidence that they were actually composed later, probably in the Middle Kingdom, and were ascribed to great men of the Old Kingdom to give them an additional level of authority.[2] Again, like the Pyramid Texts, they are so different from the texts to be translated here that they deserve treatment in volumes dedicated to this specific genre. A further religious text sometimes attributed to the Old Kingdom is the so-called Memphite Theology on the Shabaka Stone in the British Museum (EA 498). Current opinion is that this text is a later composition, and it is thus omitted.[3]

This book concentrates on a wide range of texts, most of which are often ignored in volumes of translation—those found in the temples, tombs, and remains of administrative centers in Egypt of the Old Kingdom. It would be wrong to label them in a blanket fashion as "documentary texts," since so many of them come from tombs and hence act as self-conscious quasi-religious texts and were also intended to present the owner in a favorable light in his passage to the afterlife (see also §4.1 below).

While far less written material has survived from the Old Kingdom than from the other great periods that followed it, the texts translated in this book are only a selection to permit the reader to understand the breadth and depth of the written output of this great period.

1.2 Selection and Presentation Criteria

The selection of texts for the volume began inevitably with those included in *Urkunden des alten Reichs* ("Urk I" = Sethe 1933, see further below §2.1) but has since expanded considerably beyond that. It was never my intention to aim at completeness, and I have tried to resist the temptation to provide a comprehensive sourcebook for the Old Kingdom. All the principal series of publications that include Old Kingdom material have been examined, as have collections of material and translations such as Kloth 2002 and Roccati 1982. However, it would also be true to say that the library has not been trawled through from A to Z.

I have tried to include all the well-known texts of a biographical nature, as well as royal decrees and private legal texts, although a few have been omitted because they are so broken as to be incapable of meaningful reconstruction.[4] Most administrative texts, written as they were on papyrus, not the sturdiest medium, have not survived the centuries well, but I have attempted to give the reader a "feel" for such texts. The Old Kingdom is not rich in religious texts outside those in the pyramid chambers, but I give some samples to show the important place the temples of the kings of the third to sixth dynasties played in the development of such inscriptions.

Lists of names and titles are frequent in the Old Kingdom, and it was felt that the reader should be spared more than a sample; I have not, however, shirked from translating titles in full where they appear in the course of other featured texts, but this book is not intended to be a source book for the prosopography of the Old Kingdom. Hence objects like cylinder seals and sealings, as well as most graffiti (but compare §6.9), are omitted.

The same is true of tomb inscriptions of a more formulaic or repetitive nature; I have tried to cover all the broad variants of texts, including examples of the absolutely standard along with the more unusual ones. Far more standard formulae have been included as part of other texts than was the original intention, but they do serve to impress on the reader the ubiquity of certain types of text. Thus not every text on a given wall or monument is translated, in part to avoid the repetition of too many formulae.

A particular category of text that tends not to feature in books of translations is the caption inscriptions that accompany so many scenes in tombs. Because of the interdependence of text and image in Egyptian representational art,[5] they are best studied where a large selection of illustrations can be made available. Nonetheless, a small cross-section of these fascinating texts is translated here in an attempt to convey the range of scenes, liveliness, and modes of expression.

The date range is broadly third to eighth dynasty, but a small number of texts here are in all probability of the First Intermediate Period and thus outside the strict date period of this volume. They are included largely because of their appearance in Urk I or another collection of texts, but those which add little or nothing to what is known from other texts are deliberately omitted.[6] I have tried not to compromise excessively any future volume in this series on texts of the First Intermediate Period.

Reconstructions are employed where they appear plausible, and they are indicated where they will not be too disruptive to the reader. I indicate editions and principal translations of the texts and have inconsistently attempted to note translations of significant parts of them, but I do not mention every translation of a snippet of a text. For the latter, the reader is encouraged to consult (the indexes of) the scholarly studies that translate many isolated sections of these texts (in particular, Edel 1944, Edel 1955–64, Doret 1986, Kloth 2002, as well as Sainte Fare Garnot 1938). No material which is unpublished or not in press is included here, and minimal comments are offered so as not to burden the texts with an excess of notes.

A considerable bibliography is available for a number of the texts, but in general I have decided against giving most of it, preferring instead to indicate the versions or editions of the text I have used plus other translations, collections of bibliography, and significant other scholarly contributions. The reader is thus urged to look at those editions plus Porter and Moss 1974–81, Kloth 2002, and Roccati 1982 for more detail. The exception is for significant material not in those publications. For each text I have also tried to indicate its date and site of origin, as well as its present location if different.

2. Previous Work on Old Kingdom Texts

2.1 Collections and Translations of Large Bodies of Old Kingdom Material

Only one work exists in English which attempts the same scope as the present book, namely, the first volume of Breasted's *Ancient Records* (Breasted 1906–7). This monumental work includes in its first part many of the texts in the present volume. Breasted's work was a remarkable achievement, appearing as it did before anyone had assembled even a list of basic texts, and he would surely be gratified and astonished that it is still referred to almost one hundred years later. The number of texts known has expanded greatly since his time, and at that point the study of Egyptian was in its infancy, scientific research into the Egyptian language only having really started in the last quarter of the nineteenth century.

In 1897 the great Berlin project to produce a dictionary of ancient Egyptian began (Erman and Grapow 1926–53; work toward a second edition continues in Berlin). This dictionary was to be based wholly on a new and wide-ranging collection of texts rather than just relying on what had gone before. Scholars from all nations were invited to contribute to various areas of the corpus of Egyptian textual material, and one of those most heavily involved was Kurt Sethe, who became professor at Göttingen in

Germany in 1900. He first put his skills to work on texts of the Old Kingdom and in 1903 produced *Urkunden des alten Reichs* ("Documents of the Old Kingdom" = "Urk I" or Sethe 1903), 152 pages of autographed texts from the Pyramid Age. A trip to Egypt in 1904–5 caused him to concentrate his text-collecting efforts for some time on the eighteenth dynasty, and he next produced *Urkunden der 18. Dynastie* ("Documents of the Eighteenth Dynasty") in 1906–9.

These two titles were part of the series Urkunden des ägyptischen Altertums, which, with contributions by others, eventually covered large areas of the texts of the Old, Middle, and early New Kingdoms, as well as the Greco-Roman period, and the principle of collecting texts has been continued by others into the missing periods. These volumes include most of the basic texts from these periods known when they were compiled. The standard form for the Urkunden is to write texts from left to right in horizontal lines, inserting gaps and line breaks to give pointers for the parsing of the text.[7] They are still standard reference works today, even though it is now generally preferred that the texts be studied in facsimile rather than in a form so much removed from the original arrangement. In 1933 Sethe published a second edition, this time of 308 pages, of the *Urkunden des alten Reichs* (Sethe 1933). This collection of texts has provided the starting point for the present book.

Since Breasted, the only compendious set of translations produced of Old Kingdom texts is that in French in Roccati 1982. The translations are still up to date, and the bibliography for most items is very full. That book does not, however, include the royal decrees and the private legal documents, two of the most intriguing groups of texts of the Old Kingdom. Since 1982, most of the extant Old Kingdom letters were translated in Wente 1990 in the Writings from the Ancient World series. There is without doubt a need for modern English translations of these texts.

2.2 Translations of Egyptian Literature in English Incorporating Some Old Kingdom Texts

It is a sad reflection of the undue prominence of textual study in Egyptology that texts termed "literary," however broadly one defines literature in an Egyptian context, tend to be those which have been translated and studied the most, despite their relatively restricted number when compared to more "documentary" texts.[8] Some of the longer biographical texts of the Old Kingdom do appear in a few of the standard books of translations of this type, but the principal inclusions from that epoch tend to be the Pyramid Texts and the wisdom literature (see above). The first such volume was Erman 1923, translated into English by Blackman as Erman 1927. Erman's selection ranged from the Pyramid Texts to the New Kingdom but did not include any of the Old Kingdom texts translated here. A similar selection of material was translated in Simpson 1972; the most recent revision (Simpson 2003) includes three Old Kingdom biographical texts. Between 1973 and 1980, Miriam Lichtheim published the three volumes of her *Ancient Egyptian Literature*, which still remains the principal set of translations to cover the longer texts of the whole of Egyptian history; the first volume includes a number of the biographies translated in the present volume (Lichtheim 1973). A subsequent volume by the same author on (mainly) Middle Kingdom biographies also includes a few additional Old Kingdom examples (Lichtheim 1988).

2.3 The Study of Old Kingdom Texts

A summary of the history of study of Old Kingdom texts may be found in Goedicke 1973–74. The texts from the Old Kingdom that have received the widest attention over the years are those deliberately excluded from the scope of the present volume, that is, the Pyramid Texts and the wisdom and instructional texts.[9] Studies have been made of various groups of texts; for example, Goedicke produced two volumes on what are perhaps the most difficult texts of the period, the royal decrees and the legal texts (Goedicke 1967a; 1970), and Kahl, Kloth, and Zimmermann 1995 is a collection of material from the third dynasty. Expedition inscriptions and some royal letters have been examined in Eichler 1993 and 1991a. Offering formulae (Barta 1968; Lapp 1986) and offering lists (Barta 1963) have been studied as part of research into these types of inscriptions over the wider historical span of all of ancient Egypt. The biographical texts have otherwise received the widest attention, in the contexts of phraseology (Edel 1944; Kloth 2002), development and antecedents (Kloth 2002; Baines 1999a), or in a broader context than just the Old Kingdom (Lichtheim 1988; Gnirs 1996; 2001). Lastly, it is difficult to imagine a more significant advance in our knowledge of administrative texts than Posener-Kriéger's compendious treatment of the original find of papyri from Abusir (Posener-Kriéger 1976) plus her subsequent studies of other texts on papyrus (see further below). Posener-Kriéger's unexpected and regretted passing in

1996 has robbed us of early publication of other administrative texts, notably the Gebelein papyri.

3. Historical Matters

3.1 Outline

This is not the place for more than an outline of the history of the Old Kingdom. Readers are asked to refer to the chronological table for most points and to note that the whole question of the absolute chronology of ancient Egypt is not treated in this book.[10] §3.2 considers the question of the calculation of dates within the Old Kingdom.

It is conventional to begin the epoch with the third dynasty (ca. 2707–2639 B.C.), as the reign of Netjerikhet Djoser, the first or second king, saw the beginning of large-scale building in stone, a technical achievement which characterizes the Old Kingdom. In fact, like so many of the classic dynastic divisions, there seems to be no clear family reason for making a break between the second and third dynasties, as the kings in question were closely related. One of our main sources for chronological history, the Turin Canon,[11] makes no division but does write the entry for the reign of Djoser in red ink, suggesting that this also might have been considered a turning point by the Egyptians.

Relatively little is known about the history of the third dynasty, in complete opposition to what is known about its architectural achievements. After the Step Pyramid of Djoser at Saqqara, most of the monuments appear never to have been completed. The successors of Djoser were Sekhemkhet and Khaba, and the last king of the dynasty was probably Qaihedjet Huni, who may or may not have been involved in the building of the pyramid at Meidum, just north of the Fayum. The successor of Huni was Sneferu, first king of the fourth dynasty (ca. 2639–2504 B.C.), although there is again no clear family break in contemporary records.

Sneferu is recorded in the Palermo Stone (no. 1) as raiding Nubia, and it is quite likely that incursions started by Egyptian kings in the first dynasty meant that this area was depopulated from then until later in the Old Kingdom (Trigger et al. 1983: 62–63; Nordström 2001); a graffito of Sneferu's from Khor el-Aquiba (no. 76) can be interpreted as referring to an expedition contributing to the depopulation, perhaps for labor needed in Egypt. He certainly built two pyramids at Dahshur and had a significant involvement in that at Meidum. Sneferu survived in Egyptian mythical memory as a beneficent king, whereas his son and successor, Khufu (Greek Kheops), was recalled as a tyrant; these aspects are best known from the late Middle Kingdom Papyrus Westcar.[12] Perhaps the sheer size of Khufu's funerary monument, the Great Pyramid at Giza, meant to later Egyptians that he must have been a despotic ruler to have constructed something so large. Little is known about Khufu himself, but it is quite clear that the vast amount of pyramid building going on at this time contributed to the development of a strong central administration to enable such work to proceed. Khufu's son Djedefre built his pyramid at Abu Roash to the north of Giza, but his successor, another of Khufu's sons, called Khafre (Greek Khephren), returned to Giza to construct his funerary monument; construction of the Great Sphinx at that site is usually attributed to him (but see Stadelmann 2003 for the view that it might have been constructed by Khufu). Some family instability is evident in the later years of the fourth dynasty, as there is some evidence for a couple of short reigns either side of the last two main rulers, Menkaure (Greek Mykerinos) and Shepseskaf (no. 82).

Continuity of the bloodline seems to have been ensured into the fifth dynasty by a queen named Khentkawes, called several times the mother of two kings of Upper and Lower Egypt (no. 278). Although the last two known royal tombs of the fourth dynasty did not rival those of the earlier rulers, the fifth dynasty (ca. 2504–2347 B.C.), starting with its first king Userkaf, adopted more modest designs for its pyramids. The reason for this is unknown, but it may not have been so much economic as a change in emphasis to the building of more temples; one such manifestation is the beginning of a series of six "sun temples," dedicated to the king and the sun god just north of the predominant royal burial site of Saqqara/Abusir.[13] The cult of the sun had been growing in influence since the middle of the fourth dynasty, when, for example, Re, the name of one of the principal forms of the sun god, became a standard part of the royal names (§3.3).

Changes in the way in which the administration was structured are evident at this time. While previously the royal family had filled many of the offices of state, private individuals were increasingly promoted to high levels, perhaps to reduce the chance of strife within the royal family which may be evident in the fourth dynasty. While the tombs of many fourth-dynasty officials are relatively close to their kings at Giza, more of a separation was observed in the fifth, with the majority at Saqqara while most pyramids were at Abusir (compare Roth 1988). Private tombs became more elaborate, and there is an increase in the number of texts (§6.5.3). Increasing levels of decoration are attested in royal temples, and in two of these, those of Neferefre and Neferirkare at Abusir, substantial remains of administrative archives were uncovered (§6.4). The number of rock inscriptions in the Sinai and elsewhere suggest a growth in expeditions abroad (§§6.3, 6.10).

The construction of sun temples seems to have ceased in the reign of Izezi, the penultimate king of the dynasty, who also built his pyramid at the relatively little-used site of South Saqqara—although how much should be read into either development is debatable. Also about this time a somewhat changed attitude to provincial officials is seen; whereas the provinces (Egyptologists tend to use the term "nome" from the Greek νόμος) had before been mostly administered from the capital, more tombs of important persons are now found outside Memphis. This may indicate not so much a shift to decentralization but rather an attempt to govern and exploit these regions more effectively, as some of these officials came originally from the Memphite region. The last king of the dynasty, Unas, was the first king to inscribe the Pyramid Texts on the walls of the burial chambers of his pyramid at Saqqara; tombs of some of his high officials were built adjacent to his pyramid complex. After Unas, the Turin Canon makes its first clear break, which coincides with the rise of the sixth dynasty (ca. 2347– 2216 B.C.).

Even if there was a family change, and some Egyptologists actually link Unas more with the sixth than the fifth dynasty, the Old Kingdom continued apparently much as before. Teti, the first king, built a pyramid at Saqqara, around which clustered the tombs of his high officials. A possible ephemeral king called Userkare might have reigned for a short while after Teti, and an argument has been advanced for some instability in the early years of the sixth dynasty, involving assassinations and palace intrigues (Kanawati 2002a). However, the longish reign of Pepy I ensured a measure of stability, and this king seems to have carefully modified the balance of power of provincial officials to prevent anyone becoming too powerful. He also built a series of temples throughout Egypt at major cult centers (§6.2), which might have included some of the first stone examples of such structures, which had previously mainly been made of mud brick (the use of stone had previously been concentrated on funerary temples and tombs designed for eternity). He may also have conducted military campaigns on the borders of Egypt (no. 256). His son Merenre had a short seven-year reign, after which he was succeeded by the child king Pepy II, who may have been a son of either of his predecessors (no. 281). Tradition holds that Pepy was six years old at accession and lived to be one hundred years old. Recent chronological studies have questioned this reign length, although it would still have been considerably longer than the Egyptian average (von Beckerath 1997: 151).

The first signs of internal weakness that may eventually have put an end to the strong centralized Old Kingdom possibly appear at this time (ca. 2250 B.C.). This subject is much debated (for example, Müller-Wollermann 1986), but likely systemic weakness coupled with economic and political problems in the long reign of Pepy II, together with possible changes in climate, may have contributed to the eventual demise. It has been hotly debated whether the increasing prominence of provincial officials might have contributed to central weakness, but I suspect that it was not until the center itself became weak that there is some truth to this. This systemic weakness is suggested by the appearance of two ephemeral kings (one, Nitocris, a woman, although not attested in any contemporary record [but but see now Ryholt 2000 for her possible removal from the list of kings]) at the end of the sixth dynasty, and then by the two succeeding dynasties consisting of a series of very short reigns (ca. 2216–2170 B.C.). The Koptos decrees (§6.3.2) suggest that Memphis at least held nominal control over the country until the end of the eighth dynasty, but at some point around 2170 B.C. central control disintegrated, the kingship passing to the governors of Herakleopolis, a town just to the south of the Fayum. The next approximately 160 years are termed the First Intermediate Period.

3.2 Dating Events in the Old Kingdom

3.2.1 Methods of Dating Years

The concept of absolute dating, together with the naming of historical periods such as "Old Kingdom" and "First Intermediate Period," is modern, and the terminology used is largely due to the nineteenth-century A.D. passion for cyclical history. The Egyptians seem at all times to have dated documents and monuments in terms of the point in the reign of the present king, with only the vaguest of methods (by our standards) for referring to the passage of time. Redford distinguished three ways of viewing time in the age of the pyramids: (1) "today under king X" (the present); (2) "in the time of king Y" (someone in the past); and (3) "in the time of Re" (divine mythical past). His opinion is that as society had never failed before the end of the Old Kingdom, there was little imperative to develop any further views (Redford 1986: 127–43). This is not to deny a sense of history among the Egyptians,[14] which clearly developed more as time advanced, but it would be wrong to assume that they were as obsessed with chronology and dating as we are at the beginning of the third millennium A.D.

The concept of dynasties derives from a history of Egypt written in Greek by the Egyptian priest Manetho in the third century B.C. He divided the kings into groups which he called dynasties; the use of that (Greek) word was no doubt influenced by its use to describe Greek ruling families. Manetho must have had access to archival sources, which just might have had their origins in an interpretation of a document such as the Turin Canon (Málek 1982).

Dating may have started out at the beginning of Egyptian history by naming the years based on events; the recurrence of certain events of inspection or the like probably gave rise to the principal dating system employed in the Early Dynastic Period and Old Kingdom. This was apparently based around a recurring census of the cattle of Egypt within the reign of a king, the first of which would have taken place not long after his accession to the throne, presumably as a way of establishing and announcing the authority of the new ruler.[15] Numerous examples of such dates will be found among the translations. Thus a document might be dated "the year of the x-th occasion of the count of the cattle," sometimes, but not always, accompanied by the name of a king; this is frequently abbreviated to "year of the x-th occasion." The problem with understanding this system is of knowing the frequency of these counts. From the Palermo Stone (no. 1) it would appear that the normal interval between these counts was two years (at least in the Early Dynastic Period[16]), supported generally by the appearance of many examples of "the year *after* the x-th occasion of the count of the cattle." Thus it has become normal practice for many Egyptologists to double the cattle-count number, adding one if necessary, to obtain the regnal year for an Old Kingdom royal date.

However, it would not be ancient Egypt if there were not problems with this analysis of the data (see particularly Nolan 2003, and discussions in Baud 1999b and Helck 1994: 106–10). Reign lengths in the Turin Canon cannot always be reconciled with the contemporary dates. To be sure, there is not a complete set of year/cattle-count dates for most kings, but there are also examples where the extant number of cattle counts flatly contradicts the Turin papyrus if a biennial count is assumed. The two best examples are the reigns of Sneferu and Pepy I.

The highest certain cattle count for Sneferu appears now to be twenty-four (no. 80), yet the space allocated to him in the Turin Canon gives him twenty-four years. Many writers believe that there is a problem with the Turin figure, and it is indeed suspicious that the year count is the same as that of the preceding reign (Huni presumably). That there may be an irregularity in the system of counts here is confirmed by the Palermo Stone, where counts seven and eight occur in successive years (no. 1; Wilkinson 2000: 143–46; Spalinger 1994: 281–83); in the most recent discussion of the reign length, Krauss suggests thirty-one years as a likely duration, which I find more convincing than simply multiplying the twenty-four known counts by two to reach forty-eight years.[17] Likewise the highest count known for Pepy I is twenty-five (no. 71), yet he is only apparently given twenty years in the Canon. In this case there are various feasible solutions, in addition to the possibility that the Canon is hopelessly corrupt at this point: for example, the existence of another king, such as Userkare, whose years Pepy might have taken over,[18] or the possibility that the forty-four years which seems to be allocated to Merenre in the Turin Canon is partly his.[19] It is also possible to dispute other reign lengths.[20]

The correct approach to adopt when faced with this seemingly contradictory evidence is not to see it from a modern and very rigorous point of view but rather to take a flexible and more relaxed attitude to it as surely would have been taken by the Egyptians. *They* knew what the date meant, and that mattered more than anything else; perhaps cattle counts happened as needed, with an original preference for every other year. Some sort of centralized archive must also have existed, or else the king lists we have could not have been compiled, but it is impossible to over-stress that the Egyptian attitude to dating was very different from our own.

Nolan 2003, which appeared as this book was being finalized, takes a new approach. The "festival of Thoth" probably happened every three years in an intercalary month need to resynchronize the lunar and civil calendars; this festival was a time for bringing together the cattle, and this might just account for a pattern in which counts were skipped completely every third year (Nolan 2003: 91–94). This interesting idea does of course have major implications for Old Kingdom chronology and still seeks to impose a rather rigorous framework on something which might just have been more flexible in practice.

3.2.2 Sed Festivals

One of the better-known Egyptian festivals, attested from the Early Dynastic Period onwards, is the *Sed* festival or jubilee. The festival seems to have been one of renewal of the king's powers and involved a series of separate ritual events, which sometimes apparently took place in buildings especially constructed for the purpose in the royal mortuary complex. The best example is perhaps the various dummy buildings in the southwestern area of the Step Pyramid enclosure of Netjerykhet Djoser (third dynasty) at Saqqara.[21]

There are many references to the festival in Old Kingdom texts in this book, and scenes relating to this festival may be found in other sources, notably the sun temple of Niuserre (von Bissing 1905–28; reconstruction of one part in Kaiser 1971). The "traditional" time at which this festival was enacted was in the thirtieth year of the king's reign, after which it could be reenacted at three-year intervals (Amenhotep III of the eighteenth dynasty is a good example). But there are documented examples of the first festival taking place during reigns which are known to have been of shorter duration (Nebtawyre Mentuhotep IV, eleventh dynasty, and Hatshepsut, eighteenth dynasty). The position in the Old Kingdom is not entirely clear, largely due to the lack of dates, and is also tied in with the problems of the frequency of the cattle count used for dating years. In particular, Netjerykhet Djoser is usually allocated a reign of about twenty years; the *Sed* festival of Pepy I apparently took place in the year after the eighteenth count (no. 64); and some chronologies (although not that followed here) allow Niuserre a reign of less than thirty years (for example, Shaw 2000: 480). Against this, Pepy II certainly had two *Sed* festivals (no. 53). However, we must not overlook the possibility that the frequency of this festival was not settled in the Old Kingdom and also that some kings might have undertaken building work for a festival which they never were able to celebrate.

3.2.3 The Different Seasons

The Egyptians marked the beginning of the solar year with the helical rising of the star Sothis early in our January. The Egyptian civil calendar was composed of twelve months of thirty days each, with five extra "epagomenal" days added at the end of the year to round the total to 365. This of course is roughly a quarter-day short of the true solar-year length, and this meant that every four years the Egyptian calendar moved one day ahead of the solar year. Hence a civil calendar month which originally formed part of what we would now call "winter" could occur in autumn, then in summer, then in spring, and finally, after about 1,460 years, the beginning of the civil year would become briefly synchronized with the beginning of the solar year again.

The subject of calendars is complex, and this is not the place to go into more detail.[22] The above broad characterization should enable the reader to understand how the names of the seasons appear in the translations. The Egyptians had three seasons of four months each, named *Akhet*, *Peret,* and *Shemu,* perhaps originally indicating respectively the periods which included the inundation, the emergence from the inundation and growing season, and the ripening and harvesting season. But giving these modern names like "inundation," "winter," and "summer," which are tied to well-fixed natural conditions or phenomena, is found in far too many publications and is rather meaningless with the movement of the calendar. Hence I prefer to use the ancient terms for the seasons.

3.3 Royal Names

Egyptian kings of all periods had up to five different names. Their order of appearance in the royal titulary approximately reflects their chronological introduction. Each also represents a different aspect of kingship.[23]

The Horus Name: this is the oldest royal name, most distinctively written within a rectangular *serekh* (the bottom of which is probably a stylized representation of the wall of a mud-brick palace) surmounted by a falcon. The falcon represents the god Horus, who, as the son and successor of Osiris, the first king of Egypt, is identified with the king. This name is first found in association with rulers of the late Predynastic Period and in the Old Kingdom still functions very much as the "official" name of the king—it is used, for example, on royal decrees and in formal rock inscriptions in preference to the other names.

The *Nebty* or "Two Ladies" Name: written following the hieroglyphic pair of the vulture goddess Nekhbet, the protective goddess of Upper Egypt, and her Lower Egyptian counterpart, the cobra goddess Wadjet. It identifies the king with these tutelary deities of the "Two Lands" and is first found in the first dynasty (reigns of Aha and Djet). It also emphasizes the essential religious duality of the kingship, expressed most clearly in rituals like the "uniting of the Two Lands."

The Gold or Golden Horus Name: earlier just written with the sign for "gold" , and later with a falcon on top; an additional hieroglyph can be placed with the falcon to make it distinctive for an individual, such as and , or the falcon may be doubled or tripled. The significance of the name is not completely clear, but it might involve a play on a similar-sounding word (the Egyptian for "gold" is *nub* or *nebu*) for "burn" or "glow" and be an allusion to the sun and also to the sky, emphasizing the connection of the king with these elements. The earliest association of the "Horus" and "gold" signs is in the first dynasty reign of Den.

Cartouche Names: the final two names are written in "cartouches" , loops, originally of rope, which are apparently so named from their seeming resemblance to the cartridges (French *cartouche*) used by Napoleon's troops in Egypt. They are in fact horizontal or vertical extensions of the *shen* sign 𓍶, which symbolizes all that the rule of the king encircles. As the Horus name was the principal name form in use for much of the Old Kingdom, the uses of these names tend to be somewhat restricted, and the full titulary is rarely seen in the period covered by this book. Cartouches appear particularly with the title 𓇓𓏏𓆤𓏏, *nesut-bity,* translated here "king of Upper and Lower Egypt," and sometimes "dual king," the two signs representing respectively the (mythical) kingships of each of the lands of which Egypt was traditionally composed; the Upper Egyptian 𓇓 came to be used for the general word 𓇓𓏏𓈖 "king." The other main use is in contexts where the king is to be thought of as deceased, as, for example, in titles associated with mortuary cults. In this context no kingly title is placed with the cartouche. The two cartouches function roughly as follows.

The *prenomen*: usually a name taken by the king on his accession to the throne, which tends to express some indication of his power or aspirations. It is most frequently throughout Egyptian history compounded with the name of the sun god Re. The *nomen*: from later evidence, this was almost certainly the king's personal name. From the fourth dynasty, the cartouches were often accompanied by the epithet 𓅭𓇳, "son of Re" (the sun god); although from later times the position of this is usually before the second cartouche, in the Old Kingdom its position is not fixed, as it sometimes appears after the cartouche or even inside it (von Beckerath 1999: 25–26).[24]

The first king clearly seen with a cartouche is probably Huni, the last king of the latter dynasty, and it is only with his successor Sneferu that it becomes common (only one cartouche name is used).[25] However, antecedents of the *nomen* have possibly been noted in the first dynasty,[26] and there is a possible cartouche of Nebka, once thought to be the first king of the dynasty but now more probably to be moved later (Dreyer 1998).

Until the appearance of two different cartouches in the fifth dynasty, it is assumed that these early cartouches exhibit the personal name, the *nomen* (but see also n. 25 above). The king must have had a personal name from birth, and that a note of these was kept is suggested by the later king lists, which list the early rulers only by names in cartouches which are otherwise hardly, if at all, attested in contemporary records. Perhaps the best known of these early names is that of the builder of the Step Pyramid: known on contemporary monuments as the Horus Netjerykhet, in later lists he appears with the cartouche name Djoser.

The two cartouches appear together for the first time in the reign of

Neferirkare Kakai of the early fifth dynasty, and from that time on it is presumed that the theophoric names ending in -re are the throne names (*prenomen*). Thus all elements of the titulary can be found in the fifth dynasty, although the first appearance of all in the same inscription is probably in that of Pepy I in the sixth dynasty (no. 64 E). In the Old Kingdom the Horus, *Nebty,* and Golden Horus names are often the same, while in later periods they are all different, and there is much more flexibility in the order in which the various elements appear at this time than later, and some are often omitted. Here is a titulary of Izezi of the fifth dynasty, which omits one of the cartouches:

"The Horus *Djedkhau,* the king of Upper and Lower Egypt, the Two Ladies *Djedkhau,* the Golden Horus *Djed,* Djedkare, may he live for ever" (no. 60 D).

The word *djed* used in these names means "stable, stability, enduring"; thus *Djedkhau* means "stable of appearances," "appearance" referring to the king manifesting himself on the throne of Egypt.

A number of inscriptions on objects such as stone vessels giving just the titularies of kings are included here (chapter V).

3.4 Dating Private Monuments

Despite the importance of determining how official dates were established in the Old Kingdom, it is a fact that the majority of records from the Pyramid Age (or from any section of Egyptian history for that matter) do not bear explicit dates. While the simple fact of nonsurvival is doubtless significant, in ancient Egypt, as in many societies before our own, there was not the "obsession" with dating seen today. Furthermore, the surviving contexts often do not require dates—most material comes from funerary sources, and tombs were not constructed to give the birth and death dates of their owners but had a much more complex function revolving around bringing them to new life and providing sustenance and shelter for their souls.

This relative lack of explicit dating evidence has meant that, as tombs are the sources of most texts from the Old Kingdom, considerable energy has been expended in the second half of the twentieth century A.D. on dating them. Various methodologies have been tried with varying degrees of success. The basic method is to build up a group of tombs which can be dated independently and then to use features of those tombs to date others with similar features but without explicit dating indications. Techniques tried on this body of material include the use of title sequences (Baer 1960), iconography (Cherpion 1989), and tomb size (Kanawati 1977a), as well as incorporating and refining dating as part of other studies, such as scene orientation (Harpur 1987), administration (for example, Kanawati 1980; Martin-Pardey 1976; Strudwick 1985), the royal family (Baud 1999a), and the history of particular reigns (Kanawati 2002a).

One of the principal problems for Old Kingdom tomb dating is that although royal names are to be found in a considerable number of tombs, many do not date to the reign named. In particular, titles which incorporate the names of kings can be held at a much later date, as they indicate income from some estate or office conferred on the holder (see §5.2.3) or some other involvement in a cult which still functioned at that time. Another difficulty is the extent to which monuments which might appear at first glance to be early Old Kingdom are actually from the later part of the epoch and are deliberately "archaizing" in nature. That particular problem was examined in Cherpion's study of iconography as a dating criterion; her results encouraged her to believe that more reliance could be placed both on names and on the actual antiquity of presumed archaizing monuments than had been believed before (Cherpion 1989: 139–44).[27]

4. Literary and Linguistic Aspects of Old Kingdom Texts

4.1 The Importance of Context

One of the great advances in the study of all Egyptian material in the second half of the twentieth century A.D. was a move away from taking Egyptian texts and artifacts automatically at face value and assessing them too much in relation to the norms of modern society. This was replaced with an insistence on careful consideration of the context for which they were made before invoking them in any particular argument. So, for example, while it is possible to view Egyptian sculpture as "art" and judge it accordingly, such objects were made to be used in a particular place, usually a temple or tomb, and this would give them a particular level of meaning; function was as important as form, and while it would be wrong to deny that "art for art's sake" existed in Egypt, there is nothing comparable to the practice of collecting art so common in Western society since classical times.

Likewise, it is all too easy to take a text at face value and interpret it literally. Much work has been done on literary texts in this regard, with the result that it has been shown that, for example, using Middle Kingdom wisdom literature to tell us about the chaos and recovery of the period of the ninth to twelfth dynasties is simply wrong.[28] With monumental texts such as form the principal subject of this volume, the likely location (usually tomb or temple) in which they were set up has first to be ascertained, and the likely purpose of that monument recognized. The great state temples, although we know next to nothing about their inscriptions in the Old Kingdom, were principally devoted to restating and celebrating the relationship between the king and the gods, by which the natural cosmic order was maintained: to put it simply, the king ensured that the gods received the attention they deserved and needed, and they in return ensured that Egypt was safe and provided for. Hence it was ideologically impossible for anything which contradicted this to be shown; when in the New Kingdom, kings particularly listed their military achievements in temples, nothing other than total victory over the enemy could be described. Similarly, a tomb can be viewed as the deceased's house of eternity in which he presented himself and the milieu in which he lived to this world and to the next. He had to be shown in an ideal fashion, and, if his texts contain anything which appears to be remotely "(auto)biographical" in nature, the reader has to learn to distinguish idealizing generalized expressions from those which might actually reveal something about his life or career; if the text falls into the latter category, his achievements were of greater importance than the manner by which he obtained them. Some such issues relating to the texts of Weni (no. 256) are considered in Eyre 1994; however, it needs to be pointed out now that new discoveries have shown how Weni was himself bending the truth to suit a self-portrait he wanted to project. Eyre's point that Weni is presenting himself as a "self-made man" has been somewhat undermined by the discovery that his father was a vizier (Richards 2002: 90).

The reader should thus be suspicious of taking much of what survives at face value and without question. While this can induce an attitude of extreme cynicism, when judiciously exercised it avoids falling into some of the pitfalls of earlier commentators. Interpretation always brings with it the possibility of misinterpretation, and doubtless we will be equally guilty of making our own errors which will be corrected by a future generation.

4.2 Are the Texts Herein "Literature"?

Defining literature is an issue over which much study and research has been expended in fields far broader than Egyptology (see, for example, Loprieno 1996b; Parkinson 2002: 22–29). However, there is no doubt that the texts which form the subject of this volume are not "literary" in the manner of the stories and instructions which form the (later) core of Egyptian *belles lettres* (compare comments in Gnirs 1996: 192–94; Assmann 1991: 189). That said, many texts come from tomb contexts where their purpose was anything other than factual recounting of events, and thus there is scope for a broader interpretation as literature; Assmann 1996 argues for the literary aspect of the tomb itself, from a later perspective than the Old Kingdom. It has certainly been proposed that a number of Old Kingdom texts fall into the category of "prehistories" of literature (Baines 1999b) or run parallel to literary concepts (Baines 1997: 142).

4.3 Are the Texts in Verse or Prose?

The possibility that Egyptian texts might be written in anything other than prose was first raised seriously in a series of publications by Gerhard Fecht in the 1960s.[29] Fecht's analysis is based on locating an underlying meter, as the texts are not usually written in such a way as to indicate an obvious verse structure. The exception to the latter are the so-called verse points, small red dots found in some New Kingdom papyrus texts (most recently Tacke 2001) but which are now known to go back to at least the late Middle Kingdom (Parkinson 1997: 10). These may mark off certain stress points for recitation, perhaps to help those who did not have the innate sense of spotting the stress in the structure, but they do not always coincide with the suggestions of Fecht. A differing analysis of these texts into "thought couplets," pairs of verse lines, has been proposed by John L. Foster.[30]

Fecht's theories have been accepted by many, sometimes in revised forms,[31] and the more intriguing issue is now the extent to which verse was used in Egyptian texts. Some have argued that the great Egyptian "literary" compositions, such as stories and wisdom literature, were written in verse, others in prose.[32] However, was it used in monumental texts, particularly those which form the principal subject of this volume? At a simplistic level, sometimes the use of a fixed structure, in which a certain phrase is repeated, can be used to argue in favor of it; such a section is seen in the biography of Weni in this volume (no. 256).[33] However, it has been argued that versification can be detected even in rock inscriptions of the Middle Kingdom (Leprohon 2001a; 2002).

Fecht's position on the use of meter in the Old Kingdom is far less explicit when compared with that from the First Intermediate Period onwards, from which date he argues that the system remained largely unchanged for the rest of Egyptian history (Fecht 1965: 21–22; 1993: 82). The clearest mention of his views on the Old Kingdom would appear to be Fecht 1968: 50, where he draws attention to two changes between the Old Kingdom and the First Intermediate Period, noting that the text of Ankhtyfy from Moalla is to be scanned in the earlier style.

Although the last word is far from being written on textual metrics, it cannot be denied that when reading and translating the tomb texts for this volume, the formal and ritual contexts of the tomb texts seem eminently suitable for translation into a verse-like structure that could be recited if needed. The use of blank verse also produces a printed form which distinguishes it from the more earthly structure of administrative texts and which is easier to read on the page than continuous prose and thus is less likely to be skipped over by the reader.[34] Hence I have adopted this form of rendering for most tomb texts and for those from temples, although I have tended not to put lengthy title strings occurring within these texts into such structures, mainly to distinguish them from the rest.

4.4 Old Kingdom Egyptian and Its Characteristics

The first studies of the language which the Egyptian scripts were used to write did not allow for the possibility that it might have had several different phases. As research progressed, however, it soon became clear that it was not homogenous and that the grammar of the hieratic documents was not necessarily the same as that of the hieroglyphs on the monuments. In fact, the form of the language used for monumental hieroglyphic inscriptions changed relatively little after the Middle Kingdom, while the spoken language is more closely reflected in papyrus documents in which far more significant developments can be seen.[35]

The written language of the Old Kingdom, usually called Old Kingdom Egyptian or Old Egyptian, stands near the beginning of this development.[36] The majority of surviving written materials from this period are monumental texts carved in stone, while documents on papyrus, more likely to reflect the language used on an everyday basis, are restricted to administrative texts, legal texts, and a few letters (§§6.4, 6.6, 6.12). Although forms can be recognized in letters which are not seen in the monumental texts, it is nonetheless reasonable to think that the vernacular and monumental forms of Egyptian were closer at this than at any subsequent period. An interesting issue for all periods of the language, and one yet to receive much study, is the extent to which local dialectical variation is reflected in writing (Edel 1955–64: 11–12; Peust 1999: 33–34;[37] one specific example, Roquet 1979). The dialects present in Coptic perhaps hint at the variety which might have existed earlier (compare Loprieno 1995: 40–50; Loprieno 1982).

Old Egyptian is the forerunner of what is always regarded as the classic phase of the Egyptian language, Middle Egyptian. Middle Egyptian is associated very much with the Middle Kingdom, but it also remained the language of monumental inscriptions until the disappearance of hieroglyphs; it is also the form most commonly taught to beginning students.[38] The differences between Old and Middle Egyptian are nowhere near as marked as in the transition between Middle and Late Egyptian (the latter being the vernacular language of the New Kingdom and overwhelmingly found in nonhieroglyphic documents).

This is not the place to characterize Old Kingdom Egyptian in detail, and thus I shall just mention a few salient points, concentrating on those which distinguish it from Middle Egyptian. Although translations of the Pyramid Texts are excluded from this volume, the language they employ is Old Egyptian, and these comments are derived from them as well as the monumental texts. An excellent summary of the characteristics is provided in Edel 1955–64: 8–11.

4.4.1 Phonetics

Twenty-five different basic phonemes are in use in the Old Kingdom, each of which can also be associated with a hieroglyph; see the tables in Gardiner 1957: 27; Loprieno 1995: 15; Allen 2000: 14. These mostly remain unchanged with the exception of *z* and *s*. These two sounds are kept quite distinct in Old Egyptian, but in Middle Egyptian they can be used more or less as interchangeable graphic variants of *s*, and *z* as a separate sound more or less ceased to exist. There is no indication in Old Egyptian of the convergence of *t* and *ṯ* or *d* and *ḏ* which is seen increasingly in Middle and Late Egyptian. There are other less common changes seen in the course of the Old Kingdom, for example, the occasional change of to . The consonants of Old Egyptian are described in Edel 1955–64: 48–66.

This is an appropriate moment to comment on how Egyptian words are presented in this book. No one really knows how ancient Egyptian was pronounced, not helped by the fact that the majority of the vowels and vowel-like sounds were not written. It is conventional in scholarly works to transliterate Egyptian words using romanized versions of these phonemes, complete with various diacritical marks. Thus the verb "to hear" in §4.4.2 is written *sḏm* in scholarly contexts, and the subject of §5.3.1 *imȝḫw*. However, I believe that it is against the spirit of the Writings from the Ancient World series to present words regularly in such a user-unfriendly form, so I employ hypothetical vocalized forms used by most Egyptologists, in these two cases *sedjem* and *imakhu*. The reader should realize that these might bear only limited resemblance to the original pronunciation, if indeed any at all.

4.4.2 Writing

One of the difficulties of any form of the hieroglyphic script for the student is the variable ways in which the same word can be written, often not helped by the need to fit a monumental text into a specified area. Old Egyptian exhibits far more flexibility in written forms than the later stages; in some cases such flexibility can be rather cryptic, but in many other cases more fully written forms are found which have helped in understanding the reading and development of the later phases. As one example, 𓄔𓅓, the normal Middle Egyptian writing of the verb *sedjem* "to hear," can in the Old Kingdom also be written 𓋴𓍑𓄔𓅓, 𓋴𓍑𓄔, 𓋴𓄔𓅓, or 𓋴𓄔.

Egyptian is a language which expresses many of the verbal inflections and also possession by the use of pronouns suffixed to words. Thus "I hear" might be *sedjemi* and "he hears" *sedjemef*, and "my house" *peri* and "his house" *peref*.[39] One characteristic form of Old Egyptian which does not survive long beyond the sixth dynasty (and in fact can sometimes be seen at that date, for example no. 167) is the practice of not writing the indication of the first-person suffix *i*, most commonly written in later times as 𓀀; thus Middle Egyptian 𓄔𓅓𓀀 *sedjemi*, "I hear" would more normally be written just 𓄔𓅓 in Old Egyptian. It is such a common feature that I do not place first-person pronouns thus supplied in parentheses in my translations, although sometimes of course it is not certain whether the suffix is to be understood. The most common example in the translations is perhaps when the owner refers to "this tomb," which could equally be "this tomb of mine." Compare comment below on the omission of 𓀀 in names.

A related graphic arrangement central to Old Kingdom representations is a varying use of a determinative[40] with personal names. In the simplest and most common usage in later periods, the name of a male individual would be followed by the determinative of the seated man ( ) and the name of a female by the hieroglyph of a seated woman ( ); the former of these can be replaced in a funerary context by (at least) , , or . Hence the name Ptahhotep might be written or in the New Kingdom. However, it is normal in Old Kingdom tomb scenes for the name to appear without determinative ( ). The reason for this is to be found in the close relationship between hieroglyphs and Egyptian art, in that names so written are usually accompanied by a large figure of the holder of the name, which serves as the determinative; for the same reason, a statue can be regarded as the determinative to the name in the accompanying inscription. There are some exceptions, but these tend not to relate to the principal figures in the tomb.[41] That this principle applies primarily to tomb scenes can be shown by the general prevalence of determinatives with names in administrative papyri and letters translated in this volume. Whether this practice is in any way related with the omission of the suffix *i* observed above is uncertain.

One characteristic graphic form of Old Egyptian is the writing of the plural. In Middle Egyptian, it is normally indicated with three strokes, horizontal or vertical, ııı or ⁝ , but earlier it is most commonly achieved by three repetitions of the determinative of the word. Thus the word *seru* "officials" might be in Middle Egyptian and in Old Egyptian. Egyptian also possessed a "dual" form, indicating two of something and usually expressed by a doubling of the determinative (a common example is *peruy,* "the two houses"). This is more common in Old than Middle Egyptian, and certain dual forms of Old Egyptian are not subsequently found or are used later mainly to give a spurious impression of antiquity.

4.4.3 Grammar

Negation is one area of Old Egyptian where differences can be seen from Middle Egyptian. This is not the place to explain the complex issues of negation in ancient Egyptian, but let it suffice to say that there are two basic forms common in both phases of the language, the use of groups read *n* ( ) or *nen* ( ), and the so-called negative verb *tem* ( ). A writing of the former as *ny* ( ) appears in Old Egyptian, which also has two further not uncommon negations *w* ( ) and *nefer n* ( ); each tends to have specific usages. is more or less unheard of in Middle Egyptian, while appears only in archaic phrases, and the role it fulfilled tends to be taken later by . These latter two, particularly , can be very troubling to those new to texts of the Pyramid Age.

There are a number of changes in the narrative verbal system from Old to Middle Egyptian. As these are mostly too detailed for the present volume, the reader is referred to Doret 1986: 181–87. Changes in the use of the dual have been noted in §4.4.2, and a number of particles and other words which do not survive into Middle Egyptian are mentioned in Edel 1955–64: 9–10.

4.5 Scripts

Like the language which they write, Egyptian scripts are complex. Two principal forms only need concern the reader of this volume. The majority of texts come from monuments in stone, on which it was customary to use the full hieroglyphic writing system. These were the "god's words" and were to survive for perpetuity, usually on stone but sometimes carved in wood. The earliest hieroglyphs from Egypt are now thought to date to at least 3400 B.C. and are the earliest written forms in the world.[42]

However, for the majority of daily and official documents, a more cursive script was employed, which wrote the same language rapidly and in a more cursive manner, as befits pen or brush and ink on (typically) papyrus rather than the sculptor's chisel on stone. This script is known as hieratic, and, in its various phases, it was the writing of daily life from at least 3000 B.C. until the mid-first millennium B.C., when it gave way to an even more cursive script we term demotic. The oldest hieratic is known from pot inscriptions before the first dynasty; originally derived from hieroglyphs, it soon developed its own forms. It is the script normally used for writing documents on papyrus, such as letters and the administrative documents from Gebelein and Abusir. It is also found on labels and (with a larger brush and usually in red) on stones for use in building work. A summary of Old Kingdom hieratic may be found in Goedicke 1988a.

5. Particular Points of Translation

Translating Ancient Egyptian, which we still understand imperfectly, into a modern language with totally different structures is a challenge, and it is all too easy to fall into producing a translation which makes it clear for one's academic colleagues how the text has been understood but which is stilted and off-putting to the general reader. The aim of Writings from the Ancient World is to produce clear readable English, and this is without doubt the greatest challenge of this volume. Thus where there is a clear conflict between reflecting the precise nuances of the original and making it comprehensible, I have mostly not hesitated to choose the latter.

In general, any individual problems with translations are noted with the text, but a number of general points of a longer nature which apply to all texts are worth making here.

5.1 Grammar

5.1.1 Second Tenses

Our comprehension of Egyptian grammar is constantly evolving and changing, and there is still no one fully accepted approach. The major points of controversy have always resided with the verb. For many years, Egyptian verbs were treated in a manner broadly similar to the verbs of Indo-European languages and translated in a similar manner. Then in a series of studies commencing in 1944, H. J. Polotsky proposed a theory in which what we consider verbs were largely to be understood as either nouns, adjectives, or adverbs and were made into what we might consider finite verbs by a series of "transformations" or "transpositions."[43] This is not the place to describe this, but the part of the theory which particularly affects the translator is the so-called second tense or emphatic form, in which the verbal form throws the stress of the sentence on an adverbial phrase. Polotsky proposed that such forms be translated by a "cleft sentence"; thus, using an example from the biography of Nekhebu (no. 198),

which had for many years been translated as "his majesty favored me because of it in the presence of the officials," can be rendered as "it was *in the presence of the officials* that his majesty favored me because of it," the italicized phrase being the stressed one. This may have done much for revising our understanding of Egyptian, but it did nothing for elegant translation. One particular problem is that the cleft sentence is more at home in some languages than others; it sits much better with French than English, for example. Judicious use of adverbs or adverbial phrases in the text can help avoid this. Hence I translate this example rather freely as "his majesty favored me for it right in the presence of the officials"; the word "right" is added to try and place the stress in the correct place.

I have not tried to indicate every such second tense in the text but have translated them judiciously, doing so where a stress can be made without making the English seem unnatural.[44] I realize that this leaves me open to a charge of inconsistency. However, it must be pointed out that the "standard theory" has itself been undergoing reevaluation in the 1990s, and the move at present is at least some way back in the direction of the good old-fashioned verb, although there are at present no straightforward descriptions to which the reader can be referred.[45]

5.1.2 The Infinitive

A distinctive method in ancient Egyptian of introducing a descriptive or narrative event is to begin a sentence with the infinitive form of the verb (Edel 1955–64: 344–61; Loprieno 1995: 88–89; Allen 2000: 159–74). The Egyptian infinitive is neutral in respect to tense, aspect, and voice; examples of such a use here include captions to larger tomb scenes (for example, no. 303) as well as in parts of funerary formulae (for example, no. 126). Although it is not exactly idiomatic English I have generally followed the Egyptian structure and translated such phrases as "Watching . . . by <the tomb owner>" or "Crossing the heaven so perfectly in peace" rather than completely recasting such sentences as "<the tomb owner> watches . . ." or "May he cross. . . ."

5.2 Titles

As so many texts of the Pyramid Age come from tombs, in which the personality of the owner is the most important feature, it is inevitable that titles figure prominently. The subject of Egyptian titles of the Old Kingdom is complex, and the sequences are rather long in some cases, but it has been felt that it better gives the feeling of the original text if the titles are not omitted and thus I translate them where possible.[46] Egyptian titles tend to appear in strings, sometimes quite lengthy ones in tombs and commemorative inscriptions, with the name of the holder at the end; in administrative contexts usually only one title is found plus the name. The following paragraphs offer some comments on the more important groupings of titles.

5.2.1 Honorific titles

It is conventional to divide Old Kingdom titles into two main groups, those expressive principally of rank or status, usually termed "honorific titles," and those which appear to relate to actual administrative functions. The border between these two is often blurred, not helped by our imperfect understanding of the titles themselves—there is precious little evidence available for the functions of most of them, especially the higher that one looks in the social structure of Egypt.

As a general rule in a title sequence, the honorific titles come first, indicating the owner's place in the social and courtly hierarchy, followed by the administrative ones. Comparison of the honorific titles with the various titles of nobility in Britain is instructive, where "duke," "lord," and so on indicated not just social status but also standing at court. The meaning of many of the honorific titles is very uncertain, but it should always be remembered that many (perhaps all) may originally have indicated some specific function at the royal court and may indeed have continued to do so—the lack of courtly records makes it difficult to understand. To make a further comparison with titles still in use in Britain, I note first the office of "Black Rod," the official who is responsible for running the House of Lords; second, examination of the titles of the British royal heralds, a group of offices which go back to the fifteenth century A.D., reveals the existence of titles still held today with such exquisite names as "Garter Principal King of Arms," "Rouge Dragon Pursuivant," or "Bluemantle Pursuivant."[47] With these in mind such Egyptian honorific titles as "Staff of Nekhen" or "Administrator of (the vineyard) Horus is the star at the top of heaven" are perhaps more comprehensible, or at least sound less odd!

Two of the most common titles require brief explanations: *iry pat* , also read *ra pat,* is sometimes translated "hereditary noble," although this translation does not convey the full meaning. The word *pat* expressed nobility as a religious or mythological concept rather than indicating any social class within the administration, and its counterpart for the ordinary people was *rekhyt.*[48] *iry pat* thus means either "concerned with the *pat*" or (read *ra pat*) "mouth of the *pat*"; either way it expresses the most senior noble rank and usually appears first in a title sequence. It is occasionally applied to women.

The title *haty-a* is also difficult to translate in a way to make its significance clear. Literally perhaps "foremost of arm," translations vary from the very European "Count" to the Arabic "Omda." It usually follows *iry pat* as the second highest of the common honorific titles, but its significance is not really understood. While in later periods it remains an honorific title, it is also often combined with the name of a town and understood as "mayor."

The difficulty of translating both *iry pat* and *haty-a* means that I have decided to leave them in these italicized forms in the text. Another difficult honorific title is , applied to both men and women. I have followed the older style of understanding as "royal acquaintance," *rekh-nesut* (Baud 1999a: 107–13), but a case can be made for the meaning "property custodian of the king" (*iry-khet nesut,* most recently Bárta 1999).

5.2.2 Administrative Titles

In general, more is known about the meaning of administrative titles. There seem to have been one or two men at the head of the administration, to whom it has become conventional to give the Ottoman appellation "vizier" (Egyptian , *tayty zab tjaty*). Ranged under him were a group of great state offices, the principal of which dealt with the logistics of organizing work, finances, food supply, the bureaucracy itself, and legal matters (Strudwick 1985). A range of subordinate offices can be seen for most of these, although it does seem clear that in Egypt in general there was a relatively limited number of regular set titles; rather, it appears that a number of offices were created to suit individual situations and individual people. Although Egypt is credited with creating the concept of bureaucracy, readers should be wary of making too many comparisons with modern systems; it should never be forgotten that the power of the king was absolute and the path to high office was as much due to one's standing with him as birth or ability.

Most administrative titles are reasonably clear in their meaning. One which, however, is not is that which I give in the text by its Egyptian name, *khenty-she* (Roth 1988–91; Roth 1995: 40–43; Posener-Kriéger 1976: 577–81; Andrassy 1994; Baud 1996; Andrassy 2001). This title appears in numerous contexts. For example, viziers and other senior officials can be *khenty-she* of the royal pyramid, while lesser tomb-owning officials can be *khenty-she* of the Great House. Further, *khenty-she* of very lowly status, who would never have had the inscribed tombs which so much concern us in this volume, also appear in various administrative documents, for example, as dependents of various institutions in the Royal Decrees (§6.3.2) and also carrying out duties in the temples covered by the Abusir Papyri (§6.4). Finding a meaning for the title which encompasses all these functions is difficult—translations used include "tenant," "guard," and "attendant" (compare Jones 2000: 691–94)—but one common denominator seems to have been service on the king. Thus while the lower *khenty-she* would actually have served in royal establishments, the duties of those of the vizier class would have been largely ceremonial, and conferment of the title would also have brought some extra income as with the priestly titles discussed below.

5.2.3 Priestly Titles

I place these in a separate category as these are not necessarily what they seem. In the title strings of many officials are found offices such as "priest of (king) N" or "priest of the pyramid of (king) N," or "priest of Re in [solar temple name of a specific king]." These priests are thus almost always attached to an aspect of the mortuary cult of a king or to his sun temple (fifth dynasty only), and we are fortunate enough to have parts of the administrative archives of two of these temple complexes at Abusir (the Abusir Papyri, §6.4), which also, incidentally, show that the solar temples were very much bound up in the economies of the royal mortuary complexes.

Examination of these archives show many individuals working within the temples, and yet it is immediately apparent that these people are not the same as those bearing the titles "priest of <king whose temple it was>" and the like in their tombs. What then was the association of the higher officials with the temple? It is of course possible that they were high officials in the priestly caste or the administration of the temple, but more likely is that such titles indicated that the holder was in receipt of a benefice from the king which brought a share of income from that particular institution, without necessarily specifying what, if any, function they had to perform (Posener-Kriéger 1976: 576–77). One suspects that one of the reasons for the multiplicity of titles exhibited by many officials was that each of them brought some income and thus were indicative of his wealth and importance.

Titles of priests of individual deities are relatively few in number. One apparent such title, "priest of Maat," is found almost exclusively in the titles of legal officials, and thus is probably more concerned with the execution of the concept of Maat than necessarily with a specific cult of that deity. Two titles which are usually taken as indicating high priests of specific cults are "Great Controller of Craftsmen" and "Great Seer of Heliopolis," the cults being those of Ptah and Re respectively.[49] We know next to nothing about the roles of these individuals, not even whether these were primarily a financial sinecure like the other titles, although the "Great Controller of Craftsmen" (one or two in number) is seen involved in the procurement of tombs and architectural elements in two texts in this volume (Debehen [no. 200] and Nyankhsekhmet [no. 225]). Lastly, the title "overseer of priests" in the provinces was usually a mark of one of the senior administrators of a nome, as well as any religious functions it may have encompassed.

5.2.4 "King's Son" or "King's Daughter"

The title of "king's son" or "king's daughter" is not in the Old Kingdom simply confined to offspring of rulers. Rather, it seems also to have become yet another honorific title granted to certain important individuals, and this usage is recognized in the language by addition of the suffix "bodily" in many cases. This might refer more accurately to true offspring of the king, but even this can be challenged.[50] For example, Inti (no. 285) is called "eldest king's daughter of his body" of the pyramids of both Teti and Pepy I. The mention of the pyramids may well indicate her principal sources of provision; she was perhaps a daughter of Teti and was accorded considerable prominence under her brother Pepy I and thus bore one title in an honorific manner (Callender 2002a).

5.3 Other Issues

5.3.1 imakhu

One of the most difficult words to treat in tomb texts is *imakhu* (, feminine *imakhut* , is probably the commonest writing; from the late Old Kingdom the form changes to *imakhy*). A typical usage is that a person is *imakhu kher* ( ) someone; I translate *kher* as "in the sight of," "before," or "in relation to." That person could be a god, a king, or even another individual, such as of a wife to her husband. Older styles of translations tend to express this relationship between the parties as "honored one" or "revered one," as this seemed to fit the context, for example, "honored one in the sight of the king," and indeed it may have this meaning from the Middle Kingdom onwards. Helck, however, pointed out that examination of examples from the Old Kingdom showed that it was of an overwhelmingly practical nature, indicating that the subject would be "provided for" by the other. This in particular refers to funeral provisions, above all the supply of goods and foodstuffs.[51] This emphasizes and brings firmly into focus the importance of patronage and personal associations in Egypt in relation to basic economic functions; the patron need not be alive but only to have an establishment still operating which could provide for his dependents. There are also hints that a man's state of *imakhu* could potentially be compromised by some incorrect actions: "[Never] did I abuse my authority over anyone, as I desire that my name be perfect in the sight of the Great God and that my state of *imakhu* exist in the sight of all men" (no. 216).

Thus the term "honored one" gives completely the wrong idea for texts of the Old Kingdom, but "(s)he who has been provided for" hardly trips off the tongue. The solution adopted is to use *imakhu* in the translation.[52]

5.3.2 hem

Egyptian texts of all periods refer to the king using the word 𓄓𓏺, *hem*, as in "Then his (= the king's) *hem* did (something or other)" or "My *hem* has ordered (something or other)." It has always been traditional in English to translate this term as "majesty," in the manner used of referring to British royalty in formal documents. However, Egyptian royal terms are complex and relatively specific in their usage, and *hem* does not refer to the majestic element of the king but rather to his physical presence, his "person" or "incarnation" (Goedicke 1960a: 51–68; Baines 1995: 132). This has unfortunately led to translations of the form "*his person/incarnation* did (something or other)," which sounds rather alien in a book claiming to present translations in readable English. Since this is also a formal term of address, there seems to be no better-sounding substitute than the old term "majesty" adopted in this book.[53]

5.3.3 The Offering Formula

Few funerary monuments do not include one or more offering formulae beginning 𓇓𓊵𓏏𓊪𓂞, *hetep di nesut*, "an offering which the king gives"[54] (see Gardiner 1957: 170–73 and Leprohon 2001c for an introduction to this). These formulae usually consist of two major parts: the first names those who are to give what is referred to in the second part of the formula, usually the king (never further specified) and other gods, and the second part consists of a description of what is wished for as a result of making the offering formula. The latter can take the form of physical offerings or wishes for certain things to happen on passing into the next world.

The formula suggests that the king theoretically could (or originally did) monopolize the giving of offerings to private cults; it may even have gone so far as to indicate the permission of the king for the tomb to be in the necropolis.[55] The nature of the relationship between the king and the gods named in the first part of the formula is disputed. Some believe that the "offering which the king gives" is given to the gods named, so that they then give the benefits of the second part to the deceased person. The other view holds that it is both the king *and* the other gods who make the offering and that together they give the benefits of the second part. I have opted here for the second of these two translations, on the grounds that the verb "give" is often repeated after the divine names. It is, however, likely that the first interpretation became the preferred one from the end of the Old Kingdom (Leprohon 1990).

The most consistently wished-for item in the second part of the formula is for "invocation offerings" 𓉐𓏏𓊃𓏤, *peret-kheru* and variations thereon.

The phrase so translated literally means something like "the going forth of the voice": in other words, that someone may speak the standard offering formula for the tomb owner. The basic items are bread, beer, oxen, and fowl, plus alabaster (jars) and (items of) clothing. The objects given usually come in thousands. To save a few words, I have opted for the traditional translation of "a thousand of bread, a thousand of alabaster" and so on, rather than the fuller "a thousand (loaves of) bread, a thousand (vessels) of alabaster." The wish that offerings be made on the occasions of major festivals, plus the catch-all of "every daily festival," is also very common.[56]

The other possible phrases in this part of the formula are very numerous and include wishes for burial and successful passage into the next world, to note but two of them, but there are many unusual phrases. For example, two of the most common are "that he be buried in the perfect West, having grown old perfectly," and "that he may travel on the perfect ways of the West upon which the *imakhu* travel." Among the more intriguing ones is "that he may receive his document," almost suggesting the existence of a bureaucracy of the next world. These phrases may be understood either as dependent on the offerings in the first part or as separate wishes for the deceased; I do not pretend to have been consistent in translating this relationship.

The texts in this book show how the phrases develop in the course of the Old Kingdom; they become even more varied in the Middle and New Kingdoms, and sizeable scholarly studies have been devoted to them (Barta 1968; Lapp 1986). There are many examples translated herein. I trust that the frequency of such formulae in this book gives the impression of their ubiquity in tombs, without trying the patience of the reader.

5.3.4 Egyptian Nomes

It is conventional within Egyptology to refer to the various ancient provinces by the term "nome," from the Greek νόμος. Upper and Lower Egypt were both divided into twenty-two such provinces, the boundaries of which varied somewhat over time.[57] The first nome of Upper Egypt was in the south, and the (modern) numbering runs north; sometimes the east and west banks of the Nile were parts of different nomes, but the ordering of the Lower Egyptian nomes is not so easy, and in fact they appear in different orders in some lists. The extent of some nomes changed and became more fixed in the course of the Old Kingdom. One such example is the "Eastern" nome, which we number the fourteenth nome of Lower Egypt, but which seems to have had a "northern" and "southern" part in the earlier part of the Old Kingdom (compare no. 111 and comments in Jacquet-Gordon 1962: 109–11 and Helck 1974a: 187–88).

Each nome was named in ancient times rather than numbered, and the suffix "of Upper/Lower Egypt" is a modern addition, but the reading of the names of some of these provinces is not certain.[58] For the sake of the reader it has been decided mostly to translate references in texts in the form "the n-th nome of Lower/Upper Egypt" rather than a transcription of the Egyptian name, so as better to enable the reader to locate the province in question; occasionally, to improve clarity, the name of the principal city is included if likely to be understood by the reader and significant to the text. An exception to this is in number 31, the only complete list of Upper Egyptian nomes in this book, where the opportunity has been taken to give all the probable names and some indication of the approximate modern location.

5.3.5 Pyramid Names

A similar issue to that of naming the nomes is found with the names of royal pyramids. Most constructions concerned with a king had special names compounded with the royal name,[59] and the pyramids are the best examples of this. These names can be left in a transliterated form or translated: for example, the Great Pyramid at Giza is named *akhet Khufu,* "the horizon of Khufu." For the sake of simplicity in the translations, I have used rather the circumlocution "the pyramid of Khufu" and given the full translated names of the pyramids in the Chronological Table on page xxvii; I have left the cartouche the same as that used in the text, with the addition of "I" or "II" where the name is that of Pepy. It should be noted that it became common from the end of the fifth dynasty often to refer to kings by the names of their pyramids (Kuhlmann 1982), found here for example in a number of the texts of queens of that date.

6. Principal Types of Text Translated in This Volume

The following is an outline survey of the texts translated in this volume, with notes on broader issues than can be accommodated within the comments on each text. However, the more detailed studies noted should be consulted wherever possible.

Readers should bear the remarks above under "The Importance of Context" (§4.1) in mind when considering these different groups. Many texts can be fitted into more than one category, and these notes analyze the types of text more closely than is possible in the groupings used in the translations.

6.1 Historiographic Texts

Throughout Egyptian history, let alone the Old Kingdom, there are relatively few texts which can be regarded as straightforwardly historical in nature, insofar as the concept of history to most readers is that prevalent in the Western world. Egyptian history is reconstructed using a mixture of archaeological and incidental textual evidence; the ancient near contemporary historical narrative of a Thucydides, Livy, or Bede hardly exists for the land of the Nile. The nearest are the writings of Manetho, composed in Greek by an Egyptian priest in the third century B.C., and which have survived only in extracts reproduced by other ancient writers, such as Josephus and Africanus. This text is primarily a list of kings with the occasional narrative section, but is of immense historical importance to Egyptology as it is there that the basic system of dynasties originates and because so much has been founded on it (see Redford 1986, especially 203–332).

Two annalistic texts exist for the Old Kingdom which purport to present a year-by-year account of some aspects of the surviving reigns (the Palermo Stone, no. 1, and the much-damaged sixth-dynasty annals from Saqqara, no. 3). These records tend to concentrate on relating religious events such as the creation of statues, divine boats, and so on and only occasionally mention something of a (to our eyes) broadly historical nature; the fact they were inscribed in stone, and thus set up most likely in a temple, should also encourage the reader to consider them in contexts where confirming relationships with the gods was more important than simple historical fact. The manner in which the original documents pertaining to these annals were stored is perhaps revealed by parts of third-dynasty pots found at Elephantine, which may have each contained papyrus records for a specific year (no. 2).

Most of the known lists of kings are later in date, and the most relevant of these are the Royal Canon of Turin and the Abydos list, both of the New Kingdom.[60] The Turin Canon, a papyrus of the Ramesside period, provides a basic structure with reign lengths for the Old Kingdom and is broadly supported by the Abydos list, in the temple of Sety I; the latter is particularly important as it gives the names of rulers who must be of the seventh and eighth dynasties, although its temple context should never be overlooked, since its main purpose was to stress the legitimacy of Sety, who is shown offering to his predecessors. Hence such a king list is as important for what it reveals about the official attitude to history as what it says about the names of the kings (compare n. 14 above). Some short king lists have been found in Old Kingdom tombs (nos. 5, 6), but their purpose is not to impart history but to emphasize the number of kings under whom the deceased was rewarded or honored, and hence stress his importance.

For other texts of historical import one has to comb through the different types of inscriptions in this book to discern material of interest. This is of course the staple of historical research, and, given how context can affect a source (§4.1), it must always be controlled by reference to other material remains and archaeological sources.

6.2 Temple Texts

Compared with the great mass of inscriptions from temples from the New Kingdom on, and particularly those from the Greco-Roman period, there is little material from the Old Kingdom. As in the Middle and New Kingdoms, there were two principal groups of temples, those of the cults of the major deities and those of the mortuary and solar cults of the kings themselves. Little of the former from the Old Kingdom has survived: the state temples are assumed to have been built mainly of brick, with limited use of stone,[61] while stone was overwhelmingly reserved in temple construction for the monuments of a mortuary nature; for the present purpose, the solar temples of the fifth dynasty can be regarded as almost an extension of the mortuary complex, and the close economic interdependence of solar and mortuary temples is clear from the Abusir papyri. Doubtless the choice of stone had much to do with the permanence with which such structures were viewed at the time. Kings might expect to renew the state temples periodically for an ongoing cult, but they would want their funerary monuments to last forever from the start and thus built them accordingly.

Very little is thus known of the decorative and textual program of temples in the first category; the texts of Netjerykhet Djoser from Heliopolis (no. 7) are perhaps something of an exception, although, as they are of stone, one is compelled to wonder whether they too originated in a temple dedicated to the cult of the king for perpetuity rather than "just" that of the sun god. However, whatever their origin, they show temple motifs and texts well developed by 2690 B.C. Doubtless blocks from other state temples of the Old Kingdom lie buried under or in later temples or were quarried for use elsewhere; for example, the evident interest of Pepy I in the cult of Hathor of Dendera is surely indicative of his having built more than just a soul chapel at the site.[62] On the subject of soul chapels, important parts of two have survived from Bubastis (no. 13); mention of a number of others will be found in Fischer 1958b.

Far more survives from the mortuary and solar temples. Quarrying and time have taken their toll, but some substantial parts of the mortuary temples of Netjerykhet Djoser (no. 7), Sahure (no. 10), and Pepy II have survived, as have parts of the solar temple of Niuserre (no. 11, plus the "Room of the Seasons" [Edel and Wenig 1974] and the *Sed* festival reliefs [Kaiser 1971]). The homogeneity of these texts is astonishing; traces of the standard phrases for the next three thousand years can be seen at the beginning of the third dynasty, and basic scenes which we see clearly in the temple of Sahure repeat themselves through the Old Kingdom and well beyond; I think particularly of the images of smiting enemies, first seen on ivory and wooden labels of the first dynasty and in stone from the fifth dynasty (at least) until the Roman period. Nonetheless, changes can be detected in the decorative content and religious stress between the scenes of Sahure and Pepy II, leading to an increased sacralization in the latter (Baines 1997: 145–52).

6.3 Inscriptions Set Up by or on Behalf of Kings

6.3.1 Rock Inscriptions

From early in their history Egyptians kings sent expeditions abroad in search of raw materials and other resources to maintain and enhance their culture. Quarries at sites like Aswan and Toshka in Nubia were exploited for hard stones like granite and diorite, the Wadi Hammamat for its greywacke, and Hatnub for its Egyptian alabaster, while the Sinai was a source of turquoise and copper. It became customary to leave inscriptions on the rocks in some of these places. In the Old Kingdom they often took the form of a largish relief of the king shown dominating over (often smiting) the non-Egyptian population which lived in that area, accompanied by simple texts and occasionally a date. These inscriptions range from at least the third dynasty to the end of the Old Kingdom, illustrate the power of Egypt at that time, and were doubtless intended to remain as a reminder of this for the local population.

From the later Old Kingdom the royal inscription is often accompanied by a record of the expedition itself (§6.10). It is improbable that the king accompanied most of these missions, but a number of inscriptions on the rocks in the area of the First Cataract, from the island of Elephantine southwards, might attest actual journeys by the king to his boundaries or formal ceremonies at his boundaries when he was on a military expedition (nos. 50, 51, 52), although they could equally be a statement of the royal role. A number of inscriptions relate to the royal *Sed* festival and will be found scattered among the rock inscriptions of kings, particularly Pepy I and II.

These texts provide incidental information such as dates and, very occasionally, details of why the expedition was there. Most are, however, accompanied by general expressions which outline the role of the king, such as "smiting of the Bedouin," rather than referring to any specific historical event.

It should of course be noted that there are references to visits abroad which do not have corresponding expedition inscriptions. These include references to such exotic places as Byblos and Punt (nos. 1, 241, 245).

6.3.2 Royal Decrees

The royal decrees of the Old Kingdom are a group of remarkable sources on the organization and administration of various institutions. There can be little doubt that they are copies of original administrative documents on papyrus set up in stone within the institution concerned, not least as the texts themselves tell us this (for example, Koptos B, no. 24). Indeed, fragments of documents in the same style have been noted among the Abusir Papyri from the pyramid temple of Neferefre (no. 18). The requirement for the surviving copies can be explained by the need to set down literally "in stone" that which had been decreed for the institution in question. In these cases the caution expressed above about temple context should not be applied too rigorously.

It would appear that royal decrees were one of the main systems by which orders of state, actually or nominally from the king, were passed on to officials. The issuing of decrees is mentioned both within the royal decrees themselves (nos. 24, 25, 26) and also in some of the biographical texts (nos. 200, 212, 232, 243, 267). These cover varied topics such as instructions, duties, and, of course in the tomb context, rewards.

The layout and structure of one of the royal decrees is presented together with its translation (no. 17). These texts are complex documents, very compactly written, and often with an ambiguous structure (Helck 1974b: 10–26; Goedicke 1964; 1967a; Hays 2000). Understanding the context of some phrases can be difficult, as (presumably to save space) they are often written once and then have to be understood as working with several relevant clauses subsequently presented. The reader will appreciate the potential level of difficulty with these texts if the not uncommon failure of comprehension of our own modern administrative documents is kept in mind; how much more trouble are we likely to have with an administrative system only understood at a very superficial level? One challenge of translating these texts is the extent to which this very compact structure should be reproduced or the key phrases repeated to make the text more comprehensible; I have adopted both solutions at times.

The decrees are of a number of types. They show, for example, the appointment of officials (no. 35); the setting up of a royal foundation for a specific purpose, such as the funerary offerings of the king's mother Iput at Koptos (by Pepy I, no. 21) or an estate for Pepy II in Koptos (no. 26); the establishment of a chapel for a governor (no. 28); or else the exemption of various temple dependents and lands from taxes or compulsory duties (such as the Dahshur Decree of Pepy I, no. 20). Exemptions also form a significant part of the decrees setting up new establishments. From the latter it seems right to deduce that major institutions such as temples and their associated lands and staff were not automatically free of an obligation to pay taxes to the state or immune from having their employees taken away for compulsory corvée labor and other tasks. Such a deduction is supported by statements such as that in the biography of Harkhuf that supplies were to be provided for him from storerooms and temples which were not exempt when he was bringing the famous pygmy back to the Residence (no. 241).

The issue of just how many temples were so exempted is intriguing, but little is known about Old Kingdom temples other than mortuary temples and chapels for the royal *ka* spirits (see §6.2). The extant exemptions apply to the various temples at Koptos, to some of the royal mortuary foundations in the Memphite area, and to temples at Abydos. Perhaps it is not unrealistic to assume that most temples of the royal cult were likely to have had such exemption decrees, as were other ones where the king had, or wanted to cultivate, a particular association. Given the general poor state of preservation of most temple sites, surely more must originally have existed. The preservation of a group of decrees from Koptos, reused as later building material, is particularly fortunate as it has enabled wider study of this genre of text over the period from the reign of Pepy I to the end of the eighth dynasty.

There is a particular concentration of decrees bearing the names of Neferkauhor, one of the last kings of the Old Kingdom, all of which with surviving dates appear to have been sealed on the second month of the *Peret* season day 20; from one (Koptos P, no. 38) this appears to have been in the first year of the king's reign. This is extremely significant, as this is apparently the new king asserting his authority in the city, and several of the documents are concerned with the appointments of the officials Shemay and Idi to posts, whom we know to have been there since the time of Pepy II; it is perhaps not unreasonable to speculate that such (re)appointments or promotions were, given the system of patronage on which the Egyptian administration was founded (compare Strudwick 1985: 342–44), a feature of many if not all royal accessions. The same official, the sole companion Inyotef son of Hemi, was sent along by the king (presumably) to see to the execution of each of these decrees.

Such documents have survived only from Koptos. While it is interesting to speculate whether Neferkauhor's cultivation of a powerful local family of Koptos may have much to do with the weakened state of kingship in Upper Egypt (Hayes 1946: 21–23), I find it hard to believe that these decrees were unique. Rather, we have benefited from a chance survival at Koptos. Also from Koptos, and here placed with some uncertainty at the end of the royal decrees, are two texts which may be cult inventories and which may also be of royal or private origin (no. 40).

Certain of the decrees illustrate the longevity of some cults. For example, the Dahshur decree of Pepy I is for the pyramid city of Sneferu, who died some three hundred years earlier, while there is a decree of Pepy II for the cult of Menkaure (at a similar distance in time).[63] See also comments below about the cults in the Abusir papyri (§6.4).

6.4 State Administrative Texts

Administrative texts of the Old Kingdom are restricted almost totally to those from Abusir. Those which exist were written on papyrus (summary in Posener-Kriéger 1973–74), a material which does not survive except in dry conditions, and it is no coincidence that these examples come from desert contexts.

The Abusir finds come from two of the mortuary temples of the kings of the fifth dynasty. The first and largest find of papyri relates to the mortuary temple of Neferirkare (ca. 2483–2463 B.C.). Most were found in 1893, as a result of illicit excavations at the pyramid by local inhabitants, although a few fragments were found in the subsequent German excavations by

Borchardt in the area. Most papyri found their way to the Cairo Museum and major museums in Europe. The Neferirkare papyri are comprehensively presented and studied in Posener-Kriéger and de Cenival 1968 and Posener-Kriéger 1976.

These documents date from the mid-fifth to the mid-sixth dynasty, with most belonging to the end of the fifth,[64] and show that the temple complexes to which they relate continued to operate for more than a century. They are our main source relating to all aspects of the management of the cult of the king during the Old Kingdom. They paint a complex picture of duty rosters, lists of offerings, and accounts, as well as letters, passes, and other documents, and show that the mortuary temple of Neferirkare was actually part of a larger economic complex which included that ruler's sun temple and also other institutions.[65] Goods, the income of the cults, were moved backward and forward between these different institutions to supply their various needs. A large number of lowly officials who worked in these temples appear in the text, together with the occasional higher official whose funerary offerings probably depended in some part on his relationship with the temples (see also §5.2.3).

More such material has recently come to light. The Czech team working at Abusir discovered further papyri in the temple of Neferirkare's wife Khentkawes and then in the temple of Neferirkare's short-lived successor Neferefre.[66] While not as numerous as the earlier discoveries, these documents contain a number of useful texts which in particular clarify some points unclear in the Neferirkare papyri. These newer discoveries are substantially similar to the older ones and attest a considerable degree of homogeneity across the archives.

6.5 Texts from the Tombs of Officials

The reader should compare comments at the beginning of §6 about the possibility that a text may fit into many different categories. A very simple index attempts to help the reader access texts which fit into more than one type. Note in particular that many of the legal texts in §6.6 come from tombs.

6.5.1 Standard Formulaic Inscriptions in Tombs

These fall into several groups, and elements can appear in conjunction with offering formulae as well as with biographical texts, plus those in §6.8. My terms for these groups are in italics.

The most ubiquitous is the essential prayer for offerings, the *hetep di nesut* formula, with its range of possible component phrases; this has been noted above (§5.3.3). Another category is usually termed the *appeal to the living,* normally beginning "O you who live on earth . . ." (Sainte Fare Garnot 1938). If these latter texts are to be believed, the tomb owners hoped that visitors to a cemetery would leave some offerings in the tomb for their spirits, or at least say a prayer that offerings be made—which presumably had the same effect. Similar exhortations are made to the priests whose job it was to care for the tomb and the spirits who resided in it, in particular the lector priests. A most unusual example of this text type is that of Shemay in the Wadi Hammamat (no. 66), where reciting an offering prayer to Shemay is said to guarantee successful return home to the traveler who finds the inscription.

More often than not these appeals are accompanied by *warnings to robbers and the impure,* although they can exist independently. These expressions forbid, sometime backed up by threats,[67] damage to the tomb or entry to those who are in some sort of impure state. The latter impurities are usually not always indicated, but it is clear that a major concern was the consumption of taboo foods before entry; doing any of the things mentioned would reduce the effectiveness of the tomb as a home for the owner's spirits, thus thereby contradicting Maat, and it is thus hardly surprising that the spirits would want redress. It is these threats, characteristic of the Old Kingdom, which might be at the origin of the concept of the "mummy's curse," so favored by Hollywood. The most graphic is "I shall seize his neck like a bird's," and the formula usually ends with the announcement that the deceased will be judged with the evildoer in the court of the Great God (most likely the sun god or Osiris, but perhaps sometimes even the king).

6.5.2 More Unusual Types of Text in Tombs, Other Than Biographies

A small but significant group of *payment texts* tell us in a few words that the tomb owner built his tomb with his own means, or paid off his craftsmen, who are always said to be satisfied with what was done for them. These texts raise interesting questions as to how one came by a tomb in the Old Kingdom. Did a man pay for it himself, or did the king (or a noble) provide it indirectly through his employment or payment to the owner (compare discussion of *imakhu* in §5.3.1; see Eyre 1987: 24–25)? These texts come more often than not from the (small) tombs of less elevated officials, and so they could be interpreted as saying that theirs was the exceptional route to a tomb or perhaps that they would not normally have been among those able to have such a construction.

Not infrequent are brief inscriptions which were put up by others as *commemorations* of the deceased. These most usually take the form of a text by a son or spouse indicating that they built or finished the monument for the deceased after the latter had died. Most are quite short and are often accommodated on one column of a doorway or one element of a false door. The longest (hence somewhat exceptional) and best known is that of Senedjemib Mehi, who completed his father Inti's tomb while the latter lay in the embalming workshop (no. 232). The irregular appearance of such texts again surely implies that the situation to which they refer is not the normal one and that it was usual to have one's tomb in place at death. I am of the opinion, however, that the Egyptians tended for the most part to postpone the construction of their tombs until they felt themselves to be in the financial or social position which enabled them to have the best possible place of burial; compare comments in Strudwick 1985: 343. Other changes in tombs relating to expansion after further promotion have since come to light; I think particularly of the tomb of Mehu (no. 220).

There is a small group of texts from *sarcophagi* of the sixth dynasty which appeal to the good nature of those setting the lid in place to do it well so that things will go well with them. These seem to have appeared only in tombs in the Teti pyramid cemetery at Saqqara.

6.5.3 Private (Auto)biographical/Commemorative Texts from Tombs

This category of text is perhaps the best known from the Old Kingdom. Every Egyptian tomb has a variety of functions and probably played an important role during the life of the owner, not just after his death (Assmann 1991: 183–86). An important function is to commemorate, present, and promote the identity and personality of the owner, and it has also been argued that textual material such as biographies helps to represent aspects of the tomb owner which cannot be depicted in a pictorial manner (Baines 1999b: 20–21). For the purposes of this book, I place under the heading of "Biographies" those texts (all bar one from tombs) which have at their center the person and deeds, real or ideal, of the tomb owner, rather than the many other texts which are principally concerned with the needs and function of the tomb itself, and which are mostly covered in §6.7 and §6.8 below. This modern analytic distinction, one which the Egyptians themselves would surely never have comprehended, is in itself not always clear-cut.

The following is a brief summary of the development of the biography.[68] Plausible antecedents to the classic biographical text accompanied by an enumeration of titles can be traced back to stelae of the First Dynasty and move through the wooden panels of Hezyre in Cairo to the first Old Kingdom text of any length, that of Metjen at the beginning of the fourth dynasty (no. 108; Baines 1999a). The latter is mostly concerned with legal matters (in addition to its commemorative function), and the first text which presents something of a narrative is that of Debehen from the end of the fourth dynasty or the beginning of the fifth (no. 200; from that discussion it will be seen that this text has also been dated much later).[69] More informative (to modern eyes) but still quite short biographical texts appear from about this time on, such as those of Ptahshepses and Nyankhsekhmet (nos. 226, 225); longer texts are first seen in tombs in the later fifth dynasty, continuing into the sixth. Particularly characteristic of the fifth-dynasty biographies is the stress on the king and the subject's interaction with him (compare Baines 1997; 1999b).

After the later fifth dynasty, the most extensive biographical texts come principally from sites outside the Memphite necropolis, from the tombs of the rulers or most senior officials in those places. While many of these are mostly "ideal" in nature (see below), a number reveal fascinating glimpses into the activities of these officials, while others tell us a little about the officials' relationship to the king. The best known are those of Weni from Abydos (no. 256) and Harkhuf from Aswan (no. 241); the former is the longest such text from this period and relates matters of potential domestic and national interest, as well as shedding a little light on Egypt outside the confines of the Nile Valley. The texts of Harkhuf concentrate above all on his visits deep into Africa, culminating in the well-known letter from Pepy II to bring a pygmy back to the Residence. Less well known, but equally insightful in terms of the treatment of favored officials, is the biography of Sabni from Aswan (no. 243), in which he retrieved his dead father from Nubia and both received honors from the king. In general, these sixth-dynasty biographies do not center around the subject's connections with the king, as did those of the previous dynasty.

Just before the middle of the sixth dynasty, the first hints of the somewhat different biographical texts of the First Intermediate Period can be seen, such as the personal intervention of the tomb owner in problems and the helping of the disadvantaged from his own means.[70] The biography of Qar of Edfu (no. 247) is one of the first such inscriptions. The small selection of texts translated here from Urk I which probably belong to the very end of the Old Kingdom or a little later show how these texts developed in a rather short period (for example, Henqu from Deir el-Gebrawi [no. 269] and Mery I at Hagarsa [no. 264]).

Seeking a reason for the introduction of these new biographical elements is not easy. Moreno Garcia 1998: 158–60 speculates whether in these texts can be identified early indications of some of the problems and instabilities which might have contributed to the eventual collapse of central authority at the end of the Old Kingdom, such as famine and abuse of power. This of course assumes that we take the content of these texts at face value, although I cannot help but feel that they are essentially little more than a development of the older idealizing phrases. Might it not be too fanciful to see in these writings perhaps the first stirrings of what was to become the motifs underlying much of the wisdom literature of the Middle Kingdom (see n. 28 above)?

It is unclear why these more extensive biographical texts should have flourished in the provincial cemeteries in the sixth dynasty. It used to be said that this was illustrative of the decline of central power in the Old Kingdom, but this view is now somewhat out of favor. Perhaps there were more formal constraints on what could be placed in tombs in the much larger northern courtly cemeteries, or perhaps the exuberance and initiative of those who might have been promoted from the capital to positions in the provinces might have been expressed in their texts.

The (auto)biographical inscription, in which the deceased tells us more about himself, is thus largely a product of the fifth dynasty. These inscriptions may be divided into two broad categories, those which form the "ideal" biography, composed of a number of largely standard phrases which indicate what the ideal person should have done, and those which apparently describe experiences which relate to that individual only (the "event-based" biography). Assmann sees these two types of biographies as clearly dealing with two different worlds, "wisdom" (ideal biography) and "historical discourse" (the event-based biography); he also observes that the latter sort of material remains the preserve of private inscriptions until the late Second Intermediate Period (Assmann 1991: 186–87).

By now the reader will have noted that for these texts I use the terms "autobiography" and "biography" more or less interchangeably, with a preference for the second. Although many are couched in the first person, none are really autobiographies in our sense of the term, unless we really believe that the tomb owner composed them. Rather, I suspect he discussed the content with a scribe who then assembled the type of basic text he wanted, following current preferences. Kloth considers the question of authorship (Kloth 2002: 257–60) and has pointed out one possible text of the "ideal" genre which was almost certainly composed by the subject, the expedition inscription of Anusu (no. 75); however, the biography of Washptah (no. 235) must have been assembled by others after his death. The former text is particularly unusual, as it is the only one of this biographical genre to appear outside a tomb.

For either type of biography, the comments above about the importance of context must be remembered. These are above all tomb texts, documents whose main purpose was to fit into the function of the tomb in relation to the afterlife of the deceased. Whether or not the person carried out the deeds of the ideal biography is irrelevant; that he pronounced that he did them was what mattered. There is no reason to think that the intriguing events in the event-based, more personal biographies did not happen, but they are not placed in tombs for any historical or documentary reason which we would recognize; they are set there with the aim of presenting the image of the deceased and stressing his personality and importance. The latter is illustrated most clearly either where it is commanded by the king that such an event should be recorded in the subject's tomb or in the importance attached to the "rewarding" sections of text which invariably follow the brief account of the successful completion of some deed or other commanded by the king.

Classic phrases which characterize an ideal biography are usually translated "I went out of my house, I went down into my nome"[71] and "I gave bread to the hungry and clothes to the naked" and so on; see Kloth 2002: 54–128 for these phrases (a number are collected in Lichtheim 1992: 9–19). A range of such phrases are encountered in these texts, but all are concerned to illustrate that the deceased did what was required of him and also to show his righteous nature. In Egyptian terms, they illustrate that his deeds conformed to the concept of Maat, which must, in the most general sense, indicate the existence of a basic set of moral expectations in Egypt, and that there were certain expectations of behavior toward one's fellow man, especially among the tomb-owning classes. Many texts contain unique expressions of these ideas, showing that there was a role for framing individual ideas, and sometimes it is difficult to decide whether to treat a text as an ideal biography or one of more specified content. In addition, a number of texts append the occasional ideal biographical phrase to texts of other categories, including those of the more individualized biographies. For example, some of the earliest such ideal phrases are found in conjunction with warning and payment type phrases for the tomb of queen Khamerernebty II at Giza (no. 277).

But the texts from the Old Kingdom which tend to attract the attention of the modern reader above all others are the more individualized biographical texts (Kloth 2002: 128–220). The earliest examples, such as those of Debehen, Nyankhsekhmet, Washptah, Rewer, and Ptahshepses, tend to concentrate on specific instances where they interacted with the king. Further fifth-dynasty texts stress particular associations with the king and also the donation of various parts of their tomb equipment. A change in biographies may perhaps be detected in the reign of Izezi: in particular, letters purporting to be from the king are found within biographical texts (see also §6.12), and a number of highly unusual phrases and personal stories of contact with the king make their appearance (texts of Senedjemib Inti [no. 232], Reshepses [no. 100], and Kaiemtjennet [no. 212]).[72]

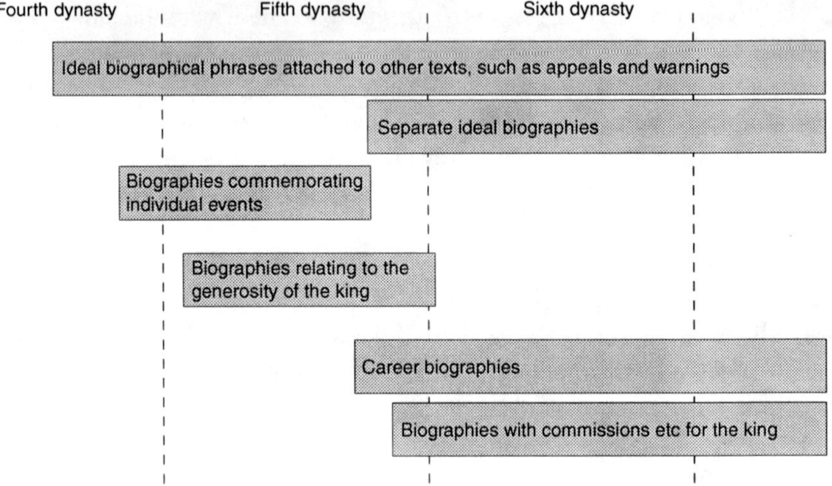

Fig. 2: The development of the Old Kingdom biography over time. Diagram adapted and modified from Kloth 2002: 285.

From the end of the fifth dynasty, biographies begin to appear which purport to present very rough outlines of the official's career reign by reign ("career" biographies), and these continue into the sixth dynasty.[73] The earliest examples of the best known type of biographical text, those in which missions and campaigns are carried out for the king, also begin to appear at this time and continue into the reign of Pepy II (see Eyre 1994 for an examination of how the text of Weni might be used for historical information, although see also my comment in §4.1 on how one aspect of this has been undermined by archaeological discoveries).

Figure 2 gives an impression of the spread of these biographical types during the Old Kingdom.

6.5.4 Captions

Tombs of the Old Kingdom are replete with depictions which are often termed "scenes of daily life," showing agricultural and craft activities and the like, as well as butchery and the bringing of offerings. The meaning of these scenes can be complex and has been studied for the Old Kingdom primarily by Altenmüller;[74] they provide a complex mix of representations of the sustenance necessary for the souls of the deceased and also illustrate his importance, the projection of his personality into the next world, and the expression of his hopes of rebirth in a variety of ways.[75] Such scenes, above all in the Old and Middle Kingdoms, are very frequently accompanied by captions or labels of three broad types. These texts are in addition to the names and titles which label figures in the scenes and which are normally not translated in this volume.

First, in conjunction with a large figure of the tomb owner beside the activities, there is usually a brief text beginning "Watching" or "Viewing" which describes what the owner is supposed to be doing and also serves to characterize the scene in question.[76] A second type is a long single line of text running over a row or series of figures which describes what they are doing; this most commonly begins with "bringing," "accompanying," or "dragging" something or other shown in the scene. These texts are there to characterize the scenes (lest there should be any doubt), although they do not explain their significance or reason for inclusion—*that* would have been obvious to an ancient Egyptian.

The third and most intriguing to the modern viewer are individual short texts above and around individuals or small groups of figures, and which are assumed to indicate the sort of things people might say in these contexts. I find it difficult to believe that there is not a lot more to these short texts than meets the eye, but a further meaning is not always clear. For example, some of these texts appear with some frequency and might indeed have some religious purpose, such as the "song of the herdsman" (no. 314) or the text which sometimes accompanies cattle crossing a canal (no. 302). Some, such as the carrying chair scene (no. 318) and the harpers' songs (no. 301), perhaps implicitly express the wish, seen so much more clearly in later texts, for a return to earth (Altenmüller 1978; 1984–85). But most appear to be commands and responses.

Let us assume with caution for the moment that the majority are possibly representation of what real Egyptians might have said. The difficult nature of many of these captions—they are very compressed and our understanding of the grammar is often little better than a guess—does tend to support an origin in everyday speech. One only has to look at the ungrammatical nature of much modern conversation to believe that this is the nearest we will come to the real speech of the day. The first study of these texts was Erman 1919, followed by Montet 1925 and Junker 1943. For the Middle Kingdom and later there is Guglielmi 1973. There is, however, a need for an up-to-date study of the captions of Old Kingdom texts.

6.5.5 Miscellaneous Texts from Tombs

Pot labels: the German excavations of 1959–73 in the necropolis of Aswan, in the area known as Qubbet el-Hawa, brought to light a mass of pottery of the late Old Kingdom which was not just intended to hold food offerings for those who had died but which also bore inscriptions indicating the contents, for whom they were intended, and by whom they were donated, plus one text which may indicate the cost of burial at this time (no. 325). The concentration of such pottery seems quite astonishing, as labels are found on later pots, but not with the specific nature of these examples.

Lists: an Old Kingdom box made to contain linen bears a list of its contents at various times in its use-life (no. 329), and a number of other short texts found on linen and boxes are included. Several tombs, primarily from the early Old Kingdom, also exhibit lists in stone of the ideal amounts of this material to be offered to the deceased, and one of these is translated here (no. 327). The most common tomb list is the offering list, given in a large grid of compartments on the walls of many mastabas; one example is translated here (no. 328). The shorter lists which appear on the panels of false doors and other offering places are not included.

Miscellaneous tomb inscriptions: among these is the unique inscription of the king's favorite dog Abutyw, who was buried and given funerary offerings in the manner of a human servant (no. 324). I also include a couple of examples of interesting *title sequences,* which would otherwise be omitted (nos. 321, 323).

I reiterate what was mentioned at the beginning of §6.5, that these varying elements, or even parts of them, can be mixed in ways which render relatively few sets of texts alike. Again I imagine the tomb owner choosing what he wanted or could afford with the scribes who worked with the crew constructing the tomb.

6.6 Private Legal Texts[77]

Private "legal texts" deal principally with agreements made between private individuals or groups of people, usually whereby a certain stipulation is made and often penalties are noted for noncompliance with the agreement. One seems to be a dispute about an inheritance, two deal with purchases of houses, a few serve the function of wills, while the majority are concerned with the owner's tomb, mainly allocations of parts of it and rules for the priests who were to look after the cult of the deceased's spirits. With the exception of two house purchases from the Gebelein papyri (no. 102) and a difficult legal text from the Aswan area (no. 103), all are preserved copies in stone of presumed papyrus originals. Like the royal decrees, they were doubtless intended to stand as a reminder of the permanence of the agreement made; while many are incorporated into the decorative programs of tombs, others might have taken the form of slabs or stelae set up in the area of the tomb of the person concerned. Although most are placed in tombs, there is no reason to believe that their context should have any undue influence on how they should be interpreted, as they pertain to the maintenance of the tomb and cult.

In common with the royal decrees, their linguistic complexity partly reflects "legalese" and partly our lack of understanding of the underlying culture. Both groups of texts use terms which do not commonly appear out of these two contexts and for which the functions have to be deduced; the translations adopted here are often speculative, but the inherent awkwardness of some modern legal English has at least allowed me to feel that a few problematic phrases can be left in. Readers are encouraged to study the text editions for more information.

The structure of many of these documents can again be complex. As an example, one of the house purchase decrees (no. 121) writes the texts in such a way as to try and illustrate the relationship between the parties concerned. See also the individual texts for more information.

The regulations relating to mortuary cults are perhaps the most intriguing of these texts. They tend to concentrate more on specifying what the members of the priesthood should not do rather than how the cult itself is to be carried out, presumably because that was self-evident to the Egyptians while the prohibitions were not. Their main concern seems to be to ensure that the priests should not appropriate resources set aside for the cult for their own purposes. The best examples are perhaps those of Kaiemnefret, Nyankhkhnum and Khnumhotep, and Nykaiankh; Nykaiankh, the longest (no. 110), also specifies how much land is to be set aside for those involved in the running of his cult. The will texts of Tjenti also apply to how his wealth should be used for the benefit of various cults (no. 115). Other interesting texts include the specification by Idu Seneni of a shaft in his tomb for his wife (no. 105), Wepemnefret giving a chapel in his tomb to his son (no. 116), and the detailed geographical spread of the estates of Nykaure which are being willed away in both Upper and Lower Egypt (no. 111).

What is particularly intriguing about all these texts is their relative infrequency; put differently, why should these particular officials have had such inscriptions? Some of this, notably the lack of papyrus documents, can be laid at the door of the lottery of preservation, but eighteen texts on stone among the hundreds of known tombs from the Old Kingdom is a very small number. Are we to assume that the remaining officials did not make such documents, perhaps as there was a standard set of regulations and these are the unusual ones, or that the majority may have executed them on papyrus only and did not feel they had to be placed in their tombs, or did not have the space for them? I am not sure that we will ever know, although the latter explanation seems the more likely, perhaps paralleling the manner (still not understood) in which an official selected scenes for his tomb. Is it significant that only one text (no. 104) comes from the tomb of an official of the highest rank in the Old Kingdom?

6.7 Private Administrative Texts

Only one private administrative archive has yet been found from the Old Kingdom, that discovered at Gebelein (just south of Thebes) by an Italian mission in 1935. These documents, with a couple of exceptions, have yet to be published, and the much regretted death of their editor in 1996 has delayed their appearance.[78] Six rolls of papyrus were found inside a box in the Old Kingdom cemetery. The texts include lists of people, as well as accounts related to cereals, dates, and linen, and there are two house purchase texts translated here (no. 102). These documents relate to the administration of a private estate and are at present unique. They appear to be earlier in date than the Abusir papyri, and a date of the "year after the eleventh occasion" might place them in one of the reigns of the major rulers of the fourth dynasty.[79]

6.8 Texts of Women

It is rather fashionable to place stress on the role of women in ancient cultures in an attempt to redress the male-orientated studies of so much of the past two hundred years. Nonetheless, as relatively few texts over the whole of Egyptian history belong to women, it is worthwhile to include a section on inscriptions set up for them in the Old Kingdom.

The texts translated here range from the tombs of queens and princesses, through the mother of the high official Mereruka (no. 296), to those of lower standing.[80] Note that there are some legal texts involving women, for example, the inscription of Pepy (no. 113). There is also the extraordinary titulary of Nebet from Abydos, in which she appears to have held some of the highest state offices (no. 295).[81] But there are no texts of a biographical nature.

The far lower number of texts of women when compared to those of men from the Old Kingdom may be a reflection of a lower level of priority given to educating women (Baines and Eyre 1983: 81–85), but it is far more likely that it is just a consequence of the fact that most women were buried in the tombs of their husbands and thus shared in their texts. The phraseology of most texts is identical to that for men. The principal differences, other than the gender of the forms, are in the deities mentioned in the offering formulae: the goddesses Hathor and Neith are more prominent in these inscriptions than they would be in those of men, suggesting that women were likely to seek benefits from female as well as male deities.

Leaving aside monuments of queens and princesses, there are nonetheless probably more inscribed and decorated parts of tombs dedicated to women surviving from the Old Kingdom than from all other periods. A selection of tomb chapels or false doors solely mentioning women are translated here. In comparison, for example, among the hundreds of New Kingdom tombs at Thebes there is not one which seems to have been built for a woman alone nor which possesses an offering place specifically for the wife of the tomb owner. Rather, she appears in the scenes which primarily concern her husband. Why this should be so is difficult to answer; perhaps it is just a cultural change (see further Callender 2002b; examination of examples in one cemetery Roth 1995: 44).

6.9 Graffiti

The majority of texts often termed "graffiti" are either grouped under another category of text in this book or are omitted. A graffito is in its simplest form a "scratching" and thus must apply to sketches or drawings as well as texts engraved in this way or in ink or paint.[82] Material from the

Old Kingdom which might come under this heading can mostly be placed in five principal groups:

1. rock inscriptions of kings
2. names and titles only of individuals
3. texts with some continuous sense as well as including names
4. marks left by builders and laborers on building stones
5. rock drawings

Most graffiti forming part of 1) and 3) are considered here as expedition inscriptions (§§6.3.1, 6.10), while a selection of 4) is considered in §6.11. It is not normally the intention of this book to translate names and titles alone, but only when they form part of a longer text—hence 2) are largely omitted. The reader should consult Peden 2001 and Eichler 1993 for examples of names and titles in graffiti of the Old Kingdom not translated in this book. Group 5) is of course outside the scope of the present publication.

Inscriptions which can be classified as graffiti in the Old Kingdom are a mixture of official record, practical identification, and private scribbling. As will be seen below, the leaving behind of an official record in the course of an expedition became quite normal practice in the later Old Kingdom, and such "graffiti" are rather elaborate, only warranting the use of the term in its strictest sense—they are not devoid of a sense of "social restraint" which has been argued as typifying the true graffito (Peden 2001: xxi). Builders' marks are of course primarily for identifying who should move blocks and other matters which are unclear to us, and this leaves the isolated names and titles as the principal examples of "true" graffiti devoid of a sense of social restraint and fulfilling the need of some individuals for commemoration of themselves in a certain spot without indication of a reason. Whether the vast increase in graffiti in later times is due simply to improved levels of literacy is to me less than certain.

Three sets of texts are included here as graffiti. The first (no. 87) has been interpreted as indicating the date of the death of Pepy II. I include it under that heading only as there is no other category into which to put it, although it could also be just a little more than a more involved quarry or mason's mark placed on a block.

Otherwise two (groups of) rock inscriptions are considered as graffiti. One particularly interesting group is found in the Wadi Hilal at el-Kab. These are neither expedition inscriptions nor simple graffiti but seem to be writings on the walls of the wadi by priests who worked in temples in the area. Most consist of names and titles only, but the extracts translated here (no. 88) are eulogistic and have almost the ring of the same self-justification and glorification as the ideal tomb biographies. They fit into none of the above categories very easily; they also might suggest that there are further such inscriptions to be found in the vicinities of similar temples. The other text is the unique inscription set up at Hindallab by Henbabai, which appears to allude to quarrymen cultivating their own food at the quarry site under the protection of Khnum (no. 89).

6.10 Expedition Inscriptions

From very early in their history, kings sent expeditions away from Egypt, often outside the main Nile valley, to obtain raw materials. Often some sort of record was left on the rocks of the area where it had stayed or worked. Sometimes there were two parts to the inscription, one a formal one with the names of the king (§6.3.1) and another indicating something, however meager, about the job in question and enumerating all or some of the members of the expedition.[83] Most frequently, however, only the second is found, and these records tend to increase in size and frequency after the Old Kingdom.

Using those from the Wadi Maghara in Sinai as an example (no. 54ff.), fourth-dynasty visits are represented by a depiction of the king smiting foreigners accompanied by his names and texts relating to the smiting, without further specification. In the later fifth dynasty the text "A royal commission made by . . ." with names begins to be added. The appearance of dates with the inscriptions is not consistent. One text of the reign of Izezi in the Wadi Maghara is particularly interesting (no. 60) since it would appear to be not only the earliest extant attempt at indicating more about the expedition but also as it may recall an oracular pronouncement.

Other texts appear in various places in the Eastern Desert and in Nubia, where Egyptian expeditions traveled on commissions of an unspecified nature or indeed military natures. Some of the latter can be compared with the biographical texts from Aswan of the later sixth dynasty for more detail on the sort of expeditions being undertaken; indeed, Sabni and Mekhu in a Tomas inscription are known from their tombs at Aswan. Two most unusual inscriptions included in this section are those of Anusu (no. 75), which would appear to be the employment of standard biographical phrases known in such a context, and that of Shemay (no. 66), with its appeal to the living in a similar unlikely context.

6.11 Builders' or Quarry Marks

The astonishing output of building work during the Old Kingdom could not have happened without a high degree of organization of labor and logistics; the office of "overseer of all works of the king" must have been of the highest importance (Strudwick 1985: 240–50; Krejčí 2000; see also Lehner 1997). With the amount of building stone on the move, it was essential to indicate where stone was going and who was to move it. On many blocks information relating to the origin, the intended destination of the blocks, or the names of those who were responsible for the operation was painted, usually in red; this information has usually (ironically) been revealed only by subsequent damage and depredations to the structure. Such marks rarely consist of more than a few signs, often completely opaque to us, but they perhaps bring us somewhat closer to the ancient laborers and masons than the finished monuments themselves.

These texts, if we can even call them that, fall into two or three groups. Many marks of the Old Kingdom appear to be just signs and marks rather than complete phrases which identified the blocks to the ancients, but their meaning is not at all clear to us, and they are not susceptible to translation here.[84] A number give dates. Other marks on pyramids or tombs seem to give measurements and perhaps relate to how the blocks might have been laid out in quarries prior to construction (Arnold 1991: 20–21); a possible description of a curved vault is presented here (no. 78).

However, other slightly longer phrases, a selection of which is translated here, show dates, the names of work crews, and the so-called phyle subdivisions which operated the system. The names of the crews are sometimes playful and amusing ("the drunks of Menkaure"), and they occasionally show royal crews working on private monuments (no. 84). The system of organizing men into groups to which Egyptologists give the name "phyles" perhaps began with work crews and then developed to underpin the grouping of temple staff into similar bodies. This became fundamental to some aspects of the organization of society in the Old Kingdom (Roth 1991; Verner 2003).

A particularly interesting subset of these crew names are those which appear in the reliefs of fifth-dynasty pyramid temples, in particular in the best-preserved of these, that of Sahure (no. 83). It will be seen from the translations that the same crew names appear in the inscriptions and in the reliefs, and the interesting question this poses is whether these are indeed the same persons (compare Roth 1991: 141–42). Verner believes that the figures shown on the causeway reliefs took part in ceremonies celebrating completion of the building work (Verner 2003: 446). While this is indeed possible (although the reliefs would have been carved before the ceremonies they are supposed to show), the specific context of the reliefs, peopled as they are with primarily divine and royal figures, is vastly different from the milieu of the persons whose labor built the pyramids. I cannot help but feel that the crews in the reliefs can also be interpreted as a part of the mythical world of the divine king, logically organized according to a system of earthly organization, with any earthly ritual version played out by specifically chosen actors (presumably priests or officials), rather than by the similarly named gangs on the pyramid construction site.

6.12 Letters

Letters in any literate culture potentially offer very personal insights into the society in which they are written and into the minds of the writers. Relatively few have survived from the Old Kingdom, and most of those that have come down to us have already been translated in this series (Wente 1990); the preface to that volume should be consulted as a general introduction to Egyptian epistolary texts. However, the scope of the present survey is much enhanced by their being also translated here, and I have also taken the opportunity to place some of them within other groups according to their context (legal documents, administrative texts, and so on). This is particularly true for the so-called Elephantine archive, which might have originally all been found in the same area and are of broadly similar date (Goedicke 1988a: xix; see nos. 96, 97, 98, 103).

The normal medium for letters in Egypt was ink on papyrus, but since the publication of Wente's volume some fascinating letters to the governors of the oases have appeared which were written on small mud tablets (no. 99). This presumably was dictated by the availability of writing materials, as papyrus would have been something of a luxurious commodity in the oases, and these documents should serve as a warning that other types of material might have existed.

There are different groups of letters. Letters purportedly from kings were occasionally carved on the walls of the tomb owner to whom they were sent (Reshepses [no. 100], Senedjemib Inti [no. 232] and Harkhuf [no. 241]; see generally Eichler 1991a). The special context of the tomb should at least urge caution about overinterpretation. These tomb letters may have something of a literary nature about them (compare Baines 1999b: 24–30), and I cannot help but be suspicious as to whether they reflect real correspondence. Two of these tombs containing letters date to the reign of Izezi of the later fifth dynasty, and, while the king might have had a hand in their composition (Baines and Eyre 1983: 77), I find it difficult to concur with Wente's suggestion that Izezi might have been something of a letter-writer and may have inspired this particular aspect of the genre (Wente 1990: 6). That they may reflect some formalized interplay between ruler and favored subjects seems more likely (Baines 1999b: 20–24), perhaps based on some event which triggered the exchange—for example, the pygmy brought back from Nubia by Harkhuf (no. 241). They are not common, and their appearance in the later fifth dynasty probably has as much to do with the more general expansion of biographical texts which was taking place at that time (§6.5.3). Perhaps this mini-genre was only a experiment of the time or one employed only by some favored officials. I would not question that decrees were the principal method by which commands were passed on from the king (see §6.3.2), but these examples are so specialized that one should be healthily suspicious as to whether they represent real correspondence, given their context.

Most other letters are of types more familiar to the modern reader, that is, administrative notes, complaints, and so on. They are not always easy to understand, since information about the background to the events is almost always lost. Nonetheless, they offer a fascinating insight into more ordinary lives than can be gained from the multitude of tomb inscriptions in this volume.

A very special category of these writings is that known as "Letters to the dead." A number of letters on a variety of media, all placed in the tomb, ranging from the late Old Kingdom down to at least the New Kingdom, show living family members writing to deceased relatives asking them to help with a problem. It is clear that it is often felt that the dead relatives might be acting against the living, and so they are sometimes asked as to what the living have done to them to deserve the problems in which they find themselves.

The fact that family could expect a deceased relative to help emphasizes just how little separated the world of the living and the dead in ancient Egypt and how easily a person could mentally move back and forth between the two. This closeness of the two worlds is something that modern Western society appears to have lost in the past couple of hundred years, since it was very much present in the Western medieval mindset, and it can still be seen in village society in modern Egypt.

Most of the extant "Letters to the dead" are later than the Old Kingdom, but the two oldest examples of the genre are included here (no.

101). Translations of a fuller range of examples will be found in Wente 1990: 211–19, and in French in Guilmot 1966; the basic set of texts is Gardiner and Sethe 1928.

7. A Final Word

I hope the reader will now appreciate the place of these texts within the Old Kingdom and will be able to turn to the ancient words themselves. I have endeavored to place each text briefly in its context, but without too much in the way of interpretation, the place of which is in a formal edition or study. I hope that the translations bring the reader closer to the Egyptians of the Old Kingdom.

8. Conventions

[ ]	enclose translations of restored text. Text within these brackets in italics is particularly speculative.
( )	enclose words not in the original but added to ease the translation. Text within these parentheses in italics is usually an explanatory note.
...	indicates gaps in the text or untranslatable words; frequently used with [ ].
< >	enclose words or parts of words omitted in the original text.
(?)	follows words or phrases of which the translation is doubtful.
(1) etc.	are line numbers to aid reference to the original longer texts, only added where meaningful or helpful; they are usually the line numbers as given in one of the editions. It should be noted that these numbers cannot always coincide with line breaks due to the differing grammatical structures of Egyptian and English.

Notes

1. Djedefhor (or Hordjedef) was a son of Khufu, builder of the Great Pyramid, and has a tomb in the adjacent cemetery. Ptahhotep was a vizier of Izezi and possessed a tomb at Saqqara, west of the Step Pyramid. Kaigemni was a vizier of Teti and owned a large tomb adjacent to that king's pyramid at Saqqara (no. 210).

2. See Parkinson 1991b, with further bibliography. Translations of all three, Lichtheim 1973: 58–80; for Ptahhotep, see also Parkinson 1997: 246–72.

3. See Junge 1973 for an attribution to the Third Intermediate Period, and Schlögl 1980: 110–17 for a date in the nineteenth dynasty. Translation, references and some notes in Lichtheim 1973: 51–57.

4. The following are the principal biographical omissions. From the Memphite area: Smenekhuptah Itwesh (James 1974: 14–15, pl. XX (38–40); translation Roccati 1982: 129–30), Ptahshepses (Vachala 1993), Khnumenti (Brovarski 2001: 116, fig. 80). Provincial: Iteti Shedu from Deshasha (Urk 1:89–90; Kanawati and McFarlane 1993: 49, pl. 45a); Kaihap Tjetiiqer at Hawawish (Urk 1:265; Kanawati 1980–92: 1:18–19, fig. 19); Nyankhpepy at Meir (Blackman 1914–53: 5:6, pl. IV).

5. See in particular the work of Henry G. Fischer, especially Fischer 1986: 24–46.

6. Thus I include the biography of Henqu from Deir el-Gebrawi (no. 269) but not that of Menankhpepy from Dendera (Urk 1:268–69).

7. Hieroglyphs in fact can be written either right to left or left to right and also in vertical columns, and there are no parsing breaks.

8. A good example of the prominence of this study among scholars may be gained from an important collection of essays published in the mid-1990s, from which an excellent overview of the literary texts may be gained (Loprieno 1996).

9. The bibliography on these texts is constantly expanding, so I content myself with some general references. For the Pyramid Texts, see Allen 2001; for the Wisdom texts, see Foster 2001b for general remarks, and Raver 2001 for the individual papyri.

10. Readers are referred to publications such as Shaw 2000 for a more detailed overview of Egyptian history, and Kemp 1989 should be read by anyone seeking insights into the development and functioning of ancient Egyptian society. For a general book on the Old Kingdom, I recommend Malek 1986 and Metropolitan Museum of Art 1999, the latter the catalogue of a remarkable exhibition which traveled to Europe and North America in 1999–2000; pp. 3–11 of this book contain a summary of the history of the Old Kingdom by Jean Leclant. Arnold 1999 is a more popular book on the same exhibition. Another excellent catalogue concentrating on Old Kingdom material from Giza is Markowitz, Haynes, and Freed 2002. A "cultural" perspective on the Old Kingdom will be found in Assmann 2003: 46–77.

11. Gardiner 1959; translation of the Old Kingdom section Roccati 1982: 31–35. The verso of this much damaged papyrus of the nineteenth dynasty, now Turin N.1874, appears to contain a list of gods who originally ruled Egypt, followed by mortal kings from around the beginning of the first dynasty to the beginning of the New Kingdom, with reign lengths. Spalinger 1994 and Verner 2001 present lists of contemporary dates and compare them with the king lists, as well as discussing the validity of the cattle-count system.

12. Parkinson 1997: 102–27; Lichtheim 1973: 215–22.

13. Only two of these temples (of Userkaf and Niuserre) have been certainly identified. See Stadelmann 2000: 540–42 for the argument that the Userkaf temple might have been modified for use by Sahure and Neferirkare.

14. Works which cover this topic include Kemp 1989: 20–27; Baines 1989; Redford 1986: 127–63; Aufrère 1998. A primarily literary approach will be found in Ver-

nus 1995. As this book was being edited, the essays in Tait 2003 became available but have not yet been incorporated into the text. Ryholt 2000 discusses new readings for some of the later names in the Old Kingdom.

15. Note that the first year of a new reign would be called "year of uniting the Two Lands." Chaos potentially assaulted Egypt on a change of ruler, and thus a reassertion of the mythical and religious unity of the two traditional lands of Upper and Lower Egypt was necessary to ensure that Maat was reestablished. For examples, see no. 38 or no. 116. Compare Baines 1995: 126.

16. The best is the reign of Nynetjer of the second dynasty (Wilkinson 2000: 119–29, fig. 1), although the reader should compare the comments in Nolan 2003: 77–78.

17. Krauss 1996, against Stadelmann 1987, basing his arguments on both the cattle counts and calculations of the rate of construction of the pyramids of Sneferu. See also Krauss 1998a.

18. Discussion in Spalinger 1994: 303–6. Two to four years, perhaps longer, are suggested for Userkare by Baud and Dobrev 1995: 53, 59–62. Kanawati 2002a: 158 suggests a period of only a year or so.

19. This number of years seems to be confirmed by the latest examination of the papyrus (Ryholt 2000: 91).

20. For example, the reign of Teti, which then further affects the reign of Pepy I and successors: Kanawati 2000; Kanawati and Abder-Raziq 2000: 21–23.

21. See Kemp 1989: 59–62; for more detail, see Martin 1984; among important publications is Hornung and Stahelin 1974.

22. Overview, Spalinger 2001a and 2002. Parker 1950 is still the fundamental work.

23. See Leprohon 2001b; Allen 2000: 64–66; Quirke 1990: 9–27; Baines 1995: 121–28; and von Beckerath 1999: 1–33 for more information on all these different names. For a survey of Egyptian kingship itself, see the essays in O'Connor and Silverman 1995. The royal names of the fourth dynasty are considered in Dobrev 1993.

24. David Silverman elaborated on the position of this epithet in his paper at the 2004 conference "Old Kingdom Art and Archaeology."

25. Dobrev 1993: 195–98 argues that both classes of cartouche *do* exist in the fourth dynasty, although the same name-form is used in each.

26. The Greek Menes, the traditional name of the first king of Egypt, might be the personal name of one of the early kings. There is also an occurrence of *nesut-bity* before a name, Merpabia, on a document of Adjib of the first dynasty (see Quirke 1990: 23).

27. A thoughtful and generally positive review of her work may be found in Malek 1991; a supportive study is Baud 1998; a statistical examination of the results is Seidlmayer 1997. Seidlmayer presented a statistical examination of the use of royal names in dating at the 2004 conference "Old Kingdom Art and Archaeology."

28. See generally, Lichtheim 1973: 6–7; more specifically, Junge 1977. For similar issues relating to the story of the Eloquent Peasant, Parkinson 1991a.

29. Principally Fecht 1965. Some of the principles, and his response to criticism of them, are contained in his English article Fecht 1993. Surveys of the state of metrical analysis in 1996 and 2002 are provided in Burkard 1996 and Parkinson 2002: 112–17.

30. A summary of this will be found, with further references, in Foster 1988: 70.

31. For the English reader, perhaps the most useful analysis is Lichtheim 1971–72.

32. Compare opinions of Lichtheim 1971–72 and Parkinson 1997: 10–11.

33. Perhaps the best-known example is the central section of the so-called Poetical Stela of Thutmose III from the eighteenth dynasty (Lange and Hirmer 1968: pl. 145). The text is studied in Osing 1999.

34. I would like to thank Richard Parkinson for this very shrewd observation.

35. Loprieno 1995, although written for the reader with a knowledge of linguistics, is perhaps the least difficult means of obtaining an overview of all phases of the language. There are of course numerous grammars of Egyptian in different modern languages, which can be divided into those whose aim is to teach and those which are primarily analytical. These, like our understanding of the language, are updated periodically. Some of the principal ones in English are noted below.

36. Edel 1955–64 is the standard analytical grammar of Old Egyptian. There are a number of other important studies which relate to Old Egyptian, such as Silverman 1980; Allen 1984; Doret 1986.

37. Peust 1993: 33 n. 15 summarizes theories on the geographical origins of the different forms and stages of the Egyptian language.

38. There are many Middle Egyptian grammars available in different languages. For English, the standard reference grammar, although very out of date in many respects, has for many years been Gardiner 1957. At the time of writing, the most up-to-date grammar in English is Allen 2000.

39. The use of suffixes as one method of expressing possession will be familiar to those acquainted with other Semitic languages.

40. Hieroglyphs "which are placed at the end of words and mark them off as belonging to a lexical or semantic group" (Parkinson 1999: 58).

41. Fischer 1973a. The interdependence of hieroglyphs and art is described in Fischer 1986, especially pp. 24–46.

42. Books dealing with Egyptian scripts are legion; for good introductory coverage with illustrations, I suggest Parkinson 1999.

43. This is known as the "standard theory" of Egyptian. Readable summaries are Depuydt 1983 and Allen 2000: 405–6.

44. I especially wish to thank my editor, Ronald J. Leprohon, for encouraging my awareness of these forms, as it is far too easy not to give them fair weight just because they are rather alien to the English language.

45. See Loprieno 1995: 9–10; the linguistically inclined reader might care to read some of the references he gives. Some changes are conveniently summarized in Allen 2000: 407–8.

46. An accessible summary of the administration of the Old Kingdom is Leprohon 1995. Many works deal with the titles, their meaning, or how they fit into the Egyptian administration, for example Baer 1960; Kanawati 1977a; 1980; Martin-Pardey 1976; Strudwick 1985. Jones 2000 is an index of titles of the period.

47. See the Web site of the College of Arms, http://www.college-of-arms.gov.uk/About/04.htm As an example of their modern courtly function, current holders of these titles appeared in the processions organized around the service of thanksgiving for the Golden Jubilee of Queen Elizabeth II in London on 4 June 2002.

48. Compare Helck 1959: 5–15; also Baines 1995: 133. Helck saw the *pat* as perhaps indicating the people of what became the dominant cultural influence after the political unification of the lands, and the *rekhyt* as those who were dominated. Further references in Baud 1999: 105 n. 2.

49. See Freier 1976 for an alternative view of the first of these titles.

50. See Schmitz 1976: 159–71 for a survey of these titles in the Old Kingdom. Further comments in Jánosi 1997.

51. Helck 1956. Summary of the position in English in Eyre 1987: 22–24. See also Málek 1986: 75–76. James P. Allen in his paper at the 2004 conference "Old Kingdom Art and Archaeology" suggested that the sense of *imakhu* might be more the concept of "association with" others rather than primarily "provision."

52. Jansen-Winkeln 1996 attempts to reconcile these two different senses of the expression. For consistency, I write *imakhu* whether the form is *imakhu* or *imakhy*, whether masculine or feminine.

53. For an attempt to associate this use of the word *hem* with the similar word for "servant," see Hofmann 2001.

54. Or perhaps "has given": see Satzinger 1997 for consideration of the verb forms used.

55. Suggestion made by James P. Allen in his paper at the 2004 conference "Old Kingdom Art and Archaeology."

56. Summary of festivals: Spalinger 2001b; comments on development of these lists in the Old Kingdom: Spalinger 1996: 110–69.

57. For an overview, see Martin-Pardey 1999. The approximate nome boundaries are marked on the maps in Baines and Malek 2000. A standard fuller reference work is Helck 1974a.

58. A major collection of nome names appears in the sun temple of Niuserre: Edel and Wenig 1974, pl. 4–7; translation Roccati 1982: 62–63.

59. See, for example, the hall of Sahure in the inscriptions of Nyankhsekhmet (no. 225) and the palace of Izezi in those of Senedjemib Inti (no. 232).

60. See n. 11 above for the Turin Canon; the Abydos list has never really been properly published—compare Redford 1986: 18–21. A recent source for the names of Egyptian kings is von Beckerath 1999. Compare Spalinger 1994 on dated texts of the Old Kingdom.

61. See, for example, the surveys of temples in Kemp 1989: 65–83 and O'Connor 1992. Large granite blocks bearing the names of Khufu and Khafre, for example, from Bubastis (London, BM EA 1097–98: Naville 1891: pl. XXXII) and Lisht (Metropolitan Museum of Art 1999: 263–64), could have come from Giza or attest the existence of further structures of which we are unaware.

62. See the survey in Fischer 1968: 37–54.

63. See discussion by Kemp in Trigger et al. 1983: 92–96.

64. Posener-Kriéger 1976: 483–91.

65. Baud 2000 makes an additional comparison between the administration of the mortuary cult and that of the royal ceremonial palace.

66. See Verner 1984: 75–76; 1994: 166–70; and 2002: 145–50 for the discovery. See Posener-Kriéger 1983; Posener-Kriéger 1985b; 1985c; 1988–91; 1991; 1995 for more detail.

67. See Morchauser 1991, especially pp. 145–57. A different, more anthropological, approach is taken in Nordh 1996. See Silverman 2001 for an introduction to curses in ancient Egypt.

68. The first study of the wider aspects of Old Kingdom biographies is Kloth 2002; pp. 229–48 give an account of development. Previous studies have tended to concentrate on their structure (Edel 1944) or have considered the Old Kingdom as part of the whole genre (Lichtheim 1988; Gnirs 1996). An accessible account is Gnirs 2001. See also Baines 1999a and Schott 1979 on their antecedents and history.

69. No. 239, possibly of the reign of Khufu, does indicate the possible existence of biographical-like texts in that time.

70. Gnirs 1996: 223–25 surveys the biographies of the First Intermediate Period.

71. Other intriguing translations of this pair of phrases have been put forward, suggesting that the word translated "nome," Egyptian *sepat,* might actually refer to the "cemetery" (Goedicke 1955) or even the area where the afterlife was thought to be (mentioned in James P. Allen's paper at the 2004 conference "Old Kingdom Art and Archaeology"). Thus this text could indicate the passage from one life to the next; see Kloth 2002: 54–56 for a discussion. One of the problems is that it is unclear to what extent *sepat* means more than "nome" in the Old Kingdom, although if one were to be buried not very far from where they lived, as we assume most Egyptians were, the cemetery would be in their nome. One of Allen's theses is that the cemetery was the location of the nonroyal afterlife in the Old Kingdom; I have adopted the potentially controversial translation "into the afterlife."

72. To be added to these probably is the biography of Smenekhuptah Itwesh, which seems to have a number of unusual phrases but which has been omitted from this volume due to its very broken nature (James 1974: 14–15, pl. XX (38–40); translation Roccati 1982: 129–30).

73. A precursor to this type of biography is that of Ptahshepses (no. 226) of the reign of Niuserre; each reign in which he lived receives a brief mention.

74. Altenmüller 1992 is an overview article, and there are several further papers, including Altenmüller 1978; 1984–85; 1989; 2002b in the present bibliography.

75. See Kamrin 1999 for such an analysis of a Middle Kingdom tomb, and Manniche 2003 for comments on the meaning of scenes in the New Kingdom. Both give instructive pointers to the interpretation of their precursors in the Old Kingdom.

76. With regard to a possible deeper meaning for this scene type, they may also be a representation of the communication of the deceased with the world of the living (Fitzenreiter 2001).

77. There is of course a large body of literature dealing with Egyptian legal matters. References to this material will be found within other works quoted here, particularly Goedicke 1970, Logan 2000, and Menu 1985.

78. A summary of the contents of the papyri will be found in Posener-Kriéger 1975. Other related articles are Posener-Kriéger 1979; 1994a. The box in which they were found is described in Posener-Kriéger 1994b, and the papyri themselves are now in Cairo, JE 66844. When this book was in proof, a publication of the photographs and Posener-Kriéger's transcriptions appeared (Torino 2004), but it has not been possible to study any of the additional texts.

79. There is one other account document of the Old Kingdom, also unpublished, that was found at Sharuna in Middle Egypt and now in Berlin: Posener-

Kriéger 1973–74: 30 and Goedicke 1988a: xviii–xix (the publication by Goedicke referred to in the latter has not appeared).

80. A number of interesting notes on women in the Old Kingdom, including their prominence or otherwise in tombs, may be found in Fischer 2000. Some titles of royal women are considered by Kuchman 1977 and Málek 1979–80: 229–30.

81. See Fischer 1976a: 69–75 for some other administrative titles of women in the Old Kingdom.

82. A survey of textual graffiti in hieroglyphs or hieratic is Peden 2001; Old Kingdom examples are considered on pp. 4–13.

83. Various aspects of Old Kingdom expeditions are studied in Eichler 1993; Eichler 1994 considers the cultic role played by inscriptions in the wish for a successful return home.

84. For example, in the unfinished pyramid of Sekhemkhet (Goneim 1957: 2–9, pl. XI–XIII), at Dahshur (Stadelmann and Sourouzian 1982), and in the sun temple of Userkaf at Abusir (Haeny 1969: 39–47). An overview of all marks known at the time is provided in Haeny 1969: 23–39; more recently discovered marks include the intensively studied mastaba of Ptahshepses at Abusir, not translated here (Verner 1992; 1985). Some from the pyramid of Pepy I at South Saqqara are considered in Dobrev 1994 and 2003. For detailed examination of Middle Kingdom material from Lisht, see Arnold 1990.

II

Annals and Lists of Kings

See notes in chapter I, §6.1.

1. The Palermo Stone and Associated Fragments

The Palermo Stone and associated fragments in London and Cairo are the remains of an annalistic (year-by-year) record on stone which originally ran from perhaps before the first dynasty to at least the fifth. The surviving text is very damaged, with significant gaps. It is very much a record of certain official, overwhelmingly religious, events. Assuming that the original on which the surviving fragments are based was contemporary with the Old Kingdom, the stone itself is much later in date, perhaps twenty-fifth dynasty or later. It was not unusual for the later epochs to renew or recodify earlier documents, not least so that the kings of that period could be seen to be emphasizing their legitimacy and heritage. The Shabaka Stone in the British Museum is another example of such a record which purports to be a copy of an older worm-eaten document (chapter I, §1.1).

Only the fourth- and fifth-dynasty sections of these annalistic fragments are translated here. The surviving entries for this period are much longer than those for the earlier dynasties. Each year was contained in a compartment, bounded by the hieroglyph { *for "year." Measurements given under many compartments are assumed to be the height of the Nile flood for that year.*

I follow the structure of Sethe (although I do not assume his reconstructions to be automatically correct), as it is the only synoptic text available and it is otherwise impossible to obtain an overall view of the whole. Wilkinson's book should be used to understand the history and relationships of the different fragments, although I would question a number of his readings and his use of earlier editions, and lament the nature of his documentation (compare Baud 2003). Much of the text is badly damaged and hard to read, and there are wide differences in the readings of different scholars; hence this translation is at best an attempt to give the flavor of the original.

Many references in this text are obscure, and I have tried to keep notes to a minimum.

Any cattle-count information in the header is reiterated for ease of reference. To aid the reader who wishes to follow the editions, I use the following abbreviations for the publications in the source list: S = Urk I *page with Sethe's section number in ( ); W = Wilkinson 2001.*

Sneferu

S 235 (1); W 233 (Count 2)

... his mansion
... [the estate of] Sneferu: date-palms (?)
... silver and lapis-lazuli. The second occasion of the count.
(*Nile height*): 3 cubits

S 236 (2); W 234

... the *per-wer*
... the *per-nu*. The *senuti* shrine.
[Fashioning of] a statue (called) Nebmaat[1] ...
(*Nile height*): 3 cubits, 5 palms

S 236 (3); W 140–41 (5th Count?)

[Fashioning] "two children [of the king of Lower Egypt"] (*perhaps two sacred vessels?*). [Fifth occasion of the count (?)]

S 236 (4); W 141–43

Construction of a ship of *meru* wood (*of type or name*) "adoring the Two Lands," of 100 cubits; and of sixty royal boats of the "sixteen" type.[2]
Hacking up the Nubians;[3] bringing back 7,000 captives and 200,000 cattle and herds.
Construction of the "mansions of Sneferu" in Upper and Lower Egypt.
Bringing forty ships full of cedar/pine wood.
(*Nile height*): 2 cubits, 2 fingers

S 236 (5); W 143–4 (7th Count)

Setting up 35 estates[4] with people and 122 cattle-farms.
Construction of one ship of cedar/pine wood (*of type or name*) "adoring the Two Lands," of 100 cubits, and two ships of 100 cubits of *meru* wood.
Seventh occasion of the count.
(*Nile height*): 5 cubits, 1 palm, 1 finger.

S 237 (6); W 144–46 (8th Count)

Erection of (the building [?]) "High is the white crown of Sneferu" at the southern gate and of (the building [?]) "The red crown of Sneferu" at the northern gate.
Making of doors of cedar/pine wood for the royal palace.
Eighth occasion of the count.
(*Nile height*): 2 cubits, 2 palms, 2¾ fingers

S 237 (7); W 146

effectively destroyed

S 237 (8)

... [nth occasion of the count of the cattle and] herds.
(*Nile height*): ... 2 palms

S 237 (9); W 235–36

Appearance[5] of the king of Upper Egypt, fourth occasion of the running of the Apis.[6]
Fashioning of a gold statue of Horus Nebmaat, inscribing the gods (*hieroglyphs*).
Bringing from the land of the Tjemehu (Libya) 1,100 captives and 13,100 (*or possibly* 23,100) small cattle.
Returning from hacking up the fortress of Ida (?).
...

Sneferu or Khufu

S 237 (10); W 215–16

S considers this of the reign of Sneferu, and W that of Khufu.
Fashioning a statue of the Horus ...
Sneferu/Khufu ... with his towns ...

Khufu

S 238 (1); W 223

... (*statue of a goddess*) ... (*statue of king in red crown*) 14
... Khufu ...
... 100 cubits
... 10,300 ...
...
(*Nile height*): 3 (?) cubits, 6 palms, 3½ fingers

S 238 (2); W 237
[The king of Upper and Lower Egypt] Khufu
[For …] he set up a monument …
made of lapis-lazuli …
as his monument … totally … which was found (?) …

Probably Khufu

S 238 (1–middle); W 224–25
[Appearance of the king of Lower Egypt] …
Construction …
Setting up …
Fashioning and opening the mouth of [statues] of Horus Khnum-[Khufu (?)] and of [all] the gods

S 238 (2–middle); W 225–26
Appearance of the king of Lower Egypt …
Following[7] …
Name (?) …

Djedefre

S 238 (1–lower); W 228–31
W's reading of the arrangement is quite different from S.
20 boats (?)
the seal-bearer of the king of Lower Egypt and scribe of the gods
20 cubits and two fingers: a block of granite for the royal burial chamber (*or*) a block of granite from the mansion of gold
The king of Upper and Lower Egypt Djedefre. For Bastet … he set up a monument … in …

[Menkaure (Last Year of)][8]

S 239 (1–lower); W 149
[four months] 24 days

Shepseskaf

S 239 (2); W 149–51
[seven] months 11 days

Appearance of the king of Upper and Lower Egypt; uniting the Two Lands, going around the Two Lands, festival of the diadem; fashioning of two images of Wepwawet; following of the king (by) the gods who unite the Two Lands.[9]

Khenty-she (?) choosing the site of the pyramid of Shepseskaf
... Upper and Lower Egypt, the *senuti* shrine, 20 daily
... 1,624 ... 600
(*Nile height*): 4 cubits, 3 palms, 2½ fingers

Userkaf

S 240 (1); W 217–18 (Year after the 1st Count)

Coming with heads bowed: 303 bag-carriers.[10]
Tribute which they brought to the pyramid of Userkaf: 70 female foreigners.
Year after the first occasion of the count of the cattle.

S 240 (2); W 218–19

The king of Upper and Lower Egypt Userkaf.
For (*the following*) he set up a monument:
The *bas* of Heliopolis:

Divine offerings were set up for them (being)
4,252 measures of bread and beer,
40 oxen, (*possibly*) 4 ibex,
132 geese, (*possibly*) 12 ducks,
on the first occasion of the festival[11] of reversion and on the occasion of every festival for the breadth of eternity.

Re:

44 arouras of land ...

Hathor:

23 arouras of land ... from ... who dwells in the pyramid of Userkaf and in ...

(*Nile height*): 3 cubits, 2 palms, 2 (or 2½) fingers

S 241 (3); W 152 (? Year after 2nd Count)

Third occasion of making the inventory of the house of Horus and Seth ...
[Year after the second occasion of the count (?)]

S 241–42 (4) W 153–58 (3rd Count)

The king of Upper and Lower Egypt Userkaf.
For (*the following*) he set up a monument:
The *bas* of Heliopolis:
    20 measures of bread and beer on every sixth-day festival …
    35 (*or* 36) ⅞ arouras of land, ½+¼+⅛ *ta* measure[12] of land, from (?) of Userkaf.
The gods of *Nekhenre:*
    24 arouras of land from … of Userkaf,
    two oxen and 2 *set* geese every day.
Re:
    44 arouras of land from the nomes of Lower Egypt.
Hathor:
    44 arouras of land from the nomes of Lower Egypt.
The gods of the estate Djebaty:
    54 arouras of land. Erection of his pedestal (?) for the temple in Pe in the sixth nome of Lower Egypt.
Horus:
    2 arouras of land. Building his temple.
Nekhbet of the divine palace of Upper Egypt:
    10 measures of bread and beer daily.
Wadjet of the *Per-nu* shrine:
    10 measures of bread and beer daily.
The gods of the divine palace of Upper Egypt:
    48 measures of bread and beer daily.
Year of the third occasion of the count of the cattle.
(*Nile height*): 4 cubits, 2½ fingers

S 242 (5); W 158–59

[The king of Upper and Lower Egypt Userkaf.
For (*the following*) he set up a monument:]
[Re (?)]
    1,705 arouras + 1½ + 12 cubits (?) of land in Lower Egypt.
[Min (?)]
    …

Sahure

S 242–43 (1); W 220–21

[The king of Upper and Lower Egypt Sahure.
For (*the following*) he set up a monument:]

Fashioning and opening the mouth in the [mansion of gold] of six statues of Sahure.
First occasion of making the inventory of the house of Horus and Seth, the year of going round ...

S 243 (2); W 221
The king of Upper and Lower Egypt Sahure.
For (*the following*) he set up a monument:

S 243–45 (3); W 160–66
[The king of Upper and Lower Egypt] Sahure.
For (*the following*) he set up a monument:
[... the souls (?)] in Heliopolis:
the son of Re (?) ... 200 *wab*-priests ... the divine barque ...
Nekhbet in the *per-wer*
800 measures of divine offerings daily.
Wadjet in the *per-nezer*
4,800 measures of divine offerings daily.
Re in the *senuti* shrine:
138 measures of divine offerings daily.
Re in the divine palace of Upper Egypt:
40 measures of divine offerings daily.
Re in the roof-temple:
74 measures of divine offerings daily.
Hathor of *Sekhetre:*
4 measures of divine offerings daily.
Re of *Sekhetre:*
24 arouras of land in the tenth nome of Lower Egypt.
(He of) Mesen:[13]
1 aroura of land in the ninth nome of Lower Egypt.
Sem:[14]
2 arouras, 2 *kha,* 4 *ta* of land in the tenth nome of Lower Egypt.
Khentyiatef:[15]
2 arouras, 2 *kha*, 6+¼+⅛ *ta* of land in the tenth nome of Lower Egypt.
Hathor in the *ra-she* of Sahure:
2 arouras, 2 *kha*, 6 *ta* ¼, 4 cubits of land in the fourteenth nome of Lower Egypt.
Hathor in the pyramid of Sahure:
2 arouras, 2 *kha* [¼] of land in the seventh/eighth nome of Lower Egypt.

The white bull:

13 (or 23) arouras, 2 *kha,* ¼, 10 cubits of land in the southern part of the fourteenth nome of Lower Egypt.

Third occasion of making the inventory of the house of Horus and Seth.

Year after the second occasion of the count.

(*Nile height*): 2 cubits, 2¼ fingers.

S 245 (4); W 166–67

The king of Upper and Lower Egypt [Sahure.

For (*the following*) he set up a monument:]

The ennead [in] the house of divine writings, the *senuti* shrine and for Horus in the royal palace (or) the roof-temple of Horus ...

...

S 245–46 (5); W 168–71 (Year after 7th Count)

[The king of Upper and Lower Egypt Sahure.]

For (*the following*) [he set up] a monument:

...

Re:

... arouras of land in Lower and Upper Egypt.

Hathor:

204 arouras (*or* 8 *ta* measures [?]) of land in Lower and Upper Egypt.

Seshat in the "school of the nobility":[16]

2 *kha* 4 *ta* measures of land in Lower and Upper Egypt.

What was brought from:

The terraces of turquoise:[17] 6,000 pieces of copper (?)

Punt: 80,000 measures of myrrh, 6,000 pieces of electrum, 2,900 pieces of malachite, 23,020 measures of unguent (?)[18]

...

Year after the seventh occasion of the count. Nine months and 23 days.[19]

Neferirkare

S 246 (1); W 172

Horus Userkhau, king of Upper and Lower Egypt, the Two Ladies Khaem-nebty, (Golden Horus) Sekhemu ...

S 246–48 (2); W 172–76 (First Year)

Two months and seven days.

Fashioning (statues) of the gods, uniting (the Two Lands), going round the wall.

The king of Upper and Lower Egypt Neferirkare.

For (*the following*) he set up a monument:
The ennead in the house of divine writing and the *senuti* shrine:
(in the) first nome of Lower Egypt, the estate/town "Neferirkare is beloved of the ennead," 3 arouras, 3 *kha* of land, under the control of his estate of the *meret* temple (?) "the mansion of the *ba* of Neferirkare" (?).
The souls of Heliopolis and the gods of Kheraha:[20]
(in the) fourteenth nome of Lower Egypt, the estate/town "beloved of the souls of Heliopolis is Neferirkare" (1)10 arouras, 1 *kha* of land
(in the) southern part of the fourteenth nome of Lower Egypt, 352 arouras, 2 *kha,* 2 *ta* ½ + ¼ of land under the control of the two "great seers"[21] and of the priest and office-holders, which derives totally from the divine offerings which are exempted in the manner of divine lands;
Re and Hathor:
an offering table in the "wall of the fortress of the sovereign (?)" set up daily with 210 portions of divine offerings; two storerooms and a set of dependents were set up for it.
Fashioning and opening the mouth of a standing statue of electrum of Ihy, which was followed to (the temple of) Hathor (lady) of the sycamore (who dwells in [?]) the *meret* temple of Sneferu.
Re ... in the roof-temple (?):
It was done for him likewise (?) ...
(*Nile height*): 3+ cubits

S 248 (3); W 177–78 (5th Count)

...
[The king of Upper and Lower Egypt Neferirkare.
For (*the following*) he set up a monument:]
Fashioning and opening the mouth in the mansion of gold (of) a bronze (statue [?] of) Neferirkare
Re in *Setibre*:
A canal going round (?)
Huni:
... arouras of land ...
Fifth occasion [of the count]

S 248–49 (4); W 179–80

Appearance of the king of Upper and Lower Egypt.
Erection of the *maaty* (solar) barque at the southern corner [of *Setibre*].
The king of Upper and Lower Egypt Neferirkare.

For (*the following*) he set up a monument:
Re and Horus in *Setibre*:
  the evening and the morning barque (in) copper (each) six cubits.
the souls of Heliopolis:
  electrum ... (?)
Ptah south of his wall:
  land ...
Wadjet of the southern town:
  electrum ...

2. Three Annalistic Vessel Inscriptions from Elephantine

Two beer jars were found on Elephantine island near the third-dynasty step pyramid in 1981. From the information they bear in black ink, it has been suggested that they contained papyri, the outline of the contents of which was written in ink on the pots. While not annalistic in the manner of the Palermo Stone, they do represent a very ancient example of such year-by-year recording of commodity deliveries. The possible count date on the first example has been suggested to be of Huni, the last king of the third dynasty. Inscriptions A and B are on the same vessel; C is on two sherds. For a different interpretation of text C, see Kaplony 2002.

A.

Year of:
The following of Horus; eleventh occasion of the count of the herds of Heliopolis.[22]
Grain, 25 *heqat* measures.

B.

[Year of:]
The following of Horus; construction in stone ...
Receiving ... the overseer of grain and cattle ...

C.

[Year of:]
Appearance of the king of Upper Egypt and the king of Lower Egypt; third occasion of fighting the robbers (?); injury[23] to (?) the great of affection, Djefatnebty.
(For the) controller of the estate "the crusher of the lands," 30 *heqat*.
(For the) overseer of the ship Heneni, malt (?) 17 (?)
Received malt ...; the desert which produces gold ...

3. Annals on the Sarcophagus of Ankhesenpepy from South Saqqara

The lid of the sarcophagus of Queen Ankhesenpepy, probably the mother of Pepy II, was found in excavations of Jéquier in 1931–32. Both sides of its lid (which itself may not originally have belonged with the base) bear very abraded inscriptions which on close examination proved to be annalistic texts of the sixth dynasty. While not as well preserved and informative as the Palermo Stone and associated fragments (no. 1), it does shed some more light on the sixth dynasty. Its structure appears to have consisted of long titularies of kings indicating the areas for different reigns, and then compartments which deal either with individual years or cattle counts. It seems that the period covered by the upper surface (recto) ran from the reign of Teti to that of Merenre; the other side (verso) ran presumably from Merenre into the reign of Pepy II, although Dobrev 2000 raises the possibility that it might have instead been inscribed in the fifth dynasty. Its historical importance is all the greater for possibly including the very obscure reign of Userkare. For the other texts on the sarcophagus see no. 281. The sarcophagus is now in Cairo, JE 65908.

Royal Titularies

Horus Seheteptawy, king of Upper and Lower Egypt, he who pacifies the Two Ladies, gold Horus "he who unites," the son of Re, Teti; mother of the king of Upper and Lower Egypt, Zeshzeshet.
[Horus … Userkare (?)]; mother of the king of Upper and Lower Egypt …
Horus Merytawy, king of Upper and Lower Egypt, the beloved one of the Two Ladies Merykhet, the triple Golden Horus [Meryre *or* son of Re, Pepy]; mother of the king of Upper and Lower Egypt, Iput.

Individual Zones (Recto)

Each probable compartment seems to have had a horizontal line captioning it with the expression:

King of Upper and Lower Egypt X. For … he set up a monument …

The second phrase is one that is found in the Palermo Stone (no. 1) and in many subsequent texts (no. 15), and is a particular set phrase used by royalty in monumental inscriptions to describe events and deeds, not just of a constructional nature; what follows here are the descriptions of these. The editors of the text divide visible inscribed areas into "zones," as the original divisions are for the most part gone. The texts are very broken, and only a selection of zones and lines is given here, without indications of every break and restoration.

Zone A3

King of Upper and Lower Egypt [son of Re] Pepy; for … he set up a monument …

Coming of those who carry out commissions for …

Coming of the expedition …

Coming with bowed heads of the pacified Nubians …

Coming with bowed heads of the pacified Nubians … when they have brought … [*next line began similarly*]

… (*something*) of best quality … honey …

… four jars of honey (on the occasion of [?]) the festival of Re …

Creation[24] in the chapel of the south[25] on the occasion of the New Year festival in the temple …

Creation in the chapel of the south … a statue of Pepy (*of a certain material*) … a statue of Pepy (*of a certain material*) …

Creation … of a statue

… a young cow … honey …

Zone B1

A list of offerings of animals

Zone E7

Traces of a date that must refer to Pepy I: the year after the twenty-third occasion of the count of the cattle.

Zone E8

Traces of a date that must refer to Pepy I: year of the twenty-fifth occasion of the count of the cattle.

Zone F1

As well as the standard formula, a list of offerings, including "the offering which the king gives," "lapis-lazuli," "bread (?)," "cattle (*possibly*) 6,420" *and so on. This list is closed by this text*:

Year of uniting the Two Lands, count of the cattle.[26]

Zone F2

[*a god?*] … in the double-pillared hall … 30 oxen …
Seth … in the double-pillared hall … oxen …
Wadjet … 5 oxen …
[*a god?*] in the double-pillared hall … offerings 2 + x oxen …

Zone F3

First (*or* second [?]) occasion of the count of the cattle …

Zone F6

This begins with the remains of several columns of offerings.
… Nefertum …
[(for) the ennead] in the house of the divine words in the double pillared hall, incense; (for) Heryshef, incense …
[offerings]
[*a god?*]—he has loved what has been done for him, (it being) … 60 oxen … (according) to that which has been said …
[offerings]
[(for) *a god?*] incense, 200 (two types of birds), 32 *baqt* jars of *setj-heb* oil; (for) Khentyimentyu …
(for) the king of Upper and Lower Egypt [Djed]kare …
… 5,000 [lost], two broad collars of silver, [X] sacks of eye-paint;
for Khentykheti …
(for) the king of Upper and Lower Egypt [name lost] …

Zone F7

Mention of a series of boats, of the king and of gods, specifically Ptah.

Individual Zones (Verso)

Zone A2

(offerings)
… the foundation of Horus …
coming of those who carry out commissions together with those of the golden boat; bringing 4,400 + x …
Coming with heads bowed of the pacified …, who have brought …
Coming with heads bowed of the pacified …
Coming with heads bowed of the pacified …

4. A Writing Board from Giza

The content of this board is in four sections: royal names, divine names, place names, and sketches of birds and fish; the texts are each repeated a number of times. It was presumably some sort of writing exercise; there is no apparently logical selection to the royal names. From tomb G 1011 in the Western Cemetery (PM III^2, 52). Now Cairo, JE 37734. Fifth or sixth dynasty.

Bedjau (*possibly a name for Hetepsekhemwy, a king of the second dynasty*)
Djedefre (*fourth dynasty*)
Khafre
Sahure (*fifth dynasty*)
Neferirkare

5. A List of Kings in the Tomb of Sekhemkare at Giza

From tomb LG 89 in the central field at Giza (PM III^2, 233–34). A caption from this tomb will be found as no. 315. Early fifth dynasty.

On the Top of a False Door

The *imakhu* in the sight of his father the king, and in the sight of the Great God, and in the sight of:
the king of Upper and Lower Egypt Khafre
the king of Upper and Lower Egypt Menkaure
the king of Upper and Lower Egypt Shepseskaf
the king of Upper and Lower Egypt Userkaf
the king of Upper and Lower Egypt Sahure

6. Royal Names from the Tomb of Netjerpunesut at Giza

The tomb is in the central field at Giza (PM III^2, 278). Early fifth dynasty.

In the sight of Djedefre I was a possessor of *imakhu*
In the sight of Khafre I was a possessor of *imakhu*
In the sight of Menkaure I was a possessor of *imakhu*
In the sight of Shepseskaf I was a possessor of *imakhu*
In the sight of Userkaf I was a possessor of *imakhu*
In the sight of Sahure I was a possessor of *imakhu*

Notes

1. The Horus name of Sneferu.

2. Either perhaps of sixteen lengths (perhaps of ten cubits each), or with sixteen oars, or perhaps sixteen structural ribs.

3. Compare no. 76 from Khor el-Aquiba.

4. Translated in Malek 1986: 68.

5. The verb *kha,* translated "manifest" or "appear," refers to the formal appearance of the king in a particular role or ceremony. See the text of Rewer (no. 227) for another example.

6. Possibly in origin a festival associated with the fecundity of the land and/or the level of the inundation, and perhaps here and later associated with a royal renewal celebration (Otto 1938: 11–14; Helck 1966; Baines 1995: 130–31).

7. The "Following of Horus" is attested in earlier parts of the stone.

8. This year compartment is divided to show the change of reign during the period it covered.

9. A series of events, mostly attested elsewhere on the stone, that were performed at and around the time of the coronation.

10. See Altenmüller 1995 for this section and for the identity of these persons; they may have been exiled Egyptians. The number 303 is not certain.

11. This follows Sethe; also possible is Wilkinson's "New Year festival and on every subsequent New Year's festival."

12. This adding together typifies the Egyptian approach to fractions of a unit. The *ta* measure is a division of an aroura (see glossary).

13. Perhaps a strange writing of this Delta place name, associated with the cult of Horus.

14. This deity is obscure.

15. A relatively obscure Memphite divinity, perhaps an aspect of Ptah. See Leitz 2002: 5:778.

16. Or "the house of the royal acquaintances." See Grdseloff 1943: 120 n. 5 and Baud 1999a: 113–18.

17. Probably Sinai; this term is certainly used for it in later times.

18. Blocks recently discovered at Abusir show that a visit to Punt was depicted in the reliefs of the causeway of Sahure (paper presented at the 2004 "Old Kingdom Art and Archaeology" conference by Tarek el-Awady).

19. Thus, with Neferirkare (2), this adds to a whole year and shows the point during the year when Sahure died. Thus the first year of Neferirkare includes numerous events for the beginning of a reign.

20. A location associated with Heliopolis, the site of the conflict of Horus and Seth (*aha* in the name means "fighting"), and a cult place of the ennead of Heliopolis. Probably to be identified with the site of Babylon in Old Cairo.

21. The title usually translated "high priest of Heliopolis." Compare the "great controller of craftsmen" title of the high priest of Ptah (no. 200 or no. 225).

22. Not the usual way of referring to a count (chapter I, §3.2), but perhaps a local variation?

23. It would be rather unusual for an official record to recount such a negative

act, so the meaning of this word might be unknown. The name of the queen is otherwise unattested.

24. This is used in the Palermo Stone often for the fashioning of a statue or the like.

25. A reference to the national shrine of Nekhbet, the protective goddess of Upper Egypt.

26. This expression is well known as indicating the accession of a new king; on the Palermo Stone (no. 1) it often appears part way through a year. Here it must refer to the accession of Merenre. Traces of this king's titulary are possibly to be seen in the "he set up a monument" label above.

III

Texts from Temples

See notes in chapter I, §6.2.

7. Reliefs of Netjerykhet Djoser

A. Stela from the Step Pyramid Enclosure at Saqqara

One of a series of stelae, perhaps embedded in conical structures and possibly erected before construction of the pyramid to mark out the area of the complex (Lauer 1936–39: I, 187–89). PM III^2, 407; other examples in Firth and Quibell 1935: II, pl. 86–87. Now Chicago, Oriental Institute OIM 13652.

Anubis, who dwells in the sacred land.
She who sees Horus, the king's [daughter](s), Inetkaues and Hetephernebty.

B. Reliefs in Underground Parts of the Step Pyramid Enclosure at Saqqara

These six famous reliefs are located under the Step Pyramid (P) or under the South Tomb (S). The symbolism is complex but may represent a series of elements in the Sed *festival of royal renewal.*

(P) *King standing wearing white crown*: Standing (in) the Upper Egyptian shrine of Horus of Behdet.
(P) *King running wearing white crown*: The white palace of the Great ones.
(P)(S) *King running wearing white crown*: Creation/dedication[1] at the southwest (corner of the) broad court.
(S) *King standing wearing red crown*: Standing (in) the Lower Egyptian shrine of Horus of Letopolis.
(S) *King standing wearing white crown*: Standing (in) the *per-wer* shrine.

C. Reliefs from a Temple at Heliopolis

i. These reliefs come from a chapel of Netjerykhet at Heliopolis, found reused in the foundations of a later building. Now in Turin 2671/21, 2671/20.

a. The king's daughter(s), who see Horus, Inetkaues and Hetephernebty.
b. (*with a figure of a god, see below*) I give life, stability, dominion, and joy for ever.

ii. This text appears adjacent to a number of seated divinities (one translated as b above) and appears to be more or less the same for each one. The following is a composite translation.

Speech: This most (?) perfect house of eternity (?) is this which I have made … I have done this …
Speech: To him have I given all life which is in my sight; to him have I given all dominion [which is in my sight].
Speech: I have allowed that he make (multiple) *Sed* festivals.
Speech: I have set him up as my heir of this [which I have made].
Speech: With respect to all things which he desires, [everything which he] has said [is done].
I give life, stability, dominion, and joy for ever.

8. From the Temples of Sneferu at Dahshur

The following texts are taken from pillars in the valley temple of the southern "Bent" pyramid of Sneferu. Text A might have been oriented toward a most unusual depiction of trees.

A.
Sneferu.
Horus Nebmaat.
The Golden Horus.
Viewing the growing of the flourishing cedar/pine trees and the flourishing myrrh trees.

B.
Sneferu.
[Horus Nebmaat]
Viewing the pens of the living antelopes.

9. Block from the Mortuary Temple of Userkaf at Saqqara, Reused at Lisht

The Userkaf mortuary temple at Saqqara was excavated in 1928–28, 1948–56, 1977–79, and 1992–93, and was finally published in Labrousse and Lauer 2000. This block was reused at Lisht and is still set into the pyramid of Amenemhat I,[2] *and is not in the previous publication; for other examples of reused blocks, see Metropolitan Museum of Art 1999 and Goedicke 1971, and nos. 12 and 120. This scene probably showed the king taking part in a temple ritual.*

Two Columns at Left

... Bastet and Shesmetet.

... returning from (?) the temple of Bastet in the ship "He who controls the *rekhyt*s."

Above and Behind Falcon at Top

He of Behdet, the Great God, the colorfully feathered one, who has come forth from the horizon; the perfect god, the lord of appearances.

Below Wing of Falcon, above Cobra

Wadjet, the inhabitant of Pe, mistress of the *per-nu.*

Center

The perfect god, the lord of cult activity, the Horus Irmaat, the king of Upper and Lower Egypt Userkaf.

Bottom Right, above Vulture

Nekhbet, the white one of Nekhen, may she give life.

Line at the Bottom of the Block, Part of the Scene Below

May she give life, stability and dominion, all joy and health for ever.

10. Texts from the Temple of Sahure at Abusir

Many fragments of scenes and inscriptions have survived from the mortuary temple of Sahure, showing the king, gods, and various other scenes. Many of the temple texts are paralleled in the later temple of Pepy II at South Saqqara; the latter are not translated in this book.

From the Mortuary Temple Itself

A.

The scene shows the goddess Seshat with depictions of a number of possible Libyan rulers and their families of various types plus large numbers of cattle, donkeys, sheep, and goats.
Above a depiction of Seshat writing: She who dwells in the house of the god's documents; she who dwells in the "school of the nobility."
In front of Seshat: Writing down the number of captives brought from all the foreign lands.

At the bottom are two standing deities:
The western goddess: Speech: To you have I given the chief of the Libyans.
Ash, lord of Libya: To you have I given every perfect thing which is in the foreign land.

B.

Two pairs of registers survive; in the upper of each pair is a row of deities bringing foreign captives (in the lower register of each pair, attached by ropes to the gods) to the king. Among the deities are "he of Ombos," *recognizable also as Seth, and another with the caption* "lord of all foreign lands" *(could apply perhaps to the Seth figure). Among the captives are Libyans, Asiatics, and inhabitants of Punt (none so described in texts).*
Three columns of text at left include the speeches of the gods:

1. To you have I given all the rebels together with all the provisions which are in every [foreign land], together with every perfect thing which is in my possession.
2. To you have I given every western and eastern foreign land together with all the Pillar people and all the Bedouin who are in every foreign land.
3. To you have I given all life and dominion, all health, all joy, and all stability, so that you may be at the head of all the living *kas*, for you have appeared on the throne of Horus for ever.

C.

King shown as a sphinx trampling over enemies. Various epithets above and behind the king:
Above the back of the sphinx:
… the lord of the Two Lands, Sahure, given all life and dominion; (he is)

Thoth, the lord of the Pillar people, (he is) Sopdet, lord of the foreign lands, who treads on the rebels.

Above and to the left of the vulture (presumably a representation of the Upper Egyptian goddess Nekhbet) over the last inscription:
… [she of outstretched] wing (*literally* "arm"), she who ties together the bows.[3]
Horus strong of arm, who acts with his own arm, the lord of the Two Lands. Given all life and stability, all health, all joy so that he may be at the head of all the living *kas* for ever.

D.

A series of boats with their crews adoring an image of Sahure (now lost)
Upper subregister: [Praise to you] Sahure, beloved of Thoth, lord of the foreign lands.

Praise to you Sahure, followers/guide (?) …

Lower subregister: Praise to you Sahure, the god of the living whose perfection we see (*or*) let us see your perfection.

Praise to you Sahure. [We] have seen [your perfection (*or similar*)].

Praise to you Sahure, the perfect one, the Horus, lord of the foreign lands.

E.

A scene of Sahure standing before Nekhbet and Khnum and being suckled by the former.
Above the king: [Horus] Nebkhau, [king of Upper and Lower Egypt] Sahure, given life for ever.
Above Nekhbet: [Nekhbet], the white one of Nekhen, [mistress of the divine mansion of] Upper Egypt, mistress of the *Per-wer*.
After the above epithets, perhaps a speech of the god: [All life and dominion] which are in my sight are for your nose, for ever.
Between both gods: May all protection and life be around (*literally* behind) him, may he be healthy, for ever.
Above Khnum: he who dwells in the "House of protection," the lord of Her-wer (*Antinoe*), he who dwells in the cataract city, lord of the house of Khnum.

F.

Remains of a speech by a god adjacent to registers of divinities:
[To you have I given] … all [(*enemies or foreigners of some type*)] under

your sandals. I have collected together the hearts of all the *rekhyt* people for you, and I have brought for you all the perfect things which are mine.

G.

Scenes showing processions of deities and corpulent figures bringing (in effect) all the good things of the land to the king:

[To you have I given] … all joy, all offerings, and every perfect thing which is in Upper Egypt, for you have appeared as the king of Upper and Lower Egypt, may he live for ever.

[To you have I given] … and every perfect offering which is in Lower Egypt for you have appeared as king of Upper and Lower Egypt, may he live for ever.

H.

The king offers to Bastet:

Above and in front of the king: the Horus Nebkhau, the perfect god, lord of the Two Lands. Offering *mimi*[4] *to Bastet.*

Speech of Bastet:

Speech: To you have I given all life and dominion, all health, and all joy for ever.

Bastet, the mistress of Ankhtawy,[5] mistress of Habes … mistress of the Two Lands in all her places.

Above the destroyed figure of the goddess is a cartouche of Thutmose IV of the eighteenth dynasty, indicating that the temple was restored at that time (compare his better-known stela in front of the sphinx at Giza).

From the Causeway of Sahure

I.

This publication also includes a scene of emaciated persons (Hawass and Verner 1996: fig. 2a, Taf. 55), together with the one from the Unas causeway. For the latter see also Schott 1965.

Teams of men holding ropes: … [dragging/pulling] the pyramidion of the pyramid of Sahure by the two boat crews …

11. Festival Offerings Calendar for the Sun Temple of Niuserre at Abu Gurob

The sun temple of Niuserre (Egyptian Shezepibre*) is one of only two such temples to have survived, the other being that of Userkaf (no. 85), although* *the Abusir papyri (no. 90) tell us much about the similar temple of Neferirkare. The temple of Niuserre was excavated at the beginning of the twentieth century, and many fragmentary scenes have survived. Not translated in this book are the hieroglyphs accompanying the well-known scenes of the so-called "Room of the Seasons" (Edel and Wenig 1974).*

These fragments were originally set up at the gateway of the valley temple and were ranged on the left and right sides of the door. The text is the only surviving such calendar of festivals from the Old Kingdom. Allowing for the restorations, it shows the range of festivals, both regular and occasional, which took place in the temple. Many of these festivals appear in the lists in tombs elsewhere in this book.

The reconstructions used are those of Helck, mostly used here without question, although they are very extensive, and the text given in his plates does not always quite equate with what he translates. These reconstructions are also not marked except where Helck has reconstructed text not shown in his plates.

Inscription A

His majesty has ordered the establishment of divine offerings specifically for his father Re in *Shezepibre* for the festival offerings:
On the day of the opening of the year: 1,000 *pezen* bread, 1 ox, 10 fowl, honey, milk, all sweet things;
On the day of the *Wag* festival, first month of the *Akhet* season, day 19: 1,300 portions of bread and beer, an ox;
On the day of the Thoth (?) festival, first month of the *Akhet* season, day 20: 1,300 portions of bread and beer, an ox for the divine offerings of Hathor. On the barque of Hathor his majesty accomplished the escort trip …
… the estate "it makes Niuserre live" in the first nome of Lower Egypt;
On the day of the *Sadj* festival of the *Akhet* season … stretching the cord, making bricks, breaking the earth, providing sand for the foundation,[6] executing work for the two Great Houses of the palace;
On the day of dressing Anubis, who is on his mountain, second month of the *Akhet* season, day … : 1,300 portions of bread and beer, an ox;
On the day of the excursion of Re in *Shezepibre*,[7] second month of the *Akhet* season, day 29: 1,300 portions of bread and beer, an ox …
…
On the day of raising the dish of the burnt offerings, third month of the *Akhet* season …: 1,300 portions of bread and beer, an ox;

On the day of "taking to the rivers (?)" in the evening of the third month of the *Akhet* season, day … : offering 30,000 portions of bread and beer and ten oxen;
On the day of the festival of Sokar, fourth month of the *Akhet* season, day 26: dragging (the image) of Sokar. On the barque of "he who is in his cavern"[8] his majesty accomplished the escort trip; 1,300 portions of bread and beer, an ox;
On the day of the excursion of Re in *Shezepibre*, fourth month of the *Akhet* season, day 29: 1,300 portions of bread and beer, an ox;
On the first day of the year, first month of the *Peret* season, day 1: 1,300 portions of bread and beer, an ox;
On the day of the *Rekeh* festival, second month of the *Peret* season, day 9: 1,300 portions of bread and beer, an ox;
On the day of the excursion of Re in *Shezepibre*, second month of the *Peret* season, day 29: 1,300 portions of bread and beer, an ox;
On the day of the excursion of Re in *Shezepibre*, third month of the *Peret* season, day 29: 1,300 portions of bread and beer, an ox;

…

… fourth month of the *Peret* season, day 27: 1,300 portions of bread and beer, an ox;

…

On the day of inspecting the granary (?) …

…

… stretching the cord, making bricks, breaking the earth, providing sand for the foundation, executing work in *Shezepibre* …

…

… His majesty (re [?])constructed this temple of *Shezepibre* in stone, for his majesty had found its columns had been erected in wood and its walls of brick;[9] his majesty erected the obelisk in stone 20 cubits wide and 20 long and … high …

…

anew his majesty excavated a lake, set out with sycamore trees …

…

… [His majesty set up: gold (?)] 107 vessels, [silver (?)] 19 vessels, bronze 8 altars, Asiatic copper […] vessels

…

… [*in the estates* … "Niuserre …"],[10] "Re makes Niuserre prosper," "Re loves what Niuserre does," "Re is the peace of Niuserre" …
… [*the estates*] "the delight of the Two Ladies," "the *inet* estate of the Golden Horus Netjeri (*Niuserre*) belongs to Re," "Re causes Niuserre to be

excellent," "Re is the peace of Niuserre (?)," "... of the Golden Horus Netjeri (*Niuserre*) belongs to [Re]" ...

... His majesty acted particularly in accordance with what he should do for the offering table of Re in every place where Re is; offering 30,000 portions of bread and beer, ... oxen, a jar of honey, a bowl for *shat* cakes;

On the day of the coming forth of Min, first month of the *Shemu* season, day 11: 1,000 *pezen* bread, an ox, ten geese, a jar of honey, *sekhet* grain, wheat, and every sweet thing;

On the day of the excursion of Re in *Shezepibre*, first (?) month of the *Shemu* season, day 29: 1,300 portions of bread and beer, an ox;

On the day ... second month of the *Shemu* season ... On the barque of Re in *Shezepibre* his majesty accomplished the escort trip: 1,300 portions of bread and beer, an ox;

On the day of [the festival of Bastet (?)], second month of the *Shemu* season [day 18: 1,300 portions of bread and beer, an ox; (?)]

[On the day of ... festival, second month of the *Shemu* season, day ...]: 1,300 portions of bread and beer, an ox;]

On the day of the excursion of Re in *Shezepibre*, second month of the *Shemu* season, day 29: 1,300 portions of bread and beer, an ox;

On the day of ... [his majesty provided (?)] a boat inlaid with green stone, ten *Wekh* standards[11] of lapis lazuli, 100 steering-oars of cedar/pine ... His majesty acted particularly in accordance with what he should do for the offering table of Re in every place where Re is; offering 30,000 portions of bread and beer, oxen (?), a jar of honey, a bowl for *shat* cakes;

On the day of the month of the *Sadj* festival of the *Shemu* season, an escort trip ...;

On the day of the excursion of Re in *Shezepibre*, third month of the *Shemu* season, day 29: a priestly allocation (?) of 1,300 portions of bread and beer, an ox;

On the day of the excursion of Re in *Shezepibre*, fourth month of the *Shemu* season, day 29: 1,300 portions of bread and beer, an ox;

... as a *wab*-priest (?) ...

...

... the five epagomenal days ...

...

... a jar of honey, a jar of milk, and *ished* fruit for Re when he makes an excursion in *Shezepibre*

...

... [*perhaps* his majesty set up offerings[12]] in detail: 108,000 portions of bread and beer, 7,720 *pezen* loaves, 1,002 oxen, 1,000 fowl ...

… *long gap*
… 1,000+ perfect wheat *shat* cakes, a jar of honey, priestly allocation (?) of
… from Lower and Upper Egypt …
… *long gap*
… at every beginning of the year, 1,000 *pezen* bread …
…
… [His majesty acted particularly in accordance with] what he should do for his offering table of Re in all these places in Lower Egypt …

Inscription B

Much more damaged than the above one; it may have been shorter.
…
… milk, a pot of honey, a bowl for *shat* cakes …
…
On the day of "taking to the rivers (?)," third month of the *Akhet* season … *pezen* bread 1,000, an ox, ten fowl;
On the day of …
…
…
… stretching the cord, making bricks, breaking the earth, providing sand for the foundation, executing work [in] …
…
… in stone, embellished with electrum, and doorways of granite did his majesty construct … (*dimensions include*) 10 + x cubits upon the reveals of the door; fashioning and opening the mouth[13] in the House of Gold of (statues of) Re and Hathor, making … of electrum …
…
… length of 7,000 cubits, width [10]6 cubits, height 22 cubits on each side
… an altar for Re of electrum …
…
… 30 arouras north of … 200 arouras …
…
… vessel of faience on the (?) festival of the fourth month of the *Akhet* season, day 25: 1,300 portions of bread and beer …
…
… 2 oxen …
On the day of giving the ten day festival of the Great One: 1,000 *pezen* bread …
…

... for all his festival offerings: 1,000 portions of bread and beer, one *iua* ox, ten oxen, a gazelle;
On the day of the reversion of offerings[14] (?) for his festival offerings, one ox;
On the day of ...
On the day of the reversion of offerings (?) ...
...
... two *iua* oxen, 100 oxen, two gazelles, provisioning ...
...
... first month of the *Shemu* season ...
...
... every month, 20 oxen, 50 goats (?) ...

12. Blocks from the Causeway of the Pyramid of Unas at Saqqara

The two major temples of Old Kingdom pyramid complexes, called the mortuary temple (by the pyramid) and the valley temple (usually at the edge of the cultivation), were linked by a processional causeway. Most of these have been destroyed, but that of Unas at Saqqara is in quite good condition (and has been quite sympathetically restored in modern times); there was an amount of decoration on the walls. Much of this is unpublished. A famous block bearing figures of emaciated people is mentioned under the Sahure temple (no. 10).

A. Caption to Boats

Arrival from Elephantine loaded with granite columns for the pyramid temple of the son of Re, Unas.
Arrival from Elephantine loaded with granite cornices (*or* lintels)[15] for the pyramid temple of the son of Re, Unas.

B. Block Reused at Lisht

See also nos. 9 and 120 for reused blocks from this site.
This is an isolated block perhaps with a part of a "historical" text recovered from the pyramid of Amenembat I at Lisht.
(1) ... the royal children, the sole companions ...
(2) ... the royal nobles, the seal-bearers of the god ...
(3) ... the overseers of the expedition who are in (*or*) those who are in ...
(4) ... secrets concerning their hearts ...

(5) … they fall on their faces (?) …
(6) … [giving] praise to the son of Re, Unas …
(7) … the might (*or* "the *bas*") of the son of Re, Unas are nobler than …
(8) … Words spoken: To you have I given the perfect appearances (as king) …
(9) … Words spoken: To you have I given might …

13. Texts of Pepy I and Teti from Tell Basta

Tell Basta, ancient Bubastis, was clearly an important place in the Old Kingdom. It was and remained the cult center of the cat-goddess Bastet, whose name is found in two temple inscriptions translated here (nos. 9 and 10). The most important Old Kingdom monument is a soul (ka) *chapel of Pepy I. See el-Sawi 1979: fig. 4 for a plan of the site. Pepy and other kings almost certainly erected numerous such chapels around Egypt, but this is the only one preserved to any extent (compare Fischer 1958b).*

Pepy I

A. Entrance Lintel with Scene of Pepy I Receiving an *Ankh* (Life) Sign from Bastet

Either side of winged sun-disc at top: He of Behdet, lord of Mesen.
Lion-headed goddess: Bastet. Giving all life.
King: The king of Upper and Lower Egypt, the son of Re, Pepy, the perfect god, given life.
Figure of goddess: Hathor, mistress of Iunet (Dendera).
Priest at right: To you have I given life and dominion. The Iunmutef priest ("pillar of his mother").
Above corpulent Nile god at left: (*The personification of*) Lower Egypt, master of provisions.
Either end of scene: Horus Merytawy, the king of Upper and Lower Egypt, the Two Ladies Merykhet …

B. Inner Gate, Lintel and Jambs

(Long) live the Horus Merytawy, king of Upper and Lower Egypt, the son of Re, Pepy, the perfect god, given life.
(Long) live the Two Ladies Merykhet, the triple Golden Horus, beloved of all the gods.
(Long) live the soul chapel of Pepy in Bubastis.
On jambs: (*R*) the *Akhet* season; (*L*) Hapy/the inundation.

C. Other Pillar and Lintel Fragments Mainly Repeat the Names of the King. For Example:

The son of [Atum], lord of Heliopolis and of [Hathor], mistress of Dendera, Pepy, the Two Ladies Merykhet. the triple Golden Horus, [Mery]re …

D. Remains of a Pillar from a Chapel of Teti

Horus [Seheteptawy …], the soul chapel of Teti.

14. A *Sed* Festival Monument of Pepy II

A most unusual monument, dealing with a small section of the Sed *festival; some of the scenes in it are paralleled in the sun temple of Niuserre at Abusir. The deities depicted are discussed in Schott 1974. Now in Cairo, CG 1747.*

Side 1—Scenes of the King in the *Sed* Festival Kiosk

At top, winged sun disc: The Behdetite.
King in red crown: Horus Netjerykhau, son of Re, Pepy, may he live like Re for ever.
King in white crown: Neferkare.
Anubis fetish: He who is in his wrappings.
Below kiosk: First occasion of the *Sed* festival, may he achieve life like Re for ever.
At bottom are the tops of speeches of goddesses.

Side 2—King with Various Goddesses

Caption: (For a statue of) electrum, making the "opening of the mouth" in the mansion of gold in the mansion "Great of perfection is Re" for the first occasion of the *Sed* festival.
King: Horus Netjerykhau, king of Upper and Lower Egypt Neferkare, given life, stability, and dominion.
Goddess: May she give all life and dominion, all stability like Re for ever.
The same text is found with another goddess
At right, in front of goddess: Speech: To you have I given (the ability to make) millions of *Sed* festivals, all life, dominion and health, and joy like Re; (the goddess) Menet,[16] may she give all life and dominion …

15. Building Inscriptions from Temples

These are characterized by the use of the phrase "he (=king X) set up a monument … ," which phrase can be used of more than just construction projects (see the Palermo Stone [no. 1] and the Sixth Dynasty Annals [no. 3]). The following is a selection of other Old Kingdom examples.[17] *See also the Menkaure decree of Shepseskaf (no. 16).*

A. Izezi, Found in the Pyramid Complex of Niuserre at Abusir

Renewal inscriptions of one king for another are not common in the Old Kingdom; rather, we think of them from the New Kingdom. Now Berlin 17933.

Horus Djedkhau, the king of Upper and Lower Egypt, the Two Ladies Djedkhau, the Golden Horus Djed, Djedkare.

For the king of Upper and Lower Egypt [Niuser]re he set up a monument …

B. Pepy I, for His Wife Nubwenet in Her Pyramid Complex at South Saqqara

The king of Upper and Lower Egypt, the son of Re, Pepy, may he live for ever.

For his beloved royal wife of the pyramid of Pepy I, she who sees Horus and Seth, the great favorite, the great of affection, the companion of Horus, his beloved royal wife Nubwenet, he set up a monument.

C. Pepy I, for His Wife Meretites in Her Pyramid Complex at South Saqqara

… For his beloved royal wife, the *imakhu,* the royal wife Meretites, he set up a monument.

D. Pepy II, for His Wife Iput in Her Pyramid Complex at South Saqqara

(Long) live the Horus Netjerykhau, the king of Upper and Lower Egypt Neferkare, given life.

For the *iry pat,* royal wife, eldest king's daughter of the pyramid "Neferkare is established and living," Iput, he set up a monument.

An almost identical but more damaged text was inscribed for Pepy's wife Wedjebten.

E. Pepy II, from a Stela in Ain Asil in Dakhla Oasis

Now in the museum at Balat.

… in the oasis in (?)… he set up a monument

Notes

1. Perhaps of a statue at this location?

2. A considerable number of Old Kingdom blocks were taken to Lisht and reused in and around the pyramid complex of Amenemhat I of the twelfth dynasty. A shortage of building stone seems an unlikely explanation, and the most plausible reason is perhaps that incorporation of blocks from an older age which in many ways Amenemhat was trying to emulate helped to legitimize the newer regime (see Goedicke 1971: 1–7).

3. Presumably a reference to the Nine Bows, the traditional enemies of Egypt.

4. An uncertain product, probably grain-based. In the Old Kingdom it seems to be found just in temple contexts like this, but in the New Kingdom it is listed among granary products.

5. Part of the Saqqara necropolis, said to be that near the Serapeum.

6. These are all stages in the foundation ceremony for a building such as a temple.

7. Evidently a regular occurrence, although Helck does observe that there is not always sufficient room for it every month.

8. A serpent deity, referred to at least twice in the Pyramid Texts and evidently regarded as an enemy of the king (PT 245 and 682; translation in Faulkner 1969: 57, 128). For the "evil eye" of the snake in the Pyramid and Coffin Texts, see Borghouts 1973: 140–42.

9. This sentence, if the reconstructions are correct, appears to suggest that Niuserre rebuilt the temple from some temporary construction. Or did he take an earlier structure and modify it to be his own temple?

10. This very damaged section almost certainly consisted of the setting up of a number of funerary domains for the benefit of the temple (compare Jacquet-Gordon 1962: 158–59). There are a number of isolated signs that appear to belong to the names of the nomes in which the estates were set up.

11. See a text in the Abusir Papyri (no. 90E).

12. Or possibly even a total?

13. Compare the Palermo Stone (no. 1).

14. Otherwise unknown; Helck also translates it as "striking the *wedjeb*."

15. The meaning of this word is not clear, but it seems to refer to an architectural feature at the tops of walls (Spencer 1984: 278–81).

16. A sky goddess, lion-headed; possibly also a protective deity for the royal pyramid complex. See Leitz 2002: 3:286–87.

17. These texts for all periods have been studied by Grallert 2001; her Old Kingdom examples are on pp. 581–82.

IV

Royal Decrees

See notes in chapter I, §6.3.2. The reader is encouraged to examine the original editions for discussion of the many difficult terms and expressions in these texts, as notes have here been kept to a minimum. Line numbers are not always added in very damaged or complex examples, and the numbers I have allocated do not always concur with those published, for example, in Urk I.

16. Decree of Shepseskaf from the Pyramid Temple of Menkaure at Giza

This is the earliest decree to survive from the Old Kingdom. Dated to the first year of Shepseskaf's reign, it suggests that it was set up at least partly as part of his pious completion of the earlier temple—it would appear that Menkaure died before the complex was complete and that Shepseskaf finished off the temple in brick rather than stone for the sake of speed (Reisner 1931: 29–31). It is just possible that this decree is a later copy of an original document, suggested by the prominence of the cartouche name at the top of the decree, which is rather strange for the Old Kingdom. However, its rather unusual structure perhaps argues for an early date for the original, before the more established forms had evolved. The fragments are now in the Egyptian Museum in Cairo (Temp. no. 26.2.21.18).

Horus Shepseskhet, the year after the first occasion of the count of the cattle and herds ... which was done in the presence of the king himself.
The king of Upper and Lower Egypt Shepseskaf.
For the king of Upper and Lower Egypt [Menkaure] he set up a monument[1] (in the form of) a *pekher* offering ... in the pyramid of Menkaure ...
With regard to the *pekher* offering brought for the king of Upper and Lower Egypt [Menkaure] ... priestly duty [is done] with respect to it for

ever. ... [it should never be taken away by someone] in the course of his duty for ever ... the pyramid of Menkaure ... burial ... the pyramid of Menkaure. [My/his majesty] does not permit ... servants ... priests [*the last part is too damaged to admit of understanding*]

17. Decree of Neferirkare from Abydos

Compared with later periods, little is known in inscriptional terms about the temples and cults of Abydos in the Old Kingdom (but see Brovarski 1994a; 1994b; Kemp 1977: 186–89; O'Connor 1992; see also before no. 255). Although the site later became the cult center of Osiris, the Egyptian god of the Dead par excellence, the earliest appearances of his name are in the fifth dynasty, and the pre-eminent deity for much of the Old Kingdom was Khentyimentyu "foremost of the Westerners," a god of the dead subsumed into Osiris in the course of the period. Temples on a mound adjacent to the cultivation now known as Kom es-Sultan extend back at least into the Early Dynastic Period and were excavated by Petrie in 1901–2, when this decree and others (nos. 19, 22) were found. This decree makes no mention of the specific temple or deity to which it applied; like so many Egyptian texts, this would have been totally obvious to all concerned and did not need to be mentioned. It is now in Boston, MFA 03.1896.

The complex line structure of this decree is schematically laid out in fig. 3 and a drawing is reproduced as fig. 4.

(1) Horus Userkhau (Neferirkare)
(2) A royal decree (to) the overseer of priests, Hemwer:[2]
(3) I do not empower any man (*to do any of the following*);

- (4) to take away any priest (5) who is in your nome (6) for the purpose of compulsory labor and any (other) work (7) of the nome, with exceptions for carrying out the cult rites (8) for his god in the temple where they take place, (9) and for maintaining the temples (10) in which they (*the rites*) are;
- (13) to levy the corvée for any work on (14) any god's field (15) on which priestly duty is done by (16) any priest;
- (17) to take away any dependents who are on (14) any god's field (15) on which priestly duty is done by (16) any priest (18) for the purpose of doing compulsory labor and any (other) work of the nome.

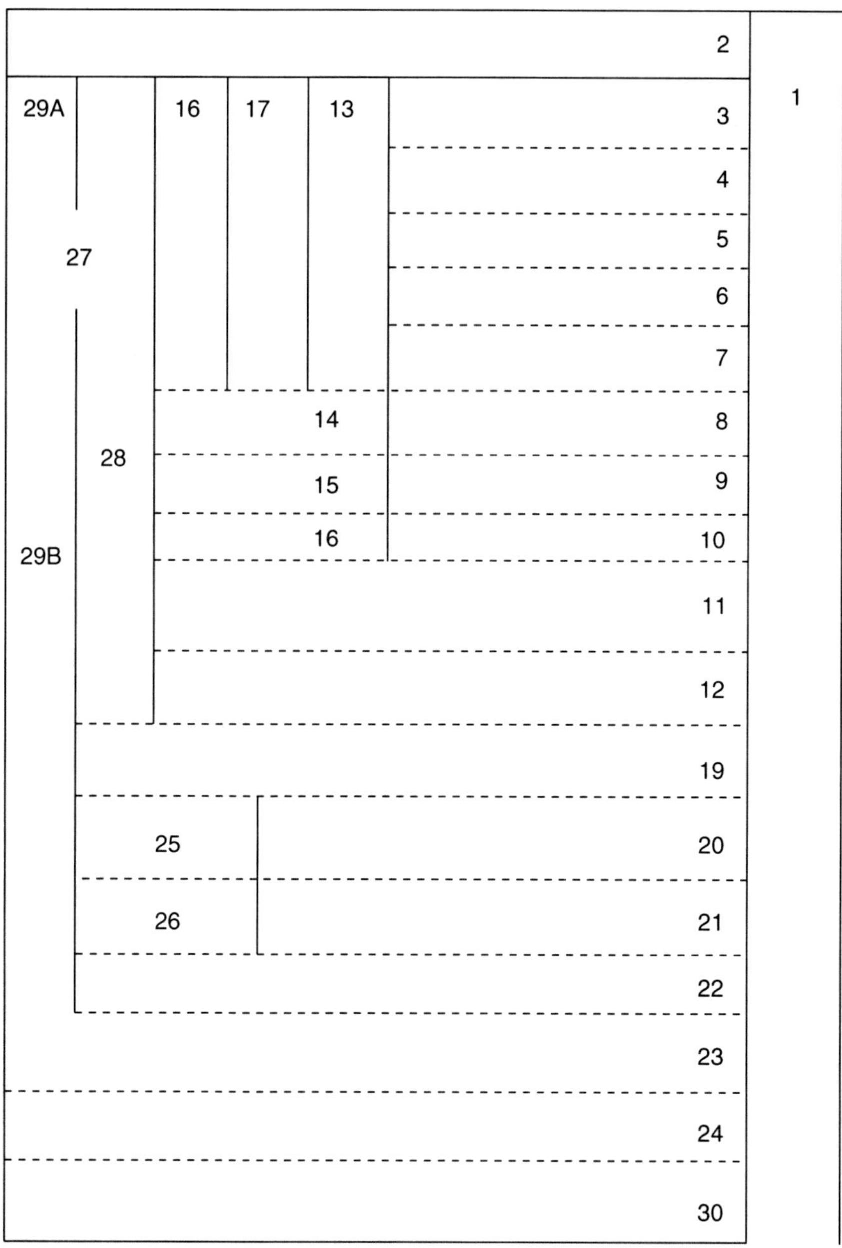

Fig. 3: Layout of Decree of Neferirkare (no. 17; adapted from Leprohon 1985: 50). Solid lines represent line divisions present on the original; broken lines are added for the remainder to assist the reader.

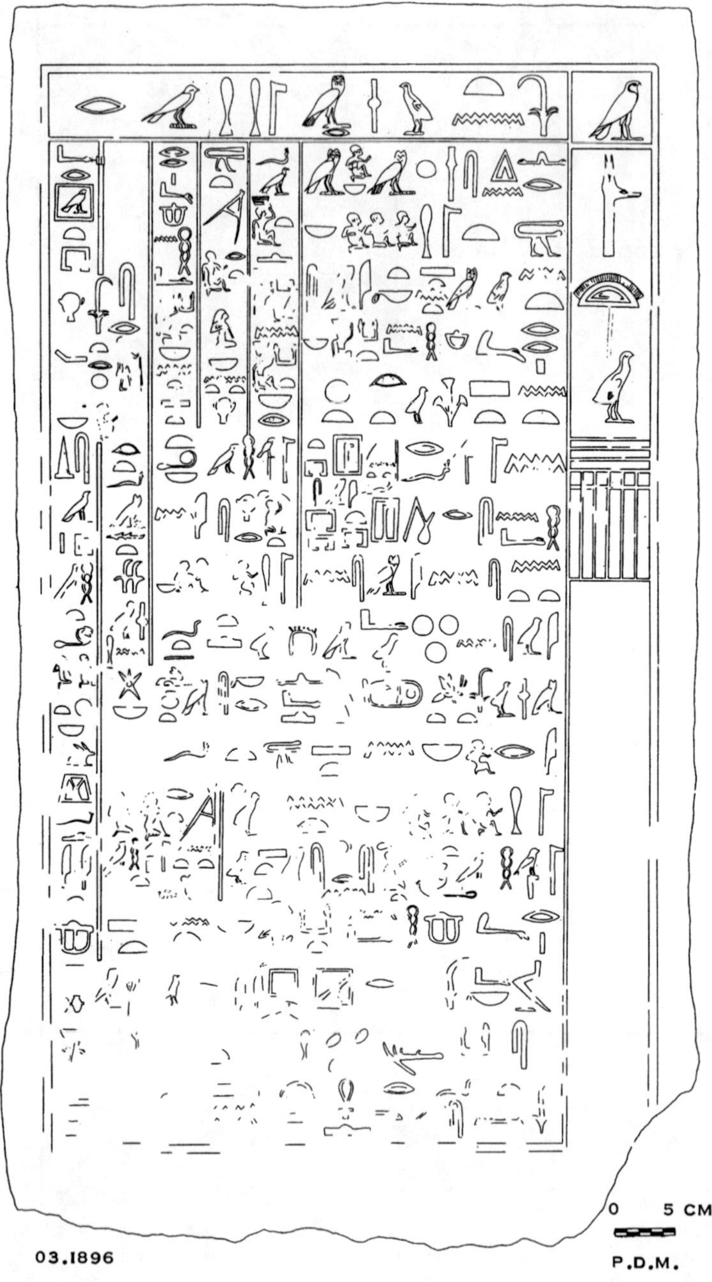

Fig. 4: Decree of Neferirkare (no. 17). Drawing by Peter D. Manuelian. Reproduced by permission of the Museum of Fine Arts, Boston.

(11) They are (all) exempted for all time (12) through the royal decree of the king of Upper and Lower Egypt Neferirkare; you do not have any legal claim against it with respect to any duty.

(19) With regard to any man of the nome who shall take away

- (20) any priest who is on (21) the land of the god who does priestly service in that nome;
- (25) the dependents (26) who are on any god's field;

(22) for the purpose of compulsory labor and any work of the nome, (23) you shall send him to the Great Mansion and he shall be made to work in the stone quarry, (24) and to harvest barley and emmer wheat.[3]

(27) (And with regard to) any noble, royal acquaintance, or person concerned with reversionary offerings (28) who shall act counter to this decree of my majesty (29a) which has been registered in the Great Mansion, (29b) (his) house, land, people, and everything he owns shall be taken away and he shall be put onto compulsory labor.

(30) Sealed in the presence of the king himself (on) the second month of the *Shemu* season, day 11 (*at least; could be higher*).

18. Two Decrees from the Abusir Papyri of Neferefre

A discovery of Old Kingdom papyri was made at Abusir in 1982 by the Czech mission working on the pyramid and temple of Neferefre (chapter I, §6.4). These two documents provide papyrus examples for the layout of the stone royal decrees. The particular topic of the examples presented here is very limited, being permissions from the king for certain named individuals to have access to the royal offerings of the pyramid—in other words, to take from the royal offerings for their own use, a form of payment. B is, of course, reconstructed on the basis of A. Both fragments now Cairo, JE 97348. Dated to the reign of Izezi. For other Abusir papyri see nos. 90, 91, and 92.

Document A

Recto

(1) Horus Djedkhau.

(2) A royal decree to the supervisors of the *wab*-priests and *khenty-she* in the pyramid of Neferefre, (3) (which relates to) Iry, the son of the companion (of the king) Semenptah and Ankhizi, the son of the *khenty-she* Ankhizi:

(4) Give [them] access [to ...] (5) of the invocation offerings of the king of

Upper and Lower Egypt Neferefre (6) in the pyramid of Neferefre (7) in the same manner in which the *wab*-priests and *khenty-she* (8) have access.

Verso

(1) Sealed in the presence of the king himself (*date lost*).
(2) The two leaders (of the temple personnel [?]) will distribute the loaves [in accordance with your legal document].

Document B

Recto

[(1) royal name destroyed].
(2) A royal decree to the supervisors of the *wab*-priests and *khenty-she*, (3) (which relates to) the two sons of Nykanezut (4) and to Ankhhaf:
[(5) Give them access ... (6) of the funerary offerings of the king of Upper and Lower Egypt Neferefre] (7) in the pyramid of Neferefre (8) in the same manner in which the *wab*-priests and *khenty-she* (9) have access.

Verso

(1) Sealed in the presence of the king himself, fourth month of the *Akhet* season, day 27.
(2) (*In red ink*)[4] Year of the fifteenth occasion, fourth month of the *Akhet* season, day 28.
(3) (*In red ink*) The elder of the palace Rehotep, the assistant of Nisuuser, Sedjertep, and the companion Nisuuser.
(4) (*In red ink*) The inspector of ...

19. Decree of Teti from Abydos

Now in London, BM EA 626.

(1) Horus Seheteptawy.
(2) A royal decree (for) ...
(3) With regard to that which you said to my majesty which has gone forth ...
(4) concerning of the reckoning of cattle and all labor therein ... [I do not (?)] permit ...
(5) The fields and people are exempted for Khenty[imentyu for eternity (?)] ... (6) through the decree of the king of Upper and Lower Egypt Teti, may he live for ever and for eternity. A decree is now made (7) for [the

haty-a, sole companion], seal-bearer of the king of Lower Egypt, overseer of Upper Egypt Nykauizezi, [son of the overseer of Upper Egypt, Re]shepses,[5]
(8) that he is charged with accounting these things completely (?).
(9) Sealed [in the presence of the king himself] (on) the third month of the *Akhet* season, day 3.

20. Decree of Pepy I from Dahshur

This is the longest and most complex of all the Old Kingdom decrees: in addition to its internal interest, at least one of the named recipients is known, and one of their names has also been erased. It has been speculated that the latter may have something to do with a possible conspiracy in the reign (Kanawati 2002a; a so-called harem conspiracy is noted in the biography of Weni [no. 256]). The structure of the document is complex, with a number of key phrases at the beginnings and in the middles of sections given once only in the original but that must in English be repeated with the subordinate clauses to make it at all intelligible; for this reason I consider that numbering the lines in this translation would be too confusing and complex. It was found in the village of Shinbab on the edge of the cultivation near Dahshur (Borchardt 1905: 1–2; PM III², 876). Now Berlin 17500.

Horus Merytawy.
Year of the twenty-first occasion, first month of the *Peret* season, day 23.
A decree to:[6]
[the overseer of the royal document scribes], the vizier [*name cut out*]; the overseer of works Meryptahmeryre; the charmed of arm, Ihykhent; the overseer of the *khenty-she* Weni; the overseer of commissions of the divine offerings Khenu; the sole companion Ihyempermeryre; the overseer of the house of reversionary offerings Meri; the inspector of foreigners and overseer of Medja, Iam, and Iertjet[7] ...

Main Section I

[With regard to] the king of Upper and Lower Egypt Sneferu in the two pyramids of Sneferu, my majesty has decreed (as follows):

that these two pyramid towns be exempted on his behalf from performing any work for the house of the king, from being taxed for the office of the Residence, or from (the performance of) any assignation (or work) or from the continuation of (such) assignations put forward by anyone;

that all the *khenty-she* of these two pyramid towns be exempted on his behalf from that which any emissary requires, whether on water or land, whether going upstream or downstream;

that it is forbidden to allow the cultivation of any field of these two pyramid towns whether as cultivation through the dependents of any royal wife, king's son, companion, or official, or as a requisition by any pacified Nubian,[8] unless it is done by the *khenty-she* of these two pyramid towns;

that it is forbidden that any *khenty-she*[9] of these two pyramid towns, who has been or will be on their register, be taken away by any man or by any pacified Nubian (just) because they were with them before. They have no legal right thereto;

that it is forbidden to include female children and the provisions of *neheru* cattle in any *djeba* levy in these two pyramid towns;

that it is forbidden to bring anyone from these two pyramid towns to dig canals in the *ra-she* of the pyramid of Ikauhor;[10]

that it is forbidden to reckon (*with a view to taxing them*) the canals, pools, wells, watering places, and trees in these two pyramid towns;

that it is forbidden that any pacified Nubian should come along with the intention of carrying out requisitions in these two pyramid towns;

that it is forbidden for any man who is beholden to these pacified Nubians to enter into the *wab*-priesthood, monthly priesthood or to eat any rations in the temple which is in these two pyramid towns;

the revision of the documents of these two pyramid towns in accordance with what the census has ordered for these two pyramid towns;[11]

that the (number of) all *khenty-she* of these pyramid towns be kept up (*literally* "caused to be complete") and that the children of all who remain be recruited to the register.

Main Section II

Do not grant any land, priesthood, or property (of these two pyramid towns) to anyone who is attached to another pyramid town, unless they are also attached to these two pyramid towns.

Do not commit the services (?) of any *khenty-she* of these two pyramid towns on the word of any man except for something which is decreed and known about in advance.

Concluding Section

My majesty has made these exemptions in these two pyramid towns in this manner particularly through the wish that the duties of *wab*-priest, monthly

priests, and whatever is done for the god (are carried out) in these two pyramid towns of the king of Upper and Lower Egypt Sneferu, in the [two] pyramid towns "Sneferu appears in glory" [as what is commanded on behalf of the] life, [prosperity, and health of the king of] Upper [and Lower Egypt] Meryre, [may he live for ever.]
[Sealed in the presence of the king himself.]

21. Decree of Pepy I from Koptos (Koptos A)

Excavations in the temple of Min at Koptos revealed a large group of royal decrees of Old Kingdom date, slabs of stone subsequently reused in later buildings. They form the largest group of such documents known and are a mixture of decrees for the main temple and for other smaller monuments. They range in date from this one relating to a chapel of Iput, the mother of Pepy I, to those of the very last kings of the eighth dynasty and are a very important set of sources for the late Old Kingdom. It has become conventional to number them Koptos A–T; some of the most fragmentary ones are omitted here.

The scene at the top of this decree shows the king offering to an ithyphallic figure of Min, with Iput standing behind. Iput was a wife of Teti and had a pyramid adjacent to that of her husband at Saqqara (no. 280). It is now in Cairo, JE 41890.

Around Scene and Immediately Below

Above the god: He of Koptos.
Above the king: Meryre, the perfect god, lord of the Two Lands.
Above the queen: The royal mother, Iput.
Below scene: (1) Beloved of he who gives life, stability, and power for ever. (2) The occasion of the first *Sed* festival; may he achieve life like Re.

Main Text

(1) The soul chapel of the royal mother Iput, in Koptos in the Koptite nome.[12]
(2) I have ordered the exemption of this soul chapel [and its priests (?)], (3) dependents, cattle, and goats [and there are no grounds for suit against it. With regard to] (4) any emissary who shall travel upstream on any mission, my majesty does not permit (5) him to burden the soul chapel in any way. Nor does my majesty allow that the (6) "following of Horus" take advantage of it. My majesty has commanded that this soul chapel be

exempted. (7) My majesty does not permit the levying of any tax, which is calculated for the Residence in this soul chapel.

22. Decree of Pepy II from Abydos

The upper part of this stela is lost. This text, in addition to the interest it bears about statues in the temple, has a number of possible structural interpretations (I do not give line numbers for this reason). For further comments on the building in which these statues might have resided, see Brovarski 1994b: 15–20. Three fragments from this decree are now in Toronto, Royal Ontario Museum 905.2.120.[13]

[My majesty has commanded the offering of half] an ox, a *meret*-jug of milk, and one-eighth portion of an ox for every festival therein (*the temple*) for:

- The service of the overseer of priests of this temple;
- The statue of Neferkare which is in the temple of Khentyimentyu;
- The statue of the royal mother of the pyramid of Neferkare Ankhesenpepy which is in the temple of Khentyimentyu;
- The statue of the royal mother of the pyramid of Merenre Ankhesenpepy which is in the temple of Khentyimentyu;
- The statue of the vizier Djau.

The soul priests of their funerary estates, who are exempt in the manner of the slaughtered divine offerings, (they it is) who shall perform their priestly duties. I do not permit that they carry the royal offerings or the offering of a private individual for the breadth of eternity.

Sealed in the presence of the king himself, third month of the *Shemu* season, day 8.

23. Decree of Pepy II from the Valley Temple of Menkaure at Giza

Pepy II here reasserts the rights of one of his predecessors. It would appear from this text that, in addition to the royal cult, three private cults were associated with the temple and benefited from it. Now Boston, MFA 47.1654.

(1) Horus Netjerykhau.

Year of the thirty-first occasion, third month of the *Akhet* season, day 6.

(2) A royal decree to [the overseer] of the pyramid town of Menkaure ... , (for the benefit of)

- (3) the *iry pat,* eldest king's son, Nemtyemzaf: (his) altar;
- (4) the *haty-a,* sole companion, charmed of arm, Imapepy: (his) altar;
- (5) the *haty-a,* sole companion, overseer of the *khenty-she* of the Great House, Khnumhotep: (his) altar.

(6) (With regard to) the lector priest, scribe of the phyle, Ishefi,[14] (7) he is the [overseer of the pyramid town (?) and responsible for (?)]

- (8–9) ... in the pyramid town
- everything which is reckoned with regard to the broad hall and the festival (?)
- the distribution of the divine offerings and ... in the pyramid town of Menkaure.

(10) No man has a right relating to it except for the aforementioned[15] Ishefi in accordance with this decree for ever.

(11) You do not have the authority to permit men of this troop (12) of the pyramids of Neferkare and Merenre and of these chapels (?) to go forth to remove property from the aforementioned pyramid town. My majesty has ordered the exemption and protection of this pyramid town (13) so that the property thereof should not be taken by any man.

(My) majesty has done this (?) particularly in relation to the (ordinary) priestly duties and the monthly priestly duties (14) [to offer] incense and the sealed things of the god [in the temple of Menkaure (?)], may he live for ever, (15) according to the command of the king of Upper and Lower Egypt Neferkare, may he live for ever and for eternity.

(16) Sealed in the presence of the king himself ...

24. Decree of Pepy II from Koptos (Koptos B)

Now in Cairo, JE 41893. For Djau mentioned in the address, see nos. 22 and 257.

(1) Horus Netjerykhau.

Year after the eleventh occasion, second month of the *Shemu* season, day 28.

(2) A royal decree for the overseer of the pyramid town, the vizier, the overseer of scribes of royal documents, Djau; the *haty-a,* the overseer of Upper Egypt, Khui; the overseer of priests, the inspector of priests, and all the chiefs of the Koptite nome (*fifth of Upper Egypt*).

(3) [With respect to] the overseer of priests and inspector of priests of Min in Koptos of the Koptite nome; all the dependents of the possessions of the estate of Min; the functionaries of the entourage and daily service of Min; the workmen and builders of this temple (4) who are there (in service).
My majesty does not permit that they be set to the royal corvée (*or the like*), (5) in cattle pastures or donkey pastures, in with other animals, in the administration of the guards, or in any duty or any tax imposition (6) which is reckoned in the royal estate, for the breadth of eternity. Their exemption within Koptos (7) is renewed today by command of the king of Upper and Lower Egypt Neferkare, may he live for ever and for eternity.
(8) With regard to:

- (9) an overseer of Upper Egypt who shall make a levy on them

or

- (10) any chief, (11) great one of the tens of Upper Egypt, (12) overseer of phyles of Upper Egypt, (13) overseer of commissions, (14) royal acquaintance, (15) overseer of payments, or (16) overseer of royal colonists (17) who shall take them on way for a levy which is brought into effect

(18) for the offices of (19) royal levies, reversionary offerings, documents, and sealed matters and to set them to (do) any work (20) of the house of the king, it is a conspiracy akin to rebellion!
(21) With regard to a levy of the nome which is brought before the overseer of Upper Egypt for his attention (22) after it has been brought before the officials, my majesty has commanded that he search out (23) the names of these priests and functionaries of this temple.
(24) [With regard to] any official, royal document scribe, overseer of scribes of fields, overseer of scribes of everything which is sealed, (25) or functionary, who shall receive a levy or who shall write out orders to enlist (26) the names of the overseer of priests, the inspector of priests, functionaries, followers or watchmen of Min, dependents (27) of the endowment of the estate of Min, those of the *per-shena* estate, or these builders of Min in Koptos (28) in the Koptite nome for any work of the royal house, (29) it is a conspiracy akin to rebellion!
(30) The king of Upper and Lower Egypt Neferkare, may he live for ever and for eternity, has commanded (31) that this document be put into the form of this decree and set up as a decree in (32) hard stone at the gate of Min in Koptos in the Koptite nome, (33) so that the functionaries of this nome should see (it) and that they do not take away (34) these priests for any work of the royal estate for the breadth of eternity.
(35) With regard to this which is said to my majesty that decrees of the king

have been sealed for Upper Egypt, in relation to the execution of required works (36) for the king in the form of every transport or every digging work which is ordered to be carried out in the aforementioned Upper Egypt—in this case, it is said in these decrees (37) "no exemption is to be made in respect of the exempted towns which are in the aforementioned Upper Egypt." My majesty does not allow that any people of the estate of Min of Koptos in the Koptite nome (38) should perform such required works of transporting or digging which are to be done in the aforementioned Upper Egypt.

The king of Upper and Lower Egypt Neferkare, may he live for ever and for eternity, has commanded (39) that they be exempted on this matter for Min of Koptos for the breadth of eternity.

My majesty requires that the royal decrees be acted upon relating to earlier exemptions for Min of Koptos, (40) and you should act in respect of his exemptions! My majesty does not permit that any emissary of any official come forth onto the mound of the estate of Min.

As the king of Upper and Lower Egypt Neferkare lives, may he live for ever and for eternity, you should not take them away (41) for any work with the exception of performing their priestly duties for Min of Koptos. It is a matter dear to the heart of Neferkare that things be carried out in accordance with the wording of this decree.

And indeed, any official or functionary (42) who does not carry out matters in accordance with the wording of this decree accepted in the "hall of Horus"[16] in relation to that which my majesty has ordered to be done—my majesty does not permit them to serve as priests in the pyramid of Neferkare for ever.

(43) With regard to any field or plowed lands set up for the benefit of the priests of this temple, my majesty has commanded that they be exempted (in the manner of) all possessions of Min (44) of Koptos.

This is renewed today as a decree on behalf of the king of Upper and Lower Egypt Neferkare, may he live for ever and for eternity.

(45) Sealed in the presence of the king himself.

25. Decree of Pepy II from Koptos (Koptos C)

This text closely parallels Koptos B in many passages, but the physical arrangement is rather different. Now in Cairo, JE 41491.

(1) [Horus Netjerykhau.

Year] after the twenty-second occasion.

(2) [A royal decree] … [(to the) scribe] of the fields of the [Koptite nome] … (with regard to) [the overseer of] priests, the inspectors (of priests) and all followers, builders and dependents of the estate of Min …
(3) My majesty [does not permit] that they be placed in the royal corvées of the cattle pastures, donkey pastures, pastures of other animals, in the administration of the guards or in any duty or any tax imposition which is reckoned in the royal estate, for the breadth of eternity. (4) [Their exemption within] Koptos is renewed today by command of the king of Upper and Lower Egypt Neferkare, may he live for ever and for eternity, for the breadth of eternity.
(5) [With regard to:]

- (6) [an overseer of Upper Egypt who shall make a levy on them]

or

- (7) any chief, great one of the tens of Upper Egypt, overseer of phyles of Upper Egypt, overseer of commissions, royal acquaintance, overseer of payments or overseer of royal colonists (8) who shall take them on for a levy which is brought into effect

(9) for the offices of (10) royal levies, reversionary offerings, documents, and sealed matters (11) and to place them to (do) any work of the house of the king, it is [truly] what the king hates.
(12) With regard to a levy of the nome which is brought before the overseer of Upper Egypt for his attention after it has been (13) brought before the officials, my majesty has commanded that he search out the names [of the priests] (14) of this temple.
With regard to any official, royal document scribe, overseer of scribes of fields, overseer of scribes of everything which is sealed, or functionary who shall receive a levy or who shall write out orders to enlist [the names of the overseer] of priests, (15) the inspector of priests, functionaries, followers or watchmen of Min, dependents of the endowment of the estate of Min in Koptos for any work of the royal house, (16) it is doubly truly what the king hates.
The king of Upper and Lower Egypt Neferkare, may he live for ever and for eternity, has commanded (17) that this document be put into the form of this decree and set up as a decree in stone at the gate of Min in Koptos, (18) so that the functionaries of this nome should see (it) and that they do not take away the priests of this temple for any work of the king for the breadth of eternity.
(19) With regard to this which is said to my majesty that decrees have been sealed for the aforementioned Upper Egypt, to the effect of the carrying

out of required works for the king (20) (whether it be)

- in the form of every transport or every digging work which is ordered to be done in the aforementioned Upper Egypt;
- in the control of (?) the overseer of Upper Egypt: gold, copper, decorative items (?);
- for the requirements of the "house of life": the annual requirements of rations and animal feed, offerings, ropes and bindings, animal skins;
- for the $19^5/_8$ arouras of land and the rights of plowing;
- for all taxes and all works which are due on water and on land

—(these) are what is ordered to be done in the aforementioned Upper Egypt.

(21) For it is said with respect to these decrees: "no exemption is to be made in relation to the exempted towns which are in the aforementioned Upper Egypt." (22) My majesty does not permit these priests to do these things which are ordered to be done in the aforementioned Upper Egypt.

(23) The king of Upper and Lower Egypt Neferkare, may he live for ever and for eternity, has commanded that they be exempted and protected for Min of Koptos (24) for the breadth of eternity.

My majesty requires that the decrees for their exemption from earlier times (25) be carried out for Min of Koptos, and you should act in respect of these matters. My majesty does not permit that any emissary of the overseer of Upper Egypt or any official come forth onto the high ground (26) of Koptos … the house of Min.

As the king of Upper and Lower Egypt Pepy Neferkare, may he live for ever and for eternity, lives, endures, and is healthy, (27) you should not take them away for [these purposes (?)] … for taxing property in relation to them or to reckoning property in relation to them, with the exception of performing their priestly duties (28) for Min of Koptos. It is a matter dear to the heart of Neferkare, may he live for ever and for eternity, that things be carried out in accordance with the wording (29) of this decree.

And indeed, any overseer of Upper Egypt or any official or any emissary or any functionary who does not carry out matters in accordance with the wording of this decree (30) shall be taken to the "hall of Horus." My majesty does not permit them to serve as priests in the pyramid of Neferkare for ever.

(31) Sealed in the presence [of the king himself], fourth month of the *Shemu* season, day 28.

26. Decree of Pepy II from Koptos (Koptos D)

See Koptos C for some parallel phrases. The decree is preserved in four fragments, now Cairo, JE 43052, and New York, MMA 14.7.10, with one fragment seen once with a dealer in Luxor. The uncertain relationship of the fragments precludes numbering the lines.

Horus Netjerykhau.
A royal decree to the *haty-a,* sole companion, overseer [of priests (?)] …
The king of Upper and Lower Egypt Neferkare, may he live for ever, has ordered the exemption and protection of the estate "Min strengthens Neferkare" which belongs to the *per-shena* estate, together with all the dependents [who are on it] … and it is renewed with effect from today under every …, together with the son of a son … [the estate "Min strengthens Neferkare" which belongs to the *per-shena* estate]
My majesty does not permit [(the taking away for any compulsory service)] which is reckoned within this nome, whether it be (any of these):

- carrying or transporting;
- the requirements of the overseer of Upper Egypt: gold or copper;
- the needs of the house of life: the annual requirements of rations and animal feed, offerings, ropes and bindings, animal skins;
- plowing rights, any taxes, any (compulsory) works which are due on water and on land, which are ordered to be done in the aforementioned Upper Egypt.

My majesty does not permit the raising of levies on the dependents [of this *per-shena* estate], (whether) for any *perer* levy, any duty or any labor, any other *perer* levy, or any requirement for the divine offerings of another (estate).
My majesty does not permit that they do these things except where they are in place for the needs of … of the offerings of the *per-shena* estate for the priestly service and the carrying out of the monthly duties and the protection of sealed things of the god in the temple of Min in Koptos for the breadth of eternity.
With regard to: [every overseer of Upper Egypt], [every] chief, [every] great one of the tens of Upper Egypt, [every] overseer of the phyles [of Upper Egypt], [every] overseer [of commissions], [every] royal [acquaintance], [every] overseer [of crews (?)], [every] overseer [of the king's people]
who shall carry out their levy … [for any *perer* levy], for any duty or labor … in relation to another *perer* levy or in relation to another duty

- in the (following) chambers: of … , of the royal documents, of the sealed documents, of the house of redistribution of offerings, of [the house of documents],
- or [to set them to any other work of the house of the king]

[it is truly what the king hates].

[With regard to a levy of the nome which is brought] before the overseer of Upper Egypt so that [it may be dealt with by him after] it has been brought before the officials: my majesty has commanded that he remove the names of the dependents of this *per-shena* estate from (the document pertaining to this levy) … [nor does my majesty permit (?)] the recruitment of a man [from it (?)]

With regard to any official of any scribe of the king's documents … any … any … any … or any functionary who shall take their levy or who shall write an order … so that the names of the dependents of this *per-shena* estate are placed on it for a *perer* levy … , for [any work] of the king, for another … or for the divine offerings of another (estate), …—[in truth, in truth, it is what the king hates].

[With regard to[17] this which is said to my majesty that decrees of the king have been sealed for Upper Egypt, in relation to the execution of required works for the king in the form of every transport or every digging work which is ordered to be carried out in the aforementioned Upper Egypt—in this case, it is said in these decrees "no exemption is to be made with] respect to the exempted towns which are in the aforementioned Upper Egypt." My majesty does not permit that it apply to this *per-shena* estate for the breadth of eternity.

My majesty does not permit that any emissary of the overseer of Upper Egypt or any official go onto the mound of this estate "Min strengthens Neferkare" except to exempt and to protect this temple.

With regard to any overseer of Upper Egypt, any official, any emissary, or any scribe who does not act in accordance with the words of this decree, he shall be taken into the "hall of Horus" and (?) he shall be taken away from his land (?); my majesty does not permit that he do priestly service at the pyramid of <Neferkare> nor in any city which is in your charge/on the register [for ever].

My majesty has ordered the erection of a wooden pole from the southern foreign lands in this new town.

My majesty has ordered that this decree be set up as a white stone decree at the gateway of the temple of Min in Koptos under the control of the overseer of fields of this town and the overseer of the storeroom of the aforementioned *per-shena* estate and of the sons of the sons of men.

I have had the sole companion Idi attend in respect of this matter.

27. Decree of Pepy II (?) from Koptos (Koptos G)

The damage to this fragment means that we cannot be certain whether this decree was set up by Pepy II for his own cult or refers to one of his successors. Sethe in Urk I and Hayes 1946: 5 prefer a later king, but Goedicke 1967a opts for Pepy II. The sense of the document is also not very clear, but it is included here as it presents a number of interesting views on the ways such foundations were set up. The decree is now in Cairo, JE 41892.

(1) [A royal decree to (?)] the *haty-a*, the overseer of Upper Egypt, the overseer of priests …
(2) The statue "the king of Upper and Lower Egypt Neferkare is justified" in Koptos … [Min in] the Koptite nome:[18] the "offering which the king gives" which is given to it to be its divine offerings which are set up in the house/estate of the king
(3) … as a decree on behalf of the king of Upper and Lower Egypt Neferkare, may he live for ever and for eternity, which is renewed today. The three *arouras* of land in the nome of Koptos
(4) … its allocation should be chosen from the pieces of *remen* land which are composed of those fields which are inundated on an annual basis
(5) … and he should set its name as the estate "Min strengthens Neferkare" which belongs to the *per-shena* estate and its loads (?) ten times (*sense unclear*). The dependents for this *per-shena* should be raised from the dependents of
(6) … the estate/house of the king. If he is not aware of his document which the Residence has drawn up, then it shall be renewed through a decision of the officials who come
(7) … these fields are to be used for the divine offerings thereof for Min of Koptos as a daily endowed offering in addition to the rites of every (other) festival
(8) … there, which is endowed for the statue of Neferkare, justified, (which is made) of Asiatic copper, colored pastes and gold, which (materials) come to this temple daily
(9) … this … loads (?) ten times in relation to the 30 arouras of land which are the share of the *haty-a,* sole companion, overseer of priests, Idi in the nome of Koptos
(10) … You shall make this division of land of the aforementioned *per-shena* together with the chiefs, rulers of the towns, and the tribunals of the

fields (and you shall do it with) cymbals, (11) [*sendu* cloth, the slaughtering of cattle and fowl as is done for] the perfect festival of a god.
The *haty-a,* sole companion, overseer of priests, Idi shall be the overseer of [the aforementioned (?)] *per-shena* ...
(12) ... the king's people of the aforementioned *per-shena* shall work under his charge. With regard to the statue which is part of the division arising from the *sekhet* land
(13) ...

28. Decree of Pepy II from Dakhla Oasis

For the context, see notes before no. 273. The decree was found against a brick wall in a building at Ayn Asil, perhaps the soul chapel referred to in the text. For more on these structures in Dakhla, see Ziermann and Eder 2001: 309–56.

(1) Horus Netjerykhau.
(2) A royal decree to the boat commander, the ruler of the oasis, the overseer of priests [...][19].
(3) My majesty has commanded (both) the building for you of a soul chapel in the oasis, and the establishment for you of soul priests dedicated to provisioning you. (4) This has been previously done for your father, the ruler of the oasis Khentyka, (son of) Desheru, (son of) Iduwy,[20] (5) and you shall act in accordance with these instructions.
(6) I have had the deputy overseer of the *khenty-she* of the Great House, the envoy, Ankhunas attend in relation to it.
(7) Sealed in the presence of the king himself, month 4 of the *Shemu* season, day 3.

29. Decree of a Successor of Pepy II from Saqqara

The name of the king on this decree is lost, but it has to be one of the successors of Pepy II. This decree was found in the mortuary temple of Neith, wife of Pepy II, and concerns two queens. Ankhesenmeryre was the mother of Pepy II, and Neith was one of his wives and presumably the mother of his successor. Texts of these queens may be found as nos. 281 and 282. It is now Cairo, JE 56370. It is unclear whether the upper part of the decree bore text.

(1) Horus ...tawy, may he live for ever. Year of uniting the Two Lands, fourth month of the *Shemu* season, first day
(2) A royal decree ...
(3) My majesty has commanded the exemption and protection of the priests and the soul priests of the estates, towns, fields, storerooms, and dependents (4) of the king's mother Ankhesenmeryre the elder and the king's mother Neith, from carrying out all forms of work and corvée. (This is done) in the wish that they are able to perform priestly duties, carry out the monthly festivals, and enact the divine offerings in the sanctuary of these two king's mothers for the breadth of eternity.
(5) [(This is enacted) through a decree on behalf of the king of Upper and Lower Egypt] (*name lost, ending in* -re), may he live for ever and for eternity.
(6) Sealed in the presence of the [king] himself.
(7) ... giving bread against your document.[21]

30. Decree of Horus Kha . . . from Koptos (Koptos H)

The identity of Horus Kha... is not clear, but from the address to Shemai, who appears in many of the late eighth-dynasty decrees and from whose tomb comes no. 249, he must be one of the relatively ephemeral kings at the end of the Old Kingdom. Von Beckerath 1999: 68–69 assigns it to Neferkaure from the Abydos king-list. Part is now in New York, MMA 14.7.14, and part in Cairo, number unknown.

(1) Year of the fourth occasion ...
(2) Horus Kha ...
(3) A royal decree to the [ ] seal-bearer of the king of Lower Egypt, overseer of Upper Egypt, overseer of priests, stolist of Min, Shemai.
(4) My majesty has commanded that there be furnished ...
(5) and there be furnished this amount for the divine offerings ...
(6) in the charge of ...
(7) to the temple of Min of Koptos [in the Koptite nome (?)]
(8) With regard to when the god is satisfied ...
(9) and when the god is satisfied ...
(10) whoever shall be overseer of the storeroom shall do ...
(11) transport of the pure offerings ...
(12) I have had [(*someone*) come along on this matter].
(13) [Sealed in the presence of the king himself] year [(*rest of date lost*)].

31. Decree of (Probably) Neferkauhor from Koptos (Koptos I)

The name of the king on this decree is lost, but it is ascribed to Neferkauhor on the basis of the address to Shemai and Idi. It would appear from the damaged ending that it might have referred to Shemai's duties and the passing on of them to his son Idi. Neferkauhor, whose name is found on more of the Koptos decrees than any other ruler, is an otherwise little-known king who reigned at the end of the eighth dynasty. It would seem likely that all these decrees were made on the same day of the first year of his reign (no. 38). Now Cairo, JE 43053.

[Horus Netjerybau]
[A royal decree to [*compare other decrees for possible titles*] overseer of the pyramid town, vizier, overseer of Upper Egypt, overseer of priests, stolist of Min, Shemai.
An uncertain number of columns missing
... in the aforementioned Upper Egypt in which you are. ...
... [*perhaps* "as was done" (?)] in the time of my predecessors. [My majesty] lets you know that the aforementioned Upper Egypt, which is under your supervision, consists of the nomes whose names are:[22]

Modern number	*Ancient Egyptian name*	*Significant towns or places (ancient or modern)*	*Other names by which it is sometimes known*
1	Ta-sety	Aswan/Elephantine	
2	Wetjezet-Hor	Edfu	
3	Nekhen	el-Kab/Hierakonpolis	
4	Waset	Luxor	
5	Gebtiu	Qift (Koptos)	"Koptite nome"
6	Iqer	Qena/Dendera	
7	Bat	Hu	
8	Ta-wer	Girga/Abydos	"Thinite nome"
9	Khenty-minu	Akhmim/Sohag	
10	Wadjet		
11	(Uncertain)		
12	Iatfet	Deir el-Gebrawi	
13	Nedjfet khentyt	Asyut	
14	Nedjfet pehtyt	el-Qusiya/Meir	
15	Wenet	Deir el-Bersha/Hatnub	"Hare nome"

Modern number	*Ancient Egyptian name*	*Significant towns or places (ancient or modern)*	*Other names by which it is sometimes known*
16	Mahedj	Zawiyet el-Meitin/ Beni Hasan/Tehna	"Gazelle nome"
17	Input		
18	Anty	Kom el-Ahmar	
19	Wabwy (?)	Oxyrhynchus	
20	Naret khentyt	Beni Suef/Sedment	
21	Naret pehtyt	Meidum/Atfih	
22	Medjenit	Lisht	

Truly my majesty has arranged on your behalf that they be totally in the charge of the overseer of Upper Egypt [in the aforementioned Upper Egypt (?)].

With regard to any official, with regard to … [with regard to] any [judge (?)] and overseer of scribes, with regard to [any] … and with regard to any functionary … who are in the aforementioned Upper Egypt, they are to act under your supervision.

With regard to … who are under your supervision so that I unite for you the aforementioned Upper Egypt in its entirety … in the aforementioned Upper Egypt that he undertake sealing (?).

With regard to any official in your charge (?) who shall do … in every position which is therein

… (?) You are to act alone with the *iry pat, haty-a*, seal-bearer of the king of Lower Egypt … overseer of Upper Egypt … the aforementioned Idi …

[Sealed in the presence of the] king himself. …

32. Decree of Neferkauhor from Koptos (Koptos J)

A very damaged text, the sense of which is not fully clear. The first part appears to be honoring the wife of Shemai. The right-hand fragment (with the royal name) is in New York, MMA 14.7.13; the other fragment was possibly seen with a dealer in Luxor.

[Horus Netjery]bau.

A royal decree to the father of the god, the beloved one of the god, the *iry pat*, royal [foster child, *compare other decrees for possible titles*, Shemai.]

Regarding [your wife], the eldest daughter of the king, the sole royal ornament Nebet:

Now, she is the eldest daughter of the king, sole royal ornament … foremost of the other women of the royal … (there is not [?]) her like through the wish of the *haty-a* (?) [*perhaps title and name of someone like Shemai?*] … the overseer of the expedition Kheredni is to do guard duty (for her) … I have had the sole companion [Inyotef son of] Hemi attend [on this matter].

My majesty has commanded that you shall organize the making of a barque for the "god of the two powers"[23] of … cubits … Residence which is in that nome under the charge of … in … crew/retinue … barque for the "god of the two powers" therein annually … on the command in respect of (?) the king of Upper and Lower Egypt Neferkauhor Khuiwika, may he live for ever [and for eternity.]

[I have had] the sole companion In[yotef] son of Hemi attend [on this matter].

[My majesty has commanded] you to give and take away offices … [from he who shall do] anything which you dislike … to its limits/end …

33. Decree of Neferkauhor from Koptos (Koptos K)

The present location of this decree is unknown. For the tomb and chapel of Shemai, see no. 249.

(1) Horus Netjerybau.

(2) A royal decree to the father of the god, the beloved one of the god, the *iry pat,* overseer of the pyramid town, vizier, overseer of document scribes of the king, overseer of priests, stolist of Min, Shemai.

(3) My majesty has commanded that there be raised for you 12 inspectors of soul priests for the soul chapel … (4) of your funerary estate, who will do priestly duties for you and who will carry out the monthly festivals for you.

My majesty has commanded (5) that there be raised for you 12 inspectors of soul priests for the soul chapel of your funerary estate which is in the temple (6) of Min of Koptos.

My majesty has commanded that there be raised for you (7) 12 inspectors of soul priests for the "upper" soul chapel of your funerary estate.

My majesty has commanded (8) that there be raised for you 10 inspectors of soul priests to perform the rites for you in the year of [your burial (?)].

(9) My majesty has commanded that there be raised for you 10 (*possibly* 12 [?]) inspectors of soul priests for your wife, (10) the eldest daughter of

the king, the sole royal ornament Nebet, to do priestly duties for her (11) and who will carry out the monthly festivals for her in her soul chapel (and [?]) in [your (?)] soul chapel (?)
(12) My majesty has commanded that [these] inspectors of soul priests will be raised (13) from the dependents of your funerary estate and the raising …
(14) families in the nome of Koptos …
(15) of your funerary estate. Afterwards it is to be placed …
(16) in the registry …
(17) I have had the sole companion [Inyotef son of Hemi] attend on this matter.
(18) Sealed in the presence of the king himself, second month [of the *Peret* season, day 20].

34. Decree of Neferkauhor from Koptos (Koptos L)

Now in Cairo, JE 41895.

(1) Horus Netjerybau.
(2) A royal decree to the seal-bearer of the king of Lower Egypt, the sole companion, the first under the king, the scribe of fields of the eighth, fifth, ninth, seventh, and sixth nomes of Upper Egypt:[24]
(3) You are to go down to the marshland along with the father of the god, the beloved one of the god, the *iry pat,* foster child of the king, (4) overseer of the pyramid town, vizier, overseer of royal document scribes, *haty-a,* overseer of Upper Egypt, sole companion, chamberlain, (5) herdsman of Nekhen, chief of Nekheb, lector priest, overseer of priests of Min, Shemai.
You are to make the document for the allocation (6) of the estate "Min of Koptos makes Neferkauhor live" in the Koptite nome in its entirety, in that place in which you were told (to make it). (7) You are to make this allocation really well, so that my majesty shall be informed, and you will be favored for it. For (8) he (*Shemai?*) has made a command with regard to a command for himself to make this division with cymbals, *sendu* cloth, the slaughtering (9) of oxen and fowl, as (is done) for the perfect festival of a god.
You shall work with him (10) as one and set up this allocation in writing which is to be set out in many copies (*literally* "documents"). You shall inspect (?) it (11) for the father of the god, the beloved one of the god, the *iry pat,* foster child of the king, overseer of the pyramid town, vizier, over-

seer of royal document scribes, (12) *haty-a,* overseer of Upper Egypt, overseer of priests of Min, Shemai. It shall be put into a place of sealed documents and taken (13) to the land-registry. I have seen to it that the sole companions Hemi and Inyotef attend on the matter.
(14) Sealed in the presence of the king himself, second month of the *Peret* season, day 20.

35. Decree of Neferkauhor from Koptos (Koptos M)

This decree was last seen with an antiquities dealer.

(1) Horus Netjerybau.
(2) A royal decree to the beloved one of the god, the *iry pat,* overseer of the pyramid town, vizier, overseer of Upper Egypt, overseer of priests, stolist of Min, Shemai.
(3) (With regard to) your son, the *haty-a* and overseer of priests Idi, (4) he is (now) *haty-a,* seal-bearer of the king of Lower Egypt, overseer of Upper Egypt, and overseer of priests (5) south as far as the first nome of Upper Egypt, and north to the seventh, and under his command do the *haty-a,* the seal-bearers of the king of Lower Egypt, (6) the sole companions, the overseers of priests, the chiefs and the rulers of towns, and (7) their associates operate. My majesty has commanded that he serve as an official (8) and that he should carry out his duties in these nomes in accordance with your commands, (9) and that he serve as your spokesman. No man has any legal claim against this. (10) My majesty has made you aware of these nomes—(11) their individual names are Ta-sety, Wetjezet-Hor, Nekhen, Waset, [Gebtiu,] (12) Iqer, and Bat (*Upper Egypt nomes 1–7*). He and [you] shall work together [as one].
(13–14) I have had the [sole companion Inyotef son of Hemi] attend [on this matter] ...
(15) [Sealed in the presence of] the king himself [second month of the *Peret* season, day 20].

36. Decree of Neferkauhor from Koptos (Koptos N)

Assigned to Neferkauhor, as the day and month are common to a number of decrees. It was presumably addressed to Shemai. From the double mention of Inyotef son of Hemi it would appear that there were two decrees inscribed on this stone. The present location of the decree is unknown.

[I have had the sole companion] Inyotef [son of] Hemi [attend] on this matter.
[*someone* ... is] a celebrant in [the temple of Min of Koptos] under the charge of your son [the *haty-a,* overseer of Upper Egypt, overseer of priests], Idi. No [man] has any legal claim [against this]. ... he should carry out ... totally.
[I have had] the sole companion Inyotef son of Hemi [attend] on this matter.
Sealed [in the presence of the king himself] second month of the *Peret* season, day 20.

37. Decree of Neferkauhor from Koptos (Koptos O)

In this decree Idi appears to be being prepared to take over from his father Shemai, although the latter is evidently still in office from this and other decrees. Much depends on whether one crucial word is translated "successor" or "spokesman." The decree is now in New York, MMA 14.7.11.

(1) Horus Netjerybau.
Sealed in the presence of the king himself, second month of the *Peret* season, [day 20].
(2) A royal decree to the *haty-a,* overseer [of priests ... Idi].
(3) You are *haty-a,* overseer of Upper Egypt, overseer of priests in the aforementioned Upper Egypt [which is] (4) under your supervision south to the first nome of Upper Egypt and north to the seventh; the *haty-a,* overseers of priests, chiefs, (5) and rulers of towns who are in post shall operate under your oversight as the successor/spokesman of your father, (6) the father of the god, beloved one of the god, *iry pat,* overseer of the pyramid town, vizier, overseer of scribes of royal documents (7) [... *further titles*, Shemai].
[No] man [shall have any claim against it].

38. Decrees of Neferkauhor from Koptos (Koptos P and Q)

The texts of these two decrees were placed on the same stone and thus presumably relate to documents of the same ruler. Only part of each survives; the object is now in New York, MMA 14.7.12.

Decree P

[His majesty has commanded that you should see to the placing of the words of this decree (*or similar*) at the] gateway to the temple of Min [of Koptos in the Koptite nome (?)] for eternity.

I have had the sole companion Inyotef son of Hemi [attend] on this matter.

Sealed in the presence of the [king] himself, the year of uniting the Two Lands, second month of the *Peret* season, day 20.

Decree Q

(1) [Horus Netjerybau]

(2) [A royal decree to] …

(3) Now you are the sole companion, celebrant in the temple (4) [of Min of] Koptos under the supervision of your brother, the *haty-a,* overseer of Upper Egypt, (5) Idi. No man has any legal claim against it. (6) … is under the charge of your father, the father of the god, beloved one of the god, *iry pat,* foster child of the king, (7) vizier, overseer of document scribes of the king, *haty-a,*(8) [overseer] of priests Shemai.

I have had the [sole companion] Inyotef [son of Hemi[25] attend] (9) on this matter.

(10) [Sealed in the presence of the king himself, the year of uniting the Two Lands, second month of (?)] the *Peret* season, day 20.

39. Decree of Horus Demedjibtawy from Koptos (Koptos R)

Horus Demedjibtawy is unknown other than in this decree; his cartouche name is possibly Wadjkare, found at the end of this decree. He was almost certainly a king of the eighth dynasty, but exactly where is uncertain (von Beckerath 1999: 70–71; other possible attestations will be found in Hayes 1948). The decree is now in Cairo, JE 41894.

(1) Horus Demedjibtawy.

(2) A royal decree to the father of the god, the beloved one of the god, the *iry pat,* foster child of the king, overseer of the pyramid town, vizier, stolist of Min, Idi.

(3) With respect to all people of this whole land

- (4) who shall do anything bad or evil against any of your (5) statues,[26] (6) offering stones, (7) soul chapels, (8) wooden items, or (9) monuments (10) which are in any temple or sanctuary—(11) my majesty does not permit (12) that their property or that of their fathers remain therein, (13) nor that they shall join with the *akhs* in the necropolis, (14) nor that they exist among the living [upon earth].

- (15) who shall damage or ruin (16) things which are associated with (17) your funerary foundation (18) which are noted in the land-registry or (19) which are made for your statues (20) which are in the sanctuaries of Upper Egypt—(whether) (21) fields, (22) bread, beer, (23) meat, (24) or milk (25) which were set up for you in a deed—(26) my majesty has not decreed that they exist among the *akhs* in the necropolis,[27] (27) but rather that they be bound and fettered under the control of the king and (28) Osiris and of their city god.

With respect to any chief or official who does not carry out punishment (29) in his nome against any man who shall do these things until the king, vizier, or officials come by—(30) he has no right to his office or his seal, he has no right to any of his property, and his children have no right to it (either). (31) He who is to remain as an official is he who shall take precautions against the execution of these things.

Have this command written down; see to it that it is taken (32) to every chief of Upper Egypt and that it is made into a stone decree at the gateway of [every temple] (33) in which you have monuments—so that the sons of the sons of men see (it) [throughout the breadth of eternity].

(34) I have seen to it that the overseer of the *khenty-she* of the Great House attend, whom Wadjkare … sent …[28]

40. Lists of Offerings for Cults from Koptos

Both these similar texts belong to the eighth dynasty or even later (Fischer 1996: 270). They consist of lists of cult objects plus various other phrases that might relate them to the royal decrees. However, as Fischer points out for the second document, the phraseology suggests that the document was made by a private person, perhaps the overseer of priests (Fischer 1996: 269 n. g). Note that a fragment of another such document in Lyon (1969.170) is published in Goedicke 1995; Koptos Decree E (Goedicke 1967a: 228–3) might even be another.

A.

The provenance of this object is deduced from the frequency of the name of the god Min in the text. The date at the beginning could be of the same Neferkauhor so prominent in the Koptos Decrees (above). The actual offer-

ings are arranged in four columns of ten rows, many of which are damaged; only a selection is given below. The text is difficult and damaged and susceptible to various interpretations. Now in Cairo, JE 43290.

Year of the (first) occasion, fourth month of the *Akhet* season, day 25, the day of the half-monthly festival.

... Min and the *iry pat,* king's son, stolist of Min, Hetepkaminu is associated with the inspectors of soul priests of [this temple] in their entirety; may he carry out the cult activity for Min, for the mother of Min, (for) Thoth, and (for) the gods who are in this temple. The list of offerings (is as follows):

(I include only the second column of items which is complete)

gold and copper pieces: 7 *ab* vessels
copper: 33 *ab* vessels
lapis-lazuli fragments: 40
turquoise fragments: 1,040
silver fragments: 40
gold fragments: 40
hez vessels: 4; fire-tongs 2
clothing (of) *paqt, shesr,* and *aat:* very great quantity
incense, natron and myrrh: very great quantity
collars decorated with lapis-lazuli: 36

The storerooms of Min and the storerooms of the mother of Min shall receive milk jars; the estates of Min and the mother of Min are to provide [divine offerings (?)] for Min ...

Made into rope[29] and sacks (?) 160 and (?) 700 (?) ...

The property of Min is to be set up: cattle and servants ...

(for) year 2 (?), available for annual needs: ...

B.

A similar object to the last, with the remains of fewer items but parts of a longer continuous inscription. It is just possible that it might originally have named Hetepkaminu of the other document. Its present location is unknown.

Imported wood
shepset vessel
Ivory censer

... With regard to any *khenret* personnel of the temple ...

... on behalf of the *iry pat,* king's son, lector priest, controller of those who are among the gods, overseer of [priests (?)] ...

... It so happened that the majesty of this god came by water ...
... Year [1], second month of the *Shemu* season, day 1, accompanied ...
... I have exempted the priests of this temple from ...
... in this temple formerly. I have acquired *henu* chests of ...
... for the sons of their sons, for the children of [their] children ...

Notes

1. See the Palermo Stone (no. 1) and the collection of examples in no. 15.

2. This person is otherwise unknown and is not to be confused with a later man from Abydos (Brovarski 1994a: 104–6). Note that the address "to" the official was expressed by reversal of the hieroglyphs for "royal decree" so that they faced the name of the recipient.

3. As the text is damaged it is not impossible that this could be construed a little differently and imply that the offender's harvest would be given to another.

4. The red entries appear to be administrative additions made by these three people, presumably when the document was received and filed in the temple.

5. For the two persons named here, see nos. 145 and 100. The filiation suggested is not certain.

6. The list of people is quite damaged, and I am for the most part following the version of Goedicke. For the possibility that the vizier could be the Rewer whose tomb at Saqqara was defaced, see Kanawati 2002a: 115–16. The Weni in this text might be the owner of the well-known biography (no. 256).

7. These Nubian place names appear in the biographical texts of Harkhuf (no. 241); compare also Goedicke 1960b.

8. Nubians who presumably had been taken away from their homeland and forcibly resettled in Egypt so as no longer to present a threat; could the term perhaps be translated "naturalized" in this context? They were probably used as mercenaries to reinforce Egyptian military strength (compare also Goedicke 1960b: 63).

9. Goedicke argues for this not being the title seen before but rather something like "outsider."

10. The pyramid of Menkauhor, location unknown. This decree is an argument for it being in the Dahshur area, while Berlandini 1979 has argued for it being near the pyramid of Teti at Saqqara; the latter argument has been challenged by Malek 1994.

11. See Römer 2002.

12. The literal order of this sentence in the original is "the Koptite nome, Koptos, the royal mother Iput, the soul chapel." It is an example of what is known as "diminishing progression," whereby the text moves from the larger items down to the smaller: see Fischer 1973b.

13. These were identified by Kei Yamamoto. I wish to thank Ronald J. Leprohon for passing this information to me. Personal inspection showed that the surviving texts are as in Goedicke.

14. The interpretation of the text below this name is very uncertain; Baer's copy shows slightly more than the published ones.

15. I thank Ronald J. Leprohon for suggesting that *pen* "this" together with some nouns in texts with legal status can sometimes be translated in this rather formal and legalistic manner.

16. A term for an audience hall of the king in which it is presumed some of these decrees were issued. See also Moreno Garcia 1997: 129–32.

17. The first half of this section is reconstructed from Koptos B; it may of course not have been totally the same. The fragment in New York begins at the end of the reconstruction.

18. Another example of "diminishing progression" (compare n. 12 above); the literal order of the text is the reverse of the translation.

19. The name was probably never given, although Goedicke disagrees. Could the probable omission of the name have anything to do with it being set up in the soul chapel of one particular official?

20. Or "your fathers, the rulers of the oasis Khentyka, (his son) Desheru, and (his son) Iduwy"; commentators are divided as to whether the text refers to one or three persons. I follow Leprohon and Ziermann/Eder.

21. A unique phrase and unclear.

22. See chapter I, §5.3.4. This is the only full list of Upper Egyptian nomes in this book, and the opportunity has been taken to present them here with further information. The names of the nomes are given in the original in running text, and the tabular arrangement is to help the reader. This is of course not a gazetteer of these provinces.

23. Or a god called Iagi, perhaps originally an oasis deity; see Fischer 1957.

24. The nome order perhaps reflects their respective importance at the time, religiously, politically, or economically.

25. I am not sure if there is enough space for all this reconstruction.

26. A possible statue of Idi has been identified in Munich, ÄS 1568 (Fischer-Elfert and Grimm 2003: 78–80, pls. XXVI–XXVII).

27. This sheds an interesting sidelight as to the extent to which the king might have played a role in ensuring the survival of the spirits of the dead; could this also be tied in with the concept of *imakhu* and the "offering which the king gives" formula? Compare comments in Willems 1990: 39 and Assmann 1992: 151–52.

28. The cartouche of Wadjkare without the customary "king of Upper and Lower Egypt" perhaps argues for this being part of a private name rather than that of a king.

29. These are referred to in Koptos decree C of the reign of Pepy II (no. 25).

V

Objects Bearing Royal Names

Many of the following are stone vessels, for which see further the article by Arnold and Pischikova in Metropolitan Museum of Art 1999: 121–31.

41. Statue of Netjerykhet from Saqqara

On the base of a royal statue of Netjerykhet Djoser from the Step Pyramid, now Cairo, JE 49889. This is the only possible contemporary mention of the famed architect of Djoser.

Horus Netjerykhet.
The twin (?) of the king of Lower Egypt.
The seal-bearer of the king of Lower Egypt, first under the king, administrator of the great estate/mansion, *iry pat*, great seer, Imhotep, controller of sculptors, maker of stone vessels (?).

42. Offering Stand of Khafre

Now New York, MMA 07.228.24.

The offering table of Re.
Horus Userib Khafre, the king of Upper and Lower Egypt, Useremnebty (*Two Ladies name*), Golden Horus Sekhem, Khafre, given life like Re for ever.

43. Vessels of Izezi

A. Alabaster Jar, London, BM EA 57322

Horus Djedkhau.
The king of Upper and Lower Egypt Djedkare.
(*below both*) Given life for ever, beloved of the Two Ladies.

Now in the time of Izezi, royal adornment (for every) ten days: *ibu* oil, ¾ of a *dut* measure.[1]

B. Alabaster Libation Vessel, Paris, Louvre E 5323

First occasion of the *Sed* festival of the king of Upper and Lower Egypt Djedkare, beloved of the *bas* of Heliopolis, given life, stability, and all joy for ever.

44. Sistrum of Teti

Now New York, MMA 26.7.1450.

On the Top of the Sistrum

The king of Upper and Lower Egypt, the son of Re, Teti.
Horus Seheteptawy.
The Two Ladies Sehetep.
The Golden Horus Sema.
May he be given life and dominion for ever.

On the Shaft

The king of Upper and Lower Egypt, the son of Re, Teti, beloved of Hathor mistress of Dendera, given life eternally.

45. Objects of Pepy I

A. Alabaster Vessel, Berlin 7715

Horus Merytawy.
The king of Upper and Lower Egypt, the son of Re, Pepy.
The pyramid of Pepy I.
May he be given life, stability, and dominion for ever.
The first occasion of the *Sed* festival.

B. Alabaster Vessel, Paris, Louvre N 527

The king of Upper and Lower Egypt Meryre, may he be given life for ever.
The first occasion of the *Sed* festival.

C. Alabaster Vessel, Paris, Louvre E 5356

The king of Upper and Lower Egypt Pepy, the son of Hathor mistress of Dendera.

Horus Merytawy.
The Two Ladies Merykhet; the triple Golden Horus.
May he be given life and dominion for ever.

D. On a Jar in Cairo

Horus Merytawy.
The king of Upper and Lower Egypt, son of Re, Pepy.
The [Two Ladies] Merykhet; the triple Golden Horus.
May he be given life and dominion for ever.
Outside the rectangle with the names
The first [occasion] of the *Sed* festival, may he be given life and dominion for ever.
The house of the king (*presumably the home of the vessel?*).

E. Alabaster Monkey Vessel, New York, MMA 1992.338

It would appear that this vessel was a gift from the king to a favored woman. Monkey vessels had particular associations with rebirth, through the maternal image of the female monkey with its young. See also Arnold and Pischikova in Metropolitan Museum of Art 1999: 128; Fischer 1993 has further references to this type of object.

The *khenty-she* of the pyramid of Meryre.
The first occasion of the *Sed* festival.
Nykhasutmeryre.

F. Faience Plaque from Elephantine

German excavations on the island of Elephantine have revealed a number of inscribed objects of the Old Kingdom, of which this is one example.

The king of Upper and Lower Egypt, the son of Re, [Meryre]; given all life, stability, and dominion [for ever].
Horus Merytawy. First occasion of the *Sed* festival.

46. Objects of Merenre

A. Alabaster Vessel, Paris, Louvre E 23140b

The king of Upper and Lower Egypt Merenre.
Horus Ankhkhau.
The Two Ladies Ankhkhau; the double Golden Horus.
May he be given life and dominion for ever.

B. Ivory Box, Paris, Louvre N 794

On the lid: Horus Ankhkhau, the king of Upper and Lower Egypt, the Two Ladies Ankhkhau, the double Golden Horus, Merenre, may he live for ever.
On the front of the box: Horus Ankhkhau.
The king of Upper and Lower Egypt Merenre.
The Two Ladies Ankhkhau.
Given life for ever.

47. Vessels of Pepy II

A. Alabaster Vessel, Paris, Louvre N 657

The king of Upper and Lower Egypt Neferkare.
Horus Netjerykhau.
First [occasion] of the *Sed* festival.
Given life like Re.

B. Alabaster Vessel, Paris, Louvre N 648ab

Horus Netjerykhau.
The king of Upper and Lower Egypt Neferkare.
May he live like Re.
In one cartouche on the lid: (Long) live the Horus Netjerykhau, king of Upper and Lower Egypt Neferkare, given life.

Note

1. The volume of the vessel is said to be 10 cm^3.

VI

Rock Inscriptions of Kings and Expedition Leaders

See notes in chapter I, §6.3.1.

In the Region of Elephantine

48. Inscription of Unas at Elephantine

Horus Wadjtawy, the king of Upper and Lower Egypt Unas, lord of the foreign lands, given life and dominion for ever, beloved of Khnum, given life for ever.

49. Naos of Pepy I from Elephantine

From the area of the temple of Satet. Now Paris, Louvre E 12660.

Top: May the king of Upper and Lower Egypt Meryre live, may he live like Re.
Sides: Horus Merytawy, the king of Upper and Lower Egypt Meryre, beloved of Satet, may he live like Re.

50. Inscription of Merenre to the South of the First Cataract

The king of Upper and Lower Egypt Merenre, beloved of Khnum, lord of the cataract region.
Year of the fifth occasion, second month of the *Shemu* season, day 28.
A visit from the king himself, when he stood at the far end of (*literally* "behind") the foreign lands:

the rulers of Medja, Irertjt, and Wawat kissed the ground and gave great praise.

51. Inscription of Merenre near Philae

The perfect god, lord of the Two Lands: Horus Ankhkhau, the king of Upper and Lower Egypt Merenre, beloved of Khnum, lord of the cataract region, may he live like Re.
A visit from the king himself, when he appeared at the far end of the foreign lands to see that which is in the foreign lands:
the rulers of Medja, Irertjt, and Wawat kissed the ground and gave great praise.

52. Inscriptions of Merenre and Pepy II on Elephantine

In a rock niche in the temple of Satet, from the German excavations on the island.

A.
Year of the fifth occasion, second month of the *Shemu* season, day 24.
A visit from the king himself, when he made prisoners of the rulers of the foreign lands: the king of Upper and Lower Egypt Merenre, may he live for ever.

B.
The king of Upper and Lower Egypt Neferkare, may he live for ever.

53. Inscription of Pepy II at Elephantine

The king of Upper and Lower Egypt Neferkare, may he live for ever.
Second occasion of the *Sed* festival.

In the Sinai Peninsula

The Sinai was a major source of copper and turquoise for Egypt during the Pharaonic period. The principal site exploited in the Old Kingdom was the Wadi Maghara, roughly in the center of the peninsula, from which most of the following inscriptions come (Nicholson and Shaw 2000: 62–63,

149–50). Remains of a settlement of this date and of copper smelters have been found. Most of these inscriptions are effectively brief captions to individual figures of the king or other persons.[1]

54. Inscription of Netjerykhet in Wadi Maghara

Horus Netjerykhet.
Behind king: given all dominion, stability, life, and joy for ever.
Above and behind a male figure: the overseer of the expedition, boundary official of the foreign land Ankhyotef (?). A first royal commission … given to him from this mountain (?).

55. Inscription of Sneferu in Wadi Maghara

Now Cairo, JE 38568.

Horus Nebmaat, the king of Upper and Lower Egypt, the Two Ladies Nebmaat, the Golden Horus Sneferu.
Sneferu the Great God, given all dominion, stability, life, and health and all joy for ever.
Over smiting scene: Subduing the foreign lands.

56. Inscription of Khufu in Wadi Maghara

Khnum-khufu,[2] the Great God.
Smiting the pillar-people, the Bedouin.
May [all] protection and life be behind [him].
At the right: Horus Medjedu, the king of Upper and Lower Egypt, the Two Ladies Medjedu, the double Golden Horus.
Either side of a divine standard: The Horus, strong of arm. Given [dominion … for ever].

57. Inscriptions of Sahure in Sinai

A. In Wadi Maghara

Now Cairo, JE 38569.

Horus Nebkhau, the king of Upper and Lower Egypt Sahure, given life for ever.
The Great God.
Smiting the Bedouin and/of all the foreign lands.
Subduing all the foreign lands.

B. In Wadi Kharig

The Wadi Kharig is a site about 15 km north of Wadi Maghara.

Horus Nebkhau.
The king of Upper and Lower Egypt Sahure, may he live for ever.
Thoth, the lord of terror, the subduer of Asia.

58. Inscription of Niuserre in Wadi Maghara

Now Cairo, JE 38570.

Horus Setibtawy Niuserre, given life for ever.
The Great God, lord of the Two Lands, king of Upper and Lower Egypt, Two Ladies Setib, Golden Horus Netjer, Niuserre, son of Re, beloved of Wadjet, he who subdues all the foreign lands, given life.
Above king smiting: Smiting the Bedouin of all the foreign lands, the Great God, lord of the Two Lands.
At the right is a depiction of a large libation vessel: above it:
Thoth, lord of the foreign lands, who has made pure libations (*There is possibly a depiction of Thoth to the left of the king*).
On the vessel:
King of Upper and Lower Egypt Niuserre, given all life and health, all joy for ever.

59. Inscription of Menkauhor in Wadi Maghara

Now Cairo, JE 38566.

Horus Menkhau, king of Upper and Lower Egypt Menkauhor, given life, stability, and [dominion for ever].
A commission carried out by …

60. Inscriptions of Izezi in Wadi Maghara

A.

Horus Djedkhau, son of Re, may he live for ever.
[The king of Upper and Lower Egypt, the Two Ladies] Djed[khau, Golden Horus Djed], Djedkare beloved of Wadjet and the spirits of [Pe].
[Given life], all health, and [all] joy [for ever].
A royal commission carried out by … kau …

B.

Year of the ninth occasion of the count [of all] the cattle …
Horus Djedkhau, king of Upper and Lower Egypt Djedkare, may he live for ever.
Subduing all the foreign lands.
Smiting the ruler of the foreign land.
A royal commission [carried out by …]

C.

This is probably the earliest extant example of an expedition inscription consisting of more than just a depiction of the king, and it is also one of the most intriguing. The most recent study of the text suggests that it is perhaps the first recorded example of a divine oracular indication that success would be achieved on such a mission, in this case to extract semiprecious stones, especially turquoise, from Sinai. The inscription is now believed to be destroyed.

Horus Djedkhau, the king of Upper and Lower Egypt, the Two Ladies Djedkhau, the Golden Horus Djed, Djedkare, may he live for ever.
The year after the third [*possibly fourth*] occasion of the count of the cattle and all the herds.
Divine authority was given to the finding of semiprecious stone in the writing of the god himself, (and was enacted) in the broad court of the temple *Nekhenre*.[3]
A royal mission was sent under the command of the boat captain Nyankhkhentykhety to the hills of turquoise; he carried it out, together with:

The overseer of officials Nemtyiu, Ptahshepses, Sabi.
The judge and scribe Ptahuser.
The scribe of copper (?) Khunes.

The controller of a crew of recruits Abdu, Merynetjerizezi, Nyankhmin, Heru.
The overseer of foreigners (*name lost*).
The deputy overseer of foreigners Nykaiankh.
The supervisor of officials Washka, Hetepni, Nysobek.
plus illegible text of further, perhaps subordinate, officials.

D.
This text may just be associated with the previous one.

The king of Upper and Lower Egypt Djedkare, son of Re, Izezi, may he live for ever.
A royal commission carried out by the overseer of official Sedhetepi, son of the mistress of the house Merythathor, together with 1,400 men and the inspector of officials Seneni Idu.

61. Inscriptions of Pepy I in Wadi Maghara

The king of Upper and Lower Egypt, the Two Ladies Merykhet, Meryre, given all life for ever.
Horus Merytawy.

Scene of King Running Wearing the Red Crown

At top (falcon): the Behdetite, the perfect god, lord of the Two Lands.
First occasion of the *Sed* festival; placing the *sekhet* scepter four times.
May protection and life be behind him.

Scene of King Smiting Wearing the White Crown

The perfect god, lord of the Two Lands, Pepy, the Horus strong of arm.
The Great God.
Smiting and subduing the Bedouin of all the foreign lands.
Given all life.

Expedition Inscription

Year after the eighteenth occasion, fourth month of the *Shemu* season, day 5.
A commission carried out by the overseer of the expedition Abdu and the overseer of the expedition Ankhmeryre.
The captains of the boat crew and overseer of the pool:
Sebekhotep and Ihy.

The judge and overseer of scribes Shafti.
The pilots and overseers of foreigners
  Nykaiankh the elder
  Nykaiankh
  Senedjem.
The boat captain and overseer of officials, Hemi.
The inspector of the boat Abdu.
The chief of recruits Khuit.
The judge and scribe Nyptah.
by Khuenptah (?).[4]
The director of ten, Nefertkhuf.
The chiefs of recruits
  Hor...
  Wadjy
  Ankhu.
The overseer of ten Sepseny (?).

62. Inscriptions of Pepy II in Wadi Maghara

This scene is immediately adjacent to the previous one of Pepy I, doubtless a very deliberate decision.

Scene of the King and His Mother at the Top

Year of the second occasion of the count of all the cattle and herds of Lower and Upper Egypt.
Horus Netjerykhau, Neferkare, may he live for ever.
The king of Upper and Lower Egypt, the Golden Horus Sekhem, Neferkare, may he live for ever like Re.
The mother of the king of Upper and Lower Egypt, the pyramid of Neferkare, his beloved royal wife of the pyramid of Meryre, Ankhesenmeryre, she who is beloved of all the gods.

Expedition Inscription

A royal commission which was sent with the seal-bearer of the god Hepy to the terraces of turquoise.
The captains and overseers of pools Nybakptah and Wedjai.
The overseer of scribes Senedjem.
The captains and overseers of foreigners Ankhmeryre and Nykaiankh.

The captains and overseers of officials Iqeri, Ankhefkhnum, and Hemu.
The judge and scribes Djaty and Khentykheti (?).
The controllers of a crew of recruits Hemi and Senedjem.
The deputy overseer of foreigners Ikhuf.

In the Wadi Hammamat

The Wadi Hammamat, which runs east from Qift (Koptos), just south of modern Qena, was an important trade route to the Red Sea. Its quarries also provided greywacke, a medium-hard stone (Nicholson and Shaw 2000: 57–58).

63. Inscription of Ity

Ity is thought to be a possible birth name for the probably ephemeral king Userkare, who seems to have succeeded Teti in the early sixth dynasty (Baud and Dobrev 1995: 60).

Year of the first occasion, fourth month of the *Akhet* season, day 2.
The boat captains Ipi and Nykauptah came to carry out work for the pyramid of Ity in the company of 200 sailors, 200 masons, total 400 men.
Separate but probably part of the same text: The overseer of the expedition Ihyemzaf; the overseer of the expedition Irenakhet.

64. Inscriptions of Pepy I

A.
The king of Upper and Lower Egypt Meryre, the perfect god, lord of the Two Lands.
Horus Merytawy Pepy, beloved of the gods.
The first occasion of the *Sed* festival.
Depiction of the king before the god Min
Horus Merytawy, the king of Upper and Lower Egypt, Meryre, he who lives like Re.
The first occasion of the *Sed* festival, may he be given life for ever.
(*before depiction of Min*) The lord of Koptos.

B.

Ankhmeryremeryptah Nekhebu is well known from a biographical text in his tomb (no. 198).

The year after the eighteenth occasion, third month of the *Shemu* season, day 27.
The king of Upper and Lower Egypt Meryre, may he live for ever.
The first occasion of the *Sed* festival.
A royal commission carried out by the overseer of all the works of the king, the sole companion, the royal master builder in the two houses, Ankhmeryremeryptah and his son, the lector priest Ankhmeryremeryptah, along with:
The seal-bearers of the god
Ikhi
Ihu.
The assistant overseers of craftsmen
Khuenptah
Khuenhor
Qar
Neferi
Tjetji.
The royal acquaintances and overseers of builders
Amtjensu
Tjetji
Inkhi.

C.

The year after the ... occasion ...
A royal commission carried out by the overseer of all the works of the king, the sole companion, the royal master builder in the two houses, Ankhmeryremeryptah.
The overseer of commissions of the divine offerings in the two houses, the first under the king, the judge and inspector of scribes Zezi.
The scribe of the royal documents Khenu.
The judge and supervisor of documents Khui.
The seal-bearer of the god Ihu.
The seal-bearer of the god Ikhi.

D.

The king of Upper and Lower Egypt Meryre, may he live for ever; first occasion of the *Sed* festival.

A royal commission carried out by the overseer of all works of the king, the sole companion, the royal master builder in the two houses, Ankhmeryremeryptah, together with:
The deputy overseer of craftsmen, the royal noble Meryrekhuenhor.
The royal acquaintance, overseer of builders of the pyramid, Ankhemtjenenet.
The deputy overseer of craftsmen, the royal noble Meryreneferherenptah and his son Sankhptah and the inspector of scribes Zezi.
(*list of other persons involved*)
The sole companion Khuenptah.
The overseer of works Ankhmeryremeryptah.
His son, the lector priest Ankhmeryremeryptah.
His eldest son the overseer of gold Neferrenpet.
The royal noble Khuenhor.
The overseer of foreigners Nedjemib, Twau, Ihy.
. . .
The first under the king of the Great House, the overseer of sweet things (?) Hetepsen (?)
The royal noble, overseer of foreigners, Senedjemib.
His son the royal noble and overseer of foreigners Khuenhor.
Idy.
Din.
Hepy.
The overseer of the pool (?), the pilot Ankhemiunu.
The overseer of the pool (?), the inspector of the boat, Khui.

E.

Horus Merytawy, the son of Re, given life for ever.
The triple Golden Horus, the Two Ladies Merykhet, Pepy, may he live like Re.
The king of Upper and Lower Egypt Meryre; the first occasion of the *Sed* festival.
A royal commission carried out by the seal-bearer of the god Ikhi and his son, the captain of the boat crew Ikhi.
The assistant overseers of craftsmen of the Great House
Nefermeryre
Khuenptahmeryre
Khuenhormeryre
Neferherenptahmeryre
Sankhptahmeryre.
The overseer of builders of the pyramid Tjetji.

65. Expedition Inscription of Djaty

The identity of King Imhotep is unknown, but the text would nevertheless appear to be an Old Kingdom product. The king is placed in the eighth dynasty by von Beckerath 1999: 70–71.

(1) A commission carried out by the eldest king's son, the seal-bearer of the god, overseer of the expedition Djaty called Kainefer, (2) who is concerned for his subordinates on the day of fighting (3) and who foretells the coming of the day of attack through his council.
(4) I was more distinguished than a multitude of men, for I carried out works for King Imhotep (5) with (6) 1,000 men of the Great House and 100 stonemasons, (7) 1,200 sailors and 50 specialists (?) (9) from the Residence. (8) His majesty had this large troop of men come from the Residence, (10) and I carried out this work for grain payments and for all sorts of linen; his majesty gave (11) (supplies of) 50 oxen and 200 goats for every day.
(12) The inspector of the Great House, Inyotef.
(13) The scribe of the boat of Min, Mereri.

66. Expedition Inscription of Shemai

Sixth dynasty.

(1) O you who live and who shall come to this desert and desire
to return to Upper Egypt laden with their tribute for their lord,
(2) you should then say: "a thousand of bread, a thousand of beer,
a thousand of oxen, a thousand of fowl, a thousand of alabaster,
a thousand of clothing, and a thousand of every perfect thing
for the seal-bearer of the king of Lower Egypt,
the sole companion, the lector priest, the judge and overseer
of scribes Shemai."

67. Expedition Inscriptions Relating to Tjautyiqer

These three texts all relate to expeditions for the same Upper Egyptian official, Tjautyiqer. Kanawati 1980: 119–21 places him in the eighth dynasty and suggests he might be the same as the better-known Tjauti from Koptos (see further Fischer 1964: 47–48; Martin-Pardey, 1976: 227). These texts are clearly on the boundary of our time period, either in the reign of an eighth-dynasty king or even a little later.

A. Idi

(1) Year of the first occasion, third month of the *Shemu* season, day 2.
Arrival of the sole companion, overseer of cattle, Idi, (2) to extract a block of stone for the beloved one of the god, the *iry pat, haty-a,* lector priest, sole companion, (3) overseer of Upper Egypt, overseer of priests, stolist of Min, Tjautyiqer.
I extracted for him a block of stone (measuring) 12 cubits (4) with 200 men. I came back with (= *was paid*) two oxen, 50 goats, and five pots of animal fat.

B. A Different Idi

(1) Fourth month of the *Shemu* season, day 3.
Arrival of the seal-bearer of the king of Lower Egypt, the sole companion, inspector of priests, keeper of secrets of the seal-bearer of the god, Idi, (2) to extract a block of stone for the beloved one of the god, the *iry pat, haty-a,* lector priest, sole companion, overseer of priests, overseer of Upper Egypt, stolist of Min, Tjautyiqer.
(3) I extracted for him two blocks of stone (4) each measuring 10 cubits long by 3 cubits wide.

C. Heqeq

(1) Fourth month of the *Shemu* season, day 3.
Arrival of (2) the seal-bearer of the king of Lower Egypt, judge and mouth of Nekhen, elder of the portal, (3) overseer of everything commanded in the Residence, Heqeq, whose perfect name is Meri.
(4) I extracted two blocks of stone of … (5) [cubits] for the beloved one of the god, the *iry pat,* overseer of Upper Egypt, overseer of priests, stolist of Min, Tjautyiqer.

68. Inscriptions of Tjetji

Late sixth dynasty.

A.

A commission carried out (by) the seal-bearer of the king of Lower Egypt, sole companion, seal-bearer of the god, overseer of the expedition, overseer of the hunting-country (?), overseer of gold (*or* of foreigners), overseer of all the southern foreign lands, overseer of the "Narrow Doorway,"[5] who places the fear of Horus in the foreign lands, Tjetji.

B.

Tjetji was from Aswan, and the following titles come from his tomb at Qubbet el-Hawa.

The *haty-a*, seal-bearer of the king of Lower Egypt, seal-bearer of the god, sole companion, lector priest, he who brings the products of the southern foreign lands to the king, Tjetji.

Hatnub

One of the major alabaster quarries in Egypt, located not far from Amarna in the fifteenth nome of Upper Egypt. See generally Klemm and Klemm: 216–19; Shaw 1986; Nicholson and Shaw 2000: 59–60. What Egyptologists normally term "alabaster" is more correctly either travertine or calcite.

69. Inscription of Khufu

Horus Medjedu, the king of Upper and Lower Egypt Khufu.
At top (falcon): the Behdetite.
Behind figure of king: May protection, life, stability, dominion, and joy be behind (him) for ever.

70. Inscriptions of Teti

A.

Horus Seheteptawy, may he live for ever; the king of Upper and Lower Egypt, son of Re, Teti, given all life for ever.
Year after the sixth occasion, third month of the *Shemu* season …
The overseer of [the expedition (?)], Akhet and the pilot (?) of the ship, Meru [speak]:
That which we have carried out is this work for the king of Upper and Lower Egypt Teti, may he live for ever,
with 300 men and controllers … who are from the Residence.
60 (of these) men were making [boats (?)] in the fifteenth nome of Upper Egypt …
wrapped in materials (?) from the new estates.

...
living animals which are ... so that they might be eaten (?) ... (*perhaps a specification of time?*) ... for the noble *ba*s of Teti.

B.
Horus Seheteptawy, may he live for ever; the king of Upper and Lower Egypt, son of Re, Teti, given life.
List of names and titles—row 1
The judge and boundary official Nykhnum.
The scribe of the boat Khuenkhnum.
The member of the crew Nysuptah.
The captain Mehu.
The overseer of the workshop (?)
Nedjemib.
Nyankhminu.
Khenu.
... wib ...
List of names and titles—row 2
... of the boat ... [*hacked out*]
The inspector Hatywadj
The overseers of officials Khety (?) and Ankhteti.
The overseer of ten men ...
Ankhteti.
[*Hacked out*]
i...w
Qa[r].
Shedi.
Ankhi.
Neferheri.
Blank.
Iy.
They speak: we have carried out this work for the king of Upper and Lower Egypt Teti, may he live for ever.

71. Inscriptions of Pepy I

Horus Merytawy, the king of Upper and Lower Egypt Meryre; given life for ever.
First occasion of the *Sed* festival.
Year of the twenty-fifth occasion,[6] first month of the *Akhet* season ...

[A royal commission carried out by] the sole companion, the great one [of the five of the house of Thoth (?)] …
The first under the king, keeper of secrets …

The following section is in Urk I but may be a later addition as the title "great chief" is not known in this area until the First Intermediate Period (Eichler 1993: 39 n. 37).

The controller of the two thrones, the overseer of the palace, true overseer of Upper Egypt, great chief of the fifteenth nome of Upper Egypt, Khuu's son Nyankhseskhnum.

72. Inscription of Merenre

Horus Ankhkhau, the king of Upper and Lower Egypt Merenre.
At top (falcon): the Behdetite.
In front of king: The perfect god, lord of the Two Lands.
Behind figure of king: May all protection and life be behind him like Re for ever.
Year after the fifth occasion.
A mission which the *haty-a* [overseer of Upper Egypt, sole companion, Weni (?)] carried out.

73. Inscriptions of Pepy II

A.
Horus Netjerykhau
Year of the fourteenth occasion, first month of the *Akhet* season, day 23.
The seal-bearer of the god Nemtyiu speaks:
I went down to Hatnub to quarry four alabaster offering-tables, after I had constructed two barges at *Rakheny*.
With me were the crews of the boats which were with me: the captains Khesef, Seri, Imai; the inspector of boats Nehsi, Derkhesef, Wentua, and twenty *sem* priests and officials.

B.
The inspector of boats Neferha's son Derkhesef speaks:
Your servant went down with 1,000 men of Sh… following me; 80 men then traveled north on the route of the *meret* temple of Sneferu; I went down having constructed a barge myself. I brought it back when the water was high, having provided well for my crew.

C.

The seal-bearer of the king of Lower Egypt, the overseer of the alabaster (quarry), Sankhy and his son, the officer, the overseer of the expedition, Khuy, (say):

I went down to this Hatnub with 100 men; (that quarry) was being worked with 1,000 men (*or,* they worked harder than 1,000 men). The overseer in it …

D.

The king of Upper and Lower Egypt Neferkare.

… Neferkare …

… of the mansion, the companion … speaks:

I was sent to Hatnub by the *haty-a* …

I organized the sending of 300 blocks of alabaster in one day (*or* [n] days) … with my team … I went down to this desert with 1,600 men and my colleagues, the companions Djehuty (?) and Impi and the first under the king of the Great House, the scribe of the estate, Meri. This work all was carried out [for the nobility of the *ba*s of Neferkare.]

… youths (of three different places) numbering 500, 600, and 500 …

and the stones went down through the efforts of this team all at one go … and I loaded up two boats measuring 80 (cubits) for the estate of the *haty-a*, the sole companion, the overseer of the *khenty-she* of the Great House, the overseer of estates Idi and for the … of five, Khuit.

E.

Horus Netjerykhau, the king of Upper and Lower Egypt Neferkare, may he live for ever.

Year after the thirty-first occasion, first month of the *Shemu* season, day 20. The fifteenth nome of Upper Egypt …

… the sole companion, the overseer of the *khenty-she* of the Great House, lector priest, overseer of priests, Ankhkhnum, whose perfect name is Ankhy, speaks:

I was sent from the Residence to carry out work at Hatnub. I quarried 2,000 (?) blocks of alabaster—they were brought into being and placed [in boats (?) …] in accordance with what had been ordered in the Residence … and they were placed in barges which were … in my charge at Hatnub … and were at the Residence in … days … from the aforesaid Hatnub by my father, the sole companion, lector priest, overseer of priests Ankhkhnum.

F.
The pilot Ser speaks:
After I had been to Behekes, I went down to this Hatnub. No one else like me had been found to have done this.

Nubia and the Deserts

74. Graffito in the Wadi Dungash in the Eastern Desert

Sixth dynasty.

A water source.
22 people.
They came to this mountain; their forced labor was organized by the royal noble and overseer of foreigners, Senu.

75. Graffito in the Bir Mueilha (Wadi Umm Hoda) in the Eastern Desert

This inscription is most unusual as it is the only rock text probably written by someone on an expedition which employs some of the standard biographical phrases from tomb inscriptions; it is thus also probably the only such text certainly composed by the person whose name it bears (above, chapter I, §6.5.3). It will also have had a cultic purpose (Eichler 1994). Probably reign of Pepy II.

The king of Upper and Lower Egypt Neferkare, may he live for ever.
The scribe Anusu speaks:
I organized the excavation of this water-hole.
I gave water to the thirsty, and I gave bread to the hungry.
I did not let anything bad happen there,
for I am satisfactory in the sight of my lord.

76. Two Inscriptions from Khor el-Aquiba

Khor el-Aquiba is located about 80 km north of Abu Simbel. Some Old Kingdom graffiti were found there during the Nubian rescue campaign in the

1960s. There is some dispute as to the date; they were originally dated to the fifth dynasty, but Helck in particular has pointed out that the title used for "governor" is an early form, and he would place them in the fourth dynasty. He links them with records of the Palermo Stone (no. 1), in which Sneferu brought many prisoners from Nubia, perhaps to supply labor for the expanding economy of Egypt.

A.

The governor (?) of the seventeenth nome of Upper Egypt, Khabaubat came with an expedition of 20,000 men to hack up Wawat.

B.

The governor (?) of the northern part of the fourteenth nome of Lower Egypt, Zauib: 17,000 Nubians were taken.

77. Inscriptions at Tomas

Tomas is located in lower Nubia, about 200 km to the south of Aswan. The texts date to the sixth dynasty.

A.

(29) I was sent to open up the land of Irertjet for the king of Upper and Lower Egypt Neferzahor, may he live for ever. The inspector of the *khenty-she* of the Great House, overseer of foreigners, Khunes.
(30) I was sent to open up the southern foreign lands for Horus Merytawy Neferzahor, may he live for ever. The inspector of the *khenty-she* of the Great House, overseer of foreigners, Iyhenaef.
(28) I was sent in the time of the triple Golden Horus Neferzahor. The inspector (of *khenty-she* [?]) of the Great House, overseer of foreigners, Idi, in the charge of Iyhenaef.
The following are extracts of inscriptions with brief snippets of text or names:
(5) … to pacify the southern foreign lands.
(9) the *imakhu* in the sight of Pepy, the *imakhu* in the sight of Teti, Sabi, the royal noble, overseer of the *khenty-she* of the Great House, inspector of the *khenty-she* of the Great House, overseer of foreigners, overseer of foreigners (*sic*), lord of the southern land of Nubia, Sabi.
(18) Year of the sixth occasion, third month of the *Shemu* season: a commission which the overseer of the expedition … undertook …

B.

Sabni is the official of the same name with a tomb at Aswan, and Mekhu is his father. See no. 243 for the biographies of Sabni and his son Mekhu II.

The seal-bearer of the king of Lower Egypt, sole companion, lector priest, overseer of foreigners, [who brings joy to the heart of] the king, overseer of the foreign lands of his lord in Iam, Irertjet, Wawat, keeper of secrets of all that is spoken ... who places the fear of Horus [in the southern foreign lands], overseer of the expedition from Zetjau,[7] Inyotef whose perfect name is Mekhu;

his son, his beloved, the sole companion, lector priest, keeper of secrets of all that is spoken in relation to the narrow door of Elephantine, Sabni.

The royal noble, the overseer of foreigners of Zetjau, Horkhuni;

His son the royal noble, the overseer of foreigners, Gebi.

Notes

1. The examples translated are of those kings represented by more than just their names; the Horus names of Sekhemkhet (Giveon 1974; Eichler 1993: 37) and Zanakht (Metropolitan Museum of Art 1999: 176–77) are also present, and there are shorter inscriptions of many of these kings which reveal nothing further and are not included here.

2. The full form of the royal name usually just written as "Khufu."

3. This indicates that the oldest of the sun temples was still important towards the end of the fifth dynasty, when such temples were no longer being built.

4. This is at the end of a section of the inscription, and the next names are differently cut. Perhaps it was the name of the man who wrote the record, but it could also be interpreted as the name of another "judge and scribe."

5. Perhaps the entry point to Upper Egypt from Nubia at Elephantine? Compare titles with these words in Jones 2000: 158–59, 634.

6. I see no reason to follow Eichler's belief that this part of the inscription does not belong with the names of Pepy I (Eichler 1993: 39).

7. This Nubian/Sudanese state appears in the Harkhuf inscription (no. 241).

VII

Quarry and Constructional Marks and Phyle Texts

See notes in chapter I, §6.11.

78. Construction of a Curve at the Step Pyramid at Saqqara

A diagram on a flake of limestone found in the area of the Step Pyramid. It seems likely that it illustrates a way of working out a crude arc, supported by the remains of a curved saddleback construction in the same area. Now in Cairo, JE 50036. Presumably third dynasty.

1 cubits, 2 palms, 1 fingers.
2 cubits, 3 palms.
3 cubits.
3 cubits, 2 palms, 3 fingers.
3 cubits, 3 palms, 2 fingers.

Fig. 5: Flake of limestone from the Step Pyramid (no. 78). Gunn 1926: 198, fig.1.

79. Dates from the Pyramid of Meidum

The pyramid of Meidum was certainly completed by Sneferu and may have been started by him or his predecessor Huni. Its blocks bear a mixture of year-dates and other marks, many of the latter being phyle marks. These are just some examples assumed to belong to Sneferu.

A.

Year of the thirteenth occasion.
Year of the eighteenth occasion.
Year of the twenty-third occasion, second month of the *Shemu* season.
One group of signs appears to say "brought to the south corner."

B.

Year of the seventeenth occasion, second month of the *Peret* season, day 24 (?).
Year of the seventeenth occasion, second month of the *Peret* season.
Year of the seventeenth occasion, third month of the *Peret* season, day 30 (?).
Year of the fifteenth/seventeenth occasion, third month of the *Shemu* season, day 8.

80. Dates from the Red Pyramid of Dahshur

These dates are quite critical for determining the length of the reign of Sneferu. See Stadelmann 1987 and 1980 for the possibility of a reign of forty-eight years; against this, see Krauss 1996 and 1998a.

Setting in place at the western corner, year of the fifteenth occasion …
Year of the fifteenth occasion, second month of the *Peret* season, day 14.
Year of the sixteenth occasion, third month of the *Peret* season …
Year of the twenty-fourth occasion.
Year of the twenty-fourth occasion, … *Peret* season …

81. Giza Pyramid Crew Names

These texts were usually painted in red on blocks and probably indicate which blocks were being moved by which crews of workmen. Note that these names can also be taken as referring to the king or as exhortations; many of the phyles are further divided into subsections by the use of single hieroglyphs, not usually translatable. These have been omitted from the following. There are also various other marks and also cubit levels (Reisner 1931: 273–77, plan XI and XII; Arnold 1991: 20–21). A general discussion of phyles may be found in Roth 1991; see *Roth 1991: 119–45 for a discussion of how these crews might have worked in pyramids.*

Khufu (Horus Name Medjedu)

The crew "The pure ones of Horus Medjedu."
The crew "Horus Medjedu is the one who purifies the Two Lands."
The crew "The companions of Horus Medjedu."
The crew "The pure ones of Khufu."
The crew "The white crown of Khnumkhufu is pure."

Menkaure

The crew "The drunks of Menkaure," phyle *wadjet*.
The crew "The drunks of Menkaure," phyle *nedjes*.
The crew "The companions of Menkaure," phyle *wadjet*.

82. Crew Name from the Unfinished Pyramid at Zawiyet el-Aryan

The unfinished pyramid at Zawiyet el-Aryan, between Giza and Abusir, is thought to belong to an otherwise unknown king of the fourth dynasty, whose name may have been Nebka.

"The instructors of Nebka" (?)

83. Crew Names and Other Related Texts from Abusir

See generally Verner 2003. The following are among the better-preserved names.

A. Pyramid Complex of Sahure

i.

Men bending forward; context unclear but perhaps associated with scenes of receiving gold or the like.

The crew "The beloved ones of Sahure."

ii.

Men bending forward; some are possibly dancing.

The crew "The skilled ones of Sahure."
The crew "The companions of Sahure."
The crew "The noble ones of Sahure."

The crew "The followers of Sahure."
The crew "(Those engaged by [?]) the decree of Sahure."

B. Pyramid Complex of Neferirkare

The following are examples of names and dates on the pyramid blocks, presumably indicating officials in charge of these parts of the work.

The first under the king, the lector priest, Ipi.
Fourth month of the *Shemu* season, day 21: the companion Ankhirptah; the judge and boundary official Teti.
The king's son, the first under the king, Rehotep.

C. Pyramid Complex of Neferefre

These crew names are painted on blocks.

The crew "The companions of Neferefre"
The crew "The beloved ones of Neferefre"
The crew "The servants of Neferefre"
The crew "Neferefre is the lord of stability"

D. Pyramid Complex of Niuserre

These crew are shown in the temple reliefs.

The crew "The companions of Niuserre"; the crew "the beloved ones of Niuserre."

84. Quarry Marks from Private Tombs at Giza

A. Meresankh III at Giza

See other texts from this tomb for an introduction (no. 276).

Year of the seventh occasion, fourth month of the *Peret* season, day 10.
Year of the seventh occasion, fourth month of the *Peret* season, day 20; she who is great of affection, Hetepheres.
Third month of the *Shemu* season, day 21; she who is great of affection, Hetepheres.

B. Mastaba G VI S at Giza

Mastaba G VI S was one of a row of very large tombs immediately to the south of the Great Pyramid, south of the famous boat pits. It is likely that they were built in the reign of Menkaure (Horus Kakhet), and not all were used in the period immediately following construction. The owner of this mastaba is unknown, but at least one other original owner of the others was a Prince Djedefkhufu, suggesting that they were intended for high officials. These translations are but a selection of the originals.

i.
Third month of the *Peret* season, day 23, the crew "the little ones of Horus Kakhet," phyle *nedjes.*

ii.
The crew "the little ones of Horus Kakhet," phyle *wadj.*

iii.
Phyles *wadj* and *nedjes,* 4; the crew "the little ones of Horus Kakhet," phyles *wadj* and *nedjes,* 4.

iv.
The crew "the little ones of Horus Kakhet," phyles *setj* and *nedjes.*

v.
The crew ["the little ones of Horus Kakhet,"] phyles *setj* and *nedjes*; year (?), third month of the *Peret* season …

vi.
Year of the eleventh occasion … month of the *Peret* season, day 10 + x.

C. Dates from Mastaba of Hemiunu at Giza

These dates presumably relate to the reign of Khufu, in whose time Hemiunu was vizier, and are on stone blocks used in the construction of the mastaba in the Western Cemetery. Some notes on Hemiunu are in Metropolitan Museum of Art 1999: 229–33. Tomb G 4000 in the Western Cemetery (PM III², 122–23). Early fourth dynasty.

(1, 2) Year of the tenth occasion, first month of the *Shemu* season, day 10 (*two blocks, one with a damaged date, so could be a few days later*).
(3) Year [of the nth occasion], fourth month of the *Peret* season, day 10 + x.
(10) Year of the eighth occasion, third month of the *Shemu* season, day 20 or 22.
(12) Year of the tenth [occasion], fourth month of the *Peret* season, day 23 or 24.

85. Phyle Texts from the Sun Temple of Userkaf at Abusir

Four small stone tablets were found in the debris around the sun temple of Userkaf (Nekhenre) at Abusir. They indicate such divisions of labor and were perhaps inscribed to mark various stages of progress in the work. It has been observed, as these tablets provide dates higher than otherwise known for Userkaf, that the building might have been continued or completed under one of his successors.[1]

A.

Year of the fifth occasion, first month of the *Akhet* season.
Beginning of work on the construction of the upper part of the temple of Re in *Nekhenre*, at the northern part on the part of the *ka* section of the *nedjes* phyle.

B.

Year of the fifth occasion, third month of the *Peret* season.
The western part for section *djed* of the *imy-nefert* phyle. 22 measures.[2]

C.

Year of the fifth occasion, fourth month of the *Shemu* season.
Construction at the north by the *ka* section of the *nedjes* phyle. 23 measures.

D.

Year after the fifth occasion, second month of the *Peret* season.
The *nefer* division of the *wer* phyle, at the south. 40 measures.

86. Brief Texts of Phyles That Appear in the Decoration of Tomb Chapels

A. Obelisk of Ptahhotep Desher from Saqqara

Now in Cairo, CG 1308. Mid–late fifth dynasty.

The *haty-a,* vizier, Ptahhotep Desher.
That which the *imy-nefret* phyle made.

B. Scene in the Tomb of Ptahshepses at Abusir

Block now Berlin 14105. Reign of Niuserre or thereabouts.

Bringing the *setjat* boxes of the two parts of the *wadjet* phyle—the inspector of soul priests Khnumhotep.

C. Tomb of Ankhmare at Giza

Tomb in the Eastern Cemetery (G 7837+7843; PM III[2], 206). Probably fifth dynasty. See no. 191 for another text from this tomb.
Above a line of offering bearers

The phyle of soul priests which is in its month on duty.

D. On a Block from the Tomb of Akhethotep Hemi/Nebkauhor at Saqqara

Some of the larger tombs of the late fifth and early sixth dynasties had their own phyles of priests, and this block indicates that each of the five might have had its own storeroom. See nos. 195 and 104 for longer texts from this tomb.

The storeroom of the *wer* phyle in the charge of the judge and elder of the doorway, the supervisor of soul priests Bebi and the assistant supervisor of soul priests Imi.

E. Possible Preparations for a Circumcision from the Tomb of Ankhmahor at Saqqara

Roth makes the intriguing suggestion that this largely ignored scene relates to a possible initiation ceremony for phyle membership which began at the time a male was old enough to be circumcised. See nos. 197, 302, and 322 for more texts from this tomb.

Bringing *menkhet* cloth to the festival for the circumcision at the *tep-mer* (head of the canal [?][3]) by the soul priests.
In front of many of the men carrying boxes in the scene: "the favored one of the phyle *imy-weret / imy-nefret / wadjet /setj /nedjes.*

Notes

1. Kaiser 1956: 108–11 argued that this might have happened under Neferirkare, although Posener-Kriéger 1976: 519–20 considered this unlikely. However, the argument that the temple might have been reused has been reopened in Stadelmann 2000: 540–42; Verner 2001: 388–90 makes a case for completion of the temple under Sahure.

2. These figures are hard to follow. Edel suggested that they might relate to the number of men involved, but such a designation of men by the hieroglyph 𓂝 would be strange; Roth suggests that it might be better to associate it with some measure of work completed.

3. Roth 1991: 65 n. 15 notes that until relatively recently some circumcision rites in Egypt and Nubia were performed near the river.

VIII

Graffiti

See notes in chapter I, §6.9.

87. A Graffito on the Pyramid of Pepy II at South Saqqara

This text seems to refer to a burial, and it has been suggested that the person in question was Pepy II. The problem is that this has to be reconciled with the ninety-year reign traditionally given to the king. This problem is discussed in Goedicke 1988d; for other contemporary sources on the length of the reign of Pepy, see Spalinger 1994: 307–8, 315. See also chapter I, §3.2 for comments on Old Kingdom dates.

Year of the thirty-first occasion, fourth month of the *Peret* season, day …
Burial … in burial …
All rites were given to him therein of the best …

88. A Selection of Graffiti from el-Kab

Several hundred rock inscriptions, mostly of the Old Kingdom, have been located in the Wadi Hilal, to the east of the ancient town of Nekheb, modern el-Kab. These inscriptions mostly concern priests involved in local cult temples, notably the Upper Egyptian per-wer *shrine in el-Kab itself, and also an "upper temple," which might indicate an older structure in the area now occupied in the valley by the temple of Amenhotep III. Most inscriptions name personnel and give their titles; a few tell us a little more and are translated here. This selection of graffiti date to the sixth dynasty.*

A. Inscription N5

(1) [*Date missing*]
(2) The first under the king, inspector of priests Ibi's son, the first under the king, inspector of priests, Bekheni speaks:

I am a priest and keeper of secrets (3) of the upper temple, the beloved one of his father and the favored one of every *djasti*[1] with whom I carried out the duties of a priest (4) in this temple since the time when I was sent. For I am one whose entry in this temple is awaited, (5) the beloved one of his colleagues, the favored one of (every) priest and his crew in this temple. For I am one whose character is prominent (6) in this desert temple since I set foot in it.

B. Inscription N6

(1) The inspector of the *khenty-she* of the Great House, Nefershememi's son, the first under the king, inspector of priests, Sebekhotep's (2) beloved son, the first under the king of the Great House, inspector of priests, Bekheni, the *imakhu* in the sight of the Great God's (3) beloved son, the first under the king, overseer of musicians, Baq speaks:
This servant (4) was among the priests who went out to (take part in) the *djeser-ta* festival[2] of Nekhbet this year. (5) This servant carried out the priestly hourly duty successfully in relation to everything, so that the *djasti* (6) who was in charge favored (me) more than on any other occasion when it had been done in this desert land before.
For I am one who is awaited (7) in this desert in relation to every commission sent out. For the *djasti* and the priests (8) wish that Nekhbet mistress of Nekheb (*el-Kab*) favor them, and they speak my perfect name while I am alive (9) [and say] "a thousand of bread, a thousand of beer" while I am in the necropolis. For I am the beloved one (10) of the priests and the favored one of his colleagues.

C. Inscription N9

Day of the rejuvenation of the year.[3]
(1) The inspector of priests Nefershemem's son, (2) the first under the king, inspector of priests, overseer of herds Merery's (3) son, the first under the king, inspector of priests Memi's (4) [son], the priest, keeper of secrets of the seal-bearer of the god (5) [Merer]y speaks:
'The servant (*the speaker*) (6) was among the priests who went forth (7) … to the *djeser-ta* festival this year. (8) The servant carried out successfully the duties of the priest."

D. Inscription O54

(1) The first under the king, inspector of priests, overseer of herds of *netjert* cattle, (2) Ignes' son, the first under the king, inspector of priests (3) Inyotef speaks:

I am (4) one favored of the *djasti* and of the priest, (5) (for) with them I have carried out the duties of a priest (6) in this temple since I set foot in it.

E. Inscription O65

(1) The inspector of priests Kameni's son, (2) the inspector of priests Sabni's son, the deputy overseer of the temple Shu's son, (3) the inspector of priests of the soul chapel of Meryre, inspector of priests of what is in the *per-nu* shrine (4) ... whose perfect name is Nebniankhmeryre (5) [speaks (?)] [I am one favored of] the *djasti* and of the priest, (6) (for) [with them] I have carried out the duties of a priest in this temple since I set foot in it. For I am (7) ...[a keeper (?)] of the secrets of this temple (8) in this temple since I set foot in it.

F. Inscription O74

(1) Made in the desert of the upper temple, year of the second occasion, third month of the *Akhet* season, day 15.
(2) The inspector of hairdressers of the Great House, *djasti*, overseer of priests (3) Nyankhhor's son, the inspector of priests Kameni's (4) son, the first under the king, inspector of priests Shesemui's son, (5) the first under the king, inspector of priests, scribe of the temple, Nyankhmeryre's beloved son, (6) the first under the king, inspector of priests, scribe of the temple, whose perfect name is Ankhu, (7) Nebniankhmeryre.
(8) The first under the king, scribe of the temple, (9) Idui's (10) beloved son, (11) the royal acquaintance, he who pursues legal proceedings, whose perfect (12) name is Fereri, Ankhmeryre, (13) speaks:
I am a priest and keeper of secrets of this temple. (14) I am one whose coming is awaited among the priests, (15) the favored one of the priests.

G. Inscription O144

(1) Made in ... fourth month of the *Akhet* season, day 10.
(2) The sole companion, *djasti,* Merpepy speaks:
(3) The office of *djasti* was passed on to me (in) the year after the first occasion.
The last line is rather damaged.

89. A Graffito from Hindallab

Hindallab is a small quarry site just to the north of Qubbet el-Hawa on the west bank of the Nile at Aswan. This unusual graffito is probably late Old

Kingdom; the name Henbaba(i) is found among the Qubbet el-Hawa inscriptions (no. 325 ix).

The seal-bearer of the king of Lower Egypt, sole companion, lector priest, Henbabai.
His son, the royal noble, overseer of foreigners, Heqaib.
With regard to a man who shall work or quarry in this hill of the lord of the two banks, the ancient one,[4] he shall not die if he pours water on the land and cultivates his grain. May his god make his *ka* live.

Notes

1. A title attested only in el-Kab, perhaps meaning an "advisor" or similar. See Vandekerckhove and Müller-Wollerman 2001: 333–35.

2. Literally "the festival of the sacred land." Almost certainly a celebration local to el-Kab (Vandekerckhove and Müller-Wollerman 2001: 43).

3. A term attested only in el-Kab, which might perhaps refer to the period in the year when priests such as these went out into the deserts to perform rites (Vandekerckhove and Müller-Wollerman 2001: 36–37).

4. Almost certainly Khnum, the god of the cataract region.

IX

State Administrative Texts

See notes in chapter I, §6.4.

90. Selections from the Abusir Papyri from the Neferirkare Temple

See chapter I, §6.4 for an introduction to these texts. Two letters from this archive will be found as no. 92. It is likely that most texts without explicit dates come from the reign of Izezi.

From the Beginning of Papyrus Rolls

A.

Now Paris, Louvre E 25416a. Reign of Izezi.

Year of the sixteenth occasion of the count of [all] the cattle and herds [of Lower and Upper Egypt.]

Horus Djedkhau …

Duty roster for those on night duty (in) the pyramid of Neferirkare.

For the use of the following three headings, see the duty roster below.

Date

Division of service

Duty

B.

Now Cairo, CG 58062, frame 2.

[Year of the nth occasion of the] count of [all] the cattle and herds [of Lower and Upper Egypt.]

Horus … [may he achieve] millions of *Sed* festivals …

Duty roster for the priests and *khenty-she* (in) [the pyramid of Neferirkare]

C.

Now London, BM EA 10735, frame 10. Reign of Izezi.

Year of the fourteenth [occasion] of the count of all the cattle and herds [of Lower and Upper Egypt.]
Horus [Djedkhau]

D.

Now Cairo, 602, frame V.
[Year of the nth occasion of the count of] all the cattle and herds of Lower and Upper Egypt.
Horus ... , may protection and life be behind him for ever.

E. Service List for the Festival of Sokar

Allocation of duties to a group of priests taking part in this festival. Some are to carry out purifications and others to carry certain ritual and valuable objects. No descriptions of the rituals themselves are given. Now Paris, Louvre E 25416c, and Cairo, 602, frame X. Probably reign of Izezi (Posener-Kriéger 1976: 60).

Year of the third occasion, fourth month of the *Akhet* season, day 25: the service list for the day of the festival of Sokar was drawn up for phyle *tawer*, section *was*.
Column A:
Those who make purification in the temple:
Kaiemwab, Merydjehutykakai, Weha.
Column B:
Those in charge of the two *Wekh*[1] *standards:*
Wekh called "the one which ascends to Re"
the priest Ankhkakai
the *khenty-she* Nitawykakai and Merydjehutykakai the younger.
Wekh called "the one which joins itself to Re"
the priest Ipi
the *khenty-she* Merydjehutykakai the younger, son of Merydjehutykakai the elder, and Ima.
(those in charge of) the *Teba*:[2]
Irenakh
Meni.
Column C:
those concerned with the invocation offerings in the festival hall:[3]
(Items of) silver:
one *shat* basin—the priest Nedjemankh
one *hezmeni* ewer—the priest Ipi

one *zenbet* vase—the *khenty-she* Nitawykakai
one *andju* bowl—the *khenty-she* Ankhkakai.
(Items of) Asiatic copper:
one offering table—Merydjehutykakai
two *hez* vases—Ni[...]kakai son of Weha
one *aperet* vase—
one *nesmet* jar
one upper part of a censer
one lower part of a censer
one *andju* bowl.
Incense: one *afdjet* box
Sesher linen: two pieces
Nefer linen: six pieces

Entry Passes

F.

This document is a palimpsest—it was written over an earlier text which was erased. A number of more broken but similar texts are discussed in Posener-Kriéger 1976: 475–77. Now London, BM EA 10735, frame 19. Probably reign of Izezi (Posener-Kriéger 1976: 491).

The deputy overseer of priests, Werka; the "brother of the funerary estate" and priest Irenptah.
Let him be allowed access to the container of the invocation offerings of the king of Upper and Lower Egypt Neferirkare in the king's mortuary temple in the same manner as access is granted to the *wab*-priests and *khenty-she*.

G.

This small fragment does shed some light on the filing aspect of the administrative practices of the temple. Now Cairo, 602, frame V.

Copy in a box of written documents.
No man or craftsman can enforce any judicial act against it.

H. Delivery Note

Now Cairo, CG 58063, frame 3. Reign of Unas.

Year of the sixth occasion, second month of the *Shemu* season, day 28.
I have had brought to you (the following) supplies for the pyramid of Kakai, which have been noted in writing:

des jugs of *hedjet* drink	11	
des jugs of *peru* drink	11	
des jugs of *hedjeret* drink	10	
[*hetja* bread]		*A pointed loaf*
[*hetjat* bread]		*Variant of the above*
khemed bread	10	
pezen bread	4	*An oval loaf*

Transferred to the *khenty-she*
Kakai.[4]

I. Beginning of a Duty Roster

No attempt is made here to represent precisely the lines and compartments of the original and the location of the text within the latter; the original is also written from right to left. The duty roster in fact spreads over pls. LXXXIV–LXXXVI of the publication but is too large to reproduce successfully in full here. See Posener-Kriéger 1976: Tableau III after p. 57 for a full presentation. Blank areas are intended to indicate approximately where the papyrus is damaged. Now Berlin 15726 and 21001. Probably reign of Izezi. *See table on p. 169.*

J. Part of a Duty Roster

No attempt is made to represent precisely the lines and compartments of the original and the location of the text within the latter. In particular the names do not line up under the column headings—I have done that here for simplicity; the text is also written from right to left in the original. Blank areas are intended to indicate approximately where the papyrus is damaged. A number of columns are omitted between the two parts of this table. Only part is presented here; see Posener-Kriéger 1976: Tableau II after p. 57 for a full presentation. Now London, BM EA 10735, frame 7. Reign of Izezi. *See table on pp. 170–71.*

Date	Division of service		Those who (*specified in subsequent columns*)		
			After (*specified in subsequent columns*)		
	Duty		Lector priest	Hairdresser of the Great House	Priest
Names of those on duty			Tyu	Ankhmare	…
Second	day	1	x	x	
month of	day	2	x	x	
the *Akhet*	day	3	x	x	
season	day	4	x	x	
	day	5	x	x	
	day	6	x	x	
	day	7	x	x	
	day	8	x	x	
	day	9		x	
	day	10			
	day	11			
	day	12			
	day	13			
	day	14	x		
	day	15			
	day	16			
	day	17			
	day	18			
	day	19			
	day	20			
	day	21			
	day	22			
	day	23			
	day	24			
	day	25			
	day	26			
	day	27			
	day	28			
	day	29			
	(last day)				

Those who carry out the cult rites around the pyramid				Receiver of the writings after carrying out the rites for the king's mother Khentkawes	
Day rites		Night rites			
Priest	*khenty-she*	Priest	*khenty-she*		
				Nefernemtut	
Phyle *imy-nefret* section *hat*		*Phyle imy-nefret* section *hat*			
Nakhti Nefersemen Khuwinefer Nakhti Khuwinefer Nakhti				x	x
Khuwinefer Nefersemen NakhtiIri				x	x
Nakhti Shededi Meri Nisuqed Nakhti				x	x
Khuwinefer Nakhti Iri Shededi Meri				x	x
Nakhti Iri Khuwinefer Shededi Meri				x	x
Khuwinefer Khuwinefer Iri Khuwinefer Iri				x	x
Nakhti Nefersemen Iri Nakhti Khuwinefer				x	x
Nefernemtut Khuwinefer Shededkakai Nisuba				x	x
Nakhti Khuwinefer Nefersemen Nakhti Nefersemen				x	x
Nakhti Khuwinefer Iri Nefernemtut Inkhi				x	x
Khuwinefer Nefersemen Nakhti Nakhti				x	x
Nefernemtut Shededi Meri Iri				x	x
Khuwinefer Nefersemen Nakhti Nisuba				x	
Nakhti Khuwinefer Nefersemen Khuwinefer Iri				x	
Khuwinefer Khuwinefer Shededi Nisuba				x	
	Nefersemen Meri Nakhti			x	
	Khuwinefer Nakhti Shededi			x	
	Nefersemen Iri Nefernemtut			x	x
Nefernemtut Khuwinefer Iri Khuwinefer				x	x
Khuwinefer Nefersemen Nefersemen Nakhti				x	x

See continuation on next page

Continuation from previous page

Second month of the *Shemu* season, day 18			
Dresser	Purifier	Decorator	Censer
The (royal) statues			
(statue wearing white crown)	*(statue wearing red crown)*	*(statue wearing* nemes)	
khenty-she			
Iri	Nefer-nemtut-kakai	Sheded-kakai	Priest Sankhenptah
in attendance			

	Gate-keepers				
Lector priest Tyu	Nakht-kakai	Nefer-semen-kakai	Khuiwi-nefer-kakai	Men-kau-kakai	Inkhi

91. List from the Abusir Papyri from the Neferefre Temple

For general information about the Abusir Papyri and the recent finds, see chapter I, §6.4. Longer discussions about the objects in this temple list in the publication and Posener-Kriéger 1976. This papyrus is now in Cairo, JE 97348.

A.

Total of (this) category of article:	80	
Wooden heron[5]	1	
Wooden hippopotamus (?)[6]	1	

B.

Total of the totals of (each) category, arranged by name

Khetem box	100	
Hen box	42	*A rectangular box with four feet*
Ritual clothing	6	
Zenbet vessel	6	*A spouted metal vase*
Carrying table	9	
Barques	2	
Carrying-plates for offerings	13	
Djebau box	7	*Not unlike a* hen *box*
Tema box	2	
Imyt-ra scepter	4	*Perhaps used in the "Opening the Mouth"?*
Mat scepter	2	*A scepter of authority?*
Nemtet stick	5	*A walking stick?*
Semiprecious stone	6	
Wooden heron	1	
Wooden hippopotamus (?)	1	
Entire reckoning of the house of cloth	206	*Perhaps a room in the temple*

Notes

1. A standard in the form of a column with an open papyrus flower at the top, surmounted by a solar disc flanked by a pair of uraei, as described in an adjacent text (Posener-Kriéger 1976: 65–66). Other representations show that two feathers may have been on top of it. It is likely that these two emblems evoke the solar

aspect of the deceased king—particularly understandable in view of the fact that the Sokar festival was here being celebrated in the royal mortuary temple—and indicate that the king may have taken part in this ritual (Posener-Kriéger 1976: 550–51). One of these columns is also mentioned in the festival calendar in the sun temple of Niuserre (no. 11).

2. Less certain in nature than the *Wekh*, this object may be associated with the cult of Hathor, which deity played an important part in the Sokar festival (Posener-Kriéger 1976: 66–68, 551).

3. In the central sanctuary of the mortuary temple (Posener-Kriéger 1976: 68–69).

4. Perhaps part of a personal name or the name of the pyramid.

5. Perhaps a statue in a series of deities used in a ritual in the temple, dealing with the ascension of the king to the sky (Posener-Kriéger 1991: 296–97).

6. Reading uncertain; if a hippo, then it could be concerned with the ritual of destroying the hippopotamus, known from one or two Old Kingdom references and more fully described in the temple of Edfu (Posener-Kriéger 1991: 297–98).

X

Letters

See notes in chapter I, §6.12.

On Papyrus or Other Non-stone Media

92. Letters in the Abusir Papyri from the Neferirkare Temple

Both letters are presumably part of a correspondence archive and do not necessarily relate directly to the administration of the temple of Neferirkare. From the similarities of phraseology it is not impossible that they both related to the same dispute. The sense of the second letter is particularly obscured by its broken nature.

A.

This papyrus is now Berlin 11301. Reign of Izezi.

(1) [May your heart be made pleasant in the sight of Ptah south of his wall (*or* Ptah-Sokar)], in the sight of Khentytjennet, in the sight of Djedshepses,[1] in the sight of all the gods. May they permit that you thrive; may they do for you daily everything perfect, along with everything which you desire …
(2) … to you, as I had proceeded to the place where I am as I am so annoyed … for I had seen to it that you were satisfied when I provided the items of bread and beer, although I got none. I am like …
(3) … in the records of those who have been judged (*or* "the judges" [?]). Did I not come back from the officials at the gate of the Great Mansion? Did I not come back … ?
(4) … I have complained via the government agents, as Re, Hathor and [all] the gods desire that Izezi live for ever and for eternity, concerning the case of receiving transport payments (?) …
(5) … I have gained access to it (above all) through the kindness of

Ankhnebef. May … not say … the young men, known as the temple youth, are doing well …
(6) … for it is the wish of the inspector of priests Ipi … in Tura. You it is who shall remember …

B.

The letter occupies both sides of the papyrus. Now London, BM EA 10735, frame 4, it probably dates to the reign of Izezi.

Recto

(1) Second month of the *Shemu* season, day 1[6]
(2–3) The scribe of a (divine) barque phyle Horemzai
(4) The scribe of a (divine) barque phyle …
…
(5) He said to …
(6) you … forage (?)
(7) in giving you payment …
(8) which you carried out (in a hostile manner) against the house of the *khenty-she* Djef[au] …
(9) For I am fearful of you …
(10) greatly. But I shall have him give you an ox …
(11) For there is no one reckoning …

Verso

(1) … the letter-carrier and inspector …
(2) … [insofar as Re,] Hathor, and all the gods [desire that] Izezi be in …
(3) … every official sent to the place …
(4) … to you … in order to give you items [of bread and beer (?)] …
(5) … you used to place for yourself your declaration via [the government agents (?)] …
(6) … Second month of the *Shemu* season, day 16: it was arranged to be brought to you …

93. A Sixth-Dynasty Letter, Probably from Saqqara

Known as Papyrus Boulaq 8, this letter is now in Cairo, CG 58043. Reign of Pepy I.

(1) [Year after the nth occasion] third month of the *Akhet* season, day 5.

(3) [the sender addresses] [Meh]u
(5) ... your agent. Why are you remaining at home? This Mehu (6) has arrived to where I your servant am; should misfortune come (7) upon me your servant and this my associated female servant? I swear[2] by the eyes of Mereri my lord: (8) the heart of this female servant of Mereri leaps when she sees (9) the messenger of her lord. Indeed, Mehu has set down in this letter (10) which I had brought to me his legal commitment regarding (his responsibility) in sustaining her.
However, a little honey and *ished* fruit it is that are the requirements of the family (11) of my fellow servant, the assistant of the Great House Iren-akhet. I spoke of the matter relating to him to the messenger of your agent (12) especially with reference to his being appointed as scribe of the phyle of the *meret* temple of (king) Neferzahor; he was ejected therefrom (13) due to what had been omitted from the assignment orders of the messenger of your agent. Surely Mereri my lord (14) would want to keep the mistress of the female servant of the funerary estate happy by listening to my words (15) regarding this fellow servant. Come to me, come to me, as fast as my lord can!

94. A Protest to the Vizier from Saqqara

This letter was found torn in two, and it has been suggested that this might have resulted from the vizier's reaction to it! It was found within the Step Pyramid enclosure in 1925 and is now in Cairo, JE 49623. Sixth dynasty.

(1) Year of the eleventh occasion, first month of the *Shemu* season, day 23.
(2) The overseer of the expedition speaks:
(3) The letter of the vizier has been brought to this your servant,[3] to effect that the division of troops of Tura should be brought (4) to the Western Enclosure[4] so that they may be fitted with clothes in his presence. (However), this your servant protests at (such) unusual requests;[5] for indeed the letter-carrier (5) is about to come to Tura with the (stone) barge, while your servant has to spend six days at the Residence (6) along with this division until it is clothed. It is (this) which gets in the way of your servant's work, since but one day (7) needs to be wasted for the clothing of this division.
So speaks your servant. Inform the letter-carrier![6]

95. Part of a Letter Regarding Work on a Pyramid, Probably from Saqqara

Now Cairo, JE 52001A. Probably reign of Merenre.

Either the Writer or the Addressee of the Note

The inspector/foreman of the property of the granary of the Residence, the lector priest Ankhpepy.

The Note Itself

… [of] the pyramid of Merenre, which is made in excellent fashion … of stone; in accordance with my orders I have spent a year at the pyramid of Merenre, which is indeed prospering …

96. The "Crimes of Sabni," from Elephantine

As with so many letters, the missing context does not help us. Sabni, possibly the person of the same name whose biography is translated as no. 243, has clearly committed some offense of which both the parties here are aware. The first editor detected an innate lack of trust between both parties to the letter. This is one of a number of fragments of papyrus of late Old Kingdom date found in illicit excavations at Elephantine at the end of the nineteenth century (see chapter I, §6.12). Now Berlin 8869. Possibly eighth dynasty (see Edel 1970a: 117).

(1) (To)[7] the *haty-a,* the seal-bearer of the king of Lower Egypt, the sole companion, the seal-bearer of the god, Iruremetju.
(2) (From) the overseer of the expedition, Merrenakht, son of Kahotep, son of the sole companion, lector priest Sebekhetepi.
(3) I have given my attention to the matter about which you[8] sent the sole companion and overseer of the estate Hetep, because (4) I do not wish to do anything you dislike. If you have sent to me (5) so that you let it be known about the crime which has been committed against me, then matters are in order. However, if you have done (6) this to make fighting break out because you have seen the two foreign lands … me … (7) I see whether you really love the *haty-a,* the seal-bearer of the king of Lower

Egypt, the sole companion, the overseer of priests Sabni (8) more than me. For it is good that one love trueness of voice more than crookedness over a long time, and this is an occasion for attending (9) to all the transgressions of the aforesaid *haty-a*. He is not one who eats his own produce.[9] Insofar as you and I are as one (11) that the aforesaid *haty-a* should not shake off this crime which he has committed, (10) you have vouched for me in the hall of Horus.

(12) Furthermore, the sole companion and overseer of the estate Hetep has seen that I did not make myself available to the troops of Medja and Wawat (13) so that I did not do what you dislike.

(*Address on exterior*): The *haty-a,* the sole companion, overseer of priests of Re, Iruremetju.

97. A Letter about Complaints over Farming

The letter, perhaps originally from Elephantine (see chapter I, §6.12), is now in Turin CG 54002. It perhaps dates to the reign of Pepy II or later. The translations of Roccati and Wente disagree quite widely on the meaning of the text.

(1) [*date all but destroyed*] day 3 ...

(2) [*Perhaps* It is ... who addresses ... of] Memi

(6) ... cultivated for ...

(8) ... He said to me that you have had (9) one (*or* ten [?]) *heqat* of emmer wheat sown in the third nome of Upper Egypt ... which the aforesaid Memi cultivated (10) alongside the companion and overseer of priests ... in Imiotru (*modern Rizeiqat*) (11) in the charge of the sole companion Shemai. Now the sole companion Senkau (12) has come to this nome. [*perhaps* He employed me (?)] within the farm, (13) cultivating the dry lands with one man's (allotment) of emmer wheat and his (allotment) of Upper Egyptian barley. Now (14) your claim is wrong in relation to ... [and I shall proceed (?)] to judgment. (15) Come to the farm's landing place (?), and my agent ... in order to let you know how evil (16) are the transgression and insolence of those with false claims.

(17–18) (*either*) If indeed I hold you captive for the officials I will be acting in a way to gain your disapproval (*or*) Beware of the officials as I shall act in a way that you will not like.

98. Fragments of Letters from the Elephantine Archive

All are probably late Old Kingdom, although the address of the Strasbourg fragments has something in common with the Heqanakht Papyri of the late eleventh/early twelfth dynasty. See chapter I, §6.12 for the Elephantine archive.

A.

The translation here is an amalgam of the beginning of a number of fragments in Strasbourg, Berlin, and Munich.

A son speaks to his father: May your state of health be like (that of) the living one million times (*or* "[may it be said] one million times").

B. Fragment of a Letter in Brooklyn

Now Brooklyn 47.218.18.

A son speaks to his father, whom he loves, may he live, prosper, and be healthy …
May Ptah south of his wall make your heart pleasant while you are alive … while your state of *imakhu* exists perfectly in the sight of the *ka* of Neferkare …

99. Letters from the Oasis of Dakhla

Excavations since 1987 have revealed approximately thirty small letters from the area of the palace at Ayn Asil. Unlike the other letters of the Old Kingdom, either on papyrus or surviving in stone versions of possible papyrus originals, these are made of small pieces of mud and inscribed using a bone stylus. Two examples have so far been published. For a popular article on Ayn Asil, including mention of these letters, see Soukiassian 1997. See also notes before no. 273.

A.

As with so many letters, the context of this one is lost; we have no idea as to the identities of the sender and recipient.

This servant speaks: inform the letter-carrier who is in the counsel that the builder[10] has not yet arrived at Rudjet[11] to prepare the way for the ruler of Demiu.[12] May the *ka* of the letter-carrier[13] order that a builder be sent.

B.

This is considered by the excavators as more of a brief internal note than a letter. Again the context is nonexistent.

The royal noble and messenger Rensi to the seal-bearer Rensi:
I have sent him ... for the children of the ruler. Make these accounts for the overseer of the estate Rensi.

Letters from Tombs

See also letters within the longer texts of Senedjemib Inti (no. 232) and Harkhuf (no. 241).

100. Letter from Izezi in the Tomb of Reshepses at Saqqara

The tomb of Reshepses is to the north of the Step Pyramid (LS 16: PM III^2, 494–96); it dates to the reign of Izezi.

(1) Royal decree for the vizier, overseer of royal document scribes, Reshepses.
(2) My majesty has seen this wonderful letter which you have had brought to me in the palace on this perfect day in which the heart of Izezi is truly pleased (3) with what he truly loves. Seeing this letter of yours is what my majesty desired above all else, for you indeed know how to say what my majesty loves better than anything, and what you say is more pleasing to me than anything else. (4) My majesty knows full well that you desire to say everything which my majesty loves.
(5) O Reshepses: I say to you millions of times: (7) (you are) one whom his lord loves, (8) one whom his lord favors, (9) one who is close to his lord, (10) the keeper of secrets of his lord; (11) truly I know that Re loves me as he has given you to me. (12) As Izezi lives for ever, you should say all your desires to my majesty (13) in your letters immediately this day, and I shall see to it that they are executed immediately.

Letters to the Dead

101. Two Letters to the Dead

See chapter I, §6.12, for general notes on these texts. The subject matter of both is complex, and as we do not know the context it is not easy to deduce the precise problems. In the Cairo linen the trouble is clearly being caused by third parties, but in the Qau bowl the miscreant is thought to be the writer's dead brother. Note the similarities of phraseology in both texts. See the editions for more comments on the context.

A. On Linen, Perhaps from Saqqara

Now Cairo, JE 25975. The JE entry apparently indicates that it came from the sixth-dynasty tomb of Sankhenptah at Saqqara (PM III², 672).

(1) A sister addresses her brother,[14] and a son addresses his father. Your condition is like that of he who lives a million times! May Ha, lord of the West,[15] and Anubis, lord of burial, act for you in the way she (*wife*) and he (*son*) desire!

(2) This (letter) is a reminder of the fact that the agent of Behezti came for (some) leather when I was sitting by your head when Irti's son Iy was summoned (3) to vouch for the agent of Behezti, and that you said "keep him hidden for fear of the elder Iy. May the wood (4) of this bed beneath me rot (?) if a man's son is barred from his household property."

But now, look, Wabut has come (5) along with Izezy; they have devastated your house, and they have seized everything which was in it with the specific aim of enriching Izezy. (5) They wished to ruin your son while enriching the son of Izezy. She has taken Iazet, Iti, and Anankhi away from you; (7) she is taking away your personal attendants after taking everything which was in your house.

(8) Can your heart be calm about this? I wish you would bring (me) to you so that I might be there at your side in preference to seeing your son dependent on the son (9) of Izezy. Wake up your father Iy against Behezti! Rouse yourself and make haste against him! (10) You know that I come to you here on the matter of litigation with Behezti and Aai's son Anankhi. Rouse yourself against them, (11) along with your ancestors and brothers and your friends so that you might overthrow Behezti and Aai's son Anankhi.

(12) Remember what you said to Ireti's son Iy: "the houses of the ancestors should be protected" when you (also) said "a son's house is (his) son's

house." May your son set up your house in the way you set up the house of your father!
(13) O Sankhenptah my father, may it please you to have Ini summoned to you to seize the house of Anankhi born to Wabut!

B. On a Bowl from Qau in Upper Egypt

This text dates probably to the end of the Old Kingdom or First Intermediate Period. Now London, University College UC 16163.

Inside

(1) Shepsi addresses his father Iyenkhenmut:
(2) This (letter) is a reminder of your going to the prison (?) at the place where Sen's son Hetepu was when you brought (3) the leg of an ox and when I, your son, arrived there with Newaef, and when you said "Welcome the two of you (?), sit down and eat (4) meat." Am I being injured in your presence, when I, your son, have neither said nor done anything, by my brother whom I buried, whom I brought back from I ... , (5) whom I placed among his tomb-companions? (I did this) in spite of the fact that (the value of) 30 *heqat* of Upper Egyptian barley in the form of a loan was still outstanding against him: a loincloth, a jug, six *heqat* of Upper Egyptian barley, (6) a bundle of (?) flax, a *mehet* cup; indeed I did for him that which had never been done (before). He has acted against me, your son, particularly wrongfully, (7) since you said to me, your son, "All my property is to remain (actually) with my son Shepsi."
See, my fields have been taken away by (8) Sher's son Henu. See, he (*Shepsi's brother*) is with you in the same city; (9) arrange for litigation to be made against him as you have witnesses with (you) in the same city. (10) Can the man who wields the javelin be joyful while his rulers are repressed?[16]

Outside

(1) Shepsi addresses his mother Iyu:
(2) This (letter) is a reminder of this which you said to me, your son: "Bring me quails that I may eat them"; and I, your son brought you (3) seven quails and you ate them (all). Am I being injured right in your presence so that my children are discontent with me, your son who is (himself) ill? (4) Who will pour water for you?[17] If only you would decide between me and Sebekhotep, whom I brought from another town to be buried in his town (5) among his tomb-companions, having given him funerary clothing. Why does he act against me, your son? I have neither said nor done anything wrong to him. (6) Wrongdoing is painful to the gods!

Notes

1. These are two of a number of relatively obscure Memphite deities, which are also to some extent aspects of Ptah. See Baines 1988: 124–33 with reference to an earlier study by Kees.

2. Literally "as the eyes of Mereri live for me"; a not unusual pattern of oath making.

3. A polite circumlocution used in letters by an inferior to a superior; sometimes translated "this your humble servant"; its literal meaning is "the servant there." See other such terms in the Sabni letter (no. 96) and the el-Kab graffiti (no. 88).

4. Almost certainly the Step Pyramid enclosure.

5. "Protests at the use of out-of-the way places" has been the more common translation of this phrase.

6. See Piacentini 2002 for this title.

7. It is possible that the addressee and sender could be reversed: Eichler 1991b: 22–24.

8. The terms I translate "I" and "you" are substituted for the expressions "your brother there" and "your scribe," as it is clear that these are respectful circumlocutions used by the parties involved. They do, however, indicate social equality between the correspondents. See also Eichler 1991b: 25–26.

9. Meaning "does not live off his own means." Smither 1942: 18–19 contrasts this strongly with the ideal at about this time of living off one's own resources and not off others.

10. Pantalacci translates "potter."

11. Perhaps on one of the tracks leading out of the oasis.

12. Seemingly a non-Egyptian toponym; it might indicate that the Egyptians were putting their knowledge at the disposal of those outside the oases.

13. An unusual expression in letters, but known from other sources, so probably just an expression of deference.

14. "Sister" and "brother" are normal terms used familiarly in ancient Egypt of a husband and wife to each other.

15. A necropolis god who appears far less frequently than Anubis (see Leitz 2002: 5:10–11).

16. Following Wente; perhaps this is a saying of the time.

17. A reference to the son maintaining the mortuary cult of his deceased mother.

XI

Private Legal Texts

See notes in chapter I, §6.6.

On Papyri

102. House Purchases from the Gebelein Papyri

See chapter I, §6.7, for the Gebelein Archive. There is some disagreement among Egyptologists as to who is the seller and who is the purchaser in these two texts. They are structured so that one almost can imagine the parties and their witnesses standing together, the witness coming in as the middle man in the deal. The (to us) relatively small amounts of cloth being offered in exchange for a house indicate that fine cloth was an expensive commodity. The papyrus is now in Cairo, JE 66844. Fourth dynasty.

A.

The year after the third occasion of the count of the cattle of Lower and Upper Egypt, third month of the *Peret* season, day 26 in Inerty-Inpu (*Gebelein*)

First Party

I present my part of the deal, a house 16 cubits long and 15 wide.
The royal servant Nefer.

Witness to the Transaction

As the king lives, Netjersen ensures that Maat should be enacted, and I am satisfied concerning it.

Second Party

I present my part of the deal: a piece of cloth of 15.5 cubits.
The royal servant and "brother of the funerary estate" Iri.

B.

[The year] after the second occasion of the count of the cattle [of Lower and Upper Egypt], the [nth] month of the *Akhet* season, day 20 [+ x], sealed …

First Party

I present my part of the deal, being a house of 16 cubits long and 11 wide. The royal servant Iu …

Witness to the Transaction

As the king lives, I shall ensure that Maat should be enacted, and I am satisfied concerning it …

Second Party

I present my part of the deal: a piece of cloth of 24 cubits (*the rest is lost*).

103. A Dispute over an Inheritance from Elephantine

The papyrus is now Berlin 9010, part of the Elephantine archive from Aswan (see chapter I, §6.12). Probably late Old Kingdom.

This unique document is most probably a judgment handed down resulting from a problem of inheritance. This translation tends to follow Sethe's edition more than Goedicke's; the subheadings added are my own to make it easier for the reader to follow the text.

Part of the Submissions Made by the Parties

(1) … the aforementioned Sebekhotep has brought a document relating the words of the royal noble and overseer of foreigners User, that he should carry out his task for (2) his (*User's*) wife and his children, whereby all his property is in his control until all the children (3) of the aforementioned User are satisfied therewith—the older one according to his greater (age), the younger one according to his younger (age).
The aforementioned Tjau has said that this is not the case, (4) that his father has in no way done it (*made such an agreement*).

The Verdict of the Court

If the aforementioned Sebekhotep can bring three excellent witnesses who are convincing on this matter (5) and who shall make (this oath) "May your might be against him, O god"[1] in relation to this document which is in agreement with that which the aforementioned User said on the matter,

(6) then matters will remain in the hands of Sebekhotep, for he has brought these three witnesses who say on this matter in their presence (7) "The aforementioned Sebekhotep is the beneficiary."
If he does not bring these three witnesses to speak on this matter (8) in their presence, then everything belonging to the aforementioned User shall not remain with him but (rather) remain with his son, the royal noble and overseer of foreigners, Tjau.

On Stone in Tomb Contexts

104. Legal Text from the Tomb of Akhethotep Hemi/ Nebkauhor at Saqqara

For the chapel, see no. 195; some captions are also translated in no. 301. This text is very broken, and we cannot really obtain the sense, but it is not unlike some of the other series of prohibitions and punishments in such texts that relate to the administration of his funerary cult. It is presented on a line-by-line basis because of the damage; although the latter is extensive, it is too important to omit. Late fifth or early sixth dynasty.

Horizontal Line at Top

The *iry pat, haty-a,* vizier, seal-bearer of the king of Lower Egypt, sole companion, administrator of (the vineyard) "Horus is the star at the top of heaven,"[2] keeper of secrets of the House of the Morning, chief lector priest, charmed of arm, *haty-a,* scribe of the divine documents, ...

Vertical Columns

(1) He has made an order ... (*understand,* "for a will" *or similar*)
(2) With regard to the phyle of soul priests ...
(3) They should make the invocation offerings ...
(4) in respect of their requirements ...
(5) in respect of that which they do for me in accordance with ...
(6) to carry out his monthly duties for my invocation offerings ...
(7) He has no documentary claim against my house, my fields, and their workers; (8) rather, he should be thrown out of it ... [With regard to his son] (9) he should not replace him in ... [making offerings (?)]
(10) With regard to any soul priest of the funerary estate ...
(11) who shall go off to other people ...

(12) and who does not come back to make the monthly offerings for me …
(13) they shall give [that which is in his portion of income] to the excellent son …
(14) in the manner in which I have done myself, since it has happened …
(15) and who does not come back to make the monthly offerings for me …
(16) They should bring [their] wives and family …
(17) concerning the invocation offerings which (are present) for me in the necropolis …
(18) who shall take them for *shaw*[3] …
(19) in the will for me in …
(20) together with the father of …
(21) for another priestly duty …
(22) With regard to these soul priests …
(23) levied in connection with a commission …
(24) for any son or brother who is given for …
(25) except for those who are soul priests …
(26) With regard to any soul priest of my funerary estate who speaks or who proceeds [against a colleague of his] …
(27) who comes to the soul priests of [the funerary estate (?)] … [he is proceeded against (?)] (28) in the name of the king and [his share (?)] is taken away [from him (?)] …
(29) they have power over …
(30) for the burden of the soul priests …
(31) about which I have spoken in this will[4] …
(32) that which I have given them in this will …
(33) I do not permit anyone to have power over them, their children, and … for the breadth of eternity, (34) except when he himself should go …
(35) With regard to an official, a noble one, an official of the Great House, granary, treasury, or the house of documents, or a man of the house of sealed documents …

105. Inscription above a Shaft in the Tomb of Idu Seneni at el-Qasr wa es-Sayed

Reign of Pepy II. See no. 252 for the biography from the tomb.

Seneni speaks:

(1) In respect of this shaft which I made,
(its) mouth (measuring) 6 + x cubits [and with a depth of] 3 + x cubits,[5]

(2) which I have given to my beloved wife Asenkai,
I shall prevail (legally) against any man (3) who shall take it away from the aforementioned Asenkai.
I shall be judged with them by the Great God, (4) the lord of heaven.
I shall seize their necks like a bird's.
I am an excellent and potent *akh*; I know (5) all the secrets of the words of the god,
through which one is transfigured in the necropolis. …
I do not permit (6) any man to have control (over it) who goes down into (robs [?]) it,
for [I have buried my beloved wife (7) Asenkai] therein.
I am the owner of the tomb according to [my document].
(8) I did this for the aforementioned Asenkai because of the greatness of her state of *imakhu* in (9) my body.
She has not uttered a sentence which has repulsed my heart; she was not angry while she was alive.

Asenkai speaks:

(10) I am a priestess of Hathor, the beloved one of her whole town.
In respect of any person who shall take this shaft from me,
I shall be judged with them by the Great God.

106. Block Bearing a Legal Text of (Possibly) Kaiemnefret

This is perhaps one of the most exhaustive documents relating to the setup and governance of the priests who looked after the funerary estates. It is probably from the tomb of the Kaiemnefret family at Giza of the middle to late fifth dynasty (see PM III², 263–64). Now in Cairo, CG 1432.

(*The beginning is lost*)
(1) when he was alive and on his feet, being a sole companion, chief of Nekheb, one who does guard duty on the king every day, the sole companion, chief of Nekheb, the boundary official of the estate "Horus is the star at the top of heaven" … (*this would have included further titles and ended with his name*)
(2) … (with regard to [?]) these soul priests of my funerary estate:
(3) … in accordance with all the commands I have made concerning it.
I do not permit that [children, brothers], (4) sisters, or any of those born of supervisors of soul priests, deputy supervisors of soul priests, or soul priests have any power over [the fields], (5) personnel, or anything which I

have set up for them so that invocation offerings can be made for me therefrom while they, their children, (6) their brothers, and their sisters are able to perform service.

The exception (to this) is (what is needed) to make the invocation offerings [for me there in the necropolis, in] (7) my tomb of eternity which is in the (area of) the pyramid of Khafre, in accordance with the setup of the fields, the personnel, and everything [which I have set up for them, so that invocation offerings can be made for me] (8) therein.

I do not permit that any soul priest of my funerary estate should have power of disposal of the land, personnel, or [anything which I have set up for him, so that invocation offerings can be made for me] (9) therein, whether that be by selling to any person or by transferring it to any person by means of a will, except for giving [it to his son alone (*or*) his excellent son] (10) to be his share together with the soul priesthood, so that (these) remain with these soul priests.[6]

With regard to any soul priest of my funerary estate who shall repudiate [*lost, but perhaps* the fields, personnel, or anything] (11) belonging to my invocation offerings which were given to me by the king so that I might be *imakhu*, part of his share shall be taken away from him and allocated to the share [of the phyle to which he belongs].

(12) With regard to any soul priest of my funerary estate who shall go to law against his colleague and who makes a complaint that (that colleague) should be ejected from the job of soul priest [with the aim that he take his part] (13) of the share by means of it: the fields, personnel, or anything which I have given to him, so that invocation offerings can be made for me therefrom shall be taken from him [*lost but probably something to do with the officials*] (14) therein who shall make an end for him not going to law in the presence of the officials [on the matter of the fields, personnel, and anything which I have done] (15) for the soul priests of my funerary estate so that invocation offerings can be made for me therefrom in my tomb of eternity which is in the necropolis in (the area of) [the pyramid of Khafre].

[With regard to] (16) any soul priest of my funerary estate who shall go into the presence of the officials (to transfer) to another duty[7] [*lost, perhaps* if] (17) the officials [permit] he shall go to another duty, (but) his part of his share (still) belongs to the phyle in which he was—[I do not permit him to take (anything)] (18) from the fields, personnel, or anything which I set up for them to enable the invocation offerings to be made for me therefrom in my tomb in [the necropolis in (the area of) the pyramid of Khafre]. (19) He shall go off only with his body.

With regard to these fields which the king gave to me so that I might be *imakhu* ... , [*lost, but perhaps* they belong to the soul priests] (20) so that invocation offerings can be made for me therefrom in the necropolis.

With regard to everything which is produced in that which I have given them,[8] [*lost and uncertain, but perhaps* it shall be divided up in the place in which] (21) judgment is given, and the share for those who belong (?) to these phyles shall be one-tenth; this shall be done ... (22) so that invocation offerings can be made for me therefrom in the necropolis, in my tomb of eternity in (the area of) the pyramid of Khafre.

[With regard to the towns[9]] (23) of my funerary estate which the king gave me so that I might be *imakhu*, and which are exempted for the purposes of (providing) invocation offerings in accordance with the list (?) ... [*a crucial phrase lost*] [soul priests of (?)] (24) my funerary estate who make invocation offerings for me therefrom in my tomb of eternity in the necropolis in (the area of) the pyramid of Khafre, [in respect of the fields, personnel,] (25) and everything which I have set up for them.

With regard to the towns of my funerary estate which are handled by priests, priestly services shall be done in relation to them ...

107. Provision of a Doorway by Khenemti in the Tomb of Iarti at South Saqqara

This is an intriguing document, as the double orientation of the text does not obviously make any link between Khenemti's office and the provision of the doorway. Interpretations of the second text vary widely; my translation mostly follows that of Menu. The text is on a lintel of the chapel of Iarti (PM III², 674). Now in Cairo, CG 1634. Reign of Merenre or later.

Texts in Front of Figures Facing Right

The sole companion, overseer of the *khenty-she* of the Great House, Iarti.

An offering which the king gives for invocation offering for the sole companion and lector priest, Iarti.

Wab-priest of the 200 of the pyramid of [Merenre], overseer of the harim, Iarti.

The sole royal ornament, priest(ess) of Hathor, his beloved wife, the *imakhu* Merti.

His beloved eldest son, sole companion, and lector priest Merenresoneb.

Text of Khenemti, Presenting a Leg of Meat to the Figures on the Left

The guardian of the tomb, the soul priest Khenemti, speaks:

My lord appointed me as assistant of the soul priest.
He organized that I succeed him as soul priest.
This doorway was bought for a *daiu* measure of cloth.[10]

108. Decrees Setting Up the Estates of Metjen from His Tomb at Saqqara

The texts of Metjen are probably the earliest ones to expand beyond the listing of offerings, names, and titles; in addition, we find a complex and frankly difficult series of statements about the founding of his funerary property over Egypt. I follow the structure of Gödecken that the texts are perhaps taken from an original series of decrees setting up these foundations; I do not translate most of the titles outside the immediate context of these "decrees." The chapel is now Berlin 1105. Early fourth dynasty.

Decree I

(To) the ruler of the nome, leader of the land, overseer of commissions of the eastern part of the sixth nome of Upper Egypt (regarding) the judge in charge of offering, controller of the great estate of the third and fourth/fifth nomes of Lower Egypt, overseer of the troops of the western border:
He has bought 200 arouras of land from many royal colonists.[11]
He has given 50 arouras of land to (his) mother Nebesneit when she set up her will for the children, and their share was set down in a royal document for every office.[12]

Decree II

(To) the controller of the mansion of Huni in the second nome of Lower Egypt:
He was given together with his son 12 arouras of land with dependents and herds of cattle.

Decree III

(To) the leader of the land, ruler of the nome, overseer of commissions in the seventeenth nome of Upper Egypt, overseer of messengers:
(regarding) the sixteenth nome of Lower Egypt, 4 arouras of land in Baseh (with) dependents and all things which are contained in a decree of the scribe of the office of provisioning; while he is (still) on earth, it was given

to (his) only son and it was seen to that the decree was brought into his presence.[13]

Decree IV

(To) the overseer of commissions of the fourth/fifth and third nomes of Lower Egypt:

12 "foundations of Metjen" have been founded for him in the fourth/fifth, sixth and second nomes of Lower Egypt (along with) their products for him in the dining room. These have been bought for 20 arouras of land from many royal colonists, (along with) 100 portions of funerary offerings which come daily from the soul chapel of the royal mother Nymaathap[14] (and with) a walled estate 200 cubits long and 200 broad, set out with fine trees, and a large pool made in it; it was planted with fig trees and vines.

It is written down in a royal document, and their names are (recorded likewise) on (this) royal document.

The trees and the vines were planted in great numbers, and the wine therefrom was produced in great quantity (*or* "of great quality"). A garden was made for him on land of 1 *kha* and 2 *ta* within the enclosure, which was planted with trees.

(It was named) Iymeres, a "foundation of Metjen," and Iatsobek, a "foundation of Metjen."

The property of his father the judge and scribe Inpuemankh was given to him, without wheat and barley and the property of the estate, but with dependents and herds of donkeys and pigs (?).

He was promoted to first of the scribes of the office of provisioning and overseer of the office of provisioning;

He was promoted to be the "strong of voice" among those involved in agricultural production[15] when the boundary official of the sixth nome of Lower Egypt was in charge of the judge and supervisors of reversionary offerings in the sixth nome of Lower Egypt, who should take the job of judge and "strong of voice,"

and he was promoted to be overseer of all linen products of the king;

and he was promoted to be ruler of the Per-Desu and the towns which are under the same control (?);

and he was promoted to be the boundary official of the people of Buto and controller of the estate of Per-Sedjaut and Per-Sepa and boundary official of the fourth/fifth nome of Lower Egypt and controller of the estate of Senet and the nomes under the same control, controller of Per-Sheptjet, and controller of the towns of the Great Mansion of the southern lake (*the Fayum*).

The "foundations of Metjen" have been founded out of what his father Inpuemankh gave him.

109. Agreement with Soul Priests from the Tomb of Nyankhkhnum and Khnumhotep at Saqqara

The tomb of Nyankhkhnum and Khnumhotep is most unusual in that while most Egyptian tombs were built for one person, it seems here that two colleagues pooled their resources and built a particularly beautiful tomb, discovered in 1964. The tomb was constructed between about 2400 and 2350 BC and was subsequently destroyed by the construction of the causeway of the pyramid of Unas. This text relates to agreements for the maintenance of the funerary offerings for the tomb owners and describes the penalties for noncompliance. Some captions are also translated from this tomb (no. 309).

Nyankhkhnum and Khnumhotep, inspectors of manicurists[16] of the Great House and possessors of *imakhu* in the sight of the Great God, speak:

- (1) With regard to these brothers and these soul priests who deal with the invocation offerings for us (2) and who act on our behalf in the necropolis: they shall not let our children, our wives, or (3) any people have power over them. They are to deal with the invocation offerings for us together with (those of) (4) our fathers and mothers who are in the necropolis.
- With regard to any soul priest (5) who shall sell his share to anyone: everything which has been given to him shall be taken (6) from him and shall be given (instead) to the soul priests of his phyle.
- With regard to any soul priest who shall be reassigned (7) to another priestly duty: everything which has been given to him shall be taken from him and shall be given instead to (8) the soul priests of his phyle.
- With regard to any soul priest who shall start proceedings against his fellow priests, (9) whether it be coming forward with a complaint about his carrying duties or producing a document for the discontinuation of the invocation offerings of the owners of this funerary cult: (10) all of his share shall be taken from him and given instead to that soul priest against whom he started proceedings.

(11) We have made all these (arrangements) above all so that you make these invocation offerings excellent (12) for the *akh* spirits, for the owners of this cult, and for those who are in the necropolis.

110. Texts of Nykaiankh from Tehna

Other texts of the Old Kingdom make mention of setting up arrangements for cults after the death of the owner, but none are so extensive as these texts of Nykaiankh. He appears to have had two tombs, the second cut when he was more elevated than the first, in which also his parents are more prominent. In both tombs great efforts were expended to detail how the cults should be set up and organized. Tehna is a little to the north of Minya in Middle Egypt; the tombs are of the early fifth dynasty.

A. Earlier Tomb

Titles of the Tomb Owner

The overseer of the Great Mansion, the priest of Hathor who dwells in *Ra-inet,* the possessor of *imakhu* in the sight of the god, the royal acquaintance Nykaiankh.

Inscriptions over Engaged Statues on the Rear Wall of the Tomb

Overseer of the estate, Heti (*father of the deceased*).
The royal acquaintance, Debet (*mother of the deceased*).
My father and mother—while they were proceeding to the West, I made this (tomb) for them in the place of *imakhu* in the sight of the god.
Her eldest son, the overseer of the Great Mansion, the royal acquaintance Nykaiankh.
The royal acquaintance Nefertkau.

Setting Up of His Funerary Cult

(1) A decree which the royal acquaintance Nykaiankh made (2) in his house, from his own mouth while he was alive:
(3) With regard to all my children, I have set things up for them from that from which they benefit. I do not permit that any one of them be empowered to give away what I have done on his behalf through a will or by gift to any relative, (4) with the exception of where he has a son—he may give (it) to him. They should operate under the charge of my eldest son with respect to the way they carry out the rites for me.
I am one who has set up my heir for the day on which I travel to the West—may that be a long way off!
(5) That soul priest (6) who carries out cult activity on my behalf under his supervision—(7) he it is who shall organize them in relation to my invocation offerings daily, at the beginning of the months, at the half-months, and in (every) festival throughout the year.

I do not empower them to take away (anything or anyone) for any work other than that of the daily invocation offerings.
(8) If he does take (them) away for any work which is not (related to) my invocation offerings, then I do not give him control over these soul priests with respect to any work apart from my invocation offerings.

B. Later Tomb

Introduction

(1) The overseer of the estate of the Great Mansion, (2) overseer of the new towns, (3) overseer of priests of (4) Hathor mistress of *Ra-inet,* (5) royal acquaintance, Nykaiankh.
(6) His wife, the possessor of *imakhu* (7) in the sight of Hathor, Hedjethekenu.
(8) He made a command for his children to serve as priests for Hathor mistress of *Ra-inet.*

Service for Hathor

(9) These are the priests whom I have set up from among the children of my funerary estate, so that they might serve as priests for Hathor.
Two arouras of land were set up by the majesty of Menkaure for these priests so that they might serve as priests for it.

Adjacent to the previous text is this table of persons:[17]

<table>
<tr><td colspan="4">The royal acquaintance, overseer of the estate of the Great Mansion, Nykaiankh, his wife, the royal acquaintance Hedjethekenu, and her children</td><td></td></tr>
<tr><td rowspan="2">the royal acquaintance Hedjetheknu, possessor of imakhu</td><td rowspan="2">(F)[18]</td><td colspan="2">Time of the year[19]</td><td>Fields</td></tr>
<tr><td>First month</td><td rowspan="4">The Akhet season</td><td>5 arouras</td></tr>
<tr><td>The royal document scribe, Hemhathor</td><td>(M)</td><td>Second month</td><td>5 arouras</td></tr>
<tr><td>Shepseswabhathor</td><td>(M)</td><td>Third month</td><td>5 arouras</td></tr>
<tr><td>Nysuakhethathor</td><td>(M)</td><td>Fourth month</td><td>5 arouras</td></tr>
<tr><td>Shepseshathor</td><td>(M)</td><td>First month</td><td rowspan="4">The Peret season</td><td>5 arouras</td></tr>
<tr><td>Wabkauhathor</td><td>(M)</td><td>Second month</td><td>5 arouras</td></tr>
<tr><td>Qasuthathor</td><td>(M)</td><td>Third month</td><td>5 arouras</td></tr>
<tr><td>Khabauhathor</td><td>(M)</td><td>Fourth month</td><td>5 arouras</td></tr>
</table>

<table>
<tr><td colspan="2">Khentysutkathor</td><td>[ ]</td><td>[First] month</td><td rowspan="6">The Shemu season</td><td>5 arouras</td></tr>
<tr><td colspan="2">Rainet</td><td>[ ]</td><td>[Second month]</td><td>5 arouras</td></tr>
<tr><td colspan="2"></td><td></td><td></td><td></td></tr>
<tr><td colspan="2">His share is one-tenth of everything that enters the temple over and above bread and beer
The priest Hemhathor</td><td>(M)</td><td>Third month</td><td>5 arouras</td></tr>
<tr><td>Royal acquaintance</td><td>Merrekhkha</td><td>(M)</td><td rowspan="2">Fourth month</td><td>5 arouras</td></tr>
<tr><td>Soul priest</td><td>Kheshka</td><td>(M)</td><td></td></tr>
</table>

a. (M)ale or (F)emale depiction.
b. The argument has also been made that this may be the term for the five "epagomenal days" (chapter I, §3.2.3)

(25) The majesty of Userkaf it was who ordered that I should carry out priestly service for Hathor mistress of *Ra-inet*.
With regard to anything which shall come into the temple, I am the one who shall perform priestly service in relation to these things and the reversionary offerings which relate to the temple.
(26) Those children of mine are those who shall do priestly service for Hathor mistress of *Ra-inet* in the manner in which I myself have done, when I have gone to the West as a possessor of *imakhu*. [The fields (?)] are in the care of these children of mine.

Funerary Cult of Khenuka

(27) These people are those who shall make the invocation offerings for the royal acquaintance Khenuka, his father, his mother, his children, all his successors:

Adjacent to the previous text is this table of persons:

<table>
<tr><td colspan="2">Time of the year</td><td rowspan="2">Royal acquaintance, Merrekhkha
Soul priest, Kheshka</td></tr>
<tr><td>First month</td><td rowspan="4">The Akhet season</td></tr>
<tr><td>Second month</td><td>The priest Hemhathor</td></tr>
<tr><td>Third month</td><td>Rainet</td></tr>
<tr><td>Fourth month</td><td>Khentysutkathor</td></tr>
</table>

First month	The *Peret* season	Khabauhathor
Second month		Qasuthathor
Third month		Wabkauhathor
Fourth month		Shepseshathor
First month	The *Shemu* season	Nysuakhethathor
Second month		Shepseswabhathor
Third month		The royal document scribe, Hemhathor
Fourth month		the royal acquaintance Hedjetheknu

(41) These children of mine are those who shall make the invocation offerings at the *Wag* festival, the festival of Thoth, and the daily festivals, for the royal acquaintance Khenuka, his father, his mother, his children, all his successors.

Part of Another Text

(1) The overseer of the estate of the Great Mansion, (2) the royal acquaintance Nykaiankh, (3) the possessor of *imakhu*; (4) the royal acquaintance Hedjethekenu.

(5) He has spoken with his mouth regarding the matter of his children, while he was on his feet and alive (6) in the sight of the king.

Details of the Funerary Cult of Nykaiankh

A number of individuals, including those named in the lists above, are shown behind the deceased. Each scene shows a pair of figures making offerings or carrying them, and are captioned by the line "his assistants" and the name of an overseer of soul priests. Names include those of Shepses and Khentysut.

The soul priests are in the charge of these children of mine.

I do not permit that permission is granted to take them away for any priestly duty with the exception of the (making) of invocation offerings which are divided up in the estate of this (4) … these soul priests. With regard to these children of mine who shall carry out any (other) work using these soul priests, or with regard to any man who shall interfere (with them), I shall be judged with him.

Text over a Statue Group

The overseer of the estate of the Great Mansion Nykaiankh; his wife the royal acquaintance Hedjethekenu; his daughter and his son made this for him in accordance with their (*literally* "his") state of *imakhu* in his sight.

Over three figures:

The possessor of *imakhu* in the sight of Hathor, the royal acquaintance Akhetnub;
The inspector of royal document scribes, royal acquaintance Nyankhsy;
The overseer of the Great Mansion, the possessor of *imakhu* in the sight of the Great God, the royal acquaintance Nykaiankh.

C. Inscriptions Relating to His Son as Heir

These are mostly too damaged to make sense.

i.

(1) … I have not given them bread and beer from my will. He who is my successor …
(2) … in my will so that they shall act in these matters for this my heir in the manner in which I have acted myself for them.
(3) The priest Hemhathor.

ii.

(1) … his son … may he give to him what he has done …
(2) … this my son is my heir; may invocation offerings be there for this my son …

iii.

(1) [With regard to any child of mine: He is not to give anything which I have done for him to any man except for that which concerns] my son …
(2) in respect of invocation offerings daily …

iv.

(1) … [With regard to any soul priest: He is not to give] …
(2) … [He is not to give them anything therefrom] …

v.

… the royal document scribe Hemhathor; he is my heir who is in my place, the possessor of all my property.
… Hemhathor; he is my heir, the possessor of all my property, an *imakhu* …

vi. (Child Standing in Front of Wife of Nykaiankh)

Her eldest son, his father's *imakhu,* the royal document scribe Hemhathor.

111. Record of the Disposal of the Estates of Nykaure in His Tomb at Giza

Nykaure was a son of Khafre and a lesser wife. He was a vizier, presumably in the time of Menkaure. This text sets out the distribution of a part of Nykaure's wealth among his wife and children, that from his "funerary domains" (compare no. 319). The tomb is in the Central Cemetery (LG 87; PM III², 232–33). Late fourth dynasty.

Year of the twelfth occasion of the count of the cattle [and herds] …
The king's son Nykaure is setting down (these) instructions while he is still alive on his feet and not ill.
I give: (*This is arranged in a tabular fashion*)
to the royal acquaintance, Nykanebty: in (*name lost*) nome, (*two estates compounded with the name of Khafre*);
to his son, the royal acquaintance, Nykaure: in the north of the fourteenth nome of Lower Egypt, (*three estates compounded with the name of Khafre*);
to his daughter, the royal acquaintance, Hetepheres: in the fourteenth nome of Lower Egypt, (*one estate compounded with the name of Khafre*), and in the north of the fourteenth nome of Lower Egypt, (*one estate compounded with the name of Khafre*);
to his daughter, the royal acquaintance, Nykanebty the younger (*plus possibly another name now erased*): in (*name lost*) nome, the estate "[the *ba* of] Khafre is great," and in the sixteenth nome of Upper Egypt, (*four estates compounded with the name of Khafre*);
to his beloved wife, Nykanebty: in the twelfth nome of Upper Egypt the estate "Khafre is perfect," in the twentieth nome of Upper Egypt (*one estate compounded with the name of Khafre*), and the house/tomb/estate of his daughter in the pyramid of Khafre …

112. Disposition of the Funerary Estate of Penmeru in His Tomb at Giza

The text shows how one's funerary offerings could come both from one's own estate and from the reversion of offerings from a high official. From tomb G 2197 in the Western Cemetery (PM III², 82–83). Late fifth dynasty.

The royal *wab*-priest, the priest of Menkaure, the overseer of soul priests, Penmeru speaks:

With regard to my brother of my funerary estate, the soul priest Neferhotep and his children of father or mother,[20] they are to be the soul priests of my funerary estate responsible for the invocation offerings for my tomb of eternity in the necropolis of the pyramid of Khufu; they are also those who bring to me the reversionary offerings of my sovereign, the vizier Seshem-nefer.[21]
[With regard to] the one *kha* measure of land which I have given to him and these his children, I do not empower any person to have authority over him and these his children; I do not empower any son of mine and any children of mine to have authority.
He shall give 5 *ta* measures of land for the invocation offerings of the royal acquaintance Meretites.[22]

113. Part of the Dispositions of Pepi, Possibly from Giza

Berlin 14108. Probably fifth dynasty.

The dependent of the funerary estate of the royal mother Hetepheres,[23] the soul priest Tjenti's daughter Pepi speaks:
With regard to these children given to me by the aforementioned father of mine in his will, I do not permit that any person should have power over them.
The soul priest But (*there follows the beginnings of the names of seven more persons, doubtless witnesses to the above statement*)

114. Instructions for the Funerary Priests of Sennuankh from Saqqara

Tomb east of the Step Pyramid (D 52: PM III², 582). Perhaps middle fifth dynasty. The ends of each line are damaged; I incorporate the restorations of Sethe and Goedicke.

(1) These soul priests of my funerary estate and their children and indeed the children of their children who will be born to them throughout eternity ... [*perhaps* "they will provide me with my funerary offerings"].
(2) I do not empower them to sell or will away (anything) to anyone, but rather they should pass on to their children what is their share [together with the soul priesthood, so that (these) remain with these soul priests].[24]
(3) With respect to any soul priest among them who should leave or who is taken away to perform another priestly duty, everything which I have

given to him should go to the soul priests of his phyle; I do not permit … [*perhaps* "him to have the power to take away with him anything I have given him"].
(4) With respect to any soul priest among them who shall go to law against his colleague, everything which I have given him shall be taken away, and indeed it shall be given to the soul priest against whom he went to law. I do not permit him to have the power … [*perhaps* "to carry out the making of offerings for me"].

115. Instructions for the Cult of Tjenti and His Family from Giza

Exact find-spot not known (PM III^2, 308). Now Cairo, JE 57139. Sixth dynasty.

With regard to the invocation offerings which have come to me from the "house of the king"[25] in the form of barley, wheat, and clothing, it is my wife, the royal acquaintance Tepemnefret, who will provide my invocation offerings, for she is *imakhu* in my sight.
With regard to the first of two fields which provide the invocation offerings for my mother, the royal acquaintance Bebi, it now belongs to my wife, the royal acquaintance Tepemnefret. She is the one who shall make the invocation offerings for me and my mother, the royal acquaintance Bebi. I it was who begged them (*the plots of land*) from the king for my own *imakhu* provision. I am her eldest son, her heir; I it was who buried her in the necropolis.
(For)

the soul priest Neferher	3 *ta* measures of land	3 *heqat* of grain
the soul priest Iufi	3 *ta* measures of land	3 *heqat* of grain
the soul priest Seneb	3 *ta* measures of land	3 *heqat* of grain
the soul priest Persen	1 *ta* measure of land	3 *heqat* of grain

shall be provided from the property of Tepemnefret, and I have set up her property for these soul priests from a small aroura.[26] Should they not remain in the associated "Mansion of the *ka*" which is under the control of my wife, the royal acquaintance Tepemnefret, then it (*the land*) will revert to the ownership of my wife Tepemnefret.
With regard to the invocation offerings for my mother, the royal acquaintance Bebi consisting of barley and wheat from the granary, and clothing from the treasury, my "brother of the funerary estate" it is, the soul priest

Kaiemnefret, who shall provide the invocation offerings there for my mother, the royal acquaintance Bebi and for myself.
As regards the second of these two fields which provide the invocation offerings for my mother, the royal acquaintance Bebi, it shall belong to my "brother of the funerary estate," the soul priest Kaiemnefret. He it is who shall provide the invocation offerings there for my mother, the royal acquaintance Bebi and for myself.

116. Wepemnefret Grants His Son Rights to Use Parts of His Tomb at Giza

This text was surely placed in the tomb so as to be a reminder to all that the author's wishes were to be respected. Examination of the tomb shows that the northern chapel indeed belongs to Iby; the shaft aligned with that chapel can reasonably be assumed to be the one mentioned in this text. From his tomb in the Central Cemetery (PM III², 281–82). Middle to late fifth dynasty (see Verner 2001: 405, n. 304).

Year of the uniting of the Two Lands, third month of the *Peret* season, day 29. The sole companion, Wep (*the "perfect name" of Wepemnefret*), speaks:
I have granted for ever to my son, the lector priest Iby, the northern burial place (*shaft*) together with the northern tomb (*chapel*), together with the invocation offerings which will be in my tomb of eternity of the necropolis. (This is done) that he might be buried in it and that invocation offerings might be made for him therein. For he is (my) *imakhu*. No brother, no woman, no child shall have any rights in relation to it, with the exception of my eldest son, the lector priest Iby, to whom I have granted it.

117. From the False Door of Yotefnen from Giza

Found in the Western Cemetery, in debris north of tomb G 2041 (PM III², 69). Now Cairo, JE 56994. Sixth dynasty.

I made this in accordance with my state of *imakhu* in the sight of my lord, and I caused that the craftsmen thank the god of the necropolis in relation to that which I did in this matter in exchange (for their work): the inspector of those concerned with matters of the granary, the controller of measurers, Yotefnen.

The paid employees[27] of the funerary estate will bring their invocation offerings for me in the necropolis in exchange for a sealed and registered service agreement.

118. Fragment of a Document Relating to a Mortuary Estate from Saqqara

Stored in the tomb of Kairer at Saqqara; PM III², 652. Late fifth-early sixth dynasty (?). The further fragments 2–5 are even less comprehensible!

Fragment 1

… [with regard to] every [dignitary], every official, and every functionary [who shall …]
… who shall designate a male or female servant [of mine] …
… who shall make/give soul priests [of mine] …
… who shall conduct …

119. Purchase of a Plot of Land for a Tomb from Saqqara

Adjacent to the fragmentary text translated here is the figure of a standing woman and two vessels, so it may have come from the decoration of a tomb. It is also important for shedding some small light on the process of tomb provision in the Old Kingdom: the writer was not buying land for building a tomb, but rather land that would provide an income for his or her cult. The text is on a slab found near the valley temple of Unas and is now in a storeroom there. See PM III², 652. Probably fifth to sixth dynasty.

[With regard to the land (?) for] this soul chapel which I have bought from the maker of sweet things Perhernefert, the extent being one-thirtieth of an aroura: the price will be paid by my daughter, the royal acquaintance …

120. A Legal Fragment Found Reused at Lisht

This slab must come from a tomb in one of the Old Kingdom Memphite cemeteries (compare other reused blocks nos. 9 and 12). This text should perhaps be compared with the better-preserved texts presented in this book. Found reused in a Middle Kingdom tomb; the object is presumably still at Lisht. End of fifth dynasty.

(1) ... every town ...
(2) ... the inspector of soul priests and the deputy overseer of soul priests and [these soul priests ...
(3) ... I do not permit] that anyone change the boundaries of any piece of land (for) they are registered. If they (*the soul priests*) should be taken away [for any task other than the making of invocation offerings for me]
(4) they should resign from any (claim on a) funerary estate, any place of habitation or any town ...
(5) ... [all property which I have given] him should be transferred to a sole companion and royal noble who has an interest in these matters, and [it shall be (?)] taken away ...
(6) ... for they are registered to the funerary estate ...
(7) [I do not permit (?)][28]
(8) that they—they themselves, their children, or siblings—seal any sealed document,
(9) or that they—they themselves, their children, or siblings—give away anything in a will,
(10) along with anything which I have given them (11) in relation to these invocation offerings which I have set up, or that they might go to (12) any service of any other person ...
(13) [I do not permit (?) that] the deputy overseer of soul priests, these soul priests ...
(14) ... celebrating monthly festivals ...
(15) ... together with ...

121. Sale of a House, Found at Giza

Only a few documents from the Old Kingdom deal with sales of property. The original surely would have been on papyrus (compare the Gebelein documents in no. 102) and was also put down in stone; this may have served to identify the house to which it related and to ensure that the wishes were carried out, possibly as the full agreed price might not have been paid at this point.[29] *The document is structured in such a way that the statements of the two parties are separate and then joined by the sale price of the house and the mention of witnesses, whose names are found at the end (the headings given are mine and not in the text). The degree of uncertainty present in some of these translations is encapsulated here by the fact that there has not been total agreement as to who is the purchaser and who the buyer. The text is on a stela found near the temple of the Sphinx. Now in Cairo, JE 42787. Probably fifth to sixth dynasty.*

Statement by the Seller

[The *mehenek* Serf]ka speaks: I bought this house, for which I paid 10 *shat*,[30] from the scribe Tjenti. (The deal) was sealed in the land registry in the presence of the court of magistrates of the pyramid of Khufu and many witnesses of Tjenti of the phyle of Kaiinpu.

Specification of Price

One piece of four-measure cloth[31]	3 *shat*.
One wooden bed	4 *shat*.
One piece of two-measure cloth	3 *shat*.

Notes on the House Being Sold

Of very upright construction, unfinished roof of sycamore wood.

Statement by the Purchaser

The scribe Tjenti speaks: "As the king lives, I shall act correctly, and you shall be satisfied in this matter with regard to what shall happen to everything in this house, since you have already paid for it."

Witnesses

The stonemason Mehu; the soul priest Iyni; the soul priest Sabni, the soul priest Nyankhhor.

Notes

1. Perhaps the king (Green 1980).

2. A classic Old Kingdom honorific or courtly title, which goes back at least to the reign of Netjerykhet Djoser at the beginning of the third dynasty. I presume it originally pertained to a special estate of the king, to be appointed to which was a great personal honor. Whether that estate continued in existence or whether the title just became a mark of importance of court is uncertain. Compare comments in the introduction in chapter I, §5.2.1; other examples in nos. 106 and 153.

3. Uncertain term.

4. This complex term, *imyet per*, seems to be used to deal with not just a transfer of property but also conferring the right to bequeath it further. See most recently Logan 2000.

5. When the tomb was excavated in 1975, the mouth was found to measure 3 × 2 m and be approximately 3 m deep. See Säve-Söderbergh 1994: pl. 5, p. 32.

6. See Edel 1966 for this passage.

7. The term translated as "duty" seems to refer to the general term for an obligation such as being a soul priest.

8. The funerary estate.

9. The various places which provide offerings for the tomb and which are often shown in personified form in some tombs (no. 319).

10. This might also be a term for a kilt or loincloth. "Bought" is literally "exchanged"—Egypt was fundamentally a barter/exchange economy.

11. For this designation, perhaps referring to a type of farmer, see the references in Jones 2000: 489. Other examples will be found in this book in the texts of Nesutnefer (no. 321) and the Koptos decrees B and C (nos. 24, 25).

12. Following Baud and Farout 2001: 43–45.

13. Following Baud and Farout 2001: 45–47.

14. Probably the wife of Khasekhemwy, last king of the second dynasty, and mother of kings of the early third.

15. For this obscure title, see Jones 2000: 488.

16. It may seem surprising that such a remarkable tomb as this is owned by manicurists. However, readers should bear in mind that anyone who was permitted to carry out manicure and pedicure on the king was one to be trusted and (potentially) be highly honored. Tjy (no. 150), the owner of one of the most beautiful tombs at Saqqara, was a royal hairdresser who then rose to high state office.

17. This simplification of the arrangement is taken from Urk I; the original layout may be seen in Fraser 1902: pl. 4.

18. (M)ale or (F)emale depiction.

19. The argument has also been made that this may be the term for the five "epagomenal days" (chapter I, §3.2.3). See most recently Manuelian 1986: 4–9.

20. A strange expression, perhaps legalese; could it mean "male or female"?

21. The owner of a large mastaba tomb in the Western Cemetery, vizier in the reign of Izezi. His chapel is now in Tübingen: Brunner-Traut 1995 and Gamer-Wallert 1998.

22. The wife of Penmeru. This whole sentence seems not to be connected directly to the rest of the text but is presumably a command for Neferhotep.

23. Perhaps the wife of Sneferu and mother of Khufu whose tomb was found at Giza in 1926 (Reisner and Smith 1955).

24. See Edel 1966 for this passage.

25. Literally "the king, from the house."

26. Half the size of a normal aroura, Baer 1956: 116.

27. This unique term has been translated as "slave," but the word is also the same as that used for "exchange" several times in this text and seems more likely to mean "paid labor."

28. Reconstruction of Goedicke. A different reconstruction is suggested in Fischer 1961: 50: "[With regard to any funerary priest] who will seal (something) by seal … to (someone) (or) who will give (something) as a deed … to (someone)."

29. See Fischer 1980b: 13–16 for some simpler stelae marking houses or land.

30. A unit of measurement known best from the New Kingdom, when it appears to have been one-twelfth of a *deben* and perhaps weighed 7.6 g of copper. See Janssen 1975: 102–8.

31. Compare the Old Kingdom linen lists (nos. 329, 330).

XII

A Selection of Offering Formulae and Titles

See notes in chapter I, §6.5.1.

122. From the Tomb of Kaiemsenu at Saqqara

This tomb is northwest of the pyramid of Teti (PM III², 541–42). Probably fifth dynasty.

The overseer of the granary, who does what his lord desires every day, the overseer of the granary, royal acquaintance, Kaiemsenu.

(1) An offering which the king gives
that he may give every invocation offering from the royal estates:
grain from the granary, clothing and *merhet* oil from the two treasuries ...
(2) sweet things from the *per-aqet,* pieces of meat from the gate-chamber,
(in fact) all the invocation offerings which should be given to an *imakhu* ... (3) from the royal estates for the breadth of eternity.
The priest of Re in *Setibre,* [priest] of the pyramid of Neferirkare ... ,
(4) *wab*-priest of the pyramid of Niuserre, overseer of the granary, the *imakhu* ... [Kaiemsenu].

123. From the Tomb of Kaipure at Saqqara

Originally north of the Step Pyramid, the chapel is now in Philadelphia, Pennsylvania University Museum E 15729 (PM III², 455–56). Late fifth or early sixth dynasty.

Left Outer Jamb

(1) An offering which the king gives
that this his tomb may be given to him and that he may be buried in it,

having grown old perfectly (2) as an *imakhu* in the sight of the Great God, a possessor of burial.
The overseer of the treasury of the Residence, Kaipure.

Left Inner Jamb

(1) An offering which the king gives
and an offering which Anubis, who dwells in the divine tent-shrine, gives
that invocation offerings may be given to him within:
(2) grain from the two granaries, clothing from the two treasuries,
merhet oil from the two chambers, and sweet things from the house of the *ished* tree.
(3) The overseer of the treasury, Kaipure.

124. Formulae from the False Door of Mereri at Saqqara

These formulae are to be understood as following on from "offering which the king gives" formulae on the architrave and on the inner jambs of the door which are not translated here. The texts of Ptahhotep II (no. 126) are similar.

The tomb is located west of the Step Pyramid (PM III^{2}, 607–8). Mid sixth dynasty.

Left-hand Outer Jamb

(1) Proceeding to his house of eternity in great peace,
for indeed he is an *imakhu* in the sight of Anubis, lord of the sacred land,
after invocation offerings have been made for him (2) upon the offering place,[1]
after he has traversed the lake (*in the next world*),
and after his transfiguration by the lector priest and the embalmer,
for his state of *imakhu* is great.
Mereri.

Right-hand Outer Jamb

(1) Crossing the heaven in great peace,
and going forth to the top of the mountain of the necropolis.[2]
May his document be handed over by his ancestors and by his *kas*,[3]
(2) for he is the foremost of the possessors of *imakhu*.

May invocation offerings be made for him
upon the offering place in his house of eternity.
For indeed he has grown old most perfectly in the sight of Osiris.
Mereri.

125. Formulae in the Tomb of the Physician Nyankhre at Giza

The tomb is south of the Great Pyramid (LG 55: PM III[2], 223). Late fifth or early sixth dynasty.

False Door

Outer Jamb Left

... the *imakhu* in the sight of the king in the double granary, the double treasury, at the doorway of the kitchen,[4]
and in every place from which the invocation offerings of the king are made.
The physician of the Great House Nyankhre.

Outer Jamb Right

... in the Opening of the Year festival, the festival of Thoth, the first day of the year festival,
the *Wag* festival, the festival of Sokar, and every daily festival,
for the physician of the Great House Nyankhre.

Inner Jamb Left

(1) The physician of the Great House, the companion of the house, he who does what his god favors every day, priest of Anubis who dwells in *Sepa*.
(2) [The chief of reversionary offerings] in the Mansion of Life, physician of the Great House, keeper of secrets of the king wherever he is.
Nyankhre.

Inner Jamb Right

(1) [The physician of the Great House], priest of Heka, priest of Horus *imy-senut*, keeper of secrets of his lord every day.
(2) The *imakhu* in the sight of his lord, the *imakhu* in the sight of the Great God, *wab*-priest of the king.
Nyankhre.

126. Formulae from the False Door of Ptahhotep II in His Tomb at Saqqara

In a tomb west of the Step Pyramid (PM III², 600–604). Late fifth dynasty.

Upper Lintel

(1) An offering which the king and an offering which Anubis,
who is on his mountain, who is in his wrappings,
who dwells in the divine tent-shrine, give
that he may be buried in the necropolis,
having grown old most perfectly.
(2) An offering which Osiris gives
that invocation offerings may be made for him
in the Opening of the Year festival, the first day of the year festival,
the *Wag* festival, the festival of Thoth, the great festival,
the *Rekeh* festival, every monthly and half-monthly festival and daily.
(3) The first under the king, staff of the *rekhyt*, pillar of *kenmut,* judge and boundary official, he of the foremost seat, priest of Maat, follower of Duau, first under the king, Ptahhotep.

Panel

He has made the crossing of the canal/pool,
having been transfigured by the embalmer.
Ptahhotep.

Lower Lintel

Right: (1) The first under the king, staff of the *rekhyt,* great one of the tens of Upper Egypt.
(2) The *imakhu* in the sight of the Great God, Ptahhotep.

Left: (1) The judge and boundary official, one of the foremost seat.
(2) The *imakhu* in the sight of Osiris, Ptahhotep.

Inner Right Jamb

(1) An offering which the king gives and an offering which Osiris,
lord of Busiris, foremost of the Westerners, gives
that invocation offerings may be made for him every day.
(2) The judge and boundary official, he of the foremost seat, he who loves Maat, her *imakhu,* controller of the great ones of the tens of Upper Egypt, controller of the broad hall.
(3) Ptahhotep.

Inner Left Jamb

(1) An offering which the king gives
and an offering which Anubis, who dwells in the divine tent-shrine, who is on his mountain, gives
that he may be buried in the necropolis, having grown old perfectly.
(2) The first under the king, staff of the *rekhyt*, priest of Maat whom she loves, the *imakhu* in the sight of the Great God.
(3) Ptahhotep.

Outer Right Jamb

(1) Crossing the heaven so perfectly in peace;
proceeding to the mountain of the necropolis,
so that he may be taken possession of by the ancestors and by his *kas*,
(2) the foremost one, possessor of the state of *imakhu*,
and so that invocation offerings might be made for him
at the offering place in his house of eternity.
For he has grown old most perfectly in the sight of Osiris, the first under the king, Ptahhotep.

Outer Left Jamb

(1) Proceeding to his house of eternity in a very perfect manner,
for his state of *imakhu* exists in the sight of Anubis, who dwells in the necropolis,
after invocation offerings have been made for him (2) at the offering place,
after crossing the canal/pool,
after having been transfigured by the lector priest and the embalmer;
for his state of *imakhu* is very great in the sight of the king and of Osiris, the first under the king, Ptahhotep.

127. Formulae on the Sarcophagus of Sedjefaptah Called Fefi from Giza

A tomb in the Central Cemetery (PM III^2, 285). Fifth or sixth dynasty.

(1) An offering which the king and an offering which Anubis,
who dwells in the divine tent-shrine, give
that Sedjefaptah might be buried in a very perfect manner
in that which he has made for himself.
(2) An offering which the king and which Anubis,
lord of the sacred land, give

that Fefi be buried in a place of *imakhu* in the sight of the god and of men.

128. From the Tomb of Sekhemka at Saqqara

On the lintel of a false door. Tomb west of the Step Pyramid (PM III², 596). Middle fifth dynasty or later.

(1) An offering which the king and an offering which Anubis give
that invocation offerings may be made for him
in the form of a prepared offering
at the monthly and half-monthly festivals for the breadth of eternity;
(2) so that he may be given grain from the granary,
clothing from the two treasuries,
pieces of meat from the gate-chamber,
(so that he may be) among the *imakhu* in the sight of the god.
(3) The judge and mouth of Nekhen, Sekhemka.

129. Formulae of Sneferunefer II from Saqqara

On a lintel in his tomb north of the Step Pyramid (E 7: PM III², 468). Now Cairo CG 1421. Late fifth dynasty or later.

(1) An offering which the [king]
and which Osiris, who dwells in Busiris, in all his places,
and which Anubis, who dwells in the divine tent-shrine,
who is in his wrappings, lord of the sacred land, lord of Sepa, give
(2) that he may be buried in the necropolis in the Western Desert,
having aged most perfectly,
(3) and that invocation offerings may be made for him in every daily festival
and that invocation offerings may be given to him from the Residence:
(4) grain from the two granaries, clothing from the two treasuries,
merhet oil from the two chambers, (5) *wah* fruit from the *per-aqet*,
and every sweet thing from the house of the *ished* tree.
(6) The deputy overseer of priests of the pyramid of Djedkare,
overseer of singers of the Great House, Sneferunefer.

130. Formulae from the False Door of Tepemankh at Saqqara

Tomb north of the Step Pyramid (D 10: PM III², 483). Late fifth or early sixth dynasty.

Lower Lintel (the Upper One Is Missing)

(1) An offering which the king gives
that he may go down into this his tomb,
(2) having grown old most perfectly in the sight of the Great God;
the sole companion Tepemankh.

Inner Right Jamb

(1) Traveling in peace to his tomb of the necropolis,
having grown old most perfectly as an *imakhu*.
(2) The first under the king, his true beloved, who does everything commanded of him in writing, whom the god loves, Tepemankh.

Inner Left Jamb

(1) Officiating at the offering place,
so that invocation offerings might be made for him,
and that he might be taken possession of by his *ka*s and by the ancestors.
(2) The sole companion, who is in the heart of his lord, who very truly delights his lord in everything which he loves, Tepemankh.

Outer Right Jamb

(1) Proceeding to his tomb of the West,
having crossed over in the *weret* boat,
having been led to the booth prepared in accordance
with the writings of the skills of the lector priest.
(2) An offering which the king gives and an offering which Anubis gives
that he may travel on the perfect ways of the West upon which
the *imakhu* travel in peace and in the sight of the Great God.
(3) The priest of the pyramid of Unas, first under the king, true overseer of commissions, true judge and boundary official, true judge and inspector of scribes, true judge and scribe, sole companion, Tepemankh.

Outer Left Jamb

(1) Going forth to the top of the mountain of the necropolis,
having traversed the pool (*or* canal[5]),
having been transfigured by the lector priest,
for whom (every)thing has been done by the embalmer
in the sight of Anubis (*i.e., being mummified*);
(2) An offering which the king gives and an offering which Anubis gives
that invocation offerings may be made for him
in the Opening of the Year festival, the festival of Thoth,
the first day of the year festival, the *Wag* festival,
the festival of Sokar, the great festival, and every daily festival.
(3) The inspector of priests of Hathor (in) the *meret* temple of Unas, *haty-a*, true sole companion, lector priest, keeper of secrets of the king wherever he is, sole companion, Tepemankh.

Notes

1. This offering place might be on top of the mastaba tomb, at or near the mouth of the shaft. One may be illustrated in the tomb of Debehen (no. 200: Hassan 1932–60: IV, fig. 122), and the remains of one have possibly been excavated at Dahshur (Alexanian 1998; Alexanian 1999: 36–38).

2. An allusion to Anubis, the necropolis god, one of whose epithets is "he who is upon his mountain."

3. This "document" appears occasionally in these texts. Should we see this as a reference to some sort of administrative procedure needed for a tomb or burial, or perhaps as something more conceptual, since the god is shown taking it? It seems plausible that it might conveniently cover both senses, in a practical and religious manner.

4. Suggestion of Junker; literally "gateway of the chamber."

5. Perhaps a reference to such as in the boat texts (no. 317).

XIII

Appeals to the Living and Warnings to Evildoers and the Uninitiated

See notes in chapter I, §6.5.1.

131. Texts of Ankhi Called Intji from His Tomb at Saqqara

Poor publication of this tomb hampers this translation, but Ankhi, as well as possessing some unusual titles, exhibits many unusual phrases in his warning texts and formulae. There are some parallels between the latter and those of Ptahhotep II (no. 126) and Tepemankh (no. 130). The tomb is northwest of the Step Pyramid (PM III^{2}, 608–9). Probably early sixth dynasty.

On Front of a Series of Figures on the Entrance Lintel

(1) The priest of the pyramid of Teti.

(2) The metal-worker of the Great House, controller of mottled snakes,[1] Ankhi.

(3) The priest of the pyramid of Unas.

(4) The metal-worker of the Great House, controller of mottled snakes, Ankhi.

(5) The *imakhu* in the sight of the Great God, Ankhi.

(6) The metal-worker of the Great House, overseer of the two houses of gold, Intji.

Facade Left

... he shall support any man in the noble court of his fathers, which belongs to the Great God, for him who shall do this.

I shall see to it that he is transfigured in the sight of the Great God,
and that he is perfect in the sight of those who are on earth.

Facade Right

[With regard to] every workman, every stonemason, or every man
who shall (do) evil things to this tomb of mine of eternity
by removing bricks or stones from it,
no voice shall be given to him in the sight of any god or any man.[2]

Either Side of Niche Containing False Door

The true metal-worker, Ankhi, speaks:
(1) Officiating at the offering place, after having crossed the pool,
when his document has been received by the perfect West
(2) when he (*or* his document) might be taken possession of by the Western Desert.
For I am a *akh* better prepared (with) magic than any other person.
I did not take the property of any weaker man (3) by force or strength,
for I wish to be *imakhu* in the sight of the Great God lord of the West.
O lector priest, *imakhu* in the sight of Anubis
(4) May your heart be sweet in relation to the king!
Do not desist from your reading of the transfigurations!
I know the royal decree made for an *akh*.

132. Texts from the Tomb of Ankhwedja Itji at Giza

Tomb in the Western Cemetery (PM III², 167); probably sixth dynasty.

Remains of an Ideal Biography

(1) … *imakhu* twice in the sight of the god and in the sight of the king, who has reached …
(2) … that which the god opposes;
I have spoken what is right; I have done what is right,
that which the [god (?)] loves …

A Warning to Robbers

The scribe in the presence, Itji, speaks:
With regard to any person
who shall take stones from this tomb of mine of the necropolis,
I shall be judged with them on this matter by the god.
For I am an excellent *akh* who knows his spells.

133. Lintel in the Tomb of Herymeru at Saqqara

The tomb is near the causeway of the pyramid of Unas (PM III², 626). The cult of this king seems to have continued into the sixth dynasty and beyond. Sixth dynasty.

Line of Larger Hieroglyphs at Top

(1) The priest of the pyramid of Unas, *khenty-she* of the pyramid of Unas, the *imakhu* in the sight of the king of Upper and Lower Egypt, the Golden Horus Wadj, Unas, supervisor of *khenty-she* of the Great House, Herymeru.

Formulae

(2) An offering which the king and an offering which Anubis,
who dwells in the divine tent-shrine, who is in his wrappings,
who is on his mountain, lord of the sacred land, give
that he might be buried in his tomb of the necropolis
as an *imakhu* who loves the god;
may the West stretch out her arms to him
as he is one who has done what is satisfactory
and who has reached the state of *imakhu*.
The sole companion, overseer of the *khenty-she,* Herymeru, whose perfect name is Merery.
(3) May he be united with the land, may he cross the heavens,
may he ascend to the Great God,
may his *ka* dwell in the presence of the king,
may his *ba* endure in the presence of the god,
may his document be taken by the god to the pure places,
as (is done) for one whom his father loves and his mother favors.
(4) An offering which the king and which Osiris give
that he may make a perfect journey
on the perfect ways on which the *imakhu* travel,
that he may be followed by his *ka*,
that he may be led on the holy ways,
that his *ka*s may be excellent in the sight of the king,
and that where he resides may be pure in the sight of the god.
(5) An offering which the king and which all the gods of the West give
that invocation offerings may be made for him in the *Wag* festival,
the New Year festival, the festival of Sokar, the great festival,
the *Rekeh* festival, the festival of the appearance of Min,
the *Sadj* festival, the monthly and half monthly festivals,
and in every perfect daily festival,

for the *imakhu*, (6) supervisor of *khenty-she* of the Great House, Herymeru.

He speaks:

I am an excellent *akh*, one who knows things,
a speaker of perfection and a repeater of perfection.
I have never said or done any evil thing in relation to anyone,
for I am one who loves *Maat* in the sight of the perfect god
and in the sight of men.
But with regard to any man (7) who shall do anything evil to my tomb,
or who shall enter it with the intention of stealing,
I shall seize his neck like a bird's, and I shall be judged with him in the court of the Great God.
However, with regard to any person
who shall make invocation offerings or shall pour water,
they shall be pure like the pureness of god,
and I shall protect him in the necropolis.

134. Offering Table of Ishetmaa from Saqqara

This table was found outside the mastaba of Khentika Ikhekhi near the pyramid of Teti (PM III², 511; no. 216); Ishetmaa is almost certainly the man of the same name shown in the reliefs of that tomb (see James 1953: 68), and it would appear from this text that one of his privileges as a dependent of that great man was to have his priests look after his offerings and presumably his tomb after his death. Middle sixth dynasty or later.

(1) An offering which the king and Anubis, who is on his mountain, give
to the *imakhu*, the overseer of the office of the *khenty-she* of the Great House, Ishetmaa.
(2) With regard to any soul priest of the sole companion Khentika
who shall not make the invocation offerings,
I shall make him lose his job (*or* "make him resign").
(3) The overseer of the office of the *khenty-she* of the Great House Ishetmaa.
(4, right): A thousand of bread, beer, cakes, alabaster, clothing, incense for Ishetmaa.
(5, left): A thousand of (*five different types of fowl, not further specified*) for Ishetmaa.

135. Text of Khenu from Saqqara

This little-known tomb has not been seen since its discovery by Mariette. The owner bore a number of courtly titles and other, more unusual, ones concerned with the oversight of linen. From tomb D 6 at North Saqqara (PM III², 488–89). Perhaps late fifth dynasty.

Text on an Unfinished False Door (Repeated Twice)

(1) ... [overseer] of linen, overseer of fringed cloth of the king, the companion, keeper of secrets of the House of the Morning;
(2) ... which he loves, keeper of secrets of the words of his god, who is in the heart of his lord, the *imakhu* in the sight of his lord;
(3) ... the overseer of the "breakfast" of the king wherever he is, overseer of measuring gold of the king, overseer of the chamber of the *Ames* scepter;
(4) ... With regard to any man who shall do anything (bad) to this (tomb)
which I have made so as to be *imakhu* in the sight of my lord,
I shall be judged with him in the place where judgment is.
The sole companion, chief of Nekheb, Khenu.

A Formula on the False Door

An offering which the king and which Geb and Anubis,
who dwells in the divine tent-shrine wherever he is, give
that there may be given to him invocation offerings,
for the sole companion, chief of Nekheb,
the *imakhu* in the sight of the Great God,
who has reached the state of *imakhu* in the sight of his god.

136. Texts from the Tomb of Khui at Saqqara

In the Teti pyramid cemetery (PM III², 519). Reign of Pepy I.

Entrance Thickness Left

(1) The sole companion and lector priest Khui speaks:
(2) Beloved of the king and beloved of Anubis, who is on his mountain,
is every lector priest who shall come to me
and make for me the transfigurations and offerings
(3) in accordance with that secret writing of the skills of the lector priest.

Recite those transfigurations,
be equipped in the manner in which you should act
for any royal noble like me.
(4) For I am an excellent *akh*;
I know all the excellent magic spells
(5) which should be known by every excellent *akh*
(6) buried in a tomb in the necropolis, in the Western Desert.

Entrance Thickness Right

(1) O you who live on earth, the *imakhu* who love the god,
and who shall pass by this tomb of mine of the necropolis,
may you give bread, beer, (2) and water from that which you possess!
If you have none, then you shall speak with your mouths
(3) and offer with your hands:
"a thousand of incense, (4) a thousand of alabaster and clothing,
oxen and fowl, oryxes and antelopes,"
so you shall say.
(5) For I am an excellent *akh*,
and I shall be his supporter in the necropolis.
(6) The sole companion and lector priest Khui.

137. Text of Khuit, Perhaps from Saqqara

Now in Basel, Museum für Völkerkunde III 6206. Perhaps late Old Kingdom.

(1) [(*Address to the living*)] [may] they [say]
"a thousand of bread, a thousand of beer,
a thousand oxen, a thousand fowl,
a thousand of alabaster, a thousand items of clothing
for the ruler of the estate, the companion, the lector priest, the scribe of magical protection, the *imakhu* Khuit.
(2) … I am a speaker of perfection and a repeater of perfection,
in order that it go well with me in the sight of (3) [the Great God …
I am an effective *akh* (?)] in the necropolis.
I am the beloved one of his father and the favored one of his mother,
whom his siblings love.
(4) The ruler of the estate, the sole companion, Khuit.
(5) The lector priest, scribe of magical protection, Khuit.

138. Architrave of Mehi from Saqqara

The small mastaba of Mehi is to the north of those of Kaigemni and Mereruka in the Teti pyramid cemetery. The text has a number of unusual features. This architrave has a complex discovery and publication history. Reign of Teti to Pepy I.

(1) An offering which the king and an offering which Anubis give
that he may be buried in the necropolis, in the Western Desert,
having grown old most perfectly,
and that his state of *imakhu* may exist in the sight of Teti,[3]
doubly in peace, in the sight of the Great God
as a possessor of the state of *imakhu*.
The overseer of the office of *khenty-she* of the Great House, Mehenes called Mehi, the beloved one of his father, [Mehi].
(2) An offering which the king and Osiris give
for his invocation offerings in the festival of the opening of the year,
the festival of Thoth, the festival of the first of the year,
the *Wag* festival, the festival of Sokar,
and the daily festivals for the extent of time,
so that his state of *imakhu* might exist in the sight of his children.
The royal noble Mehenes called Mehi, the favored one of his mother, [Mehi].
(3) An offering which the king and an offering which Anubis give
that he may travel in peace upon the perfect ways of the West
on which the *imakhu* travel,
in the sight of all the gods of the West (*or,* "the gods lords of the West"),
as one whom the king favors, as one who does what is peaceful,
as one who reaches the state of *imakhu*,
as one who speaks Maat, which the god loves.
The overseer of the office of the *khenty-she* of the Great House, Mehi.
(4) O you who live on earth, the *imakhu* in the sight of the Great God,
who shall pass by this tomb:
pour water, make invocation offerings from that which you have!
If you have nothing,
(then) speak with your mouth and offer with your hands:
"a thousand of bread and beer, a thousand of alabaster,
a thousand oxen, a thousand fowl and vegetables

for the *imakhu* in the sight of the Great God,
the overseer of the office of the *khenty-she* of the Great House, Mehi."
(5) I am a speaker of perfection and a repeater of perfection,
one who carries out Maat, which the god loves.
I am one who makes peace and who reaches the state of *imakhu*.
With regard to any person who shall make invocation offerings,
I shall support them in the necropolis in the West.
For I am an excellent *akh*, an equipped magician (?)
beloved of men and favored of the god,
an *imakhu* in the sight of the king.
The companion of the house, the keeper of secrets, Mehi.
(6) I made this tomb actually while I was alive and on my feet,
as the favored one of the king and a beloved one of men;
I paid the masons so that they were satisfied with it,
and I decided between two parties as far as I could
so that they were both satisfied.
The mouth of the sealers of the Great House, Mehi.
(7) He who loves the king and who is *imakhu* before the Great God
and who shall be perfectly buried in the necropolis
is he who shall pass by this tomb and shall say:
"bread and beer for Mehenes called Mehi, born of Khenit."
May you say that I was indeed an *imakhu*
in accordance with what used to be said (when I was) on earth;
that I was one who existed (according to) Maat
and who made peace and reached the state of *imakhu*.
The overseer of the office of the *khenty-she* of the Great House, Mehi.
(8) (*Column at the end*) The *imakhu*, the overseer of the office of the *khenty-she* of the Great House, Mehi.

139. Inscriptions over the Entrance to the Tomb of Mereri at Saqqara

The tomb of Mereri is another of those in the Teti pyramid cemetery that have been deliberately damaged. I only translate the last line of the inscription here as the rest are formulae well represented elsewhere. Perhaps early reign of Pepy I.

O you *imakhu* who live on earth:
one who loves the king is he who shall say

"a thousand of bread, a thousand of beer,
a thousand of geese and cattle,
a thousand of alabaster, a thousand of clothing for … Mereri."

140. Text of Meru Called Bebi from Saqqara

Original position unknown (PM III^2, 694). The chapel is now Brussels E.2243. Sixth dynasty.

The overseer of the *khenty-she* of the Great House, Bebi, the *imakhu* in the sight of Merenre, lector priest, scribe of magical protection, Meru whose perfect name is Beb(i).

[With respect to anything bad done to my tomb]
by the soul priests of my funerary estate,
I shall be judged with them by the Great God, lord of the West
in the place where Maat is.
For I am a lector priest … [*perhaps* who knows his spells (?)];
I know all the transfigurations (which are needed) for myself in the necropolis.
I shall drive out their descendants,
I shall not permit that their doorways be founded,
I shall not let [them/their people (?)] live …

141. Lintel of Nedjemib from Saqqara

From his tomb to the west of the Step Pyramid (E 14: PM III^2, 611). Now Cairo CG 1732. Sixth dynasty.

(1) An offering which the king gives
and an offering which Anubis,
who dwells in the divine tent-shrine, gives
for his perfect burial in the necropolis, in the Western Desert.
(2) An offering which the king gives
and an offering which Osiris, lord of Busiris, gives
that invocation offerings may go forth for him
(in the) *Wag* festival, (3) in the festival of Thoth,
in the great festival, in the *Rekeh* festival,

at the Opening of the Year, in the First of the Year,
and in every festival.
(4) O you who live upon earth and who shall pass by this tomb:
Pour water for me!
I am a keeper of secrets.
(5) (Make) invocation offerings come forth for me from what you have!
I am the beloved one of men.
I never was beaten in the presence of any official (6) since I was born.
I never stole the property of any person.
I am one who does that which everyone favors.
(7) The overseer of metal-workers of the Great House, royal *mehenek,* Nedjemib.

142. Texts from the Tomb of Nenki from Saqqara

This tomb was located west of the pyramid of Pepy II at South Saqqara (PM III², 686). The lintel was in Leipzig (Inv. 359) but is now lost. Reign of Pepy II.

Lintel

(1) The mouth of Nekhen, priest of Maat, who satisfies the king when paying homage to him,[4] who makes speech right, keeper of secrets of hearing (matters) alone in the six Great Mansions, (2) the *imakhu* Nenki, speaks:

With regard to this tomb of mine
which I made in the West (in) the necropolis,
I made it (in) a pure place in the midst (thereof);
With regard to any noble, (3) any official or any man
who shall remove any stone or any brick from this tomb of mine,
I shall be judged with him by the Great God.

Jamb

(1) I shall seize his neck like a bird's;
I shall place fear (among) all the living upon earth
(2) on behalf of the *akh*s who are in the West
and are far away from them.
The *imakhu*, the true mouth of Nekhen, Nenki.

143. Texts at the Entrance to the Tomb of Nyankhpepy at Saqqara

The arrangement of the lintel with the offering formulae illustrates the complex manner in which such a text can be arranged; it has similarities with that of Iyenhor no. 208. At the end of the warning to robbers is also an interesting later addition. The tomb was probably usurped during the later Old Kingdom. It is adjacent to the causeway of Unas (PM III², 630–31). Late sixth dynasty.

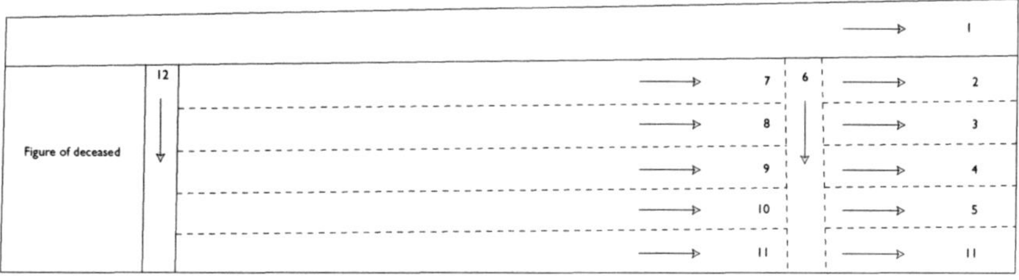

Fig. 6: Lintel of Nyankhpepy (no. 143). Upper, from Hassan 1976: II, fig. 3. Lower, schematic diagram of text arrangement.

Lintel with Formulae (See Fig. 6)

Top line

(1) The *imakhu* in the sight of the king of Upper and Lower Egypt Unas, the *imakhu* in the sight of Anubis, who is upon his mountain, Nyankhpepy; the *imakhu* in the sight of the Great God Ptah-Sokar, Nyankhpepy.

First area of formulae

(2) An offering which the king gives and an offering which Anubis who is upon his mountain, who is in his wrappings, gives;

(3) An offering which the king gives and which Osiris
who dwells in Sepa gives;
(4) An offering which the king gives and which Anubis
who dwells in the divine tent-shrine, the lord of the Two Lands, gives;
(5) An offering which the king gives and which Osiris
who dwells in the Thinite nome gives;
(6) for the sole companion, lector priest, Nyankhpepy,
(7) that he may receive a perfect burial in the necropolis,
as one who does what is satisfactory,
and who is well prepared and *imakhu*.
May the god take his document and place it in the holy places
of the perfect West (8) among all the noble *akh*s
in respect of (his) state of *imakhu*
in the sight of the Great God Ptah-Sokar, Nyankhpepy.

Second area of formulae

(9) An offering which the king and the Great God give
that he might become a possessor of a perfect burial in the necropolis,
and that invocation offerings may be made for him
during the *Wag* and Thoth festivals, and in every daily festival.
(10) An offering which the king and all the gods of the West give
that he might travel on those perfect ways
upon which the *imakhu* travel.

(11) The sole companion, lector priest, royal noble; the sole companion, overseer of the *khenty-she* of the Great House, keeper of secrets of all commands, overseer of the two pools of the Great House, the *imakhu* in the sight of the Great God, Nyankhpepy.
(12) The sole companion, lector priest, royal noble, Nyankhpepy.

The Warning to Robbers (Right Jamb)

(1) The sole companion, lector priest, royal noble, Nyankhpepy speaks:
With regard to any man who shall do anything evil
to this tomb of mine (2) of the necropolis,
or who shall take a stone from its appointed place,
I shall contest with him in the noble and excellent court
(3) of the Great God, the lord of the necropolis.
I shall seize his neck like a bird's,
and the fear of me will be instilled in him,
so that the living (4) on earth shall be fearful of (5) excellent *akh*s.
I am an excellent *akh;*
(6) no excellent magic is ever hidden from me.

(7) and, with regard to excellence,
I am a lector priest who knows what to do.

Just in front of the figure of Nyankhpepy is a very interesting later insertion or graffito, which is probably to be translated like this:

You have locked me up, you have beaten my father; I am now happy, as how can you escape my hand? My father is satisfied.[5]

The Appeal to the Living (Left Jamb)

(1) The sole companion, lector priest, royal noble speaks:
O you who live on earth, the *imakhu* who love the god,
(2) and who shall pass by this tomb of mine:
pour water and beer for me from that which you possess.
(3) If you have nothing,
(4) then you shall speak with your mouth (5) and offer with your hand
bread, beer, oxen, fowl, incense (6) and pure things
for the royal noble, companion of the house, scribe Nyankhpepy.

144. Texts on the Pillars of the Tomb of Nyhetepptah at Giza

Tomb G 2430 in the Western Cemetery (PM III², 94–95). Late fifth or early sixth dynasty. The reconstructions are mostly those of Altenmüller.

Southern Pillar, East Side

(1) [Beloved of the king and of Anubis
is] the lector priest who shall come to this my tomb of eternity[6]
to carry out the rites in accordance with
(2) [those writings of the skills] of the lector priest.
May the (acts of) preparation be carried out for me
particularly in accordance with what is on his papyrus roll.
May everything excellent and noble be carried out for me
(3) [through the priestly offices of the lector priest.
May] invocation offerings [be made] for me
while I am alive on my two feet above all
in accordance with what should be done for any great noble.
(4) [May invocation offerings be made for my father] and mother
in accordance with their state of *imakhu*
in the sight of the majesty of my lord.
(5) The overseer of the *khenty-she* of the Great House, Nyhetepptah.

Southern Pillar, North Side

(1) May all excellent and noble things be done for me
as should be done for an *imakhu* of the king.
(2) [An offering which the king gives and] an offering which Anubis,
who is on his mountain, lord of the necropolis, gives
that invocation offerings may be made for him daily for ever.
(3) [The overseer of] *khenty-she* [of the Great House], overseer of weapons of the royal documents (?), the *imakhu* in the sight of the king, (4) [the judge and boundary official (?), overseer of] the noble places of the Great House, controller of the palace, keeper of secrets of his lord.
(5) The overseer of the two pools of the Great House, Nyhetepptah.

Northern Pillar, East Side

(1) [An offering which the king, Anubis], who dwells in the divine tent-shrine,
and Osiris, lord of the necropolis, give
that he may be excellent, well-prepared and noble in the desert.
(2) [May invocation offerings be made for him] daily
for ever as a possessor of *imakhu* in the sight of the god.
He has carried out Maat perfectly (3) [for her lord].
He has given satisfaction to the one who loves it daily,
being respectful of the rites, for it is something perfect.
(4) [The *imakhu* in the sight of] Maat who dwells in the Western Desert,
a possessor of offerings in the perfect fields of eternity.
(5) The judge and boundary official of the Great House, Nyhetepptah.

Northern Pillar, South Side

(1) [May everything be done for him
in accordance with] those [writings] of the skills of the lector priest.
May he be transfigured into his transfigured state,
and may well-prepared offerings be made for him daily.
(2) [An offering which the king and Anubis, lord of] the necropolis, [give]
for burial in this tomb, having grown old perfectly as an *imakhu*.
(3) [He speaks:]
I am *imakhu* in the sight of Osiris, the Great God.
I am *imakhu* in the sight of every sovereign for whom I did guard duty.

(4) [The companion of the house], controller of the palace, keeper of secrets of the king wherever he is, who is in the heart of his lord, whom his lord loves.

(5) The overseer of the *khenty-she* of the Great House, Nyhetepptah.

Northern Pillar, North Side

(1) [He speaks:
May] all excellent and noble things [be done for me]
through the priestly offices of the lector priest,
(as) for an *imakhu* in the sight of the Great God.

(2) [The overseer of] *khenty-she* [of the Great House], overseer of weapons of the royal documents (?), who is in the heart of his lord, keeper of secrets of his lord, (3) [companion of the house, controller of the palace, overseer of] the noble places of the Great House, the *imakhu* in the sight of the king, who acts in accordance with the favor of his lord daily, (5) Nyhetepptah.

(4) [His beloved wife], his *imakhu,* the royal acquaintance, priestess of Hathor wherever she is, possessor of *imakhu* in the sight of his husband, (5) Khamerernebty.

145. Inscriptions at the Entrance to the Tomb of Nykauizezi at Saqqara

Nykauizezi probably began his career in the reign of Unas, as he is mentioned in that king's causeway inscriptions and rose to prominence in the reign of Teti. The decree of that king from Abydos (no. 19) is addressed to him. His tomb in the Teti pyramid cemetery was found in 1979, and the remains of a male aged forty to fifty, almost certainly Nykauizezi, were recovered. The date here, should it belong to Teti, has caused some rethinking of the late fifth and early sixth dynasties (Kanawati and Abder-Raziq 2000: 22–23, Verner 2001: 412). Early sixth dynasty.

Left of Entrance

[With regard to anyone who shall enter] this tomb
not being pure like a *wab*-priest of a god
(or, like the purity needed for a god),
I shall make a punishment for them
in excess of the great evil (they have done).

Right of Entrance

But if any soul priest of my estate makes invocation offerings for me
in a pure state for me so that his heart is confident in this matter,
I shall hold his hand (support him) in the necropolis and in any tribunal.

Beneath a Fowling Scene, in Ink

Year of the eleventh occasion, first month of the Akhet season, day 20: burial in the necropolis (of) the *iry pat,* seal-bearer of the king of Lower Egypt, Nykauizezi.

146. Text of Pehenwikai from Saqqara

From the jambs of a false door in his tomb north of the Step Pyramid (D 70: PM III², 491–92). His tomb was examined by Lepsius in the 1840s but has not been seen since. Mid fifth dynasty.

Right Jamb

... [With regard to any man who shall approach] this statue in an impure state,
or with regard to any man who shall approach these statues[7] in an impure state,
I shall be judged with him in the place where judgment is.
I never did anything evil to the property of any person.

Left Jamb

... [I made this tomb of mine] actually as an *imakhu* in the sight of the king.
[With regard to] any person who shall enter it in an impure state
and/or shall do evil things to it after this which I have said,
I shall be judged with them in the place where judgment is.

147. Inscription on Blocks of Reherytep Iti from Saqqara

The references to the vizier Kaigemni suggest that the owner was most probably a dependent of that great man, and thus set up a tomb for himself in the area of that of his master. These blocks were found during the excavation of the cemetery around the pyramid of Teti (PM III², 546). Sixth dynasty.

A.

(1) An offering which the king and Osiris, Lord of Abydos give
that invocation offerings may be made
(2) for the *imakhu* in the sight of Ptah-Sokar,
beloved one of his father, (3) favored one of his mother,
whom his brothers (4) and sisters love.
The first under the king of the Great House, royal noble, Iti;
(5) the *imakhu* in the sight of the vizier Kaigemni,
(6) the lector priest, chief of secrets, Reherytep whose perfect name is Iti.

B.

(1) [O] you who live upon earth and who shall pass by this tomb,
as [...] favors you (2) ...
(3) [Beloved of Osiris] is he, whether a lector priest or any man,
who shall give me bread and beer (4) from that which you possess.
If you have none, (5) then [you] shall say:
"A thousand [of bread], a thousand [of beer], a thousand oxen,
a thousand fowl, a thousand of alabaster and a thousand of clothing
for the royal noble, regular one of the phyle, Iti."
(6) [With regard to] a lector priest who is excellent, equipped, and prepared
and who shall read (7) [on behalf of] any man
and who shall cause invocation offerings to be made for me,
(8) [I shall] be his helper (9) [in] the court/tribunal of the Great God.
(10) The first under the king of the [Great House], Iti.

148. Texts on False Door of Sekhentyuka and Nyankhsheret from Giza

Perhaps from a tomb of similarly named persons in the Central Cemetery (PM III², 251–52). Now Frankfurt, Liebieghaus, 1638. End fifth dynasty.

Left Outer Jamb

... he who shall do evil things to this (tomb of mine)
[shall not be a possessor] of the state of *imakhu* in the sight of the king;
I shall be judged with him on the matter
by the Great God, lord of the Western Desert.

Right Outer Jamb

May it go well for you my successors,
may (you) be true of voice my ancestors;
with regard to that which you do to this (tomb of mine),
the like shall be done to your funerary property by your successors.

149. Texts from the Tomb of Tjetu at Giza

Tomb G 2001 in the Western Cemetery (PM III², 66–67). Fifth or sixth dynasty.

Architrave over the Entrance of the Tomb
Upper Line (Small Hieroglyphs)

The first under the king of the Great House, Tjetu (speaks):

Beloved of Anubis, beloved of Osiris
and beloved of the king and their god
are those who give[8] bread and beer
for the owner of this tomb from that which you possess;
if you have nothing,
then speak with your mouths and offer with your hands.
I am a beloved one of his father, a favored one of his mother;
I am …

Lower Line (Large Hieroglyphs)

Overseer of the pyramid town of the pyramid of Khufu, inspector of *wab*-priests of the pyramid of Khufu, first under the king of the Great House, the *imakhu* in the sight of Osiris, Tjetu.

Vertical Framing Text in the South of the Portico

… an excellent lector priest, one who knows his spells.
I am one who knows all the excellent magic (through which) he is transfigured in the necropolis.
With regard to any man
who shall take or who shall remove stones or bricks
which form part of this tomb of mine,
I shall be judged (with him) in the tribunal of the Great God;
I shall make an end for him on account of this matter,
and I shall see life (again [?]) on earth.
The first under the king of the Great House, Tjetu.

Texts on the Northern False Door
Top

(1) An offering which the king and which Anubis,
who is on his mountain, who is in his wrappings,
lord of the sacred land, give
that he may be buried (2) in the Western Desert,
having grown old most perfectly,
that he may reach land, that he may cross the heavens.

Outer Left Jamb

(1) May invocation offerings be made for him
in the festival of the opening of the year, in the festival of Thoth,
in the first day of the year festival, in the *Wag* festival,
and in every perfect festival.
(2) May he ascend to the Great God, may he be followed by his *ka*s,
may the desert extend her hand to him.
The first under the king of the Great House, Tjetu.

Inner Left Jamb

(1) The sole companion, lector priest, (2) the *imakhu* in the sight of the Great God,
(3) Tjetu whose perfect name is Kanesut.

Outer Right Jamb

(1) The overseer of the town of the pyramid of Khufu, inspector of *wab*-priests of the pyramid of Khufu,
(2) sole companion, lector priest, the *imakhu,* Tjetu.

Inner Right Hand

(1) The sole companion, the overseer of the *khenty-she,*
(2) the *imakhu* in the sight of Ptah-Sokar,
(3) Tjetu.

150. Inscription in the Tombs of Tjy and Mereruka at Saqqara

The following text appears in very similar and damaged versions in two famous tombs at Saqqara. They appear to be sufficiently similar that they can be conflated and presented as one text. There are some further frag-

ments of the text, but they are too broken to translate here. The numbering is based on the text of Tjy, following Wild 1959; restorations are not marked. The tomb of Tjy is at North Saqqara and dates to the mid to late fifth dynasty (D 22: PM III², 468–78), while that of Mereruka is by the pyramid of Teti and dates to the reign of Teti or Pepy I (PM III², 526–34).

(1) (*Titles and name*) speaks:
(2) With regard to any person who shall enter this my tomb of eternity
in an impure state, having eaten something abominable
which is an abomination to an *akh* who has gone to the necropolis,
(3) and who are not pure at the time when they should be pure
as in the temple of a god,
then I shall be judged with them on this matter
by the Great God in the place where judgment truly is.
(4) I am an excellent *akh*, keeper of secrets
of the divine words of the skill of the lector priest,
and all excellent and noble rites shall be done for me,
as should be done for an excellent person who is among the *akhs*,
(5) by means of the priestly duties of the lector priest.
I am initiated in all the secrets of the house of divine documents;
I know all the rites by which an *akh*
who has gone to the necropolis is transfigured;
(6) I know all the rites by which he is prepared
in the sight of the Great God;
I know all the rites by which he ascends to the Great God;
I know all the rites by which he is ennobled in the sight of the Great God.
(7) However, with regard to any man who shall enter this my tomb of eternity
who is pure at the time as he should be in the temple of the Great God,
I shall be his supporter
in the court of his noble ancestors (8) of the Great God;
I shall act as one who works in the fields
I shall never let anything happen which he hates for ever;
I shall never let anything critical of him happen for ever
in the sight of the Great God
(9) … there together with the invocation offerings
of the funerary estate daily for the breadth of eternity.
(10) …

(11) … I say this to all people who shall enter this my tomb of eternity for ever,
whether they be … or … or … or sole companions
who are noble in the sight of the king,
for indeed I am in this state of nobility.
(12) … He who loves Anubis is the lector priest
(13) who shall enter this my tomb of eternity to carry out the rites for me.
Read for me (the words of) transfiguration and preparation …

151. Stela of Nipepy from Abydos

From his tomb in the central necropolis. Now in Cairo, CG 1579. Middle sixth dynasty or later.

(1) O you who live upon earth, servants like myself;
(2) those who shall be in the entourage of the god are (3) those who shall say:
"a thousand of bread, a thousand of beer,
a thousand oxen, and a thousand fowl
for (4) the true *haty-a,* charmed of arm, controller of the two thrones,
controller of the black vase, (5) sole companion, keeper of the diadem, Nipepy."

To the Side Are Two Vertical Columns of Titles

(1) The inspector of priests of the pyramid of Pepy I, the seal-bearer of the king of Lower Egypt.
(2) The inspector of priests of the pyramid of Merenre, the overseer of the royal house.

Notes

1. This unusual title has a number of interpretations: see Jones 2000: 468.

2. A unique phrase for the Old Kingdom, meaning that he will lose any right to appeal. Does it look forward to the later expressions like "true of voice" for justification in the afterlife?

3. The name of Teti was inscribed on a separate piece of stone, possibly as a result of changing the royal name from another, perhaps Userkare. See Kanawati 2002a: 94–95.

4. See the inscription of Mekhu II for another example of this term (no. 243C).

5. Drioton 1952. The sense of this is not particularly clear, but one wonders

whether whoever wrote this bore some sort of grudge against Nyankhpepy, and was expressing a hope that matters would be resolved in the next world.

6. This expression, found many times in this book, can be interpreted two ways. *Djet* is one of the words for "Eternity," but a similarly written word in the Old Kingdom refers to one's "funerary estate" and is seen particularly in the title "brother of the funerary estate" or in the legal texts that refer to setting up requirements for such foundations. The problem is that either translation makes sense in the context and the reader should be aware of this.

7. Pehenwikai is clearly differentiating between two different statue groups here, but the lack of more information about the tomb makes it difficult to understand. There are different determinatives for the statues.

8. Literally "say"; I have used this translation to make a contrast with the next part of the text.

XIV

Commemorative and Dedicatory Texts

See notes in chapter I, §6.5.2.

152. From the Tomb of Ankhires and Medunefer at Giza

Tomb G 4630 (PM III², 133–34) in the Eastern Cemetery. This false door is now in Cairo, CG 57189.

The scribe of the house of the god's documents, the stolist of Anubis, follower of the Great One, follower of Tjentet,[1] Ankhires.

Lintel
His eldest son it was, the lector priest Medunefer, who made this for him.

Left and Right Outer Jambs

An offering which the king and which Anubis,
who dwells in the divine tent-shrine, give for burial in the West,
having grown old most perfectly.
His eldest son it was, the lector priest Medunefer,
who acted on his behalf when he was buried in the necropolis.
The scribe of the house of the god's documents, Ankhires.

This Ankhires is probably the son of another Medunefer; on the false door of the latter (Curto 1963: fig. 32) it also says, "his eldest son Ankhires speaks: I am the one who made this for my father."

153. Text on a Statue of Ankhirptah, Perhaps from Saqqara

Now in Cairo, CG 376.

The sole companion, keeper of secrets of the House of the Morning, administrator of the domain "Horus is the star at the top of heaven,"

Ankhirptah. The sole companion, keeper of secrets of the House of the Morning, who is in the heart of his lord, whom his lord loves, Ankhirptah.
His beloved wife, the royal acquaintance Nubiret speaks:
I made this particularly for my beloved husband whom I loved and who loved me, the sole companion Ankhirptah.

154. Text on Offering Basin of Hebi from Giza

Now Leipzig 3140. From a tomb in the Western Cemetery (PM III², 108). Sixth dynasty.

His son it was, the scribe Renefer, who acted on his behalf when he was in the necropolis.
The overseer of the estate, overseer of soul priests, Hebi, the *imakhu* in the sight of his lord Hebi.

155. Texts from the False Door of Inikaf at Giza

Found out of context in the Western Cemetery (PM III², 108). Sixth dynasty.

Left Outer Jamb

The inspector of craftsmen of … Ankhhaf speaks:
I made [this] for my father and mother.

Left Inner Jamb

The overseer of the craftsmen of the weavers' shop Inikaf; [his] eldest son it was who acted on his behalf, the inspector of … Ankhhaf.

156. Text from the Tomb of Inpuhotep at Giza

Tomb in the Western Cemetery (PM III², 106–7). Sixth dynasty.

Entrance Lintel

His son it was, the inspector of embalmers, who acted on his behalf, when he was proceeding to the funerary estate (in) the necropolis, Inpuhotep.

West Side of Entrance

His eldest son, the embalmer Zehi, speaks:
I acted on behalf of my father, the *imakhu* in the sight of the Great God, the royal acquaintance, the embalmer, Inpuhotep.

157. Text over the Entrance Doorway of the Tomb of Iy at Giza

Tomb in the Central Cemetery (PM III², 285). Late fifth dynasty or later.

(1) An offering which the king gives and an offering which Anubis who dwells in the divine tent-shrine gives
that he may be buried in the necropolis, in the Western Desert,
having grown old most perfectly in the sight of the Great God.
(2) His wife it was, his beloved, his *imakhu,* who acted on his behalf
so that he might be *imakhu* in her sight
when he was buried in his tomb (*literally* "property") of the West.
(3) The royal acquaintance, the steward Iy; his wife Heknu.

158. Texts on a Wooden Door Panel from the Family Tomb of Kaiemhezet at Saqqara

From his tomb to the west side of the pyramid of Teti (PM III², 542–43). Now in Cairo, JE 47729. Probably fifth dynasty.

At Top

(1) An offering which the king and which Anubis,
who dwells in the divine tent-shrine, give
that invocation offerings may be made for them
at every season of the year.

(2) The children of the royal master builder Senefankh.
(3) The royal master builders, the great ones of censing in the land of the eighth nome of Upper Egypt:

(4) Kaiemhezet, (5) Kapunezut, (6) Memi, (7) Hetepka.
(8) The judge and boundary official Khentyka.

Beside and below Figure

(9) I made this (tomb) for my elderly father and for my brothers particularly so that invocation offerings might be made for them and myself in my tomb (*literally* "property"). (10) The overseer of builders, Kaiemhezet.

Smaller figure: (11) the overseer of builders, Hetepka.

Behind the main figure: (12) Presented and made (by) the sculptor Itju. (13) The "brother of his funerary estate," the overseer of builders, Hetepka. (14) Given to him from the town Gerget-Hem-djefau in the twentieth nome of Upper Egypt (*Herakleopolis*): 2 arouras of land.

159. Texts from the Tomb of Kaiemrehu at Saqqara

Mariette's copy indicates that the two top lines might have been altered, but it is impossible to confirm this. Tomb C 25; position and present location unknown (PM III^2, 690). Middle to late fifth dynasty.

(1) An offering which the king gives
and an offering which Anubis gives
(2) that he may be buried in the necropolis, in the Western Desert,
having aged most perfectly as an *imakhu* in the sight of the Great God
and an *imakhu* in the sight of Osiris, who dwells in Busiris;
(3) and that he might travel upon the perfect ways
on which the *imakhu* travel,
attaining the offerings that the *imakhu* seek,
doing that which his god favors.

(4) The sole beloved companion, controller of the booth of the Great House,[2] overseer of the cool rooms of the Great House, overseer of the abundance of the fields of offering of the king, possessor of *imakhu* in the sight of his lord every day, (5) overseer of the mansion of the cattle, Kaiemrehu.

(This) was what his eldest son, his *imakhu*, the official and supervisor of scribes, Hetep, did for him so that he might be *imakhu* in his sight when he goes to his *ka*.

The sole companion Kaiemrehu.

160. Commemoration of the Scribe Seni in the Tomb of Kaihap at Hawawish

Caption to a man standing adjacent to a scene of the tomb owner fishing. Kanawati makes the intriguing suggestion that a sculptor called Seni in the tomb of Ibi at Deir el-Gebrawi could be the same man (Kanawati 1980–92: II, 13). He also makes stylistic comparisons between these and other tombs of approximately the same date, suggesting that the Kheni mentioned here was the son of Kaihap (Kanawati 1980–92: II, 13–15). Kaihap dates to the reign of Pepy II.

The outline draughtsman Seni speaks:
I it was who decorated[3] the tomb of the *haty-a* Kheni.
I alone it was who decorated this tomb.

161. Dedication on a Relief Panel from the Tomb of Kaihersetef at Saqqara

Reliefs from this tomb are in several museums, but the original location of the chapel is now lost (PM III², 693). This is a panel that probably fronted the serdab, *as this text is written around a slot at the top. The remainder of the panel shows a scene of the deceased and his wife seated at table, with three rows of people below. Now in Cairo, CG 1566. Probably sixth dynasty.*

Everyone who shall see this—they should thank the god for this.
The possessor of *imakhu,* his beloved wife Ib.
The scribe of the house of documents, scribe of royal commands, Kaihersetef.

162. From the Texts on the False Door Niche of Kainefer from Dahshur

The tomb is east of the northern pyramid of Sneferu (PM III², 893). Probably early fifth dynasty, but see Baud 1999a: 83–92, 592 for a fourth-dynasty date. Now in London, BM EA 1324 and Paris, Louvre E 11286.

With regard to this (tomb), his eldest son it was, the royal acquaintance Kaiwab, who acted on his behalf while he was in the necropolis, having gone to his *ka*.
His son, the royal acquaintance, priest of Sneferu, keeper of secrets, Kaiwab made this (especially) for him.

163. Text at the Entrance to the Tomb of Khufuhotep at Giza

Tomb LG 76 in the Eastern Cemetery, in the escarpment to the east of the Great Pyramid (PM III[2], 212). Probably fifth dynasty or later.

His eldest son, the supervisor of *wab*-priests, the overseer of the *ges*-[*per*] (?) ... it was who acted on his behalf when he was buried in the necropolis, acting for Khufuhotep.

164. Text of Medunefer from His Tomb at Giza

Tomb in the central field (PM III[2], 258). Middle fifth dynasty or later.

(1) An offering which the king and which Anubis,
who dwells in the divine tent-shrine, give
that he may be buried in the necropolis of the Western Desert,
as a possessor of *imakhu* in the sight of the Great God,
having grown old most perfectly.
The supporter of Duau, the strong one among the gods, keeper of secrets of the Great House, the possessor of *imakhu* in the sight of his god, physician of the Great House, royal acquaintance,
Medunefer.
(2) The supporter of Duau, Medunefer: the son of his sister, the overseer of soul priests Senmereri, it was who made this (tomb) for him when he was buried in the necropolis having aged most perfectly, through the desire that people see (this) and thank the god for it.

165. Commemoration of Workmen in the Tomb of Nebemakhet at Giza

These rare texts accompany the figures of two workmen who worked on the tomb of this son of Khafre. Tomb in the Central Cemetery (LG 86; PM III[2], 230–32). Mid to late fourth dynasty.

His *mehenek*, who inscribed this his tomb, the outline draftsman, Semerka.
His *mehenek*, who made this his tomb as a work-project, Inikaf.

166. Offering Basin of Nefer

Now Berlin 11665. Provenance and date uncertain.

[An offering which the king gives] and an offering which Anubis,
who dwells in the divine tent-shrine, who is in his wrappings,
lord of the sacred land, who is on his mountain, gives
for burial in the necropolis in the desert of the West,
having grown old perfectly in the sight of the Great God.

The overseer of the southern mansion Nefer.
His eldest son Neferseshemptah it was who acted on his behalf when he was in the necropolis so that invocation offerings might be made.
[His] eldest [son] Neferseshemptah it was who acted on his behalf so that invocation offerings might be made in the monthly festivals, the half-monthly festivals and in every daily festival, for ever.

167. Text of Neferseshemptah from Saqqara

The tomb of Neferseshemptah and Sekhentyu (PM III², 645) is one of a group built in an area subsequently selected for the site of the causeway of the pyramid of Unas (see also texts from the tombs of Nefer and Kahay [no. 330] and Nyankhkhnum and Khnumhotep [nos. 109, 309]). Unusual for the Old Kingdom, much of the decoration is paint on a mud plaster, seemingly referred to in this text. The understanding of the inscription is far from certain. Mid fifth dynasty.

(1) [The overseer of goldsmiths Neferseshemptah] speaks:
Now I acted on behalf of my father Kaidebeh[4]
when he was buried (2) [with (?)] Sekhentyu after many years (of life).
I affixed a smooth surface of ochreous earth
particularly decorated with writing and drawings.
(3) I never found someone (else) for whom it was done;
(thus) a son is useful for his father.

168. Text of Nyankhsokar, Perhaps from Giza

On an offering slab or similar, seen with a dealer at Giza in 1907.

The under-supervisor of officials Nykare speaks:
I made this for my father, the inspector of officials Nyankhsokar, particularly so that invocation offerings might be made for him therein consisting of bread, beer, oxen, fowl and every daily item.

169. Text from the False Door of Nykauptah from Saqqara

Exact provenance unknown (PM III², 744–45); now in Manchester, University Museum 10780. Mid fifth dynasty or slightly later.

His "brother of the funerary estate" it was who acted on his behalf, while he was buried in the perfect West among the *imakhu*.

170. Inscription of Pepysoneb in the Tomb of His Father Memi at Hawawish

These inscriptions are of additional interest as it appears the second one might have been covered up to give precedence to the one at the top of the scene. Kanawati believes they both refer to the same man, although they could also be seen as one son supplanting another. Probably early to middle reign of Pepy II.

Top of Scene

His [eldest] beloved son, the *haty-a,* seal-bearer of the king of Lower Egypt, sole companion, chief under the king, overseer of commissions, Pepysoneb whose perfect name is Seni, speaks:
I it was who decorated this my father's tomb when he had gone to his *ka*.

In Front of Figure

The chief under the king, seal-bearer of the king of Lower Egypt, Ty, speaks:
It was I who made this …

171. Texts of Sehetepu from His Chapel at Saqqara

Chapel in the tomb of Kaiemsenu (no. 122; PM III², 541). Perhaps late fifth dynasty.

Lintel

(1) An offering which the king and an offering which Anubis,
who dwells in the divine tent-shrine, give
for burial in the necropolis, having aged perfectly,
a possessor of *imakhu* in the sight of the Great God.

(2) The priest of Re in *Setibre*, priest of Neferirkare, *wab*-priest of the pyramid of Sahure, overseer of the granary: (3) his two sons it was, the chief of the granary, Kaiemsenu, and the judge and inspector of scribes, Washptah, who acted on his behalf when he was buried in the necropolis, (4) Sehetepu.

False Door
Left Outer Jamb

... the overseer of the places of offerings of provisions, Sehetepu.
His son acted on his behalf, the judge and inspector of scribes, keeper of secrets, *wab*-priest of the king, royal acquaintance, Washptah.

Right Outer Jamb

... [the overseer] of the granary, possessor of *imakhu* in the sight of the Great God, Sehetepu.
His son acted on his behalf, the chief of the granary, overseer of the abundance of all provisions of the king, Kaiemsenu.

172. Libation Basin of Shedy from Saqqara

Now Zürich, Museum Rietberg RAG 6, presently on loan to Basel, Antikenmuseum.

(*outside)* An offering which the king and an offering which Anubis,
who dwells in the divine tent-shrine, give
for burial in the necropolis in the Western Desert
(for him who belongs to) the dwarfs, Shedy.
The overseer of dwarfs of the god's palace, Shedy.

His eldest son it was, he who belongs to the dwarfs, Nebiemtjenenet, who acted on his behalf when he was buried in the necropolis after many years (of life).

(*inside*) The libation basin in which invocation offerings are made for (he who belongs to) the dwarfs, Shedy.

173. Texts in the Tomb of Tepemankh II at Saqqara

Tomb north of the Step Pyramid (D 11: PM III[2]*, 483–84). Middle fifth dynasty. Tepemankh held an unusually large range of titles concerned with kings and royal establishments. See also texts of his wife Nubhotep (no. 298).*

A. From the False Door of Tepemankh's Son Hemmin (Cairo, CG 1417)

The seal-bearer of the divine documents of the Great House Tepemankh (it was) who made this for my eldest son, the seal-bearer of the divine documents, Hemmin, when he was a child.

B. Some Titles from Tepemankh's False Door (Cairo, CG 1564)

Left

(1) *wab*-priest of the pyramid of Sahure, keeper of secrets.
(2) Custodian of linen of the Great House, property custodian of the Great House.
(3) Priest of Khufu, overseer of the seal.
(4) *wab*-priest of the pyramid of Sneferu, controller of all letter-carriers.
(5) *wab*-priest of the pyramid of Menkaure, priest of Wadjet.
(6) *wab*-priest of the pyramid of Khafre, custodian of the divine image.
(7) Tepemankh.

Right

(1) Seal-bearer of the divine book, elder pillar of Anubis, priest of Seshat.
(2) Priest (of Re in) *Nekhenre*, keeper of secrets, priest of Anubis of the divine tent-shrine.
(3) Inspector of seal-bearers of the divine book, priest of Horus (in) *Nekhenre*.
(4) *wab*-priest of the pyramid of Userkaf.
(5) Letter-carrier of royal documents of the Great House, keeper of secrets.
(6) Priest of Hathor, priest of Menkaure, (he who is in [?]) the palace of the Residence.
(7) Tepemankh.

174. Text at the Entrance to the Tomb of Tjenti at Giza

Tomb LG 77 in the escarpment to the east of the Great Pyramid (PM III[2], 212). Fifth or sixth dynasty.

Over the Door

The royal acquaintance, the *imakhu* in the sight of the king, the overseer of … Tjenti.

To the Left

His eldest son, the overseer of soul priests, the scribe Iutenptah it was who made this for him when he was buried in the perfect West, in accordance with what had been said to him while he (*his father*) was alive and on his two feet.

175. Dedication on a Jamb from the Tomb of Tjetji at Giza

This is an outer jamb of the false door of Tjetji's parents Ramu and Tjentet (BM EA 568, James 1961: 16, pl. XVI). The exact location of the tomb is uncertain, but it is perhaps from the east part of the Central Cemetery (PM III[2], 302–3). Now London, BM EA 157C. Fifth or sixth dynasty.

His son, the overseer of the pyramid of Khafre, the royal acquaintance Tjetji it was who acted on behalf of his father and his mother when they were buried in the Western Desert.

176. From a Stela of Tjezi at Giza

This stela is of a most unusual shape, and the word used in the text to describe it may be associated with words for "tower" or "watchtower." Whether Tjezi felt that this unusually shaped monument afforded him extra protection while in his tomb is uncertain. From tomb D 220 in the Western Cemetery (PM III[2], 117). Now Cairo, JE 57174.

The royal acquaintance, the overseer of craftsmen Tjezi, speaks:
So that I might to be buried in this (tomb), I made this "tower" while I was ill and being treated by the *wab*-priest.

177. Text of Ty from Hawawish

Some alterations have been made to the first text here; Ty may not have been the original owner. Middle sixth dynasty.

An offering which the king gives by[5] Osiris, lord of Abydos,
for the *imakhu,* the sole companion, inspector of priests, overseer of the *per-shena,* Ty.

His daughter, the royal noblewoman Nefertjenet, and his brother, the sole companion Tjery, it was who made this on his behalf when he had gone to the perfect West.

178. Text from the Tomb of an Unknown Person

On a false door seen in a dealer's shop. Date uncertain; perhaps fourth dynasty.

[The possessor of] *imakhu* in the sight of the Great God, whose son made this for him when he was in the West.
Ikhi speaks:
I made this for my father actually while he was traveling to the West on the perfect ways upon which the *imakhu* travel.

Notes

1. Both these deities may be associated with Heliopolis; the "Great One" may be Re or Atum, and Tjentet is a bovine god, sometimes identified with Hathor, and particularly venerated at Heliopolis.

2. A series of relatively unusual titles, about which little is known, although it seems fairly clear that they were concerned with provisioning the king's household.

3. This word in Egyptian (*zesh*) is the basic verb for "to write" and the noun for "scribe."

4. I follow the interpretation of Fischer 1978: 51 against Moussa and Junge 1975: 24.

5. For another example of this rare variation see no. 289.

XV

Texts Relating to Payment of Workmen and Tomb Acquisition

See notes in chapter I, §6.5.2.

179. From the Tomb of Abdu at Giza

From the doorway of this tomb in a small cemetery northwest of the Great Pyramid (PM III², 51), excavated in 1949–50. These tombs did not form part of the large cemeteries laid out for the officials and relatives of Khufu and then of Khafre, but more recent excavations by Zahi Hawass in the area have shown that the Abu Bakr tombs were part of a larger cemetery of officials of broadly comparable low rank. Probably sixth dynasty, but the case has also been made for many of these tombs belonging to the fourth dynasty.

Right Jamb of Entrance

(1) I made this tomb right in the city of my lord,[1]
on account of my being *imakhu* in the sight of my lord.
I never said an evil thing about anyone in the presence of any official.
(2) I caused the craftsmen who made this tomb to praise the god,
(as) I had provided them with everything which they had requested from me,
because of my desire to be (seen as) excellent in the presence of the Great God.

Left Jamb of Entrance

(1) The overseer of the estate Abdu speaks:
A man who loves Anubis is he who shall enter this tomb

and make bread and beer be there,
and who shall speak the rituals therein (2) which transfigure (me)
in accordance with what is usually done in a tomb.

180. Text of Akhetmehu from His Tomb at Giza

This tomb (G 2375, PM III², 87) was a mid sixth dynasty insertion into the group of mastabas of the Senedjemib family (nos. 198, 232).

Left

The judge and elder of the doorway, the *imakhu,* Akhetmehu, speaks:
(1) With regard to this my tomb of eternity, it was made for bread and beer;
every workman who worked on it thanked all the gods for me.
(2) I gave them clothing, oil, copper and grain in great quantity,
so that they said
"O every god of the necropolis, we have had our fill, and our hearts are at peace,
(3) because of the bread and beer which Akhetmehu, the *imakhu*, has given us."
I went down into this my tomb, having reached old age
in the company of (4) the children of my children;
my eldest son is in my place.
That which is done is the (doing) of the god for his *imakhu*,
for him who has done Maat, which the god loves.

Right

The overseer of the house of weapons, judge and elder of the doorway, the *imakhu,* Akhetmehu, speaks:
(1) The beloved one of the king and the beloved one of Anubis, lord of the necropolis,
is he who shall not enter this my tomb of eternity in an impure state
(2) having eaten abominable things which the *akh* abominates—
(he is) the one who has traveled to the necropolis as an *imakhu* of the Great God.
(3) With regard to any soul priest of my funerary estate
who shall make invocation offerings for me in a pure state,
whose hearts are (as) attentive as when they are pure in the temple of the Great God—

(4) I shall be their support in the tribunal of the noble ancestors.
All transfiguration and noble rites are done for me.

181. Statue Inscription of Memi from Giza

From tomb D 32 in the Western Cemetery (PM III², 110). Now Leipzig 2560. Fifth dynasty.

Left Side

The royal *wab*-priest Memi, speaks:
I had these statues made by the sculptor who was satisfied by the payment which I made him for them.

Right Side

The royal *wab*-priest Memi; may he travel on the perfect ways upon which the *imakhu* travel.

182. Text of Meni, Probably from Giza

Probably associated with a tomb in the Western Cemetery (PM III², 107–8). Now München, Staatliche Sammlung, Gl. 24. Perhaps sixth dynasty.

Before the Deceased on a Panel of a False Door

(1) With regard to any man who made (2) this for me,
he is never angry.
(3) With regard to a craftsman or (4) quarryman,
I have satisfied him.
(5) The elder of the house, Meni. Nysumerut (*his wife*).

On a Lintel of a Second False Door

The elder of the house, Meni speaks:
May the crocodile be in the water, and the snake be on the land
against him who shall do anything to this (tomb);[2]
I never did anything to him, and it is the god who shall judge him.

183. From the Tomb of Merankhef at Giza

From a false door of Merankhef's wife Neferhetepes in their tomb in the Central Cemetery (PM III², 278–79). Sixth dynasty.

Left

He speaks
with regard to any craftsman who carried out work for me,
I caused them to thank god for me
in relation to the payment which I gave them

Right (Inner)

… and live with you afterwards.
With respect to anything which you do to this (tomb) …

Right (Outer)

… my lord; he speaks:
may he travel upon the perfect way,
an *imakhu* in the sight of the Great God.
You have never given/caused …

184. Inscriptions of Merkhufu from Giza

The tombs in this small cemetery in the cliff east of the Great Pyramid (PM III[2], 213–14) are rather difficult to date. Merkhufu's titles relate to kings of the fourth dynasty, although this does not automatically mean that the tomb is of that date.

Architrave over the Entrance

(1) An offering which the king and which Anubis,
who dwells in the divine tent-shrine, give
for burial in the Western Desert, having grown old most perfectly
(and being) a possessor of *imakhu* in the sight of the Great God
(2) (and) that invocation offerings be made for him
(in) the festivals of opening the year and the first of the year,
the festival of Thoth, the *Wag* festival,
the monthly and half-monthly festivals, and every daily festival,
for the overseer of the youths of the Great Mansion (3) Merkhufu.

Drum of Entrance

The priest of Khafre, priest of Menkaure, *wab*-priest of the king, royal acquaintance, overseer of the office of royal youth (?), the possessor of *imakhu* in the sight of his lord, Merkhufu.

Left Entrance Jamb

(1) Merkhufu, the possessor of *imakhu* in the sight of Menkaure;
My lord did this for me especially so that I might be *imakhu*.
(With regard to) him who shall do anything evil to it (*the tomb*),
(2) I shall be judged with him on this matter by the Great God.
I satisfied the craftsman in respect of that which he did.

Lintel over False Doors inside Tomb

The inspector of priests of the king's mother, overseer of youths of the Great Mansion, royal acquaintance, the possessor of *imakhu* in the sight of the Great God, he who does that which his lord loves every day, Merkhufu.

185. Texts from the False Door of Nefer at Giza

Found reused covering shaft S 576 in the Western Cemetery (PM III², 154). The door is now Hildesheim 2403. Fifth or sixth dynasty.

Right

With regard to him who shall do anything evil to this (tomb), he and I shall be judged by the god.

Left

I made this particularly from gifts of offerings which my lord made to me in relation to my state of *imakhu* in his sight. No craftsman was ever upset with me over it.

186. Inscriptions of Nymaatre from His Tomb at Giza

Tomb in the Central Cemetery (PM III², 282–84). Late fifth dynasty.

A. On Left-hand Pillar

The overseer of singers of the Great House Nymaatre speaks:
Beloved of the king and of Anubis, lord of the necropolis,
is he who shall not enter this my tomb of eternity in an impure state,
having eaten abominable things
which an *akh* in the necropolis abominates.
Regarding this tomb of mine,
which I made as a result of my state of *imakhu* with the king,
any workman (*involved*), I gave (him) what he demanded for it.

B. On Right-hand Pillar

The overseer of singers of the Great House Nymaatre speaks:

The beloved one of the king is the lector priest who will come to this my tomb of eternity

to carry out the rites in accordance with those secret writings of the skills of the lector priest.

Recite for me … [spells for the use of] that natron.

The king has ordered the carrying out for me of all the rites of transfiguration;

I am *imakhu* in the sight of every sovereign for whom I have done guard duty.

C. Also above the Remains of an Offering Bearer

They bring the reversion of the divine offerings … of the mother of the king of Upper and Lower Egypt … of the overseer … of the [pyramid] of Niuserre.

D. (See No. 191 for Other Examples of This Type)

Reconstructions here are not marked.

(1) The overseer of singers of the Great House Nymaatre speaks:

(2) Going home in peace,
after seeing (3) the work done on his tomb of the necropolis …
(4) With regard to my tomb of eternity,
I made it as a result of my perfect state of *imakhu*
(5) in the sight of the king;
I gave to every craftsman who worked on it
a very large payment (6) of all types of linen,
and they thanked all the gods for me on account of it.

187. Text on the False Door of Nysuredi from Giza

This false door is unusual in that it has a frontal depiction of the deceased in relief, perhaps to be associated with examples of tombs with statues standing in or striding out of doors and niches. It is in tomb G 5032 in the Western Cemetery (PM III², 145). The door is now in Boston, MFA 21.961. Sixth or perhaps fifth dynasty.

Left Outer Jamb

The scribe Nysuredi speaks:

I have never done an evil thing (to) any person;
(with regard to) anyone who shall do (any)thing to this (*the tomb*),
(it) shall be protected from them.

Right Outer Jamb

The scribe Nysuredi speaks:

I made this (tomb) expressly from my very own property;
it is the god who shall judge him who shall do (evil) things to it.

188. Inscriptions of Remenuka from His Tomb at Giza

Tomb in the Central Cemetery (PM III[2], 261–62). Sixth dynasty.

(1) The beloved one of the king and of Anubis, who is on his mountain,
is he who shall not inflict damage on (?) that which is in this tomb of mine
which relates to persons who have gone to the West.
With regard to this tomb of mine of eternity,
(2) I made it particularly as a result of my perfect state of *imakhu*
in the sight of men and of the god.
I never took away anything which was brought by another man
to this tomb of mine, as I am mindful of the judgment in the West.
(3) This tomb was made for me specifically
in exchange for bread and beer
which I gave to the workmen who made this tomb.
For indeed I have given to them
a large payment of all sorts of linen which they requested,
and they thanked the god for it.
(4) The *imakhu* in the sight of the Great God Remenuka.

189. Architrave of Tetiseneb Called Iri from Saqqara

The small mastaba of Tetiseneb was one of a number of smaller monuments added to the cemetery around the pyramid of Teti, probably in the reign of Pepy I. The name Iri has been placed over another name.

(1) [An offering which the king gives] and an offering which Anubis,
who is on his mountain, who dwells in the divine tent-shrine,
lord of the sacred land, who is in his wrappings gives
that he may be buried in the necropolis in the Western Desert,
having grown old most perfectly as an *imakhu* in the sight of the king.
The priest of the pyramid of Teti, Iri.
(2) An offering which the king gives and an offering which Osiris,
who dwells in Busiris gives, that invocation offerings be made for him
in the festival of Opening the year, the festival of Thoth,
the festival of the first of the year, the *Wag* festival, the festival of Sokar,
the great festival, the *Rekeh* festival and every daily festival.
(3) An offering which the king gives and an offering which Anubis,
who is on his mountain, gives
that he might travel on the perfect ways of the West
on which the *imakhu* travel doubly in peace in the sight of Osiris
for he is a speaker of perfection and a repeater of perfection.
(4) Regarding this tomb which I made in the necropolis,
the king it was who gave me its location
as I was/so that I might be an *imakhu* in the sight of the king,
for I always do what his lord favors.
I paid the stonemason (5) who made it for me
so that he was satisfied with it (*the payment*).
I did the work within it (*the tomb*) with my own hand
together with my children and my siblings.
The scribe of the king's documents of the Great House, the *imakhu* Iri.
(6) The *khenty-she* of the pyramid of Teti, judge and boundary official, he who judges in noble places of the Great House, … royal noble Tetiseneb whose perfect name is Iri.

190. Inscription of Zeftjwa in Berlin

This is a fairly minimal biographical inscription, on the right and left jambs of a false door, now Berlin 15126. The lintel (not translated here), with the names and titles, is in Paris, Louvre E 31859. Provenance unknown. Perhaps fourth dynasty.

Right-hand Text

(1) The royal acquaintance Zeftjwa speaks:

I made this (my tomb) from my own true means;
(2) never did I take anything from another concerning it,
and never did I do anything evil to another man.

Left-hand Text

(1) (With regard to) any man who shall do anything evil to this (tomb) of mine,
I shall be judged (2) with him by the Great God.
I never inflicted evil on any man, in spite of my power.[3]

191. Scenes of Visiting the Tomb from Giza

See Roth 1994 for a study of this group of texts.

A. Tomb of Neferkhuwi

Tomb G 2098 in the Western Cemetery; late fifth dynasty. The text is heavily reconstructed; this is not marked in the translation.

(1) Going home in peace,
(2) having seen the work done (3) on his tomb of the necropolis.
(4) This his tomb was made for him
(5) as a result of his perfect state of *imakhu* in the sight of the god.
(6) With regard to his tomb,
every craftsman (7) who worked on it was given a very large payment,
(8) and they thanked all the gods for him.
(9) The overseer of the *khenty-she* of the Great House,
(10) Neferkhuwi.

B. Tomb of Nymaatre: See No. 186

C. Tomb of Ankhmare

The tomb is in the Eastern Cemetery (G 7837+7843; PM III^2, 206). Probably fifth dynasty. Line numbers are not marked as the lines are very short. See no. 86 for another text from this tomb.

Going home in peace, having seen the work done on his tomb of the necropolis. The responsible one of the granary, Ankhmare.

192. A Nameless Tomb from the Teti Pyramid Cemetery at Saqqara

A text on a fragment of a lintel, found in the area of smaller tombs in the cemetery. Perhaps late reign of Teti.

Upper Part

(1) An offering which the king gives …
(2) I made this tomb of mine …
(3) I satisfied the craftsmen who …
(4) O you who live on earth and are *imakhu* …

Lower Part

(5) for the first under the king, overseer of the Great Mansion, controller of scribes of petitioners, judge and boundary official, judge …

193. Texts from a Monument of an Unknown Man in the British Museum

The central part of a false door of unknown provenance, now London, BM EA 1186. Fifth or sixth dynasty.

(1) I made this particularly for bread and for beer.
(With regard to) him who shall do anything to this (*the tomb*),
the crocodile shall be against him (2) [in the water,
and the snake shall be] against him on land.[4]
I never did anything evil (to) men.

Notes

1. Presumably the necropolis of the pyramid city of Khufu.
2. Compare the similar phrases in no. 193 and associated comment.
3. Compare Fischer 1996: 271.
4. See Willems 1990: 34–35 and Assmann 1992: 152–53 for these phrases. Although the context is very different, readers may be interested in the New Kingdom story of the "Doomed Prince" who was threatened by three fates, two of which were the crocodile and the snake (Lichtheim 1976: 200–203). No. 182 is a not dissimilar text.

XVI

Biographical Texts from the Memphite Region

See notes in chapter I, §6.5.3. See chapter XVII for biographical texts from cemeteries outside the capital city of Memphis.

194. Text from the Tomb of Akhethotep at Saqqara

Mastaba chapel now in Paris, Louvre E 10958 (PM III², 634–37; Ziegler 1993). Recent excavations at Saqqara have located the original position of this chapel, adjacent to the causeway of Unas. Mid to late fifth dynasty.

(1) His majesty had his son,
the sole companion, charmed of arm, Sankhuptah,
bring for him malachite and lapis lazuli
in the form of a broad collar, a *shenu* collar and an *ankhet* counterpoise,
and also an *izen* pendent[1] of malachite to be placed around his neck,
as well as two oxen from the island,
as a reward for having educated him to the satisfaction of the king.
(2) The sole companion, charmed of arm, *heqa-a,* controller of the two thrones,
(3) priest of Horus *imy-shenut,* priest of Heka, favorite (?) of Anubis,
(4) priest of Khnum wherever he is who dwells in the house of life,
(5) lector priest, he who is in charge of the secrets of the House of the Morning,
(6) the superior of the great ones, the companion Akhethotep.

195. Text from the Tomb of Akhethotep Hemi/ Nebkauhor at Saqqara

This large tomb was probably built by Akhethotep in the reign of Unas and was reused in the sixth dynasty by Nebkauhor (see PM III², 627–29). Thus the texts could have been set up by either man and it is not easy to separate them.[2] *The biography contains a number of unusual phrases, which the damage to the text makes very hard to understand. Legal (no. 104) and caption texts (no. 301) from this tomb are also in this book.*

A. Main Ideal Biographical Text

(1) The beloved one of (2) the king, (3) Osiris, (4) Anubis and (5) Khentyimentyu
(6) is any inspector of soul priests, (7) assistant inspector (of soul priests), (8) scribe of a phyle,
(9) or (ordinary) soul priest (10) of my funerary estate
(11) who carries out the rites
in accordance with (12) these instructions
which I have made (13) while I was alive and on my feet.
(14) For I am one who speaks, I am one who acts,
(15) I am one who is remembered …
(16) by many people. I never spent the night … his majesty.
(17) With regard to any man (18) with whom I was angry,
(19) or who did something which irritated me
(20) or (did) something hateful,
(21) I it was myself who pacified him.
(22) With regard to any man about whom I knew
(23) that they were locked up in the Great Mansion,
(24) or were beaten in the Great Mansion,
(25) or were punished on guard duty,
(26) I did not …
(27) I never blocked any path
(28) I never went above traveling by foot or by boat
(29) I never did what any of his rivals loved
(30) I never excused the evil of another (man) in the presence of his majesty
(31) I never[3] made any command or any will in any place except for …

B. On a Block Originally on the Facade of This Mastaba

(x + 1) His majesty commanded that the outline draughtsman go out …
(x + 2) together with the Nubians and the Libyans who go forth …

196. False Door Inscriptions of Ankhkhufu from Giza

The singer Ankhkhufu was not (to modern eyes) a particularly important official, but I assume that his relationship with the king, presumably from performing at court, caused the (unnamed) king to reward him with this false door. From tomb G 4520 (PM III[2], 129–30); the false door is now Boston, MFA 21.3081. Probably later fifth dynasty.

Right-hand Inner Jamb

(1) His majesty had this done for him
as a mark of his state of *imakhu* in the sight of his majesty
(2) while he was still alive and on his feet.
The *khenty-she* of the Great House, the singer, Ankhkhufu.

Left-hand Inner Jamb

(1) The work was done close by the king himself in the doorway of the audience hall,
(2) and thus his majesty saw what was done daily on it there every day.
Ankhkhufu.

Left-hand Outer Jamb

(1) An offering which the king gives and which Anubis
who dwells in the divine tent-shrine gives
that he may be buried in the necropolis.
(2) The *khenty-she* of the Great House, singer, overseer of singers of the Great House,
(3) overseer of flautists, beloved of his lord, who loves his lord,
(4) who speaks every perfect thing to his lord, the *imakhu* in the sight of his lord, the royal acquaintance,
(5) the delight of his lord daily, the royal acquaintance Ankhkhufu.

Right-hand Outer Jamb

(1) An offering which the king gives and which Anubis
who dwells in the divine tent-shrine gives
that she may be buried in the necropolis, (2) in the Western Desert,
having grown old most perfectly in the sight of the god, the possessor of *imakhu*,
(3) the priestess of Hathor mistress of the sycomore,
the priestess of Neith opener of the northern ways,
(4) that invocation offerings be made for her
in the festival of Thoth and in the *Wag* festival,
(5) the royal acquaintance Djefatka.

197. Text of Ankhmahor from Saqqara

The tomb of Ankhmahor is approximately contemporary with the other two tombs in the "Street of Tombs" near the pyramid of Teti (PM III[2], 512–15), those of and Neferseshemre (no. 226) and Neferseshemptah (no. 223). This tomb is particularly famous from the apparent presence of a circumcision scene in it (no. 302). Other texts from this tomb are nos. 322 and 86. Early sixth dynasty.

Left Side of Facade

(1) [The overseer of] all [works] of the king in all the land, chief under the king, overseer of the Great Mansion, controller of royal scribes, Ankhmahor whose perfect name is Zezi, (2) speaks:
(3) [May things be perfect for you] my successors;
may matters be prosperous for you my ancestors.
With regard to anything you shall do to this tomb of mine of the necropolis,
(4) [I shall do the like] to your (funerary) property.
For I am an excellent and knowledgeable lector priest;
no excellent magic is ever hidden from me.
(5) [With regard to] any persons who shall enter this tomb in an impure state,
having consumed the abomination (6) which is abhorrent to an excellent *akh*,
and not having purified themselves according to the manner
in which they should be pure for an excellent *akh*,
one who regularly did what his lord favored—
(7) [I shall seize his neck] like a bird's and put fear in him
so that the spirits and those on earth see and are fearful of an excellent *akh*;
(8) he and [I shall be judged] in that noble court of the Great God.
But with regard to any man
who shall enter (9) [this tomb] in a pure state
and with whom I am satisfied,
I shall be supportive of him in the necropolis
and in the court of the Great God.

Right Side of Facade

(1) [The overseer of] all works of the king in all the land, Ankhmahor whose perfect name is Zezi, speaks:

(2) [O lector priest who] shall come into this tomb of mine
to perform the rites of transfiguration
in accordance with that secret writing of the skills of the lector priest
(3) … the king … his name,
recite for me that which will glorify me (?)
(4) … equipped …
recite for me that which will glorify me for I am equipped
(5) … in an excellent matter which you know …
I never said anything evil to the king (6) …[4] against a god.
The [text] shall be read out for me
(7) … through the desire to be perfect before the god and before men.

198. Texts of Ankhmeryremeryptah Called Nekhebu from Giza

These biographical inscriptions are one of the most important of the Old Kingdom for learning about those who directed the organization of labor. Nekhebu was a member of the family of Senedjemib Inti (no. 232), although his precise relationship is uncertain. It describes steps in his career, although it does not quite cover promotion to his highest offices. The more conventional appeals to the living are actually rather unusual and fulsome.

The chapel had been more or less dismantled and the inscriptions have had to be restored from a jumble of blocks. These texts were probably originally on either side of a doorway. For comments on Nekhebu and on the information from these texts: Strudwick 1985: 113, 241–43; Brovarski 2001: 32–33. Most reconstructions of Sethe and Dunham are not marked. From tomb G 2381 in the Western Cemetery (PM III^2, 89–91). Now Boston, MFA 13.4331 and Cairo, JE 44608. Reign of Pepy I.

Boston Text (MFA 13.4331)

(1) The sole companion, royal master <builder (?)>, Ankhmeryremeryptah, speaks:

(2) I was a worker of Meryre, my lord.
His majesty sent me [to direct all the works of the king,
and I acted] to the satisfaction of his majesty in Lower and Upper Egypt.
His majesty sent me to direct the construction (3) of soul chapels
for his majesty in Lower Egypt,[5] the *ges-per* of the mansion,
my northern limit being in the City of the Pools in the Akhbit of Horus,
and my southern limit being at the pyramid of Pepy I.

I came back only when I had finished.
(4) I [erected (?)] the soul chapels there, built the hall,
and I placed wood on it composed of timber felled in Lower Egypt.
I came back only when it had been finished through my efforts,
and his majesty favored me for it (5) right in the presence of the officials.
His majesty gave me *nub-ankh* amulets and bread and beer in large amounts,
and his majesty had one of the divisions of the Residence
come to me with it until they reached my gate.
(6) (This all happened) as I was more excellent in his sight
than any other royal master <builder (?)>
whom his majesty had (previously) sent
to deal with a *ges-per* of the royal estate.
His majesty sent me to lay out a canal in the Akhbit of Horus
and to excavate it.
(7) I excavated it in a period of three months,[6]
so that when I came back to the Residence it was already full of water.
For this his majesty favored me,
and his majesty gave me *nub-ankh* amulets and bread and beer,
as I was one whom his majesty favored highly
with regard to what he had sent me to do,
(8) having done everything which I was sent to do.
His majesty sent me to Kis[7] to excavate his canal (?) for Hathor-in-Kis.
I acted (9) and excavated it so that his majesty favored me for it.
Then I came back to the Residence and his majesty favored me highly,
and gave me *nub-ankh* amulets and bread and beer.

Cairo Text (JE 44608)

(1) [The sole companion, the royal master <builder (?)>,
Ankhmeryremeryptah,] speaks:
(2) [I was a worker of] Meryre, my lord.
His majesty sent me to direct work on his monuments in Heliopolis,
and I acted to the satisfaction of his majesty.
I spent six years there directing work,
and whenever I came to the Residence his majesty favored me for it.
Everything I did came about through the vigilance I practiced …
(3) … there in accord with what I myself know.

His majesty found me (originally) just as one of many builders,
and his majesty appointed (me) as inspector of builders,
overseer of builders and the leader of a phyle;
(then) his majesty appointed me as royal master builder
and first under the king and royal master builder;
(then) his majesty appointed me to be sole companion
and royal master builder in the two houses.
His majesty acted above all through the greatness of his favor for me.
(4) I am the beloved one of his father
and the favored one of his mother.
I never gave them reason to punish me on any matter
until they went to their tomb of the necropolis.
I am one favored of his siblings.
Now I was working with my brother, the overseer of works (*name lost*)
[When he did (*something or other, possibly his first promotion?*)]
I wrote, I carried his palette.
When he was appointed as inspector of builders,
I carried his measuring rod (?).
(5) When he was appointed as overseer of builders,
I was his companion (?).
When he was appointed royal master builder,
I was in charge of his town for him,
and I did everything excellently for him.
When he was appointed as sole companion
and royal master builder in the two houses,
I took charge of all his property for him,
as there was more in his house than that of any noble.
When (6) he was promoted to overseer of works,
I followed up on all of his commands to his satisfaction in these matters.
I looked after matters for him in his funerary estate
for a period of more than twenty years.
Never did I beat any man there so that he fell as a result of my action;
never did I enslave anyone therein.
With regard to anyone therein (7) with whom I dealt,
I am he who propitiated them;
I never slept in a state of anger with anyone.
I it was who gave clothing, bread, and beer
to everyone who was naked and hungry there.
I am the beloved one of everyone;

I never said anything evil against any man
to a king or someone in power.
I am one favored of his father and mother
and of the noble ones in the necropolis
(8) for making invocation offerings for them
and for conducting all the festivals for them—
in the *Wag* festival, the festival of Sokar, the first of the year festival,
the festival of Thoth, the festival of opening the year,
the first of the month festival and the last of the month festival,
and in every perfect festival made at every season of the year.
O soul priests of the *imakhu*:
do you wish that the king favor you
and that you shall be in the state of *imakhu*
in the sight of your lords and fathers in the necropolis?
(Then) you shall make invocation offerings (9) of bread and beer
as I have done for your fathers themselves.
Since you wish that I intercede on your behalf in the necropolis,
then teach your children the words of making invocation offerings
for me on the day of my passing there.
I am an excellent *akh*;
I know everything through which I may become transfigured in the necropolis.
O you who live on earth and shall pass by this tomb,
if you wish that the king might favor you
and that you may be *imakhu* in the sight of the Great God,
(10) [then do not] enter this tomb as you are tainted …
on account of your impurity.
With regard to any man who shall enter therein
in a hostile manner after this (I have said),
I shall be judged with him by the Great God;
I shall destroy their descendants and their doorways on earth.
O you who live on earth and who shall pass by this tomb,
do you desire that the king favor you
and that you be *imakhu* in he sight of the Great God?
Then you shall say
"a thousand of bread and a thousand of beer for Nekhebu, the *imakhu*."
You shall not destroy anything in this tomb,
for I am an [excellent] and prepared *akh*.
With regard to any man who shall destroy anything in this tomb,

I shall be judged with them by the Great God.
For I am speaker of perfection and a repeater of perfection.
I never spoke anything evil against any man.

199. Text of Bia from Saqqara

Bia built his tomb (PM III², 623) in the cemetery in front of the pyramid of Unas and near the mastaba of the vizier Mehu (no. 220), whom he served. Four inscriptions from the chapel were recovered during excavations in 1939–40. Late sixth dynasty.

Lintel, Left-hand Side

(1) O you who live on earth, soul priests of the estate of my lord.
As my lord favors you every day,
you shall give bread, beer, and water,
the reversionary offerings of my lord.
(2) I am one of you, a speaker of perfection and a repeater of perfection.
I never said anything evil against anyone;
I never seized anything from any poor man.
With regard to any man
(3) who shall make invocation offerings for me—
no matter whether a brother, a son, any person, a scribe—
and who shall pass by this tomb
(4) and who shall read (the inscription on) this doorway,
I shall be his support in the court of the Great God.
I am an excellent and true lector priest.
(5) The *imakhu*[8] in the sight of his lord, the royal noble, the companion of the house, Bia.

Lintel, Right-hand Side

(1) An offering which the king gives and an offering which Anubis,
lord of the sacred land, who dwells in the divine tent-shrine, gives
that he may cross over to the perfect West
(2) among the *imakhu* who love the Great God,
that he may join with the earth and cross over the heavens,
(3) and that Re may take his hand at the pure places.
For I am an excellent and truthful *akh*;
(4) I am the beloved one of his father
and the favored one of his mother every day.
(5) The royal noble,[8] the companion of the house, Bia.

Left Side Piece of the False Door

(1) An offering which the king has given[9]
and an offering which Anubis, who is on his mountain,
lord of the sacred land, who dwells in the divine tent-shrine, has given
that invocation offerings may be made for him
in the necropolis of the Western Desert.
(2) An offering which the king has given
and an offering which Khentyimentyu has given
that invocation offerings may be made for him
in the first of the year festival, the opening of the year festival,
the festival of Thoth, (3) the *Wag* festival,
the festival of Sokar and the great festival,
so that his voice may be true in the sight of the Great God
and excellent in the sight of his lord[10]
as one who has made the offerings and sought out the state of *imakhu*;
(4) that he may proceed on the perfect ways of the West,
that he may be united with the land,
that he may cross over the heavens
and that he may ascend to the Great God as an *imakhu*,
(5) that he may be followed by his *ka*s doubly in peace
in the sight of Osiris, lord of Busiris,
that the West may give him her hands.
(6) I am the beloved one of my father, the favored one of my mother,
an *imakhu* in the sight of his lord daily—
they used to say (7) when they saw me coming in the door
"he is one truly *imakhu*"—so they said about me.
(8) The *imakhu* in the sight of Anubis, who is on his mountain, and in the sight of Osiris, lord of Busiris, (9) the royal noble, companion of the house Bia.

An Upright Slab

(1) The *imakhu* in the sight of Anubis, who is on his mountain, who is in his wrappings;
(2) The *imakhu* in the sight of Osiris, lord of Busiris;
(3) The *imakhu* in the sight of the Great God, lord of the West;
(4) The *imakhu* in the sight of Ptah-Sokar;
(5) The royal noble, companion of the house Bia.

200. Text of Debehen from Giza

The text records the construction of the tomb as a favor from Menkaure, and as such is one of the earliest texts to describe specific events in the life of the owner. There is some controversy about the date; Kloth 2002: 38–39 puts it not before the middle fifth dynasty, suggesting that various features of the decoration and the type of the biography (and one rather questionable section of text) might indicate that the scenes were erected posthumously by Debehen's son. The phrasing of the text almost reads as if it was set up as a royal decree, but whether this means it should be dated later or be seen as a very early example of a biography is unclear. The tomb is in the Central Cemetery (PM III², 235–36).

(1) …
(2) He speaks:
With regard to this tomb of mine,
it was the king of Upper and Lower Egypt,
Menkaure [may he live for ever] who gave me its place,[11]
while he happened to be on the way to the pyramid plateau
(3) to inspect the work being done on the pyramid of Menkaure.
… The [royal master] builder [came]
with the two Great Controllers of Craftsmen[12] and the craftsmen,
(4) to be present at it in order to inspect the work done on [the temple (?)];
[he arranged for] 50 craftsmen to do the work on it daily
and they were assigned the (5) completion of the *wabet*.
His majesty commanded that they were not to be taken for any work-duty,
other than carrying out work on it (*the tomb*) to his satisfaction.
(6) His majesty also ordered the clearance of the building-site (?)
[especially for the construction of (?)] this tomb of mine.
His majesty ordered [*that someone come (?)*] …
(7) for the clearance of the building-site …
[His majesty ordered] that two seal-bearers of the god come;[13]
they said/his majesty said …
(8) [*large gap*] … gold was given to them (?) …
(9) [*large gap*] … the two Great Controllers of Craftsmen.
His majesty decided to pay a visit to the work which had been assigned (10) …
Stone was brought from Tura with which to clad the temple

(11) as well as a double false door and entrance doorway for this tomb of mine.
Two boats with the two Great Controllers of Craftsmen
and the royal master builder it was who came (12) … [*large gap*] …
bringing for me a statue to receive offerings[14] … [*large gap*]
(13) … every … daily.
Now it is finished on the desert with its statue shrine
(14) … [*large gap*] …
together with two other statues which were authorized, one of which was …
(15) [*large gap*] … the festival of the Apis bull in the divine tent-shrine
(16) … [*large gap*] … He did this through the wish
that his state of *imakhu* exist in the sight of his lord
(17) … [*large gap*] … [I was beloved (?)] of [my father] and my mother,
and I protected (?) them
(18) … [*large gap*] … green and black eye-paint … a document (?) …
(19) at the door of the office.
Then I requested … of all types from Lower Egypt,
in particular from the sixth nome (the place) called Iatmen.
(20) A royal decree was made for the overseer [of all works of the king that the craftsmen (?)] should make it,
a tomb 100 cubits long (21) and 50 cubits in breadth and five cubits [high (?)] …
larger than that which my father (could have [?]) made when he was alive.
His majesty commanded … (22) …

201. Inscription on the False Door of Geref from Saqqara

Located near the tomb of Mereruka in the Teti pyramid cemetery. Early sixth dynasty.

A. Architrave

First three lines of formulae omitted.

(4) I made this tomb actually while I was alive on my feet,
as one whom the king favored, one whom men loved;
I gave payment to the stonemasons so that they were satisfied therewith …
(5) I judged between two litigants to their satisfaction in matters over which I was in control.

He who loves the king it is, an *imakhu* in the sight of the Great God
and who shall be buried perfectly in the necropolis who shall pass by this tomb of mine …
(6) and who shall say: "bread and beer for Geref called Itji born of Meretites"
and who shall say that I am indeed an *imakhu*
in accordance with what was said on earth,
that I existed making peace and seeking the state of *imakhu* …

(7) The priest of the pyramid of Teti, overseer of the two cool rooms of the Great House, overseer of every royal "breakfast" which the sky gives and the earth creates, overseer of the two fields of reeds of offerings, overseer of marshlands … Geref.

B. Left Outer Jamb of False Door

(1) Every man shall be *imakhu* who shall say:
(2) "bread and beer for the royal nobleman Geref,
who is known as Itji, engendered/born of Tjatbed,
whose perfect name is Itji."
(3) For I am an *imakhu* in accordance with what was said on earth.
I am one who exists having made peace and having reached the state of *imakhu*.
Geref.

202. Texts from the Tomb of Hetepherakhet at Saqqara

The tomb of Hetepherakhet was located at Saqqara, west of the Step Pyramid (D 60, PM III^2, 593–95), and like a number of the mastabas there was sold to foreign museums in the early years of the twentieth century; it is now in Leiden, Rijksmuseum F.1904/3.1. Later fifth dynasty.

Entrance Inscription Left

(1) The judge and mouth of Nekhen Hetepherakhet speaks:
I made this tomb from my own true property;
I never took the property of any person.
(2) With regard to any person who worked therein for me,
they worked on it thanking the god for me very greatly for it.
They made this (3) particularly for bread, for beer, for clothing,
for *merhet* oil, for wheat and barley, (all) in great quantity.
I never did anything (4) by force against any person,

for the god loves a good nature.
I am *imakhu* in the sight of the king.

Entrance Inscription Right

(1) The judge and elder of the portal Hetepherakhet speaks:
In a pure place on the side of the West was where I made this tomb of mine,
where there was no (2) tomb of any man,
so that the property of one who has gone to his *ka* could be protected.
With regard to any person
who shall enter (3) this tomb of mine in an impure state,
or who shall do anything evil to this,
I shall be judged with him on this matter (4) by the Great God.
As a result of my state of *imakhu* in the sight of the king I made this tomb,
and a sarcophagus was brought for me.

203. Pillar Text from the Tomb of Hetepherenptah

The provenance is unknown but is doubtless the Memphite region. Now Cairo, CG 15048. The date is somewhat disputed, ranging from the end of the third dynasty to the sixth; the latest study suggests that it is not earlier than the middle fifth dynasty (Kloth 2003).

Three sides of this pillar are covered with archaizing titles, not translated here.

The chief lector priest, great seer, overseer of crews, overseer of all marshlands.
An "offering which the king gives" of a carrying chair was made for him.
The youths it was who carried him in it following the king.
Never was (the like) done for any man.
Hetepherenptah.

204. From the Left Jamb of the False Door of Hetepu at Saqqara

A fragment of an ideal biography found reused in the late necropolis west of the Step Pyramid. Sixth dynasty.

...
I carried out Maat for her lord.
I judged (between) two litigants to their satisfaction.

...
I am a speaker of perfection and a repeater of perfection,
for I wish that it go well with me in the sight of the god.

205. Inscriptions of Hezi from Saqqara

The tomb of Hezi has suffered some deliberate damage to the names and titles in ancient times. Hezi appears also to have been one of those rare officials who were promoted to high office after much of his tomb had been completed (he became vizier). These texts are intriguing, not least for the number of unusual phrases and expressions they contain. The tomb is in the Teti pyramid cemetery; early to mid sixth dynasty.

Lintel

(1) An offering which the king and an offering which Anubis,
who is on his mountain, who dwells in the divine tent-shrine,
who is in his wrappings, lord of the sacred land give
that he may be buried as an *imakhu* in the sight of the king
in his tomb of the necropolis in the Western Desert,
having grown old most perfectly
as an *imakhu* in the sight of the Great God,
among the *imakhu* in the sight of the king and in the sight of the god.
(2) An offering which the king and an offering which Osiris, lord of Busiris give
that he may travel doubly in peace
upon the ways which are made holy of the West,
upon which the *imakhu* travel,
that he may ascend to the Great God, the lord of heaven,
to make offerings and to seek the state of *imakhu*.
(3) An offering which the king and an offering which Anubis, who dwells in Sepa, give
that invocation offerings may be made for him
in the necropolis in the Western Desert,
that he may be transfigured by the lector priest
through the secret writings of the house of the god's words
in the opening of the year festival, the festival of Thoth,

the first of the year festival, the *Wag* festival, the great festival of Sokar,
the festival of the coming forth of Min, the *Rekeh* festival,
in the monthly and half-monthly festivals and daily.

(4) The *imakhu* in the sight of the West [Hezi][15] speaks:
I went forth from my town, I went down into the afterlife;
I acted in accordance with Maat for my lord,
whom I made satisfied in accordance with that which he desires.
I never said anything evil against any man to any powerful person;
I judged between two litigants
so that they were satisfied in matters where I was in charge.

(5) The judge and scribe of Maat ... judge and inspector of scribes, regular one of the phyle, ... judge and overseer of scribes, keeper of secrets of judgment ... , royal document scribe in the presence, keeper of all the secrets of everything which is ordered, the *imakhu* ...

(6) The inspector of priests and deputy inspector of priests of the pyramid of Teti, *khenty-she,* the *wab*-priest, scribe of the *phyle* ... , first under the king, staff of the *rekhyt,* pillar of *kenmut,* overseer of the Great Mansion, overseer of commissions of the divine offerings in all of (?) Lower and Upper Egypt, overseer of the chamber of the *meret*, overseer of the chamber of sealed documents and of the house of reversionary offerings ...

Western Reveal of the Entrance

(1) He speaks:
I was a judge and scribe of the time of Izezi;
I was a judge and inspector of scribes of the time of Unas;
it was Teti my lord who appointed me judge and boundary official
(2) and who appointed me first under the king.
His majesty permitted that (this) be done for me
as his majesty knew my name
from when I took the (office of) scribe from his hands,[16]
as there was no helper whom he recalled
and of whom it was said that he was a wise man.
(3) I carried out the role of a scribe in the presence of his majesty
actually at the forefront of the scribes,
and I carried out the role of an official in the presence of his majesty
actually at the forefront of the officials.
(4) His majesty regularly had me go down to the barque to carry out guard duty,
and had me to come to the ways, and had gifts prepared for me[17]

as is normally done for a chamberlain or a first under the king,
even though I was (only) a judge and boundary official,
with the like not being done for any of my equals.
Because of my efficiency, his majesty used to ask my advice (5) among the officials,
even though I was only a judge and inspector of scribes,
for he knew my name was valued more highly than that of any other servant.

Eastern Reveal of the Entrance

(1) He speaks:

With regard to any man who shall enter this tomb
after he has eaten the abominations which an *akh* abominates
and/or who has had sexual intercourse with women,
(2) I shall be judged with him in the tribunal of the Great God.
I am a more excellent *akh* than any other;
I am a better prepared *akh* than any other.
(3) I know everything which is excellent, whereby an *akh* is excellent,
and what is potent,
whereby an *akh* which is in the necropolis is effective.
I am one whom his father favored, (4) and the beloved one of his mother, the support[18] of his family.
I have organized the creation of one room in this tomb
(5) so that invocation offerings can be made in it,
although I am capable of creating it with many rooms.
Those who hate entering it or being associated with it
never work for me so that it (stays) pure for me.

206. Facade Text from the Tomb of Idu at Giza

The sixth-dynasty tombs of Qar (no. 313) and Idu lie to the east of the queens' pyramids of Khufu. They are of a father and son and form one of the few inserted later tombs in this area of the cemetery. These texts are placed over the entrance to the tomb of Idu (tomb G 7102, PM III², 185–86). The orientation of the upper text is of particular interest, as the top line runs from right to left, and the text wraps round and continues left to right. Early to middle sixth dynasty.

Upper Text

(1) (Idu) speaks:
I came forth from my town, I went down into the afterlife;
I carried out Maat for her lord,
I propitiated the god in accordance with what he desires;
I said what was perfect and repeated what was perfect;
I spoke and acted truly:
I gave bread to the hungry, and clothes [*text wraps and changes direction*] (2) to the naked;
I was respectful of my father and kind to my mother as far as I was able;
I never said anything evil, unjust or devious against any man,
through desire of being happy and to have a clear character,
and that I may be *imakhu* in the sight of the god and of men for ever.

Lower Text

(1) An offering which the king gives and which Anubis,
who dwells in the divine tent-shrine, who is on his mountain,
who is in his wrappings, the lord of the sacred land, gives
for a perfect burial in the necropolis,
and an offering which Osiris gives[19]
that he may be buried perfectly in his tomb which is in the necropolis;
that he might travel on the perfect ways,
(2) that he might be followed by his *ka*s,
that his document might be received by the Great God,
that he might be guided upon the holy ways on which the *imakhu* travel,
and that he might be raised up to the Great God as an *imakhu*,
(3) for he is one who loves the Great God,
a possessor of the state of *imakhu*
and a possessor of a perfect burial in the necropolis;
and that invocation offerings be made for him in abundance in the West,
and that he might be greatly transfigured by the lector priest and the embalmer,
(4) in the opening of the year festival, in the festival of Thoth,
in the first day of the year festival, in the *Wag* festival,
in the festival of Sokar, in the great festival, in the *Rekeh* festival,
in the *Sadj* festival, in the festival of the coming forth of Min,
(5) in the half-monthly and monthly festivals,
in the seasonal festivals, in the ten-day festivals,

in every great festival daily;
(*the offerings shall be*) a thousand oryx, a thousand cattle,
a thousand *ra* geese, a thousand *tjerep* geese, a thousand (6) *zet* geese,
a thousand *se* geese, a thousand pigeons, a thousand of alabaster,
a thousand of clothing, a thousand of bread, a thousand cakes,
a thousand of beer from the pure (offerings) of the Great God,
for the overseer of commissions of the divine offerings in the two houses,
the *imakhu* in the sight of the Great God,
(7) the first under the king, staff of the *rekhyt,* pillar of *kenmut,*
keeper of secrets of judgment, priest of Maat,
royal document scribe in the presence,
overseer of scribes of the dependents,
the *imakhu* in the sight of Anubis, who is on his mountain, who is in his wrappings,
(8) the royal document scribe in the presence, overseer of the scribes of the dependents, Idu.

207. Text of Ipi from Saqqara

This block was found at Saqqara in the 1920s (PM III[2], 569), and is a part of a damaged biographical inscription; the beginnings and ends of lines are incomplete. Probably late Old Kingdom.

(1) … the *imakhu* in the sight of Anubis, who is on his mountain, Ipi,
the overseer of "kissing the ground" …
(2) … of his mother, Ipi, the overseer of "kissing the ground,"
who was in post as [seal-bearer] of the king of Lower Egypt …
(3) … and established in Lower Egypt, who is in the heart of his lord,
he who gives judgment …
(4) … alone. I always have done what the king commanded and what people love;
I gave bread to the hungry, clothes [to the naked] …
(5) … [I am] *imakhu* in the sight of men;
I am the beloved one of his father and the favored one of [his] mother …
(6) … [O you who live upon] earth, those who come after (me), *khenty-she, wab*-priests …
(7) … king commands … favored …

208. Lintel from the Tomb of Iyenhor at Saqqara

Tomb adjacent to the causeway of Unas (PM III[2], 630). Late sixth dynasty. The arrangement of the lintel has similarities with that of Nyankhpepy (no. 143).

(1) An offering which the king gives and an offering which Anubis
who is in his wrappings, who dwells in the divine tent-shrine, gives
that he may be buried in the necropolis, in the Western Desert,
having grown old very perfectly as an *imakhu* in the sight of Unas.
The sole companion Iyenhor.
(2) An offering which the king gives
and which Osiris, who dwells in Sepa, gives
that invocation offerings may be made for him
in the form of an "offering which the king gives"
in every place of the Residence.
The *imakhu* in the sight of the Great God, the lector priest Iyenhor.
(3) An offering which the king gives and which Anubis,
lord of burial in the necropolis, gives
that he might be followed by his *ka*s among all the *akh*s.
The *imakhu* in the sight of Anubis, the royal noble Iyenhor.
(4) An offering which the king gives
and which Osiris, who dwells in Busiris, gives
that he may travel on the perfect ways of the West
on which the *imakhu* travel, as one who makes offerings,
the *imakhu* Iyenhor.
(5) May he be united with the land, may he cross the heavens,
may he ascend to the Great God,
may the god receive his document at all the pure places.
The *imakhu* in the sight of the god, whom men praise,
the overseer of the office of the *khenty-she* of the Great house
Iyenhor.

(6) He speaks:

I am the beloved one of his father, the favored one of his mother.
I am an [excellent] *akh* who knows magic.
Men know that I am an excellent lector priest.
(7) The royal noble Iyenhor.

The following additional column of hieroglyphs is placed after the first part of the above four "offering which the king gives" formulae:

for the sole companion, lector priest Iyenhor.

209. Inscription of Izi from Saqqara

This text is not unlike that of Bia (no. 199), in which the owner addresses his fellow priests, and it also comes from the same area of the Unas cemetery at Saqqara (PM III², 626). Sixth dynasty.

(1) O you *wab*-priests and *khenty-she* of the pyramid of Unas,
(2) and servants of the estate of my lord:
I am Izi, one of you.
(3) Perform priestly service for Unas and Unas shall favor you;
perform priestly service for him
(4) and you shall be buried in the necropolis
having spent years as *imakhu*.
(5) Give me water, bread and beer, me, Izi, for I am one of you,
one who works in the fields, who speaks utterances,
(6) (and also to) my father Kaitepet and my mother Setibi.
I am an excellent scribe who knows the rites.
(7) With regard to any man who shall give me water, bread, and beer which are our due,
I shall go on their behalf (8) into the place where the *akh*s are
and I shall be behind him in the court of the Great God.

210. Texts from the Tomb of Kaiaper at South Abusir

Objects from the tomb of Kaiaper have been on the art market throughout the twentieth century A.D.*; inscriptions known from it in the late 1950s were published in Fischer 1959 (translation of some Roccati 1982: 115–16); compare PM III², 501. The site of the tomb was located in Egyptian excavations in 1989. Early fifth dynasty. The reconstructions are not marked here.*

(1) I made this (tomb) (2) when I was a possessor of the state of *imakhu* in the sight of the king.
(3) I made this (tomb) from my own (4) true property … (5) of any man.
I never spoke (6) anything evil about any person
(7) I never took the property of (8) any person
(With regard to [?]) he who shall do anything (9) to this (tomb),
he shall be punished (10) by the Great God, the lord of judgment.
(11) The judge and boundary official, Kaiaper.

211. Texts from the Tomb of Kaiaper at Saqqara

The tomb is located in one of the outer sections of the Teti pyramid cemetery, which continued on from the Street of Tombs of Neferseshemre, Ankhmahor, and Neferseshemptah. Reign of Teti or of Pepy I. No. 322C is a sarcophagus text from here.

The *iry pat, haty-a,* overseer of the *ges-per*, first under the king,
Kaiaper speaks:
(1) One who loves the king
and one who loves Anubis, who is on his mountain,
is any man or soul priest (2) who shall pass along this route,
whether going north or south, and who pours water for me
(3) or who gives bread and beer to me from that which you possess.
If you have no bread or beer with you,
(4) then you shall speak with your mouth and offer with your arm:
"a thousand of bread and beer, (5) a thousand *ra* geese, a thousand
tjerep geese,
a thousand *zet* geese, a thousand *ser* geese, a thousand pigeons,
(6) a thousand oryx, a thousand oxen and (measures) of incense
for the overseer of the *ges-per*, first under the king, overseer of the
Great Mansion, (7) the *imakhu* in the sight of the king, Anubis, who is
on his mountain, and the Great God, lord of the West.

Ideal Biography on North Entrance Thickness:

(1) I came forth from my town, I went down into the afterlife;
I carried out (2) Maat for her lord,
I propitiated the god in respect of that which he loves;
(3) I gave bread to the hungry, clothes to the naked,
and I ferried to land (4) him who had no boat.
I am a speaker of perfection and a repeater of what is desired,
(5) the *imakhu* in the sight of the Great God,
(6) the *iry pat,* overseer of the administrative district, Kaiaper.

212. Inscriptions of Kaiemtjennet from His Tomb at Saqqara

This badly damaged text, consisting of four blocks in addition to the titles of the deceased at the entrance, is one of the most intriguing biographies of the

Old Kingdom, as many phrases and events recounted in it are unique. Most of the reconstructions in [ ] are simplified from the longer suggestions of Schott and are more like those of Roccati; rather than being attempts at formal restorations, they restore the sense, *not the* length, extent, or actual wording *of what might have been there. Hence this translation is in places no more than a paraphrase of the possible original content of the text. The numbering of the blocks themselves follows Sethe, but the sequence and line numbering follow Schott. Tomb D 7 at North Saqqara (PM III², 489). Reign of Izezi.*

A.

(a) The king's son, sole companion, seal-bearer of the god, overseer of all works of the king, who loves his lord, overseer of all commands of the king, who places the fear of Horus in the foreign lands.
(b) [The king's son, seal-bearer of the god in] the two great ships, overseer of all commands of the king, who loves his lord, ... of two boat-crews, who is in the heart of his lord, the overseer of the expedition, the *imakhu*.
(c) ... the overseer of instructors of the royal children *or* the overseer of pilots, Kaiemtjennet.

E.

(1) ... I was noble in the sight of his majesty
(2) ... his majesty ... valuable things
(3) [were given to me] ... in accordance with his majesty's wish in relation to it
(4) [his majesty sent me out to put down the rebels in] ...
(5) [I brought *various important people*] to the Residence as captives
(6) [I took the grain from their] threshing floors and cut down
(7) [their trees and devastated their fields] ... and their grain did not grow and there was nothing [in] this [land (?)].
(8) A royal decree was brought to me to command me
(9) [to accompany the prisoners as there were] many women among them. I came to the Residence
(10) [and his majesty favored me] more than anything. Then his majesty had carried out under my charge
(11) [*some building project or other*] this flooring (?)

B.

(1) [I made ...] for this temple which was finished off with inscriptions,
(2) [and I put in place an overseer of] workmen and an overseer of builders,

(3) [and these floors] remained under the structure of this temple.
(4) … the structure was built and the floor was not damaged.
(5) … Then his majesty said “Tell me a thousand of your wishes,”
(6) [and he thanked *a goddess, perhaps Hathor*] for I had done what he favored inside her temple
(7) [His majesty promoted me to overseer] of pilots, for I was but a lowly oarsman (at that time).
(8) … I was one who saw [what was coming] …
(9) [and his majesty placed me] among the companions
(10) [he said] “you think a great deal” *or* … I was very thoughtful. Then his majesty had [*someone*] come
(11) [and he said] “you shall speak to the ship’s crew so that they proceed to the Residence”
(12) … among the foremost ones and I heard
(13) … “You are indeed a very strong man and you shall do more than a thousand strong men”
(14) … therein myself due to (the fact that) I am more valuable in the sight of his majesty than anything.

D.

(1) [His majesty was sailing in boats together with a sphinx and its base] as it happened that we were sailing in the two great ships
(2) … the men [took *the base*] and it was placed in its perfect place of eternity
(3) … the master of all the works [said] “I need to know the number of
(4) [cubits needed for moving this sphinx] when it is to be placed in its perfect place of eternity on a base of five cubits.”
(5) [His majesty summoned me.] Then his majesty said “Look at what is the matter with this sphinx.”
(6) [I gave the answer] so that it was as when the shadows run away at daybreak without
(7) [I took over the work] likewise, constructing it of bricks
(8) [Then his majesty said “you have carried out this work] to the delight of my majesty over it. For my majesty brought you along to deal with it, as my majesty knew [that you were capable”]. …

C.

(1) … Djedkare, and they were satisfied with it. It happened that there was a trip to see it on another occasion
(2) [His majesty said “Let us go and I shall] do for you everything

which is done for a servant who loves his lord." It happened that [a storm and darkness] arose,

(3) ... and I could not find a man who could follow the route because of the storm.

(4) [Nonetheless, his majesty ordered that the voyage continue] on the river, on that day of desperately foul weather.

(5) [His majesty said "You have sailed the vessel] to the delight of my majesty over it. For you are a true sailor

(6) [and you are not fearful] of a great storm on the river."

(7) [His majesty backed me in this difficult journey] from beginning to end, and it went well for him, and nothing happened to him.

(8) [When we reached the Residence, his majesty favored me] very greatly. Then his majesty said "It was like the voyage of Re on the Great Lake"

(9) [and he had me initiated] in the secret matters in the Great Mansions. Then his majesty said

(10) ["I shall reward you"[20]] and the vizier Reshepses[21] was summoned into the court council. Then his majesty said

(11) ["When the storm came up] you it was who saw to it that I was saved from it and taken away from it.

(12) [*A specification of a reward, perhaps something for his tomb?"*] Then the vizier Reshepses went away on this matter

(13) [(?) to Tura (?)] ... and I followed at the stern of the great boat to the place

(14) [where we landed.] ... Then his majesty had invocation offerings set up for me from all parts of the Residence,

(15) [*specification of other items*] *idmy* and *sezef* linen[22] of two cubits. The *haty-a* saw to the setting up of these grants.

(16) [This was done ...] because of my vigilance in matters night

(17) [and day (?) for I did what his majesty favored ...] even though I was but a young sailor.

213. Texts from the Facade of the Mastaba of Kaigemni at Saqqara

Kaigemni was the first of a large group of officials of the reigns of Teti and Pepy I to build a tomb in the area of the pyramid of Teti (tomb LS 10, PM III^2, 521–25). He was a vizier of Teti, although his career began in the reign of Izezi. After the Old Kingdom he was treated as a wise man, and a later *wisdom text ("The Instructions of Kaigemni") was ascribed to him (chapter I, §1.1). I follow here the text of Edel without marking his reconstructions.*

Right of the Tomb Entrance

At the top are the remains of an offering formula in four lines.

A.

(1) (*over figure*) The vizier Kaigemni speaks:
(2) A contemporary[23] of Izezi.
In the time of Unas I served as a judge and boundary official,
and his majesty favored me more than anything.
(3) When I came to the Residence,
his majesty favored me because of it more than anything.
The majesty of Teti, may he live for ever, proceeded to the Residence.
(4) … for his majesty knew their names in the bodyguard
as his majesty ordered everything
which his majesty desired (5) to be done in the six Great Mansions.
With regard to everything which (6) his majesty ordered
to be done correctly in the six Great Mansions,
(7) it happened right through my actions,
as (8) his majesty desired very much that everything he commanded be done right.

B.

(1) (*over figure*) The vizier Kaigemni speaks:
(2) The majesty of Teti my lord, may he live for ever, appointed me
as overseer of every office of all the priesthoods of the Residence,
for I was firm of purpose for his majesty
in respect of everything which his majesty had ordered to be done,
(3) through my excellence and my nobility in the sight of his majesty.
O [you who live on earth (?)] …
do true things for the king, for Maat is what the God loves;
speak true things to the king, (4) for Maat is what the king loves.
O … do not say to him anything evil in the form of lies against me to the king,
for the sovereign knows my character and my conduct,
and I am firmer of purpose for his majesty
than any of his officials who have existed in this land.
For I am a speaker of truth and a repeater of perfection
in all matters which the king loves.

For I it is who desires that it go well for me
in the sight of the king and in the sight of the Great God.
(5) For I it is who desires that I might be *imakhu*
in the sight of men and in the sight of the Great God.
I judged between two litigants so that they were (both) satisfied;
I provided for him who was in need of help,
(6) and I drove away sadness from him who was troubled.
With regard to any man who shall enter this my tomb not having purified himself,
(7) I shall seize his neck like a bird's so that the living see (it)
and are fearful (8) of an excellent and equipped *akh* who knows the rites.
I shall be judged with him in the tribunal of the Great God.
(9) I am an excellent and equipped *akh* who knows the rites.
I know all the excellent secrets of the god's words.

214. Part of a Lintel of Kaihap Tjeti

Kaihap was probably the first of the nomarchs to be buried in the Hawawish cemetery near Akhmim in the sixth dynasty (reign of Pepy II). However, these two blocks perhaps come from an earlier tomb in the Memphite region.

(1) The seal-bearer of the king of Lower Egypt, sole companion, lector priest, stolist of Min, overseer of priests, the *imakhu* Tjeti, (2) speaks:
As a youth, I tied the headband under the majesty of Pepy;
(3) when I was judge and boundary official
I was appointed to be first under the king.
I was appointed as companion (4) and overseer of priests,
and every companion in the city was in my charge;
then I was appointed as sole companion
(5) in the sight of the majesty of Pepy.
When I was appointed as sole companion,
I was allowed to enter the royal house—
(6) (this) was not done as a favor for any other person.
Favors were done for me greatly
(7) by the Residence under the majesty of Merenre.
I was promoted to stolist of Min …

215. Texts from the Tomb of Kaikherptah at Giza

Tomb G 5560 in the Western Cemetery (PM III[2], 166–67). Early sixth dynasty. This text shows an interesting series of reversals of the hieroglyphs, which are perhaps only to be explained as alternating the orientation of the text columns for some uncertain effect (Fischer 1977: 49–52, fig. 52).

In the Chapel

A number of fragments of a ideal biographical text from the tomb:

(1) … doubly truly *imakhu* in the sight of the god and in the sight of the king, one who traveled/lived …

(2) … what the god opposes; I spoke truly and I acted truly, that which [the god] loves …

In the Burial Chamber

(1) The beloved one of the king and Anubis (2) is the lector priest
who shall carry out the rites of transfiguration for an *akh*
in accordance with those (3) secret writings of the skills of the lector priest.
For I am an excellent and well-loved scribe,
(4) perfect of heart and peaceful of place,
(5) one who does not spend the night
(7) being angry (6) (with) anyone about matters.
(8) The judge and overseer of scribes Kaikherptah.

216. Texts from the Tomb of Khentika at Saqqara

The tomb of the vizier Khentika, adjacent to the pyramid of Teti (PM III[2], 508–11), is probably later in date than the "Street of Tombs" and was started in the reign of Teti and completed in that of Pepy I. Large parts of the texts are missing as a result of the damage suffered by the tomb; the reconstructions translated here are mostly those of James. A sarcophagus text will be found as no. 322B.

Ideal Biographical Texts on the Tomb Facade

Text A

More than 50 percent of the top of the text is missing

(1) [*Name and titles of Khentika missing*] speaks:

(2) … may Osiris, lord of Busiris, lord of the West, favor them;
every lector priest
(3) … for the breadth of eternity,

in accordance with what should be done for any royal noble, my like
(4) … shall be satisfied, he being well prepared.
Incense is to be burned (*literally* "made") for me,
so that I might be in the state of being well prepared
(5) [according to those writings of] the secrets of the god's words of the skills of the lector priest. For I am
(6) … [there is nothing] kept secret from me in the writings of the house of the god's books. For I am a keeper of secrets
(7) … I know everything which an excellent *akh* should know, who should proceed (8) [upon the perfect ways of the West (or) into the necropolis]
… the Great [God], lord of the necropolis. I know every way
(9) … For I am initiated into all the secrets of the house of the god's books of the palace
(10) … [I was more favored] in the sight of the majesty of my lord than anything else
(11) … of this inscription which is upon this tomb of mine
[lines 12–15 lost]
(16) … I shall be …
(17) … of the Great God, the lord of the necropolis …

Text B

Large section in the center and bottom right lost

(1) The chief lector priest, the sole companion Ikhekhi (2) speaks:
(3) The inspector of priests of the pyramid of Teti …
(4) With regard to every person who shall enter this tomb of mine
[of the necropolis in their state of impurity,
(5) having eaten] these [abominations]
which excellent *akh*s [who journey to the West] abominate …
(6) not having purified themselves according to the manner
in which they should be to enter a temple of [a god.
(7) I shall be judged with them] about it in the Western Desert,
in the tribunal of the Great God …
(8) his equals; an end shall be made for him in relation to it concerning this evil …
(9) [and I shall seize] his neck like a bird's.
I shall seize … the land. I shall place fear of me therein,
(10) so that those who are living on earth may see (it)
and may fear the excellent *akh*s who shall travel to the West
(11) [Moreover, I know] every secret and excellent duty
[which is performed by (?)] every excellent lector priest.

For I am initiated (12) into every secret of the job of the embalmer;
I know …
(13) But with regard to every lector priest or soul priest
who shall perform for me all this (14) which I have said
upon this tomb of mine of the necropolis,
I shall be their supporter (15) in the necropolis;
I shall not let anything they hate happen for ever.
(16) If I am seen on the road by anyone, (then)
(17) "Look (it is) Ikhekhi, the *imakhu* in the sight of Anubis who is on his mountain" shall be what they say on any road.

Text C

Upper parts mostly missing

(1) … the sole companion, the embalmer of Anubis, the favored one of Anubis, the stolist of Anubis, lector priest

(2) … [keeper of secrets] of the king wherever he is, overseer of every royal estate

(3) … [keeper] of the secrets of every royal command, Khentika, whose perfect name is Ikhekhi, speaks:

(4) … all persons who shall pass by this tomb of mine
(5) [of the necropolis, give bread] beer and water from that which you possess
(6) … [and if you have nothing]
then you should speak with your mouth and offer with your hand
(7) ["a thousand of bread and beer, a thousand oxen and fowl,]
a thousand of incense and alabaster, a thousand of clothing and *ra* geese
(8) … [a thousand of …] and pigeons, and a thousand of everything which is sweet,
all seasonal offerings, fowl, oxen, oryxes and joints of meat, pure things
(9) [for … the overseer of] *khenty-she* [of the Great House],
keeper of secrets of that which is seen alone
(10) … [noble] in his name, in his nobility, in his office, the *imakhu*
(11) … [in the sight of Anubis …] who is on his mountain,
who is in his wrappings, lord of the sacred land, Ikhekhi.
(12) … [the *imakhu* in the sight of] Osiris, lord of Busiris, Khentika
(13) … [in his] nobility (as) an *imakhu* in the sight of the Great God
(14) … this my [tomb] of the necropolis for all the living
(15) … in order to pour libations
(16) … [the sole companion] the embalmer of Anubis Khentika"—so you shall say.

Text D

Upper parts mostly missing

(1) [The *iry pat*], *haty-a,* [chief lector priest], *sem* priest, sole companion, embalmer of Anubis, favored one of Anubis, keeper of the great ones, Ikhekhi (2) [speaks:

I came forth from my town, I went down from my] nome,
I carried out Maat for her lord,
I satisfied the god with regard to that which he loves.
(3) … [Never] did I abuse my authority over anyone,
as I desire that my name be perfect in the sight of the Great God,
and that my state of *imakhu* exist in the sight of all men
(4) … [I judged between two litigants to their satisfaction.
Where I had authority,
I rescued the wretched one] from the one who is stronger than he.
(5) … [I gave bread to the hungry, clothes to the naked,
a crossing-over to him who had no] boat,
a burial to him who had no son;
I made (6) … [a boat for him who did not have a boat.
I was respectful to] my father, and I was kind to my mother.
I brought up [their] children
(7) … [I provided for the orphans (?)] … powerful at all times.
I never said anything wrong (8) … [about any person to his superior.
I did this because I wish to attain] the life-span of my ancestors.
Respect for me will remain in the sight of the man
(9) … [who has done service for me on account of the provisioning I have set up for him;
I ensured they were satisfied]
so that my (funerary) property shall well and truly exist in the sight of men in this land.
(10) … [for I desire] that I shall be *imakhu*
in the sight of the Great God, lord of the West and in the sight of men
(11) … For I am *imakhu* in of Ptah south of his wall, Ikhekhi.
(12) … all men in the majesty of the court council.
I begged this from the majesty of my lord.

217. Text of Khenu from Saqqara

Tomb adjacent to the causeway of Unas (PM III[2]*, 625–26). Sixth dynasty or possibly later.*

(1) The royal noble of the Great House, Khenu, speaks:
(2) [O you *khenty-she* of (3) the pyramid of Unas,]
whom Unas loves and whom Unas favors,
whom the king loves and whom Anubis favors,
(4) [bring for me invocation offerings
from] the reversionary offerings of Unas your lord,
and your children will do likewise for you.
For I am a servant of Unas,
(5) [who speaks truly and acts truly] toward anyone,
a speaker of perfection and a repeater of perfection.
I have never spoken or done anything evil to anyone,
for I wish that it will go correctly for me in the sight of the god
and perfectly for me in the sight of men.
(6) [With regard to any man who shall enter] this burial place
in order to make invocation offerings for me,
to pour water for me, or to make an offering by reciting,
I shall support him in the tribunal of the Great God.

218. Text of (Another) Khenu from Saqqara

Khenu stresses his efficiency in bringing back stones in a very short period; Fischer calculated that he would have to have traveled at roughly 5.5 km/hour day and night to have achieved this! Fischer also comments that the style of this block is very similar to an anonymous one mentioning Teti (no. 237) and could be from the same tomb. I follow Edel in some of the reconstructions of the missing upper fragment. This text was last seen in a storeroom in 1953; part of it has since appeared on the art market. End of the fifth dynasty.

(1) [His majesty sent me to Elephantine to bring back granite columns (?);
I brought them from] Elephantine for the majesty of Unas in seven days
(2) [*perhaps a date and a location where they landed* …] his majesty favored me for it.
(3) [His majesty sent me to … to bring back … ;
I brought it back in (only)] four days
as (I am) one who is very efficient (*literally* “one who comes and goes”).

His majesty had me
(4) … for what I had done.
I did not permit that any stone go off [to any other building (?)]
(5) … He has spoken, the royal noble, overseer of the office of the *khenty-she,* Khenu.

219. Inscriptions of Khuiwer from Giza

This text is found in virtually identical copies on either side of the entrance reveals of the chapel. The graphical variations between the two copies suggest either that one sculptor executed each side or that he worked slightly differently in different directions. Tomb LG 95 in the central field (PM III², 254–55). Probably middle fifth dynasty.

(1) I went forth from my town, I went down into the afterlife;
I spoke what was right there and did what was right there.
May it go well with you who come after me,
and may you my ancestors be "true of voice."
(2) With regard to those of you who shall do anything (evil) to this (tomb),
then I shall do likewise to your property to affect those who come after you.
For I never did harm (to) anyone,
and I never since birth caused that any man
spend the night (3) being angry with me on any matter.
I am one who proceeds peacefully,
one who does (what is necessary to be) *imakhu,*
the beloved one of his father, the beloved one of his mother,
(4) an *imakhu* in the sight of those who are with him,
one who is pleasant in the sight of his siblings,
the beloved one of his servants, one who never did harm to anyone.

(5) The royal acquaintance, scribe of the king's documents of the Great House, judge and overseer of scribes, judge and inspector of scribes of the two Great Mansions which are in the western part of the Residence, controller of scribes of petitioners,
(6) he who judges in the chamber, he who acts protectively toward the shade,[24] judge and inspector of scribes of commissions, inspector of scribes of the house of reversionary offerings, overseer of the place of provision,
(7) controller of scribes of petitioners in the great tribunal, overseer of the

west side (*crew*) of the great pyramid site, overseer of the expedition of recruits, who hears (8) the words in every secret (matter) of the king, Khuiwer.

An offering which the king and Anubis give
that he may travel on the perfect way (*sic*) of the West
on which the *imakhu* travel.
(8) I have reached old age most perfectly,
I am pure upon the perfect way as a possessor of *imakhu*
in the sight of the Great God,
the judge and inspector scribes Khuiwer.

220. Architraves from the Tomb of Mehu at Saqqara

The tomb of Mehu near the pyramid of Unas (PM III², 619–22; Altenmüller 1998; Kloth 2002: 19 [37]) was probably built in the early sixth dynasty but went through a number of constructional phases, and it was discovered in 1992 that the architrave at the present entrance superseded one set up earlier. Readers should note the similarities and differences between the two, as one was clearly replacing the other; for example, a son also appears with Mehu in the later one only. For captions from this tomb see no. 306. The tomb dates perhaps to the reign of Teti to that of Pepy I.

A. Earlier Architrave

(1) The tomb of the overseer of the *ges-per*, first under the king, Mehu, which the *haty-a* Shepsipuptah gave him while he was alive on his feet; truly he is in his heart who loves his name.

(2) An offering which the king gives,
an offering which Anubis, who dwells in the divine tent-shrine, gives,
and an offering which Anubis, who is on his mountain,
who is in his wrappings, lord of the sacred land, gives
for his burial in his tomb in the necropolis in the Western Desert,
having grown old most perfectly.
(3) An offering which the king gives
and an offering which Osiris, lord of Busiris, gives
that invocation offerings may be made for him
in the form of an "offering which the king gives" daily
at the opening of the year festival, the first day of the year festival,
the festival of Thoth, the *Wag* festival, the festival of Sokar,

the great festival, the *Rekeh* festival, the seasonal festivals,
and the monthly and half-monthly festivals.
(4) An offering which the king gives
and an offering which Khentyimentyu, lord of the Thinite nome
(*eighth of Upper Egypt*), gives
that he may be united with the land, that he may cross the heavens,
and that he may ascend to the Great God in the Western Desert;
an offering which the West gives
that he may go into it (*the West*) in his perfect name.
(5) An offering which the king gives and an offering which Anubis,
who is on his mountain, who dwells in the divine tent-shrine gives
that the skills of the lector priest and the job of the embalmer
may be performed for him,
so that (he) may be transfigured by the lector priest
through the excellent writings of the god's words
which report (?) that he is loved by the people (?).

(6) The *iry pat*, *haty-a*, vizier, overseer of all works of the king, sole companion, overseer of the *ges-per*, first under the king, the *imakhu* in the sight of the king, the *imakhu* in the sight of the bull of Mendes.

(7) I came forth from my town, I went down into the afterlife,
having become a great one, having grown old;
I carried out Maat which is what the god loves;
I propitiated the god in respect of all that which he loves;
I made invocation offerings for the *akh*s;
I was respectful of my father and kind to my mother.
(8) I buried him who had no son; I ferried him over who had no boat;
I rescued the wretched man from the (more) powerful one;
I gave the share of the father to his son.
(9) It so happens that men say when I pass them by:
"Look, he is an *imakhu* and the beloved one of the god," so they say.
For I am an excellent and well-prepared *akh*;
I know all the excellent magic.

(10) (*vertical*) The *imakhu*, overseer of the *ges-per*, first under the king, Mehu.

B. Later Architrave

(1) The tomb of the overseer of the *ges-per*, first under the king Mehu, which the *haty-a* Shepsipuptah gave him while he was alive on his feet … (*compare earlier text above*).

(2) An offering which the king gives,
an offering which Anubis, who dwells in the divine tent-shrine, gives,
and an offering which Anubis, who is on his mountain,
who is in his wrappings, lord of the sacred land, gives
that he may be buried in the necropolis,
having grown old most perfectly.
(3) An offering which the king gives
and an offering which Osiris, lord of Busiris, gives
that invocation offerings may be made for him
in the form of an "offering which the king gives" daily
at the opening of the year festival,
the first day of the year festival and every daily festival.
(4) An offering which the king gives
and an offering which Khentyimentyu, lord of the Thinite nome (*eighth of Upper Egypt*) gives
that he may be united with the land, that he may cross the heavens,
and that he may ascend to the Great God.
(5) The *iry pat*, *haty-a*, vizier, overseer of all works of the king, overseer of the *ges-per*, first under the king, the true *imakhu*.
(6) It so happens that all men say when I pass them by:
"Look, he is an *imakhu* and the beloved one of the god,"
so they say about me.

(7) (*vertical*) The overseer of the *ges-per*, first under the king, the true *imakhu*, Mehu.

221. Text of Mersuankh from His Tomb at Giza

The small chapel of Mersuankh in the Central Cemetery (PM III^2, 269–70) is close to that of the important early-fifth-dynasty official Rewer (no. 227). This text shows that he looked after the cult of Rewer and benefited from it. End fifth dynasty.

False Door

Top

An offering which the king and an offering which Anubis,
who dwells in the divine tent-shrine, give
that he may be buried in the necropolis having reached old age.
Mersuankh, who loves life.

Left Side

Attendant of the funerary estate of the companion Rewer, overseer of youths of the Residence, overseer of all his property of the Residence and of the gateway, Mersuankh.

Right Side

The companion Rewer—
I am his *imakhu* more than any other man;
an *imakhu* of his lord is an *imakhu* of the god.
I never did anything evil to any man.

222. Texts of Metjetji, Probably from Saqqara

The location of the tomb of Metjetji has been lost. Elements of it, including statues, came onto the art market in about 1947 and were purchased by a variety of institutions in Europe and North America. Textual and stylistic indications indicate that it came from Saqqara (the area west of the Step Pyramid has been suggested, PM III^2, 646–48), and it probably dates to the sixth dynasty, although an argument has also been made for it belonging to the ninth dynasty (Munro 1994).

The longer texts on the facade, while not individual biographical texts, use a number of phrases rarely or not at all seen elsewhere. Some parts are clearly unfinished. All texts given below are incomplete at the top, and the restorations are somewhat tentative.

Left Side of Facade (Toronto, Royal Ontario Museum 953.116.1)

(1) … [I am … whom his father loved],
an *imakhu* whom his mother favored;
I transported them to the perfect West,
with them thanking god for me
as they had been provided with the daily offerings.
(2) … for them.
I transported them to the perfect West,
having requested for them burial/sarcophagi from the Residence
as "an offering which the king gives"
(3) … [so that they were][25] *imakhu* in the sight of the king.
I never let them see anything (bad)
from the time when I was a child until their burial in the perfect West.

(4) … [I was beloved of] everyone;
I never did anything which could anger anyone since I was born
when speaking of all the works of the king which I have done.

(5) (*horizontal*) The royal noble, overseer of the *khenty-she* of the Great House, Metjetji.

Right Side of Facade (Berlin 32190)

(1) [O you who] live and who are upon earth, praise the king,
so that you may live and be watchful regarding his works;
guard his commands, do what he desires!
It is better for him who does (2) [it than for him for whom it is done].
He is *imakhu* who loves the god.
He is prosperous because of it;
may his passage though the whole of his life be good—
it is beneficial for him in the sight of the god
(3) [in the beautiful necropolis of the West (?)]
O you who come across this tomb of mine,
your heart shall be pleasing to Osiris, the lord of burial, when you say:
"May pure bread and beer be given
to the overseer of the office of the *khenty-she* of the Great House,
Metjetji."
(4) [May your heart be pleasant] to Anubis, lord of the West,
when you make invocation offerings from that which you possess
which can be used for invocation offerings for an *akh*.
For I am an excellent *akh*,
I am an excellent scribe for whom things should be done.
(5) … There is no bread or beer for the man who rebels against him
in the necropolis (or [?]) (6) [who acts against (?)] any *akh* buried in the
perfect West.
(7) [With regard to myself (?)]
I am *imakhu* in the sight of the *akh*s in the necropolis
(8) [and approval of me is in the mouth of] the officials and of men—
it is an excellent thing to give bread and beer
to those who are in the necropolis.
(9) [With regard to every son of mine,] every brother of mine,
and every man of my funerary estate
who shall come to make invocation offerings for me
(10) … I shall let him know that it is excellent
that he make invocation offerings for the *akh* in the necropolis.

(11) (*horizontal*) The royal noble, overseer of the office of the *khenty-she* of the Great House, Metjetji.

Entry Door Side Wall Left (Horizontal Text at Top and Vertical at Left); Kansas City, Nelson-Atkins Museum 52-7/1

[*Probably one or two lines lost, at least*
I am the beloved one of his father and the favored one of his mother]
(1) I am *imakhu* in the sight of men,
I am the beloved one of the multitude.
(2) With regard to any man who saw me, anywhere,
["he is an *imakhu* and the beloved one of the god," so they say[26]].
(3) The overseer of the office of the *khenty-she* of the Great House, Metjetji.

Entry Door Side Wall Right (Horizontal Text at Top and Vertical at Right); Kansas City, Nelson-Atkins Museum 52-7/2

[*Probably one or two lines lost, at least*
With regard to every man who worked on this tomb of mine, I paid him]
(1) for he had worked on it using copper from my funerary estate;
(2) I gave them clothing and permitted them
to live off the bread and beer of my funerary estate,
(*now vertical*) and because of it they thanked the god for me.
(3) The overseer of the office of the *khenty-she* of the Great House, Metjetji.

223. Texts from the Tomb of Neferseshemptah at Saqqara

The tomb of Neferseshemptah in the so-called Street of Tombs, adjacent to the pyramid of Teti (PM III², 515–16), is approximately contemporary with the other two tombs in that street, those of Ankhmahor (no. 197) and Neferseshemre (no. 224); there are many similarities in this text with the ideal biography of Neferseshemre. Neferseshemptah lived on into the reign of Pepy I, as is seen from one area of his tomb, although Kanawati has argued that the area of the tomb of the reign of Pepy I actually was built for Neferseshemptah's son (Kanawati 2002a: 108–10). The reconstructions translated here are those of Edel. Reign of Teti or a little later.

On the Tomb Facade

(1) … inspector of priests of the pyramid of Teti, *khenty-she* of the pyramid of Teti

(2) … pillar of *Kenmut,* overseer of commissions of the divine offerings, Wedjahateti Neferseshemptah Sheshi.[27]

(3) [I came forth from my town, I went down into the afterlife;
I carried out] Maat for her lord;
I satisfied him with regard to that which he loves;
I spoke perfection, I repeated perfection;
(4) [I chose the right moment,
for I love perfection to be there for the] people.
I judged between two litigants to their satisfaction.
Where I had authority,
I rescued the wretched one from the one who is stronger than he.
(5) [I spoke Maat, I carried out Maat
I gave bread to] the hungry, clothes to the naked,
I ferried over him who had no boat, I buried him who had no son;
I made a boat for him (6) [who did not have a boat;
I provided for] the orphans;
I never said anything evil against any person to his superior;
(7) [I did this because I wish to attain the lifespan] of my ancestors.
Respect for me will remain in the sight
of the man who has done service for me
on account of the provisioning (8) [I have set up for him];
I ensured they were satisfied for I desire that I shall be *imakhu*
in the sight of the god and in the sight of all men.
So says the *imakhu* of the god
(9) … the *imakhu* in the sight of Osiris, Neferseshemptah.

224. Texts from the Tomb of Neferseshemre at Saqqara

The tomb of Neferseshemre is one of the earliest among those of a large group of officials of the reigns of Teti and Pepy I in the area. It is the first in the "Street of Tombs" by the pyramid of Teti (PM III^2, 511–12). Reign of Teti.

Entrance Recess

(1) … places that invocation offerings may be made for him
in the necropolis in the Western Desert,
he who is true to the heart of Osiris, lord of [Busiris]
(2) … he who is true to the heart of Anubis, lord of the West,
that invocation offerings may be made for him in the necropolis as an *imakhu* …

(3) … [an *imakhu*] in the sight of the perfect West,
as an *imakhu* in the sight of all the gods of the West,
as an *imakhu* [in the sight of] …
(4) … [that] he [may be buried] in his tomb of the necropolis in the Western Desert,
having grown old most perfectly as an *imakhu* in the sight of the king;
(5) … perfect [ways],
that he may be guided by his *ka*s
on the holy ways upon which the *imakhu* travel.
(6) The *imakhu* in the sight of the king,
the *imakhu* in the sight of Osiris, the *imakhu* in the sight of Anubis.
An act of uniting with the perfect West for the *iry pat* Neferseshemre.
(7) The inspector of priests and *khenty-she* of the pyramid of Teti, *haty-a,* vizier, overseer of document scribes of the king, overseer of all works of the king, overseer of the two treasuries,
(8) overseer of the two *wabet*s, overseer of the two houses of gold, overseer of the two chambers of the royal ornament, overseer of Upper Egypt,
(9) overseer of the *ges-per*, overseer of the two granaries, overseer of commissions of offerings,
(10) overseer of the Residence, overseer of the two chambers of the sealed documents, Neferseshemre.
(11) Overseer of the two cool rooms of the Great House, overseer of what the sky gives and the earth creates, overseer of all vegetation,
(12) first under the king, staff of the *rekhyt*, pillar of *kenmut*, overseer of the six Great Mansions, Sheshi.

Ideal Biography from the Middle Jambs of the False Door (same on Both Sides)

(1) I came forth from my town, I went down into the afterlife;
I carried out Maat for her lord;
I satisfied him with regard to that which he loves;
I spoke Maat, I carried out Maat;
I spoke perfection, I repeated perfection;
I chose the right moment,
for I love perfection to be there for the people;
(2) I judged between two litigants to their satisfaction.
Where I had authority,
I rescued the wretched one from the one who is stronger than he;
I gave bread to the hungry, clothes (to the naked),

I ferried over him who had no boat,
(3) I buried him who had no son;
I made a boat for him who did not have a boat.
I was respectful to my father, and I was kind to my mother
I brought up their children.
So he speaks, he whose perfect name is Sheshi.

Ideal Biography from the Inner Jambs of the False Door
Left

(1) Proceeding to his funerary estate most perfectly, in peace,
for his state of *imakhu* exists in the sight of Anubis,
foremost of the Westerners, lord of the sacred land
after invocation offerings have been made for him
(2) upon the offering place
when he has crossed the pool,
when he has been transfigured by the lector priest
for his state of *imakhu* is very great in the sight of the Great God.

(3) The vizier, overseer of royal document scribes, overseer of all works of the king, first under the king, staff of the *rekhyet,* pillar of *kenmut,* overseer of every royal "breakfast" (4) [Nefer]seshem[re].

Right

(1) Crossing the heavens in peace very greatly;
going to the top of the mountain of the West;
grasping his arm by his ancestors [and by his *ka*s]
(2) (and by) the possessor of *imakhu,*
when invocation offerings have been made for him
upon the offering place in his funerary estate,
when he had grown old most perfectly in the sight of Osiris.

(3) The vizier, overseer of royal document scribes, overseer of all works of the king, first under the king, staff of the *rekhyet,* pillar of *kenmut* (4) [Neferseshemre].

225. Inscriptions of Nyankhsekhmet from Saqqara

These texts occupy most of one of the best-made false door stelae in an Old Kingdom tomb of a noble. The text is of exceptional interest as it relates to the making of the door, and it is highly important as one of the earliest biographical texts in existence (Baines 1999b: 22–24 and Baines 1997: 136–38). Tomb north of the Step Pyramid (D 12: PM III², 482–83). The false door is now in Cairo, CG 1482. Early fifth dynasty.

Left-hand Text

(1) The chief physician Nyankhsekhmet addressed his majesty:
"How I wish that this *ka* of yours, beloved of Re,
would order that a stone false door be made
(2) for that tomb of mine in the necropolis!"
His majesty had two false doors[28] of Tura stone brought for him,
(3) and they were placed inside the audience hall
called "Sahure appears wearing the White Crown."
The Great Controller of Craftsmen[29] and a (4) workshop of craftsmen
were then set to work on them in the presence of the king himself.
This work was carried out daily,
(5) and the results were apparent every day in the court council.
His majesty arranged for pigment to be placed on them,
and they were decorated in blue.[30]

Right-hand Text

(1) Then his majesty spoke to the chief physician Nyankhsekhmet:
"As I breathe and as the gods love me, may you go to the necropolis
having reached a great age as an *imakhu*!
Adore the king greatly, and thank every god for Sahure,
(3) for he is wise, together with the entire retinue.
Every pronouncement of his majesty is immediately realized.
(4) The god gave him knowledge of things
while he was still in the womb as he is nobler than any god.
Do you love Re?
(5) Then thank every god for Sahure who has done these things."
I am his *imakhu*; I have never done anything evil to anyone.

226. False Door of Ptahshepses from Saqqara

This false door consists of a large lintel and an unusually arranged series of jambs, each consisting of only one vertical column of text. It seems probable *that each column of text dealt with a specific reign; although I identify these kings here more cautiously than did Sethe, it would appear that Ptahshepses lived a long life. I follow the reconstructions of Dorman 2002. From tomb C 1 north of the Step Pyramid (PM III^2, 464). Door now in London, BM EA 682 and Chicago, Oriental Institute OIM 11048. Early to middle fifth dynasty.*

Right of Center of Door

(1) [A child born in] the time of Menkaure,
he grew up among the royal children in the palace of the king,
inside the royal harem.
He was more valuable in the sight of the king than any child.
Ptahshepses.
(2) [A youth who tied the headband[31] in] the time of Shepseskaf,
he grew up among the royal children in the palace of the king,
inside the royal harem.
He was more valuable in the sight of the king than any youth.
Ptahshepses.
(3) … of Userkaf.
His majesty gave him his eldest royal daughter, Khamaat, as his wife,
for his majesty wished that she be with him more than with any other man.
Ptahshepses.
(4) … [the great controller of craftsmen in the two] houses of Sahure,
one more valuable in the sight of the king than any servant;
he embarked on every boat, he did guard duty,
and he entered upon the ways of the southern Palace in every festival [of appearance].
Ptahshepses.

Left of Center of Door

(1) (*reign of Neferirkare?*)
… [he was more valuable in the sight of the king than] any servant,
as keeper of secrets of every task which the king desired to be done.
He who makes perfect the heart of his Lord every day.
Ptahshepses.
(2) (*reign of Shepseskare?*)
… [he was more valuable in the sight of the king than] any servant.
When his majesty favored him because of the things (which he had done),

his majesty allowed him to kiss his foot—
he did not allow him to kiss the ground.
Ptahshepses.
(3) (*reign of Neferefre?*)
... [he was more valuable in the sight of the king than] any servant,
and he embarked on the barque (named) "supporter of the gods"
in every festival of appearance,
the beloved one of his Lord.
Ptahshepses.
(4) (*reign of Niuserre?*)
... [who is] in the heart of his Lord, the beloved one of his Lord,
the *imakhu* of Ptah, who does what his god desires,
who keeps every craftsman sweet in the sight of the king.
Ptahshepses.

227. Inscription of Rewer from Giza

This inscription from the tomb of Rewer in the Central Cemetery (PM III^2, 265–69), one of the largest private tombs at Giza, is one of the most intriguing of the Old Kingdom. It appears that Rewer may have tripped over a staff held by his king, Neferirkare and that the king pronounced over him that everything was well and that this event should be inscribed in his tomb. Either Rewer had to be magically "cleansed" of his unintentional contact with the king, or else the king absolved him in this life and the next for having disrupted the ceremony. Comments on the relationship with the king displayed in this text in Baines 1999b: 23–24; 1997: 138–40. Reign of Neferirkare or later.

Note that Rewer also had a more idealized biography, which is too damaged to be translated here (Hassan 1932–60: I, 15, pl. XII).

(1) The king of Upper and Lower Egypt, Neferirkare,
appeared[32] as the king of Lower Egypt
on the day of taking the prow-rope of the god's boat.[33]
(2) Now the *sem* priest Rewer was at the feet of his majesty
in his noble office (3) of *sem* priest and keeper of ritual equipment.
The *ames* scepter (4) which his majesty was holding
blocked the way of the sem priest Rewer.
His majesty said to him, (5) "Be well!"—thus spoke his majesty.

His majesty said: "it is the desire of my majesty
(6) that he be very well, and that no blow be struck against him."[34]
For indeed he was more valuable (7) in the sight of his majesty than any man.
His majesty then commanded
that it be placed in writing (8) on his tomb of the necropolis,
and his majesty had a (9) document about it made for him,
written in the presence of the king himself,
(10) in the workshop of the Great House,
so that it was written (11) in his tomb of the necropolis
in accordance with what had been [said].

228. Inscriptions of Sabu Ibebi from Saqqara

Sabu was an important official in the Memphite region, as the high priest of Ptah in the time of Unas and Teti. The false door is particularly large and impressive. The phraseology has some parallels with the earlier texts of Ptahshepses (no. 226). Tomb to the north of the Step Pyramid (PM III^2, 460–61); the false door is now in Cairo, CG 1565. Early sixth dynasty.

Entrance Right

(1) The great controller of craftsmen of Unas, one more valuable in the sight of the king than any servant (2) when he embarks on any boat, who does guard duty, [who enters] the ways of [the palace of Upper Egypt in the festivals, (3) Sabu, whose perfect name is Ibebi].

Entrance Left

(1) The *imakhu* in the sight of the king, who does what he favors, who loves his lord, (2) the great controller of craftsmen in the two houses on the day of the festival, the priest of Ptah, the priest of Sokar, (3) Sabu, whose perfect name is Ibebi.

From the False Door

Formulae on the Lintel

(1) An offering which the king gives
and an offering which Osiris gives
that he may travel upon the perfect ways,
that he may be followed by his *ka*s

and be given his document by (his) *ba*,
that he may journey on the ways which are made holy
on which the *imakhu* travel,
that he may ascend (to) the Great God,
(2) lord of the West, lord of the pure places,
among the noble *imakhu* who love the Great God;
(*all this so that he*), an *imakhu,* may be the possessor of a perfect burial in the necropolis,
that invocation offerings may be made for him
in great quantity in the necropolis,
and that he may be very well transfigured
(3) by the lector priest and by the embalmer
in the New Year festival, in the festival of Thoth,
in the first of the year festival, in the *Wag* festival,
in the festival of Sokar, in the great festival, in the *Rekeh* festival,
in the *Sadj* festival, in the festival of the coming forth of Min,
in the monthly and half-monthly festivals,
(4) in the seasonal festivals and the ten-day festivals and daily;
(these offerings are) a thousand of alabaster, a thousand of clothing,
a thousand oryxes, a thousand oxen, a thousand gazelles, a thousand ibex,
a thousand small cattle and all pure things, a thousand *ra* geese,
a thousand *tjerp* geese, a thousand *zet* geese, a thousand *senedj* geese,
a thousand pigeons (5) and all pure fowl, a thousand (jugs) of wine,
a thousand *ished* fruit, a thousand figs, a thousand of all sweet things,
a thousand vegetables and everything daily throughout eternity
for the *imakhu,* (6) (*vertical*) the great controller of craftsmen on the day of the festival, Sabu.

Left

(1) A contemporary of the son of Re, Teti, may he live for ever;
the great controller of craftsmen,
one more valuable in the sight of the king than any servant
as keeper of secrets of all works which the king desires to be done;
he who makes perfect the heart of his lord every day,
the great controller of craftsmen, Sabu.
(2) The great controller of craftsmen, the royal *mehenek,*
keeper of secrets of the king wherever he is,

the *imakhu* in the sight of the king,
great controller of craftsmen in the two houses on the day of the festival,
he who makes all craftsmen sweet,
(3) the *imakhu* in the sight of every sovereign,
who does guard duty for him, he who belongs in the affection of his lord,
who is in the heart of his lord, the beloved one of his lord,
the *imakhu* of Ptah, who does what his god desires daily in the sight of the king.

Right

(1) A contemporary of the son of Re, Teti, may he live for ever;
the great controller of craftsmen,
one more valuable in the sight of the king than any servant
when he goes down to any boat, who does guard duty,
who enters onto the ways of the palace of Upper Egypt in every festival of appearances,
the great controller of craftsmen in the two houses on the day of the festival, Sabu.
(2) Then his majesty favored me, and he had me enter the Residence,
and he placed attendant youths in every place where I went.
Never was the like done for any servant or equal by any sovereign,
(3) because his majesty loves me more than any servant,
because I do what he favors every day,
because my state of *imakhu* exists in his heart.
I am excellent in the sight of his majesty
as I find the way into all the secrets of the Residence,
and I am a noble one in the sight of his majesty.

On Both Inner Jambs

(1) An offering which the king gives and an offering which Anubis gives
that invocation offerings go forth for him from the two granaries,
from the two treasuries, from the two chambers of the royal ornament,
(2) from the house of supplying provisions,
from every place of the Residence from which invocation offerings should come forth.

(3) The *imakhu* in the sight of Osiris, great controller of craftsmen in the two houses on the day of the festival (in) the palace, priest of Ptah, Sabu.

229. Inscriptions of Sabu Tjeti from Saqqara

These broken but intriguing texts are from the surviving parts of his false door from tomb E 3 to the north of the Step Pyramid (PM III², 463), close to that of Sabu Ibebi (no. 228). Parts now in Cairo, CG 1709, 1756. Reign of Pepy I or later.

Middle Jamb

(1) … before. A contemporary of his majesty,
his majesty promoted me to be (2) [the great controller of craftsmen, I alone] …
… the temple of Ptah south of his wall, wherever he is, was under my control.
Indeed never had (3) [a great controller of craftsmen been in this position on his own[35] since antiquity] …
… Sokar in his *shet* sanctuary, all property of the god and every duty
which two great controllers of craftsmen would have done/do regularly.

Right Jamb

(1) … Indeed never was the like done for any great controller of craftsmen
in the lifetime (2) [of any ruler] …
… for the *ges-per* of the temple
in accordance with the wishes of his majesty.
His majesty promoted me
(3) … workers (?) under my charge,
while their offices were like those of their (4) noble fathers …
… workers (?) under my charge, that which was to be done in all the land,
while the heart of his majesty was stronger than anything which was to be done there.

230. Inscriptions from the Tomb of Sankhuptah Called Nyhetepptah at Saqqara

Tomb in the Teti pyramid cemetery, behind the tomb of Kaigemni. Reign of Teti to Pepy I.

Facade, West of Entrance

Priest and *khenty-she* of the pyramid of Teti, sole companion, lector priest, great censer, keeper of secrets of magic, Nyhetepptah.

Nyhetepptah speaks:
(1) I was a youth [*perhaps* "in the time of king X"]
(2) on all her/its ways, (3) in every place of heaven
(4) in her/its canals, in her/its wells, (5) in all the ways
(6) and everything beneficent and excellent in the sight of the Great God.
(7) The sole companion, lector priest, (8) [Sankhuptah].

Facade, East of Entrance

Priest and *khenty-she* of the pyramid of Teti, sole companion, lector priest, great censer, great physician, Sankhuptah.

Nyhetepptah speaks:
(1) I am a well-prepared *akh*; I am/was …
[With regard to any man (?)]
(2) who shall [not (?)] enter herein being pure
(3) as he should be pure when entering the tomb (4) of an excellent *akh*,
he shall not possess his *ka*,
(5) he shall not be perfect in the sight of the god,
(6) he shall not be buried in the necropolis.
(7) The sole companion, great physician, (8) [Sankhuptah].

231. Inscriptions of Sekhemankhptah from Giza

Tomb G 7152 in the Eastern Cemetery (PM III^2, 191). Mid fifth dynasty.

Central Recess of False Door

(1) [… I came from] my town, I came forth into the afterlife,
I went down into this tomb of mine;
I (always) spoke Maat, and I carried out Maat which the god loves, and I judged (well).
The first under the king, Sekhemankhptah.
(2) […] strong man at the correct place.
I did not allow that a noble take for himself the property of a poor man.
I made this tomb with the aim of being *imakhu*,
for I had done what is right.
The sole companion, Sekhemankhptah.

232. Texts from the Mastaba of Senedjemib Inti at Giza

The inscriptions of Senedjemib are some of the most extensive from the Memphite necropolis and are composed of a mixture of biographical texts with unusual features and letters from the king. They are perhaps somewhat "literary" in nature and shed light on the interplay between the king and his highest officials (Baines 1997: 141–42; compare introduction §6.5.3). The tomb (G 2370, PM III², 85–87) is just to the northwest of the Great Pyramid and dates to the reign of Izezi.

i. Principal Biographical Texts (Numbers of Brovarski)

Reconstructions are not usually marked—see Brovarski 2001 for more detail.

A1.

(1) The *iry pat, haty-a,* vizier, overseer of royal document scribes, (2) overseer of all works of the king, overseer of the six Great Mansions, (3) overseer of the two granaries, overseer of the two treasuries, (4) overseer of the two chambers of the royal ornament, overseer of the armory, (5) overseer of every office of the Residence, overseer of the royal children.

(6) (I have spent) five years, four months, and three days now under Izezi.
(7) During (this) time I have been more valuable in the sight of Izezi
than any like me in my capacity as keeper of secrets of his majesty
and as one who is in the heart of his majesty in every matter
(8) which his majesty is desirous of doing.
During (this) time his majesty was praising me
concerning all the works which his majesty has ordered to be done,
as I always acted in accordance with the wishes of his majesty
concerning these things.
(9) Izezi gave me a necklace of malachite (?)
(*perhaps*) through the greatness of favor of (?) his majesty
when he was in the document office,
when it happened that (10) I was in attendance in the grounds (of the palace).
His majesty had it tied upon my neck …
and his majesty saw to it that I was anointed with unguent
(11) and that my skin was cleansed in the presence of his majesty

by an inspector of hairdressers of the Great House,
a chief of Nekheb and the keeper of the diadem.
Never had the like been done in the presence of the king for any man,
(12) for I was more valuable, excellent and beloved
in the sight of Izezi than any like me.
(13) Izezi made for me a decree
which his majesty wrote with his own hand in order to favor me
(14) for everything which I had done nobly, perfectly and excellently
in relation to his majesty's wish concerning it.

A2.

(1) A royal decree to the vizier, overseer of royal document scribes, (2) overseer of all works of the king, Senedjemib.

(3) My majesty has seen this letter of yours which you wrote
to let my majesty know everything which you have done
in relation to the setting out and the inscriptions/decoration
(4) of the *meret* temple of Izezi in the precinct[36] of the Great House.
Have I been correctly informed?
Do not let it be said that it is a case of (just) (5) gratifying Izezi!
Let my majesty know the truth about it immediately!
And if it is (yet) to happen,
you are one (6) who speaks what Izezi desires
more than any noble who has come into being in this land.
(7) I know that you are highly important to me,
since my majesty is aware that every ship should be on an even keel;
the speech of the overseer of all works of the king (8) is pleasing to me,
(for) truly it informs Izezi.
If only you could come to me
as you always deal with these things (9) so very well.
You have acted (on my behalf [?]) on millions of occasions
so that my majesty should love you, and assuredly I do love you.

B1.

(1) A royal decree (2) to the vizier, (3) overseer of royal document scribes, (4) overseer of all works of the king, (5) Senedjemib the elder.

(6) Note has been taken of this letter of yours
which you prepared for the king at the council chamber
in order to let my majesty know
that a royal decree has been brought to you regarding …

and you it is who speaks to my majesty
that you shall work on the precinct
in accordance with what was said to you in the court council …
(7) … work in the court council in your absence,
and now you are saying to my majesty that you are going to …
the *Sed* festival.
Now my majesty desires to hear these words of yours very much …
(8) … I will not cause you trouble;
the *ka* of Izezi will not put you into the arms of your foe …
You it is to whom my majesty commits everything which my majesty announces,
since the overseer of all works of the king is mentioned
(9) as soon as a work project is looked at in the court council.
For you are …
on account of the vigilance which he has carried through night as day
so as to carry out everything which (10) my majesty ordered therein daily.
(11) Because he has given you to me is why I know that Re loves me.

B2.

(1) A royal decree to the vizier, overseer of all works of the king, (2) overseer of royal document scribes, Senedjemib the elder.

(3) My majesty has seen this ground plan
which you have had brought for consideration in the court council
for the precinct of the broad court
(4) of the palace "it belongs to the *Sed* festival of Izezi."
Now you say to my majesty
that you have planned it as (5) 1,000 cubits long and 440 cubits wide,
in accordance with what was said to you in the court council.
How (well) you know how to say what Izezi desires above all else!
(6) Surely the god made you (just) for the joy of Izezi!
My majesty is aware that you are more skilled
than any overseer of works (7) who has come into being in this whole land.
A great deal has been done through you
so that what I desire above all else might be done.
You have indeed acted as (8) controller millions of times
and you shall be the overseer of all works of the king.
(9) O Senedjemib the elder,
I do love you and it is known that I love you.

(10) Year of the sixteenth occasion, fourth month of the *Shemu* season, day 28.

C.

(1) The *iry pat,* true *haty-a,* overseer of all works of the king, (2) sole companion, first under the king, royal master builder in the two houses, (3) Senedjemib Mehi, speaks:

I made this (4) for my father the vizier, overseer of all works of (5) the king, overseer of document scribes of the king, overseer of the two treasuries, overseer of the royal ornament, overseer (6) of the two granaries, Senedjemib.

The next seven columns are too damaged to translate, although they end with the words "in the court council."

(14) A document was made for him therein.
The majesty of my lord commanded that there be made (15) decrees
to assemble together the officials and six crews
who are (concerned) with the apportionment of the divine offerings of "the Wall"[37]
(16) so that there might be set up for him a share of the duty
which my father claimed formerly, once the harvest had been brought,
from the apportionment of the divine offerings
in Lower Egypt and Upper Egypt, (namely) the share of the duty
(17) … (18) …
(19) … the pyramid of Izezi concerning it
(20) … this soul chapel which I made
(21) … which is beneficial to him in every respect
(22) as he had a document for these towns/estates[38]
so that it might be done (23) anew for him today.
His majesty has had decrees sealed on this matter with the document seal.
(24) He set up soul priests;
I had (*the decrees*) put in writing (25) in outline upon this his tomb,
and they were cut out by the sculptor.
(26) The instructions in them were recited to me directly
according to the decisions of the court council.
Then I begged (27) from my lord
that a sarcophagus from Tura be brought for him (28) for this his tomb.
I acted on his behalf for one year and three months

when he was in the embalmers' workshop (29) in his funerary estate
which is in (the necropolis of) the pyramid of Izezi.

D. (Accompanied by a Depiction of a Boat with the Sarcophagus)

(1) I begged from my lord
that a sarcophagus be brought for him (2) from Tura;
the majesty of my lord had an overseer of the expedition
and an overseer of officials cross (the river)
with the specific aim of bringing back this sarcophagus from Tura
in a great cargo vessel of the Residence.
(3) … The overseer of the expedition and the overseer of officials (4) crossed over.
Everything was done (5–6) for these troops
(7) as had been ordered (8) in the Residence.
(9) … this sarcophagus and its lid were brought from Tura
right to the town of the pyramid of Khufu (10) and placed in his tomb,
having been ferried over from Tura
(11) and placed on its allocated place[39] (12–13) in five days (14) of transit.
(15) His majesty made decrees (16) relating to them
so that they are favored (17) above all else,
while they were making (18) letters daily to let (19) his majesty know
that this sarcophagus (20) was on its way
so that it might rest in its (allocated) place.

ii. Inscription on the North Side of the Portico

Probably a speech of Senedjemib Mehi.

(1) [The majesty of my lord had produced for me] every secret requirement
which I had requested for my father the true vizier (2) [Senedjemib], …
as he was more valuable in the sight of the king than any (other) of his nobles,
(3) as he was more important [in his sight than any of his great ones] …
(4) … I was excellent in the sight of the majesty of my lord
so that I was listened to on every matter.
Then [his majesty] said …
(5) … [the true *haty-a* and] overseer of all works of the king, Senedjemib.

iii. On a Thickness of a Doorway; Son before His Father

(1) … drawn as an outline
(2) … which is done for a great noble
(3) … the *imakhu* in the sight of every god, he for whom his son shall do the like Senedjemib (Mehi).

233. Texts from the False Door of Seshemu at Giza

Tomb in the Central Cemetery (PM III², 260). Sixth dynasty.

Below Panel

(1) The *imakhu* in the sight of Osiris, the *imakhu* in the sight of the Great God, (2) the royal acquaintance of the Great House, overseer of the office of the harem, keeper of secrets, (3) Seshemu.

Left Outer

[An offering which the king and which] Anubis [give]
that invocation offerings may be made for him
in the festival of the opening of the
the first day of the year festival, the festival of Thoth,
the *Wag* festival, and every daily festival.
Seshemu.

Left Inner

(1) An offering which Anubis gives
that he may join the land at the perfect West as an *imakhu*;
(2) the *imakhu* in the sight of the king and the officials.
(3) Seshemu.

Right Outer

[I have gone forth from] my house,
I have gone down from my town,
I carried out Maat which the god loves;
I never did an evil thing to anyone.
Seshemu.

Right Inner

(1) An offering which Osiris gives
that he may travel doubly in peace upon the (2) perfect
on which the *imakhu* travel in t he sight of the Great God.
(3) Seshemu.

234. Inscriptions of Seshemnefer IV and His Son Ptahhotep from Giza

The owner is usually called Seshemnefer IV to distinguish him from others (unrelated) of the same name. His tomb is part of a family complex at the southwest corner of the Great Pyramid (PM III², 223–28), including chapels for his son Ptahhotep and a woman Hetepheres (no. 292). Ptahhotep employed an almost identical ideal biography to his father's; he placed it on the inner jambs of his false door, while on his father's door it was on the central niche. Included here is a small fragment of biography that seems to relate to Seshemnefer IV and one that may relate to Ptahhotep. Late fifth and early sixth dynasties.

Extract from the False Doors (Seshemnefer a, Ptahhotep a)

(1) I came from my town, I came forth into the afterlife,
and I have been buried in this tomb of mine.
I (always) spoke what was right
which is what the god loves every day.
(2) It is a good thing.
I always used to say in the presence of the king
that which was good for men;
I never said anything evil against any person
in the presence of the majesty of my lord.

Fragment of Biographical Text (Seshemnefer b)

(1) … when I was ill in my office
(2) [(*perhaps*) the news was taken to the king,[40] who caused doctors to come …]
and I was soon cured and was back in the Residence …

Two Fragments of a Biographical Text Perhaps from the Tomb (Ptahhotep b)

(*larger block*) … the pyramid of [Teti]
… carrying out work therein
… every … more than any of his nobles
(*smaller block*) … more valuable in his sight than any of his nobles

235. Inscriptions of Washptah from Saqqara

The biographical inscriptions of Washptah are, along with those of Debehen, Nyankhsekhmet and Rewer, the earliest of the genre from the Old Kingdom. They show the beginning of the narrative genre of this type of text and the already clearly stylized interplay between officials and the king (Baines 1999b: 23–24; 1997: 138–40). This very broken inscription shows that Washptah was probably taken ill in the presence of the king, and describes the favor the king showed to him as a result of this unusual event. Many of the reconstructions are guesswork. The tomb was located north of the Step Pyramid; the inscriptions translated here are now in Cairo (CG 1569, 1570, 1674, 1702, JE 55937) and Aberdeen (1560, 1558a–c). Reign of Neferirkare.

A. Right Side of Entrance Doorway

(1) His eldest son it was who acted on his behalf,
the first under the king, staff of the *rekhyt,* Nesutmerynetjer,
when he was in his tomb of the necropolis.
(2) … [in] *Setibre* when Neferirkare was inspecting its perfection
(3) … [in every] secret [matter]. Now then he went forth upon them
(4) … he fell. His majesty had people support him
(5) … an emergency treatment (?) [was brought to him].
Now, the royal children saw
(6) … and when they saw they trembled with fear.
(7) … were at the emergency treatment (?).
Now then his majesty favored him because of it,
as when his majesty saw him lying on (*literally* kissing) the ground
(8) … [he said to him] … "Do not kiss the ground, kiss my foot."
When the royal children and companions who were in the court council heard
they trembled with fear.

B. Right Side of Facade

(1) … [Now when peace had returned to the] Residence,
his majesty had the royal children, the companions,
lector priests and physicians come along,
(2) … and they said to his majesty [to bring texts (?)] …
Then his majesty had the chest of writings brought

(3) … illness (?)[41] …
They said to his majesty that he had lost consciousness[42]
(4) … [then his majesty] prayed to Re on the *she* structure[43]
… above all else.
His majesty said "He did everything above all in accordance with my wishes
whenever he came to the Residence."
(5) … immediately, without anything like this having happened before
… and he prayed to Re
(6) … in the heart of his majesty thereby above all else.
… [*perhaps* His majesty ordered that it be placed] in writing on his tomb
(7) … and there were filled for him eight vessels of alabaster
[with sacred oils (?) and placed in] a sealed box of ebony.
Never (8) [was the like done for (?)] any man since the beginning of the world.
It was said … which were placed on him.
(9) … [His majesty placed a life-giving amulet (?)] on his nose,
for it was desired that this (tomb) be made for him above [all else]
… those … which were filled … [with (?) …]
(10) … in the *ra-she* of the Great House,
and the hairdressers [prepared his body (?)]
and his majesty had him anointed in the presence of his majesty.

C. Left Side of Entrance Doorway

(1) His eldest son it was who acted on his behalf,
the first under the king, staff of the *rekhyt,* Nesutmerynetjer,
when [he was in his tomb of the necropolis].
(2) … [His majesty had] made for him a carrying chair
(3) … [and arranged for] ten men to carry him in it as a gift (?). When
(4) … inside the Great House. When he was put down on the ground in it
(5) … guard his majesty (?). Then he ordered that he go
(6) … [*some title*], the royal nobles and all the troops in the Residence
(7) … [*a pyramid, perhaps that of* Sahure]. Then his majesty commanded an *iry pat* that it be placed in writing upon [his tomb] …
(8) … his majesty; his majesty was praising him for it
and he prayed to the god (*gave thanks* [?]) very greatly indeed …

Below text: the vizier, sole companion, keeper of the diadem, lector priest, overseer of the embalming workshop, who is in the heart of his lord, Washptah.

D. Left Side of Facade

(1) … of white limestone in the area of the *she* structure of eternity
which is in the area of the pyramid of Sahure …
(2) … he had 200 pieces of royal linen brought
from the *she* of the Great House.
Then his majesty had …
(3) … their … of flowers. Then his majesty had …
(4) … the *tjezet* chests of the duration (of the existence) of the booth of purification[44]
along with the needs of the [skills of the lector priest][45] …
(5) … His majesty had it done for him
(6) … king. Never was the like done for any dignitary before.
(7) … Then his majesty sat down to eat
(8) … and he had given to him foodstuffs from everything
which had been brought in the majesty of the court council.
Then [he] said …
(9) … that was given to Washptah;
when his majesty placed an *ankh* amulet (?) on his nose (?)
(10) … the royal children and companions
who were in the court council were very joyful.

Below text: the overseer of all works of the king, chief lector priest, scribe of the divine documents, elder of the *senut* shrine, Washptah.

236. A Fragment of a Biography from West of the Step Pyramid at Saqqara

Probably sixth dynasty.

(1) … the majesty of my lord … me on this matter.
I carried out (matters) in such a way
that (2) my lord favored me on account of it,
as I was more excellent in the sight of his lord than any of my peers.
His majesty used to give gold to me
due to the greatness of his favor for me,
the controller … of the Great House …

237. Anonymous Biographical Fragment of the Reign of Teti from Saqqara

Fischer 1975: 33 associates this with the style of the block of Khenu no. 218 from the Unas causeway. Exact provenance unknown. Now in Cairo, CG 1433. Perhaps early sixth dynasty.

(1) … I acted so that his majesty favored me [greatly] on account of it …
(2) … [His majesty had] me enter the Residence and I did guard duty for the sovereign …
(3) … His majesty had the companion Rewer go forth and thank [the god on this matter] …
(4) … A contemporary of Teti, my lord, [may he live for ever] …
(5) … His majesty sent me to control the works in his soul chapel and in Tura …
(6) … I made a gateway there while I was controlling works …
(7) … West …
(8) … the estates and new towns of [the pyramid of Teti] …
(9) … barley and emmer … His majesty had me travel north …
(10) … clothing and every priestly duty of …
(11) … traveled to the Residence …

238. Block Found near the Pyramid of Teti at Saqqara

Found in excavations in the 1920s (PM III², 547); present location unknown. Mid sixth dynasty.

(1) An offering which the king gives and which Anubis, who is on his mountain … [gives] …
(2) for the *imakhu* in the sight of the Great God …
[He speaks:]
(3) In the time of [*probably* Teti] I entered into (service in) the Residence.
I acted … (4) under Meryre (*Pepy I*), and I served as lector priest under Merenre …

(5) The *imakhu* in the sight of Ptah, the first under the king of the Great House …

[With regard to] any man who shall take stone from this tomb, or who shall enter not in a pure state …

239. Block from Giza

This text says very little but is one of the few inscriptions that can almost certainly be dated to the reign of Khufu (Horus and Nebty names Medjedu). Found west of the Great Pyramid; now Turin 1853 (PM III², 177). Early fourth dynasty. The translation assumes, quite possibly incorrectly, that there was nothing below the surviving ends of columns 2 and 3, which cannot be proven.

(1) The Two Ladies, Medjedu …

(3) In this town of my lord (2) did I make this tomb of mine …

240. Text of an Unnamed Person from Giza

This text from the Western Cemetery (PM III², 179), although fragmentary, tells of a rather unusual event in the life of an official, whereby the king helped him in the execution of his duties. An unexpected intervention by the king is often the subject of all or part of a biographical text of the fifth dynasty; see, for example, the texts of Rewer (no. 227) and Washptah (no. 235).

Line at Top

(1) *Only the cartouche of Khufu remains; it seems probable that this was part of a title, such as* "priest of Khufu" *or* "*(holder of some office)* at the pyramid of Khufu"*; that it is a name is improbable.*

Main Text

(2) Now with regard to the period when he was ill,

his majesty had brought for him a carrying chair from the Residence

(3) so that he might supervise from it the work for which he was responsible.

His majesty also had set up for him an escort

(4) of (men of) the Residence
who would accompany him when he entered the Residence (?).
(5) When he was in the *ra-she* the followers …
(6) of the Great Mansion … cause to enter …
(7) … of the Great House people (?) with his son …
(8) … place where it happened …
(9) …

Notes

1. The "broad collar" (*weskhet*) is that which is seen commonly in Old Kingdom and later tombs; a form of it is worn by Akhethotep in this scene. The nature of the other items of jewellery is rather less clear. It is intriguing to note that the excavations in his tomb at Saqqara produced at least one unusual object, which it is tempting to relate to this text (Christiane Ziegler, paper at 2004 conference "Old Kingdom Art and Archaeology"). See Andrews 1990 for an introduction to Egyptian jewellery.

2. For the titles, compare Strudwick 1982. Kloth 2002: 4, 22 is of the opinion that text A was inscribed by Nebkauhor and text B by Akhethotep.

3. It is not clear whether the "never" at the top of this section of text applies to this last column also. Goedicke translates it as nonnegative.

4. Roccati suggests a reconstruction in this gap along the lines of "about anyone, in line with my state of *imakhu* with the god."

5. For an example see no. 13.

6. A guess.

7. El-Qusiya in Middle Egypt. See biography of Pepyankhheryib (no. 270).

8. At this point the text changes from sunk to raised relief, perhaps indicating two phases of decoration and sense or two different craftsmen.

9. The form is rather unusual—could the scribe have really been attempting a past tense in the formula?

10. Almost certainly the vizier Mehu and not the king.

11. Following Edel 1955–64: 442 against Urk I.

12. The principal title of the high priest of Ptah at Memphis. It refers to the ancient association of Ptah, the god of Memphis, with craftsmen and creation. This example of its use, one of the earliest, shows that a close association still existed between the religious and craft role of this office. See on the title, Maystre 1992 (alternative view in Freier 1976). Compare also the biographies of Nyankhsekhmet and Ptahshepses (nos. 225 and 226).

13. Men with this title are frequently seen in expedition inscriptions (see below chapter VI); this mention of these men would tie in with the mention of quarries a little later on.

14. See Fischer 1963: 27.

15. The names of the owner have been erased on this lintel.

16. Whether this means every official received offices personally from the king

is otherwise unknown but is doubtless highly plausible (at least above a certain level).

17. "Guard duty" refers to attendance on the king, in this context presumably when the king was either traveling or taking part in a specific ritual; "come to the ways" is unclear, but the gifts are clearly those for loyal service.

18. For this unusual epithet, see Fischer 2001: 45–47.

19. It is relatively unusual for a new offering formula to start in the middle of a line of text; they usually begin at the start of a line or column. The line here is particularly long.

20. Schott 1979: 450 makes the interesting restoration that this lacuna might have referred to a letter or decree being made out for Kaiemtjennet. See introduction §6.12 for a brief consideration of royal letter-writing at this time.

21. See no. 100.

22. Compare the linen lists below nos. 329 and 330.

23. Edel 1953a: 213–17 makes an argument for translating this word as "honored" or something like it; I have followed the more conventional translation (compare Brovarski 2001: 91 note e).

24. Almost certainly the person of the king.

25. It is also possible to suggest for this "through the excellence of my state of."

26. A guess; compare, for example, the texts of Mehu (no. 220).

27. It is rather unusual for an Old Kingdom Egyptian to have three names.

28. There was, as far as is known, only one place for a false door in the tomb; Baines 1997: 136 suggests that this may be hyperbole based on the idea of the king always having to give more than requested.

29. See n. 12 in the biography of Debehen (no. 200).

30. The false door as it is now has few traces of the colors left; the faces of the male figures show remains of red; the reed and basket hieroglyphs show traces of green, and the only obvious blue in September 2002 was on the hieroglyph for a swallow. Kloth 2002: 213 n. 922 suggests it means that the sunk parts of the decoration were done in this manner as were apparently the Washptah inscriptions (no. 235); she translates this word as "lapis-lazuli."

31. A certain stage in growing up and in the passage toward manhood.

32. See n. 5 on the Palermo Stone (no. 1).

33. The nature of the ceremony being conducted here is not at all clear; it might be a solar ritual or perhaps a festival like the *Sed* festival. See the discussion in Allen 1992: 16.

34. This is a crucial phrase, as it has also been translated along the lines of "I did not strike him," which is interpreted as the king attempting to counteract any ill effects of being hit by the power immanent in his scepter and himself. Allen's translation, followed here, suggests that Rewer not be punished for what had happened.

35. The office of the high priest of Ptah seems to have been mostly split between two men, as shown in the texts of Nyankhsekhmet (no. 225) and Debehen (no. 200). Thus something unusual and noteworthy was happening here, assuming Sethe's reconstructions to be correct. See Maystre 1992: 51–60.

36. For the complex meaning of the word *she*, which can also mean "pool" and the like, see Brovarski 2001: 97–98.

37. Probably a circumlocution for the "White Walls" of Memphis; Brovarski 2001: 103 (h).

38. Presumably those that supply the income referred to in the "duty" and "divine offerings."

39. I have varied from Brovarski 2001: 108-9, n i. here, wondering if the word he translates "bed" should be associated with the similar verb *ḥnq,* meaning "donate," "allocate," and cognates (Wb III:117 ff.).

40. Some sort of association with the king must have been intended, as otherwise a text simply about being ill would not have appeared in the tomb. Compare the inscription of Washptah (no. 235).

41. A word here [illegible] is left untranslated in all versions. I have no suggestion to offer unless it is an early example of the medical condition noted in Wb I:11.2. This might perhaps fit the context.

42. Probably meaning that he died.

43. A part of the economic area of palaces or temples; see Posener-Kriéger 1976: 616–19.

44. See captions in the tomb of Qar (no. 313).

45. Following Brovarski 1977: 111.

XVII

Biographical Texts from the Provinces

See notes in chapter I, §6.5.3. The majority of texts presented here from outside the area of the capital city of Memphis come from Upper Egypt, although there are a handful from Lower Egypt and the oasis of Dakhla. The texts from each province are listed in south to north order by nome, ending with Dakhla oasis. For each site, only specific studies relating to Old Kingdom material are mentioned. For more general considerations of the areas in the Old Kingdom, see, for example, Martin-Pardey 1976 and Kanawati 1980.

Texts from the following Upper Egyptian nomes are translated in this book: 1. Elephantine; 2. Edfu; 3. Moalla; 5. Koptos, Kom el-Koffar; 6. Dendera; 7. el-Qasr wa es-Sayed; 8. Abydos, Sheikh Farag; 9. el-Hawawish, Hagarsa; 12. Deir el-Gebrawi; 14. Meir; 16. Tehna; 20/21. Deshasha.

There are a number of other Upper Egyptian nome sites with Old Kingdom tombs containing texts that are mostly brief and not translated here. These include: 3. el-Kab (Quibell 1898); 4. Thebes (Saleh 1977; note also two uninscribed mastabas dated to the fourth dynasty [Arnold 1976: 11–18]); 10. el-Hammamiya (el-Khouli and Kanawati 1990); 14. Quseir el-Amarna (el-Khouly and Kanawati 1989); 15. Sheikh Said (Davies 1901); 16. Zawiyet el-Meitin: (LD II: 105–11; Varille 1938); 18. Kom el-Ahmar Sawaris (Brodrick and Morton 1899).

Upper Egypt—Nome 1

The rock tombs at Qubbet el-Hawa on the west bank at Aswan are one of the most interesting groups of provincial tombs of the Old Kingdom. Their owners were mostly expedition leaders who supervised much of the trade and interaction with the African lands south of the First Cataract, and aspects of their exploits are frequently given in their tombs. There is extensive bibliography on the geopolitical background and the identity of the countries mentioned in these texts, for example, O'Connor 1986; 1991 (with further references).

There are also remains of a cemetery on the island of Elephantine itself, probably earlier than that at Qubbet el-Hawa (Seidlmayer and Ziermann 1992).

241. Texts on the Facade of the Tomb of Harkhuf at Qubbet el-Hawa

This is one of the two most famous biographical texts of the Old Kingdom (the other is Weni, no. 256). It shows clearly the sorts of duties expected of the leaders of Aswan and also sheds some light on the political situation in the lands to the south; from the enumeration of the lands in the different journeys some cautious deductions can be made as to geopolitical changes in the lifetime of one man. Middle sixth dynasty.

Over the Entrance

(1) An offering which the king gives and an offering which Anubis,
who is on his mountain, who dwells in the divine tent-shrine,
who is in his wrappings, the lord of the sacred land gives
that he might be buried in the necropolis of the western desert,
having grown old most perfectly
as an *imakhu* in the sight of the Great God.
... the Great God

The *haty-a*, overseer of Upper Egypt, seal-bearer of the king of Lower Egypt, sole companion, lector priest, overseer of foreigners, the *imakhu* in the sight of Ptah-Sokar, Harkhuf.

(2) An offering which the king gives
and an offering which Osiris, lord of Busiris, gives
that he may travel in peace
on the holy ways of the West upon which the *imakhu* travel,
and that he may ascend to the god, the lord of the sky,
as an *imakhu* in the sight of [the Great God (?)].

The *haty-a*, he who is in the chamber, herdsman of Nekhen, chief of Nekheb, sole companion, lector priest, *imakhu* in the sight of Osiris, Harkhuf.

(3) An offering which the king gives
that invocation offerings may be made for him in the necropolis,

and that he may be transfigured by the lector priest
in the beginning of the year festival, in the festival of Thoth,
in the first of the year festival, in the *Wag* festival,
in the festival of Sokar, in the great festival,
and in every daily festival …

for the seal-bearer of the king of Lower Egypt, sole companion, lector priest, overseer of foreigners, Harkhuf.

(4) Today I came from my town, I went down into the afterlife,
I have built my house and set up doors,
I have dug my pool, I have planted trees.
The king has favored me, and my father has made a will for me.
I am an excellent person … ,
beloved of my father and favored of my mother,
whom all his siblings always loved.
(5) I gave bread to the hungry, clothes to the naked,
and I brought to land him who had no boat.
O you who live on earth who shall come across this tomb of mine
when traveling north or south, if you shall say:
"a thousand of bread and a thousand of beer
(6) for the owner of this tomb,"
then I shall watch over them in the necropolis.
For I am an excellent and well-equipped *akh*,
a lector priest who knows his spells.
With regard to any man who shall enter this my tomb in an impure state,
I shall seize his neck like a bird's,
and he shall be judged for it by the Great God.
(7) I am a speaker of perfection and a repeater of what is desired.
I never said anything evil to any great one against any man,
because I wish my name to be perfect in the sight of the Great God.
I never judged between two parties …
in the case where a son was deprived of his father's inheritance.
(8) An offering which the king gives and an offering which Anubis,
who is on his mountain, who dwells in the divine tent-shrine, gives
that invocation offerings may be made for him in the necropolis,
for the *imakhu* in the sight of Anubis, who is on his mountain,
who dwells in the divine tent-shrine, …
the *haty-a*, lector priest … , sole companion, lector priest,
overseer of foreigners, the *imakhu*, Harkhuf.

Texts to the Right of the Entrance

(1) The *haty-a*, sole companion, lector priest, the one who is in the chamber, herdsman of Nekhen, chief of Nekheb, seal-bearer of the king of Lower Egypt, sole companion, lector priest, overseer of foreigners, he who is in charge of all matters of the Head of Upper Egypt,[1] who is in the heart of his lord, Harkhuf.

(2) The seal-bearer of the king of Lower Egypt, sole companion, lector priest, overseer of foreigners, he who brings the products of all foreign lands to his lord, who brings tribute to the royal ornament,[2] overseer of all foreign lands of the Head of Upper Egypt, who places the fear (3) of Horus in the foreign lands, who does what his lord favors, seal-bearer of the king of Lower Egypt, sole companion, lector priest, overseer of foreigners, the *imakhu* in the sight of Ptah-Sokar, Harkhuf.

(4) He speaks:

The majesty of (King) Merenre, my lord, sent me
together with my father, the sole companion, lector priest, Iri,
to Iam to open up the way to this foreign land.
(5) I made the trip in seven months,
and I brought back all sorts of perfect and luxury items of tribute therefrom;
I was favored very highly for it.
His majesty sent me a second time, (6) only this time on my own.
I took the Elephant[3] road,
and went out via Irtjet, Mekher, Tereres and Iertjetj
in the space of eight months.
I returned (7) having brought great amounts of tribute
from those foreign lands,
(8) the likes of which had never before been brought back to this land.
I returned in the region of the house of the ruler of the lands of Setjau and Irtjet,
(9) after having explored those foreign lands.
I have not discovered that this was done
by any companion and overseer of foreigners
who went previously to Iam.
(10) His majesty sent me a third time to Iam.
(11) I went out from the Thinite nome upon the oasis road,
and I found that the ruler of Iam (12) had gone away to the land of the Tjemehu

to drive them off (13) to the western corner of the sky.
I followed him to the land of the Tjemehu.
(14) I satisfied him just so that he might praise all the gods for the sovereign.[4]

[text continues to the left of the entrance]

(1) [Then I sent off an official with a man of] Iam to the retinue of Horus (*the royal court*)
to let the majesty of Merenre, my lord, know
(2) that [I had gone to the land of the Tjemehu] in pursuit of the ruler of Iam.
When I had satisfied that ruler of Iam,
(3) [I came down through ...] south of Irtjet and north of Setjau,
and I found the ruler (4) who had united Irtjet, Setjau and Wawat;[5]
With three hundred donkeys loaded with incense, ebony, *heknu* oil,
shesat,[6] (5) panther skins, elephant tusks, throw-sticks,
and all sorts of wonderful products did I travel.
When the ruler of Irtjet, Setjau and (6) Wawat saw
the strength and the number of the troop-contingent of Iam
which was coming along with me to the Residence,
as well as (my own) expedition which was traveling with me,
(7) this ruler then accompanied me, gave me cattle and goats,
and led me on the hill-paths of Irtjet,
due to the excellent manner in which I (8) had exercised vigilance,
more so than any companion or overseer of foreigners
who had previously been sent to Yam.
Now when this servant had traveled north to the Residence,
(9) the *haty-a,* sole companion, overseer of the two cool rooms Khuni
was sent to greet me with ships laden with date-wine, cakes, bread, and beer.

(10) The *haty-a,* seal-bearer of the king of Lower Egypt, sole companion, lector priest, seal-bearer of the god,[7] keeper of secrets of what has been commanded, the *imakhu* Harkhuf.

Letter from Pepy II to Harkhuf

(1) The king's own seal, year of the second occasion, third month of the *Akhet* season, day 15:
(2) a royal decree for the sole companion, lector priest and overseer of foreigners Harkhuf.

(3) Note has been taken of the content of this letter of yours
which you composed for the attention of the king at the palace,
to let it be known that you have come back successfully
(4) from Iam with the expedition which was with you.
What you have said in this letter of yours
is that you have brought back (5) all sorts of great and wonderful tribute
which Hathor, mistress of Imaau, has given to the *ka* of
(6) the king of Upper and Lower Egypt Neferkare,
may he live for ever and for eternity.
What you have (also) said in this letter of yours
is that you have brought back a pygmy who dances (7) for the god
from the land of the Horizon-dwellers,
just like the pygmy which (8) the seal-bearer of the god Werdjededba
brought back from the land of Punt in the time of Izezi.
What you have said to my majesty
is that (9) his like has never been brought back by another who did[8] Iam before.
How indeed you know (10) how to do what your lord loves and praises,
for you spend day and night thinking of how to do (11) what your lord loves and praises!
His majesty shall fulfil your (12) many excellent wishes
to benefit the son of your son for eternity,
so that everyone (13) who hears what my majesty has done for you shall say
"Was there ever the like of what was done
for the sole companion, Harkhuf (14) when he came back from Iam,
because of the concern he paid to doing what his lord (15) loves, favors and commands?."
Come north to the Residence straightaway!
Cast (everything else) aside,
bring with you (16) this pygmy who is in your charge,
whom you brought from the land of the Horizon-dwellers.
May he live, prosper and be healthy,
(17) so that he may dance for the god
and gladden and delight the king of Upper and Lower Egypt Neferkare, may he live for ever!

(18) When he goes down in your charge into the boat,
station reliable people around him (19) on deck lest he fall in the water!
When he sleeps at night,
ensure that reliable (20) people sleep around him in his quarters.
Make inspection ten times per night!
(21) My majesty wants to see this pygmy more than the tribute of Sinai or (22) of Punt.
When you draw near to the Residence,
and this pygmy in your charge (23) is alive, prosperous and healthy,
my majesty shall do great things for you,
more than what was done for the seal-bearer of the god Werdjedba (24) in the time of Izezi,
all because of the joy in the heart of my majesty at the sight of this pygmy.
(25) Orders have been taken to (every) chief of a new settlement, companion, and overseer of priests
to command that supplies be taken which are (26) in his charge
from every estate storeroom and from every temple;
I make no exemption therefrom.[9]

242. Inscriptions of Pepynakht Called Heqaib from His Tomb at Qubbet el-Hawa

This text speaks of missions both to Nubia and to the Eastern Desert. Pepynakht was an important character later in the history of Aswan; in the First Intermediate Period and Middle Kingdom he was deified and a temple set up in his honor, part of which is still visible.[10] *No. 244 is a text of his (probable) son Sabni. Middle reign of Pepy II.*

Titles above Entrance

(1) The *khenty-she* and scribe of a phyle of the pyramid of [Neferkare], seal-bearer of the king of Lower Egypt, sole companion, overseer of foreigners, Heqaib.
(2) Overseer of the pyramid town of Pepy I, sole companion, lector priest, overseer of foreigners, he who brings the products of the foreign lands to his lord, Pepynakht.

(3) The leader of the phyle of the pyramid of Merenre, he who instils the fear of Horus (in) the foreign lands, the *imakhu,* Heqaib.
(4) The *haty-a,* sole companion, he who is in the chamber, herdsman of Nekhen, chief of Nekheb, overseer of all foreigners, the *imakhu* in the sight of the Great God, Pepynakht.

Right of the Entrance

(1) The *haty-a,* seal-bearer of the king of Lower Egypt, sole companion, lector priest Pepynakht.
(2) The sole companion, he who is in the chamber, herdsman of Nekhen, chief of Nekheb, overseer of all foreigners, Heqaib.

Left of the Entrance

(1) The *khenty-she* and scribe of a phyle of the pyramid of Neferkare, sole companion, Heqaib.
(2) The *haty-a,* seal-bearer of the king of Lower Egypt, sole companion, lector priest, overseer of foreign lands, *imakhu* in the sight of the Great God, Pepynakht.

Main Inscription

(1) I am a speaker of perfection and a repeater of what is desired,
I never said anything evil to any great one against any man,
because I wish my name to be perfect in the sight of (2) the Great God.
I gave bread to the hungry, and clothes to the naked.
I never passed judgment on my fellows
(3) lest I cause my/a son to lose the property of his father.
I am the beloved one of his father, the favored one of his mother,
(4) and beloved of his siblings.
The majesty of my lord sent me to devastate the land of Wawat and Irtjet.
I did (5) what pleases my lord and killed a great number there,
including the ruler's children and the commander of the excellent Nubian force.
I brought a (6) great number of them to the Residence as prisoners,
I being at the head of the expedition, a large and strong force,
as one who is strong of heart,[11]
and my lord was delighted (7) with me
as (he was) with every mission on which he sent me.

The majesty of my lord sent me to subdue those foreign lands,
(8) and I did it in such a way that my lord was immensely pleased with me.
I brought to the Residence the two subdued chiefs of these foreign lands
along with gifts of (9) live oxen and goats chosen for the benefit of the Residence,
as well as their children and the two commanders of the Nubian forces which were with them.
(10) I outdid what had been done before by the great ones of the south/Upper Egypt
because I paid close attention to carrying out the wishes of my lord.
The majesty of my lord sent me (11) to the land of the Aamu
to bring back (the body of) the sole companion, controller of Nekhen,
Kaaper's son the overseer of foreigners Ankhti.
He had been building a reed boat there to travel to Punt
(12) when the Aamu and Sand-dwellers[12] killed him
and the armed division of the expedition which accompanied him.
(13–14) [... *missing text probably indicated he attacked*] (15) ... those Aamu.
Using the military wing of the expedition which was with me,
I drove the murderers among them away.

(16) The *haty-a*, seal-bearer of the king of Lower Egypt, sole companion, lector priest, overseer of foreigners, he who instils the fear of Horus in the foreign lands, Pepynakht, whose perfect name is Heqaib.

243. Inscriptions on the Facade of the Tomb of Sabni and Mekhu I at Qubbet el-Hawa

Sabni and his father, Mekhu I, possess a joint tomb at Qubbet el-Hawa. The first of these texts describes how Sabni dealt with the death of his father in Nubia and is accompanied by his ideal biography. Between these two texts is placed one of his son Mekhu II, relating a remarkably similar sequence of events. The location of the tomb of Mekhu II is not certain, but he could perhaps have been buried in one of the eleven shafts in his father and grandfather's tomb. These texts date to the later sixth dynasty. See no. 77B for an inscription of Mekhu I and Sabni at Tomas. Reign of Pepy II.

Inscription of Sabni

A. Main Text

[Sabni speaks:]

(1) The [royal noble Iry (?)] had the boat captains Inyotef and Mekhu
come with Hazu, a man from Behekez, to let me know
that my father, the sole companion and lector priest (2) Mekhu
had died [in Wawat].
[I set forth] accompanied by a troop of men of my funerary estate and 100 donkeys,
carrying *merhet* oil, honey, linens, faience vessels, *tjehenu* oil
and all requirements for making gifts (?) to [these] foreign lands.
(3) For these Nubian foreign lands [had requested these items from my informants],
who were in the "Narrow Doorway."[13]
I wrote letters particularly to let it be known[14] that I had set forth
to bring back that father of mine who had traveled to Wetjtj (in) Wawat.
I satisfied (4) those foreign lands [with these gifts (?)],
and I found that sole companion in the foreign land
whose name is Temetjer at the end of the estate of Zeb.
I found him upon a donkey.
I saw to it that he was transported by the troop of my funerary estate.
(5) I made for him a [wooden] coffin;
I brought it along with its [lid] especially to bring him out of these foreign lands.
I did not let any valuable item go to any Egyptian, foreigner, or Nubian
(6) in exchange for property of the Residence,
and when I came back I was favored for it.
I went down to Wetjek (in) Wawat,
and sent the royal noble Iri along with two dependents of my funerary estate as an advance party
(7) carrying ... measures of incense, ... one three-cubit long elephant tusk,
to let it be known that a seven-cubit long lion-skin
was what this father of mine had brought,
along with all the tribute which is (normally) brought from these foreign lands.
(8) I went down to place this father of mine [in his tomb] in the district.

When this Iry returned from the Residence,
he brought a decree to confer (the offices of) *haty-a,*
seal-bearer of the king of Lower Egypt, sole companion
and lector priest (on) (9) this Mekhu.
He (also) brought … two embalmers, a senior lector priest,
one who is on annual duty, the inspector of the *wabet,* mourners,
and the whole of the equipment from the *per-nefer.*[15]
He brought *setj-heb* oil from the *per-nefer,*
(10) the secrets of the two *wabets,*
… from the house of weapons, linens (from) the treasury,
and all the needs of burial which come from the Residence,
in accordance with what had been set up for the *iry pat* Mereru.
(11) When this Iry came, he brought for me a decree
that favored me in relation to it (*what Sabni had done*).
The contents of this decree:
"I shall do for you all excellent things
as a repayment for this great deed
… in bringing back your father from this foreign land."
(12) Never had the like happened before.
I buried this father of mine in his tomb of the necropolis.
Never before had anyone like him been buried in a like manner.
I traveled downstream to Memphis with the tribute of
(13) those foreign lands which this *haty-a* had brought.
I collected all the tribute which this father of mine had collected
with that previous expedition
with that expedition of mine consisting of Nubians and my own troop.
(14) This servant was then favored in the majesty of the court
council.
Then this servant praised Re for the king
regarding the greatness of the favor shown to this servant
by the followers of the king.
(15) There was given to me an *afdjet* box of *sesdj* wood
containing myrrh and (?) sweet *merhet* oil;
(also) was given linen of best quality and … clothing.
(16) The gold of favor was given to me in great quantity.
Tables of food were given to me (bearing) meat and fowl.
Then [the king] held council,
and that which I had done was recalled (17) by my lord.
Then it was said to this servant:
"Greetings! I have commanded the vizier [to organize the burial of (?)]
the chief of Nekheb (*el-Kab*),

(18) the inspector of priests Ineni …
when he was placed (?) in the southern court.
Go forth to bring this man (home [?]) immediately."
(19) Then I buried this man (*the chief of Nekheb*) in his tomb north of el-Kab,
and there was given to me x + 30 arouras of land
in Lower and Upper Egypt,
as a *khenty-she* of the pyramid of Neferkare,
as a favor for this servant.

B. Accompanying a Seated Figure of Sabni

(1) An offering which the king and Anubis, who is on his mountain,
who dwells in the divine tent-shrine, lord of the sacred land, give
that invocation offerings might be made for him
in (his) tomb of the necropolis,
(2) for the … *haty-a,* seal-bearer of the king of Lower Egypt, Sabni.
He speaks:
I went forth from my town, I went down into the afterlife,
(3) I have enacted Maat [for her lord]
I have satisfied the god in respect of that which he loves daily.
I have spoken Maat (4) for her lord,
I have done that which [the god] loves.
[I have enacted Maat] which [the god] loves;
I have satisfied him as I have let it (*Maat*) (6) go up [to her lord].

C. Inscription of Mekhu II

(1) His eldest [beloved] son, seal-bearer of the king of Lower Egypt, sole companion, lector priest, Mekhu, speaks:

(2) I traveled [with a troop of my funerary estate to pay homage[16] to the king.
When] I had paid homage, (3) [I traveled upstream to Elephantine …
Now his majesty had sent (4) my father,]
the sole companion, [lector priest, Sabni, to Iam.
When I arrived at Elephantine, I found that my father had died,
(5) having brought back] all [the tribute]
which he had collected with the expedition
which he had brought back, (6) knowing that he would be favored.
I found him there in the *wabet,*
(7) laid out in the manner of the dead in the *wabet.*
I traveled downstream to Memphis.

When I arrived (8) at the Residence, his majesty spoke:
"Invocation offerings shall be set up for your father,
and I have had a decree brought [for him]."
(9) He took care of the *haty-a,* [seal-bearer] of the king of Lower Egypt, sole companion, lector priest, Sabni (10) and also of me.
All the needs of burial were provided actually from the places of the Residence
(11) (in the same manner as would be done) for an *iry pat* in the pyramid of Neferkare
(for) the *imakhu* in the sight of the Great God, Sabni.

244. From the Tomb of Another Sabni at Qubbet el-Hawa

Sabni was a characteristic name at Aswan in the late Old Kingdom; this Sabni is not to be confused with the better-known expedition leader of the same name (no. 243). This man may have been the son of Pepynakht Heqaib (no. 242); this chapel is adjacent to that of Pepynakht, and the texts are on the sides of the entrance. Reign of Pepy II.

At Top

(1) The *haty-a,* sole companion, who repeats the words of Horus to his followers, the throw-stick of Horus in the foreign lands.

The majesty of my lord sent me to construct two great barges (2) in Wawat
so as to ship two great obelisks north to Heliopolis.
I set out for Wawat with troops of five soldiers.
The foreigners whom I had engaged[17] were on the west and east of Wawat
in order to bring back my troop of soldiers (3) successfully.
I never permitted that the sandal or bread of any man be stolen.
I constructed these two barges so that the majesty of my lord favored me for it.
For I am an excellent *akh*, one who knows his spells;
I know the spell of ascending to the Great God lord of heaven.

(4) The *haty-a,* sole companion, overseer of foreigners, keeper of secrets of the doorway of Upper Egypt, Sabni.

Vertical Column in Front of Deceased

The seal-bearer of the king of Lower Egypt, the *imakhu* in the sight of the Great God, lord of heaven, Sabni.

The following line of text is written in smaller hieroglyphs above the head of Sabni, almost as if it were a later addition.

I gave bread to the hungry, clothes to the naked.
I ferried those who had no boat in my boats.
I never stole the property of another;
I never deprived any man of his belongings.

245. Text of Khnumhotep in the Tomb of Khui at Qubbet el-Hawa

Later sixth dynasty.

The controller of the tent Khnumhotep speaks:

I went forth with my (two) lords,
the *haty-a* and seal-bearers of the god Tjetji and Khui,
to Byblos and to Punt … times;
I returned successfully after having done these lands.

Note that Khnumhotep also appears in the tomb of Tjetji at Aswan with the titles "the controller of the tent, he who does what his lord favors, Khnumhotep." *See no. 68 for Tjetji.*

Upper Egypt—Nome 2

The cemetery at Edfu is adjacent to the modern town and its famous Ptolemaic temple. The site was excavated first in a systematic manner by Alliot (for example Alliot 1935), but no systematic study of the second Upper Egyptian nome has yet been made. Kemp 1977: 189–91 has a number of observations on the layout and stratigraphy of the town site.

246. Inscriptions of Izi from Edfu

The mud brick mastaba of Izi, located approximately 150 m to the west of the great temple at Edfu, is one of very few non rock-cut tombs of important officials to have been excavated at a provincial town site. He was also the subject of a posthumous cult, as several later stelae found in the neighborhood of the tomb include prayers to him as "the living god, Izi" for the provision of their funerary offerings. At some point, presumably late in his career, he was promoted to vizier, in Upper Egypt at least; this comes from fragmentary texts not translated here. Parts of the chapel are in Warsaw, National Museum 139944 (Ruszczyc 1957) and the lintel is in Paris, Louvre E 14329. Early sixth dynasty.

Left-hand Side

The sole companion, Izi speaks:

(1) [I came forth from my town, I went down into the afterlife;
I acted perfectly] on behalf of my nome
and I said what was right (2) for [its] lord.
I judged between [two litigants] so that [they] were satisfied.
I am a speaker [of perfection and a repeater of perfection
I never (3) spoke anything evil about any man,
as I want things] to go well for me in the sight of the Great God.
I am the beloved one of his father,
(4) and the favored one of his mother.
I never [took anything from any man by violence].

Right-hand Side

The sole companion, Izi [speaks]:

(5) In the time of Izezi [I acted as] the elder of the doorway who … ;
in the time of Unas the [office] of controller of the estate was given to me.
(6) The [offices] of scribe and master of the king,
judge and boundary official and first under the king
were given to me in the time of Teti.
(7) I [did everything] this god [loved].
[The offices of *haty-a,* sole companion and] nomarch
[were given] to me (8) [by the majesty of this god, may he live for ever,
because I was more excellent and valuable in the heart of his majesty] than any of his officials.
[I was attentive] (9) with respect to all royal works
which are reckoned [in this nome (10) so that] his majesty favored me
when I had carried out a commission for the Residence.

Lintel Paris, Louvre E 14329

(1) An offering which the king gives and which Anubis gives
that he may be buried in the necropolis.
(2) An offering which Osiris, lord of Busiris, gives
that he may travel (3) on the perfect ways on which the *imakhu* travel

(4) doubly in peace in the sight of Anubis,
(5) and that he may reach land and traverse the sand
and ascend to the Great God.

(6) The sole companion, first under the king, judge and boundary official, master of royal scribes Izi.
(7) The controller of the estate, great one of the tens of Upper Egypt, the *imakhu* Izi.

247. Inscriptions of Meryrenefer Qar from Edfu

One interesting aspect of this text is that it introduces some new phrases, those referring to the care and nurture of his nome, which become central to many biographies of the First Intermediate Period (chapter I, §6.5.3). One set of formulae is omitted. Middle sixth dynasty. The sigla A–E are those of el-Khadragy's edition.

E. False Door, Left Jamb

(1) The *imakhu* in the sight of the Great God, in the sight of Osiris, Lord of Busiris, the sole companion, the lector priest Meryrenefer.
(2) The sole companion, lector priest, the *imakhu* in the sight of the king, the *imakhu* in the sight of Ptah south of his wall, (3) the sole companion, lector priest Meryrenefer, speaks:

O you who live on earth
and who shall enter this tomb of mine of the necropolis,
and who desire (4) that their god favor them,
say "bread, beer, oxen, and fowl for the *imakhu*
in the sight of Ptah south of his wall,
the sole companion, lector priest Meryrenefer."

Right Jamb

(1) The *imakhu* in the sight of the king, the *imakhu* in the sight of the Great God, in the sight of Anubis, who is on his mountain, the sole companion, lector priest, nomarch Meryrenefer.
(2) The *haty-a,* overseer of Upper Egypt, sole companion, lector priest, keeper of secrets of the House of the Morning, the *imakhu* in the sight of the Great God lord of the West.

(3) An offering which the king and which Osiris, lord of Busiris, give
that he may travel on the perfect ways on which the *imakhu* travel
doubly in peace in the sight of Anubis, who is on his mountain;

that he may be united with the land,
(4) that he may cross the sands
to his places for the *imakhu* in the sight of the Great God.
The sole companion, lector priest, nomarch Meryrenefer.

A. The Architrave

(1) An offering which the king and which Anubis,
who dwells in the divine tent-shrine, who is on his mountain,
who is in his wrappings, lord of the sacred land, lord of Sepa, give
that he may be perfectly buried in the necropolis, in the Western Desert,
[having grown old most perfectly] doubly in peace,
(and that he may travel) on the perfect ways of the West
[on which the *imakhu* travel];
the sole companion, nomarch, Qar whose perfect name is Meryrenefer.
(2) An offering which the king and which Osiris, foremost of the Westerners,
lord of Abydos, who dwells in Busiris, give
that invocation offerings may be made for him in every *Rekeh* festival,
in the *Sadj* festival, in the first day of the year festival,
in the *Wag* festival and the festival of Thoth, and in every perfect festival.
The sole companion, lector priest, overseer of the *khenty-she* of the Great House, Qar.
(3) I was a youth who tied the headband in the time of Teti,
and (then) I was taken to Pepy (I)
to be given an education among the children of the chiefs.
I was promoted to sole companion
and overseer of the *khenty-she* of the Palace in the time of Pepy.
Then the majesty of Merenre had me go south
to the second nome of Upper Egypt
as a sole companion and great chief of the nome
and as overseer of the grain of Upper Egypt and overseer of priests,
(4) through my excellence and my noble status in the heart of (his) majesty.
It fell to my lot to be the lord at the head of all the chiefs of the totality of Upper Egypt.
I was the one who judged for the whole of Upper Egypt.
I saw to it that the cattle of this nome were more (numerous)

than the cattle in the stables of the foremost part of the whole of
Upper Egypt.
The fact is that it was not found that (anything comparable was done
by) the chief who was previously in this nome;
(5) this was through my vigilance,
through my excellence in controlling matters for the Residence.
I was the keeper of secrets of all matters
which were brought from the narrow doors in the foreign lands[18]
and from the southern foreign lands.
I gave bread to the hungry and clothes to the naked
whom I found in this nome.
I gave a jug of milk from my own hand;
I measured out the grain of Upper Egypt from my funerary estate
for a hungry man whom I found in this nome;
(6) with regard to any man whom I found in this nome
burdened down with a loan of grain from another,
I paid back his creditor from my funerary estate.
I buried every man of this nome who had no son
with linen from the property of my estate.
I propitiated all foreign lands for the Residence
in accordance with my excellence
and in accordance with my vigilance in relation to this,
and I was favored in respect of it by my Lord.
I rescued the helpless one from one who was more powerful than he,
and I judged litigants to their satisfaction.
(7) I am the beloved one of his father
and the favored one of his mother, whom his siblings love.
O you who live upon earth and who shall pass by this tomb (of mine),
if you love the king, then you shall say
"a thousand of bread, a thousand of beer,
a thousand oxen, for the sole companion Meryrenefer."

Upper Egypt–Nome 3

Moalla, located to the south of Luxor, is best known for its tomb of the nomarch Ankhtyfy of the First Intermediate Period, one of the most powerful nobles in Upper Egypt at the time of the disintegration of the Old Kingdom. Little is known about it in the preceding period, however. The major site in the Old Kingdom was el-Kab (Nekheb), where there are remains of some early Old Kingdom tombs (Quibell 1898: 3–11); from there also come some sixth-dynasty graffiti (no. 88).

248. Stela of Hekenu, Perhaps from Moalla

This stela must date to the end of the Old Kingdom or later, to judge from the somewhat crude style; there also seem to be a number of errors in the text. Now Paris, Louvre E 26904.

(1) May he travel in peace twice over to his *ka,*
having grown old most perfectly,
upon the (2) perfect ways of the Western Desert
on which the *imakhu* travel.
For I am an *imakhu,* (3) the beloved one of his father,
the favored one of his mother.
I judged between two litigants to their satisfaction.
O (4) you who are on earth
who desire that they may be *imakhu* in the sight of their fathers,
say: "give food and water" to (both)
(5) the first under the king, Hekenu, son of Iku, born of Hemi,
(6) and his wife, his beloved, the royal acquaintance Sabes.

Upper Egypt–Nome 5

Other than the royal decrees (chapter IV), most material evidence from the Koptite nome dates to the end of the Old Kingdom and later (Fischer 1964).

249. Text from the Tomb of Shemai at Kom el-Koffar

Shemai and his son Idi were two of the most powerful individuals in Upper Egypt at the end of the Old Kingdom; many of the later royal decrees from Koptos, including those of Neferkauhor as here, are addressed to them (chapter IV). The discovery of the tomb of Shemai in 1981 was an important find, with this unusual and difficult inscription indicating some of what Idi did for his father. Kom el-Koffar is 1 km south of Koptos (Qift). Late eighth dynasty.

Date in the Pillared Hall of the Tomb

Neferkauhor, year of the first occasion, fourth month of the *Shemu* season, day 2: setting off for Ra-henu for the second time in order to bring noble stone from …

Inscription on a Wall

(1) Beginning of the speech of the officials throughout the nomes of Upper Egypt.

(2) The god's father, beloved one of the god, *iry pat,* foster-child of the king, *haty-a,* overseer of [Upper Egypt (?)] (3) Idi.

I established the monuments …
(4) and I made pleasant with incense
this soul chapel of my father and my ancestors
so that these soul chapels of these noble ones were like
(5) … noble and I refreshed and set up the statues of these noble ones,
these *iry pat,* which I found in a state of disrepair,
with the effect that [I brought in new statues]
(6) in the manner of those which had fallen into disrepair in his soul chapel
in accordance with his will.[19]
I looked at the tomb of my father,
the *iry pat, haty-a,* sole companion, lector priest, overseer of priests, … of Min [Shemai]
(7) … the offering places/tables were provided with excellent and perfect offerings,
and their names and their titles were placed on it,
so that they might last for eternity.
I made these stelae for them …
(8) I executed everything which he had ordered in terms of works for the necropolis,
everything which he had ordered.
I never gave him a reason to be disappointed;
I never did anything which was distasteful to him
(9) … for my part, I looked for every man who had a problem with him,
for he has let me know everyone among them who was in his house:

I have got rid of them totally, I have dispossessed [them] …
(10) from his granaries, from his treasuries, from his cattle,
from his herds, and from all his duties,
and he has been thrown out of his house
(11) … festival … stelae … of the Residence (?)

Upper Egypt—Nome 6

Dendera is an ancient site, long the cult center of the goddess Hathor and the cemetery in the Old Kingdom of the nomarchs of the sixth Upper Egyptian nome. The site was first examined by Petrie 1900; a comprehensive treatment of the area in the Old Kingdom and First Intermediate Period will be found in Fischer 1968. See Kemp 1985 for the location of the Old Kingdom town.

250. Inscriptions of Idu I from Dendera

Originally a very elaborate and wealthy tomb, what remains is badly damaged and close to incomprehensible. There are some unusual phrases in the biographical text. Reign of Pepy II.

Titles

Controller of the estate of the pyramid of Neferkare, seal-bearer of the king of Lower Egypt, sole companion …
Controller of the estate of the pyramid of Meryre, nomarch, the *imakhu* in the sight of …
Seal-bearer of the king of Lower Egypt, controller of the estate, sole companion, chief lector priest, nomarch, keeper of secrets of every secret matter which is brought to the nome, the *imakhu* in the sight of Osiris, lord of Busiris, the *imakhu* in the sight of the Great God, Idu.
The *haty-a,* true overseer of all Upper Egypt, seal-bearer of the king of Lower Egypt, sole companion, chief lector priest, nomarch, Idu.

Remains of the Biography

[An offering which the king and which Anubis] … lord of the sacred land [give]
that invocation offerings may be made for the *haty-a,* he who is in the chamber … [Idu]
… from bread and beer.

... everything excellent and splendid: oxen, herds, copper
... where my ancestors were and those before me ...
... others upon whom this office of "seal-bearer of the king of Lower Egypt" has devolved ...
... through greatness of desire within ...
... the *imakhu* in the sight of my lord. I never did ...

251. Inscriptions of Idu II from Dendera

This Idu was a successor of Idu I, probably still within the reign of Pepy II. The inscription is composed of a number of fragments, and the arrangement is questionable.

An offering which the king and Hathor mistress of Dendera give
for the sole companion ...
I judged between two litigants to their mutual satisfaction
(for) I desire that it go well for me in the sight of the Great God.
I heard the words of one whose throat was narrow,
and I kept away evil from the needy,[20]
for I wish ...
[With regard to this tomb of mine,
I satisfied all the craftsmen] who worked on it,
and they praised god (for me). ...

(*There are remains of other biographical phrases*)

Upper Egypt—Nome 7

El-Qasr wa es-Sayed (Hamra Dom) is the location of the principal cemetery of the seventh Upper Egyptian nome in the Old Kingdom. See Säve-Söderbergh 1994 for an account of the nome and of the principal tombs.

252. Texts on the Facade of the Tomb of Idu Seneni at el-Qasr wa es-Sayed

Reign of Pepy II. A legal text from the tomb will be found as no. 105. The reconstructions are those of Edel.

The inspector of priests of the pyramid of Pepy I [*haty-a,* chief of the nome, Idu]

The inspector of priests of the pyramid of Merenre, [sole companion, controller of the mansion, Idu]
The inspector of priests of the pyramid of Neferkare, [*haty-a,* seal-bearer of the king of Lower Egypt, Idu]

(1) [He speaks:
I came from my] city, I went down (2) [into the afterlife;
I carried out Maat for her lord,
(3) whom I satisfied in respect of that which he desired;
I spoke perfectly and repeated perfectly.
(4) I gave bread to the hungry, clothes to the naked;]
I ferried across the man (5) [who had no boat.
I never] acted badly to a wretched man.
(6) [I never gave cause for] any man [to be angry with me],
since I wish that [my name] may be perfect (7) in the sight of the god.
With regard to men who shall do (8) [anything bad]
to [the offering place of this tomb of mine]
or to the soul priests (9) of my funerary estate,
I shall [be judged with them by] (10) the Great God;
I shall seize [their necks like a bird's].
(11) For I am an excellent *akh*, [one who knows his spells;]
I know (12) all the secrets of the words of the god,
through which one is transfigured in the necropolis,
(13) because I have never done anything against (14) any person
(15) which would result in their doing anything (16) bad against (17) any of my (funerary) property.

I am one (18) who is beloved of men, (19) favored of his ancestors.
(20) The *haty-a,* the controller of the mansion Idu, whose perfect name is Seneni.

253. Slab of Djadjay from el-Qasr wa es-Sayed

A loose slab found in debris; it probably dates to the very end of the Old Kingdom.

(1) [O you who live on earth (+ *many possibilities*)] …
(2) … then you shall say:
"A thousand libations, a thousand of bread and beer,
a thousand oxen and fowl, a thousand oryxes
[and a thousand of every perfect thing]

(3) for the seal-bearer of the king of Lower Egypt, sole companion,
ruler of the estate, overseer of Upper Egypt,
the *imakhu* in the sight of the Great God, lord of heaven, Djadjay." …
He speaks:
(4) I made twenty boats while doing what the people of my city wanted;
I made a *zehyt* boat with provisions on it
(5) … field … for I know (how to recognize [?]) my own property (?) from that of my lord (?)
… Never did I punish (?) anyone (?) …
(6) Never did a great one summon his lord in relation to my job when I was doing it.
I am one beloved of …

254. From the Tomb of Idu Menza from el-Qasr wa es-Sayed

Late sixth dynasty.

Parts of Inscriptions on the Front of the Tomb

a. … [A tomb or shaft] which I gave to him in this desert area …
b. … [I made] this town in its entirety [live] …

Also on the Front, above a Shaft

(1) The seal-bearer of the king of Lower Egypt [sole companion, lector priest, the *imakhu* (2) … (3) … Idu Menza speaks:]

(4) …
(5) With regard to any person who shall do anything
in an evil manner against my stela or my tomb,
[I shall be judged with them] (6) by the Great God,
the lord of heaven, the lord of this desert,
and I shall be found to be justified in the presence of the [Great] God …

Opposite the Last

(1) An offering which the king and which Anubis, who is upon his mountain,
who is in his wrappings, lord of the [sacred] land, give
(2) for a perfect burial in his tomb of the necropolis
in (3) the Western Desert, in all his perfect places,
and that invocation offerings be made for him

(4) in the *Wag* festival, the *seqet* festival [(*various others lost*)] (5) daily (for) the seal-bearer of the king of Lower Egypt, the sole companion [(*rest of titles and name lost*)].

Upper Egypt—Nome 8

The burial site of predynastic rulers and kings of the first two dynasties, Abydos in the eighth Upper Egyptian nome is best known as the cult center of Osiris, the Egyptian god of the dead. Excavations in the cemeteries have been conducted since the mid-nineteenth century A.D. and continue today (see no. 256). For studies of the nome in the Old Kingdom, see Brovarski 1994a; 1994b; for some stratigraphic notes on the town and temple site see Kemp 1968; 1973; 1977: 186–89; and O'Connor 1992, and also no. 17.

There are other cemeteries in the nome; Sheikh Farag is part of the Naga ed-Der cemeteries, opposite modern Girga. This area was of considerably less national importance but was just as important locally, particularly in the late Old Kingdom and First intermediate Period.

255. Architrave of Per-shenay from Abydos

Found in the cemetery excavations without a specific provenance. Said by Frankfort to be in Cairo. Late Old Kingdom.

(1) An offering which the king and Osiris give
for the invocation offerings of the ruler of the estate and companion,
the *imakhu* in the sight of the Great God Per-shenay.
(2) He speaks:
I came from my town, I went down into the afterlife.
I am a speaker of perfection, I am a repeater of perfection.
I am the beloved one (3) of his father, the favored one of his mother.
I never violently seized the property of any person.
(4) With regard to any man who shall violently seize any of my (funerary) property,
(5) I shall be judged with them by the Great God in the necropolis
(6) when I am in the West, for they remember evil in the necropolis.
I am an excellent *akh*;

(7) I know all the excellent magic
through which one is transfigured in the necropolis;
Everything is done for me by which one is transfigured.

256. Inscription of Weni from Abydos

The biography of Weni is, with that of Harkhuf (no. 241), the best-known biographical text of the Old Kingdom and has been widely discussed, as it is important for literary and historical reasons; it is also the longest such document. Richards 2002: 82–85 observes that the unusual layout of this text parallels the arrangement of royal decrees. Now Cairo, CG 1435.[21] *Middle sixth dynasty.*

The tomb of Weni was relocated at Abydos in 1999 (Richards 2000; 2001; 2002; 2003); this slab would have been placed on the exterior of the offering chapel. Further decorated elements were found, including additional titles for Weni, such as that of vizier.

Top Line (Horizontal)

[An offering which the king gives] …
that invocation offerings may be made for him
in every daily festival from the offerings …
[a thousand of bread], a thousand of beer, a thousand oxen,
a thousand oryx, a thousand *tjerep* geese, a thousand *te* geese,
a thousand *se* geese, a thousand … geese,
a thousand (vases) of alabaster, a thousand [items of clothing (?)] …

Introductory Titles (Vertically, Facing the Main Text)

[The *haty-a*, overseer of Upper Egypt,] he who is in the chamber, herdsman of Nekhen, chief of Nekheb, sole companion, the *imakhu* in the sight of Osiris, foremost of the Westerners, Weni.

Main Text

(1) [He speaks:]
[I was a youth] who tied the headband under Teti,
when my office was that of overseer of the storeroom,
and then I became supervisor of the *khenty-she* of the Great House.
(2) [I was …] lector priest and elder of the palace under Pepy (I);
his majesty promoted me to the office of companion and supervisor of priests of his pyramid town when I held the office of …[22]

(3) His [majesty promoted me] to judge and mouth of Nekhen,[23]
as he preferred me to any of his servants.
I heard cases alone (just) with the vizier relating to all secret matters;
(4) I acted in the king's name for the royal harem and for the six great mansions
because his majesty preferred me to any of his officials, his nobles, or servants.
(5) When I requested from the majesty of my lord
that a sarcophagus of white stone of Tura be provided for me,
his majesty had the seal-bearer of the god and a boat-crew
(6) under his command cross over and bring back this sarcophagus from Tura.
He brought it himself actually in a great barge of the Residence,
together with its cover, (7) a false door, an architrave, two jambs, and an offering table.
Never before had the like been done for any servant,
(for) I was excellent in his majesty's heart,
(8) I was rooted in his heart, and his heart was full of me,
when I was judge and mouth of Nekhen.
His majesty promoted me to be sole companion and overseer of the *khenty-she*
(9) when four overseers of *khenty-she* who had been in post (before) were replaced in my favor.
I acted in accordance with what his majesty favored
when doing guard duty, preparing his way, and standing in attendance.[24]
In all respects I acted (10) in such a way that the king favored me for it above all else.
When there was a legal case in secret in the royal harem against the royal wife, the "great of affection,"[25]
his majesty had me proceed to hear it on my own.
(11) No vizier or official was present apart from myself[26]
because I was excellent, I was rooted in his heart, and his heart was full of me.
I alone, together (12) with (just) one other judge and mouth of Nekhen put it down in writing,
although I was (just) of the rank of overseer of the *khenty-she* of the Great House;
never before had anyone like me heard the secrets of the royal harem,
and yet his majesty let me (13) hear (them),

because I was more excellent in the heart of his majesty
than any of his officials, nobles, or servants.
When his majesty repelled the Aamu and Sand-dwellers,[27]
(14) his majesty put together an army of many tens of thousands,
from all of Upper Egypt, from Elephantine north to Medenyt,
from Lower Egypt, from all the Delta,
(15) from Sedjer, Khensedjer, from Irtjet Nubians, Medjay-Nubians,
Iam-Nubians, (16) Wawat-Nubians, Kaau-Nubians
and from the Tjemehu.[28]
His majesty sent me at the head of this army,
(17) in which were also these (officials):[29]
haty-a, seal-bearers of the king of Lower Egypt, sole companions of the Great Mansion, chiefs, estate controllers of Upper and Lower Egypt, companions and overseers of foreigners, (18) overseers of priests of Upper and Lower Egypt, overseers of the workroom in charge of troops of Upper and Lower Egypt and the rulers of their estates and towns, and Nubians of those foreign lands.
(19) I it was who was in charge,
while being (only) an overseer of the *khenty-she* of the Great House;
this was because of my punctiliousness,
so that no one attacked his companion,
(20) so that no one took bread or sandals from the traveler,
so that no one took cloth from any town,
(21) so that no one took a goat from any man.
I led them from the Island of the North, the Gate of Imhotep,
the district of Horus lord of *Maat*, while I was in this position (22) … everything.
I expanded (?) the numbers of these troops;
no servant had done (such) an expansion (?) (before).
This expedition returned in peace,[30]
having hacked up/ravaged the land of the Sand-dwellers;
This expedition returned (23) in peace,
having destroyed the land of the Sand-dwellers;
(24) This expedition returned in peace,
having pulled down its fortresses;
This expedition returned in peace,
having cut down (25) its figs and vines;
This expedition returned (26) in peace,
having set fire to all its houses;

This expedition returned in peace,
having slaughtered the troops there in many tens of thousands;
This expedition returned in peace,
having brought great numbers of the troops (27) therein away as captives.
His majesty favored me for it above all else.
(In fact) his majesty sent me to lead this force (28) five times, with these same troops,
to drive away the Sand-dwellers each time they rebelled.
I acted in such a way that his majesty favored me above all else.
(29) It was said that there were insurgents in those foreign lands
in the area above Gazelle Nose.[31]
So I crossed over (30) in barges with these troops;
north of the high lands of the mountain range,
(31) north of the land of the Sand-dwellers
was where I made a landing,
while half of the army was still on the road.
Only after I had apprehended them all,
slaughtering (32) every insurgent among them, did I return.
When I was in the Great Mansion as an officer and sandal-bearer,
the king of Upper and Lower Egypt Merenre, my lord, given life,
promoted me (33) to be *haty-a* and overseer of Upper Egypt,
south to the first nome and north to the twenty-second.
(He did this) because of my excellent standing in the heart of his majesty,
because I was rooted in his heart, and because his heart was full of me.
(34) When I was an officer and sandal-bearer,
his majesty favored me more than any of his officials,
more than any of his nobles,
(35) more than any of his servants,
for my watchfulness and for the guard duty I did when I was in attendance.
Never had this office been given to anyone of the status of servant before.
I acted for him as overseer of Upper Egypt in a satisfactory manner
so that a man did not do injustice to his companion/equal (by)
—(36) carrying out every task;
—assessing everything which needed assessing for the Residence in

Upper Egypt on two occasions and every regular duty which needed assessing for the Residence in Upper Egypt on two occasions;[32]
—carrying out my official duties (37) so as to make my reputation in this Upper Egypt.
Never had the like been done in Upper Egypt since ancient times;
I acted in all respects so that his majesty favored me for it.
His majesty sent me (38) to Ibhat[33]
especially to bring back the sarcophagus "Chest of the Living"[34] and its lid,
as well as a costly and noble pyramidion for the pyramid of Merenre, my mistress.
(39) His majesty sent me to Elephantine
especially to bring back a granite false door and its lintel
as well as (other) doors and associated elements of granite,
(40) and also to bring back a granite doorway[35] and lintels,
(all) for the upper chamber of the pyramid of Merenre, my mistress.
In (just) one expedition consisting of six barges,
three transport ships and three eight-oared/ribbed boats
did I travel north with (them) (41) to the pyramid of Merenre.
Never had anyone worked before at (both) Ibhat and at (42) Elephantine
during the same expedition in the time of any king.
Everything which the king had ordered
was carried out in line with what his majesty had ordered.
His majesty sent me (43) to Hatnub
especially to bring back a great offering table of Hatnub alabaster,
and I organized that this offering table was brought down
(after) seventeen days of quarrying at Hatnub.
I had it travel north in a barge;
(44) I made for it (this) barge from acacia wood 60 cubits long and 30 cubits wide,
assembled in seventeen days in the third month of the *Shemu* season.
Despite there being no (45) water on the sandbanks,
I moored successfully at the pyramid of Merenre.
Everything in my charge had come to pass
exactly in accordance with the order of the majesty of my lord.
His majesty sent (me) to excavate five canals (46) in Upper Egypt
and to make three barges and four transport ships from acacia wood of Wawat,

for which the rulers of those foreign lands of Irtjet, Wawat,
Iam and Medja (47) cut down the wood.[36]
I completed this task in the space of one year,
including filling (them) with water and the loading of large amounts of granite intended for the pyramid of Merenre.
I made a saving (?)[37] (48) for the palace because of all these five canals
because the *bas* of the king of Upper and Lower Egypt Merenre, may he live for ever,
are nobler, more efficacious and powerful than any god,
because everything always comes to pass
(49) in accordance with the order which his *ka* decreed.
I am one the beloved one of his father,
the favored one of his mother, (50) the favored one of his brothers,
the *haty-a,* real overseer of Upper Egypt, the *imakhu* in the sight of Osiris, Weni.

257. Inscription of Djau from Abydos

The family of Djau had an extraordinary position in the sixth dynasty. As this inscription shows, two of his sisters married kings of the dynasty (see further Fischer 1976a: 75 n 40 and Dobrev 2000: 385–87), and he became vizier, doubtless due to his family connections; his mother Nebet enjoyed a unique titulary (no. 295). This inscription was later reused in a well, but probably originally came from the temple of Khentyimentyu, the principal cult place in Abydos during the Old Kingdom. Now in Cairo, CG 1431. Probably early reign of Pepy II.

Three Persons at the Top of Stela

(1) The royal wife of the pyramid of Meryre, great of affection, great of praise, follower of the great one, companion of Horus, favorite of Horus; (2) mother of the king of Upper and Lower Egypt the pyramid of Merenre, Ankhesenmeryre.

(3) The royal wife of the pyramid of Meryre, great of affection, great of praise, daughter of the god, follower of the great one, companion of Horus, favorite of Horus; (4) mother of the king of Upper and Lower Egypt, the pyramid of Neferkare, Ankhesenmeryre.

(5) … their brother, the vizier Djau.

Main Inscription, Written in Retrograde Fashion

(6) The *iry pat* Djau; the stolist of Anubis Djau; the keeper of the diadem Djau; the beloved sole companion Djau; the controller of the great ones of Upper and Lower Egypt, scribe of the divine documents, controller of every divine office, stolist of Horus, follower of Min, the *imakhu* Djau.

(7) Their brother, the true *iry pat*, *haty-a* and overseer of the pyramid town, vizier, overseer of royal document scribes, servant of the *bas* of Pe, servant of the *bas* of Nekhen, chief lector priest, *sem* priest, controller of every kilt, seal-bearer of the king of Lower Egypt, embalmer of Anubis, priest of Nut, the *imakhu* in the sight of Osiris, Djau.

(8) I made this (*monument/tomb*) at Abydos in the Thinite nome
particularly because of my state of *imakhu*
in the sight of the majesty of the king of Upper and Lower Egypt Neferkare, may he live for ever,
and in the sight of the majesty of the king of Upper and Lower Egypt Meryre and the king of Upper and Lower Egypt Merenre,
(and also) through love of my nome,
in which the royal ornament Nebet gave birth to me (9) to my father,
the *iry pat*, *haty-a*, beloved one of the god,
the *imakhu* in the sight of the Great God, Khui.
O you who live on earth, every overseer of priests, every priest,
every *shesemt* or *dja* priest of the temple of the majesty of my lord Khentyimentyu;
(10) as the king lives for you,
you shall obtain for me invocation offerings from the income of this temple,
from what you do for me which is decreed,
and from what you do for me yourselves.
For you have seen my offices in the sight of the king,
for I am more valuable in the sight of the majesty of my lord
than any other dignitary [of his, than any of his officials, than any of his servants], the vizier Djau.

258. Ideal Biography from the Tomb of an Unknown Person at Abydos

Now in Cairo, CG 1650. Late Old Kingdom or later.

(1) I came from my town, I went down into the afterlife.
I am a speaker of perfection (2) and a repeater of perfection.
With regard to any person who shall do anything against my children,

I (3) shall be judged with him by the Great God in the place where judgment is.

259. Stela from Tomb 253 at Sheikh Farag

Perhaps late Old Kingdom, but could even be Middle Kingdom.

(1) An offering which the king, Anubis and Osiris of Busiris [give]
(2) that invocation offerings be made for the sole companion,
the *imakhu* in the sight of …
[He speaks: (?)]
(3) I am the beloved one of his father, the favored one of his mother,
one whom (4) his siblings love;
I made this tomb of mine, I acted as one steadfast (5) of limbs,
I acted with my own arm when I was a child
and the property of my father (6) was taken from me;
I took counsel with the great and the lesser ones when I followed them.

By the Woman (Name Possibly [Shedites])

(7) His wife, his beloved, the priestess of Hathor …
(8) One favored of the household of her husband.

Upper Egypt—Nome 9

El-Hawawish is the location of the cemetery of the town of Akhmim. The tombs there are published in Kanawati 1980–92, and the history of the area in the Old Kingdom is examined in Brovarski 1985 and Kanawati 1992. There are many more tombs there than the few samples of more interesting texts translated here. A popular work on the site is Kanawati 1988.

Hagarsa lies near the boundary between nomes 8 and 9, and Kanawati 1993: I, 7 believes it is more likely to have belonged to the latter nome. The site was first investigated by Petrie 1908, and the tombs were recorded in the 1990s in Kanawati 1993–95. One text from here is translated above (no. 170).

260. Text of Bawy from Hawawish

Mid sixth dynasty. The line breaks given are very approximate.

(1) I came from my town, I went down into the afterlife;
I acted according to Maat [for her lord (*or similar*)] …

[I am a speaker of perfection] and (2) a repeater of perfection,
one who acquires things properly,
for I desire that it go well for me there in the presence [of the Great God (?)] ...
(3) I am the beloved one of his father, the favored one of his mother,
an *imakhu* who is beloved (*or* who loves [?]) ...
(4) [I gave bread to the hungry and clothes] to the naked therein,
and I rescued him who was wretched [from one more powerful than he (?)] ...
(5) I made these inscriptions which I put together for my father,
the inspector of priests [*name lost*] ...
[With regard to any man who shall enter this my tomb (*to do something bad*)],
(6) [I shall seize] his neck like a bird's when I am ...
(7) [For I am] an excellent *akh*; all excellent magic [is known to me (?)] ...
... alone there (?).
(8) I judged [between two men] ...
(9) ... my tomb of the necropolis. I went down ...

261. Fragments of the Biography of Iy Mery at Hawawish

End sixth dynasty or later.

Biography

(1) The companion, the steward Iy, whose perfect name is Mery, speaks:
(2) ... Upper Egyptian grain to the Residence;
the like was never found with respect to another man
(3) ... of this nome, in reckoning matters/property for the Residence,
as a trusted one in the house of (the god) Min.
(4) For indeed I never took away grain which was in my charge
other than all payments relating to any works of
(5) the soul chapel of Pepy which is in Akhmim.[38]
My children ...

Commemoration

(1) His eldest son, his beloved, the companion Mery, (2) speaks:
I it was who caused the making of this tomb (3) for my father,
the inspector of priests Mery, (4) when he had gone to his *ka*.

262. Text of Nehutdesher at Hawawish

Reign of Teti to Pepy I.

(1) The sole companion, stolist of Min, overseer of priests Nehutdesher speaks:

(2) I came from [my town, I went down] into the afterlife.
I carried out Maat for her lord.
I satisfied the god (3) in respect of what he loves.
I am a speaker of perfection and a repeater of perfection,
one who acquires the property (of others) in the right manner,
as I want things to go well for me (4) in the sight of the Great God,
for I am *imakhu* thereby in the sight of men.
I set my face to men (?)
(5) I have indeed come to the necropolis ...[39]

263. Text of Qereri at Hawawish

Reign of Pepy I or later.

South Wall

(1) The inspector of priests, the first under the king of the Great House in the time of Meryre, (2) Qereri, speaks:
I have indeed come to the necropolis;
I have dug (3) a pool of 100 cubits on each side with ten sycomores thereon.
(4) With regard to any son (of mine) who shall neglect these,
he shall have no claim on my property.

North Wall

(1) I acquired a herd of breeding donkeys;
they produced (2) 200 further donkeys.
With regard to any man who shall pass upon this way,
(3) you shall say:
"A thousand of bread, beer, alabaster, and clothing (4) for Qereri."

264. Inscription from the Tomb of Mery I at Hagarsa

This fragmentary inscription of the elder Mery is not very informative, but Kanawati has shown that the text was originally much longer than had been thought by earlier scholars. Reign of Pepy II or later.

(1) The sole companion, Mery [speaks:] …

(2) I made this for myself … [due to my state of *imakhu* (?)] …

(3) in the sight of the majesty of the king of Upper and Lower Egypt Neferkare [may he live for ever …]

(4) I made two from one (?) … granary (5) of Upper Egyptian grain, which I made …

[I did not (?)][40] strike (even) a (6) dog …

[I gave bread to the hungry, clothes to the (?)] naked

(7) I am the beloved one of his [father,

(?) the favored one of his mother, beloved of (?)] his brothers (?).

(8) I am a speaker of perfection and a repeater of perfection … [Mer]y.

265. Inscription of Mery II at Hagarsa

End Old Kingdom or First Intermediate Period. Mery II or Meryaa ("Mery the great") may be a descendant of Mery I. No. 308 is a caption from here.

(1) An offering which the king gives and which Anubis …

The *imakhu* Meryaa speaks:

I am noble, (2) one of great wealth within …

… I set up for him grain (?) from Upper Egypt and grain (?) from Lower Egypt (3) and filled the treasury with everything …

… during the *Peret* season in the years of famine, my Upper Egyptian grain reached …

(4) … when I had nourished the poor …

… valleys/buildings, cattle and goat stalls. (5) I made …

… perfect for the nome … to ferry across the sleeper (*the dead?*) who had no boat.

I am one who …

(6) … I am one who speaks on behalf of the widow (*or* "speaks up for the rights of the widow" [?]) …

(7) … one who acts fairly in dealing with the words of two litigants, one who calms the fears of the downcast …

(8) … with my seal in my office of the necropolis in accordance with that which the ancestors said, those who existed before me.

(9) With regard to all my property in existence, may my name be justified …

… one whose words are listened to by the officials.

I gave bread to the hungry and clothes (10) to the naked.

What his eldest son, his beloved did for him, the owner of all his property, the *haty-a* Nuu, in words:

I entombed my father with "an offering which the king gives";
I buried him in (11) the perfect West;
I embalmed him with *sefetj* oil from the Residence
and *insu* linen from the House of Life;
I inscribed his tomb;
I erected his statues—
(all) in the manner in which an excellent heir should act,
one who is beloved of his father,
who buries his father and who is strong of arm.

Upper Egypt—Nome 12

Deir el-Gebrawi is the cemetery of this nome in the Old Kingdom. The tombs there were published in Davies 1902; since that time there has been no work at the site.

266. Texts from the Tomb of Ibi at Deir el-Gebrawi

The translation uses most of the reconstructions of Sethe in Urk I, and they are often not marked. A caption from this tomb will be found below as no. 303. Early reign of Pepy II. Note that Ibi was also the nomarch of the eighth nome of Upper Egypt (Abydos).

A. Text on the East Wall
Left

(1) An offering which the king gives and which Osiris gives …
that invocation offerings be made for the *haty-a* Ibi …
(2) the seal-bearer of the king of Lower Egypt, ruler of the estate, sole companion, great chief of the eighth nome of Upper Egypt, Ibi.

He speaks:

I was a youth who wore a headband
[in the sight of the majesty of the king of Upper and Lower Egypt Meryre;
then the majesty of] (3) my lord, the king of Upper and Lower Egypt Merenre, may he live [for ever],
promoted me to be *haty-a,* sole companion, and great chief of the eighth nome of Upper Egypt.
Then the king of Upper and Lower Egypt [Neferkare, may he live for ever, …]
promoted me to be overseer of Upper Egypt.

The real overseer of [Upper Egypt], (4) Ibi, speaks:

With regard to any person who shall enter this tomb of mine [in an impure] state,
I shall seize [his neck] (5) like a bird's;
I am an excellent and well-prepared *akh*.
I know all the secret magic of the Residence
and everything through which one is transfigured (?) in the necropolis.
[I am] (6) the beloved one of his father,
[the favored one] of his mother,
an *imakhu* in the sight of the king,
and an *imakhu* in the sight of his local god, the beloved one, Ibi.

Right

(1) An offering which the king gives and which Anubis,
who is on his mountain, who is in his wrappings, … gives …
may the West extend (2) her arms to him
… the *imakhu* in the sight of the Great God, lord of heaven, Ibi.

He speaks:

(3) … the two chambers … I never …
(4) through the greatness of my nobility …
in the twelfth nome of Upper Egypt and those who are in it.
For I gave bread to the hungry, and clothes (5) to the naked;
[I judged] between two parties so that they were both satisfied.
For [I have worked in the fields (?)] with my … , my … ,[41]
my seed, (6) my yoke of oxen and with the dependents of my funerary estate.
[*A further reference to cultivation*]
I am one favored of my mother and father (?).

B. Another Text in the Middle of a Wall; Above Are a Procession of Offering Estates, Below Some Depictions of Cattle

(1) For the *ka* of the *haty-a*, the controller of the estate, the sole companion, the chief of the king, the *imakhu* Ibi.

I did this in the towns of my funerary estate in a pure manner,
as an "offering which the king gives,"
which the majesty of my lord gave me,
in order to do [*perhaps something to do with fields?*] …
(2) with dependents of the funerary estate;
they are full of oxen, goats, donkeys …
not including the property of my father,

when I was the controller of an estate of fields of 203 arouras,
which the majesty of my lord gave me to enrich [me].

267. Inscription of Djau at Deir el-Gebrawi

This unique text recounts how Djau sought posthumous favors for his deceased father (also called Djau; compare Kanawati 1977b). Note the stress placed on the fact that the two Djaus were not buried in the same tomb through lack of means. This emphasizes the social status associated with being in the tomb-owning class. Reign of Pepy II.

(1) His eldest beloved bodily son, [who does what his father favors], (2) who is in his heart, and who belongs to his affections, the *haty-a* of the great estate, seal-bearer of the king of Lower Egypt, controller of the estate, (3) true sole companion, great chief of the twelfth nome of Upper Egypt, Djau, speaks:

I am (4) the beloved one of his father
and the favored one of his mother, (5) one whom his siblings love.
I buried (6) my father, the *haty-a* Djau, more splendidly and perfectly than all his like (7) who are in this Upper Egypt.
I begged a favor (8) of the majesty of my lord,
the king of Upper and Lower Egypt Neferkare, may he live for ever,
(9) that a coffin, clothing and *setj*-oil be provided (10) for this Djau.
His majesty had (11) wood of Lebanon brought (for) the coffin,
setj-oil, (12) *sefetj*-oil, 200 bolts of *hatyw* linen
(13) and *shemau-nefert* linen[12] for bandaging,
which were issued from the two treasuries (14) of the Residence for this Djau.
Never was the like done (15) for another of his peers.
In fact, I saw to it that I was buried in one tomb (16) together with this Djau,
particularly through the desire to be with him in one place,
(17) and not because of the lack of means to build a second tomb.
I did this from the desire (18) to see this Djau every day,
through desire of being with him in one place.
The *haty-a*, controller of the estate, the sole companion, (19) Djau.

He speaks:

O you who live upon earth, servants and peers,

he who shall say "a thousand of bread, beer, oxen, fowl,
alabaster and clothing for Djau, son of Djau"
is one whom the king loves (20) and whom their local god favors.
I begged (21) [from his majesty] the granting of the office of *haty-a* for this Djau,
and his majesty had a decree drawn up making him a *haty-a*
as an "offering which the king gives."

268. Fragment from the Tomb of Nebib at Deir el-Gebrawi

A text above a painted figure of the deceased and his wife. Late Old Kingdom.

(1) The *imakhu* in the sight of (the goddess) Mati, lady of Iatkemt,[43] the chief of secrets of the seal-bearer of the god ... Iatkemt, overseer of ... of the seal-bearer of the god, Nebib.

(2) He speaks:
I came from my town, I went down into the afterlife;
I did daily what was favored as an *imakhu* in the sight of his lord.

269. Text of Henqu from Deir el-Gebrawi

This text probably dates to the end of the Old Kingdom or slightly later. It is a difficult text and contains many phrases not seen in the other texts in this book, a sure pointer to its later date.

(1) O all men of the twelfth nome of Upper Egypt,
O nomarchs of other nomes who shall come upon this my tomb,
I am Henqu who speaks perfectly and sweetly.
(2) Pour water and give bread and beer
for the *imakhu* in the sight of Mati, mistress of Iatkemt,
and in the sight of Nemty who is in the temples of Mam,
for the *iry pat, haty-a, sem* priest, sole companion, lector priest,
nomarch of the twelfth nome of Upper Egypt, the *imakhu* in the sight of his lord Henqu.

(He speaks:)

(3) I am an *imakhu,* (4) beloved of his fathers,

(5) favored of his mothers, (6) who buries the aged,
(7) who releases your deprived ones from the ropes
(8) which you had to pull on the canal,
while you grow old in the hall of the officials.
(9) I never put a daughter of one among you into service
so that she would turn (10) her arms against me.
I did not place ten *medjeh/medju* ropes on one of you …
(11) in this place where you are.
I gave bread to all the hungry of the twelfth nome of Upper Egypt,
(12) clothes to the naked therein.
I kept its (*the nome's*) banks filled (13) with cattle, its pastures with herds.
(14) I satisfied the jackals of the mountain and the kites of the sky
with carrion (15) from the herds.
O you who love the servants who are in it (?)
(16) I carried out (the roles of) nomarch and overseer of Upper Egyptian grain in this nome.
I never harvested (?) or stood on the stair/threshing floor of any of its men (*i.e., of the nome*)
in order to dig a well for his daughter or for a downtrodden woman to go forth at the gate (?).[44]
(17) With regard to those among you who shall be too young to understand these kind words, your father shall explain it to you.
(18) I (re)established towns which had lost their spirit in this nome using specialists (?) from other nomes;
(19) those who were (just) dependents (of others) therein, I made them officials.
(20) I never deprived a man of his father's share, lest he should complain to his local god about it.
For I am one who speaks and repeats perfection.
(21) I never slandered a man to one more powerful than he,
lest he should complain to god about it.
Together with my brother, the *imakhu*, sole companion, lector priest Hemre, the *imakhu*,
I have risen (22) to be ruler in the twelfth nome of Upper Egypt.
(23) I am generous to it particularly in respect of cattle-stalls and nets for the fishermen.[45]
I reestablished all its town-sites[46] (24) with men, cattle, and herds as is right.
I did not speak lies therein …

(25) I am the (26) beloved one of his father,
(27) the favored one of his mother,
(28) one of excellent character among his brothers,
(29) a charming one among his sisters.[47]
(26a) I am one who serves as a priest for his local god,
whose mouth sets fear (27a) into his neighbors (?).
For I wish that [his] state of *imakhu* continue to exist (28a) in their sight in the place [where you are.
I made this tomb of mine (29a) beside] this noble myself for payment of cloth.[48]
(30) I am noble [in the sight of] the king, my father,
my mother, men, my siblings, the noble ones,
(31) those who are noble in the sight of the king, and their ancestors.
(32) I am an excellent and equipped *akh* in this place where I am.

Upper Egypt–Nome 14

The tombs of the Old and Middle Kingdoms at Meir form the principal necropolis seven km to the west of the ancient town of Kis (Greek Kusae, modern el-Qusiya), an important administrative center, 50 km down-river from Asyut. The tombs of the Old and Middle Kingdoms were published by Blackman 1914–53. There are a smaller number of Old Kingdom tombs at Quseir el-Amarna on the East bank (el-Khouly and Kanawati 1989). See Gillam 1991 for a general study of the nome.

270. Inscription of Pepyankhheryib at Meir

The only Old Kingdom inscription at Meir of any length is this longer-than-average ideal biography of the nomarch Pepyankhheryib, inscribed on the west wall of the courtyard of his tomb. Middle reign of Pepy II. No. 311 is a caption from this tomb.

Lintel Inscription

(1) An offering which the king and which Anubis,
who is on his mountain, who dwells in the divine tent-shrine,
who is in his wrappings, lord of the sacred land give,
and an offering which Osiris gives
that he may be united with the land of the necropolis
in accordance with his name,

that he may be buried in the necropolis,
and that invocation offerings be made [for him]
in the festival of Sokar, in the *Rekeh* festival,
in the beginning of the year festival, in the first of the year festival,
in the *Wag* festival, in the festival of Thoth,
and in the perfect festival in the sight of the Great God.

(2) The *iry pat, haty-a*, he who is in the chamber, herdsman of Nekhen, chief of Nekheb, vizier, overseer of royal document scribes, seal-bearer of the king of Lower Egypt, staff of the Apis, mouth of every inhabitant of Pe, overseer of the double granary, overseer of the two *wabet*s, overseer of the storeroom, judge and boundary official, royal document scribe in the presence, seal-bearer of the god, outline draughtsman (*or* scribe of character [?]), overseer of priests of Hathor mistress of Kis, (3) chief lector priest, *sem* priest, sole companion, lector priest, overseer of Upper Egypt in the middle nomes, chief under the king, staff of the *rekhyt*, pillar of *kenmut,* priest of Maat, keeper of secrets of everything which the king commands, who is in the heart of the king wherever he is.

Right-hand Inscription

(1) I lived to the age of 100 years[49] among the living *imakhu*
in possession of my *ka*,
and I spent much of this time
(2) as overseer of priests of Hathor mistress of Kis,
when I attended to Hathor mistress of Kis,
seeing her and carrying out the rituals for her with my own hands.
(3) I am *imakhu* in the sight of the king,
I am *imakhu* in the sight of the Great God,
I am *imakhu* in the sight of men.
I am the beloved one of his father
(4) and the favored one of his mother,
I am the beloved one of his siblings.
Serving as an official was how I spent all my life,
(5) doing good things and saying that which was liked,
so that my (good) character (*or* reputation) would reach the Great God
and so that I might grow old [perfectly/in my town].
(6) I judged two litigants to their satisfaction,
as I know that which the god desires.
I never went to bed angry with people
(7) because of their behavior toward me.

I have had the tomb[50] of an official set up right in the necropolis,
in the area (called) (8) Nebmaat, in a pure place and a perfect place,
where there had been no activity,
in which no other (9) ancestor had done (anything).
I it was who opened up this area,
and it shall function for me as a necropolis
(10) and do for me what I desire;
I paid great attention to it while I was among the living,
and now I have come to it, having grown old (11) most perfectly,
having spent my time among the living
as a result of being *imakhu* in the sight of the king.

Left-hand Inscription

(1) Until the end of the time I spent as an official
I was occupied with the function of the seal:
I never slept with the seal far from my side
from the time when I was promoted (2) to be an official.
I was never placed under guard, I was never imprisoned.
With regard to everything the witnesses said
in the presence of the officials,[51]
(3) I always came away from the matter with success,
the matter having been thrown back
on those who spoke (against me),
since I had been cleared in the presence of the officials,
(4) for they had maliciously spoken against me.
O every man who travels downstream or upstream,
(5) as the king lives for you,
as the god whom you worship lives for you,
you shall give bread and beer from that which you possess
and raise up (6) your hands and make offerings with your mouth.
With regard to those who shall act in accordance with what I have said …
(7) It shall be done in accordance with what they desire.
For I am an *akh* who is better equipped than [other] spirits
… who have existed before.
(8) I am *imakhu* in the sight of the king and in the sight of the god;
all things I have are excellent
as a result of being a *wab*-priest of Hathor mistress of Kis,
and because of doing guard duty for the goddess
(9) so that she has favored me.

O every man who travels downstream or upstream,
as the king lives for you,
as the god (10) whom you worship lives for you, you shall say
"May Hathor mistress of Kis transfigure ... the overseer of priests
Pepyankhheryib."
With regard to any man who shall say these things,
(11) Hathor mistress of Kis will fulfil their desires.
With regard to ... the god,
it is spoken as true words: I am not one who speaks as a bigmouth.

Upper Egypt–Nome 16

For texts in the tombs at Tehna, see no. 110.

Upper Egypt–Nome 20/21

Deshasha is about 120 km south of Cairo, 25 km southwest of Beni Suef, on the west bank of the Nile. The cemetery belongs perhaps with both of these nomes (compare Kanawati and McFarlane 1993: 11–14). Little is known about the nome in the Old Kingdom.

271. Inscriptions of Inti at Deshasha

This tomb is famous for what seems to be the earliest known battle or siege scene (Petrie 1898: pl. IV; Kanawati and McFarlane 1993: pl. 2, 26–27), in which Egyptians are shown fighting Asiatics and also attempting to scale a fortified town. The text that accompanies it is unfortunately too damaged to understand, but there is a not dissimilar scene in the almost contemporaneous tomb of Kaiembezet at Saqqara; the motif is next found in monuments of the later First Intermediate Period at Thebes. The text translated here accompanies a scene of Inti and his wife. Late fifth or early sixth dynasty.

Lintel Text Above

An offering which the king gives and an offering which Anubis,
who dwells in the divine tent-shrine, gives
for burial in the Western Desert,

that he may grow old perfectly as an *imakhu*
in the sight of the Great God.

… the overseer of … supervisor of the barque, controller of the perfect white crown, overseer of commissions of the twenty-first nome of Upper Egypt, Inti; his wife, his beloved, Meretminu.

Main Text

(1) [The royal acquaintance Inti speaks:]
[I made this tomb from my own true property;
I never took any] thing from any man.
(2) … with the words of any man (3) …
I never did anything evil to any man.
With regard to every craftsman,
(4) [I satisfied them] for this which they did,
and they thanked the god for me because of it,
for they loved what I had done.
(5) I set it up for them with great effort
as I wished that they would thank god for me in this matter.
(6) Beloved of Anubis is the man who shall enter this (tomb)
and thank the god therein; the like will be done for him in his tomb.
(7) With regard to any man who shall do anything evil to this (tomb)
or shall do any damage to this (tomb),
(8) or who shall [erase] the writing therein,
I shall be judged with them by the Great God, the lord of judgment,
(9) in the place of judgment.
With regard to any man who shall desire that he be buried
(10) in his own tomb (*literally* "[funerary] property")
and who will protect the property of he who has passed away—
he is an *imakhu* of the Great God
(11) and shall pass away at a great and perfect old age.
I am *imakhu* in the sight of the king,
I am *imakhu* (12) in the sight of the Great God;
I am one who loves perfection and hates what is wrong.
He who shall do what is right is one who loves the god.

Lower Egypt—Nome 9

Little has survived (or at least been excavated) of the Old Kingdom from the Delta. This has much to do with the more difficult nature of Delta excavation and the fact that cemeteries as well as town sites were mostly in cultivated areas, unlike in the Nile Valley, and thus more prone to destruction. Fischer 1976 collects a number of monuments from the end of the sixth dynasty and the First Intermediate Period; see also no. 289.

272. On the Architrave of Khnumnedjem from Busiris

Monuments from Busiris in the Delta, perhaps the original center of the cult of Osiris, are rare. This unusual composition mixes figures, formulae, and a butchery scene with a caption; for the latter see no. 305. See no. 289 for another inscription from Busiris. Present location unknown. Sixth to eighth dynasty.

An offering which the king and which Anubis,
who is on his mountain, lord of the sacred land, give
that invocation offerings may be made
for the seal-bearer of the king of Lower Egypt,
overseer of the *ges-per*, ruler of the estate, sole companion,
[first under the (?)] king, the *imakhu* [Khnumnedjem].
An offering which the king and which Osiris, lord of Busiris, give
for the *imakhu* Khnumnedjem.

Dakhla Oasis

The oases were never included among the nomes of Upper or Lower Egypt. French excavations in the latter years of the twentieth century in the area of Balat in Dakhla Oasis have revealed an Old Kingdom settlement and tombs of some of the governors of the oasis at that time. The settlement (Ayn Asil) has the potential to provide enormous amounts of useful information about this period. Also included in this volume are a royal decree (no. 28) and examples of the correspondence of the governors (no. 99). Much of this material seems to date to later in the sixth dynasty; certainly the major tombs belong to governors of the reign of Pepy II (for these see Valloggia 1986; 1998; Minault-Gout and Deleuze 1992). For comments on the links between the Residence and the oases and also on the population, see Pantalacci 1997; 1998. For comments on the administration, see Valloggia 1996.

273. Stela from the Chapel of Khentyka at Balat

This large stela is from the burial place of one of the oasis governors of the sixth dynasty. The form of the stela is somewhat unusual in that it is a double stela, each part with a figure of the deceased at the bottom; the right-hand part bears these texts, while the left carries a long offering list of ideal provisions for the dead. Now in the museum in Kharga Oasis. Later sixth dynasty.

Top, in Horizontal Lines

(1) An offering which the king gives
and an offering which Anubis gives
that he may be buried in the necropolis,
(2) and an offering which Osiris, foremost of the Westerners, gives
that invocation offerings may be made for him,
(3) (namely) the boat captain, the ruler of the oasis Khentyka,
(4) and that he may cross the land,
that he may be united with the heavens,
that he may travel (5) on the perfect ways of the sky
on which the *akh*s (6) of the *imakhu* travel,
as one who has set up offerings
(7) and who has reached the state of *imakhu*.
The *imakhu* in the sight of Osiris,
the favored one in the sight of the Great God.
(8) The boat captain, ruler of the oasis Khentyka speaks:

Vertical Columns

(1) O you who live upon earth
and who shall pass (2) by this tomb of mine:
they who shall love the king, (3) especially any scribe,
are those who read out the writing on this stela,
(4) and who shall give me bread and beer from that which you possess.
(5) If you possess nothing, then you shall make this pronouncement:
(6) "a thousand of bread and a thousand of beer
for the boat captain, the ruler of the oasis, Khentika."
(7) For I am an excellent and prepared *akh*,

and I have made this stela in the wish that (8) my perfect name
be remembered by those who live upon earth.
I am one who is *imakhu* hourly (?).[52]
(9) I gave bread to the hungry, clothes to the naked,
(10) *merhet* oil to him who had none;
I raised up Maat for him who made it.
(11) The boat captain, the ruler of the oasis, Khentika,
the *imakhu* in the sight of the Great God.
The boat captain, ruler of the oasis, the *imakhu*, Khentyka.

274. Stela from the Chapel of Khentykawpepy at Balat

This stela is the principal surviving monument from the burial place of one of the oasis governors of the sixth dynasty. It is unusual for the mention it makes of the time it took to set up parts of the tomb. Now in the museum in Kharga Oasis. Later sixth dynasty.

(1) The boat captain, ruler of the oasis, overseer of priests, the *imakhu*, Khentykawpepy (2) speaks:

O you who live upon earth, (take note):
I made this tomb of mine in the West
[... in the space of] three months,
and I erected its enclosure wall in (1 + x) months;
I set (it) up (3) with the servants of a funerary estate,
and I established payment for them
in the hope that [they would provide me with offerings].
For I am noble in the sight of the king,
and my name is better known by his majesty
(4) than all the other rulers of the oases.
I was favored by promotion to ruler of the oasis
when I was only a young man
who had (just) put on the belt in front of the great ones,[53]
(5) and I am more valuable in the sight of his majesty
than those who came before me.
I have seen to it that these two obelisks[54] of mine
are inscribed with details of what I have done for the Residence,
that which is new which has come to pass,
and my acquaintance with his majesty.

Notes

1. Probably the very southern part of Upper Egypt; perhaps a miswriting of the better-known "Head of the South," whose limits are sometimes disputed (Fischer 1968: 68).

2. A term applied to women of high status and honor; it could in this context refer to the king's wife, given the parallel with the previous clause.

3. Presumably the name of a road stretching into Nubia, on which African products, such as ivory, were brought. The state of Iam was probably south of the others he mentions (see next note). Another interpretation is "the road of Elephantine" (for example Doret 1986: 71 [example 112]).

4. This means Harkhuf paid the ruler of Iam for the wares that he was expecting to obtain from Iam—this is why he followed the ruler out into the desert, to ensure that he carried out his transactions.

5. Following the reconstruction suggested by Edel 1955: 58–59. The previous trip mentioned a ruler of two of these lands; now that he ruled three, it might be possible to argue for local disputes and the taking-over of adjacent territory.

6. An aromatic product (Edel 1984: 193).

7. A title almost exclusively given to expedition leaders.

8. Presumably this term had the same sense to the ancient Egyptians as its colloquial usage does to us.

9. See the various royal decrees for such exemptions from state-commanded duties (chapter I, §6.3.2).

10. See Habachi 1985 and Franke 1994. Most recent work on the earliest temple of Heqaib in Kaiser et al. 1999: 85–90.

11. Could this expression, *nakht-ib,* be a pun on the name Pepynakht Heqaib?

12. See further in the inscription of Weni (no. 256).

13. Presumably a term for a route that went through a pass or wadi of some sort; here doubtless the way into Nubia from Elephantine; Sabni holds a similar title in the Tomas inscription. See other mentions in the inscriptions of Tjetji (no. 68) and Qar (no. 247).

14. Presumably to his superiors or even to the king.

15. "House of perfection," another place very much associated with embalming; possibly also "house of rejuvenation" (Donohue 1978).

16. A rare expression, literally perhaps "protect the name." Discussed in Seyfried forthcoming.

17. Literally "pacified" or "satisfied"; compare the Dahshur Decree of Pepy I (no. 20 n. 8). The same word is frequently used in the payment texts to express that the workmen were paid by the tomb owner. In this context the word probably means a mixture of these ideas; hence I have used "engaged."

18. Perhaps a reference to a route out to the oases. Cf. el-Khadragy 2002a: 210 n. 24 and Fischer 1968: 12 n. 56. Compare its use in the Aswan area (for example no. 242).

19. This seems to offer better sense than Mostafa's interpretation, "as if they were in his house" (?).

20. This unusual phrase is only attested from Dendera (Kloth 2002: 85

[§ 3.3.3.7]); it appears also in the First Intermediate Period text of Menankhpepy (Urk 1:268–69).

21. Other blocks from this tomb are also in Cairo: false door CG 1574; obelisks CG 1309–10; reliefs and texts CG 1643, 1670.

22. I parse the text differently to Sethe, treating this and others like it in this text with the particle [hieroglyphs]/[hieroglyphs] as a clause subordinate to the preceding one (following Doret 1986: 25 n. 105).

23. See Callender 2000 for this primarily legal title.

24. A scene from the temple of Niuserre at Abusir may show officials performing these acts that were presumably part of the ritual of attending on the king (see Borchardt 1907: Bl. 16, and Grdseloff 1951: 131 n. 1).

25. A queenly title (see, for example, no. 276) and not a name (Lichtheim 1973: 19). The name is not given presumably because she was disgraced and naming a disgraced person in the tomb would potentially bring harm to it.

26. This is one of the extremely rare references to such goings on in ancient Egypt (compare Kanawati 2002a, especially pp. 171–73). Nothing more is known about the incident, as Weni's only reason for mentioning it was to illustrate his own importance. Circumstantial evidence possibly points to who else might have been involved; the name of the vizier in the Dahshur decree of Pepy I (no. 20) has been excised, and involvement of a vizier in such a conspiracy as this might explain (a) the Dahshur damage and (b) the omission of the vizier in the legal process. A possible candidate for the vizier is Rewer, who was buried at Saqqara (el-Fikey 1980). Kanawati's book draws attention to the number of officials buried in the Teti Pyramid Cemetery at Saqqara whose tombs have also been deliberately defaced.

27. Or "Asiatic Sand-dwellers," Aamu being later usually translated as "Asiatic." These people are perhaps one of the predecessors of the modern bedouin of the Eastern Desert. This is one of the few references to Asiatics in the Old Kingdom and one of the first to mention a campaign against them. Nothing further is known about this. Compare text of Pepynakht (no. 242); see the comment of Roccati 1982: 189.

28. Many of these Nubian places appear again in the biography of Harkhuf (no. 241); the Tjemehu lived in the Western Desert and are probably ancestors of the later Libyans.

29. Weni is making the point that he was in charge despite there being many other persons in the army who were theoretically of higher rank than he.

30. A particularly poetic interlude (compare chapter I, §4.3). It might even be possible to imagine the following lines as a song of victory chanted by the expedition.

31. The geographical term remains unknown. See various sources for discussion.

32. We do not know what these sorts of taxing or assessment cycles might have been; one wonders whether they were related to the "cattle counts," which were used as a method of reckoning regnal years (chapter I, §3.2).

33. A quarry south of Elephantine, possibly Toshka (Zibelius 1972: 74–75).

34. I assume this to be the name given to this particular sarcophagus.

35. Some of these terms for architectural elements are a little unclear, but they

are clearly for important elements of temples; in this case I am assuming that the intended destination of the Merenre pyramid is true for all of them.

36. These areas are not renowned for having an excess of wood, although the climate of the area was much less hostile then than now.

37. The sense of this word is unclear.

38. See chapter I, §6.2 and an actual example in Bubastis (no. 13).

39. Not clear, but compare texts of Qereri (no. 263).

40. This reconstruction is highly speculative, as the phrase is not attested elsewhere.

41. Two unclear and uncertain words, although the context suggests that they may have been something agricultural. This phrase is unparalleled elsewhere in the Old Kingdom ideal biography.

42. Two types of particularly fine linen. See also the linen lists in chapter XX.

43. Mati was a lion-headed local deity of the Deir el-Gebrawi region. Little is known about her in the Old Kingdom, although she was still preeminent in this locality according to the geographical lists of the Graeco-Roman temples. At Dendera she was regarded as a form of Hathor, while she was also regarded as being at the side of the god Nemty in warfare. See further, Davies 1902: 2:43; Graefe 1972–92; Leitz 2002: 3:213.

44. This is perhaps the most obscure and difficult sentence in this book! Perhaps Henqu is indicating that he never obstructed anyone else while doing his good works? Compare Janssen 1946: 2:203 (17) and Schenkel 1965: 43. I thank Ronald J. Leprohon for his thoughts.

45. A different reading of this line "I found it as stalls of cattle …" is proposed in Fischer 1968: 148 and Doret 1986: 156.

46. At this point in the text there appears to be a boxed-off area containing the words "the *imakhu* Henqu."

47. I tentatively follow Sethe's parsing of Urk 1:79.3–11, with the tops of columns 26–29 following directly on line 25, and numbering the lower parts as columns 26a–29a (followed by Edel 1955–64: 478–79).

48. I follow Fischer 1976c: 18, fig. 11, for restorations of parts of columns 27a–29a.

49. We have no way of knowing how true this is. This may be very much the ideal age that an Egyptian wished to attain.

50. Literally "property," which can be construed in a funerary sense (e.g., Edel 1955–64: §301).

51. Following Gillam 1991: 578, in preference to Sethe's and Blackman's "With regard to everything said about me in the presence of the officials."

52. The most obscure phrase in the text; Osing et al. 1982: 27–28 discusses the problem.

53. "Put on the belt" seems to be a term alluding to the rites of passage into manhood. Compare "tie the headband" in nos. 214 and 226.

54. For some Old Kingdom obelisks, see Martin 1977: 48–62.

XVIII

Texts of Women

See notes in chapter I, §6.8.

Queens

See also the titles of the two queens named Ankhesenpepy on the monument of Djau (no. 257) and those in building inscriptions (no. 15). See Jánosi 1996 for information about queens' pyramids.

275. Text Relating to Meretites I from Giza

In the mid-nineteenth century, Mariette found parts of a false door of Meretites I, the principal wife of Khufu, probably in the area of the mastaba of her eldest son, Kaiwab, in the Eastern Cemetery at Giza. The false door probably came from the queen's pyramid in which she was buried. The text survives only in hand copies. Early to middle fourth dynasty.

Horizontal Line at Top

The king's beloved wife, the follower of Horus, Meretites.

Columns

(1) The great favorite of Sneferu …
(2) The great favorite of Khufu, follower of Horus …
(3) The *imakhu* in the sight of Khafre, Meretites
(4) The king's beloved wife, beloved one of his father …
(5) Consort of him who is beloved of the Two Ladies; everything she says is done for her.
(6) …

276. Texts from the Mastaba of Meresankh III at Giza

The tomb of Meresankh (G 7530, PM III^2, 197–99) has the best-preserved chapel in the field of royal mastabas to the east of the Great Pyramid, which *cemetery was mostly reserved for relatives and descendants of Khufu. It is the oldest well-preserved tomb at Giza. Meresankh seems to have been the daughter of Kaiwab, probably the eldest son of Khufu, and Hetepheres; both persons are shown in her tomb. Bones, perhaps belonging to Meresankh, were found in the burial and suggest that she might have been about fifty at death. Dates of her death and burial are recorded, but the reign is unknown; depending on the date of her birth, her death is to be placed in either the reigns of Menkaure or Shepseskaf. She would have been married to either Khafre or Menkaure. The sarcophagus was originally made for her mother. See also quarry marks and captions from this tomb in no. 84.*

Entrance

Lintel

She who sees Horus and Seth, great of affection of the Two Ladies, follower of Horus, great of favor, the beloved one of Horus and Thoth, his companion, king's daughter of his body, royal wife, Meresankh.

Drum

She who sees Horus and Seth, great of affection, royal wife, Meresankh.

Right jamb

The king's daughter Meresankh.
Year of the first occasion, first month of the *Shemu* season, day 21.
Her *ka* rested and she proceeded to the *wabet*.

Left jamb

The royal wife Meresankh.
The year after the first occasion, second month of the *Peret* season, day 18.[1]
She went to her perfect tomb.

Sarcophagus

Top, both long sides

She who sees Horus and Seth, great of affection, great of favor, controller of the butchers of the acacia house,[2] priestess of Bapefy, consort of he who is beloved of the Two Ladies, king's beloved daughter of his body, Hetepheres.

Vertical column at each corner

I have given it to the king's daughter and king's wife, Meresankh.

277. Texts in the Mastaba of Khamerernebty II at Giza

Khamerernebty was almost certainly a wife of Menkaure. See Baud 1995 and Callender and Jánosi 1997 for more information on the tomb, located in the quarry by the second pyramid (PM III², 273–74). Later fourth dynasty. I follow Edel's reconstruction of the commemorative text.

Architrave Inscription

(1) The mother of the king of Upper and Lower Egypt, daughter of the god, who sees Horus and Seth, great of affection, great of favor, priest(ess) of Thoth, priest(ess) of Tjasepef, his beloved royal wife, king's daughter of his body, the possessor of *imakhu* in the sight of the Great God, Khamerernebty.

(2) Eldest daughter, who sees Horus and Seth, great of affection, great of favor, priest(ess) of Thoth, priest(ess) of Tjasepef, intimate of Horus, consort of he who is beloved of the Two Ladies, his beloved royal wife, king's daughter of his body, the possessor of *imakhu* in the sight of her father, Khamerernebty.

Commemoration

(1) [Beloved of Anubis is he who shall provide protection]
(2) for the property of another who has gone to [her *ka*];
(3) I have never done anything evil against [anyone].
(4) With regard to [him who shall do anything] to this (tomb),
(5) [I shall be judged with him by the Great God.
(6) I have] satisfied the craftsmen [who made this for me].

278. Inscriptions Relating to the "Khentkawes Problem"

Egyptology was astonished when a tomb was found in 1932 in the central field at Giza of a Queen Khentkawes bearing the title possibly of "mother of two kings of Upper and Lower Egypt," and then again in 1976 when the pyramid of a similarly named and titled person was located at Abusir. At the time of writing this book, the preferred interpretation is that there were two separate women with the same name, who both happened to mother two kings. The former may have been a wife of Shepseskaf, who gave birth to Userkaf and Sahure (but see no. 312 below), while the second was the spouse of Neferirkare and probable mother of Neferefre and Niuserre. The most-accessible accounts of this problem are Verner 1994: 115–31; 2002:

89–109, with further discussions in Verner 1999a; 1999b. For the complex political goings-on that may have surrounded the succession in the mid fifth dynasty, see Verner 2000.

A. Inscriptions of Queen Khentkawes at Giza

Tomb LG 100: PM III^2, 288–89.

Jambs at Entrance to the Chapel

Mother of two kings of Upper and Lower Egypt, daughter of the god, who relates every perfect thing which she has done, Khentkawes.

B. Inscriptions of Queen Khentkawes at Abusir

False Door

Top

Mother of two kings of Upper and Lower Egypt, Khentkawes.

Left and Right Jambs

Mother of two kings of Upper and Lower Egypt, daughter of the god, who sees Horus and Seth, great of affection, his beloved royal wife, Khentkawes.

Mother of two kings of Upper and Lower Egypt, daughter of the god, the follower of Horus, who sits with Horus, great of affection, Khentkawes.

Gateway

Top

Mother of two kings of Upper and Lower Egypt, daughter of the god, king's wife, Khentkawes.

Jambs

Mother of two kings of Upper and Lower Egypt, daughter of the god, great of affection, great of favor, who sits with Horus, who sees Horus and Seth, Khentkawes.

C. Inscription of Idu from Abusir Naming Khentkawes

An ink inscription on a sarcophagus, probably dating to the reign of Izezi.

Year after the seventeenth occasion, first month of the *Shemu* season (?), day 23.

A gift for the priest of Setibre, the *wab*-priest of the pyramid of Kakai, the scribe of the royal children, Idu.

The inspector of priests of the mother of two kings of Upper and Lower Egypt Khentkawes, Idu.

The judge and scribe, ruler of the great estate, *wab*-priest (?) of the pyramid of Neferefre, Idu.

279. From the Tomb of Nebet, Wife of Unas, at Saqqara

Unas constructed a double mastaba adjacent to his pyramid for two of his queens, Nebet and Khenut (PM III², 624–25). That of Khenut is rather damaged, but the scenes and texts are better preserved in the tomb of Nebet. Late fifth or early sixth dynasty.

Nebet Watches the Bringing of Wine

(*Over the queen*): She who sees Horus and Seth, great of affection, great of favor, follower of the Great One, companion of Horus, his beloved, the *imakhu* in the sight of (the king [?]), royal wife, Nebet.
(*In front of her*): Viewing the wine brought from the court council for the great of affection, the royal wife, his beloved, Nebet.
(*Behind a man holding up a papyrus*): Wine for your *ka* O mistress!
(*Above men dragging a sledge with large jars*): Dragging wine. Bringing wine for you O mistress!

280. From the Pyramid of Iput, Wife of Teti and Mother of Pepy I, at Saqqara

The pyramid complex of Iput is adjacent to her husband's pyramid (PM III², 396–97). For more detail on the complex, see Labrousse 1994; Hawass 2000: 414–19; Firth and Gunn 1926: I, 11–14.

A. On a False Door

An offering which the king and which Anubis, who is on his mountain, give
for the mother of the king of Upper and Lower Egypt, Iput,
the royal mother, Iput.
The mother of the king of Upper and Lower Egypt, Iput;
the daughter of the king of Upper and Lower Egypt, Iput,
his beloved wife, Iput.

B. From an Offering Table

An offering which the king and which Anubis, who is on his mountain, give that invocation offerings may be made for the royal mother of the pyramid of Pepy I, Iput.

C. On Some Copper Cups from the Pyramid

Invocation offerings for she who see Horus and Seth, great of affection, great of favor, beloved royal wife, Iput.

281. Texts of Two Queens of Pepy I Named Ankhesenpepy from Saqqara

There are a number of queens' tombs around Pepy I's pyramid (Labrousse and Albouy 1999). Pepy I took, for us, the very confusing step of marrying two sisters or half-sisters from Abydos, both named Ankhesenpepy; one became the mother of Merenre, the other perhaps of Pepy II (although see further below). See also nos. 22 and 257.

A. Sarcophagus of Ankhesenpepy I, Mother of Merenre, from the Pyramid Complex of Pepy II

This sarcophagus (now in Cairo, JE 65908) was installed in a group of chambers in a storeroom to the south of the pyramid of Iput. The lid has been discovered to bear annalistic texts of the sixth dynasty (no. 3); the following are the other texts on it:

Horus Merytawy, the king of Upper and Lower Egypt, Meryre, given all life for ever.
King's beloved wife, great of affection, Ankhesenpepy.
Mother of the king of Upper and Lower Egypt, daughter of the god, foster child of Wadjet, king's beloved wife, great of affection, Ankhesenpepy.

B. Lintel of Ankhesenpepy II Found in the Pyramid Complex of Pepy I

Mother of the king of Upper and Lower Egypt, the pyramid of Neferkare, Ankhesenpepy.

C. Block of Ankhesenpepy II Found in Her Pyramid Complex by That of Pepy I

This block has produced a major surprise in that it suggests that Ankhesenpepy II, having married Pepy I, might also have married his son and successor by her sister, Ankhesenpepy I! This opens the interesting possibility that Pepy II was a son of Merenre and not, as usually assumed, Pepy I.

... Royal mother of the pyramid of [Neferkare] ...
... Royal wife of the pyramid of [Meryre] ...
... Royal wife of the pyramid of [Merenre] ...
... daughter of the god ...
... Ankhesenpepy ...

282. Inscriptions of Queens of Pepy II from the Area of His Pyramid Complex at Saqqara

A. Obelisk of Neit

The *iry pat*, royal wife of the pyramid of Neferkare, his beloved.
The eldest king's daughter of his body of the pyramid of Meryre, Neit.

B. Obelisk of Iput

(*One erased column*)
The *iry pat*, royal wife of the pyramid of Neferkare, king's eldest daughter Iput.
The *iry pat*, who sees Horus and Seth, of the pyramid of Neferkare, [Iput].

C. From the Damaged False Door of Ankhesenpepy IV

A wife of Pepy II and mother of an ephemeral successor. See Dobrev 2000: 385–87 for the identity of different queens of this name; the king may be Neferkare Nebi of the eighth dynasty (von Beckerath 1999: 66 [4]).

Royal wife of the pyramid of Neferkare, beloved one of Anubis who is on his mountain ...
King's mother of the pyramid of Neferkare III ...

D. Fragments Naming Wedjebten

Fragment of text: ... pyramidion of electrum ...
Door jamb: *iry pat*, royal wife, Wedjebten: construction of a temple in ...
On a casing block: ... the son of Re, Pepy, may he live for ever—for the *iry pat* and royal wife of the pyramid of Neferkare, he set up a monument ...

Princesses

These women bear the title "king's daughter," which, as discussed in chapter I, §5.2.4, is not necessarily indicative of true royal filiation.

283. Inscriptions of Hemetre Called Hemi from Her Tomb at Saqqara

The tomb is located to the west of the Step Pyramid (PM III^2, 606). Late fifth or early sixth dynasty; she may have been a daughter of Unas.

False Door

Lintel

(1) An offering which the king gives
and an offering which Anubis gives
that she may be buried in the necropolis,
having grown old most perfectly, Hemetre.
(2) An offering which Osiris, foremost of the Westerners, gives
that invocation offerings may be made for her
in every daily festival for ever,
the king's bodily daughter, Hemi.

(3) The king's bodily daughter, who has grown old, whom he loves, the *imakhu* in the sight of Anubis, who is on his mountain, Hemetre.

(4) The king's bodily daughter, whom he loves, the *imakhu* in the sight of Hathor lady of the sycomore, Hemi.

Left Outer Jamb

(1) The priestess of the *meret* temple of Teti, king's bodily daughter, the *imakhu* in the sight of the Great God, the *imakhu* in the sight of Hathor lady of the sycomore, Hemetre.

(2) An offering which the king gives
and an offering which Anubis, who is on his mountain,
who dwells in the divine tent-shrine, who is in his wrappings,
lord of the sacred land, gives
that invocation offerings may be made for her in the necropolis
as (is done for) an *imakhu* whose perfect name is Hemi.

Left Inner Jamb

(1) The *imakhu* in the sight of Neith, opener of the ways, king's bodily daughter, Hemetre.

(2) The king's beloved bodily daughter, priestess of Hathor wherever she is, Hemi.

Right Outer Jamb

(1) She who belongs to the pyramid of Unas, king's bodily daughter, the *imakhu* in the sight of the Great God, the *imakhu* in the sight of Hathor lady of the sycomore, Hemetre.

(2) An offering which the king gives and which Anubis,
who dwells in the divine tent-shrine, who is in his wrappings,
lord of the sacred land gives
that invocation offerings be made for her in the necropolis
as (is done for) an *imakhu,* whose perfect name is Hemi.

Right Inner Jamb

(1) The king's beloved bodily daughter, the priestess of Hathor wherever she is, Hemetre.

(2) The *imakhu* in the sight of Neith, opener of the ways, king's bodily daughter, Hemi.

284. A Text of Iabtet from Giza

On a very complicated false door, which mixes depictions of the deceased with those of offering bearers and priests, one of whom, Kai, figures prominently on the door. Tomb G 4650 in the Western Cemetery (PM III², 134–35). Middle or later fourth dynasty.

[An offering which the king gives ...]
in the monthly and half-monthly festivals,
for the king's bodily daughter,
the possessor of *imakhu* in the sight of the god, Iabtet.

This was done for her by the overseer of the estate (*steward*), the overseer of soul priests Kai.

285. Texts of Inti from Her Tomb at Saqqara

This tomb, north of the pyramid of Teti (PM III², 508), was discovered in the 1920s but is now apparently lost. The formulae repay reading, since there are some unusual phrases. Inti is referred to as a bodily daughter of both Teti and Pepy I (chapter I, §5.2.4); see further Callender 2002a. Early to middle sixth dynasty.

Lintel Text on Entrance to Tomb

(1) An offering which the king gives and which Anubis,
(who dwells in) the divine tent-shrine, who is in his wrappings,
the lord of the sacred land, who is on his mountain, gives
in order that she may be buried in the necropolis,
in the Western Desert, having grown old most perfectly.
(2) An offering which the king gives and an offering which Osiris,
lord of Abydos, lord of Busiris, in all his places, gives
that she may travel on the perfect ways.
(3) An offering which the king gives for her treatment in her *wabet*
while the work of the embalmer is done to (her)
and the craft of the lector priest is carried out for her
as an *imakhu* in the sight of (the Great God [?]).
(4) An offering which the king gives
that invocation offerings may be made for her
in the Opening of the Year festival, the festival of Thoth,
the first day of the year festival, the *Wag* festival,
the festival of Sokar, every daily festival,
every monthly and ten-day festival of the year and in the *Sadj* festival.
(5) I am an excellent and prepared *akh* whose name the god knows;
she whose name the lord knows is she whose name the god knows.
I am an *imakhu* in the sight of her lord.
(6) The *imakhu* in the sight of the Great God, the king's daughter, Inti.

Titles from Other Parts of the Tomb

The eldest king's daughter of his body of the pyramid of Teti, the companion of Horus, his beloved one, the *imakhu* in the sight of the Great God, the king's daughter, Inti.
The eldest king's daughter of his body of the pyramid of Pepy I, Inti.

286. From the Saqqara False Door of Merut Called Zeshzeshet

Found in the tomb of Ptahembat, near the mastabas of Akhethotep and Ptahhotep, west of the Step Pyramid, without any indication of her relationship to him, although she is probably his spouse. Note the careful alternation of her two different names. Probably late Old Kingdom.

Top

(1) An offering which the king and Osiris give
that invocation offerings be made for her in the necropolis,
the king's daughter Merut.
(2) The king's daughter, the *imakhu* in the sight of Anubis,
who is on his mountain, Merut.
Panel: The king's daughter Merut.
Below panel: The king's eldest daughter Merut.
Drum: The king's daughter Zeshzeshet.

Outer Jambs

An offering which the king and which Anubis,
who is in his wrappings, who dwells in the divine tent-shrine give
that she may be buried in her tomb of the necropolis
(*left*) (as) an *imakhu* whose perfect name is Zeshzeshet
(*right*) as an *imakhu*, Merut.

Inner Jambs

An offering which the king gives and an offering which Osiris gives
that invocation offerings may be made for her
in every daily festival for her
(*left*) for the one whose great name is Merut
(*right*) whose perfect name is Zeshzeshet.

287. Formulae of Nensedjerkai from Her Tomb at Giza

From tomb G 2101 in the Western Cemetery (PM III^2, 72). Early fifth dynasty. Nensedjerkai was the daughter of Merib (no. 307). The structure of these formulae is similar, but the second was cut back by the space available.

Outer Architrave

(1) An offering which the king gives and which Anubis,
lord of the sacred land, who dwells in the divine tent-shrine, gives
that she may be buried (in) the necropolis, in the Western Desert,
having grown old very perfectly,
and that she may travel on the perfect ways
on which the *imakhu* travel;
(2) and that invocation offerings be made for her (on)
the festival of opening the year, the festival of Thoth,

the first day of the year festival, the *Wag* festival,
the festival of Sokar, the great festival, the *Rekeh* festival,
the *Wah-akh* festival,[3] the festival of the coming forth of Min,
the monthly *Sadj* festival, the monthly and half-monthly festivals,
and every daily festival,
for the king's daughter, the royal ornament, Nensedjerkai.

Inner Architrave

(1) An offering which the king gives and which Anubis,
who dwells in the divine tent-shrine, gives
that she may be buried (in) the necropolis, in the Western Desert,
having grown old very perfectly in the sight of the Great God,
(2) and that invocation offerings may be made for her (on)
the festival of opening the year, the festival of Thoth,
the first day of the year festival, and the *Wag* festival,
for the king's daughter, the royal ornament, Nensedjerkai.

Private Individuals

288. Dedicatory Text of Djenwen

From a false door seen in a palace in Cairo by Lepsius; date uncertain.

Left

Her son the soul priest Iunka it was who acted on her behalf while he was alive and on his two feet. He is *imakhu* in the sight of his mother—Iunka.

Right

(1) An offering which the king gives
that invocation offerings be made for her
on the day of the Opening of the Year festival, the festival of Thoth,
on the day of the first day of the year festival, the *Wag* festival,
every great festival, the *Rekeh* festival,
the festival of the coming forth of Min, and the *Sadj* festival
for (2) the royal acquaintance Djenwen
(3) who has protected the property for when she shall die.
She is an *imakhu* when she shall die.
With regard to any man who shall do anything against this (tomb),
I shall be judged with him by the Great God.

289. False Door of Hemire, Perhaps from Busiris

Some of the phraseology of this late false door is different from the texts of the main part of the Old Kingdom. See no. 272 for another inscription from Busiris. Now Cambridge, Fitzwilliam Museum, E.6.1909. Perhaps eighth dynasty or a little later.

Outer Jambs, Left

(1) An offering which the king gives by[4] Osiris, lord of Busiris
(for) bread, beer and everything pure which should be put (*literally* "goes forth")
on the offering slab of Osiris in Busiris
for the *imakhu* Hemire whose perfect name is
the royal acquaintance, priestess of Hathor, Hemi.
(2) O you who live on earth and who shall pass by on this path,
(are) you who shall say:
"It is the pure bread of Osiris (and) it is for the *imakhu* Hemi."

Outer Jambs, Right

(1) [An offering which the king and which] Anubis,
who dwells in the divine tent-shrine, who is in his wrappings,
lord of the sacred land give
that invocation offerings may be made in the *Wag* festival
and the festival of Thoth for the *imakhu* Hemire
whose perfect name is Hemi.
(2) [I am one who makes] peace and who attains the state of *imakhu,*
the favored one of her father and beloved one of her [mother],
the *imakhu* of Hathor mistress of Busiris,
Hemire whose perfect name is Hemi.

Inner Jambs, Left

(1) May she travel on the perfect ways of the necropolis
as an *imakhu* of the Great God,
Hemire whose perfect name is Hemi.
(2) With regard to any scribe who shall pass by this tomb of mine,
he it is who shall say
"bread and beer for the mistress of this tomb, the *imakhu* Hemi."

Inner Jambs, Right

(1) I am she who gives bread to the hungry and clothes to the naked,
one favored of her husband, Hemire.

(2) With regard to any man who shall say
"bread and beer for Hemi in this her tomb!"—
I am an excellent *akh* and I will not allow that evil (happen) to them.

290. Inscribed Slab of Henutsen from Saqqara

From the tomb of her son Kaiemtjenenet, exact original location unknown (PM III², 692–93). Now in Cairo, CG 1691. Fifth dynasty.

(1) An offering which the king and which Anubis
who dwells in the divine tent-shrine, give
for a burial in the necropolis
(2) as a possessor of *imakhu* in the sight of the Great God
(for) the royal acquaintance, Henutsen.

Her eldest son, (3) the official and chief of provisioning Kaiemtjennet, it was who acted on her behalf so that invocation offerings may be made for her there.

291. Inscriptions of Hetepheres from Giza

From her chapel in the tomb complex of the family of Seshemnefer IV (no. 234). Although she refers to a husband in these inscriptions, it is not clear who it was; Seshemnefer is one possibility. Tomb LG 54, PM III², 227–28. Probably sixth dynasty.

False Door

Top

An offering which the king and an offering which Anubis,
who is on his mountain, give for burial in the necropolis.

Outer Jamb Left

An offering which the king and an offering which Anubis give
that invocation offerings may be made for her in
the opening (of the year) festival, the festival of Thoth,
the first day of the year festival, the *Wag* festival …

Outer Jamb Right

An offering which the king and an offering which Anubis give
that she may travel in peace on the perfect ways
on which the *imakhu* travel
in the sight of the Great God, lord of the necropolis.

Both Inner Jambs

The royal acquaintance, the *imakhu* in the sight of the Great God, the *imakhu* in the sight of her husband, Hetepheres.

Panel

The royal acquaintance, the *imakhu*, Hetepheres.

Lower Lintel

The royal acquaintance, the *imakhu* in the sight of the Great God, Hetepheres.

Remains of an Offering Scene

The royal acquaintance, priestess of Neith, the *imakhu* in the sight of the Great God, lord of the necropolis, Hetepheres.

292. Inscriptions of Hetepheres Called Khenut from Giza

From her false door in the tomb of her husband, Nymaatre (PM III^2, 282–84), in the Central Cemetery. Perhaps late fifth dynasty.

Top

An offering which the king gives
that invocation offerings be made for her every day
so that she may be *imakhu* in the sight of the Great God,
the priestess of Hathor, the *imakhu* in the sight of her husband,
priestess of Neith, possessor of love, royal acquaintance, Khenut.

Outer Jamb Left

[An offering which the king and an] offering which Anubis [give]
for burial in the necropolis,
and that invocation offerings may be made for her among the *imakhu*,
the royal acquaintance, Khenut.

Outer Jamb Right

[An offering which the king gives and an] offering which Osiris gives
that she may travel on the perfect ways on which the *imakhu* travel,
the royal acquaintance, Khenut.

Both Inner Jambs
The royal acquaintance, Hetepheres called Khenut.

Lower Lintel
The royal acquaintance, the beloved *imakhu* of her husband, Khenut.

293. From the Stela of Iret, Said to Come from Akhmim

Now in Cairo, CG 1613. The form of this stela dates it to the very end of the Old Kingdom or later.

(1) An offering which the king and which Anubis,
who is on his mountain, who is in his wrappings, give
(2) that invocation offerings be made for the royal acquaintance,
priestess of Hathor, Iret.

(3) Her husband it was who made these inscriptions, the royal document scribe Bawy.

294. False Door of Khenit from Giza

Tomb in the Western Cemetery (PM III², 162). Probably later fifth dynasty.

Lintel

An offering which the king and which Anubis,
who dwells in the divine tent-shrine, give
that she may be buried in her (?) necropolis
having grown old perfectly.
An offering which Osiris, lord of Busiris, gives
that invocation offerings may be made for her in
the Opening of the Year festival, the festival of Thoth
and every daily festival,
the royal acquaintance Khenit.

Jambs of Door (Same Both Sides)

Inner

An offering which the king gives and which Anubis,
who dwells in the divine tent-shrine, who is on his

the lord of the sacred land, gives
that invocation offerings may be made for her every day, Khenit.

Outer

that she may travel on the perfect ways on which the *imakhu* travel,
in the sight of the lord of the necropolis,
the royal acquaintance, priestess of Hathor, Khenit.

295. Stela of Nebet and Khui from Abydos

This stela from the Central Cemetery at Abydos would not be remarkable if it were not for the extraordinarily high-ranking titulary of Nebet who is apparently granted some of the highest state offices in it, as well as having some unique titles such as "daughter" of certain gods. Fischer 2000: 37–38 discusses whether she actually might have exercised these titles, or whether perhaps her husband Khui did so. As she was the mother of the two women named Ankhesenpepy who married Pepy I (compare no. 257), most Egyptologists assume that her relationship to the king was in some way responsible for this remarkable situation. Now in Cairo, CG 1578. Middle sixth dynasty.

Left Half

(1) [An offering] which the king and which Osiris,
foremost of the Westerners, lord of Abydos, give
that invocation offerings be made for (2) the *iry pat,* the daughter of Geb, the *haty-a,* daughter of *Merhu,* (3) vizier, daughter of Thoth, companion of the king of Lower Egypt, daughter of Horus, (4) the *imakhu* in the sight of Osiris, foremost of the Westerners, lord of Abydos, (5) the *imakhu,* Nebet.

Right Half

(1) An offering which the king and which Osiris,
foremost of the Westerners, lord of Abydos, give
that invocation offerings be made for (2) the god's father, *iry pat,* overseer of the pyramid town, *haty-a,* controller of the great ones of Upper and Lower Egypt, (3) controller of the estates of the Red Crown, controller of every divine office, the *imakhu,* (4) Khui.
(5) The *imakhu* in the sight of Osiris, foremost of the Westerners, lord of Abydos, Khui.

296. False Door of Nedjetempet from Saqqara

Nedjetempet was the mother of the vizier Mereruka; her tomb is a few meters to the northeast of that of her son in the Teti pyramid cemetery. Doubtless she was only able to be buried in such an important location because of her son's rise in importance; this false door is one of the largest to have been dedicated to a woman alone. The body of a fifty-year-old woman, presumably Nedjetempet, was found in the sarcophagus. Early to middle sixth dynasty.

Upper Lintel

(1) An offering which the king gives and an offering which Anubis,
who dwells in the divine tent-shrine, who is in his wrappings,
who is on his mountain, the lord of the sacred land, gives
that she may be buried in the necropolis;
(2) An offering which the king gives and which Osiris,
who dwells in Busiris, gives
that invocation offerings may be made for her every day.

Lower Lintel

(1) The royal acquaintance, priestess of Hathor lady of the sycomore, (2) the *imakhu* Nedjetempet, whose perfect name is Iteti.

Left/right Inner Jamb

(1) The royal acquaintance, priestess of Hathor lady of the sycomore, priestess of Neith north of her wall, priestess of Wepwawet, (2) the *imakhu* in the sight of the Great God, lord of the West, Nedjetempet, whose perfect name is Iteti.

Left/right Center Jamb

(1) An offering which the Great God gives
that she may travel on the perfect ways of the West
and that she may be followed by her *ka*s,
having grown old most perfectly.

(2) The royal acquaintance, priestess of Hathor lady of the sycomore, priestess of Neith north of her wall, priestess of Wepwawet, the *imakhu* in the sight of Anubis, Nedjetempet, whose perfect name is Iteti.

Left/right Outer Jamb

(1) An offering which Osiris gives that she may be guided
on the sacred ways of the West upon which the *imakhu* travel,
and that her document may be received by the god,
and that the Western Desert may extend its arms to her.

(2) The royal acquaintance, priestess of Hathor lady of the sycomore, priestess of Neith north of her wall, priestess of Wepwawet, the *imakhu* in the sight of Osiris, Nedjetempet, whose perfect name is Iteti.

297. Inscriptions of Neferesres from Giza

From her chapel in the tomb of Nymaatre in the Central Cemetery (PM III², 282–84). Late fifth dynasty.

Lintel

(1) An offering which the king gives
and an offering which Anubis gives
for burial in the necropolis as an *imakhu* in the sight of the god;
(2) and that invocation offerings may be made for her
in every daily festival for the breadth of eternity
for she who always does what her god loves,
the sole royal ornament Neferesres.

Door Reveals, Left and Right

(1) The "brother of her funerary estate," the overseer of singers Nymaatre, it was who made for her this her tomb of eternity (2) while she was in the Residence, in the royal harem, because of her perfect state of *imakhu* in the sight of the king every day.

(3) The sole royal ornament whom he loves, (4) the overseer of the royal harem, (5) the overseer of pleasures, (6) Neferesres.

298. Texts of Nubhotep from Saqqara

On a false door in the tomb of her husband, Tepemankh (D 11; PM III², 483–84). Now in Cairo, CG 1415. Middle fifth dynasty. See also texts of her son Iunmin and her husband (no. 173).

Titles

The royal acquaintance, priestess of Hathor, priestess of Neith, Nubhotep.

Dedication

The seal-bearer of the divine book of the Great House Tepemankh it was who made this for his wife Nubhotep when she was buried in this perfect tomb.

299. Inscriptions of Rudjzas from Giza

Rudjzas is rather unusual in that she bears an apparently functional title, "overseer of weavers." Her son Mersuankh worked in the cult of Rewer (no. 227), although his titles are not translated here. From a false door in the tomb of Mersuankh in the Central Cemetery (PM III[2], 269–70). End fifth dynasty.

At Top

The overseer of youth of the Residence, Mersuankh.
His mother, the overseer of weavers, Rudjzas.

Right

The overseer of weavers of the Residence, the *imakhu* in the sight of the Great God, Rudjzas.

Left

Her son it was who acted on her behalf, the overseer of youth of the Residence, the recruit Mersuankh.

300. Texts of Shepset and Nykauhathor from Giza

In the tomb of Akhethotep in the Central Cemetery (PM III[2], 284). Shepset is probably the mother of Akhethotep, and Nykauhathor is his spouse. Both have somewhat different titles from usual. Perhaps fifth dynasty or later.

Lintel of False Door of Shepset and Husband Kainefer

An offering which the king and Anubis,
who dwells in the divine tent-shrine, give
for burial in the Western Desert, having grown old most perfectly,

and that invocation offerings may be made for her
in the festivals of the first of the year and of the opening of the year,
the festival of Thoth, the *Wag* festival and every daily festival.
The possessor of the state of *imakhu* in the sight of the Great God, the overseer of physicians, Shepset.

Lintel of False Door of Nykauhathor

(1) An offering which the king and which Anubis,
the lord of the sacred land, give
that she may be buried in the Western Desert
as a possessor of *imakhu* in the sight of the Great God;
(2) and that invocation offerings may be made for her in
the festival of the opening of the year,
at the first (festival) of the year, at the festival of Thoth,
the *Wag* festival, the great festival, the *Rekeh* festival,
the festival of the coming forth of Min,
the *Sadj* festival, and every daily festival;
(3) The royal acquaintance, the soul priest(ess) of the king's mother, Nykauhathor.

Notes

1. Comment has often been passed on the length of time between Meresankh's death and burial (nearly eight months), which contrasts strongly with the seventy days attributed to the embalming process by Herodotos, backed up by, for example, an eighteenth-dynasty reference in Theban tomb 110 (Davies 1932: 289, pl. 40, l. 9). In reality, it shows how little we know about the progress of these rites (see further Taylor 2001: 77).

2. The "acacia house" seems to have been a temple, perhaps at Heliopolis, and one of its roles was to deal with slaughtering cattle for funerals. See Edel 1970b, and compare no. 313.

3. A festival that involved making burnt offerings. Junker 1929–55: 2:116 notes that a number of ovens of the *akh* type were found in the superstructures of some tombs, suggesting that, even if they were not for the *wah-akh* festival, they must have been used for various burnt offering rituals.

4. See no. 177 for another example of this rare variant of the formula, also discussed in Fischer 1989.

XIX

Captions to Tomb Scenes

See notes in chapter I, §6.5.4. See no. 279 for a caption in the tomb of a queen.

301. Musical Scenes in the Tomb of Akhethotep Hemi/ Nebkauhor at Saqqara

The words of the harpists may refer to a festival of the temporary return of the dead to the land of the living via the offices of Hathor (compare no. 311). For information about the tomb see no. 195.

Before the first harpist:
May the house be opened in perfection for Hathor!
Before the second harpist:
Life is sweet. May your perfect protection be in the sight of Hathor every day.
Before the flautist:
Playing the flute for your *ka* every day.
Above a singer:
Greetings in life, O Hathor, may you make … live every day.
Above a man playing the double pipe:
Playing the double pipe.
Above two men playing the senet *game:*
(*Left*): Take this and I shall remove that!
(*Right*): Let me remove these pieces (?).
Above each figure in a row of men dancing:
The perfect *iba* dance (is done) for your *ka* every day.
Above three women:
The singing and clapping of the harem.
In front of each woman is: Perfect clapping.

302. From the Tomb of Ankhmahor at Saqqara

For more on this tomb see no. 197. One caption from this tomb is included under phyle texts (no. 86).

A. Men Watching Cattle Cross the River

The inscription in the tomb of Ankhmahor is the most complete example of this particular text. This is doubtless a magical spell for protection; see also the example translated here from the tomb of Mehu (no. 306).

O herdsman! You'll survive this marsh-creature[1] which is in the water, so that those (cattle) do not come into contact with that marsh-creature, for he is comes as if (he's) blind. May you survive well against him!
To the left: Repelling the crocodile.
To the right: Setting in place by the controller of the herdsmen.[2]

B. Above a Man with a (Damaged) Papyrus before the Figure of the Deceased

Reading out on his behalf the document for his burial arrangements which was given to him as an "offering which the king gives," the overseer of works, Zezi.

C. Above Some Bread-makers

Above a scribe:
Shape (*literally* "pour") those well, use the right amounts!
Above two men shaping bread:
(*Left*): Write down what I'm saying: I have made six portions of *pezen* bread.[3]
(*Right*): Watch out that you work correctly; the *reteh* bread should be in good condition.
Above two men also shaping bread:
(*Left*): Bring out another *beta* bread.
(*Right*): It's really full.

D. Above Men Smelting Metal

A standing man speaks to his four colleagues blowing in the furnace:
Look at its surface—it's a new vessel. Aim right at its base,[4] you lot, by my life!
The reply is: I'll do as you wish, look.

E. Various Captions to Butchers (Selected)

Above two men cutting the leg off an ox:

(*Right*): Stand up, mate; get this ox-leg to the offering table.

(*Left*): I'll do as you wish; I'll carry it well.

A man cutting off a leg to the left says:

Look, I'll come with you if you get on and do it today.

Above a man apparently extracting the heart of an ox and his colleague with a vessel:

(*Right*): Pure, it is pure for Zezi and for his *ka*. Bring on this vessel.

(*Left, with vessel*): Hand over the heart, hurry.

A man extracting a piece of meat:

Look, the best piece of meat. Put it on the offering table!

Above two men working on an ox:

(*Right*): Cut off the leg, by my life, and bring it to the offering table.

(*Left*): I'll do as you wish, mate.

Above two men working on a living ox:

(*Left, sharpening a knife*): Turn round the head of this ox quickly; let me get this leg off for the *ka* of Zezi,[5] my lord, the *imakhu* of Anubis.

(*Right*): I'll do as you wish.

F. Two Possible Scenes of Circumcision

This is the only possible illustration of circumcision in Egypt, and it has occasioned much discussion. See the comments in Kanawati and Hassan 1997: 49–50.

Left scene.

Above the man with the stone: Hold him still; don't let him faint/resist.

The man holding the "patient": I'll do as you wish.

Right scene.

The "patient": Cut well.

The man with the knife: I shall do it without pain.

G. Manicure and Pedicure

Manicure (customer): Do this—put some effort into it.

Pedicure (customer): Don't make it feel pain.

Answer to both is: I'll do as you wish.

303. From the Tomb of Ibi at Deir el-Gebrawi

From a scene showing craftsmen and scribes at work. See no. 266 for the biographical text. Early reign of Pepy II.

Viewing work in the craftsmen's shop (done) by the hands of every craftsman of the Residence and the assessment and reckoning of the work of every craftsman by the scribes of his funerary estate; also making an account of the work in writing (for) the *haty-a,* the ruler of the estate, the seal-bearer of the king of Lower Egypt, the real sole companion, the *imakhu* in the presence of Mati, the beloved one, Ibi.

304. From the Tomb of Kaiemnefret at Saqqara

Originally built north of the Step Pyramid (tomb D 23; PM III², 467–68), the chapel is now in Boston, MFA 04.1761 and 07.1005. Middle to later fifth dynasty.

A. Kaiemnefret Watches Two Registers of Scribes and Six of Men Bringing Cattle

Viewing the writing down of the produce which is brought in abundance from his towns of the funerary estate in Lower Egypt and Upper Egypt.

B. Kaiemnefret Watches a Series of Registers of Agricultural Activity

Viewing the cultivation of wheat, pulling of flax, reaping, loading [donkeys], threshing, winnowing, heaping.
Above a scene of scribes working and men being presented to them:
Man at right: The overseer of the estate ("steward").
Above two scribes: Reckoning the rulers (of the estates) by the tribunal of the funerary estate.
Above a bowing man being presented: Bringing a miscreant (?) before you.

305. Caption to Butchers on the Architrave of Khnumnedjem from Busiris

From Kom el-Akhdar near Busiris; present location unknown. Sixth to eighth dynasty. The formulae are translated above as no. 272.

Caption over Two Men Butchering an Ox

Right-hand man: The controller of the tent, Sabni: "Make an effort, mate."
Left-hand man: "I'll do as you wish, mate; I'll get out the best cuts (of meat)." The controller of the tent, Meni.

306. From the Tomb of Mehu at Saqqara

This tomb contains an excellent variety of captions. See no. 220 for other texts from this tomb. Reign of Teti to Pepy I.

A. Next to the Tomb Owner Watching Mainly Sailing and Agricultural Scenes

Viewing the arrival of boats, the work of the fields, and also the coming of his estates and towns of Lower and Upper Egypt (by) the overseer of the *ges-per*, beloved first under the king, Mehu.

B. Next to the Tomb Owner Watching Mainly Sailing and Agricultural Scenes

Viewing the catching of enormous quantities of fish, the work of the fields, and the distribution of fish to the teams of workers of the funerary estate (by) the overseer of Upper Egypt, the overseer of the two granaries, the overseer of the two treasuries, the overseer of the *ges-per*, beloved first under the king, Mehu.

C. Above a Man Supervising the Bundling-up of the Flax Harvest

Hurry up! I want you to keep binding—do your jobs!

D. Above Men Preparing Sacks for Transport on a Donkey

Tying up the sack; lifting up the sack.

E. Above Men Tossing Ears into a Heap

Stacking up the corn heap.
(*Left man*): My back hurts!
(*Right man*): Work and you'll be better for it!

F. Above a Scene of Men in Boats Leading a Herd of Cattle across a Ford

See comments on the similar text of Ankhmahor (no. 302A).

Herdsman! You'll survive this marsh-creature which is in the water, who comes as if (he's) blind. Don't worry about him, herdsman—your arm is above the water!

G. Above a Man Sowing

Sowing barley and emmer by the "ruler of the estate."

Note that in the same scene is part of the "Herdsman's song," translated above from the tomb of Sekhemankhptah (no. 314).

H. Above a Man Calling to His Plow Team

Come on, get moving, to work, my servants!

I. Above the Tomb Owner in a Papyrus Boat with His Son and a Number of Boatmen

Who is the man of the morning? The *ba* of Mehu is coming.[6]

J. Above Two Men in a Metal-working Scene

Where is a (good) craftsman? Hurry up, mate! Put on the scales what has been made today, or your colleague will replace (you)!
And the other replies:
I'll do what you want!

Above two further men in the same scene
Hurry up, mate! The crucible is [*rest lost*]
And the other replies:
I'll do what you want, *mehenek*, even though I'm tired from the work in this house!

K. From a Butchery Scene

Get him (*the ox*) on the ground quickly!
Slaughter him (*the ox*) immediately! Get the choice cuts on the way (to the offering place)!
Grab hold mate! Take this leg!
I'll do what you want immediately.

L. From Another Butchery Scene

General caption to a register:
The altar is (prepared) as for a perfect festival this day for the *ka* of Mehu, the *imakhu*.
A man speaks: Get away from me! Clear the way for me, quick!

M. Above a Procession of Offering Bearers

Carrying choice cuts of meat and fowl which were brought from the estates of his towns and from the locations of his soul chapels which are in Lower and Upper Egypt and in the eastern and western sides of the river, by his children, his brothers, and the soul priests of his funerary estate, for the *imakhu* in the sight of the king and the *imakhu* in the sight of Anubis, who is in his wrappings, the lord of the sacred land, the *iry pat, haty-a,* vizier, the overseer of the *ges-per*, the first under the king, Mehu.

N. Above a Procession of Offering Bearers (from the Chapel of the Son of Mehu)

Carrying gifts which were brought for him from his towns and his estates of both Lower and Upper Egypt, by his children, his brothers, and the soul priests of his funerary estate in the *Wag* festival, the festival of Thoth, and every perfect festival for the *haty-a,* the seal-bearer of the king of Lower Egypt, the overseer of the *ges-per,* the sole companion, the lector priest, the *imakhu* in the sight of the god, Ankhmeryre.

307. From the Tomb of Merib at Giza

In both examples Merib is shown being presented with various goods. The first example may illustrate how the "offering which the king gives" formula worked in practice. From tomb G 2100 in the Western Cemetery (PM III[2]*, 71–72). Most of the tomb is now Berlin 1107. Later fourth dynasty.*

North Door Reveal

Viewing the invocation offerings which the "house of the king" brings: a thousand young oxen, a thousand young antelopes, a thousand young ibex, a thousand young gazelles, a thousand ducks, and a thousand geese.

South Door Reveal

Viewing the sealed goods which the royal estate/royal house brings: *idmy* linen in measures of a thousand, 6, 4, 2, and 1; a thousand *padj* cakes of incense, a thousand pieces of incense, and green and black eye-paint, and a thousand measures of the best oils.

308. From the Tomb of Mery II at Hagarsa

A text above the deceased watching cattle. No. 265 is a biography from this tomb. End Old Kingdom or First Intermediate Period.

Viewing the enactment of the count in his own property by the *haty-a*, sole companion, lector priest, the *imakhu* Meryaa, truly. There is no exaggeration in it.

309. From the Tomb of Nyankhkhnum and Khnumhotep at Saqqara

The following is only a small selection from this tomb; I have chosen mostly the somewhat longer texts which make sense without the illustration of the scene. For another text from this tomb and notes about the tomb itself, see no. 109. A boat caption appears in no. 317. Mid fifth dynasty.

A. Hunting in the Marshes

[Passing through] the marshes, viewing all the work [of the meadows, spearing fish]. The inspector of manicurists of the Great House, the royal *mehenek* in manicure, the keeper of secrets, one whom his lord loves, Khnumhotep.

Hunting the marsh birds with a throw-stick in the marshes and in the papyrus thickets. The priest of Re in *Shezepibre,* [the overseer] of manicurists, [the *mehenek*] of the king, [Nyankhkhnum].

B. From the Burial Scenes

Above a slaughtering scene:

Bringing of the choice cuts (of meat) which are from the funerary estate for the burial.

Above men carrying out rituals in front of a statue in a shrine:

Standing before the tomb of the inspector of manicurists of the Great House Khnumhotep.

Before men setting out food and offerings:

Laying out of the invocation offerings by the embalmer.

Presentation (of wine [?]) by the embalmer.

Above men in papyrus boats accompanying a statue shrine:

Crossing over the pool which is in the embalming house (*literally* "perfect house"), doubly in peace, to his tomb of the necropolis.

C. Men Moving Statues

Above men with a standing statue:

Accompanying the perfect statues, doubly in peace in the sight of the Great God.

Ditto:

Accompanying the statues to the tomb of the necropolis, in peace.

Above men with a possible double statue:

Accompanying the statues to the tomb.

Above men dragging two special containers:
Dragging the *stjat* box during the festival of Thoth intended for invocation offerings.

D. From Scenes of Preparing Grain for Brewing and Baking

Measuring grain in the granary of the funerary estate; registering the contents of the granary.
Receiving grain by the overseer of the storeroom.
Writing in the register.
Crushing grain for *heta* bread.
Cleaning the grain.
A siever speaks to the female miller: Hurry up, you white one, I want to sieve this flour.
Response: I'll do what you want.
Heating up of *bedja* moulds for *hetjet* bread.
Checking the *bedja* moulds.
Checking the loaves.
Reckoning: Receiving the baked products from the overseer of the storeroom for the daily needs of a thousand things.

E. Garden and Related Scenes

Overall caption adjacent to Nyankhkhnum (left) and Khnumhotep (right):
Viewing the making of a *shabet* boat,[7] the papyrus plantation and the property of the funerary estate.
Boats: Cutting down trees by the shipwright.
Building the *sekhet* part of the boat by the carpenter.
Garden: Watering the garden; hacking up the ground by the gardeners.
Over a papyrus thicket: The bird pool and the papyrus thicket of the funerary estate.

F. Manicure, Barber, and Market Scenes

Manicure: Shaving the neck.
Perhaps wash up that razor.
Shaving the head.
Shaving the legs.
A vegetable seller to a young man with a baboon[8] which is stealing food:
Oi, lad, acting the boss, do you want me to bring you the owner of this?
Deals are made: Hand over your stuff as the price of my fish!
Hand over your stuff as the price of my very sweet sycamore figs.
Hand over your stuff and I'll give you perfect vegetables.

A thief is perhaps caught by a man leading a long-tailed monkey:
Grab hold, grab hold.
(*Next is rather unclear but perhaps*): Old man, not on me! Keep him on the ground!
A deal in linen: 1 + x cubits of cloth for payment of six *shat*.[9]
I'll tell you this truly—it's a *netjeru* cloth, really careful work.

G. Marsh Scenes, Including Netting Birds and Fishing

General caption, in front of Khnumhotep:
Viewing the marshes in all their aspects: the catching of fish, the trapping of birds; it is more perfect to see than anything! (*similar text in front of Nyankhkhnum*).
Above the man giving the signal to close the net:
Come on, let's go; net the birds! Come on, get a move on!
In a scene of preparing the net:
Twisting the rope by the bird-catchers of the funerary estate.
Tying the net by the bird-catchers of the funerary estate.
Repairing the net by the bird-catchers of the funerary estate.
Above a scene of men pulling fishing nets:
Look out, lads, the overseer of fishermen is watching you!
It's catching time, lads; the net's coming and it will bring a great catch!

H. Presentation of Offerings

Main caption:
Viewing the "gifts of greeting" brought from all his towns and piling up of sweet things in the "red house."[10]
The scene shows presentation of dates, figs, and other fruit, wine, and so on, including some in boats:
Transport of the sweet things for inspection.

310. Fishing and Fowling Scenes in the Tomb of Nyankhpepy Kem at Meir

Nyankhpepy also bears the names Heny and Henenit Kem. Late sixth dynasty.

Spearing Fish

The *haty-a,* seal-bearer of the king of Lower Egypt, overseer of Upper Egypt, sole companion, lector priest, overseer of priests, the *imakhu* in the sight of Osiris, foremost of the Westerners, Heny whose perfect name is Henenit Kem.

Spearing a massive catch of fish in the marshlands of Upper Egypt and Lower Egypt.

Hunting Birds with a Throw-stick

The *haty-a,* seal-bearer of the king of Lower Egypt, true overseer of Upper Egypt, sole companion, lector priest, overseer of priests, Heny whose perfect name is Henenit Kem.

Passing through the flooded fields, swamps, and all the marshes; throwing the throw-stick (at) the marsh birds and (other) fowl.

His beloved wife, the royal ornament Zetnetpepy: "Official, bring me this golden oriole!"[11]

(*His reply*): I'll do (so) and get it for you!

311. Musical Scenes in the Tomb of Pepyankhheryib at Meir

Altenmüller 1978 and Buchberger 1995 argue that the words of the harpists refer to a festival of the temporary return of the dead to the land of the living via the offices of Hathor. See no. 270 for the biographical text and more about the tomb.

Above a man playing a pipe:

The royal noble, Imyshetj; playing the pipe very well.

Above a woman playing a harp:

His beloved daughter, Peshernefert; May the golden one *(Hathor?)* appear in the great door (of the tomb).

Above a second woman playing a harp:

His beloved daughter, Meretyotef; May your *sekhmet*[12] be extolled by Horus.

Above two men playing the senet *game:*

(*Left*): The overseer of the estate, Mereri: … a good thing … Just watch me take it!

(*Right*): The royal noble, Khuenre: You have spoken too soon; the board is mine!

312. Offering Bearers in the Tomb of Persen at Saqqara

Tomb at North Saqqara (D 45: PM III^2, 577–78). Now Berlin 15004. Early fifth dynasty.

This text, behind a row of offering bearers, is a simple illustration of one of the basic economic principles of the Egyptian economy. Offerings which went to a major temple of a god or a king were then further granted to be the offerings for favored officials; once these offerings had been presented to the deceased in his tomb, they would then be used to pay his dependents and add to his overall wealth. Three funerary estates depicted in the tomb are compounded with the name of Neferhetepes and the fourth-dynasty kings Sneferu and Djedefre.

Bringing the invocation offerings for the inspector of the Great House, Persen, part of the reversionary offerings consisting of *hetja* bread, *pezen* bread, and *sefetj* oil which have traveled from the temple of Ptah south of his wall for/to the mother of the king Neferhetepes[13] every day, for the breadth of eternity.
(This) was granted to him to be his invocation offerings in the time of Sahure.

313. From the Tomb of Qar at Giza

The tombs of Qar and Idu (G 7101–2) lay to the east of the queens' pyramids of Khufu (PM III², 184–86). A text of Idu is translated here (no. 206). Early to middle sixth dynasty.

A. Block Showing People Performing Rituals

This block shows a row of men with captions explaining their activities, all of which are related to rituals done for the deceased person, either at his funeral or afterward (or both).

Above a man kneeling with his hands on a small table:
Presenting offerings by the embalmer.
Above a man with his right hand extended:
Offering by the lector priest.
Above a man reading from a papyrus:
Transfiguration by the lector priest.
Above two men, one kneeling, the other pouring:
(Dispensing) water.
Above a man holding an incense burner:
Dispensing incense.

Either side of a man with a broom in one hand and a papyrus in the other:
Bringing *rd*[14] (by) the lector priest.

B. Texts from the Funeral of Qar

This interesting scene shows, in the upper scene, a procession (doubtless with the body) to the "booth of purification," together with hints at some of the rituals, preliminary to the body being taken to the embalmers' workshop. The latter is shown in the lower register. The "booth of purification" might have been a temporary structure erected in the area of the royal valley temple, and the embalmers, while having their own workshop, may in many cases have set up inside or in the immediate vicinity of the person's tomb. See Brovarski 1977 for some of these issues.

Upper Register

At the left, a procession.
Above the first three figures:
(*Male*) The lector priest transfiguring.
(*Male*) The embalmer.
(*Female*) The mourner.[15]
To the right of them are seven pairs of men carrying a container (presumably with the body inside).
Carrying in peace to the "booth of purification" in the retinue of the *imakhu*.
To the right, three further figures like the three above.
In the center of the scene is "the booth of purification."
Left-hand compartment, which contains two chests:
The requirements of the skills of the lector priest.
Right-hand compartment, which contains four food offerings:
The requirements of the "booth of purification," a meal.
On either end of the structure is the word "path."
To the right of the structure, a man:
Transfiguring—the lector priest.
A man and a woman face each other:
Speaking by the embalmer. Speaking by the mourner.
Between the embalmer and the mourner is a small table with the same four food offerings:
A meal.
At right, two bound oxen:
Fettered.

Lower Register

At the right, seven pairs of men carry the body container:

A procession in peace to the *shabet* funerary boat, the *imakhu*, the sole companion, Qar.

To the center and left, the boat is pulled by two teams of men. Three figures are seated in the front of the boat:

The embalmer. The lector priest. The mourner.

At the front of the canopy of the boat is seated a man:

The overseer of the embalmers.

At the rear of the canopy is seated a woman:

The mourner.

Above two oarsmen at the rear of the boat:

Oh my noble Lord, sweet of love [*by whom this is said is not clear*].

The boat is pulled by two teams of men. In the upper subregister:

This pure bread of the estate of Ptah, it is for the sole companion Qar, the *imakhu*, born of Khenut.

In the lower subregister:

Anubis has made a landing place in peace especially for the overseer of the Residence Meryrenefer, born of Khenut.

In the left of the upper register are four women:

Mourning by the two acacia houses.[16]

The first three women are described as "dancing" *and the fourth one as* "clapping."

In the lower register is one woman and two men:

The woman is called "leader," *and the two men are called* "friends of the acacia house."

At the left end of the scene is what is presumably the embalming house itself. At the right is a man holding a jar:

The lector priest is attending to the house.

Another text inside the house:

The inner room of the *wabet* of attending.[17]

314. From the Tomb of Sekhemankhptah at Saqqara

The tomb chapel (D 41: PM III², 454–55) is now in Boston, MFA 04.1760. Middle to later fifth dynasty.

A. The So-called Herdsman's Song

This text is somewhat obscure. That it relates just to something said by herdsmen in the fields is surely an oversimplification, and it may indeed have slightly different interpretations in different tombs. The deity Bet is a little-known, perhaps archaic, deity of the next world but who might perhaps be a forerunner of the later deity Bata, best-known from the New Kingdom Tale of the Two Brothers.[18] *If this latter association is valid, we note from that story whereby Bata therein cuts off his phallus and throws it into the water, where it is eaten by a catfish; the whole might just be an Osirian allegory of rebirth and a return to this world, and there is indeed a reference in the Coffin Texts (spell 368) to herdsmen in the path of the deceased in the next world. The whole of the present text seems to be a spell that relies on the identification of the deceased with the seed being planted in the adjacent scene and that will then grow again into new life (Altenmüller 1989 and Meyer 1990).*

Above a flock of sheep treading in grain just sown:
West, where is *Bet*? *Bet* is in the water among the fish; he speaks with the catfish and greets the pike—*Bet* of the West.

B. Other Captions to Agricultural Scenes

General caption:
Viewing the work of the fields—cultivation, reaping, pulling flax, loading donkeys, donkeys treading the threshing floors, and winnowing.
Above a plowing scene:
Cultivation with the plow. (*Above a man*) Go forward, O go forward!
Above reapers:
I say to you: "lads, barley is there—he who reaps the best will get it."
What is this then, a careful man?[19]
Measuring grain:
Measuring barley by the assessors.
Above winnowing (by women):
Winnowing by the team of five.
Gleaning barley with a brush[20] by the team of five.
Above donkeys threshing:[21]
(*To the animals*): Get back among yourselves!
Can you see what you have done?
Above two men piling grain:
Pile it up well, and you shall prosper in life!
Stacking emmer wheat.

315. From the Tomb of Sekhemkare at Giza

For the tomb see no. 5. Early fifth dynasty.

Viewing the produce of his (estate) controllers and his herdsmen, his fowlers and his fishermen, which is brought from his towns of his estates, for the *iry pat,* vizier, chief lector priest of his father, the doorkeeper of Duau … Sekhemkare.

316. Bringing Cattle out of the Marshes in the Tomb of Tjy at Saqqara

Caption to a man with a calf on his back, leading cows out of the marshes. The use of the abusive term is most unusual! See no. 150 for the tomb.

Oh, you shit, may you get the cattle moving! Swing that calf over your shoulder of those nursing ones (*cows*) who have come forth from the papyrus marshes."

317. Boat Texts from Tombs

These scenes have an important religious role. They depict not just the presumed journey of the deceased on the ocean of the sky and visiting the important cult sites in the Delta of Buto and Heliopolis but also the actual ceremonies which might have taken place, or were thought to take place, in conjunction with the burial and wishes for further existence of the deceased. An additional interpretation has been proposed in Altenmüller 2000; 2002b: 274–81 that these boats exist in pairs and parallel the day and night barks of the kings and, hence, concern the deceased's journey across the heavens.

Such infrequent scenes from the Old Kingdom might just be precursors to the later and better-known "Journey to Abydos" and the scenes of the deceased's body being carried over to his tomb in the West in a boat with mourners. A hint of this is probably to be seen in the texts from the tomb of Kaiemankh, which seem to be a series of exhortations to the crew to follow the ideal route to the West. These latter scenes are also found in the burial chamber as opposed to the chapel, and so they might be more closely connected with the funerary aspect.

See also texts of Fetekta in no. 320C.

A. Tomb of Nykanesut at Giza

Tomb G 2155 in the Western Cemetery (PM III², 78–79). Early fifth dynasty.

Above a large wooden boat with sails:
Coming from Buto and sailing to the field of offerings in a perfect manner.
Above a papyrus boat being rowed:
Sailing to Heliopolis.

B. Tomb of Kaiemankh at Giza

Tomb G 4561 in the Western Cemetery (PM III², 131–33). Sixth dynasty.

First boat:
Keep an eye on the sail-rope, (for this is) the canal of the West—it is truly good!
Second boat:
Keep an eye on the sail-rope, pilot. Hold a good course, as you are "one of the waters." The wind of the canals (?) is behind the messenger,[22] for this is the canal of the West. Keep (your) course to port, the perfect way!
Third boat:
Keep an eye on the sail-rope, for I shall work with the man with the steering oar. Keep low to the water, boy! For port is the perfect way—pilot, hold a good course. Keep an eye on the sail-rope!

C. Tomb of Nyankhkhnum and Khnumhotep at Saqqara

i.

For other captions from this tomb see no. 309.
Go to starboard and then straight on to the perfect canal—the canal of the perfect West.
Traveling to the perfect West to be among the *imakhu*.
Go to starboard (and follow) the *menti* boat! Keep an eye on the sail-rope, for the wind is behind you, you who transmits (instructions to the steersman)!

ii.

Traveling to the perfect places to be among the *imakhu*.
Go to starboard, the perfect way!

Traveling to the field of offerings.
Go to starboard! Don't run into our *henti* boat!

318. Carrying Chair Scenes

This difficult and compact text is here presented in a synoptic translation from eight different texts. The scene with the carrying chair is without doubt an allusion to the desire to be brought back to earth after death, as obliquely expressed in this text. The men carrying the chair are perhaps "on loan" from the necropolis god mentioned in the text. It illustrates how much more there is to scenes in Egyptian tombs than sometimes thought.

> Go up to the *mehenek*, may he prosper;
> go up to the *mehenek*, may he be healthy—O <*god's name*>[23] who is upon the sand:
> present and protect what is presented to <*the deceased*>;
> make him a "Great One" as is desired,
> for it (*the carrying chair*) is more beloved when full than when empty.

319. Some Funerary Domains

A very common sight in tombs of the Old Kingdom are rows of men and women bearing offerings for the tomb owner; they also appear (much more damaged now) in the funerary temples of kings. Captions give their names; the figures tend to be only male after the fifth dynasty. A special group of these representations are known as "funerary domains/estates" or "pious foundations" as they represent personified forms of the estates throughout Egypt from which a king or official derived income and produce. Many, perhaps most, of these estates in reality belonged to the kings, and the right to income from them given to officials was at the basis of the wealth of these officials, and the passing on of this income to priests, family, and other dependents was the basis of the Egyptian economy. See, for example, Kemp 1989: 89–92, 104–7. Study of these domains, Jacquet-Gordon 1962; Butzer 1976 and Kanawati 1980 use some of the data they provide for demographic and economic purposes

The following is a selection from some better-known tombs; they combine estates with the name of the deceased and with those of kings and others.

A. Tomb of Tjy at Saqqara

See no. 150 for the tomb. Mid to late fifth dynasty.

The palace of Tjy
The beer of Tjy
The *nebes* fruit of Tjy
The wine of Tjy
Perfect things belong to Tjy
The two sycamores of Tjy
The *ished* fruit of Tjy
The milk of Tjy
The *wah* fruit of Tjy
The invocation offering of Tjy

B. Tomb of Ptahhotep II at Saqqara

The location of these estates is indicated in the inscriptions. See no. 126 for the tomb. Late fifth dynasty.

The estate of Izezi "Anubis makes Izezi live"	21st nome of Upper Egypt
The estate of Khufu	20th nome of Upper Egypt
The estate of the *ka* of Setibhor	20th nome of Upper Egypt
The foundation of Setibhor	21st nome of Upper Egypt
Great of *imakhu* is Izezi	11th nome of Upper Egypt
Perfect of life is Ikauhor	7th/8th nome of Upper Egypt
Maat loves Izezi	8th nome of Upper Egypt
... Userkaf	9th nome of Upper Egypt
The two *ba*s desire that Izezi live	12th nome of Upper Egypt
The estate of Izezi "Wadjet makes Izezi live"	[11th nome of Upper Egypt]
The estate of Sahure "Sahure is one who loves perfection"	7th/8th nome of Upper Egypt
The provisions of Kakai are stable	12th nome of Upper Egypt
The *Nekhen sanctuary* of Osiris	9th nome of Upper Egypt
The *inet* foundation of Sneferu	1st nome of Lower Egypt
The *ka*-chapel of Setibhor	3rd nome of Lower Egypt
Sneferu is firm	10th nome of Lower Egypt
The silos	2nd nome of Lower Egypt
The nurse of Ptahhotep	12th nome of Lower Egypt

320. Scenes of Pulling Papyrus

Old Kingdom scenes, going back to the fourth dynasty, show the tomb owner pulling papyrus. This is another scene that is perhaps not what it seems; marshes and swamps may have been part of the passage that needed to be traversed to return to this world and can be seen as a metaphor for creation and rebirth.[24]

A. Tomb of Meresankh III at Giza

See no. 276 for the tomb. Later fourth dynasty.

Caption to the deceased with her mother Hetepheres

Pulling papyrus for Hathor in the marshland together with her mother; they view every perfect thing in the marsh.

B. Tomb of Iazen at Giza

Tomb in the Western Cemetery (PM III², 82). Fifth or sixth dynasty.

Pulling papyrus for Hathor (in) the marshland by the *khenty-she* Iazen.

C. Tomb of Fetekta at South Abusir

Tomb LS 1: PM III², 351 plus Barta 2001. Perhaps middle fifth dynasty.

Two texts above vessels going down- and upstream:

Traveling downstream to pull papyrus for Hathor, the perfect one, mistress of the sycamore.

Traveling upstream, having pulled papyrus for Hathor, the perfect one, mistress of the sycamore.

In between these two inscriptions are:

Go to port; keep the direction of the boat steady.

Go to starboard! Don't run into our *henti* boat!

Notes

1. The crocodile who is shown lying in wait to the left.

2. Perhaps refers to the spell or even the leading of the cattle across the water.

3. The three types of bread in this scene are found as part of the standard offering list (no. 328).

4. This might be the vessel or the base of the furnace. See also Drenkhahn 1976b: 31–32.

5. There is some evidence that the first leg to be taken off an animal was sometimes cut when the animal was still alive, as abhorrent as this seems to us. The term *khepesh* is used for this leg as here, and this is the same term as used in various ritual presentations of this joint. In New Kingdom tombs and papyri, a calf is also shown with a leg missing, which may be a reference to the same; perhaps the best-known example is that in the papyrus of Hunefer (BM EA 9901/5, for example, Faulkner 1985: 54).

6. Another allusion to rebirth, as the reference to the morning must be making the comparison with the sun, which is born again in the morning. This text is a refrain of the boatmen.

7. Compare comments below on boat texts (no. 317).

8. The presence of baboons and long-tailed monkeys, while they might have been used as "guard dogs" (although not the most predictable and reliable of animals), in a market scene should perhaps make us pause and consider whether there might be more to the meaning of this scene than meets the eye. An enumeration of Old Kingdom scenes with apes in them may be found in Vandier d'Abbadie 1964.

9. A unit of value, extent unclear; I am unsure about Altenmüller's speculation that it might have been a sort of currency equivalent in snail shells (Moussa and Altenmüller 1977: 85).

10. These gifts are an important part of the invocation offerings that are central to the deceased's provision in the tomb. The "red house" appears to be an old term (from the third dynasty) for a storeroom, of which there seems to have been one for the king and one for officialdom (Moussa and Altenmüller 1977: 102). Hartwig Altenmüller presented a paper on these offerings at the 2004 "Old Kingdom Art and Archaeology" conference, in which he noted how this particular example harks back strongly to early Old Kingdom prototypes.

11. A similar but damaged scene in the tomb of Mereruka at Saqqara appears to have the wife say: "O Meri, do give me those perfect fowl, as you live for me!" (Fischer 1978: 45–46).

12. This word is rather obscure. It could be related to the word for sistrum or sistrum-player; the sistrum is a symbol of Hathor and would thus fit the Hathoric context of the scene.

13. A queen of either the fourth or early fifth dynasties. Baud 1999: 493–94 makes a strong case for her being the mother of Userkaf.

14. This refers to a stage in one of the rituals. This has been both interpreted as a ritual for cleaning away footsteps (Davies and Gardiner 1915: 93–94) or one of bringing the purification waters of Osiris (Altenmüller 1971).

15. Literally "the kite" (a hawklike bird of prey). Together with the next mourner she completes the pair of "kites," Isis and Nephthys, sisters of Osiris, who protect the mummy.

16. The "acacia house" seems to have been a temple, perhaps at Heliopolis, and one of its roles was to deal with slaughtering cattle for funerals. See Edel 1970b.

17. *Wabet* is the name for the whole building, so this might be the name for this part of the interior.

18. This will be found in all major volumes of translations; for a recent study see Hollis 1990.

19. Possibly a sarcastic urging on for the men to finish that day (Erman 1919: 22–24).

20. The distinction is between tossing the threshed grain in the area and sweeping up the debris looking for more grains.

21. See Altenmüller 1994. Altenmüller's basic argument is that the captions apply to the donkeys and not, as has been long thought, to the men supervising the work.

22. Term that probably describes a man on the boat who passes the commands back from the pilot at the front to the steersman at the rear of the boat.

23. The names Djau and Sokar are normally used. Djau may just be a rare and archaic name used for the same necropolis deity more normally called Sokar.

24. See further Altenmüller 2002a; Munro 1993: 95–118, 126–36; Wettengel 1992; Harpur 1980, all with references to further literature.

XX

Miscellaneous Texts from Tombs and Objects in Tombs

See notes in chapter I, §6.5.2 and §6.5.5.

321. Titles of Nesutnefer from His Tomb at Giza

These titles of the early fifth dynasty are rather unusual for the different offices in the provinces and capital which they exhibit. Although buried in the Memphite region, Nesutnefer seems to have functioned as the principal nome official for three provinces, two in Upper Egypt and one in Lower Egypt. Tomb G 4970 in the Western Cemetery (PM III^2, 143–44). Early to middle fifth dynasty.

Eighth nome of Upper Egypt: overseer of fortresses, leader of the land, overseer of royal colonists, overseer of commissions, controller of the estate.
Tenth nome of Upper Egypt: overseer of commissions, overseer of fortresses, overseer of royal colonists, leader of the land, controller of the estate.
Thirteenth nome of Lower Egypt: overseer of fortified enclosures, overseer of the deserts, overseer of the royal fortress, the royal acquaintance, Nesutnefer.

322. Sarcophagus Lid Texts

These texts of three officials of the sixth dynasty, all from the same area of Saqqara, offer an interesting insight into the important role of the sarcophagus. Already for many years it had been a container for the body, but these inscriptions show the ritual importance of ensuring the lid is in place, which will help the transformation of the deceased into an akh; *these are the beginning of the visibility of the burial chamber and the sarcophagus or coffin as a special environment for the dead.*[1] *Note that most hieroglyphs of human figures in these texts are incomplete, "mutilated," so that the depiction could not come to life and inflict harm on the deceased.*

A. Sarcophagus of Ankhmahor Called Zezi

Other texts from this tomb are translated as nos. 197 and 302. Early sixth dynasty.

East Side of Lid

The overseer of all works of the king in the entire land, Zezi, speaks:

> O eighty men, embalmers, rulers of the necropolis,
> and every office-holder who shall descend to this place;
> do you wish that the king favor you,
> that invocation offerings be made for you in the necropolis,
> and that you become *imakhu* in the perfect manner
> in the presence of the Great God?
> Then you should place this lid of this coffin upon its base[2] exactly
> in the excellent manner of which you are aware,
> in accordance with that which you should do for an excellent *akh*,
> so as to do what its owner favors.
> I am Zezi. one who is loved.

B. Sarcophagus of Khentika Called Ikhekhi

See no. 216 for further texts from this tomb. Early to mid sixth dynasty.

Top

The *iry pat* Ikhekhi, the *haty-a,* vizier, Khentika, the sole companion, lector priest. the *imakhu* in the presence of the Great God, Ikhekhi.

East Side of Lid

The sole companion Ikhekhi speaks:

> O lector priests and men of the *wabet,* embalmers,
> and the eighty men of the necropolis who shall descend to this place;
> do you wish that the king favor you,
> that you become *imakhu* in the perfect manner
> in the presence of the Great God,
> and that you become the owner of a burial in the necropolis?
> Then you should place this lid upon its base exactly
> in the excellent manner of (which you are aware).
> For I am Khentika, one who is loved. Then I shall be your helper.

C. Sarcophagus of Kaiaper

See no. 211 for another text from this tomb. Early sixth dynasty.

… first under the king, overseer of the Great Mansion, Kaiaper, speaks:
O lector priest, embalmer, men of the *wabet*,
and eighty men (*or* eighty men of the *wabet* [?])
… [do you wish that the] king [favor you],
and that you become *imakhu* in the perfect manner
in the sight of the Great God?
Then you shall place for me this lid on its base in an excellent manner.
I am Kaiaper, one whom is loved.

323. Titles on the Sarcophagus of Weta from Giza

From south Giza (PM III², 311). Now in Cairo, CG 1787. Late Old Kingdom.

The *wab*-priest of the king, the royal acquaintance, possessor of *imakhu in* the sight of his lord; the *khenty-she* and keeper of secrets of the pyramid of Menkaure, the leather-worker, Weta.
The assistant of the overseer of the leather-workers, keeper of secrets, who delights his lord in the activity of leather-working, Weta.
The overseer of tanning, the sandal-maker of the king, who works in matters of royal sandal-making to the delight of his lord, Weta.
The overseer of parchment who makes the leather roll of the lector priest to the delight of his lord, in accordance with what was ordered, who delights the king when it happens that he sits at the courtyard door, Weta.

324. Inscription of Abutyu from Giza

This unique text comes from a block reused in a sixth-dynasty tomb (G 2188: PM III², 81) but is probably earlier in date. It could have come from a relief showing a dog or could have been part of the dog's tomb described in the text. It was not unusual to represent and name a dog in tombs of the Old and Middle Kingdoms, but the specific reference to a tomb being created for a dog by the king is not seen elsewhere. Fifth dynasty.

(1) The dog who used to carry out guard duty for his majesty,
(2) whose name is Abutyu.
(3) His majesty ordered that he be buried

(4) and that a sarcophagus be given to him from the two treasuries
(5) (along with) a great quantity of *idmy* linen,
(6) incense and (7) *sefetj* oil.
(6–8) His majesty also had a tomb constructed for him
by the crews of (9) tomb-builders.
His majesty did this for him above all to ensure his state of *imakhu*.

325. Hieratic Texts on Pots from Qubbet el-Hawa

Edel excavated in the tombs of the later Old Kingdom to Middle Kingdom at Aswan in 1959–73. Among the finds were hundreds of pots bearing hieratic inscriptions. Most of these, of which just a handful are given here, indicate the contents of the jars and also the donor and deceased to whom they were presented. They are not common outside this site and are thus of interest for what was buried with people of this date. There is also one longer inscription that appears to indicate payments for enabling the burial of a certain person within another tomb. For some further vessels from Aswan, see el-Din 1994: 31–34.

A. Longer Text

(*interior*): List of valuables given to the possessor of this tomb by Sebekhotep concerning his burial of his father in it:

Upper Egyptian barley	2 sacks
emmer wheat	3 sacks
wah fruit	1 sack
cloth of 50 (square) cubits (*or*) kilt of quality cloth	1
copper axe	1
pure cloth	1

(*exterior*): Waemmut has given on behalf of his father; it was given as he wanted (?):[3] Upper Egyptian grain, total 4 (sacks) and two jars of *merhet* oil.

B. Shorter Jar Inscriptions

i.

Flour made from *pat*[4] for the royal noble, the overseer of foreigners, Sebekhotep.

ii.

An itet jar of *sekhet* grain, *nebes* fruit and *annut* fruit for the sole companion, first under the king, overseer of scribes of troops, Ametjenu, the great.

iii.
An *itet* jar of *sekhet* grain, *nebes* fruit and *annut* fruit for the royal ornament, Sabtes.

iv.
A *denet* jar of *sekhet* grain for the royal noble, sole royal ornament, Ipi.

v.
(For) the seal-bearer of the god, Ametjenu: *wah* fruit, *nebes* fruit and *ished* fruit.

vi.
(For) the *haty-a* Mekhu's son, the sole companion, lector priest Sabni: *wah* fruit, *nebes* fruit, and flour made from *sekhet* grain.

vii.
The royal noble, the overseer of foreigners, Khenuzu.
Nebes fruit of his funerary estate.

viii.
The royal noble, the overseer of foreigners, Khenuzu.
Flour made from *sekhet* grain of his funerary estate.

ix.
Flour made from *sekhet* grain for Henbaba's daughter Stjet-khnumhotep. Made by her brother of the (funerary) estate Sebekhetepi.

x.
Ished fruit for Ipi's daughter Senet. Made by her brother of the (funerary) estate Sebekhotep.

326. Texts on the Sarcophagus of Minkhaf from Giza

Few Old Kingdom sarcophagi are as decorated with formulae and offering lists as this one, but the contents have strong parallels with lists on offering niches and so on of the period. The vertical columns are separated by miniature offering niches, like false doors. This sarcophagus was found in the northern shaft of tomb G 7430+7440 in the Eastern Cemetery (see PM III^2, 195). Now in Cairo, JE 48852. Approximately reign of Khafre.

East Side
Horizontal

An offering which the king gives and an offering which Anubis,
who dwells in the sacred land, gives for burial in the West,
having grown old very perfectly as a possessor of *imakhu* …
the lector priest, scribe of the divine [book], Minkhaf.

Vertical

(1) An offering which the king gives
and an offering which Anubis, who dwells in the sacred land, gives
that invocation offerings be made for him,
for the king's son Minkhaf daily
(2) in the opening of the year, (at) the first of the year,
(on) the first day of the monthly and half-monthly festivals,
(at) the festival of Thoth, the *Wag* festival,
(at) every seasonal festival of the year, and daily.
(3) A thousand of incense, a thousand of every best *merhet* oil.
(4) A thousand of green eye-paint, a thousand of black eye-paint,
a thousand of natron.
(5) … a thousand of clothing …
(6) … a thousand of *te-imy-ta* bread.
(7) A thousand … a thousand *nebes* fruit bread, a thousand *wah* fruit,
and a thousand of every sweet thing.
(8) An offering which the king gives and an offering which Anubis,
who dwells in the (divine [?]) tent-shrine, gives
(for) thousands of everything which he desires daily for Minkhaf.

South Side
Horizontal

The sole companion of his father, keeper of secrets of his father, overseer of all works of the king, Minkhaf.

Vertical

(1) A libation basin, a thousand pure offering tables.
(2) A thousand of every kind of stone vessel,
a thousand libation vessels.
(3) A thousand pure *shenes* cakes, a thousand *nebes* fruit,
a thousand of every (kind of) bread daily.
(4) A thousand of every sweet thing, a thousand of every vegetable,
a thousand of beer for the king's son Minkhaf.

West Side
Horizontal

An offering which the king gives and an offering which Anubis,
who dwells in the sacred land, gives for burial in the West,
having grown old very perfectly
as a possessor of *imakhu* in the sight of the Great God,
and as a possessor of *imakhu* in the sight of his father.
The king's eldest bodily son, lector priest, scribe of the divine book, Minkhaf.

Vertical

(1) An offering which the king gives and an offering which Anubis,
who dwells in the sacred land, gives
that offerings may be established for him,
for the king's son Minkhaf daily.
(2) a thousand of Upper Egyptian grain,
a thousand of Lower Egyptian grain, a thousand of barley,
a thousand of wheat, a thousand of *besha* grain, a thousand dates,
a thousand of *dudju* flour. (*Each of these is inside a hieroglyph of a granary.*)
(3) A thousand *ra* geese, a thousand *tjerep* geese,
a thousand *set* geese, a thousand *semen* geese,
and a thousand pigeons.
(4) A thousand *shabet* boats, a thousand *wahet* boats,
a thousand *setjer* boats, and a thousand *nehbet* boats.[5]
(5) A thousand provisions, a thousand *hetjau* bread daily.
(6) A thousand *shenes* cakes, a thousand *pezen* bread,
a thousand *kemehu* bread, a thousand double-bread (?).
(7) A thousand of wine, a thousand *nebes* fruit,
a thousand *setjet* cakes, and a thousand *neheru* bread.
(8) An offering which the king gives and an offering which Anubis,
who dwells in the (divine [?]) tent-shrine, gives
that these may be established for Minkhaf daily,
the offering (?) of the soul priest.

North Side
Horizontal

An offering which the king gives and an offering which Anubis,
who dwells in the sacred land, gives
that invocation offerings may be made for him

for the opening of the year, (at) the first of the year,
(on) the first day of the monthly and half-monthly festivals,
(at) the festival of Thoth, the *Wag* festival,
(at) every seasonal festival of the year, Minkhaf.

Vertical

(1) A thousand of *setji-heb* oil, a thousand of *hekenu* oil,
and a thousand of *sefetj* oil.
(2) A thousand strips of *wenkhu* linen, a thousand *idmy* linen,
a thousand *sesher* linen, and a thousand *ma-a* linen.[6]
(3) A thousand *mesekhtyu* hooks, a thousand adzes,
a thousand axes, a thousand saws, and a thousand chisels.[7]
(4) A thousand *ha-shema* garments, a thousand *netjeret* garments,
a thousand *khesededj* garments, and a thousand *maset* garments.[8]

327. Short Offering and Linen List of Nefretiabet from Giza

Fig. 7: Slab stela of Nefretiabet (no. 327). Manuelian 2003: pl. 12. Drawing by Peter D. Manuelian.

Early offering lists on offering panels, perhaps prototypes of the later false door (without the jambs), often contain, in addition to a depiction of the deceased with an offering table and short lists of food and other offerings, a very rigidly structured ideal list of linen. This style of panel mostly dies out by about the middle of the fourth dynasty, to be replaced by the false door. The short list of offerings continues to be on the panel of false doors and is supplemented by the longer offering list (see below), but the linen lists disappear. The best known of these panels are the so-called slab-stelae found at Giza, such as this example. For these stelae in general, see Manuelian 2003; for the linen list, Smith 1935; Posener-Kriéger 1977; and Manuelian 2003: 153–60. From mastaba G 1225 in the Western Cemetery (PM III², 59–60). Now Paris, Louvre E 15591. Early fourth dynasty.

Above the Seated Figure of the Owner

The king's daughter, Nefretiabet.

Short Offering List

In front of deceased: Cool water, implements for hand washing.
Upper row: incense, *hatet* oil, green eye cosmetic, black eye cosmetic, figs, *ished* fruit.
Lower row: *sekhepet* drink, wine, *nebes* fruit, *nebes* fruit bread, *wah* fruit.

Above the Offering Table

Four hieroglyphs, probably indicating: meat, ribs, fruit, fowl.

Below the Offering Table

Left: A thousand of all clothing, fowl, and alabaster.
Right: A thousand of bread and beer; a thousand geese, oxen, and antelopes.

The Linen List

idmy linen:

100 (cubits area)	90 (cubits area)	80 (cubits area)	70 (cubits area)
1,000	1,000	1,000	1,000

sesher linen:

100 (cubits area)	90 (cubits area)	80 (cubits area)	60 (cubits area)
1,000	1,000	1,000	1,000

aat linen:

100 (cubits area)	80 (cubits area)	70 (cubits area)	50 (cubits area)
1,000	1,000	1,000	1,000

328. Long Offering List from the Chapel of Ankhmeryre at Saqqara

This is an example of a very long offering list, including the basic products that were expected to be offered to a tomb owner and that also formed the basis of the products in the offering ritual. This list lasted in modified versions for many hundreds of years. Note that the number of portions or repetitions of each item is given. The exact nature of many of these terms is not certain, and hence they are left in transliterated form. The chapel of Ankhmeryre is part of the complex of the tomb of Mehu (nos. 220, 306). Middle sixth dynasty.

water for pouring	1
fire for incense	1
setj-heb oil	1
heknu oil	1
sefetj oil	1
nekhenem oil	1
twawt oil	1
best cedar/pine oil	1
best Libyan oil	1
bags of green eye cosmetic	2
bags of black eye cosmetic	2
strips of cloth	2
fire for incense	1
libation and two cakes of natron	2
offering table	1
royal offering	2
royal offering in the broad hall	2
service	1
cakes for the morning meal	1
djuiu jar for the morning meal	1
ut bread	1
reteh bread	1
nemset jar of *desheret* drink	1
nemset jar of *khenemes* beer	1
cake and bowl for transport	1
cakes for the main meal	1
djuiu jar for the main meal	1
for this main meal	1
sut meat	1
bowl of water	2
natron	2
cakes for the morning meal	1
djuiu jar for the morning meal	1
ut bread	1
reteh bread	1
hetja bread	2
neheru bread	2
depet bread	4
pezen bread	4
cakes	4
imy-ta bread	4
khenfu bread	4
hebenut bread	4
qemeh-qema bread	4
idat bread, may it be behind you	4
paut bread	4
asher bread	4
onions	4
leg of an ox	1
iwa meat	1
zekhen meat	1
sut meat	1
ribs	1
roast meat	1
liver	1
spleen	1
ha meat	1
best meat	1
ra goose	1
white-fronted goose	1

set and *ser* geese	1	*ished* fruit	2
pigeon	1	white barley	2
zif bread	1	fresh barley	2
shat bread	1	roasted wheat grain	2
nepaut bread	1	grain	2
mezit	1	*babaut* grain	2
red beer	2	*nebes* fruit	2
red *iatet* drink (?)	2	*nebes* fruit bread	2
khenmes beer	2	*wah* fruit	2
sekhepet drink	2	all sweet things	3
pekha drink	2	all fresh foods	3
figs	2	bread halves	1
vessel of *sesher* drink	2	*pekher* offerings	3
wine	2	*pedju* bread	3
abesh wine	...[9]	choice cuts	3
imet wine	...	best things from the offering table	1
zenu wine	...	wiping of footprints and breaking of red pots	[1]
kham wine	2	reversion of the divine offerings, fire for incense	[1]
khenfu grain	2		
hebenenut grain	2		

329. Linen Lists on a Wooden Box from Gebelein

This box bears parts of three different inventories of linens which it contained at different times of its life before burial in the tomb. Many of the designations are obscure. Found in an uninscribed tomb at Gebelein in 1911. Fifth dynasty.

Inventory 1

First month of the *Akhet* season, day 22.

Good *sezwf* linen		12
Wemet linen		4
Henku linen		5
Good Upper Egyptian linen	60 cubit[10]	1
	50 cubit	1
	10 × 4 cubit	2
	10 × 3 cubit	1
	10 × 2 cubit	1

Inventory 2

Year, third month of the *Shemu* season, day 27.

Good *sezwf* linen	5	
Wemet linen	10	
Good 10 × 4 cubit linen	1	

Inventory 3

Year of the sixth occasion, first month, day 22.

Good *sezwf* linen	12	2
Wemet linen	2	
Taken out, *sezwf* linen		6
Wemet linen	5	
Good 10 × 4 cubit linen	1	
(?) 10 × 4 cubit linen	1	
(?) 10 × 4 cubit linen	3	
10 × 4 cubit clothing	(?)	1
Clothing, 50 cubit	2	
nuset linen 50 cubit	2	
Totals		
sezwf linen	8	
10 × 1 cubit (linen)	8	

330. List of Linen on a Box from the Tomb of Nefer and Kahay at Saqqara

This is from a small, well-preserved tomb with interesting wall reliefs, dedicated to a number of people, the principal of which are the two men above and their spouses. Evidence of a number of burials (including a well-preserved mummy) was found; this text comes from eight fragments of a wooden box which originally contained linen. The tomb of Nefer and Kahay is located next to (but was built before) the causeway of the pyramid of Unas (PM III², 639–41). Perhaps reign of Izezi.

Year of the sixth occasion, fourth month of the *Peret* season, day 22.
Account of the linen with the overseer of weavers Waty:

Sesher linen, balance:		10 pieces		
Sezef linen:	*shemat* material:	6 pieces		
	ma material:	6 pieces	(total)	12 pieces

Entrusted to Waty.

331. Inscriptions on Pieces of Linen from Abusir

Discoveries of inscribed mummy wrappings of the Old Kingdom are uncommon. These examples come from the burial chamber of Khekeretnebty. The second fragment is now in the Náprstek Museum in Prague (P 5609). Probably reign of Izezi. It is presumed that the names on these examples refer to the official responsible for supplying this section of linen; the reading of the linen quantities and designations is not certain.

A.
The first under the king Kahif; (his) assistant, the overseer of the house of weavers Khnumu. 10 × 1 cubits (?) Royal (linen) 30 cubits (?).

B.
The overseer of provisions, first under the king, who loves his lord, judge and boundary official, Seru (?); (his) assistant … of the house of life, the overseer of the hall. 10 × 1 cubits, 3 (?) Royal (linen) 30 cubits (?).

Notes

1. More detail in Taylor 2001: chapter 7.

2. The word translated "lid" in Egyptian is literally "door," and the word "base" is "mother."

3. Goedicke interprets this rather differently; he sees the name on the exterior as a pejorative reference to the tomb owner, as a result of a dispute about the cost of burial, insofar as that person originally wanted the amount mentioned on the exterior and ended up being given the amount on the interior.

4. Presumably a grain or other material that can be ground up.

5. Boats are not a normal item in offering lists. For some comments about boats in private tombs, see no. 317 and also Altenmüller 2002b: 274–81.

6. See the linen lists herein (for example, no. 327); also Smith 1935 and Posener-Kriéger 1977.

7. Tools are not common in Old Kingdom lists; see discussion in Smith 1933: 153–54.

8. For comments on these and other garments, see Smith 1933: 154–59.

9. The names of these wines were cut in the wrong order by the sculptor; they were subsequently corrected in paint.

10. It is difficult to express the sizes of these linen designations. Following Posener-Kriéger 1977, 10 cubit measures are expressed in these lists either by multiples of ⊥ or by multiples of a horizontal line —. Posener-Kriéger considers the first of these to represent a 10 × 1 cubit measure and multiples thereof (so that ⊥⊥ would

be 10 × 2 cubits), and that the multiples of — indicate unspecified dimensions totalling 10 cubits (thus = might represent a total surface area of 20 cubits). I have tried to distinguish between the two by calling the first 10 × 2 and the second 20. Note that Scheele 2005 appeared too late for its contents to be taken into consideration here.

XXI

Addendum

These publications have come to my attention since the original manuscript of the book was submitted. They are too interesting to be omitted, and I am grateful for being allowed to add them.

332. Warning to Visitors from the Tomb of Peteti at Giza

A cemetery, known as the "Tombs of the pyramid builders," was uncovered by chance in 1990. A series of very small tombs, yet containing quality statues and interesting reliefs, belong to men with titles which suggest they were those who designed and built some of the pyramid complexes at the site. The tomb of Peteti is a mixture of limestone and mud brick. Fourth or fifth dynasty. See nos. 182 and 193 for other examples of this rare threat formula.

Below a Figure of Peteti and Two Sons

(1) (With regard to) any person, priest of Hathor, or musician who strikes (?)
(2) who shall enter this (tomb)
(3) and who shall do something therein which is evil:
the god it is who shall protect me (4) from them.
For I am the *imakhu* (5) of his lord.
I never did an evil thing (6) to any man,
(even if) he did something to me in relation to it.
(7) The crocodile, the hippo or the lion it is who shall consume them.

Below a Figure of Peteti's Wife Nesysokar and Two Daughters

(1) (With regard to) any person
(2) who shall do anything evil (3) to this (tomb)
(or) enter therein (*with the intention of doing evil ?*):
(4) The crocodile shall be against them in (5) the water,
the snake shall be against them on land,
(6) the hippo shall be against them in the water,
(7) and the scorpion shall be against them on land.

333. Warning and Biographical Texts of Merefnebef from Saqqara

The tomb of Merefnebef, a previously unknown vizier, was discovered immediately to the west of the Step Pyramid enclosure in 1997. Early sixth dynasty.

The biographical text is particularly difficult and unusual, and because of its late inclusion in this book, the following translation should be regarded as very preliminary. Some phrases are unique, while others are preserved in other texts of the period, such as nos. 220 and 223.

Lintel over Facade

(1) An offering which the king gives, and an offering which [Anubis],
who dwells in the divine tent-shrine, who is in his wrappings,
who is on his mountain, lord of the sacred land and of Sepa, gives
that he might be buried in the necropolis in the Western desert,
having aged most perfectly,
doubly in peace in the sight of the Great God,
(as one who has made) the offerings and sought out the state of *imakhu*,
who speaks perfection and who recalls the (day of [?]) burial:
the *imakhu* in the sight of Osiris, he who is in the heart of the king wherever he is, whose great name is Merefnebef.
(2) An offering which the king and Osiris, lord of Busiris, give
that invocation offerings be made for him
in the opening of the year festival, in the festival of Thoth,
in the first day of the year festival, in the *Wag* festival,
in the great festival, in the *Rekeh* festival,
in the monthly, half-monthly and *Sadj* festivals,
and in every daily festival for the breadth of eternity,
for the *imakhu* in the sight of the Great God,
in the sight of Ptah, south of his wall, in the sight of Sokar,
whose perfect name is Fefi.
(3) With regard to any person
who shall [enter] this tomb of mine of eternity in their impurity,
having eaten the abomination which an *akh*
who has gone to the necropolis abhors,
without removing the impurity in the manner

in which they should be pure for the temple of a god—
an impediment is placed (in) their (way) by the Great God,
for they have acted in a most evil manner.
For indeed I have carried out every excellent and noble ritual,
one whose great name is Ankhunas.[1]
(4) (That which is done for [?]) an effective one among the noble *akh*s
through the duties of the effective lector priest
who knows doubly truly the rites.
For indeed I am initiated (into) the secrets of every god.
For indeed I know all the effective rituals of the *akh*s
who have gone to the necropolis as *imakhu* of the Great God
in the sight of the king.
For indeed I know all the rituals (by which) he ascends to the Great God:
the sole companion, keeper of secrets, whose great name is Merefnebef.

At the left end of the lintel are more titles of Merefnebef and a standing figure of him and his son.

East Wall of Facade: Right

(1) I am a more excellent and better prepared *akh* than [any *akh* …].
(2) an *imakhu* in the sight of the king, his favoured one.
(3) I am an excellent lector priest who knows all magical matters (better) (4) than any person.
No excellent (5) magic was ever hidden from me.
He who is a keeper of secrets (6) of the king in all matters
is him who he loves …
who does (?) what is excellent and (7) hidden
within the gateway in relation to every judgment—
(8) (this is) the one who is truly a keeper of secrets of the king.
(9) O you who pass by, [you who live!]:
(10) With regard to any person who shall do an [evil] thing
(11) to this tomb of mine in relation to the invocation offerings,
or in relation to the soul priest(s),
(12) I shall make an end for him concerning it in their presence.
(13) Fear is not put in me in regarding it,
in order that (14) those on earth see and are fearful of noble *akh*(s)
(15) who are created in this entire land.

(16) I went forth from my town, I went down into the afterlife;
(17) I have achieved greatness and reached old age;
I carried out Maat which is what (18) the god loves;
I satisfied (the god) with regard to that which he loves,
which is truly making (?) (19) invocation offerings for the noble *akhs*.
I was respectful (20) of my father, I was charming to my mother.
(21) I buried him who had no son;
I ferried him over (22) who had [no boat;
I rescued] (23) the wretched man from [the (more) powerful one];
(24) I gave the share of the father to his [son].
(25) For (the following) is what is said by [people who pass by]:
(26) ["Look, he is] an *imakhu* [and the beloved one of the god,"
so they say about me].[2]

East Wall of Facade: Left

(1) He who loves the king is he who loves (the fact that) he is alive;
(2) He who loves (the fact that) he prospers
is he who loves (the fact that) he exists (3) on this earth for ever
in the manner in which Re exists in the horizon.
(4) He who does not act against (?) the burial within (5) this tomb of mine
(is) he who does not bury (6) any (other) person within this tomb of mine (7) for ever,
whether his children, his siblings, (8) or his soul priests.
With regard to he who shall do (such things) in spite of this,
(9) I shall penalize them in relation to it, as I live for the king:
(10) he is his enemy, he is his opponent,
(11) he is the conspirator (against) him therein.
Indeed (12) I shall be judged with him on this matter
by the majesty of the Great God.
(13) Now, with regard to this tomb of mine of eternity,
which I made (14) more than anything (else)
as a result of my state of *imakhu* in the sight of the king,
(15) the king had me take its location in a pure place
(16) in the sacred land in the … enclosure of Osiris,
(17) for his majesty desired more than anything
that I should particularly ascend to the god,
for his majesty desired more than anything
that I should be transfigured in the sight of the god,

(18) for his majesty desired more than anything
that I should be noble (19) in the sight of the Great God,
for I am more noble in the sight of the king (20) than anything.
Now, with regard to this tomb of mine of eternity,
(21) I [made] it to be a solid place for my limbs in my funerary estate
(22) when I was a royal noble.
The painters (*literally* "scribes") it was (23) [who made] it truly in its midst.
The craftsmen it was who made it.
(24) The craftsmen it was who made this tomb of mine …
(25) a perfect burial (for) the companion, the controller of the palace, Merefnebef.

Notes

1. Another rare example of a man with three names; compare no. 223, also of the same period. Note that the phrase translated as "great name" at the ends of lines 1 and 4 is actually using two words for great: the first is *ren wer* and the second *ren aa*.

2. This is speculatively based on the texts of Mehu (no. 220).

List of Sources

1. Text used: Urk I, 235–49; Wilkinson 2000. Translation and important comments in Roccati 1982: 36–52; Breasted 1906–7: I, 65–72.
2. Text used: Dreyer 1987; Kahl, Kloth, and Zimmermann 1995: 168–71.
3. Text used: Baud and Dobrev 1995 (recto); Baud and Dobrev 1997 (verso). See also Dobrev 2000.
4. Text used: Brovarski 1987: 27–48, pl. I; Wildung 1969: 39–40, 94–95, 194–96, 204, Abb II, III.1.
5. Text used: Hassan 1932–60: IV, 119–20, fig. 64; Urk I, 166. Translation: Roccati 1982: 71.
6. Text used: Urk I, 166. Translation: Roccati 1982: 70–71.
7. A. Text used: Metropolitan Museum of Art 1999: 172 (4); Kahl, Kloth, and Zimmermann 1995: 74–75.

   B. Text used: Friedman 1995. See Friedman 1995; 1996 for interpretations and many further references.

   C i. Text used: Metropolitan Museum of Art 1999: 175–76 (7B–C).

   C ii. Urk I, 153–54; Kahl, Kloth, and Zimmermann 1995: 116–19; Weill 1911–12: 12–16.
8. A. Text used: Edel 1996, 200–204, Abb 1.

   B. Text used: Edel 1996, 206–8, Abb 4.
9. Text used: Metropolitan Museum of Art 1999: 318–19, 321.
10. A. Text used: Borchardt 1910–13: II, 10–15, Bl. 1. Translation: Roccati 1982: 58–60.

    B. Text used: Borchardt 1910–13: II, 18–21, Bl. 5. Part of the text and the Seth god in Priese 1991: 40–41 [25]). Translation: Roccati 1982: 60.

    C. Text used: Borchardt 1910–13: II, 21–23, Bl. 8.

    D. Text used: Borchardt 1910–13: II, 27–28, Bl. 12. Translation: Roccati 1982: 60; translation and comment in Baines 1997: 141–42.

    E. Text used: Borchardt 1910–13: II, 35–36, Bl. 18.

    F. Text used: Borchardt 1910–13: II, 99–100, Bl. 20

    G. Text used: Borchardt 1910–13: II, 108–9, Bl. 29–30.

H. Text used: Borchardt 1910–13: II, 49, Bl. 35.

I. Text used: Hawass and Verner 1996: 181, fig. 1a.

11. Text used: Helck 1977a, with references to the original publications. Some notes and other examples of most of these festivals in Schott 1950. See also comments in Sherif el-Sabban 2000: 2–8 (written without the benefit of the Helck article).

12. A. Text used: Hassan 1938: 519; Hassan 1955: 137–38, fig. 1; Goyon 1971: 13–14. Translation: Roccati 1982: 131–32.

B. Text used: Goedicke 1971: 24–26.

13. A. Text used: Habachi 1957: 14–17, fig. 2; Fischer 1968: 41, fig. 8.

B. Text used: Habachi 1957: 17–18, fig. 3.

C. Text used; Naville 1891: pl. XXXII (D).

D. Text used: el-Sawi 1979: 75–76, figs. 164–67.

14. Text used: Urk I, 114–15; Borchardt 1937–64: II, 170–72, Bl. 98. Translation: Roccati 1982: 68–69.

15. A. Text used: Urk I, 179.

B. Text used: Leclant 1992: 218–19, figs. D, E.

C. Text used: Leclant and Clerc 1997: Tav. XVI.

D. Text used: Urk I, 271–72.

E. Text used: Osing 1982: 33, Taf. 61 (28).

16. Text used: Urk I, 160; Goedicke 1967a: 16–21. See also Hofmann 2001: 126–28.

17. Text used: Leprohon 1985: 49–53; Goedicke 1967a: 22–36; Urk I, 170–72; Markowitz, Haynes, and Freed 2002: 76 (color photograph). Translation: Pritchard 1955: 212.

18. Text used: Posener–Kriéger 1985b, including other similar but more broken examples.

19. Text used: Urk I, 207–8; Goedicke 1967a: 37–40; James 1961: pl. XXXI.

20. Text used: Urk I, 209–13; Goedicke 1967a: 55–77; Borchardt 1905.

21. Text used: Goedicke 1967a: 41–54; Urk I, 214. Translation: Lichtheim 1973: 28.

22. Text used: Goedicke 1967a: 81–86; Urk I, 278–80.

23. Text used: Leprohon 1985: 156–59; Urk I, 277–78; Goedicke 1967a: 148–54. Ronald J. Leprohon has permitted me to see an unpublished copy of the text by the late Klaus Baer, for which I am very grateful.

24. Text used: Urk I, 280–83; Goedicke 1967a: 87–116. Translation of part: Lorton 1977: 8.

25. Text used: Urk I, 284–88; Goedicke 1967a: 117–27.

26. Text used: Urk I, 288–93; Goedicke 1967a: 137–47. One fragment in Hayes 1946: 7–11 (d), pl. II.
27. Text used: Urk I, 293–95; Goedicke 1967a: 128–36.
28. Text used: Pantalacci 1985. Further studies: Leprohon 1986: 55–56; Goedicke 1989; Ziermann and Eder 2001, 338–41.
29. Text used: Urk I, 307; Goedicke 1967a: 158–62.
30. Text used: Urk I, 303–4; Goedicke 1967a: 163–64 and Abb. 23 on p. 196; Hayes 1946: 11–13 (h), pl. III.
31. Text used: Goedicke 1967a: 172–77.
32. Text used: Urk I, 297–99; Hayes 1946: 13–16 (j), pl. III; Goedicke 1967a: 197–202.
33. Text used: Urk I, 302–3; Goedicke 1967a: 206–13.
34. Text used: Urk I, 295–96; Goedicke 1967a: 165–71.
35. Text used: Urk I, 300–301; Goedicke 1967a: 184–89. Translation: Wente 1990: 21.
36. Text used: Urk I, 301–2; Goedicke 1967a: 193–94.
37. Text used: Urk I, 299; Hayes 1946: 16–17 (o), Pl. IV, IVA; Goedicke 1967a: 178–83.
38. Text used: Urk I, 299–300; Hayes 1946: 17–19 (p–q), pl. V; Goedicke 1967a: 190–92, 195–96.
39. Text used: Urk I, 304–6; Goedicke 1967a: 214–25. Translation of part: Lorton 1977: 11; Verbovsek 2004: 5–6.
40. A. Text used: Goedicke 1994; comments in Fischer 1996: 267–70.
    B. Text used: Fischer 1996: 267–70; Petrie 1896: pl. XII (1).
41. Text used: Urk I, 153; Gunn 1926: 177–96; Kahl, Kloth, and Zimmermann 1995: 70–71. Comments in Lauer 1996.
42. Text used: Hayes 1953: 64, fig. 41; Fischer 1963–64: 240.
43. A. Text used: Goedicke 1957.
    B. Text used: Ziegler 1997, 464–65, fig. 1.
44. Text used: Metropolitan Museum of Art 1999: 450–51 (182).
45. A. Text used: Urk I, 97; Priese 1991: 42 (27); Hölzl 2004: 220–21 (6).
    B. Text used: Urk I, 97. Metropolitan Museum of Art 1999: 448–49 (179) and Ziegler 1997, 465, fig. 6. Further similar vessels Ziegler 1997, 465, figs. 7–8.
    C. Text used: Ziegler 1997, 465, fig. 5.
    D. Text used: possibly unpublished (author's hand copy).
    E. Text used: Fischer 1993; Metropolitan Museum of Art 1999: 446–47 (178b).
    F. Text used: Kaiser et al. 1976: 80 (b).
46. A. Text used: Ziegler 1997, 466, fig. 10.

B. Text used: Metropolitan Museum of Art 1999: 450 (181).

47. A. Text used: Urk I, 115; Ziegler 1997, 466, fig. 13.
B. Text used: Ziegler 1997, 466, figs. 11–12; Metropolitan Museum of Art 1999: 448–49 (180); (lid) Urk I, 115.

48. Text used: Urk I, 69; Petrie 1888: 12, 312. Translation: Roccati 1982: 77.

49. Text used: Ziegler 1990: 50–53; Ricke 1960: 54, n. 18.

50. Text used: Urk I, 110.

51. Text used: Urk I, 111; Petrie 1888: pl. XIII (338).

52. Text used: Kaiser et al. 1976: 79.

53. Text used: Urk I, 115; Petrie 1888: pl. XII (311). Translation: Roccati 1982: 77.

54. Text used: Gardiner, Peet, and Černý 1952–55: 54, pl. I (no. 2); Eichler 1993: 29 (2), 118; Kahl, Kloth, and Zimmermann 1995: 120–21. Translation: Roccati 1982: 240.

55. Text used: Urk I, 7–8; Gardiner, Peet, and Černý 1952–55: 56–57, pl. II (no. 5). Eichler 1993: 30 (5), 118. Translation: Roccati 1982: 241; Breasted 1905–7: I, 75–76.

56. Text used: Urk I, 8; Gardiner, Peet, and Černý 1952–55: 57–58, pl. II (no. 7). Eichler 1993: 30–31 (7), 118. Translation: Roccati 1982: 241; Breasted 1906–7: I, 83.

57. A. Text used: Urk I, 32; Gardiner, Peet, and Černý 1952–55: 58, pl. V (no. 8). Eichler 1993: 31 (8), 119. Translation: Roccati 1982: 241; Breasted 1906–7: I, 108. Now Cairo, JE 38569.
B. Text used: Giveon 1977; Giveon 1978; Edel 1978; Eichler 1993: 38 (21), 120.

58. Text used: Urk I, 53–54; *LD* II, 152a; Gardiner, Peet, and Černý 1952–55: 59–60, pl. VI (no. 10). Eichler 1993: 31–32 (10), 119. Translation: Roccati 1982: 242; Breasted 1906–7: I, 114.

59. Text used: Urk I, 54; Gardiner, Peet, and Černý 1952–55: 60, pl. IV (no. 12). Eichler 1993: 32 (12), 119. Translation: Roccati 1982: 242; Breasted 1906–7: I, 119.

60. A. Text used: Urk I, 55; Gardiner, Peet, and Černý 1952–55: 62, pl. IV (no. 15). Eichler 1993: 34 (15), 120. Translation: Roccati 1982: 244; Breasted 1906–7: I, 120.
B. Text used: Urk I, 56; Gardiner, Peet, and Černý 1952–55: 61–62, pl. VIII (no. 14). Eichler 1993: 33 (14), 119. Translation: Roccati 1982: 243; Breasted 1906–7: I, 121.
C. Text: Baines and Parkinson 1997; Urk I, 55–56; Gardiner, Peet, and

Černý 1952–55: 60–61, pl. VII (no. 13). Eichler 1993: 32–33 (13), 119. Translation: Roccati 1982: 242–43; Breasted 1906–7: I, 120–21.

D. Text used: Edel 1983: 158–63; Abb. 1a–b; Gardiner, Peet, and Černý 1952–55: 65, pl. IX (no. 19); Eichler 1993: 36 (19), 120. Translation: Roccati 1982: 244.

61. Text used: Urk I, 91–92; *LD* II, 116a; Gardiner, Peet, and Černý 1952–55: 62–63, pl. VIII (no. 16). Eichler 1993: 34 (16), 210. Translation: Roccati 1982: 245–46; Breasted 1906–7: I, 138–39.

62. Text used: Urk I, 112–13; *LD* II, 116a; Gardiner, Peet, and Černý 1952–55: 64, pl. IX (no. 17). Eichler 1993: 35 (17), 120. Translation: Roccati 1982: 246–47; Breasted 1906–7: I, 155–57.

63. Text used: Urk I, 148; Couyet and Montet 1913: 94–95 (169–71). Translation: Roccati 1982: 258; Breasted 1906–7: I, 174.

64. A. Text used: Urk I, 96–97; Eichler 1993: 71 (123–24), 124. Translation: Breasted 1906–7: I, 136.

B. Text used: Urk I, 93. Eichler 1993: 74–5 (133), 125. Translation: Roccati 1982: 259–60; Breasted 1906–7: I, 137.

C. Text used: Urk I, 94. Eichler 1993: 70 (122), 124. Translation: Roccati 1982: 260; Breasted 1906–7: I, 137–38.

D. Text used: Goyon 1957: 55–56 (21). Eichler 1993: 56–57 (82), 123. Translation: Roccati 1982: 260–61.

E. Text used: Urk I, 94–95; Couyet and Montet 1913: 72 (103). Eichler 1993: 73–74 (132), 124. Translation: Roccati 1982: 261; Breasted 1906–7: I, 138.

65. Text used: Urk I, 148–49; Couyet and Montet 1913: 103–4 (206). Translation: Roccati 1982: 258–59; Breasted 1906–7: I, 175.

66. Text used: Urk I, 149–50; Couyet and Montet 1913: 91–92 (150). Translation: Roccati 1982: 259.

67. A. Text used: Urk I, 258. Translation: Roccati 1982: 261–62; Mostafa 1987: 174–75.

B. Text used: Urk I, 259. Translation: Roccati 1982: 262; Mostafa 1987: 175.

C. Text used: Urk I, 259. Translation: Roccati 1982: 262; Mostafa 1987: 175.

68. A. Text used: Newberry 1938: 183–84; Eichler 1993: 68 (116), 124. Translation: Roccati 1982: 262–63.

B. Text used: Urk I, 141. Translation: Roccati 1982: 213.

69. Text used: Anthes 1928: Taf. 4 (Inschrift I); Eichler 1993: 38 (27), 121. Translation: Roccati 1982: 249.

70. A. Text used: Anthes 1928: Taf. 9 (Gr. 1); Eichler 1993: 41 (36), 121. Translation: Roccati 1982: 249.
    B. Text used: Anthes 1928: Taf. 9 (Gr. 2); Eichler 1993: 42 (38), 122. Translation: Roccati 1982: 249–50.
71. Text used: Urk I, 95; Anthes 1928: Taf. 4 (Inschrift III); Eichler 1993: 39 (30), 121. Translation: Roccati 1982: 250; Breasted 1906–7: I, 139–40.
72. Text used: Anthes 1928: Taf. 5 (Inschrift VI); Urk I, 256; Eichler 1993: 40 (33), 121. Translation: Roccati 1982: 250–51.
73. A. Text used: Anthes 1928: Taf. 10 (Gr. 3); Eichler 1993: 43 (39), 122. Translation: Roccati 1982: 251; part Doret 1986: 107 (example 194).
    B. Text used: Anthes 1928: Taf. 10 (Gr. 4); Eichler 1993: 43 (40), 122. Translation: Roccati 1982: 251.
    C. Text used: Anthes 1928: Taf. 10 (Gr. 5); Eichler 1993: 43–44 (41), 122. Translation: Roccati 1982: 251.
    D. Text used: Anthes 1928: Taf. 11 (Gr. 6); Eichler 1993: 44 (42), 122–23. Translation: Roccati 1982: 252.
    E. Text used: Anthes 1928: Taf. 12 (Gr. 7); Eichler 1993: 44–45 (43), 123. Translation: Roccati 1982: 252–53.
    F. Text used: Anthes 1928: Taf. 12 (Gr. 8); Eichler 1993: 45 (44), 123. Translation: Roccati 1982: 253.
74. Text used: Eichler 1998: 255–56, Taf. 31b.
75. Text used: Rothe et al. 1996: 97–98, with improvements in Goedicke 1997: 63 and Eichler 1998: 263–66, Taf. 34d. Kloth 2002: 9–10 (17). Translation of part: Kloth 2002: 238–39.
76. Text used: López 1967; Helck 1974c; Eichler 1993: 112–13 (260–61), 125. Translation, Roccati, 1982: 269.
77. A. Text used: Weigall 1907: pl. LVIII; some Urk I, 208–9; Eichler 1993: 106–11, 125. Translation: Roccati 1982: 266–68.
    B. Text used: Edel 1971b: 53–59; Eichler 1993: 112 (258).
78. Text used: Gunn 1926: 197–202; Kahl, Kloth, and Zimmermann 1995: 80–81. Compare Arnold 1991: 8–9; Kemp 1989: 139.
79. A. Text used: Posener-Kriéger in el-Khouli 1991: 17–21, pls. 7–12.
    B. Text used: Petrie et al. 1910: 9, pls. V–VI.
80. Text used: Stadelmann 1987: 233–35, 239–40, Abb. 1–4.
81. Text used: most conveniently Reisner 1931: 273–77, plan XI and XII.
82. Text used: Barsanti 1906: e.g., p. 266 (I).
83. Ai. Text used: Borchardt 1910–13: II, Bl. 52.
    Aii. Text used: Hawass and Verner 1996: 182–84; Verner 2003: 447.
    B. Text used: Borchardt 1909: 46–47.

C. Text used: Verner 2003: 448.
D. Text used: Borchardt 1907: 71, Abb. 49.

84. A. Text used: Dunham and Simpson 1974: 3, figs. 1a–d.
B. Text used: Junker 1929–55: X, 69–81, Abb. 34–35. Important comments and modification to readings: Roth 1991: 13–15, 130–32.
Bi. Text used: Junker 1929–55: X, 71–2 (1), Abb. 34.1.
Bii. Text used: Junker 1929–55: X, 72 (2), Abb. 34.2.
Biii. Text used: Junker 1929–55: X, 72 (3), Abb. 34.6.
Biv. Text used: Junker 1929–55: X, 72–4 (4), Abb. 34.7.
Bv. Text used: Junker 1929–55: X, 74–6 (5), Abb. 34.3.
Bvi. Text used: Junker 1929–55: X, 77 (9), Abb. 35.10.
C. Text used: Junker 1929–55: I, 158–61, Abb. 24.

85. Text used: Edel 1969. Important comments: Roth 1991: 133–42.

86. A. Text used: Urk I, 58; Borchardt 1937–64: I, 6 Bl. 2.
B. Text used: Roth 1991: 93–94 (2).
C. Text used: Roth 1991: 96 (6).
D. Text used: Roth 1991: 17.
E. Text used: Roth 1991: 62–66, fig. 4.1. cf. Kanawati and Hassan 1997: pl. 54.

87. Text used: Goedicke 1988d: 114–16; Jéquier 1936–40: II, 68, fig. 9.

88. A. Text used: Vandekerckhove and Müller-Wollerman 2001: 38–40, with further bibliography.
B. Text used: Vandekerckhove and Müller-Wollerman 2001: 41–45, with further bibliography.
C. Text used: Vandekerckhove and Müller-Wollerman 2001: 47.
D. Text used: Vandekerckhove and Müller-Wollerman 2001: 172, with further bibliography.
E. Text used: Vandekerckhove and Müller-Wollerman 2001: 177–78, with further bibliography.
F. Text used: Vandekerckhove and Müller-Wollerman 2001: 183–86, with further bibliography.
G. Text used: Vandekerckhove and Müller-Wollerman 2001: 210–11, with further bibliography.

89. Text used: Edel 1995; Eichler 1993: 96 (202).

90. A. selection of these texts, including sections of some of the following, is translated in Roccati 1982: 277–85.
A. Text used: Posener–Kriéger and de Cenival 1968: pls. IA (A), I (A); Posener–Kriéger 1976: 3–13.
B. Text used: Posener–Kriéger and de Cenival 1968: pls. IA (B), I (B); Posener–Kriéger 1976: 3–13.

C. Text used: Posener–Kriéger and de Cenival 1968: pls. IIA (A), II (A); Posener–Kriéger 1976: 3–13.

D. Text used: Posener–Kriéger and de Cenival 1968: pls. IIA (B), II (B); Posener–Kriéger 1976: 3–13.

E. Text used: Posener–Kriéger and de Cenival 1968: pls. XIII–XIV (A). Posener–Kriéger 1976: 59–76.

F. Text used: Posener–Kriéger and de Cenival 1968: pls. XVII (A), XVIIA (A); Posener–Kriéger 1976: 472–75. A number of more broken but similar texts are discussed by Posener–Kriéger 1976: 475–77.

G. Text used: Posener–Kriéger and de Cenival 1968: pls. LXXIII (E), LXXIIIA (E); Posener–Kriéger 1976: 479.

H. Text used: Posener–Kriéger and de Cenival 1968: pls. LIVA (A), LIV (A); Posener–Kriéger 1976: 480–81.

I. Text used: Posener–Kriéger and de Cenival 1968: pls. LXXXIVA (C), LXXXIV (C); Posener–Kriéger 1976: Tableau III after p. 57.

J. Text used: Posener–Kriéger and de Cenival 1968: pls. III–IV, IIIA–IVA; Posener–Kriéger 1976: 14–57.

91. Text used: Posener-Kriéger 1991: 293–301.

92. A. Text used: Posener–Kriéger and de Cenival 1968: pls. LXXXA (A), LXXX (A); Posener–Kriéger 1976: 451–65. Translation: Roccati 1982: 285–86; Wente 1990: 55–56.

B. Text used: Posener–Kriéger and de Cenival 1968: 37–38, pls. LXXXA (B, C), LXXX (B, C); Posener–Kriéger 1976: 465–72. Translation: Roccati 1982: 286–87; Wente 1990: 56.

93. Text used: Baer 1966; Goedicke 1967b; Goedicke 1988c. Translation: Roccati 1982: 291–92; Wente 1990: 56–57.

94. Text used: Gunn 1925; Gardiner 1927. Comments in Grdseloff 1948. Translation: Roccati 1982: 293–94; Wente 1990: 42.

95. Text used: Posener–Kriéger 1980, 83–85. Translation: Wente 1990: 57.

96. Text used: Smither 1942. Translation: Wente 1990: 58; Roccati 1982: 288–89.

97. Text used: Roccati 1968. Translation: Roccati 1982: 289–90; Wente 1990: 57.

98. A. Text used: Edel 1992.

B. Text used: Unpublished, but for this section see Posener-Kriéger 1976: 454 n. 4.

99. Text used: Pantalacci 1998a. See also general notes in Pantalacci 1996 and Pantalacci 1998b.

100. Text used: Urk I, 179–80; Eichler 1991a: 149–52. Translation: Roccati 1982: 78–79; Wente 1990: 18. Comments in Baines 1997: 141–42 on the interplay between subject and ruler.

101. A. Text used: Gardiner and Sethe 1928: 1–3, 13–16, pls. I–IA; compare Gunn 1930: 148–50. Translations: Roccati 1982: 296–97; Wente 1990: 211.
B. Text used: Gardiner and Sethe 1928: 3–5, 17–19, pls. II–IIIA; compare Gunn 1930: 150–51. Translations: Roccati 1982: 297–98; Wente 1990: 211–12.
102. Text used: Torino 2004: Tav. 5B (text A), Tav. 43 (text B); Posener-Kriéger 1979; Menu 1985: 257–59.
103. Text used: Möller 1909–12: I, Taf. II; Sethe 1926; Goedicke 1974; Priese 1991: 274 (171). Some sections translated in Doret 1986: 51 (example 79), 54 (example 87), 89 (example 155); Green 1980.
104. Text used: Hassan 1975: I, fig. 18; Goedicke 1970: 81–94, Taf. IX. Translation: of part and comments Logan 2000: 55–56.
105. Text used: Edel 1981: 15–25; Urk I, 115–17; Säve-Söderbergh 1994: 32–33, pl. 9; Goedicke 1970: 186–89, pl. XVIII. Kloth 2002, 9 (16). Translation Breasted 1906–7: I, 155.
106. Text used: Goedicke 1970: 44–67, Taf. V; Urk I, 11–15; Borchardt 1937–64: I, 112–13, Bl. 28. Translation: Breasted 1906–7: I, 91–93; part with comments: Logan 2000: 54.
107. Text used: Borchardt 1937–64: II, 101–2, Bl. 85; Goedicke 1970: 178–81, Taf. VII; Fischer 1977: 106–7. Translation of part and comments: Menu 1985: 256–57; Logan 2000: 55; see also Doret 1986: 107 (example 193).
108. Text used: Urk I, 1–7; Goedicke 1966; Goedicke 1970: 5–20, Taf. I–II; Gödecken 1976; Baud and Farout 2001: 43–47. Translation: Roccati 1982: 83–88; parts and comments: Logan 2000: 51. For a consideration of this unique text in the development of the Old Kingdom biography, see Baines 1999a, particularly pp. 29–34.
109. Text used: Moussa and Altenmüller 1977: Taf. 28, Abb. 11, p. 87–88.
110. A. Text used: Urk I, 161–63; Goedicke 1970: 144–48, Taf. XV; Edel 1981: 52–56. Comments and some translations: Logan 2000: 53.
B. Text used: Urk I, 24–32; Goedicke 1970: 131–43, Taf. XIV; Edel 1981: 38–51. Comments and some translations: Manuelian 1986 and Logan 2000: 52; Breasted 1906–7 I: 99–107.
C.i Urk I 31 a; Edel 1981:Abb. 16 c.
C.ii. Urk I 31 b; Edel 1981:Abb. 16 d.
C.iii. Edel 1981:Abb. 17 d.
C.iv. Edel 1981:Abb. 17 c.
C.v. Urk I 31 c.
C.vi. Urk I 31 d
111. Text used: Urk I, 16–17; Goedicke 1970: 21–30, Taf. III. Translation: Breasted 1906–7: I, 88–90.

112. Text used: Goedicke 1970: 68–74, Taf. VI; Simpson 1980: 24, pls. XLVIb, XLVII (both with further references).
113. Text used: Urk I, 35; Goedicke 1970: 108–12, Taf. XIb. Translation of part and comments: Logan 2000: 56.
114. Text used: Urk I, 36–37; Goedicke 1970: 75–80, Taf. VIII; Mariette 1889: 318. Translation of part and comments: Logan 2000: 54.
115. Text used: Urk I, 163–65; Goedicke 1970: 122–30, Taf. XIII.
116. Text used: Goedicke 1970: 31–43, Taf. IV; Hassan 1932–60: II, 190, fig. 219. Translation of part: Doret 1986: 78 (example 126).
117. Text used: Bakir 1978: Pl. I; Goedicke 1970: 182–85, Taf. XVIIb.
118. Text used: Goedicke 1970: 104–7, Taf. XIa; Fischer 1958a. See also Hofmann 2001: 128–29.
119. Text used: Goedicke 1970: 174–77, Taf. XVIIa; see also Menu 1985: 255–56.
120. Text used: Goedicke 1970: 113–21, Taf. XII; comment on one section: Edel 1981: 68–69.
121. Text used: Menu 1985: 251–55, fig. 1; Urk I, 157–58; Goedicke 1970: 149–73, Taf. XVI. See also Mahmud 2000–2001.
122. Text used: Urk I, 175; Firth and Gunn 1926: I, 159–64, II, pls. 62–63.
123. Text used: Silverman 1997: 170–75; Urk I, 177.
124. Text used: Hassan 1975: III, 29–33, fig. 17b.
125. Text used: Junker 1929–55: XI, 85–87, Abb. 47. Translation of part: Roccati 1982: 135.
126. Text used: Urk I, 188–89; Paget and Pirie 1898: 32–33, pl. XXXIX.
127. Text used: Urk I, 228; Hassan 1932–60: I, 101, pl. LXIV.
128. Text used: Murray 1905–37: I, pl. VII; Urk I, 176–77.
129. Text used: Urk I, 177–78; Borchardt 1937–64: I, 102, Bl. 22.
130. Text used: Urk I, 190–91; Mariette 1889: 195.
131. Text used: Goyon 1959.
132. Text used: Junker 1929–55: VIII, 133–35, Abb. 61, 62.
133. Text: Hassan 1975: III, 76–78, fig. 39.
134. Text used: James 1953: 68–69, pl. XLI, (X[242]); Edel 1981: 67–71.
135. Text used: Urk I, 34–35; Mariette 1889: 184–86.
136. Text used: Lloyd et al. 1990: 37–38, pl. 22.
137. Text used: Fischer 1992: 67–70. Kloth 2002: 27 (55).
138. Text used: Edel 1994, completing previous publications (el-Khouli and Kanawati 1988: 14–15, pl. 6; Kanawati 1984; Edel 1981: 88–94). Compare Kanawati 2002a: 93–95; Kloth 2002: 18–19 (36).
139. Text used: Kanawati and Abder-Raziq 2001: 37–38, pl. 44.
140. Text used: Urk I, 255–56; Capart 1906: pls. 1–5. Translation: Roccati 1982: 157.

141. Text used: Urk I, 75; Mariette 1889: 417; Borchardt 1937–64: II, 162, Bl. 94. Kloth 2002: 23 (46). Translation of part: Roccati 1982: 142–43; Breasted 1906–7: I, 125.
142. Text used: Urk I, 260; Gardiner and Sethe 1928: pl. X (1). Translation: Roccati 1982: 156.
143. Text: Hassan 1975: II, 4–11, figs. 2–5.
144. Text used: Urk I, 187–88; Badawy 1978: 5–7, figs. 9–11, 13–14; Altenmüller 1981: 43–50.
145. Text used: Kanawati and Abder-Raziq 2000: 33–34, 41, pls. 43–44, 50.
146. Text used: Urk I, 48–49; *LD* II, 46.
147. Text used: Urk I, 197; Firth and Gunn 1926: I, 212, II, pl. 77 [A–E]. Translation: Roccati 1982: 159–60.
148. Text used: Schlick-Nolte 1993: 21–31.
149. Text used: Simpson 1980: 8–10, figs. 12, 15–16.
150. Text used: Wild 1959; Edel 1944: 56–68. Translation: Roccati 1982: 155–56.
151. Text used: Urk I, 112; Borchardt 1937–64: II, 60, Bl. 76.
152. Text used: Curto 1963: 82–83, fig. 33.
153. Text used: Urk I, 73; Borchardt 1911–36: I, 197–98.
154. Text used: Junker 1929–55: IX, 118–20, Abb. 52.
155. Text used: Junker 1929–55: IX, 173–78, Abb. 78.
156. Text used: Junker 1929–55: IX, 159–61, Abb. 72, 74.
157. Text used: Hassan 1932–60: I, 102, fig. 172; part Urk I, 227.
158. Text used: Urk I, 206–7; McFarlane 2003, 42–44, pls. 15, 50.
159. Text: Mariette 1889: 160; Urk I, 33–34 (part only).
160. Text used: Kanawati 1980–92: I, 19, fig. 8.
161. Text used: Borchardt 1937–64: II, 35–36, Bl. 66; Urk I, 10.
162. Text used: James 1961: pl. X; Urk I, 227; Ziegler 1990: 231–37.
163. Text: Urk I, 9.
164. Text used: Hassan 1932–60: III, 117, fig. 104.
165. Text: Urk I, 16; Hassan 1932–60: IV, 137–38, fig. 78. Translation: Roccati 1982: 161.
166. Text used: Berlin 1913: 62; Urk I, 165.
167. Text used: Moussa and Junge 1975: 24–26, pl. 4a.
168. Text used: Urk I, 165.
169. Text used: Urk I, 227; Strudwick 1987.
170. Text used: Kanawati 1980–92: VII, 21–22, fig. 11; Schiaparelli 1885: 88. Translation of part: Roccati 1982: 162.
171. Text used: Urk I, 176; Firth and Gunn 1926: I, 165–66, II, pl. 63 (4, 5); McFarlane 2003, pls. 93–94, 62.

172. Text used: Fischer 1978: 47–52, with Fischer 1980a: 86; Wiese 2001: 52 (21).
173. A. Text: Urk I, 33; Borchardt 1937–64: I, 89–91, Bl. 20.
B. Text used: Mariette 1889: 198–99; Borchardt 1937–64: II, 28–30, Bl. 64. Translation: Roccati 1982: 73–74.
174. Text: *LD* II, 34 (d); Urk I, 8.
175. Text: James 1961: pl. VIII (1); Urk I, 15.
176. Text used: Urk I, 152; Brovarski 2002 with further bibliography. Translation: Roccati 1982: 135–36.
177. Text used: Kanawati 1980–92: VI, 53–54, fig. 23b.
178. Text: Urk I, 9.
179. Text used: Abu Bakr 1953: 73–74, figs. 47–48. Kloth 2002: 3 (1).
180. Text used: Edel 1953b: 327–33. Translation: Roccati 1982: 157–58.
181. Text used: Urk I, 225. Krauspe 1997: 51–53, Taf. 40–41. Translation: Roccati 1982: 161–62.
182. Text used: Urk I, 23; Scharff 1938: Taf. 12. Translation: Roccati 1982: 152.
183. Text used: Hassan 1932–60: III, 17–18, fig. 15.
184. Text used: Fakhry 1935: 19–21.
185. Text used: Urk I, 225–26; Junker 1929–55: VII, 146–49, Abb. 60; Martin 1978: 120–22.
186. Text used: Hassan 1932–60: II, 213–20, figs. 231, 232, 240; reconstruction of A and B in Edel 1944: 74–78; reconstruction of D: Roth 1994: 231, fig. 16.3. Translation, Roccati 1982: 158–59.
187. Text used: Manuelian 1994; Urk I, 226. Translation: Roccati 1982: 162.
188. Text used: Hassan 1932–60: II, 173, fig. 206. Translation of part: Doret 1986: 78 (example 125).
189. Text used: el-Khouli and Kanawati 1988: 9–10, pl. 3. Kanawati 2002a: 74–78.
190. Text used: Urk I, 71–72; Ziegler 1990: 212–14. Kloth 2002: 30 (63). Translation: Kloth 2002: 232.
191. A. Text used: Roth 1995: 146, pl. 191 and Roth 1994: 229, 232, fig. 16.1.
C. Text used: Roth 1994: 230, fig. 16.2. Kloth 2002: 43 (97).
192. Text used: Kanawati 2002a: 132–34; Kanawati and Abder Raziq 2001: 44, pl. 46b.
193. Text used: Urk I, 226; James 1961: pl. XII (1).
194. Text used: Ziegler 1993: 110–14. Kloth 2002: 4 (2).
195. A. Text used: Hassan 1975: I, fig. 17; Goedicke 1970: 94–99, Taf. X.
B. Text used: Hassan 1975: I, 60–61, pl. LIA.

196. Text used: Reisner 1942: 504–5, pl. 65b. Kloth 2002: 27 (56). Translation: Kloth 2002: 212–13; Roccati 1982: 99–100.
197. Text used: Urk I, 201–3; Badawy 1978: 14, figs. 22–23; Kanawati and Hassan 1997: 27–29, pls. 34–35; parts Sainte Fare Garnot 1938: 28–34. Kloth 2002: 10 (19). Translation: Roccati 1982: 153–54.
198. Text used: Urk I, 215–21; Dunham 1938. Kloth 2002: 16–17 (31). Translation: Roccati 1982: 181–86; Lichtheim 1988: 11–14; sections in Doret 1986: e.g., 100–101 (example 177).
199. Text used: Wilson 1954; Fischer 1965; Edel 1958: 3–9. Kloth 2002: 12–13 (13). Translation: Roccati 1982: 147–48.
200. Text used: Hassan 1932–60: IV, 168–69, fig. 118; Urk I, 18–21. Kloth 2002: 38–39 (84). Translations: Reisner 1931: 257–58; Roccati 1982: 91–93; Kloth 2002: 184–87; Maystre 1992: 223–25; Breasted 1906–7: I, 94–95. Comments, Baines 1999b: 21.
201. A. Text used: Kanawati and Abder Raziq 2001: 61–62, pl. 53.
B. Text used: Kanawati and Hassan 1996: 71–73, pl. 65.
202. Text used: Urk I, 49–51; Mohr 1943: 34–35. Kloth 2002: 27 (54). Translations: Lichtheim 1973: 16; Lichtheim 1988: 10–11; Lichtheim 1992: 10–11; Breasted 1906–7: I, 114–15; parts in Kloth 2002: 125, 127.
203. Text used: Urk I, 231; Baud and Farout 2001: 47–48; Kloth 2003.
204. Text used: Kuraszkiewicz 2002: 352–54, fig. 1, pls. 12–13.
205. Text used: Kanawati and Abder-Raziq 1999: 22–23, 37–38, pls. 52, 59; Silverman 2000. Translation of part and comments: Baud and Farout 2001: 49–54.
206. Text used: Simpson 1976b: 20–21, fig. 33; Munro 1989. Kloth 2002: 8 (12). Translation of part: Roccati 1982: 143–44.
207. Text used: Kloth 2002: 5–6 (7), 45–46, Abb, 1.
208. Text: Hassan 1975: III, 61–62, fig. 33.
209. Text used: Helck 1977b; Edel 1979. Translation: Roccati 1982: 148.
210. Text used: Bárta 2001: 158–60, based on his reconstruction.
211. Text used: Kanawati and Hassan 1996: 43–45, pls. 49–50. Kloth 2002: 35 (75).
212. Text used: Urk I, 180–86; Schott 1979. Kloth 2002: 35 (76). Translation: Roccati 1982: 118–21; some parts translated in Kloth 2002: 187–89, 194–95, 210–11.
213. Text used: Edel 1953a, with many improvements over Urk I, 194–96. Translation: Roccati 1982: 139–41; part Lichtheim 1992: 12–13.
214. Text used: McFarlane 1987: a fragment Paris, Louvre AF 9460 (Urk I, 250–51, Ziegler 1990: 270–73), joins another part Chicago, Field

Museum 31700 (Brovarski 1985: pl. VIII; Kanawati 1980–92: VI, 61, pl. 15, fig. 31). Translation of part: Roccati 1982: 170–71.

215. Text used: Urk I, 186; Junker 1929–55: VIII, 133–34, 119–20, Abb. 56. Kloth 2002: 36 (78).

216. Text used: James 1953: 36–41, pls. V–VI. Kloth 2002: 29 (60). Translation: Roccati 1982: 164–67.

217. Text used: Altenmüller 1974: 14–18. Kloth 2002: 28 (58).

218. Text used: Edel 1981: 72–75; Fischer 1975: 33–35. Kloth 2002: 28 (57). Translation: Roccati 1982: 132–33.

219. Text used: Urk I, 46–48; Hassan 1932–60: V, 240–42, fig. 101. Kloth 2002: 12 (21). Translation of part: Lichtheim 1992: 9.

220. A. Text used: Hawass 2002; Kloth 2002: 48–49, Abb 3; cf. Altenmüller 1998: 31, 89.
B. Text used: Altenmüller 1998: 87–88, Abb. 1.

221. Text used: Hassan 1932–60: I, 106, fig. 182; Urk I, 234. Kloth 2002: 17 (32).

222. Text used: Kaplony 1968; Kaplony 1976. Kloth 2002: 20–21 (39). Translation: Roccati 1982: 145–47. A number of pieces from it, with excellent photographs, including these four texts, feature in the exhibition catalogue Metropolitan Museum of Art 1999: 408–17.

223. Text used: Edel 1981: 77–84; Urk I, 200–201; Capart 1907: pls. LXXVI–LXXVII; Lloyd forthcoming. Kloth 2002: 22 (43). Translation of part: Lichtheim 1992: 13–14.

224. Text used: Urk I, 198–99; Kanawati and Abder-Raziq 1998: 24–25, 34–36, pls. 44, 58. Kloth 2002: 22–23 (44). Translation: Roccati 1982: 144–45; part Lichtheim 1973: 17; Lichtheim 1988: 6; Lichtheim 1997: 12.

225. Text used: Urk I, 38–40; Borchardt 1937–64: I, 169–73, Bl. 39. Kloth 2002: 21 (40). Translations: Roccati 1982: 96–98; Maystre 1992: 225–26; Breasted 1906–7: I, 108–9; Kloth 2002: 213 (part); several examples in Doret 1986.

226. Text used: Dorman 2002; Urk I, 51–53; James 1961: 17, pls. XVII. Kloth 2002: 15–16 (29). Translations: Roccati 1982: 105–7; Maystre 1992: 105–6, 226–31; Assmann 1991: 180–81; Breasted 1906–7: I, 115–18; part, Lichtheim 1997: 10.

227. Text: Urk I, 232; Hassan 1932–60: I, 18–19, fig. 13; Allen 1992. Kloth 2002: 23–24 (47). Translation: Roccati 1982: 101–2; some parts in Kloth 2002: e.g., 219; also Hofmann 2001: 130–32.

228. Text used: Urk I, 81–84, 177; Borchardt 1937–64: II, 31–34, Bl. 65; Mariette 1889: 373–76, 412–15. Kloth 2002: 30 (64). Translations:

Roccati 1982: 173–75; Maystre 1992: 113–15, 236–44; Breasted 1906–7: I, 131–32.

229. Text: Urk I, 84–85; Borchardt 1937–64: II, 148, 177–78, Bl. 100; Mariette 1889: 390 (copy of right jamb inaccurate). Kloth 2002: 30–31 (65). Translations: Roccati 1982: 175–76; Maystre 1992: 62–65, 247–49; Breasted 1906–7: I, 133.
230. Text used: Kanawati and Abder-Raziq 1998: 49, pl. 64. See also Kanawati 2002a: 117–19.
231. Text used: Badawy 1976: 16–17, fig. 19.
232. i. Text used: Brovarski 2001: 89–110, using restored texts in text figures 1–4. Further bibliography will be found there; see also Urk I, 59–67; Eichler 1991a: 142–49; Kloth 2002: 32–33 (69). Translations: Roccati 1982: 122–28; Breasted 1906–7: I, 121–25; Wente 1990: 18–20 (letters).

     ii. Text used: Brovarski 2001: 41–42, fig. 29.

     iii. Text used: Brovarski 2001: 43, fig. 35.
233. Text used: Hassan 1932–60: III, 80–81, fig. 69.
234. Text used: Seshemnefer: a. Urk I, 57; *LD* II, 81; Junker 1929–55: XI, 214–16, Abb. 83. Kloth 2002: 33–34 (72). Translation: Roccati 1982: 143; Lichtheim 1992: 9–10. b. Urk I, 178; Junker 1929–55: XI, 174–76, Abb. 71. Translation: Roccati 1982: 134–35.

     Ptahhotep: a. Junker 1929–55: XI, 265–68, Abb. 108. Small part in Lichtheim 1992: 9–10. b. Junker 1929–55: XI, 264–65, Abb. 107. Translation: Roccati 1982: 171.
235. Text used: Urk I, 40–45; Kloth 2002: 14 (26), Abb. 4a–d, Taf. IIa–c. Translation: Roccati 1982: 108–11; Breasted 1906–7: I, 111–13; some parts in Kloth 2002: 209–10, 219.
236. Text used: Kuraszkiewicz 2001.
237. Text used: Urk I 86–87; Borchardt 1937–64: I, 114, Bl. 28. Kloth 2002: 40 (87). Translation: Roccati 1982: 171–72; Breasted 1906–7: I, 133–34.
238. Text used: Urk I, 249–50; Firth and Gunn 1926: I, 168, II, pl. 66 (1–5). Kloth 2002: 42 (93). Translation: Roccati 1982: 169–70.
239. Text used: Urk I, 154; Curto 1963: 96 (15), Tav. XXVIII (a). Kloth 2002: 42 (94).
240. Text used: Goedicke 1959. Kloth 2002: 40–41 (89). Translation: Roccati 1982: 134; part Doret 1986: 47 (example 62).
241. Text used: Urk I, 120–31. Kloth 2002: 24–5 (49); the bibliography is extensive. Translations: Lichtheim 1973: 23–27; Roccati 1982: 200–207; Simpson 2003: 407–12; Breasted 1906–7: I, 150–54, 159–61; some sections Kloth 2002: 196–99; many passages in Doret 1986. The letter is translated in Wente 1990: 20–21 and Eichler 1991a: 152–55.

242. Text used: Urk I, 131–35. Kloth 2002: 13–14 (25). Translation: Roccati 1982: 208–11; Breasted 1906–7: I, 161–64; Lichtheim 1988: 15–16; part Lichtheim 1992: 14–15; some parts in Kloth 2002: e.g., 189–90; a number of sections in Doret 1986.

243. A. Text used: Urk I, 135–40; copy of the text by Edel and translation kindly provided by Karl Seyfried in advance of publication of the material (Seyfried forthcoming). Kloth 2002: 31 (66). Translation: Roccati 1982: 216–20; Breasted 1906–7: I, 164–69; parts, Kloth 2002: 203–8; several parts: Doret 1986.

B. Text used: Copy of the text by Edel and translation kindly provided by Karl Seyfried in advance of publication of the material (Seyfried forthcoming).

C. Text used: Copy of the text by Edel and translation kindly provided by Karl Seyfried in advance of publication of the material (Seyfried forthcoming, in which the reconstructions are discussed). Kloth 2002: 20 (38). Translation: Roccati 1982: 220; parts Kloth 2002: 208.

244. Text used: Habachi 1981: 19–22, fig. 5; Habachi 1978: 40, fig. 16. Kloth 2002: 31 (67). Translation: Roccati 1982: 214–15; Lichtheim 1988: 17–18. some parts in Kloth 2002: 202 and Fischer 1964: 30.

245. Text used: Urk I, 140–41; Newberry 1938: 182–83. Translation: Roccati 1982: 213; Breasted 1906–7: I, 164.

246. Text used: Edel 1954; Ziegler 1990: 78–81. Kloth 2002: 7 (10). Translated Roccati 1982: 178–79. Some comments and retranslations, Kloth 2002: 46–48, Abb. 2 a–c, Taf. 1a–d, suggesting that the heavy restorations of Edel might be somewhat excessive. The account of the excavation of the mastaba and the fragments is Alliot 1935: 8–38.

247. Text used: el-Khadragy 2002a; Urk I, 251–55. Kloth 2002: 34 (74). Translation: Roccati 1982: 179–80; parts: Simpson 2003: 412–13; Kloth 2002: 255–56; Doret 1986: e.g., 99 (example 173); and Moreno Garcia 1998.

248. Text used: Ziegler 1990: 204–6. Kloth 2002: 26 (52). Now Paris, Louvre E 26904.

249. Text used: Mostafa 1984–85; Mostafa 1987.

250. Text used: Urk I, 270; Petrie 1900: pls. V–VI. Kloth 2002: 8 (13). Comments Fischer 1968: 93–100; Schenkel 1965: 34–36.

251. Text used: Urk I, 271; Petrie 1900: pl. VI. Kloth 2002: 8–9 (14). Comments Fischer 1968: 100–103; Schenkel 1965: 34–36.

252. Text used: Edel 1981: 9–15; Säve-Söderbergh 1994: 28–29, pl 6a. Kloth 2002, 9 (16).

253. Text used: Säve-Söderbergh 1994: 62–63, pl. 46b.
254. Text used: Edel 1981: 25–34; compare Säve-Söderbergh 1994: 60–61. Kloth 2002: 9 (15).
255. Text used: Urk I, 263; Frankfort 1928: 235–38, pl. XX (3). Translation: Roccati 1982: 149 (129).
256. Text used: Urk I, 98–110; Borchardt 1935–64: I, 115–19, Bl. 29–30; Piacentini 1990; color photo Association Boulogne 2004: 186–87. Kloth 2002: 10–12 (20); the bibliography is extensive. Translations: Lichtheim 1973: 18–23; Roccati 1982: 187–97; Simpson 2003: 402–7; Breasted 1906–7: I, 134–35, 140–44, 146–50; Hofmann 2002; some parts in Kloth 2002: e.g., 190–94, 200–202, 214; one part Pritchard 1955: 227–28; many sections in Doret 1986. Analysis of the grammar Osing 1977; notes on palaeography el-Khadragy 2002b. Various comments on the events described in relation to the political situation in Egypt in Kanawati 2002a; compare Eyre 1994.
257. Text used: Fischer 1977: figs. 58–59; Urk I, 117–19; Borchardt 1937–64: I, 111–12, Bl. 24. Translation: Roccati 1982: 229–31; Breasted 1906–7: I, 157–59.
258. Text used: Urk I, 150; Borchardt 1937–64: II, 111. Kloth 2002: 40 (88). Translation: Roccati 1982: 149 (128).
259. Text used: Dunham 1937: 24–26, pl. VII (2); Leprohon 1985: 109–11. Kloth 2002: 41 (91).
260. Text used: Kanawati 1980–92: VIII, 40, fig. 19.
261. Text used: Kanawati 1980–92: VII, 15–16, figs. 7b, 8a; Urk I, 264. Kloth 2002: 4–5 (4). Translation: Roccati 1982: 232–33.
262. Text used: Kanawati 1980–92: VIII, 12, fig. 3b. Kloth 2002: 23 (45). Reign of Teti to Pepy I.
263. Text used: Kanawati 1980–92: VI, 48–49, figs. 20b-c; Vandier 1936. Translation of first part: Kloth 2002: 61; parts Doret 1986: 70 (example 108), 108 (example 198).
264. Text used: Fischer 1979: 44–46; Fischer 1981; Edel 1981: 75–76; Kanawati 1993–5: I, 59–60, pl. 42c. Kloth 2002: 17 (33).
265. Text used: Urk I, 266–67; Petrie 1908: pl. VI; Kanawati 1993–5: III, 32–33, pls. 7a, 35. See also Schenkel 1965: 38–40.
266. A. Text used: Davies 1902: I, 21–22, pl. XXIII top; Urk I, 142–45. Kloth 2002: 5 (6). Translation: Roccati 1982: 225–26; Breasted 1906–7: I, 169–71.

     B. Text used: Urk I, 144–45; Davies 1902: I, 22, pl. VII.
267. Text used: Urk I, 145–47; Davies 1902: II, 13, pl. XIII. Kloth 2002: 39–40 (86). Translation: Roccati 1982: 227–28; Breasted 1906–7: I, 171–73; sections in Doret 1986: e.g., 100–101 (example 177).

268. Text used: Urk I, 80; Davies 1902: II, 34, pl. XXI (A; tomb 38). Kloth 2002: 21 (41).
269. Text used: Urk I, 76–79; Davies 1902: II, 30, pls. XXIV–XXV. Translation: Schenkel 1965: 41–44; Breasted 1906–7: I, 126–27.
270. Text used: Urk I, 221–24; Blackman 1914–53: IV, pls. IV, IVA. Kloth 2002: 13 (24). Translations: Roccati 1982, 234–36; Lichtheim 1988: 18–20; some parts in Kloth 2002: e.g., 125.
271. Text used: Urk I, 69–71; Petrie 1898: 42–43, pl. VII; Kanawati and McFarlane 1993: 32–33, pls. 12, 13a, 39; part Sainte Fare Garnot 1938: 11–15. Kloth 2002: 6 (8). Translation of part: Lichtheim 1992: 11.
272. Text used: Fischer 1976b: 6–8. From Kom el-Akhdar near Busiris.
273. Text used: Osing et al. 1982: 26–28, Taf. 4, 58.
274. Text: Osing et al. 1982: 29–32, Taf. 6, 60.
275. Text used: Smith 1952: fig. 3 upper; Reisner and Smith 1955: 6, fig. 8a. Translation: Breasted 1906–7: I, 88.
276. Text used: Dunham and Simpson 1974: 8–9, 21, figs. 1e, 2, 14. Translation: Roccati 1982: 89–90.
277. Text used: Urk I, 155–56; Edel 1953b: 333–36. Part in Kloth 2002: 230–31.
278. A. Text used: Hassan 1932–60: IV, 16–17, fig. 2.
B. Text used: Verner 1995: figs 59b, 61 (hypothetical reconstructions).
C. Text used: Verner and Callender 2002: 68; Verner 1994: 87.
279. Text used: Munro 1993: 59–64, Taf. 13–14.
280. A. Text used: Firth and Gunn 1926: II, pl. 55 (1).
B. Text used: Firth and Gunn 1926: II, pl. 55 (2).
C. Text used: Firth and Gunn 1926: I, 12–13.
281. A. Text used: Dobrev 2000: 391 fig. 2; Jéquier 1933: 51, fig. 30.
B. Text used: Labrousse and Leclant 1998: 96–98, fig. 1.
C. Text used: Labrousse 2000.
282. A. Text used: Jéquier 1933: 4, fig. 1.
B. Text used: Jéquier 1933: 43, fig. 24 (similar titles on doorway fig. 22).
C. Text used: Jéquier 1933: 53, fig. 31.
D. Text used: Jéquier 1928: 18.
283. Text used: Hassan 1975: III, 4–7, fig. 2.
284. Text used: Junker 1929–55: I, 220–26, Abb. 51.
285. Text used: Málek 1979–80.
286. Text used: Moussa and Altenmüller 1980: 340–43, Abb. 12.
287. Text used: Junker 1929–55: II, 115, Abb. 7. Translation: Lichtheim 1973: 15–16.

288. Text used: Urk I, 72–73; *LD* Text I, 19.
289. Text used: Fischer 1976b: 14–22; Fischer 2000: 39–40, fig. 30; Vassilika 1995: 22–23.
290. Text used: Borchardt 1936–64: II, 137; cf. Urk I, 34.
291. Text used: Junker 1929–55: XI, 258–61, Abb. 104, 105 (with reconstructions from earlier copies of Lepsius).
292. Text used: Hassan 1932–60: II, 208–10, fig. 230.
293. Text used: Urk I, 119; Borchardt 1937–64: II, 85, Bl. 82. Translation of part: Roccati 1982: 163.
294. Text used: Junker 1929–55: VII, 241–45, Abb. 101.
295. Text used: Borchardt 1937–64: II, 59–60, Bl. 76; Fischer 2000: 36–38, fig. 27. Other references: Fischer 1976a: 74–75.
296. Text used: Kanawati and Hassan 1996: 19–20, pl. 40.
297. Text used: Hassan 1932–60: II, 204–8, figs. 225, 226. The tomb-building text is translated in Drenkhahn 1976a: 61.
298. Text used: Mariette 1889: 201; Borchardt 1937–64: I, 84–87, Bl. 19.
299. Text used: Hassan 1932–60: I, 111–12, fig. 184; Urk I, 229.
300. Text used: Hassan 1932–60: I, 81–84, figs. 143–44.
301. Text used: Hassan 1975: I, figs 2, 6–7; Altenmüller 1978: 4–5, Abb. 1.
302. A. Text used: Kanawati and Hassan 1997: 31–32, pl. 37a; Badawy 1978: fig. 24; compare Montet 1925: 69–72; translated (in an amalgamated form) Borghouts 1978: 83. Cf Dominicus 1994: 131–43.
    B. Text used: Kanawati and Hassan 1997: 40–41, pl. 45
    C. Text used: Kanawati and Hassan 1997: 33, pl. 38.
    D. Text used: Kanawati and Hassan 1997: pl. 40.
    E. Text used: Kanawati and Hassan 1997: 43–46, pl. 49.
    F. Text used: Kanawati and Hassan 1997: 49–50, pl. 55b.
    G. Text used: Kanawati and Hassan 1997: 50, pl. 55a.
303. Text used: Davies 1902: I, 18, pl. XIII.
304. A. Text used: Simpson 1992: pl. E.
    B. Text used: Simpson 1992: pl. F.
305. Text used: Fischer 1976b: 6–8.
306. A. Text used: Altenmüller 1998: 113, Taf. 18.
    B. Text used: Altenmüller 1998: 134, Taf. 30.
    C. Text used: Altenmüller 1998: 118, Taf. 22b.
    D. Text used: Altenmüller 1998: 119–20, Taf. 23b.
    E. Text used: Altenmüller 1998: 120–21, Taf. 24b.
    F. Text used: Altenmüller 1998: 141–42, Taf. 39–40.
    G. Text used: Altenmüller 1998: 143, Taf. 41a.

H. Text used: Altenmüller 1998: 142, Taf. 41b.

I. Text used: Altenmüller 1998: 144–45, Taf. 32.

J. Text used: Altenmüller 1998: 146, Taf. 42.

K. Text used: Altenmüller 1998: 161–62, Taf. 49.

L. Text used: Altenmüller 1998: 197–98, Taf. 74.

M. Text used: Altenmüller 1998: 178, Taf. 56, 60–63 (similar text p. 191).

N. Text used: Altenmüller 1998: 228, Taf. 82–83, 85 (similar text p. 239).

307. Text used: Junker 1929–55: II, Abb. 11; *LD* II, 22a–b.

308. Text used: Urk I, 267; Petrie 1908: pl. IX; Kanawati 1995: 35, pl. 37.

309. A. Text used: Moussa and Altenmüller 1977: 58–60, Abb. 5–6

B. Text used: Moussa and Altenmüller 1977: 46–55, Taf. 6–12.

C. Text used: Moussa and Altenmüller 1977: 61–66, Taf. 16–19.

D. Text used: Moussa and Altenmüller 1977: 66–72, Taf. 23, 26.

E. Text used: Moussa and Altenmüller 1977: 72–77, Taf. 20–21, Abb. 8.

F. Text used: Moussa and Altenmüller 1977: 80–83, Abb. 10. The order and layout of the market scenes is discussed in Fischer-Elfert 2000.

G. Text used: Moussa and Altenmüller 1977: 92–101, Abb. 12.

H. Text used: Moussa and Altenmüller 1977: 101–5, Abb. 13.

310. Text used: Blackman 1914–53: V, 32, 34–35, pls. XXIV, XXVIII; Fischer 1978: 44–47.

311. Text: Blackman 1914–53: IV, 31–32, pls. IX–X; see Altenmüller 1978: 5, Abb. 2.

312. Text used: Urk I, 37; Mariette 1889: 300. Translation: Breasted 1906–7: I, 109–10.

313. A. Text used: Simpson 1976b: 4–5, fig. 22a.

B. Text used: Simpson 1976b: 5–6, fig. 24; compare also a scene in the tomb of Idu, Simpson 1976b: 22–23, fig. 35. This scene is also conveniently illustrated in Lehner 1997: 26–27.

314. A. Text used: Simpson 1976a: 13, pls. D, XI, XIII.

B. Text used: Simpson 1976a: 10–16, pl. D.

315. Text used: Hassan 1932–60: IV, 111–12, fig. 58.

316. Text used: Wild 1953: pl. 114; van Walsem 1998.

317. A. Text used: Junker 1929–55: II, 66–69, Abb. 22.

B. Text used: Junker 1929–55: IV, 56–63, Taf, III–V; Kanawati 2001: pl. 37. Comments Grunert 2003: 86–90.

Ci. Text used: Moussa and Altenmüller 1977: 85–86, Taf. 25.
Cii. Text used: Moussa and Altenmüller 1977: 90–92, Taf. 30, Abb. 11.

318. Text used: synoptic text Altenmüller 1984–85.
319. A. Text used: from Jacquet-Gordon 1962: 357–65.
B. Text used: Jacquet-Gordon 1962: 398–402.
320. A. Text used: Dunham and Simpson 1974: 10, fig. 4.
B. Text used: Simpson 1980: 20–21, fig. 30.
C. Text used: *LD* Erg: XL; Harpur 1980: 58; Bárta 2001: 84.
321. Text used: Junker 1929–55: III, 172–76, Abb. 27, 28, 30; Kanawati 2002b: 32–33, 44, pl. 53. Translation: Roccati 1982: 116–17.
322. A. Text used: Urk I, 204–5; Sainte Fare Garnot 1938: 34–36; Kanawati and Hassan 1997: pl. 69a. Translation: Roccati 1982: 154–55. Discussion in Firth and Gunn 1926: I, 98–101.
B. Text used: Urk I, 205; Sainte Fare Garnot 1938: 41–42; James 1953: 65–66, pl. XXXIX. Translation: Roccati 1982: 167–68.
C. Text used: Kanawati and Hassan 1996: 48–49, pl. 55.
323. Text used: Urk I, 22; Borchardt 1937–64: II, 205–6, Bl. 110. See Junker 1957 for texts and terms; also Schwarz 2000 for background. Translation: Roccati 1982: 94–95.
324. Text used: Reisner 1936; Fischer 1966: 57. Translation, Roccati 1982: 103–4.
325. A. Text used: Edel 1987; Goedicke 1988b; Müller 2002.
Bi. Text used: Edel 1967: Taf. 104, 102/175.
Bii. Text used: Edel 1967: Taf. 132, 105/280.
Biii. Text used: Edel 1967: Taf. 140, 105/299.
Biv. Text used: Edel 1967: Taf. 160, 109/393.
Bv. Text used: Edel 1967: Taf. 172, 109/373.
Bvi. Text used: Edel 1967: Taf. 180, 109/370.
Bvii. Text used: Edel 1971a: Taf. 85, 89/50.
Bviii. Text used: Edel 1971a: Taf. 86, 89/51.
Bix. Text used: Edel 1975a: Taf. 53, 88/589.
Bx. Text used: Edel 1975a: Taf. 52, 88/587.
326. Text used: Smith 1933.
327. Text used: Manuelian 2003: 12–13, 58–62; Ziegler 1990: 187–89; Metropolitan Museum of Art 1999: 242–44.
328. Text used: Altenmüller 1998: 232–35, Abb. 33. See Barta 1963, especially pp. 82–88, for a study of offering lists.
329. Text used: Roccati 1970. For the names of the various types of linen in this and the following texts see Smith 1935; Edel 1975b; Posener-Kriéger 1976: 341–67. For some general comments on actual linen in the Old Kingdom, see Janssen 1996.

330. Text used: Moussa and Altenmüller 1971: 43–45. fig. 11.
331. Text used: Verner and Callender 2002: 47–48; photo of first example in Verner 1994: 84.
332. Text used: Hawass 2004: 29–30, figs. 6, 7, pls. 10, 11.
333. Text used: Myśliwiec et al. 2004: 70–83, pls. XIV–XVI.

Bibliography

Abbreviations used will be found on p. xxxv.

Abu-Bakr, Abdel-Moneim. 1953. *Excavations at Giza 1949–1950*. Cairo: Government Press.

Alexanian, Nicole. 1998. "Ritualrelikte an Mastabagräbern des Alten Reiches." Pages 3–22 in Guksch and Polz 1998.

———. 1999. *Dahschur II. Das Grab des Prinzen Netjer-aperef: Die Mastaba II/1 in Dahschur.* AV 56.

Allen, James P. 1984. *The Inflection of the Verb in the Pyramid Texts*. Bibliotheca Aegyptia 21/2. Malibu: Undena.

———. 1992. "Re'wer's Accident." Pages 14–20 in *Studies in Pharaonic Religion and Society in honour of J. Gwyn Griffiths*. Edited by Alan B. Lloyd. Occasional Publications 8. London: Egypt Exploration Society.

———. 2000. *Middle Egyptian: An Introduction to the Language and Culture of Hieroglyphs*. Cambridge: Cambridge University Press.

———. 2001. "Pyramid texts." Pages 95–97 in Redford 2001: III.

Alliot, Maurice. 1935. *Rapport sur les fouilles de Tell Edfou (1933)*. FIFAO 10/2. Cairo: IFAO.

Altenmüller, Hartwig. 1971. "Eine neue Deutung der Zeremonie des *init rd*." *JEA* 57: 146–53.

———. 1974. "Zur Vergöttlichung des Königs Unas im Alten Reich." *SAK* 1: 1–18.

———. 1978. "Zur Bedeutung der Harfnerlieder des Alten Reiches." *SAK* 6: 1–24.

———. 1981. "Das Grab des Hetepniptah (G 2430) auf dem Westfriedhof von Giza." *SAK* 9: 9–56.

———. 1984–85. "Das 'Sänftenlied' des Alten Reiches." *BSEG* 9–10: 15–30.

———. 1989. "Kälberhirte und Schafhirte. Bemerkungen zur Rückkehr des Grabherrns." *SAK* 16: 1–19.

———. 1992. "Zum möglichen religiösen Gehalt von Grabdarstellungen des Alten Reiches." Pages 21–35 in *Ernten, was man sät: Festschrift für*

Klaus Koch zu seinem 65. Geburtstag. Edited by Dwight R. Daniels, Uwe Gleßmer, and Martin Rösel. Neukirchen-Vluyn: Neukirchener Verlag.

———. 1994. "Die Reden und Rufe beim Dreschen in den Gräbern des Alten Reiches." Pages 9–24 in Bryan and Lorton 1994.

———. 1995. "Die 'Abgaben' aus dem 2. Jahr des Userkaf." Pages 37–48 in Kessler and Schulz 1995.

———. 1998. *Die Wanddarstellungen im Grab des Mehu in Saqqara*. AV 42.

———. 2000. "Die Nachtfahrt des Grabherrn im alten Reich. Zur Frage der Schiffe mit Igelkopfbug." *SAK* 28: 1–26.

———. 2002a. "Der Himmelsaufstieg des Grabherrn. Zu den Szenen des *zšš wꜣḏ* in den Gräbern des Alten Reiches." *SAK* 30: 1–42.

———. 2002b. "Funerary Boats and Boat Pits of the Old Kingdom." *Archiv Orientální* 70: 269–90.

Andrassy, Petra. 1993. "Das *pr-šnꜥ* im Alten Reich." *SAK* 20: 17–35.

———. 1994. "Die *ḫntiw-š* im Alten Reich." Pages 3–12 in *Ägyptische Tempel–Struktur: Funktion und Programm*. Edited by Rolf Gundlach and Matthias Rochholz. Akten der Ägyptologischen Tempeltagungen in Gosen 1990 und in Mainz 1992. HÄB 37.

———. 2001. "*ḫntj(w)-š* und kein Ende." Pages 1–18 in *Begegnungen: Antike Kulturen im Niltal. Festgabe für Erika Endesfelder, Karl-Heinz Priese, Walter Friedrich Reineke, Steffen Wenig von Schülern und Mitarbeitern*. Edited by Caris-Beatrice Arnst, Ingelore Hafemann, and Angelika Lohwasser. Leipzig: Verlag Helmar Wodtke und Katharina Stegbauer.

Andrews, Carol. 1990. *Ancient Egyptian Jewellery*. London: British Museum Press.

Anthes, Rudolf. 1928. *Die Felseninschriften von Hatnub*. UGAÄ 9.

Arnold, Dieter. 1976. *Gräber des Alten und Mittleren Reiches in El-Tarif*. AV 17.

———. 1991. *Building in Egypt: Pharaonic Stone Masonry*. New York/Oxford: Oxford University Press.

Arnold, Dorothea. 1999. *When the Pyramids Were Built: Egyptian Art of the Old Kingdom*. New York: Metropolitan Museum of Art.

Arnold, Felix. 1990. *The Control Notes and Team Marks*. The South Cemeteries of Lisht 2 = PMMA 23.

Assmann, Jan. 1991. *Stein und Zeit: Mensch und Gesellschaft in alten Ägypten*. Munich: Fink.

———. 1992. "When Justice Fails: Jurisdiction and Imprecation in Ancient Egypt and the Near East." *JEA* 78: 149–62.

———. 1995. *Ma'at: Gerechtigkeit und Unsterblichkeit im Alten Ägypten.* 2nd ed. Munich: Beck.

———. 1996. "Der literarische Aspekt des ägyptischen Grabes und seine Funktion im Rahmen des 'monumentalen Diskurses.'" Pages 97–104 in Loprieno 1996.

———. 2003. *The Mind of Egypt: History and Meaning in the Time of the Pharaohs.* Cambridge, Mass. and London: Harvard University Press. [Translation of *Ägypten: Eine Sinngeschichte.* Munich: Carl Hanser Verlag, 1996].

Assmann, Jan, Erika Feucht, and Reinhard Grieshammer (eds.). 1979. *Fragen an die altägyptische Literatur: Studien zum Gedenken an Eberhard Otto.* Wiesbaden: Dr. Ludwig Reichert Verlag.

Association Boulogne. 2004. *Des dieux, des tombeaux, un savant: En Egypte, sur les pas de Mariette Pacha.* Paris: Somogy éditions d'art.

Aufrère, Sydney. 1998. "Les anciens Egyptiens et leur notion de l'antiquité." *Méditerranées* 17: 11–55.

Badawy, Alexander. 1976. *The Tombs of Iteti, Sekhem'ankh-Ptah, and Kaemnofert at Giza.* University of California Publications: Occasional Papers, Number 9: Archaeology. Berkeley/Los Angeles/London: University of California Press.

———. 1978. *The Tomb of Nyhetep-Ptah at Giza and the Tomb of Ankhmahor at Saqqara.* University of California Publications: Occasional Papers Number 11: Archaeology. Berkeley/Los Angeles/London: University of California Press.

Baer, Klaus. 1956. "A Note on Egyptian Units of Area in the Old Kingdom." *JNES* 15: 113–17.

———. 1960. *Rank and Title in the Old Kingdom: The Structure of the Egyptian Administration in the Fifth and Sixth Dynasties.* Chicago: University of Chicago Press.

———. 1962. "The Low Price Of Land in Ancient Egypt." *JARCE* 1: 25–45.

———. 1966. "A Deed of Endowment in a Letter of the Time of Ppjj I?" *ZÄS* 93: 1–9.

Baines, John, and Christopher J. Eyre. 1983. "Four Notes on Literacy." *GM* 61: 81–85.

Baines, John and Jaromir Malek. 2000. *Cultural Atlas of Ancient Egypt.* Revised edition. New York: Checkmark Books.

Baines, John. 1988. "An Abydos List of Gods and an Old Kingdom Use of Texts." Pages 124–33 in *Pyramid Studies and Other Essays Presented to I.E.S. Edwards.* Edited by John Baines, T. G. H. James, A. Leahy, and A. F. Shore. Occasional Publications 7. London: Egypt Exploration Society.

———. 1989. "Ancient Egyptian Concepts and Uses of the Past: 3rd to 2nd Millennium BC Evidence." Pages 131–49 in *Who Needs the Past? Indigenous Values and Archaeology*. Edited by R. Layton. London: Unwin Hyman.

———. 1995. "Origins of Egyptian kingship." Pages 95–156 in O'Connor and Silverman 1995.

———. 1997. "Kingship before Literature: The World of the King in the Old Kingdom." Pages 125–74 in *Selbstverständnis und Realität: Akten des Symposiums zur ägyptischen Königsideologie in Mainz 15.–17.6.1995*. Edited by Rolf Gundlach and Christine Raedler. Beiträge zur altägyptischen Königsideologie, 1 = ÄAT 36/I.

———. 1999a. "Forerunners of Narrative Biographies." Pages 25–34 in *Studies on Ancient Egypt in Honour of H.S. Smith*. Edited by A. Leahy and J. Tait. Occasional Publications 13. London: Egypt Exploration Society.

———. 1999b. "Prehistories of Literature: Performance, Fiction, Myth." Pages 17–41 in *Definitely: Egyptian Literature: Proceedings of the Symposium "Ancient Egyptian Literature: History and Forms," Los Angeles, March 24–26, 1995*. Edited by Gerald Moers. Lingua Aegyptia. Studia Monographia 2. Göttingen: Seminar für Ägyptologie und Koptologie.

Baines, John, and Richard B. Parkinson. 1997. "An Old Kingdom Record of an Oracle? Sinai Inscription 13." Pages 9–27 in *Essays on Ancient Egypt in Honour of Herman te Velde*. Edited by Jacobus van Dijk. Egyptological Memoirs 1. Groningen: Styx.

Bakir, Abd el-Mohsen. 1978. *Slavery in Pharaonic Egypt*. Supplément aux Annales du Service des Antiquités de l'Égypte Cahier 18. Cairo: L'Organisation Égyptienne Générale du Livre.

Barsanti, Alexandre. 1906. "Fouilles de Zaouiét el-Aryân (1904–1905)." *ASAE* 7: 257–86.

Bárta, Miroslav. 1999. "The Title 'Property Custodian of the King' during the Old Kingdom Egypt." *ZÄS* 126: 79–89.

———. 2001. *The Cemeteries at Abusir South I*. Abusir V. Praha: Czech Institute of Egyptology.

Bárta, Miroslav, and Jaromír Krejčí. 2000. *Abusir and Saqqara in the Year 2000. Archiv orientální* Supplementa 9. Praha: Academy of Sciences of the Czech Republic.

Barta, Winfried. 1963. *Die altägyptische Opferliste von der Frühzeit bis zur griechisch-römischen Epoche*. MÄS 3.

———. 1968. *Aufbau und Bedeutung der altägyptischen Opferformel.* ÄF 24.

———. 1983. "Zur Lokalisierung und Bedeutung der *mrt*-Bauten." *ZÄS* 110: 98–104.

Baud, Michel. 1995. "La tombe de la reine-mère *ḫ*ʿ*-mrr-nbtj* Ire." *BIFAO* 95: 11–21.

———. 1996. "La date d'apparition des *ḫntjw-š*." *BIFAO* 96: 13–49.

———. 1998. "A propos des critères iconographiques établis par Nadine Cherpion." Pages 31–95 in *Les critères de datation stylistiques à l'Ancien Empire.* Edited by Nicolas Grimal. BdE 120.

———. 1999a. *Famille royale et pouvoir sous l'Ancien Empire égyptien.* BdE 126.

———. 1999b. "Ménès, la mémoire monarchique et la chronologie du IIIe millénaire." *Archéo-Nil* 9: 109–47.

———. 2000. "Le palais en temple: Le culte funéraire des rois d'Abousir." Pages 347–60 in Bárta and Krejčí 2000.

———. 2003. Review of Wilkinson 2000. *CdE* 78: 145–48.

Baud, Michel, and Vassil Dobrev. 1995. "De nouvelles annales de l'Ancien Empire égyptien: Une 'Pierre de Palerme' pour la VIe dynastie." *BIFAO* 95: 23–92.

———. 1997. "Le verso des annales de la VIe dynastie. Pierre de Saqqara-Sud." *BIFAO* 97: 35–42.

Baud, Michel, and Dominique Farout. 2001. "Trois biographies d'Ancien Empire revisitées." BIFAO 101: 43–57.

Berger, Catherine, and Bernard Mathieu (eds.). 1997. *Etudes sur l'Ancien Empire et la nécropole de Saqqâra dédiées à Jean-Philippe Lauer.* 2 vols. Orientalia Monspeliensia 9. Montpellier: Université Paul Valéry.

Berger, Catherine, Gisèle Clerc, and Nicolas Grimal (eds.). 1994. *Hommages à Jean Leclant.* 4 vols. BdE 106.

Berlandini, Jocelyne. 1979. "La pyramide 'ruinée' de Sakkara-Nord et le roi Ikaouhor-Menkaouhor." *RdE* 31: 3–28.

Berlin, Königliche Museen zu. 1913. *Aegyptische Inschriften aus den Königlichen Museen zu Berlin.* Vol. I. Leipzig: Hinrichs.

Blackman, Aylward M. 1914–53. *The Rock Tombs of Meir.* 6 vols. ASE 22–25, 28–29.

Borchardt, Ludwig. 1905. "Ein Königserlaß aus Dahschur." *ZÄS* 42: 1–11.

———. 1907. *Das Grabdenkmal des Königs Ne-user-re'.* WVDOG 7.

———. 1909. *Das Grabdenkmal des Königs Nefer-ir-keꜣ-re'.* WVDOG 11.

———. 1910–13. *Das Grabdenkmal des Königs S'aꜣhu-Re'.* 2 vols. WVDOG 14, 26.

———. 1911–36. *Statuen und Statuetten von Königen und Privatleuten im Museum zu Kairo, Nr. 1–1294*. 5 vols. Catalogue général des antiquités égyptiennes du Musée du Caire. Berlin: Reichsdruckerei.

———. 1937–64. *Denkmäler des Alten Reiches (ausser den Statuen) im Museum zu Kairo Nr. 1295–1808*. 2 vols. Catalogue général des antiquités égyptiennes du Musée du Caire. Berlin/Cairo: Reichsdruckerei/Organisme Général des Imprimeries Gouvermentales.

Borghouts, Joris F. 1973. "The Evil Eye of Apopis." *JEA* 59: 114–50.

———. 1978. *Ancient Egyptian Magical Texts*. Religious Texts Translation Series. Nisaba 9. Leiden: Brill.

Breasted, James H. 1906–7. *Ancient Records of Egypt: Historical Documents from the Earliest Times to the Persian Conquest*. 5 vols. Chicago: University of Chicago Press. Reprinted by Histories and Mysteries of Man Ltd in London in 1988, and by the University of Illinois Press in 2001 (latter with supplementary bibliography in vol. 5).

Brodrick, Mary, and A. Anderson Morton. 1899. "The Tomb of Pepu ankh (khua), near Sharona." *PSBA* 21: 26–33.

Brovarski, Edward. 1977. "The Doors of Heaven." *Orientalia* 46: 107–15. 1985. "Akhmim in the Old Kingdom and First Intermediate Period." Pages 117–53 in Posener-Kriéger 1985: I.

———. 1987. "Two Old Kingdom Writing Boards from Giza." *ASAE* 71: 27–52.

———. 1994a. "Abydos in the Old Kingdom and First Intermediate Period, Part 1." Pages 99–121 in Berger, Clerc, and Grimal I.

———. 1994b. "Abydos in the Old Kingdom and First Intermediate Period, Part II." Pages 15–44 in Silverman 1994.

———. 2001. *The Senedjemib Complex, Part I. The Mastabas of Senedjemib Inti (G 2370), Khnumenti (G 2374), and Senedjemib Mehi (G 2378)*. Giza Mastabas 7. Boston: Museum of Fine Arts.

———. 2002. "A Unique Funerary Monument of Old Kingdom Date in the Egyptian Museum." Pages 183–96 in *Egyptian Museum Collections around the World: Studies for the Centennial of the Egyptian Museum, Cairo* I. Edited by Mamdouh Eldamaty and Mai Trad. Cairo: Supreme Council of Antiquities.

Brunner-Traut, Emma. 1995. *Die altägyptische Grabkammer Seschemnofers III. aus Gîsa*. Mainz: von Zabern.

Bryan, Betsy M., and David Lorton. 1994. *Essays In Egyptology in Honor of Hans Goedicke*. San Antonio: Van Siclen Books.

Buchberger, Hannes. 1995. "Das Harfnerlied im Grab des *kꜣ(=ỉ)-m-ꜥnḫ* oder 'Die Riten des *sn nṯrw*.'" Pages 93–123 in Kessler and Schulz 1995.

Burkard, Günter. 1996. "Metrik, Prosodie und formaler Aufbau ägyptischer literarischer Texte." Pages 447–63 in Loprieno 1996a.

Butzer, Karl W. 1976. *Early Hydraulic Civilization in Egypt: A Study in Cultural Ecology*. Chicago and London: University of Chicago Press.

Callender, Vivienne G. 2000. "A propos the Title of *r Nḫn n z3b*." Pages 361–80 in Bárta and Krejčí 2000.

———. 2002a. "Princess Inti of the Ancient Egyptian Sixth Dynasty." *JNES* 61 (2002): 267–74.

———. 2002b. "A Contribution to the Burial of Women in the Old Kingdom." *Archiv Orientální* 70: 301–8.

———, and Peter Jánosi. 1997. "The Tomb of Queen Khamerernebty II at Giza. A Reassessment." *MDAIK* 53: 1–22.

Capart, Jean. 1906. *Chambre funéraire de la sixième dynastie aux Musées Royaux du Cinquantenaire*. Brussels: Vromant.

———. 1907. *Une rue de tombeaux à Saqqarah*. 2 vols. Brussels: Vromant.

Cherpion, Nadine. 1989. *Mastabas et hypogées d'Ancien Empire: Le problème de la datation*. Brussels: Connaissance de l'Égypte Ancienne.

Couyat, Jules, and Pierre Montet. 1913. *Les inscriptions hiéroglyphiques et hiératiques du Ouâdi Hammâmât*. MIFAO 34. Cairo: Impr. de l'IFAO.

Curto, Silvio. 1963. *Gli scavi italiani a El-Ghiza (1903)*. Centro per le antichità, e la storia dell' arte del Vicino Oriente. Monografie di archeologia e d'arte I. Rome: Centro per le antichità, e la storia dell' arte del Vicino Oriente.

Davies, Nina de Garis, and Alan H. Gardiner. 1915. *The Tomb of Amenembet (no. 82)*. Theban Tomb Series 1. London: Egypt Exploration Fund.

Davies, Norman de Garis. 1901. *The Rock Tombs of Sheikh Saïd*. ASE 10.

———. 1902. *The Rock Tombs of Deir el Gebrâwi*. 2 vols. ASE 11–12.

———. 1932. "Tehuti: Owner of Tomb 110 at Thebes." Pages 279–90 in *Studies Presented to F. Ll. Griffith*. London: Egypt Exploration Society.

Davies, W. Vivian, Aly el-Khouli, Alan B. Lloyd, and A. Jeffrey Spencer. 1984. *The Mastabas of Mereri and Wernu*. Saqqâra Tombs I. ASE 36.

de Morgan, J. 1894. *Catalogue des monuments et inscriptions de l'Égypte* I. Vienna: Holzhausen.

Depuydt, L. 1983. "The Standard Theory of the 'Emphatic' forms in Classical (Middle) Egyptian: A Historical Survey." *Orientalia Lovensia Periodica* 14: 13–54.

Dobrev, Vassil. 1993. "Les titulatures des rois de la IVe dynastie." *BIFAO* 93: 179–204. 1994. "Observations sur quelques marques de la pyramide de Pépi Ier." Pages 147–58 in Berger, Clerc, and Grimal 1994: I.

———. 2000. "The South Saqqara Stone and the Sarcophagus of Queen

Mother Ankhesenpepy (JE 65 908)." Pages 381–96 in Bárta and Krejčí 2000.

———. 2003. "Builders' Inscriptions from the Pyramid of Pepy I." Pages 174–77 in Hawass 2003: III.

Donohue, V. A. 1978. "*pr-nfr*." *JEA* 64: 143–48.

Dorman, Peter F. 2002. "The Biographical Inscription of Ptahshepses from Saqqara: A Newly Identified Fragment." *JEA* 88: 95–110.

Dominicus, Brigitte. 1994. *Gesten und Gebärden in Darstellungen des Alten und Mittleren Reiches*. SAGA 10.

Doret, Eric. 1986. *The Narrative Verbal System of Old and Middle Egyptian*. Cahiers d'Orientalisme 12. Geneva: Patrick Cramer Éditeur.

Doxey, Denise M. 2001. "Names." Pages 490–92 in Redford 2001: II.

Drenkhahn, Rosemarie. 1976a. "Bemerkungen zu dem Titel *ḫkr.t nswt*." *SAK* 4: 59–67.

———. 1976b. *Die Handwerker und ihre Tätigkeiten im alten Ägypten*. ÄA 31.

Dreyer, Günter. 1987. "Drei archaisch-hieratische Gefässaufschriften mit Jahresnamen aus Elephantine." Pages 98–109 in *Form und Mass: Beiträge zur Literatur, Sprache und Kunst des alten Ägypten. Festschrift für Gerhard Fecht zum 65. Geburtstag am 6. Februar 1987*. Edited by Jürgen Osing and Günter Dreyer. ÄAT 12.

———. 1998. "Der erste König der 3. Dynastie." Pages 31–34 in Guksch and Polz 1998.

Drioton, Étienne. 1952. "Une mutilation d'image avec motif." *Archív Orientální* 20: 351–55.

Dunham, Dows. 1937. *Naga-ed-Dêr stelae of the First Intermediate Period*. London: Oxford University Press.

———. 1938. "The Biographical Inscriptions of Nekhebu in Boston and Cairo." *JEA* 24: 1–8.

Dunham, Dows, and William Kelly Simpson. 1974. *The Mastaba of Queen Mersyankh III. G 7530–7540*. Giza Mastabas 1. Boston: Museum of Fine Arts.

Edel, Elmar. 1944. "Untersuchungen zur Phraseologie der ägyptischen Inschriften des Alten Reiches." *MDAIK* 13: 1–90.

———. 1953a. "Inschriften des Alten Reichs. II. Die Biographie des *Kꜣj-gmjnj* (Kagemni)." *MIO* 1: 210–26.

———. 1953b. "Inschriften des Alten Reichs." *MIO* 1: 327–26.

———. 1954. "Inschriften des Alten Reichs. I. Die Biographie des Gaufürsten von Edfu, Jzj." *ZÄS* 79: 11–17.

———. 1955. "Inschriften des Alten Reiches. V. Die Reiseberichte des *ḥrw-*

ḫwjf (Herchuf)." Pages 51–75 in *Ägyptologische Studien. Hermann Grapow zum 70. Geburtstag gewidmet.* Edited by O. Firchow. Deutsche Akademie der Wissenschaften zu Berlin. Institut für Orientforschung, 29. Berlin: Akademie-Verlag.

———. 1955–64. *Altägyptische Grammatik.* 2 vols. Analecta Orientalia 34, 39. Rome: Pontificium Institutum Biblicum.

———. 1958. "Inschriften des Alten Reichs (6. Folge)." *ZÄS* 83: 3–18.

———. 1966. "Inschriften des Alten Reiches XII. Zwei bisher missverstandene Erbschaftsbestimmungen in Verträgen mit Totenpriestern: Urk. I 12, 14–15 und 36, 11–12." *ZÄS* 92: 96–99.

———. 1967. *Die Felsengräber der Qubbet el Hawa bei Assuan. II. Abteilung: Die althieratischen Topfaufschriften. 1. Band: Die Topfaufschriften aus den Grabungsjahren 1960, 1961, 1962, 1963 und 1965. 1. Teil: Zeichnungen und hieroglyphische Umschriften.* Wiesbaden: Harrassowitz.

———. 1969. "Die Kalksteintäfelchen." Pages 1–22 in Edel et al. 1969.

———. 1970a. *Die Felsengräber der Qubbet el Hawa bei Assuan. II. Abteilung. Die althieratischen Topfaufschriften. 1. Band. Die Topfaufschriften aus den Grabungsjahren 1960, 1961, 1962, 1963 und 1965. 2. Teil. Text (Fortsetzung).* Wiesbaden: Harrassowitz.

———. 1970b. *Das Akazienhaus und seine Rolle in den Begräbnisriten des alten Ägyptens.* MÄS 24.

———. 1971a. *Die Felsengräber der Qubbet el Hawa bei Assuan. II. Abteilung: Die althieratischen Topfaufschriften. 2. Band. Die Topfaufschriften aus den Grabungsjahren 1968, 1969 und 1970. 1. Teil: Zeichnungen und hieroglyphischen Umschriften.* Wiesbaden: Harrassowitz.

———. 1971b. "Zwei neue Felsinschriften aus Tumâs mit nubischen Ländernamen." *ZÄS* 97: 53–63.

———. 1975a. *Die Felsgräbernekropole der Qubbet el Hawa bei Assuan. II. Abteilung. Die althieratischen Topfaufschriften aus den Grabungsjaren 1972 und 1973.* Abhandlungen der Rheinisch-Westfälischen Akademie der Wissenschaften 55. Opladen: Westdeutscher Verlag.

———. 1975b. "Beiträge zum ägyptischen Lexikon VI. Die Stoffbezeichnungen in den Kleiderlisten des Alten Reiches." *ZÄS* 102: 13–30.

———. 1978. "A Comment on Professor Giveon's Reading of the New Sahure' Inscription." *BASOR* 23: 77–78.

———. 1979. "Zum Verständnis der Inschrift des Jzj aus Saqqara. Zu Helcks Bearbeitung dieser Inschrift in *ZÄS* 104, 89–93." *ZÄS* 106: 105–16.

———. 1981. *Hieroglyphische Inschriften des Alten Reiches.* Abhandlungen der Rheinisch-Westfälischen Akademie der Wissenschaften 67. Opladen: Westdeutscher Verlag.

———. 1983. *Beiträge zu den ägyptischen Sinaiinschriften.* Nachrichten der Akademie der Wissenschaften in Göttingen. I: Philologisch-Historische Klasse, Jahrgang 1983, Nr. 6. Göttingen: Vandenhoeck & Ruprecht.

———. 1984. "Ein bisher falsch gelesenes afrikanisches Produkt in der Inschrift des *ḥrw-ḫwjf* (Herchuf)." *SAK* 11: 187–93.

———. 1987. "Eine althieratische Liste von Grabbeigaben aus einem Grab des späten Alten Reiches der Qubbet el-Hawa." *NAWG* 1987/6: 93–106.

———. 1992. "Unpublizierte althieratische Elephantine-Papyri aus Strassburg." Pages 73–81 in Gamer-Wallert and Helck 1992.

———. 1994. "Der vervollständigte Architrav vom Grab des mḥy in Saqqara." Pages 61–67 in Bryan and Lorton 1994.

———. 1995. "Ein Graffito ungewöhnlichen Inhalts mit einer aktivischen *sḏmw.f*-Form." Pages 125–32 in Kessler and Schulz 1995.

———. 1996. "Studien zu den Relieffragmenten aus dem Taltempel des Königs Snofru." Pages 199–208 in Manuelian 1996.

———, and Steffen Wenig. 1974. *Die Jahreszeitenreliefs aus dem Sonnenheiligtum des Königs Ne-user-Re.* Staatliche Museen zu Berlin. Mitteilungen aus der ägyptischen Sammlung 7. Berlin: Akademieverlag.

———, et al. 1969. *Das Sonnenheiligtum des Königs Userkaf, Band II: Die Funde.* BeiträgeBf 8. Wiesbaden: Schweizerisches Institut für ägyptische Bauforschung and Altertumskunde.

Eichler, Eckhard. 1991a. "Untersuchungen zu den Königsbriefen des Alten Reiches." *SAK* 18: 141–71.

———. 1991b. "Zwei Bemerkungen zu den hieratischen Briefen des Alten Reiches." *GM* 123: 21–26.

———. 1993. *Untersuchungen zum Expeditionswesen des ägyptischen Alten Reiches.* Göttinger Orientforschungen. IV. Reihe: Ägypten 26. Wiesbaden: Harrassowitz.

———. 1994. "Zur kultischen Bedeutung von Expeditionsinschriften." Pages 69–80 in Bryan and Lorton 1994.

———. 1998. "Neue Expeditionsinschriften aus der Ostwüste Oberägyptens. Teil II: Die Inschriften." *MDAIK* 54: 250–66.

el-Din, Mohi. 1994. "Discovery of a Tomb of the Late Old Kingdom below the Rock Tombs of Qubbet el-Hawa, Aswân." *MDAIK* 50: 31–34.

el-Fikey, Said Amer. 1980. *The Tomb of the Vizier Rēʿ-wer at Saqqara."* Egyptology Today 4. Warminster: Aris & Phillips.

el-Khadragy, Mahmoud. 2002a. "The Edfu Offering Niche of Qar in the Cairo Museum." *SAK* 30: 203–28.

———. 2002b. "Some Palaeographic Features of Weni's Biography." *GM* 188: 61–72.

el-Khouli, Ali. 1991. *Meidum*. The Australian Centre for Egyptology Reports 3. Sydney: Australian Centre for Egyptology.

el-Khouly, Aly and Kanawati, Naguib. 1988. *Excavations at Saqqara, North-West of Teti's Pyramid, Volume II*. Sydney: Ancient History Documentary Research Centre, Macquarie University.

———. 1989. *Quseir el-Amarna: The Tombs of Pepy-ankh and Khewen-wekh*. The Australian Centre for Egyptology Reports 1. Sydney: Australian Centre for Egyptology.

———. 1990. *The Old Kingdom Tombs of El-Hammamiya*. The Australian Centre for Egyptology Reports. 2. Sydney: Australian Centre for Egyptology.

el-Sawi, Ahmad. 1979. *Excavations at Tell Basta: Report of Seasons 1967–1971 and Catalogue of Finds*. Prague: Charles University.

Erman, Adolf. 1919. *Reden, Rufe und Lieder auf Gräberbildern des Alten Reiches*. APAW: Philos.-hist. Kl. 1918, Abh. 15. Berlin: Akademie der Wissenschaften.

———. 1923. *Die Literatur der Aegypter: Gedichte, Erzählungen und Lehrbücher aus dem 3. und 2. Jahrtausend v. Chr.* Leipzig: Hinrichs.

———. 1927. *The Literature of the Ancient Egyptians: Poems, Narratives, and Manuals of Instruction, from the Third and Second Millennia B.C.* Translation by Aylward M. Blackman of Erman 1923. London: Methuen. Since 1966 this book has been reprinted by Harper Torchbooks with the title *The Ancient Egyptians: A Sourcebook of Their Writings*.

Erman, Adolf, and Hermann Grapow (eds.). 1926–53. *Wörterbuch der aegyptischen Sprache*. 7 vols. Berlin: Akademie-Verlag.

Eyre, Christopher J. 1987. "Work and the Organisation of Work in the Old Kingdom." Pages 5–47 in *Labor in the Ancient Near East*. Edited by Marvin A. Powell. American Oriental Series 68. New Haven: American Oriental Society.

———. 1994. "Weni's Career and Old Kingdom Historiography." Pages 107–24 in Eyre, Leahy, and Leahy 1994.

Eyre, Christopher, Anthony Leahy, and Lisa M. Leahy (eds.). 1994. *The Unbroken Reed. Studies in the Culture and Heritage of Ancient Egypt in Honour of A. F. Shore*. Occasional Publications 11. London: Egypt Exploration Society.

Fakhry, Ahmed. 1935. *Sept tombeaux à l'est de la grande pyramide de Guizeh. Cairo:* Impr. de l'IFAO.

Faulkner, Raymond O. 1969. *The Ancient Egyptian Pyramid Texts.* 2 vols. Oxford: Griffith Institute.

———. 1985. *The Ancient Egyptian Book of the Dead.* Edited by Carol Andrews. London: British Museum Press.

Fecht, Gerhard. 1965. *Literarische Zeugnisse zur 'Persönlichen Frömmigkeit' in Ägypten: Analyse der Beispiele aus den ramessidischen Schulpapyri.* Abhandlungen der Heidelberger Akademie der Wissenschaften. Philosophisch-Historische Klasse. Jahrgang 1965. 1. Abhandlung. Heidelberg: Carl Winter Universitätsverlag.

———. 1968. "Zu den Inschriften des ersten Pfeilers im Grab des Anchtifi (Mo'alla)." Pages 50–60 in *Festschrift für Siegfried Schott zu seinem 70. Geburtstag am 20. August 1967.* Edited by Wolfgang Helck. Wiesbaden: Harrassowitz.

———. 1993. "The Structural Principle of Ancient Egyptian Elevated Language." Pages 69–94 in *Verse in Ancient Near Eastern Prose.* Edited by J. C. de Moor and W. G. E. Watson. Alter Orient und Altes Testament 42. Kevelaer/ Neukirchen-Vluyn: Butzon and Bercker/Neukirchener Verlag.

Firth, Cecil M., and Battiscombe Gunn. 1926. *Teti Pyramid Cemeteries.* 2 vols. Excavations at Saqqara. Cairo: Impr. de l'IFAO.

Firth, Cecil M., and James E. Quibell. 1935. *The Step Pyramid.* 2 vols. Excavations at Saqqara. Cairo: Impr. de l'IFAO.

Fischer, Henry G. 1957. "A God and a General of the Oasis on a Stela of the Late Middle Kingdom." *JNES* 16: 223–35.

———. 1958a. "An Early Occurrence of *ḥm* 'Servant' in Regulations Referring to a Mortuary Estate." *MDAIK* 16: 131–37.

———. 1958b. Review of Habachi 1957. *AJA* 62: 330–33.

———. 1959. "A Scribe of the Army in a Saqqara Mastaba of the Early Fifth Dynasty." *JNES* 18: 233–72.

———. 1961. "The Nubian Mercenaries of Gebelein during the First Intermediate Period." *Kush* 9: 44–80.

———. 1963. "Varia Aegyptiaca." *JARCE* 2: 17–51.

———. 1963–64. "Two Royal Monuments of the Middle Kingdom Restored." *BMMA* 22: 235–45.

———. 1964. *Inscriptions from the Coptite Nome: Dynasties VI–XI.* Analecta Orientalia 40. Rome: Pontificium Institutum Biblicum.

———. 1965. "*bꜣ* and the Deified Vizier *mḥw.*" *JARCE* 4: 49–53.

———. 1966. "An Old Kingdom Monogram: ." *ZÄS* 93: 56–69.

———. 1968. *Dendera in the Third Millennium B.C. down to the Theban Domination of Upper Egypt.* Locust Valley, New York: J. J. Augustin.

———. 1973a. "Redundant Determinatives in the Old Kingdom." *MMJ* 8: 7–25.

———. 1973b. "Further Evidence for the Logic of Ancient Egyptian: Diminishing Progression." *JARCE* 10: 5–9.

———. 1975. "Two Tantalizing Biographical Fragments of Historical Interest." *JEA* 61: 33–37.

———. 1976a. *Varia.* Egyptian Studies I. New York: Metropolitan Museum of Art.

———. 1976b. "Some Early Monuments from Busiris, in the Egyptian Delta." *MMJ* 11: 5–24.

———. 1976c. "Notes, Mostly Textual, on Davies' *Deir el Gebrâwi.*" *JARCE* 13: 9–20.

———. 1977. *The Orientation of Hieroglyphs. Part I: Reversals.* Egyptian Studies 2. New York: Metropolitan Museum of Art.

———. 1978. "Five Inscriptions of the Old Kingdom." *ZÄS* 105: 42–59.

———. 1979. "Two Old Kingdom Inscriptions Restored." *JEA* 65: 42–46.

———. 1980a. "Addenda to 'Five Inscriptions of the Old Kingdom' (*ZÄS* 105, 1978, pp. 42–59)." *ZÄS* 107: 86–87.

———. 1980b. "*Deux stèles villageoises du Moyen Empire.*" *CdE* 55: 13–16.

———. 1981. "Concerning the Restoration of a Text in the Tomb of *Mry* at Hagarsa." *GM* 84: 19–21.

———. 1986. *L'écriture et l'art de l'Égypte ancienne. Quatre leçons sur la paléographie et l'épigraphie pharaoniques.* Paris: Presses Universitaires de France.

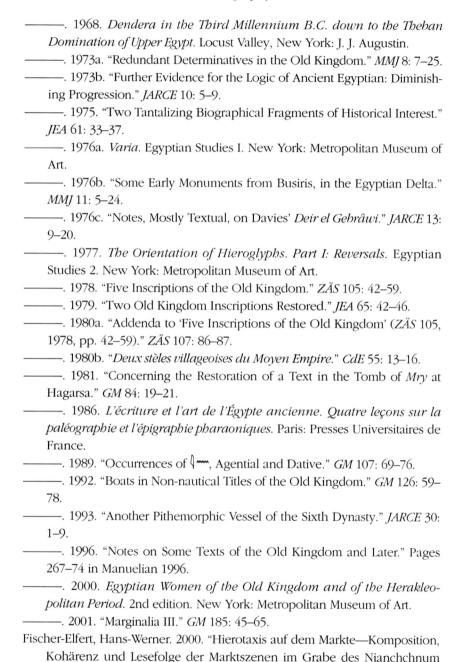

———. 1989. "Occurrences of 𓇋𓈖, Agential and Dative." *GM* 107: 69–76.

———. 1992. "Boats in Non-nautical Titles of the Old Kingdom." *GM* 126: 59–78.

———. 1993. "Another Pithemorphic Vessel of the Sixth Dynasty." *JARCE* 30: 1–9.

———. 1996. "Notes on Some Texts of the Old Kingdom and Later." Pages 267–74 in Manuelian 1996.

———. 2000. *Egyptian Women of the Old Kingdom and of the Herakleopolitan Period.* 2nd edition. New York: Metropolitan Museum of Art.

———. 2001. "Marginalia III." *GM* 185: 45–65.

Fischer-Elfert, Hans-Werner. 2000. "Hierotaxis auf dem Markte—Komposition, Kohärenz und Lesefolge der Marktszenen im Grabe des Nianchchnum und Chnumhotep." *SAK* 28: 67–82.

Fischer-Elfert, Hans-Werner, and Alfred Grimm. 2003. "Autobiographie und Apotheose." *ZÄS* 130: 60-80.

Fitzenreiter, Martin. 2001. "Grabdekoration und die Interpretation funerärer Rituale im Alten Reich." Pages 67–140 in *Social Aspects of Funerary Culture in the Egyptian Old and Middle Kingdoms.* Edited by Harco Willems. OLA 103.

Foster, John L. 1988. "'The Shipwrecked Sailor': Prose or Verse?" *SAK* 15: 69–109.

———. 2001b. "Wisdom Texts." Pages 503–7 in Redford 2001: III.

Franke, Detlef. 1994. *Das Heiligtum des Heqaib auf Elephantine. Geschichte eines Provinzheiligtums im Mittleren Reich.* SAGA 9.

Frankfort, Henri. 1928. "The Cemeteries of Abydos: Work of the Season 1925–26." *JEA* 14: 235–45.

Fraser, George W. 1902. "The Early Tombs at Tehneh." *ASAE* 3: 67–76, 122–30.

Freier, Elke. 1976. "Zu den sogenannten Hohenpriestern des Ptah von Memphis im Alten Reich." *Altorientalische Forschungen* 4: 5–34.

Friedman, Florence D. 1995. "The Underground Relief Panels of King Djoser at the Step Pyramid Complex." *JARCE* 32: 1–42.

———. 1996. "Notions of Cosmos in the Step Pyramid Complex." Pages 337–51 in Manuelian 1996.

Gamer-Wallert, Ingrid. 1998. *Von Giza bis Tübingen: Die bewegte Geschichte der Mastaba G 5170.* Tübingen: Klöpfer & Meyer.

Gamer-Wallert, Ingrid, and Wolfgang Helck (eds.). 1992. *Gegengabe: Festschrift für Emma Brunner-Traut.* Tübingen: Attempto Verlag.

Gardiner, Alan H. 1927. "An Administrative Letter of Protest." *JEA* 13 73–78.

———. 1957. *Egyptian Grammar: Being an Introduction to the Study of Hieroglyphs.* 3rd edition. Oxford: Griffith Institute.

———. 1959. *The Royal Canon of Turin.* Oxford: Griffith Institute.

Gardiner, Alan H., T. Eric Peet, and Jaroslav Černý. 1952–55. *The Inscriptions of Sinai.* Second edition revised and augmented. 2 vols. London: Egypt Exploration Society.

Gardiner, Alan H. and Sethe, Kurt. 1928. *Egyptian letters to the Dead.* London: Egypt Exploration Society.

Gillam, Robyn A. . 1991. "Topographical, Proposographical and Historical Studies in the 14th Upper Egyptian Nome." Ph.D. dissertation. University of Toronto.

Giveon, Raphael. 1974. "A Second Relief of Sekhemkhet in Sinai." *BASOR* 216: 17–20.

———. 1977. "Inscriptions of Sahure' and Sesostris I from Wadi Kharig (Sinai). *BASOR* 226: 61–63.

———. 1978. "Corrected Drawings of the Sahure' and Sesostris I Inscriptions from the Wadi Kharig." *BASOR* 232: 76.

Gnirs, Andrea M. 1996. "Die ägyptische Autobiographie." Pages 191–241 in Loprieno 1996.

———. 2001. “Biographies.” Pages 184–89 in Redford 2001: I.

Gödecken, Karin B. 1976. *Eine Betrachtung der Inschriften des Meten im Rahmen der sozialen und rechtlichen Stellung von Privatleuten im ägyptischen alten Reich*. ÄA 29.

Goedicke, Hans. 1955. “The Egyptian Idea of Passing from Life to Death (an Interpretation).” *Orientalia* 24: 225–39.

———. 1956. “Juridical Expressions of the Old Kingdom.” *JNES* 15: 27–32.

———. 1957. “A Provision-Jar of the Time of Asosis.” *RdE* 11: 61–71.

———. 1959. “A Fragment of a Biographical Inscription of the Old Kingdom.” *JEA* 45: 8–11.

———. 1960a. *Die Stellung des Königs im alten Reich*. ÄA 2.

———. 1960b. “The Title [hieroglyphs] in the Old Kingdom.” *JEA* 46: 60–64.

———. 1964. “Diplomatical studies in the Old Kingdom.” *JARCE* 3: 31–41.

———. 1966. “Die Laufbahn des *mṯn*.” *MDAIK* 21: 1–71.

———. 1967a. *Königliche Dokumente aus dem alten Reich*. ÄA 14.

———. 1967b. “Ein Brief aus dem Alten Reich (Pap. Boulaq 8).” *MDAIK* 22: 1–8.

———. 1970. *Die privaten Rechtsinschriften aus dem Alten Reich*. Beihefte zur Wiener Zeitschrift für die Kunde des Morgenlandes 5. Vienna: Notring.

———. 1971. *Re-Used Blocks from the Pyramid of Amenemhet I at Lisht*. PMMA 20.

———. 1973–74. “Hieroglyphic Inscriptions of the Old Kingdom.” Pages 15–24 in IFAO 1973–74: II.

———. 1974. “Zum Papyrus Berlin 9010.” *ZÄS* 101: 90–95.

———. 1988a. *Old Hieratic Paleography*. Baltimore: Halgo Inc.

———. 1988b. “The High Price of Burial.” *JARCE* 25: 195–99.

———. 1988c. “Papyrus Boulaq 8 Reconsidered.” *ZÄS* 115: 136–46.

———. 1988d. “The Death of Pepi II-Neferkare'.” *SAK* 15: 111–21.

———. 1989. “The Pepi II Decree from Dakhleh.” *BIFAO* 89: 203–212.

———. 1994. “A Cult Inventory of the Eighth Dynasty from Coptos (Cairo JE 43290).” *MDAIK* 50: 71–84.

———. 1995. “An Inventory from Coptos.” *RdE* 46: 210–11.

———. 1997. “Epigraphic Comments on Inscriptions from the Eastern Desert.” *GM* 159: 61–64.

Goelet, Ogden, Jr. 1986. “The Terms *śtp-Sꜣ* in the Old Kingdom and Its Later Development.” *JARCE* 23: 85–98.

Goneim, M. Zakaria . 1957. *Horus Sekhem-khet. The Unfinished Step Pyramid at Saqqara. Volume I*. Excavations at Saqqara. Cairo: Imprimerie de l’IFAO.

Goyon, Georges . 1957. *Nouvelles inscriptions rupestres du Wadi Hammamat.* Paris: Imprimerie Nationale. Librairie d'Amérique et d'Orient Adrien-Maisonneuve.

———. 1959. "Le tombeau d'Ankhou à Saqqara." *Kêmi* 15 (1959): 10–22.

———. 1971. "Les navires de transport de la chaussée monumentale d'Ounas." *BIFAO* 69: 11–41.

Graefe, Erhart. 1972–92. "Matit." Pages 1245–46 in Helck and Otto 1972–92: III.

Grallert, Silke. 2001. *Bauen–Stiften–Weihen.* ADAIK 18. Berlin: Achet Verlag.

Grdseloff, Bernard. 1943. "Notes sur deux monuments inédits de l'Ancien Empire." *ASAE* 42: 107–25.

———. 1948. "Remarques concernant l'opposition à un rescrit du vizir." *ASAE* 48: 505–12.

———. 1951. "Nouvelles données concernant la tente de purification." *ASAE* 51: 129–40.

Green, Michael. 1980. "A Means of Discouraging Perjury." *GM* 39: 33–39.

Grunert, Stefan. 2003. "Das Alte ist das Neue—Do Not Be confused about It. Randglossen einer Textaufnahme." *GM* 196: 83–94.

Guglielmi, Waltraud. 1973. *Reden, Rufe und Lieder auf altägyptischen Darstellungen der Landwirtschaft, Viehzucht, des Fisch und Vogelfangs vom Mittleren Reich bis zur Spätzeit.* Tübinger Ägyptologische Beiträge 1. Bonn: Rudolf Habelt.

Guilmot, Max . 1966. "Les Lettres aux morts dans l'Égypte ancienne." *Revue de l'Histoire des Religions* 170, no 455: 1–27.

Guksch, Heike, and Daniel Polz. 1998. *Stationen. Beiträge zur Kulturgeschichte Ägyptens. Rainer Stadelmann gewidmet.* Mainz: von Zabern.

Gunn, Battiscombe. 1925. "A Sixth Dynasty Letter from Saqqara." *ASAE* 25: 242–55.

———. 1926. "Inscriptions from the Step Pyramid Site." ASAE 26: 177–202.

———. 1930. Review of Gardiner and Sethe 1928. *JEA* 16: 147–55.

Habachi, Labib . 1957. *Tell Basta.* Supplément aux Annales du Service des Antiquités de l'Égypte Cahier 22. Cairo: Imprimerie de l'IFAO.

———. 1978. *The Obelisks of Egypt, Skyscrapers of the Past.* London/Toronto/Melbourne: J. M. Dent.

———. 1981. "Identification of Heqaib and Sabni with Owners of Tombs in Qubbet el-Hawa and Their Relationship with Nubia." Pages 11–27 in idem, *Sixteen Studies on Lower Nubia.* Supplément aux Annales du Service des Antiquités de l'Égypte, Cahier 23. Cairo: Imprimerie de l'IFAO.

———. 1985. *The Sanctuary of Heqaib*. 2 vols. AV 33.

Haeny, Gerhard. 1969. "Die Steinbruch- und Baumarken." Pages 23–47 in Edel et al. 1969.

Harpur, Yvonne M. 1980. "*zšš wȝḏ* Scenes of the Old Kingdom." *GM* 38: 53–61.

———. 1981. "Two Old Kingdom tombs at Gîza." *JEA* 67: 24–35.

———. 1987. *Decoration in Egyptian Tombs of the Old Kingdom. Studies in Orientation and Scene Content*. Studies in Egyptology. London and New York: KPI.

Hassan, Selim. 1932–60. *Excavations at Gîza*. 10 vols. Oxford: Oxford University Press/Cairo: Government Press.

———. 1938. "Excavations at Saqqara 1937–1938." *ASAE* 38: 503–21.

———. 1955. "The causeway of Wnis at Sakkara." *ZÄS* 80: 136–39.

———. 1975. *Excavations at Saqqara*. 3 vols. Cairo: General Organisation for Government Printing Offices.

Hawass, Zahi. 1994. "A Fragmentary Monument of Djoser from Saqqara." *JEA* 80: 45–56.

———. 2000. "Recent Discoveries in the Pyramid Complex of Teti at Saqqara." Pages 413–44 in Bárta and Krejčí 2000.

———. 2002. "An Inscribed Lintel in the Tomb of the Vizier Mehu at Saqqara." *Lingua Aegyptica* 10: 219–24.

———. 2003. (ed.) *Egyptology at the Dawn of the Twenty-first Century: Proceedings of the Eighth International Congress of Egyptologists Cairo, 2000*. 3 vols. Cairo: AUC Press.

———. 2004. "The Tombs of the Pyramid Builders—The Tomb of the Artisan Petety and His Curse." Pp. 21–39 in *Egypt, Israel, and the Ancient Mediterranean World: Studies in Honor of Donald B. Redford*, ed. Gary N. Knoppers and Antoine Hirsch. Probleme der Ägyptologie 20. Leiden: Brill.

Hawass, Zahi, and Miroslav Verner. 1996. "Newly Discovered Blocks from the Causeway of Sahure (Archaeological Report)." *MDAIK* 52: 177–86.

Hayes, William C. 1946. "Royal Decrees from the Temple of Min at Coptus." *JEA* 32: 3–23.

———. 1948. "King Wadjkarē' of Dynasty VIII." *JEA* 34: 115–16.

———. 1953. *The Scepter of Egypt: A Background for the Study of the Egyptian Antiquities in the Metropolitan Museum of Art. Part I: From the Earliest Times to the End of the Middle Kingdom*. New York: Metropolitan Museum of Art.

Hays, Harold M. 2000. "*wḏ*. The Context of Command in the Old Kingdom." *GM* 176: 63–76.

Helck, Wolfgang. 1956. "Wirtschaftliche Bemerkungen zum private Grabbesitz im Alten Reich." *MDAIK* 14: 63–75.

———. 1959. "Die soziale Schichtung des ägyptischen Volkes im 3. und 2. Jahrtausend v. Chr." *JESHO* 2: 1–36.

———. 1966. "Nilhöhe und Jubiläumsfest." *ZÄS* 93: 74–79.

———. 1972–92. "Maat." Pages 1110–19 in Helck and Otto 1972–92: III.

———. 1974a. *Die altägyptische Gaue.* Beihefte zum Tübinger Atlas des Vorderen Orients, Reihe B 5. Wiesbaden: Dr. Ludwig Reichert Verlag.

———. 1974b. *Altägyptische Aktenkunde des 3. und 2. Jahrtausends v. Chr.* MÄS 31.

———. 1974c. "Die Bedeutung der Felsinschriften J. Lopez, Inscripciones rupestres Nr. 27 und 28." *SAK* 1: 215–225.

———. 1977a. "Die 'Weihinschrift' aus dem Taltempel des Sonnenheiligtums des Königs Neuserre bei Abu Gurob." *SAK* 5: 47–77.

———. 1977b. "*ỉnk wꜥ jm.ṯn,* 'Ich bin ja einer von euch.'" *ZÄS* 104: 89–93.

———. 1994. "Gedanken zum Mord an König Teti." Pages 103–12 in Bryan and Lorton 1994.

Helck, Wolfgang and Otto, Eberhard (eds.). 1972–92. *Lexikon der Ägyptologie.* 7 vols. Wiesbaden: Harrassowitz.

Hofmann, Tobias. 2001. "Majestät und Diener—zur Dialektik des Begriffes ḥm." *ZÄS* 128: 116–32.

———. 2002. "Die Autobiographie des Uni ( ) von Abydos." *Lingua Aegyptia* 10: 225–37.

Hollis, Susan T. 1990. *The Ancient Egyptian "Tale of Two Brothers": The Oldest Fairy Tale in the World.* Oklahoma Series in Classical Culture 7. Norman and London: University of Oklahoma Press.

Hölzl, Christian. 2004. (ed.) *Die Pyramiden Ägyptens. Monumente der Ewigkeit.* Vienna: Verlag Christian Brandstätter.

Hornung, Erik, and Elisabeth Staehelin. 1974. *Studien zum Sedfest.* Aegyptiaca Helvetica 1. Geneva: Editions de Belles-Lettres.

IFAO. 1973–74. *Textes et langages de l'Égypte pharaonique. Cent cinquante années de recherches. 1822–1972. Hommage à Jean-François Champollion.* 3 vols. BdE 64.

Jacquet-Gordon, Helen K. 1962. *Les noms des domaines funéraires sous l'Ancien Empire Égyptien.* BdE 34.

James, T. G. H. 1953. *The Mastaba of Khentika Called Ikhekhi.* ASE 30.

———. 1961. *British Museum. Hieroglyphic Texts from Egyptian Stelae etc., Part I.* Second Edition. London: British Museum.

———. 1974. *Corpus of hieroglyphic inscriptions in the Brooklyn Museum I. From dynasty I to the end of dynasty XVIII.* Brooklyn N.Y.: The Brooklyn Museum.

Jánosi, Peter. 1996. *Die Pyramidenanlagen der Königinnen: Untersuchungen zu einem Grabtyp des Alten und Mittleren Reiches*. Vienna: Verlag der Österreichischen Akademie der Wissenschaften.

———. 1997. "Gab es Kronprinzen in der 4. Dynastie? 'Kronprinz' Iunre." GM 158: 15–32.Jansen-Winkeln, Karl. 1996. "Zur Bedeutung von *jm3ḫ*." *BSEG* 20: 29–36.

Janssen, Jac. J. 1975. *Commodity Prices from the Ramessid Period: An Economic Study of the Village of Necropolis Workmen at Thebes*. Leiden: Brill.

Janssen, Jozef M. A. 1946. *De traditioneele Egyptische Autobiografie vóór het nieuwe rijk*. 2 vols. Leiden: E.J. Brill.

Janssen, Rosalind. 1996. "The Linens of Idu II." Pages 47–58 in *Untersuchungen zu Idu II, Giza: Ein interdisziplinäres Projekt*. Edited by Bettina Schmitz. HÄB 38.

Jéquier, Gustave. 1928. *La pyramide d'Oudjebten*. Fouilles à Saqqarah. Cairo: Imprimerie de l'IFAO.

———. 1933. *Les pyramides des reines Neit et Apouit*. Fouilles à Saqqarah. Cairo: Imprimerie de l'IFAO.

———. 1936–40. *Le monument funéraire de Pepi II*. 3 vols. Fouilles à Saqqarah. Cairo: Imprimerie de l'IFAO.

Jones, Dilwyn . 2000. *An Index of Ancient Egyptian Titles, Epithets and Phrases of the Old Kingdom*. 2 vols. BAR International Series 866. Oxford: Archaeopress.

Junge, Friedrich. 1973. "Zur Fehldatierung des sog. Denkmals memphitischer Theologie, oder Der Beitrag der ägyptischen Theologie zur Geistesgeschichte der Spätzeit." *MDAIK* 29: 195–204.

———. 1977. "Die Welt der Klagen." Pages 275–84 in Assmann et al. 1979.

Junker, Hermann. 1929–55. *Giza*. 12 vols. Vienna/Leipzig.

———. 1943. *Zu einigen Reden und Rufen auf Grabbildern des Alten Reiches*. SAWW: Philos.-hist. Kl.; 2 21, Abh. 5. Vienna/Leipzig: Hölder-Pichler-Tempsky.

———. 1957. *Weta und das Lederkunsthandwerk im Alten Reich*. Österreichische Akademie der Wissenschaften. Philosophisch-historische Klasse. Sitzungsberichte, 231. Band, 1. Abhandlung. Vienna: Rudolf M. Rohrer.

Kahl, Jochem, Nicole Kloth, and Ursula Zimmermann. 1995. *Die Inschriften der 3. Dynastie. Eine Bestandsaufnahme*. ÄA 56.

Kaiser, Werner. 1956. "Zu den Sonnenheiligtümern der 5. Dynastie." *MDAIK* 14: 104–16.

———. 1971. "Die kleine Hebseddarstellung im Sonnenheiligtum des Neuserre." Pages 87–105 in *Aufsätze zum 70. Geburtstag von Herbert*

Ricke. Edited by Schweizerisch Institut für ägyptische Bauforschung and Altertumskunde in Kairo. BeiträgeBf 12. Wiesbaden: Franz Steiner.

———, et al. 1976. "Stadt und Tempel von Elephantine. Sechster Grabungsbericht." *MDAIK* 32: 67–112.

———. 1999. "Stadt und Tempel von Elephantine. 25./26./27. Grabungsbericht." *MDAIK* 55: 63–236.

Kamrin, Janice. 1999. *The cosmos of Khnumhotep II at Beni Hasan*. London: KPI.

Kanawati, Naguib. 1977a. *The Egyptian Administration in the Old Kingdom. Evidence on its Economic Decline*. Warminster, Aris & Phillips.

———. 1977b. "The Identification of *ḏꜥw/šmꜣi* and *ḏꜥw* in the Decoration of Their Tomb at Deir el-Gebrawi." *JEA* 63: 59–62.

———. 1980. *Governmental Reforms in Old Kingdom Egypt*. Warminster: Aris & Phillips.

———. 1980–92. *The Rock Tombs of el-Hawawish: The Cemetery of Akhmim*. 10 vols. Sydney: Macquarie Ancient History Association/ Australian Centre for Egyptology.

———. 1984. "New Evidence on the Reign of Userkare?" *GM* 83: 31–38.

———. 1988. *A Mountain Speaks. The First Australian Excavation in Egypt*. Sydney: Macquarie University.

———. 1992. *Akhmim in the Old Kingdom. Part I: Chronology and Administration*. The Australian Centre for Egyptology Studies 2. Sydney: Australian Centre for Egyptology.

———. 1993–5. *The Tombs of El-Hagarsa*. 3 vols. The Australian Centre for Egyptology Reports 4, 6, 7. Sydney: Australian Centre for Egyptology.

———. 2000. "A New *ḥꜣt/rnpt-zp* for Teti and Its Implication for Old Kingdom Chronology." *GM* 177: 25–32.

———. 2001. *Tombs at Giza. Volume I: Kaiemankh (G4561) and Seshemnefer I (G4940)*. The Australian Centre for Egyptology Reports 16. Warminster: Aris & Phillips.

———. 2002a. *Conspiracies in the Egyptian Palace: Unis to Pepy I*. New York: Routledge.

———. 2002b. *Tombs at Giza. Volume II: Seshathetep/Heti (G5150), Nesutnefer (G4970) and Seshemnefer II (G5080)*. The Australian Centre for Egyptology Reports 18. Warminster: Aris & Phillips.

Kanawati, Naguib, and Mahmud Abder-Raziq. 1998. *The Teti Cemetery at Saqqara. Volume III: The Tombs of Neferseshemre and Seankhuiptah*. The Australian Centre for Egyptology Reports 11. Warminster: Aris & Phillips.

———. 1999. *The Teti Cemetery at Saqqara. Volume V: The Tomb of Hesi.*

The Australian Centre for Egyptology Reports 3. Warminster: Aris & Phillips.

———. 2000. *The Teti Cemetery at Saqqara. Volume VI: The Tomb of Nikauisesi*. The Australian Centre for Egyptology Reports 14. Warminster: Aris & Phillips.

———. 2001. *The Teti Cemetery at Saqqara. Volume VII: The Tombs of Shepsipuptah, Mereri (Merinebti), Hefi and Others*. The Australian Centre for Egyptology Reports 17. Warminster: Aris & Phillips.

Kanawati, Naguib and Hassan, Aly. 1996. *The Teti Cemetery at Saqqara. Volume I: The Tomb of Nedjet-em-pet, Ka-aper and Others*. The Australian Centre for Egyptology Reports 8. Sydney: Australian Centre for Egyptology.

———. 1997. *The Teti Cemetery at Saqqara. Volume II: The Tomb of Ankhmahor*. The Australian Centre for Egyptology Reports 9. Warminster: Aris & Phillips.

Kanawati, Naguib, and Ann McFarlane. 1993. *Deshasha: The Tombs of Inti, Shedu and Others*. The Australian Centre for Egyptology Reports 5. Sydney: Australian Centre for Egyptology.

Kaplony, Peter. 1968. "Eine neue Weisheitslehre aus dem Alten Reich (Die Lehre des MTTj in der altägyptischen Weisheitsliteratur)." *Orientalia* 37: 1–62 with Zusätze und Nachträge, 339–45.

———. 1976. *Studien zum Grab des Methethi*. Monographien der Abegg-Stiftung Bern 8. Riggisberg: Abegg-Stiftung Bern.

———. 2002. "The First (Certain) Testimony for the City-name 'Sais.'" Pages 255–68 in *In Quest of Ancient Settlements and Landscapes*. Edited by Edwin C. M. van den Brink and Eli Yannai. Archaeological Studies in Honour of Ram Gophna. Tel Aviv: Ramot.

Kemp, Barry J. 1968. "The Osiris Temple at Abydos." *MDAIK* 23: 138–55.

———. 1973. "The Osiris Temple at Abydos: A Postscript to *MDAIK* 23 (1968) 138–55." *GM* 8: 23–25.

———. 1977. "The Early Development of Towns in Egypt." *Antiquity* 51: 185–200.

———. 1985. "The Location of the Early Town at Dendera." *MDAIK* 41: 89–98.

———. 1989. *Ancient Egypt: Anatomy of a Civilization*. London and New York: Routledge.

Kessler, Dieter, and Regine Schulz (eds.). 1995. *Gedenkschrift für Winfried Barta. ḥtp dj n ḥzj*. Münchener Ägyptologische Untersuchungen 4. Frankfurt am Main/Berlin/Bern: Peter Lang.

Kitchen, Kenneth A. 2001. "Punt." Pages 85–86 in Redford 2001: III.

Klemm, Rosemarie, and Dietrich D. Klemm. 1993. *Steine und Steinbrüche im Alten Ägypten*. Berlin/Heidelberg: Springer-Verlag.

Kloth, Nicole. 2002. *Die (auto-)biographischen Inschriften des ägyptischen Alten Reiches: Untersuchungen zu Phraseologie und Entwicklung*. Beihefte SAK 8. Hamburg: Helmut Buske Verlag.

———. 2003. "Die Inschrift des *ḥtp-ḥr-n(j)-ptḥ* aus dem Alten Reich: Eine phraseologische Betrachtung." Pages 225–30 in Kloth et al. 2003.

Kloth, Nicole, Martin, Karl and Pardey, Eva. 2003. "*Es werde niedergelegt als Schriftstück.*" *Festschrift für Hartwig Altenmüller zum 65. Geburtstag*. Beihefte SAK 9. Hamburg: Helmut Buske Verlag.

Krauspe, Renate. 1997. *Statuen und Statuetten*. Katalog Ägyptischer Sammlungen in Leipzig I. Mainz: von Zabern.

Krauss, Rolf. 1996. "The Length of Sneferu's Reign and How Long It Took to Build the 'Red Pyramid.'" *JEA* 82: 43–50.

———. 1998a. "Zur Berechnung der Bauzeit an Snofrus Roter Pyramide." *ZÄS* 125: 29–37.

———. 1998b. "Wenn und aber: Das Wag-Fest und die Chronologie des Alten Reiches." *GM* 162: 53–63.

Krejčí, Jaromír. 2000. "Some Notes on the 'Overseers of Works' during the Old Kingdom." *Ä&L* 10: 67–75.

Kuchman, Lisa. 1977. "The Titles of Queenship: Part I, The Evidence from the Old Kingdom." *JSSEA* 7, No. 3: 9–12.

Kuhlmann, Klaus P. 1982. "Die Pyramide als König? Verkannte elliptische Schreibweisen von Pyramidennamen des alten Reiches." *ASAE* 68: 223–35.

Kuraszkiewicz, Kamil O. 2001. "An Old Kingdom Autobiography from Saqqara." *Polish Archaeology in the Mediterranean* 13: 147–50.

———. 2002. "Inscribed Objects from the Old Kingdom Necropolis West of the Step Pyramid (with Remarks on Their White Coating)." *Archiv Orientální* 70: 351–76.

Labrousse, Audran. 1994. "Les reines de Téti, Khouit et Ipout Ire. Recherches architecturales." Pages 231–43 in Berger, Clerc, and Grimal 1994: I.

———. 2000. "Une épouse du roi Mérenrê Ier: la reine Ankhesenpépy II." Pages 485–90 in Bárta and Krejčí 2000.

———, and Marc Albouy. 1999. *Les pyramides des reines: Une nouvelle nécropole à Saqqâra*. Paris: Editions Hazan.

———, and Jean-Philippe Lauer. 2000. *Les complexes funéraires d'Ouserkaf et de Néferhétepes*. BdE 130.

———, and Jean Leclant. 1998. "Nouveaux documents sur la reine Ankhenespépy II, mère de Pépy II." Pages 95–100 in Guksch and Polz 1998.

Lange, Kurt, and Max Hirmer. 1968. *Egypt: Architecture. Sculpture. Painting in Three Thousand Years*. 4th edition. London, New York: Phaidon.

Lapp, Günther. 1986. *Die Opferformel des Alten Reiches, unter Berücksichtigung einiger späterer Formen*. SDAIK 21.

Lauer, Jean-Philippe. 1936–39. *La pyramide à degrés*. 3 vols. Fouilles à Saqqara. Cairo: Impr. de l'IFAO.

———. 1996. "Remarques concernant l'inscription d'Imhotep gravée sur le socle de statue de l'Horus Neteri-khet (roi Djoser)." Pages 493–98 in Manuelian 1996.

Leclant, Jean. 1992. "Noubounet — une nouvelle reine d'Égypte." Pages 211–19 in Gamer-Wallert and Helck 1992.

Leclant, Jean, and Gisèle Clerc. 1997. "Fouilles et travaux en Égypte et au Soudan." *Orientalia* 66: 222–363.

Lehner, Mark. 1997. *The Complete Pyramids*. London. Thames & Hudson.

Leitz, Christian (ed.). 2002. *Lexikon der ägyptischen Götter und Götterbezeichnungen*. 7 vols. OLA 110–16.

Leprohon, Ronald J. 1985. *Museum of Fine Arts, Boston. Stelae I. The Early Dynastic Period to the Late Middle Kingdom*. Corpus Antiquitatum Aegyptiacarum. Mainz: von Zabern.

———. 1986. "The Dating of the Dakhleh Oasis Epigraphic Material." *JSSEA* 16: 50–56.

———. 1990. "The Offering Formula in the First Intermediate Period." *JEA* 76: 163–64.

———. 1995. "Royal Ideology and State Administration in Pharaonic Egypt." Pages 278–80 in *Civilisations of the Ancient Near East I*. Edited by Jack M. Sasson. Peabody, Mass.: Hendrickson.

———. 2001a. "Remarks on Private Epithets Found in the Middle Kingdom Wadi Hammamat Graffiti." *JSSEA* 28: 124–46.

———. 2001b. "Titulary." Pages 409–11 in Redford 2001: III.

———. 2001c. "Offering Formulas and Lists." Pages 569–72 in Redford 2001: II.

———. 2002. "Versification in Inscription Sinai 90 from the Reign of Amenemhat III." Pages 339–48 in *A Tribute to Excellence: Studies Offered in Honor of Ernö Gaál, Ulrich Luft, Láslo Török*. Edited by Tamás A. Bacs. Studia Aegyptiaca 17. Budapest: Eötvös Loránd University.

Lepsius, Richard. 1849–59. *Denkmäler aus Ägypten und Äthiopien: nach den Zeichnungen der von Seiner Majestät dem Könige von Preussen Friedrich Wilhelm IV. nach diesen Ländern gesendeten und in den Jahren 1842–1845 ausgeführten wissenschaftlichen Expedition*. 12 vols. Berlin: Nicolaische Buchhandlung.

———. 1897–1913. *Denkmäler aus Ägypten und Äthiopien: Text*. Edited by E. Naville. 5 vols. Leipzig: Hinrichs.

———. 1913. *Denkmäler aus Ägypten und Äthiopien: Ergänzungsband*. Leipzig: Hinrichs.

Lichtheim, Miriam. 1971–72. "Have the Principles of Ancient Egyptian Metrics Been Discovered?" *JARCE* 9: 103–10.

———. 1973. *Ancient Egyptian Literature. A Book of Readings. Volume I: The Old and Middle Kingdoms*. Berkeley/Los Angeles/London: University of California Press.

———. 1976. *Ancient Egyptian Literature. A Book of Readings. Volume II: The New Kingdom*. Berkeley/Los Angeles/London: University of California Press.

———. 1988. *Ancient Egyptian Autobiographies Chiefly of the Middle Kingdom: A Study and an Anthology*. OBO 84.

———. 1992. *Maat in Egyptian Autobiographies and Related Studies*. OBO 120.

———. 1997. *Moral Values in Ancient Egypt*. OBO 155.

Lloyd, Alan B. Forthcoming. *The Mastaba of Neferseshemptah*. Saqqâra Tombs III. London: Egypt Exploration Society.

Lloyd, Alan B., A. Jeffrey Spencer, and Aly el-Khouli. 1990. *The Mastabas of Meru, Semdenti, Khui and Others*. Saqqâra Tombs II. ASE 40.

Logan, Tom. 2000. "The *Jmyt-pr* Document: Form, Function and Significance." *JARCE* 37: 49–73.

López, Jesus. 1967. "Inscriptions de l'Ancien Empire à Khor el-Aquiba." *RdE* 19: 51–66.

Loprieno, Antonio. 1982. "Methodologische Anmerkungen zur Rolle der Dialekte in der ägyptischen Sprachentwicklung." *GM* 53: 75–95.

———. 1995. *Ancient Egyptian: A Linguistic Introduction*. Cambridge: Cambridge University Press.

———, ed. 1996a. *Ancient Egyptian Literature: History and Forms*. Probleme der Aegyptologie 10. Leiden–New York–Cologne: Brill.

———. 1996b. "Defining Egyptian Literature: Ancient Texts and Modern Theories." Pages 39–58 in Loprieno 1996a.

Lorton, David. 1977. "The Treatment of Criminals in Ancient Egypt through the New Kingdom." *JESHO* 20: 2–64.

Mahmud, Osama. 2000–2001. "(Käufer und Verkäufer): einige Bemerkungen über den Kaufvertrag eines Hauses aus der 6. Dynastie." *ASAE* 76: 125–34.

Málek, Jaromír. 1979–80. "Princess Inti, the Companion of Horus." *JSSEA* 10: 229–41.

———. 1982. "The Original Version of the Royal Canon of Turin." *JEA* 68: 93–106.

———. 1986. *In the Shadow of the Pyramids: Egypt during the Old Kingdom*. London: Orbis.

———. 1991. Review of Cherpion 1989. *DE* 20: 93–100.

———. 1994. "King Merykare and his Pyramid." Pages 203–14 in Berger, Clerc, and Grimal 1994: IV.

Manniche, Lise. 2003. "The So-called Scenes of Daily Life in the Private Tombs of the Eighteenth Dynasty: An Overview." Pages 42–45 in *The Theban Necropolis: Past, Present and Future*. Edited by Nigel Strudwick and John H. Taylor. London: British Museum Press.

Manuelian, Peter D. 1986. "An Essay in Document Transmission: *Nj-kꜣ-ꜥnḫ* and the Earliest *ḥrjw rnpt*." *JNES* 45: 1–18.

———. 1994. "The Giza Mastaba Niche and Full Frontal Figure of Redi-nes in the Museum of Fine Arts, Boston." Pages 55–78 in Silverman 1994.

———, ed. 1996. *Studies in Honor of William Kelly Simpson*. 2 vols. Boston: Museum of Fine Arts.

———. 2003. *Slab Stelae of the Giza Necropolis*. New Haven and Philadelphia: Peabody Museum/University of Pennsylvania Museum.

Mariette, Auguste. 1889. *Les mastabas de l'Ancien Empire: fragment du dernier ouvrage de A. Mariette*. Publ. d'après le manuscrit de l'auteur par G. Maspero. Paris: Vieweg.

Markowitz, Yvonne J., Joyce L. Haynes, and Rita E. Freed. 2000. *Egypt in the Age of the Pyramids: Highlights from the Harvard University-Museum of Fine Arts, Boston Expedition*. Boston: MFA Publications.

Martin, Karl. 1977. *Ein Garantsymbol des Lebens. Untersuchungen zu Ursprung und Geschichte des altägyptischen Obelisken bis zum Ende des Neuen Reiches*. HÄB 3.

———. 1978. *Reliefs des Alten Reiches, Teil 1*. Corpus antiquitatum aegyptiacarum. Mainz: von Zabern.

———. 1984. "Sedfest." Pages 782–90 in Helck and Otto 1972–92: V.

Martin-Pardey, Eva. 1976. *Untersuchungen zur ägyptischen Provinzialverwaltung bis zum Ende des Alten Reiches*. HÄB 1.

———. 1999. "Nome Structure." Pages 873–74 in *Encyclopedia of the Archaeology of Ancient Egypt*. Edited by Kathryn A. Bard. London/New York: Routledge.

Maystre, Charles. 1992. *Les grands prêtres de Ptah de Memphis*. OBO 113.

McFarlane, Ann. 1987. "The First Nomarch at Akhmim: The Identification of a Sixth Dynasty Biographical Inscription." *GM* 100: 63–72.

———. 2003. *Mastabas at Saqqara. Kaiemheset, Kaipunesut, Kaiemsunu,*

Sehetepu and Others. The Australian Centre for Egyptology Reports 20. Oxford: Aris & Phillips.

Menu, Bernadette. 1985. "Ventes de maisons sous l'Ancien Empire." Pages 249–262 in *Mélanges offerts à Jean Vercoutter*. Edited by Francis Geus and Florence Thill. Paris: Éditions Recherche sur les Civilisations.

Metropolitan Museum of Art. 1999. *Egyptian Art in the Age of the Pyramids*. New York: Metropolitan Museum of Art.

Meyer, Gudrun. 1990. "Das Hirtenlied in den Privatgräbern des alten Reiches." *SAK* 17: 235–84.

Minault-Gout, Anne, and Patrick Deleuze. 1992. *Le mastaba d'Ima-Pépi*. FIFAO 33. Cairo: IFAO.

Mohr, Herta T. 1943. *The Mastaba of Hetep-her-Akhti: Study on an Egyptian Tomb Chapel in the Museum of Antiquities Leiden*. Leiden: Brill.

Möller, Georg. 1909–12. *Hieratische Paläographie: die ägyptische Buchschrift in ihrer Entwicklung von der fünften Dynastie bis zur römischen Kaiserzeit*. 3 vols. Leipzig: Hinrichs.

Montet, Pierre. 1925. *Les scènes de la vie privée dans les tombeaux égyptiens de l'Ancien Empire*. Strasbourg: Impr. Alsacienne.

Moreno Garcia, Juan C. 1997. *Etudes sur l'administration, le pouvoir et l'idéologie en Egypte, de l'Ancien au Moyen Empire*. Aegyptiaca Leodiensia 4. Liège: Centre informatique de philosophie et lettres.

———. 1998. "De l'Ancien Empire à la Première Période Intermédiaire: l'autobiographie de *qȝr* d'Edfou, entre tradition et innovation." *RdE* 49: 151–60.

———. 1999. "Administration territoriale et organisation de l'espace en Egypte au troisième millénaire avant J.-C. (V): *gs-pr*." *ZÄS* 126: 116–31.

Morschauser, Scott. 1991. *Threat-Formulae in Ancient Egypt. A Study of the History, Structure and Use of Threats and Curses in Ancient Egypt*. Baltimore: Halgo.

Mostafa, Maha F. 1984–85. "Erster Vorbericht über einen Ersten Zwischenzeit Text aus Kom El-Koffar — Teil I." *ASAE* 70: 419–29.

———. 1987. "Kom el-Koffar. Teil II: Datierung und historische Interpretation des Textes B." *ASAE* 71: 170–84.

Moussa, Ahmed M., and Hartwig Altenmüller. 1971. *The Tomb of Nefer and Ka-hay*. AV 5.

———. 1977. *Das Grab des Nianchchnum und Chnumhotep*. AV 21.

———. 1980. "Bericht über die Grabungen des ägyptischen Antikendienstes im Osten der Ptahhotepgruppe in Saqqara im Jahre 1975." *MDAIK* 36: 319–47.

Moussa, Ahmed M., and Friedrich Junge. 1975. *Two Tombs of Craftsmen*. AV 9.

Müller, Michael S. 2002. "Legale Sekundärbestattungen des späten Alten Reiches auf der Qubbet el-Hawa." *GM* 191: 67–70 and *GM* 192: 55–59.

Müller-Wollermann, Renate. 1986. "Krisenfaktoren im ägyptischen Staat des ausgehenden Alten Reichs." Ph.D. diss., Eberhard-Karl-Universität Tübingen.

Munro, Peter. 1989. "Die Inschriften auf dem Architrav des *Jdw* (G 7102). Ein Standard-Text in ungewöhnlicher Gliederung." Pages 127–58 in *Miscellanea Aegyptologica: Wolfgang Helck zum 75. Geburtstag*. Edited by Hartwig Altenmüller and Renate Germer. Hamburg: Archäologisches Institut der Universität Hamburg.

———. 1993. *Der Unas-Friedhof Nord-West. I: Topographisch-historische Einleitung. Das Doppelgrab der Königinnen Nebet und Khenu.* Mainz: von Zabern.

———. 1994. "Bemerkungen zur Datierung *mṯṯj*'s, zu seinen Statuen Brooklyn 51.1 / Kansas City 51-1 und zu verwandten Rundbildern." Pages 245–77 in Berger, Clerc, and Grimal 1994: I.

Murray, Margaret A. 1905–37. *Saqqara Mastabas.* 2 vols. ERA 10–11.

Myśliwiec, Karol, et al. 2004. *The Tomb of Merefnebef.* Saqqara I. Warsaw: Editions Neriton.Naville, Edouard. 1891. *Bubastis (1887–1889).* EEF 8.

Newberry, Percy E. 1938. "Three Old-Kingdom Travellers to Byblos and Pwenet." *JEA* 24: 182–84.

Nicholson, Paul T., and Ian Shaw. 2000. *Ancient Egyptian Materials and Technology.* Cambridge: Cambridge University Press.

Nolan, John S. 2003. "The Original Lunar Calendar and Cattle Counts in Old Kingdom Egypt." Pages 75–98 in *Basel Egyptology Prize I.* Edited by Susanne Bickel and Antonio Loprieno. Aegyptiaca Helvetica 17. Basel: Schwabe & Co.

Nordh, Katarina. 1996. *Aspects of Ancient Egyptian Curses and Blessings: Conceptual Background and Transmission.* Uppsala Studies in Ancient Mediterranean and Near Eastern Civilizations 26. Uppsala: Uppsala University.

Nordström, Hans-Åke. 2001. "A-Group." Pages 44–46 in Redford 2001: I.

O'Connor, David. 1986. "The Locations of Yam and Kush and Their Historical Implications." *JARCE* 23: 27–50.

———. 1991. "Early States along the Nubian Nile." Pages 145–65 in *Egypt and Africa: Nubia from Prehistory to Islam.* Edited by W. V. Davies. London: British Museum Press/Egypt Exploration Society.

———. 1992. "The Status of Early Egyptian Temples: An Alternative Theory." Pages 83–98 in *The Followers of Horus: Studies Dedicated to Michael Allen Hoffman 1944–1990.* Edited by Renée Friedman and

Barbara Adams. Egyptian Studies Association Publication 2 = Oxbow Monograph 20. Oxford: Oxbow Books.

O'Connor, David, and David P. Silverman. 1995. *Ancient Egyptian Kingship*. Probleme der Ägyptologie 9. Leiden–New York–Cologne: Brill.

Osing, Jürgen. 1977. "Zur Syntax der Biographie des *wnj*." *Orientalia* 46: 165–82.

———. 1999. "Zur 'Poetischen Stele' Thutmosis' III." Pages 75–86 in Assmann, Jan and Blumenthal, Elke (eds.), *Literatur und Politik im pharaonischen und ptolemäischen Ägypten. Vorträge der Tagung zum Gedenken an Georges Posener 5.–10. September 1996 in Leipzig*. BdE 127.

Osing, Jürgen, et al. 1982. *Denkmäler der Oase Dachla: Aus dem Nachlass von Ahmed Fakhry*. AV 28.

Otto, Eberhard. 1938. *Beiträge zur Geschichte der Stierkulte in Ägypten*. UGAÄ 13.

Paget, R. F. E., and A. A. Pirie. 1898. *The Tomb of Ptah-hetep*. ERA 2. [with James Edward Quibell, *The Ramesseum*].

Pantalacci, Laure. 1985. "Un décret de Pépi II en faveur des gouverneurs de l'oasis de Dakhla." *BIFAO* 85: 245–54.

———. 1996. "Fonctionnaires et analphabètes: sur quelques pratiques administratives observées à Balat." *BIFAO* 96: 359–67.

———. 1997. "De Memphis à Balat. Les liens entre la résidence et les gouverneurs de l'oasis à la VIe dynastie." Pages 341–49 in Berger and Mathieu 1997.

———. 1998a. "La documentation épistolaire du palais des gouverneurs à Balat-'Ayn Asil." *BIFAO* 98: 303–15.

———. 1998b. "Les habitants de Balat à la VIème dynastie: esquisse d'histoire sociale." Pages 829–37 in *Proceedings of the Seventh International Congress of Egyptologists*. Edited by C. J. Eyre. Leuven: Peeters.

Parker, Richard A. 1950. *The Calendars of Ancient Egypt*. SAOC 26.

Parkinson, Richard B. 1991a. "The Date of the 'Tale of the Eloquent Peasant.'" *RdE* 42: 171–81.

———. 1991b. "Teachings, Discourses and Tales from the Middle Kingdom." Pages 103–6 in *Middle Kingdom Studies*. Edited by S. Quirke. New Malden: Sia Publishing.

———. 1997. *The Tale of Sinuhe and Other Ancient Egyptian Poems, 1940–1640 BC*. Oxford: Clarendon Press.

———. 1999. *Cracking Codes: The Rosetta Stone and Decipherment*. London: British Museum Press.

———. 2002. *Poetry and Culture in Middle Kingdom Egypt: A Dark Side to Perfection*. London/New York: Continuum.

Peden, Alexander J. 2001. *The Graffiti of Pharaonic Egypt. Scope and Roles of Informal Writings (c. 3100–332 BC)*. Probleme der Aegyptologie 17. Leiden/Boston/Cologne: Brill.

Petrie, William M. F. 1888. *A Season in Egypt, 1887*. London: Field & Tuer.

———. 1896. *Koptos*. London: Quaritch.

———. 1898. *Deshasheh*. EEF 15.

———. 1900. *Dendereh 1898*. EEF 17.

———. 1908. *Athribis*. ERA 14.

Petrie, William M. F., Ernest Mackay, and Gerald Wainwright. 1910. *Meydum and Memphis (III)*. ERA 16.

Peust, Carsten. 1999. *Egyptian Phonology. An Introduction to the Phonology of a Dead Language*. Monographien zu ägyptischen Sprache 2. Göttingen: Peust & Gutschmidt.

Piacentini, Patrizia. 1990. *L'autobiografia di Uni, principe e governatore dell'alto Egitto*. Monografie di SEAP. Series Minor 1. Pisa: Giardini Editori e Stampatori.

———. 2002. "Les 'préposés aux écrits' dans l'Egypte du IIIe millénaire av. J.C." *RdE* 53: 179–96.

Porter, Bertha, and Rosalind L. B. Moss, assisted by Ethel W. Burney. 1974–81. *Topographical Bibliography of Ancient Egyptian Hieroglyphic Texts, Reliefs and Paintings III: Memphis*. 2 vols. Second edition, revised and augmented by Jaromír Málek. Oxford: Griffith Institute.

Posener-Kriéger, Paule. 1973–74. "Les papyrus de l'Ancien Empire." Pages 23–35 in IFAO 1973–74: II.

———. 1975. "Les papyrus de Gebelein. Remarques préliminaires." *RdE* 27: 211–21.

———. 1976. *Les archives du temple funéraire de Néferirkarê-Kakaï (Les papyrus d'Abousir). Traduction et commentaire*. 2 vols. BdE 65.

———. 1977. "Les mesures des étoffes à l'Ancien Empire." *RdE* 29: 86–96.

———. 1979. "Le prix des étoffes." Pages 318–31 in *Festschrift Elmar Edel. 12. Marz 1979*. Edited by Manfred Görg and Edgar Pusch. ÄAT 1.

———. 1980. "Fragments de papyrus provenant de Saqqarah." *RdE* 32: 83–93.

———. 1983. "Les nouveaux papyrus d'Abousir." *JSSEA* 13: 51–57.

———. 1985a. (ed.) *Mélanges Gamal Eddin Mokhtar*. 2 vols. BdE 97.

———. 1985b. "Décrets envoyés au temple funéraire de Rêneferef." Pages 195– 210 in Posener-Kriéger 1985a: II.

———. 1985c. "Remarques préliminaires sur les nouveaux papyrus d'Abousir." Pages 35–43 in *Ägypten—Dauer und Wandel. Symposium anläßlich des 75jährigen Bestehens des DAI Kairo am 10. und 11. Oktober 1982*. Edited by Deutsches Archäologisches Institut Abteilung Kairo. SDAIK 18.

———. 1988–91. "Aspects économiques des nouveaux papyrus d'Abousir." Pages 167–76 in Schoske 1988–91: IV.

———. 1991. "Quelques pièces du matériel cultuel du temple funéraire de Rêneferef." *MDAIK* 47: 293–304.

———. 1994a. "Les mesures de grain dans les papyrus de Gébélein." Pages 269–72 in Eyre, Leahy, and Leahy 1994.

———. 1994b. "Le coffret de Gebelein." Pages 315–26 in Berger, Clerc, and Grimal 1994: I.

———. 1995. "Fragments de papyrus." Pages 133–42 in Verner 1995.

———. 1997. "News from Abusir." Pages 19–23 in *The Temple in Ancient Egypt: New Discoveries and Recent Research*. Edited by Stephen Quirke. London: British Museum Press.

———, and Jean Louis de Cenival. 1968. *The Abu Sir Papyri Edited, Together with Complementary Texts in Other Collections*. Hieratic Papyri in the British Museum. Fifth Series. London: British Museum Press.

Priese, Karl-Heinz. 1991. *Ägyptisches Museum*. Mainz: von Zabern.

Pritchard, James B. (ed.). 1969. *Ancient Near Eastern Texts Relating to the Old Testament*. Second edition. Princeton, N.J.: Princeton University Press.

Quibell, James E. 1898. *El Kab*. ERA 3.

Quirke, Stephen. 1990. *Who Were the Pharaohs? A History of Their Names with a List of Cartouches*. London: British Museum Press.

Raver, Wendy . 2001. "'Instruction of Ptahhotep'; 'Instructions of Hordjedef'; 'Instructions of Kagemni.'" Pages 169, 173–74 in Redford 2001: II.

Redford, Donald B. 1986. *Pharaonic King-Lists, Annals and Day-Books: A Contribution to the Study of the Egyptian Sense of History*. SSEA Publications 4. Mississauga: Benben Publications.

———, ed. 2001. *The Oxford Encyclopedia of Ancient Egypt*. 3 vols. New York: Oxford University Press.

Reisner, George A. 1931. *Mycerinus: The Temples of the Third Pyramid at Giza*. Cambridge, Mass.: Harvard University Press.

———. 1936. "The Dog Which Was Honored by the King of Upper and Lower Egypt." *BMFA* 34: 96–99.

———. 1942. *A History of the Giza Necropolis. Volume I*. Cambridge, Mass.: Harvard University Press/London: Oxford University Press.

Reisner, George A., and William S. Smith. 1955. *A History of the Giza Necropolis Volume II: The Tomb of Hetep-heres the Mother of Cheops. A Study of Egyptian Civilization in the Old Kingdom*. Cambridge, Mass.: Harvard University Press.

Richards, Janet E. 2000. "Weni the Elder and His Mortuary Neighborhood at Abydos, Egypt." *Kelsey Museum Newsletter*, spring 2000: 6–9. Also available at http://www.umich.edu/~kelseydb/Publications/spring 2000/abydos.html.

———. 2001. "The Archaeology of Individuals at Abydos, Egypt." *Kelsey Museum Newsletter*, fall 2001: 4–7. Also available at http://www.umich.edu/~kelseydb/Publications/fall2001/abydos.html.

———. 2002. "Text and Context in Late Old Kingdom Egypt: The Archaeology and Historiography of Weni the Elder." *JARCE* 39: 75–102.

———. 2003. "The Abydos Cemeteries in the Late Old Kingdom." Pp. 400–407 in Hawass 2003: I.

Ricke, Herbert. 1960. *Die Tempel Nektanebos' II. in Elephantine*. BeiträgeBf 6. Cairo: Schweizerisches Institut für ägyptische Bauforschung und Altertumskunde in Kairo.

Roccati, Alessandro. 1968. "Una lettera inedita dell' Antico Regno." *JEA* 54: 14–22.

———. 1970. "Una tabella lignea inscritta da Gebelein." *Rivista del Studi Orientali* 45: 1–10.

———. 1982. *La littérature historique sous l'Ancien Empire égyptien*. Littératures anciennes du Proche-Orient 11. Paris: Les Editions du Cerf.

Römer, Malte. 2002. "Ein königlicher Befehl. Zu einer Passage im Dahschur-Dekret von Pepi I." *GM* 190: 69–74.

Roquet, Gérard. 1979. "Chronologie relative des changements phonétiques affectant [*z*] et [*r*] et dialectalismes provinciaux à l'ancien Empire. *tꜣ zrf* et *mrzt* à Hawarta/Tahna." Pages 437–62 in vol. I of *Hommages à la mémoire de Serge Sauneron 1927–1976*. 2 vols. BdE 81–82.

Roth, Ann M. 1988. "The Organization of Royal Cemeteries at Saqqara." *JARCE* 25: 201–14.

———. 1988–91. "The Distribution of the Old Kingdom Title *ḫntj-š*." Pages 177–86 in Schoske 1988–91: IV.

———. 1991. *Egyptian Phyles in the Old Kingdom: The Evolution of a System of Social Organization*. SAOC 48.

———. 1994. "The Practical Economics of Tomb-Building in the Old Kingdom: A Visit to the Necropolis in a Carrying Chair." Pages 227–40 in Silverman 1994.

———. 1995. *A Cemetery of Palace Attendants Including G 2084–2099,*

G 2230+2231, and G 2240. Giza Mastabas 6. Boston: Museum of Fine Arts.

Rothe, Russell D., George Rapp, Jr., and William K. Miller. 1996. "New Hieroglyphic Evidence for Pharaonic Activity in the Eastern Desert of Egypt." *JARCE* 33: 77–104.

Ruszczyc, Barbara. 1957. *Mastaba Izi*. Warsaw: Muzeum Narodowe w Warszawie.

Ryholt, Kim. 2000. "The Late Old Kingdom in the Turin King-list and the Identity of Nitocris." *ZÄS* 127: 87–100.

Sainte Fare Garnot, Jean. 1938. *L'appel aux vivants dans les textes funéraires égyptiens des origines à la fin de l'Ancien Empire*. RAPH 9.

Saleh, Mohamed. 1977. *Three Old-Kingdom Tombs at Thebes*. AV 14.

Satzinger, Helmut. 1997. "Beobachtungen zur Opferformel: Theorie und Praxis." *Lingua Aegyptica* 5: 177–88.

Säve-Söderbergh, Torgny. 1994. *The Old Kingdom Cemetery at Hamra Dom (El-Qasr wa es-Saiyad)*. Stockholm: Royal Academy of Letters, History and Antiquities.

Scharff, Alexander. 1938. "Die Reliefs des Hausältesten Meni aus dem alten Reich." *MDAIK* 8: 17–33.

Scheele, Katrin. 2005. *Die Stofflisten des Alten Reiches*. Menes. Studien zur Kultur und Sprache der ägyptischen Frühzeit und des Alten Reiches 2. Wiesbaden: Harrassowitz.

Schenkel, Wolfgang. 1965. *Memphis · Herakleopolis · Theben. Die epigraphischen Zeugnisse der 7.–11. Dynastie Ägyptens*. ÄA 12.

Schiaparelli, Ernesto. 1885. "Chemmis (Achmim) e la sua antica necropoli." Pages 85–88 in *Études archéologiques, linguistiques et historiques: dédiées à Mr le Dr. C. Leemans à l'occasion du cinquantième anniversaire de sa nomination aux fonctions de directeur du Musée Archéologique des Pays-Bas*. Leiden: Brill.

Schlick-Nolte, Birgit. 1993. "Scheintür von Sechentiu-ka und Ny-anch-scheret." Pages 21–31 in *Skulptur, Malerei, Papyri und Särge*. Edited by Eva Bayer-Niemeyer et al. Liebieghaus Frankfurt, Museum Alter Plastik, Ägyptische Bildwerke 3. Melsungen: Gutenberg.

Schmitz, Bettina. 1976. *Untersuchungen zum Titel s3-njswt "Königssohn."* Habelts Dissertationsdrucke. Reihe Ägyptologie 2. Bonn: Rudolf Habelt Verlag.

Schoske, Sylvia (ed.). 1988–91. *Akten des vierten Internationalen Ägyptologen Kongresses München 1985*. 4 vols. Studien zur altägyptischen Kultur Beihefte 1–4. Hamburg: Helmut Buske Verlag.

Schott, Erika. 1974. "Das Goldhaus unter König Pepi II." *GM* 9 (1974): 33–38.

———. 1979. "Die Biographie des Ka-em-Tenenet." Pages 454–61 in Assmann et al. 1979.

Schott, Siegfried. 1950. *Altägyptische Festdaten*. Akademie der Wissenschaften und der Literatur. Abhandlungen der Geistesund Sozialwissenschaftliche Klasse 10: 881–1010.

———. 1965. "Aufnahmen vom Hungersnotrelief aus dem Aufweg der Unaspyramide." *RdE* 17: 7–13.

Schulz, Renate, and Matthias Seidl. 1998. *Egypt: The World of the Pharaohs*. Cologne: Könemann.

Schwarz, Stephanie. 2000. *Altägyptisches Lederhandwerk*. Europäische Hochschulschriften. Reihe XXVIII: Kunstgeschichte, 365. Frankfurt am Main/Berlin/Bern: Peter Lang.

Schlögl, Hermann A. 1980. *Der Gott Tatenen: nach Texten und Bildern des Neuen Reiches*. OBO 29.

Seidlmayer, Stephan J. 1997. "Stil und Statistik: Die Datierung dekorierter Gräber des Alten Reiches — ein Problem der Methode." Pages 17–51 in *Archäologie und Korrespondenzanalyse: Beispiele, Fragen, Perspektiven*. Edited by Johannes Müller and Andreas Zimmerman. Internationale Archäologie 23. Espelkamp: Verlag Marie Leidorf.

———, and Martin Ziermann. 1992. "Eine Friesinschrift von einem Mastaba-Grab des Alten Reiches aus Elephantine." *MDAIK* 48: 161–76.

Sethe, Kurt. 1903. *Urkunden des Alten Reichs*. Urkunden des aegyptischen Altertums I. Leipzig: Hinrichs.

———. 1908–22. *Die altägyptischen Pyramidentexte*. 4 vols. Leipzig: Hinrichs.

———. 1926. "Ein Prozessurteil aus dem Alten Reich." *ZÄS* 61: 67–79.

———. 1933. *Urkunden des Alten Reichs*. Urkunden des aegyptischen Altertums I. Second edition. Leipzig: Hinrichs.

Seyfried, Karl-J. Forthcoming. "Qubbet el-Hawa: Stand und Perspektiven der Bearbeitung." To appear in *Texte und Denkmäler des ägyptischen Alten Reiches. Akten einer Tagung in Schloß Blankensee bei Berlin, 1.–4. Februar 2001*. Edited by Stephan J. Seidlmayer.

Shaw, Ian M. E., ed. 1986. "A Survey at Hatnub." Pages 189–212 in *Amarna Reports III*. Edited by Barry J. Kemp. Occasional Publications 4. London: Egypt Exploration Society.

———, ed. 2000. *The Oxford History of Ancient Egypt*. Oxford: Oxford University Press.

el-Sabban, Sherif. 2000. *Temple Festival Calendars of Ancient Egypt*. Liverpool: Liverpool University Press.

Silverman, David P. 1980. *Interrogative Constructions with JN and JN-JW in Old and Middle Egyptian*. Bibliotheca Aegyptia 1. Malibu: Undena Publications.

———. 1994. (ed.) *For His Ka: Essays Offered in Memory of Klaus Baer*. SAOC 55.

———. 1997. (ed.) *Searching for Ancient Egypt: Art, Architecture, and Artifacts from the University of Pennsylvania Museum of Archaeology and Anthropology*. Ithaca: Cornell University Press.

———. 2000. "The Threat Formula and Biographical Text in the Tomb of Hezi at Saqqara." *JARCE* 37: 1–13.

———. 2001. "Curses." Pages 348–50 in Redford 2001: I.

Simpson, William K., ed. 1972. *The Literature of Ancient Egypt: An Anthology of Stories, Instructions and Poetry*. New Haven and London: Yale University Press.

———. 1976a. *The Offering Chapel of Sekhem-ankh-Ptah in the Museum of Fine Arts, Boston*. Boston: Museum of Fine Arts.

———. 1976b. *The Mastabas of Qar and Idu. G 7101 and 7102*. Giza Mastabas 2. Boston: Museum of Fine Arts.

———. 1980. *Mastabas of the Western Cemetery: Part I. Sekhemka (G 1029); Tjetu I (G 2001); Iasen (G 2196); Penmeru (G 2197); Hagy, Nefertjentet, and Herunefer (G 2352/53); Djaty, Tjetu II, and Nimesti (G 2337 X, 2343, 2366)*. Giza Mastabas 4. Boston: Museum of Fine Arts.

———. 1992. *The Offering Chapel of Kayemnofret in the Museum of Fine Arts, Boston*. Boston: Museum of Fine Arts.

———, ed. 2003. *The Literature of Ancient Egypt: An Anthology of Stories, Instructions, Stelae, Autobiographies and Poetry*. New Haven and London: Yale University Press.

Smith, William S. 1933. "The Coffin of Prince Min-Khaf." *JEA* 19: 150–59.

———. 1935. "The Old Kingdom Linen List." *ZÄS* 71: 134–49.

———. 1952. "Inscriptional Evidence for the History of the Fourth Dynasty." *JNES* 11: 113–28.

Smither, Paul C. . 1942. "An Old Kingdom Letter concerning the Crimes of Count Sabni." *JEA* 28: 16–19.

Soukiassian, Georges. 1997. "A Governors' Palace at 'Ayn Asil, Dakhla Oasis." *Egyptian Archaeology* 11: 15–17.

Spalinger, Anthony J. 1994. "Dated Texts of the Old Kingdom." *SAK* 21: 275–319.

———. 1996. *The Private Feast Lists of Ancient Egypt*. ÄA 57.

———. 2001a. "Calendars." Pages 224–27 in Redford 2001: I.

———. 2001b. "Festivals." Pages 521–55 in Redford 2001: I.

———. 2002. "Ancient Egyptian Calendars: How Many Were There?" *JARCE* 39: 241–50.

Spencer, Patricia. 1984. *The Egyptian Temple: A Lexicographical Study*. London: Kegan Paul.

Stadelmann, Rainer. 1980. "Snofru und die Pyramiden von Meidum und Dahschur." *MDAIK* 36: 437–49.

———. 1987. "Beiträge zur Geschichte des Alten Reiches. Die Länge der Regierung des Snofru." *MDAIK* 43: 229–40.

———. 2000. "Userkaf in Saqqara und Abusir. Untersuchungen zur Thronfolge in der 4. und frühen 5. Dynastie." Pages 529–42 in Bárta and Krejčí 2000.

———. 2003. "The Great Sphinx of Giza." Pages 464–69 in Hawass 2003: I.

Stadelmann, Rainer, and Hourig Sourouzian. 1982. "Die Pyramiden des Snofru in Dahschur. Erster Bericht über die Ausgrabungen an der nördlichen Steinpyramide." *MDAIK* 38: 379–93.

Strudwick, Nigel. 1982. "Notes on the mastaba of *ꜣḫt-ḥtp; ḥmỉ* and *nb-kꜣw-ḥr; ỉdw* at Saqqara." *GM* 56: 89–94.

———. 1985. *The Administration of Egypt in the Old Kingdom: The Highest Titles and Their Holders*. Studies in Egyptology. London: KPI.

———. 1987. "The Overseer of the Treasury *Ny-kꜣw-Ptḥ*." *RdE* 38: 139–46.

Tacke, N. 2001. *Verspunkte als Gliederungsmittel in ramessidischen Schülerhandschriften*. SAGA 22.

Tait, J. 2003. (ed.) *"Never Had the Like Occurred": Egypt's View of Its Past*. London: UCL Press.

Taylor, John H. 2001. *Death and the Afterlife in Ancient Egypt*. London: British Museum Press.

Teeter, Emily. 2001. "Maat." Pages 319–21 in Redford 2001: II.

Torino, Museo Egizio di. 2004. *I papiri di Gebelein: scavi G. Farina 1935*. Studi del Museo Egizio di Torino I. Turin: Ministero per i Beni e le Attività Culturali, Soprintendenza al Museo delle Antichità Egizie.

Trigger, Bruce G., Barry J. Kemp, David O'Connor, and Alan B. Lloyd. 1983. *Ancient Egypt: A Social History*. Cambridge: Cambridge University Press.

Vachala, Bretislav. 1993. "Die Biographie des Ptahschepses." Pages 547–50 in *VI congresso internazionale di Egittologia. Atti*. Edited by Comitato Organizzativo del Congresso. Turin: n.p.

Valloggia, Michel. 1986. *Le mastaba de Medou-Nefer*. 2 vols. FIFAO 31. Cairo: IFAO.

———. 1996. "Note sur l'organisation administrative de l'Oasis de Dakhla à la fin de l'Ancien Empire." *Méditerranées* 6–7: 61–72.

———. 1998. *Le monument funéraire d'Ima-Pepy/Ima-Meryrê*. FIFAO 38. Cairo: IFAO.

van Walsem, René. 1998. "The Caption to a Cattle-fording Scene in a Tomb at Saqqara and Its Implications for the Seh/Sinnbild Discussion on

Egyptian Iconography." Pages 1469–85 in *Egyptian Religion: The Last Thousand Years*. Edited by Willy Clarysse, Antoon Schoors, and Harco Willems. 2 vols. OLA 85.

Vandekerckhove, Hans, and Renate Müller-Wollerman. 2001. *Die Felsinschriften des Wadi Hilâl*. 2 vols. Elkab 6. Turnhout: Brepols.

Vandier, Jacques. 1936. "Une tombe inédite de la VIe dynastie à Akhmîm." *ASAE* 36: 33–44.

Vandier d'Abbadie, J. 1964. "Les singes familiers dans l'ancienne Égypte (Peintures et Bas-reliefs) I. L'Ancien Empire." *RdE* 16: 146–77.

Varille. Alexandre. 1938. *La tombe de Ni-Ankh-Pepi à Zâouyet el-Mayetîn*. MIFAO 70.

Vassilika, Eleni. 1995. *Egyptian Art*. Fitzwilliam Museum Handbooks. Cambridge: Cambridge University Press.

Verbovsek, Alexandra. 2004. *"Als Gunsterweis des Königs in den Tempel gegeben . . ." Privat Tempelstatuen des Alten und Mittleren Reiches*. ÄAT 3. Wiesbaden: Harrassowitz.

Verner, Miroslav. 1984. "Excavations at Abusir. Season 1982—Preliminary Report." *ZÄS* 111: 70–78.

———. 1985. "Zu den 'Baugraffiti mit Datumsangaben' aus dem Alten Reich." Pages 339–46 in Posener-Kriéger 1985: II.

———. 1992. *Baugraffiti der Ptahschepses-Mastaba*. Abusir II. Praha: Universitas Carolina Pragensis.

———. 1994. *Forgotten Pharaohs, Lost Pyramids. Abusir*. Praha: Academia Skodaexport.

———. 1995. *The Pyramid Complex of Khentkaus*. Abusir III. Praha: Universitas Carolina Pragensis.

———. 1999a. "Khentkaus I, Khentkaus II and the Title *mwt nśwt bỉty nśwt bỉty* (or: *nśwt bỉty, mwt nśwt bỉty*)." *GM* 173: 215–18.

———. 1999b. "Was There a Cult of Khentkaus I at Abusir?" *GM* 173: 219–24.

———. 2000. "Who Was Shepseskara, and When Did He Reign?" Pages 581–602 in Bárta and Krejčí 2000.

———. 2001. "Archaeological Remarks on the 4th and 5th Dynasty Chronology." *Archiv Orientální* 69: 363–418.

———. 2002. *Abusir. Realm of Osiris*. Cairo–New York: American University in Cairo Press.

———. 2003. "The Abusir Pyramid Builders' Crews." Pages 445–51 in Kloth et al. 2003.

Verner, Miroslav, and Vivienne Callender. 2002. *Djedkare's Family Cemetery*. Abusir VI. Praha: Czech Institute of Egyptology.

Vernus, Pascal. 1972–92. "Name." Pages 320–26 in Helck and Otto 1972–92: IV.

———. 1995. *Essai sur la conscience de l'histoire dans l'Égypte pharaonique*. Bibliothèque de l'École des Hautes Études, Sciences historiques et philologiques 332. Paris: Librairie Honoré Champion, Éditeur.

von Beckerath, Jürgen. 1997. *Chronologie des pharaonischen Ägypten: Die Zeitbestimmung der ägyptischen Geschichte von der Vorzeit bis 332 v. Chr.* MÄS 46.

———. 1999. *Handbuch der ägyptischen Königsnamen*. Second edition. MÄS 49.

von Bissing, Friedrich W. 1905–28. *Das Re-Heiligtum des Königs Ne-woser-re (Rathures)*. 3 vols. Berlin: Duncker.

Weigall, Arthur E. P. 1907. *A Report on the Antiquities of Lower Nubia (the First Cataract to the Sudan Frontier) and Their Condition in 1906–7*. Oxford: Oxford University Press.

Weill, Raymond. 1911–12. "Monuments nouveaux des premières dynasties." *Sphinx* 15: 1–35.

Wente, Edward F. 1990. *Letters from Ancient Egypt*. Society of Biblical Literature Writings from the Ancient World 1. Atlanta, Ga.: Scholars Press.

Wettengel, Wolfgang. 1992. "Zu den Darstellungen des Papyrusraschelns." *SAK* 19: 323–38.

Wiese, André. 2001. *Antikenmuseum Basel und Sammlung Ludwig: Die Ägyptische Abteilung*. Mainz: von Zabern.

Wild, Henri. 1953. *Le Tombeau de Ti. Fascicule II: La chapelle* (Première partie). MIFAO 65.

———. 1959. "L'adresse aux visiteurs du tombeau de Ti." *BIFAO* 58: 101–13.

Wildung, Dietrich. 1969. *Die Rolle ägyptischer Könige im Bewusstsein ihrer Nachwelt. Teil I: Posthume Quellen über die Könige der ersten vier Dynastien*. MÄS 17.

Wilkinson, Toby A. H. 2000. *Royal Annals of Ancient Egypt: The Palermo Stone and Its Associated Fragments*. Studies in Egyptology. London and New York: KPI.

Willems, Harco. 1990. "Crime, Cult and Capital Punishment (Mo'alla Inscription 8)." *JEA* 76: 27–54.

Wilson, John A. 1954. "A Group of Sixth Dynasty Inscriptions." *JNES* 13: 243–64.

Zibelius, Karola. 1972. *Afrikanische Orts- und Völkernamen in hieroglyphischen und hieratischen Texten*. Beihefte zum Tübinger Atlas des Vorderen Orients, Reihe B 1. Wiesbaden: Dr. Ludwig Reichert Verlag.

Ziegler, Christiane. 1990. *Catalogue des stèles, peintures et reliefs égyptiens de l'Ancien Empire et de la Première Période Intermédiaire vers 2686–2040 avant J.-C.* Paris: Éditions de la Réunion des musées nationaux.

———. 1993. *Le mastaba d'Akhethetep. Une chapelle funéraire de l'Ancien Empire.* Paris: Editions de la Réunion des musées nationaux.

———. 1997. "Sur quelques vases inscrits de l'Ancien Empire." Pages 461–89 in Berger and Mathieu 1997.

Ziermann, Martin, and Christian Eder. 2001. "Zu den städtischen privaten *ka*-Hausanlagen des späten AR in 'Ayn Asil." *MDAIK* 57: 309–56.

Glossary

This glossary covers a number of the more important Egyptological terms found in this book as well as principal divine names and places. It also includes a few of the more common Egyptian words and building names that are not translated but rather left in italicized forms based on the Egyptian transliteration (see §4.4.1 for a note on the latter).

Abydos City in the eighth nome of Upper Egypt, cult center of Osiris. See no. 17 and before no. 255.

akh The transfigured state of the dead in the afterlife, a powerful force endowed with a creative energy, enjoying the prerogatives of gods while not actually being one. See Taylor 2001: 31–32.

Akhet season See chapter I, §3.2.3.

alabaster A yellowish translucent stone used for vessels and sometimes relief. More correctly called calcite or travertine, or "Egyptian alabaster," as it is very different from other alabasters.

Anubis Jackal deity, protector of the dead in the necropolis, and associated with embalming rituals.

aroura A Greek term for a measure of land, Egyptian *setjat*. In the Old Kingdom, it is divided into three *kha*, or 30 *ta* or 60 *remen*. Examples are seen best in the Palermo Stone (no. 1). It measured in the region of 91 m^2. See further Baer 1956.

Atum Primaeval creator god, with a cult center at Heliopolis

ba One of the spirits of a person, but in the Old Kingdom most commonly associated with the king or a god. Royal and divine *bas* encompassed the powers of the being and was the means by which they were manifest as individuals. From later texts, the *ba* of a non-royal person could separate from the body at death and visit the living, or join the gods. See Taylor 2001: 20–23.

Bastet Cat goddess, with cult center at Bubastis.

Bedouin A conventional translation of the Egyptian term *mentju,* which seems to refer to nomadic peoples in the Eastern deserts. We have no idea quite how appropriate it is. The term *iuntyu,* translated here "pillar people," refers to a similar group of people, known from the Eastern deserts and Sinai.

Bubastis Tell Basta in the Delta, near modern Zagazig.

Behdet A cult center of Horus, who is often called "the Behdetite." Horus's cult center at Edfu was called Behdet.

brother of the funerary estate This title refers to someone who was probably responsible for the management or execution of matters in the funerary estate for the deceased. See a summary of opinions and examples in Harpur 1981: 30–34.

Busiris Abusir in the central Delta, perhaps the original cult center of Osiris before Abydos became his main center.

Buto Tell el-Faraun in the Delta, traditionally made up of Pe and Dep. A site with a very long history.

cartouche See chapter I, §3.3

court council Translation mostly adopted here of Egyptian *setep-za,* often translated "palace" in this context. It may mean something more personally concerned with where the king was. See Goelet 1986 and Brovarski 2001: 95 (f).

crowns, red and white See "Two lands" below.

cubit A measure of length, 52.3 cm (20.6 in.).

epagomenal days See chapter I, §3.2.3.

ennead A group of nine deities. It particularly refers to nine major gods and goddesses, the offspring of Atum: Atum, Shu, Tefnut, Geb, Nut, Osiris, Isis, Seth, Nephthys.

false door A type of tomb stela particularly common in the Old Kingdom. Its purpose, hence its name, was to give a place through which the spirits of the dead might enter into the tomb chapel from the burial chamber to partake of offerings. Originally like a simple door with a central niche, the number of jambs and architraves multiplied as they were convenient locations for texts.

festival names Spalinger 2001b summarizes festivals in Egypt; reference should always be made to Parker 1950. Spalinger 1996: 110–69 comments on the development of these lists in the Old Kingdom.

following of Horus Attested since the Early Dynastic part of the Palermo Stone, this may be some administrative action carried out by a court retinue. See Goedicke 1967a: 48–52.

funerary estate The "pious foundation" that would form a major source of the deceased's provision of funerary offerings for his cult (Jacquet-

Gordon 1962). Frequently these offerings were granted from a royal foundation as a mark of favor (in other words, income) to an official. Compare chapter I, §5.2.3, and see no. 319 for examples. For the problem of deciding between the identically written words for "eternity" and "funerary estate," see note to no. 144.

ges-per A complex administrative term, perhaps a crown domain devoted to the intensive raising of cattle or for agricultural production, which had to give part of its income to the crown or its institutions. It can also refer to a section of the Residence directed by the vizier dealing with royal monuments. See Moreno Garcia 1999.

Great house Egyptian *per-aa,* an aspect of the royal palace. In later times an oblique way of referring to the king; almost certainly the origin of the Hebrew term "pharaoh" for the king of Egypt.

Great Mansion(s) A law court; the title of "overseer of the six Great Mansions" was probably the highest legal official in the land. Two of them are mentioned as being in the western part of the Residence (no. 219).

Hathor Goddess frequently in the form of a cow, or a woman with cow's horns. Associated with music and dancing; popular with women. Dendera was one of her main cult centers.

Hatnub See remarks before no. 69.

haty-a A noble title, see chapter I, §5.2.1.

heqat A measure of volume of about 4.5 liters.

Horus A falcon god, originally a sky god. Son of Osiris and Isis, the king is his embodiment on earth.

imakhu See chapter I, §5.3.1.

iry pat A noble title, see chapter I, §5.2.1.

ished fruit Usually identified as *Balanites aegyptica*, an edible fruit sometimes known as the "desert date."

ka One of the spirits of a person, which came into existence at birth, with some of the character of a "twin" or "double." The *ka* needed a physical form to inhabit and ideally lived with the body in the burial chamber after death. It moved into the tomb chapel to received sustenance, where it might inhabit a statue. See Taylor 2001: 18–20. "Going to one's *ka*" is a euphemism for dying.

kha measure A measure of 1,000 square cubits. See Baer 1956: 114–5

Khentyimentyu "Foremost of the Westerners," a deity with cult center at Abydos. Originally a god of the dead, whose role was gradually taken over by Osiris.

khenty-she See chapter I, §5.2.2

Koptos, Koptite nome Koptos is the Greek name for modern Quft, a village to the north of Luxor. It was the capital of the fifth Upper Egyptian nome, termed the "Koptite nome." Particularly important in this book as the find-spot for the largest single number of Old Kingdom royal decrees (chapter IV). Min of Koptos was the local god.

Lower Egypt See "Two Lands" below.

Maat A complex concept: the idea of the "correct order of things," often less correctly translated "right" or "truth." See Teeter 2001 and Helck 1972–92. For more detail, see Assmann 1995 and Lichtheim 1997. Also the name of a goddess who personifies the concept.

mastaba A rectangular flat-topped freestanding tomb particularly common in the first six dynasties in the Memphite region. Usually built of stone but sometimes of brick. The term comes from the Arabic word for "bench," often seen outside traditional houses in Egypt.

mehenek A title with different meanings in different contexts. With workmen it can refer to a royal loan-worker or specialist (no. 319 and others), including two craftsmen who worked on a tomb (no. 165), as well as the men who bear the carrying chair (no. 318). It can also be applied to an important noble, who may have had associations with craftsmen, as a special mark of favor (no. 228). See Drenkhahn 1976b: 46, 147.

Memphis Capital of Egypt in the Early Dynastic period and the Old Kingdom, located at modern el-Badrashein, about 20 km southwest of Cairo and very close to the necropolis of Saqqara.

meret temple A temple of Hathor and the reigning king; perhaps where the marriage between the king and Hathor as his queen was celebrated (Barta 1983). The location of these temples is unclear; some may have been in the palace. See further Brovarski 2001: 92–93.

Min Ithyphallic fertility god, with cult centers at Koptos and Akhmim.

nebes fruit Fruit of the Christ's thorn tree, *Zizyphus spina Christi*.

Nekhbet Vulture goddess of el-Kab, and protective deity for Upper Egypt.

Nekheb el-Kab, on the east bank of the river opposite Hierakonpolis; Nekheb was the home of Nekhbet.

Nekhen Hierakonpolis, on the west bank opposite el-Kab (Nekhen), one of the earliest power centers in Upper Egypt

Nekhenre The sun-temple of Userkaf (see no. 60C and no. 85).

nomarch Literally "great chief of <nome>," the governor of a nome.

nome From the Greek word νόμος for a "province"; used by Egyptologists to refer to each of the twenty-two provinces of Upper Egypt and the 21/22 of Lower Egypt. In no. 31 the reader will find a full list of the Upper Egyptian nomes. See further chapter I, §5.3.4.

Osiris Originally a god of vegetation, who became by the fifth dynasty the preeminent god of the dead. Cult center at Abydos, where he took over many of the functions of Khentyimentyu.

overseer of priests Used without naming a particular god, this title seems frequently to have been the most important administrative official in a provincial site until the seemingly more elevated title of "nomarch" was devised.

Pe An area of Buto, often used to characterize Lower Egypt.

Peret season See chapter I, §3.2.3.

Perfect name [Often translated "good name"]. A secondary name for an individual, as opposed to the principal "great name"; it probably expressed the characteristics and status of the owner. It dropped out of use after the Old Kingdom. See Doxey 2001; Vernus 1972–92.

per-nu shrine The national shrine of Lower Egypt, located by tradition at Buto.

per-shena Usually translated "storeroom," the term is used, for example, in the Abusir papyri to refer to the temple storerooms. However, in the Royal Decrees, the context clearly implies that it is a larger, presumably state, institution that provided directly for such royal foundations. See now the study by Andrassy 1993.

per-wer shrine The national shrine of Upper Egypt, traditionally located at Hierakonpolis.

phyle Greek word used in Egyptology to translate the Egyptian word *za,* which refers to groups of people who performed part-time service as priests or work crews. See Roth 1991: 2–4.

pillar people See "Bedouin."

pyramid names See chapter I, §5.3.5 and list in the chronology on page xxix.

Punt A land that provided incense, trees, and a variety of exotic goods for Egypt. Best known from Hatshepsut's expedition in the eighteenth dynasty, it was visited from at least the Old Kingdom (see no. 1). It is located in the area of Eritrea and Somalia and was reached by a boat journey along the Red Sea. See Kitchen 2001.

ra-she A term that appears often in decrees and particularly in the Abusir papyri, it appears to be an economic unit which provided provisions to royal temples and palaces needed for the king's funerary temple. See particularly Posener-Kriéger 1976: 616–19.

Re Form of the sun god par excellence. Sometimes shown as a man with a falcon head.

reversionary offerings the offerings which, after having been presented to the subject of the cult, then revert back and were used for the benefit of those who worked in the cult or belonged to it, or (in the case of many high officials) were designated as being able to draw on this. This system was one of the bases of the Egyptian economy.

royal ornament A courtly title held by women, some of whom claimed to be royal children, others of whom were court ladies. See Baud 1999a: 128–39.

Sed festival See chapter I, §3.2.2.

Sekhetre The solar temple of Sahure, as yet undiscovered; a number of blocks that may have been prepared for it were found in the pyramid complex of Niuserre (Verner 2000: 591–3). An alternative suggestion is that the solar temple of Userkaf was reused by both his successors: Stadelmann 2000: 540–42.

senuti shrine A building perhaps marked by snake stelae, possibly at Heliopolis (Wilkinson 2001: 137–38). Compare the doorjamb bearing a snake image from the Step Pyramid (Hawass 1994; Metropolitan Museum of Art 1999: 171).

serdab Arabic word used in Egyptology to describe a concealed statue chamber in a tomb.

serekh See chapter I, §3.3.

Seshat Goddess of writing.

Setibre The sun temple of Neferirkare. This temple has not actually been located but is thought to be in the Abusir area as it features prominently in the Abusir papyri (see chapter I, §6.4. It might have been built of brick and has now completely disappeared. Another suggestion, perhaps less likely, is that Neferirkare rebuilt the temple of Userkaf (Nekhenre) and renamed it. See further, Posener-Kriéger 1976: 519 and Stadelmann 2000: 540–42.

Shemu season See chapter I, §3.2.3.

Shezepibre The sun temple of Niuserre (see no. 11).

soul chapel A name for a small temple or chapel, not necessarily located near or at the tomb, which was devoted to the cult of the soul of the dead person. In the Old Kingdom they are known to exist for kings (no. 13, no. 88E, no. 198, no. 232, no. 237, no. 261; see also Fischer 1958b), who often had several, queens (no. 21, no. 108), and private individuals (no. 28, no. 33, no. 39, no. 119, no. 249, no. 306M; see further Franke 1994: 118–27 and n. 358 on p. 122).

stolist A priest who dresses the (image of a) god. Most commonly found with Min of Koptos but also in this book with Anubis.

Sun temple Rulers of the fifth dynasty from Userkaf to Menkauhor erected temples to the sun-god Re in the Memphite region. The remains of only two of them have been found, those of Userkaf (Nekhenre) and Niuserre (Shezepibre), both at Abu Gurob, just north of Abusir, but the names of four others are known from inscriptions. The Abusir papyri (chapter I, §6.4) provide much source material for the functioning of one of these temples, that of Neferirkare.

ta measure 100 square cubits (Baer 1956: 114–5).

Thinis, Thinite nome Thinis, probably near modern Girga, was the capital of the eighth Upper Egyptian nome, in which the town of Abydos was located. "Thinite nome" is thus a way of referring to this province.

Thoth Ibis headed god, scribe of the gods. Cult center later at Hermopolis in Middle Egypt.

Tura The principal fine limestone quarry in northern Egypt during the Old Kingdom; still a quarry site today.

Two Lands Upper (southern) and Lower (northern) Egypt; perhaps reflecting two distinct geographical, political, religious, or cultural entities which were symbolically joined together to form Egypt. The white crown of Upper Egypt is 𓋑 and the red crown of Lower Egypt 𓋔 ; together they appear as 𓋖.

Upper Egypt See "Two Lands" above.

wab-priest An order of priest, literally meaning "pure." It is a lesser priestly title than that normally translated "priest" in this book, which in Egyptian is *hem-netjer,* "servant of the god."

wabet Literally "the pure place," it seems to refer both to one of the departments of central government and also to a building of the same name which was probably located at each major necropolis and was probably a place in which embalming was performed. See Brovarski 1977.

Wadjet Cobra goddess of Buto and protective deity for Lower Egypt.

wah fruit So-called "earth almonds," *cyperus esculentus*; in English sometimes colloquially called "tigernuts."

Indexes

Names of Kings

References are to texts. They exclude king's names appearing in titles.

Bedjau, 4

Demedjibtawy, 39
Djedefre, 1, 4, 6

Huni, 79

Imhotep, 65
Ity, 63
Izezi, 15, 43, 60, 90, 92, 100, 205, 213, 232, 241, 246

Kha..., 30
Khafre, 4, 5, 6, 42
Khufu, 1, 56, 69, 81

Menkauhor, 20, 59
Menkaure, 1, 5, 6, 16, 81
Merenre, 46, 50, 51, 52, 72, 241, 247, 256, 257

Nebka, 82
Neferefre, 18, 83, 91
Neferirkare, 1, 4, 17, 83, 90
Neferkare Nebi, 282
Neferkauhor, 31, 32, 33, 34, 35, 36, 37, 38, 249
Netjerykhet, 7, 41, 54
Niuserre, 11, 58

Pepy I, 3, 13, 15, 20, 21, 45, 49, 61, 64, 71, 198, 238, 247, 256, 257, 263, 266
Pepy II, 14, 15, 22, 23, 24, 25, 26, 27, 28, 47, 52, 53, 62, 73, 87, 241, 243, 257, 266, 267

Sahure, 1, 4, 5, 6, 10, 57, 83
Shepseskaf, 1, 5, 6, 16
Sneferu, 1, 8, 20, 55, 79, 80

Teti, 3, 13, 19, 44, 70, 138, 205, 213, 228, 237, 238, 246, 247, 256

Unas, 12, 48, 6, 205, 208, 209, 213, 217, 218, 228, 246
Uncertain, 29
Userkaf, 1, 5, 6, 9, 85
Userkare, 3

Names of Persons (excluding kings)

References are to texts.

Abdu, 179
Abutyu, 324
Akhethotep, 194
Akhethotep Hemi/Nebkauhor, 86, 104, 195, 301
Akhetmehu, 180
Ankhesenpepy, 3, 281
Ankhi, 131
Ankhires, 152
Ankhirptah, 153
Ankhkhufu, 196
Ankhmahor, 86, 197, 302, 322

Ankhmare, 86, 191
Ankhmeryre, 328
Ankhmeryremeryptah, 64, 198
Ankhnespepy IV, 282
Ankhwedja, 132
Anusu, 75

Bawy, 260
Bia, 199

Debehen, 200
Djadjay, 253
Djaty, 65
Djau, 257, 267
Djenwen, 288

Fetekta, 320

Geref, 201

Harkhuf, 241
Hebi, 154
Hekenu, 248
Hemetre, 283
Hemire, 289
Hemiunu, 84
Henbabai, 89
Henqu, 269
Henutsen, 290
Herymeru, 133
Hetepherakhet, 202
Hetepherenptah, 203
Hetepheres, 291, 292
Hetepu, 204
Hezi, 205

Iabtet, 284
Iazen, 320
Ibi, 266, 303
Idi, 31, 35, 37, 38, 77
Idu, 206
Idu I, 250
Idu II, 251
Idu Menza, 254
Idu Seneni, 105, 252
Inikaf, 155
Inpuhotep, 156
Inti, 271, 285
Ipi, 207
Iput, 15, 21, 280, 282
Iret, 293
Iri, 102
Ishetmaa, 134
Iy, 157
Iy Mery, 261
Iyenhor, 208
Iyhenaef, 77
Izi, 209, 246

Kaiaper, 210, 211, 322
Kaiemankh, 317
Kaiemhezet, 158
Kaiemnefret, 106, 304
Kaiemrehu, 159
Kaiemsenu, 122
Kaiemtjennet, 212
Kaigemni, 213
Kaihap Tjeti, 214
Kaihersetef, 161
Kaikherptah, 215
Kainefer, 162
Kaipure, 123
Khabaubat, 76
Khamerernebty II, 277
Khenemti, 107
Khenit, 294
Khentika, 216, 322
Khentkawes, 278
Khentyka, 273
Khentykawpepy, 274
Khenu, 135, 217, 218
Khnumhotep, 245
Khnumnedjem, 272, 305
Khufuhotep, 163
Khui, 136, 295
Khuit, 137
Khuiwer, 219
Khunes, 77

Medunefer, 152, 164
Mehi, 138
Mehu, 220, 306
Mekhu I, 77, 243
Mekhu II, 243

Memi, 170, 181
Meni, 182
Merankhef, 183
Merefnebef, 333
Mereri, 124, 139
Mereruka, 150
Meresankh III, 84, 276, 320
Meretites, 15
Meretites I, 275
Merib, 307
Merkhufu, 184
Mersuankh, 221
Meru, 140
Merut, 286
Mery I, 264
Mery II, 265, 308
Meryrenefer Qar, 247
Metjen, 108
Metjetji, 222
Minkhaf, 326

Nebemakhet, 165
Nebet, 279, 295
Nebib, 268
Nedjemib, 141
Nedjetempet, 296
Nefer, 102, 166, 185
Nefer and Kahay, 330
Neferesres, 297
Neferkhuwi, 191
Neferseshemptah, 167, 223
Neferseshemre, 224
Nefretiabet, 327
Nehutdesher, 262
Neit, 282
Nenki, 142
Nensedjerkai, 287
Nesutnefer, 321
Netjerpunesut, 6
Netjersen, 102
Nipepy, 151
Nubhotep, 298
Nubwenet, 15
Nyankhkhnum and Khnumhotep, 109, 309, 317
Nyankhpepy, 143, 310
Nyankhre, 125
Nyankhsekhmet, 225
Nyankhsheret, 148
Nyankhsokar, 168
Nyhetepptah, 144
Nykaiankh, 110
Nykanesut, 317
Nykauhathor, 300
Nykauizezi, 145
Nykauptah, 169
Nykaure, 111
Nykhasutmeryre, 45
Nymaatre, 186, 191
Nysuredi, 187

Pehenwikai, 146
Penmeru, 112
Pepi, 113
Pepyankhheryib, 270, 311
Pepynakht, 242
Pepysoneb, 170
Persen, 312
Per-shenay, 255
Peteti, 332
Ptahhotep, 234
Ptahhotep Desher, 86
Ptahhotep II, 126, 319
Ptahshepses, 86, 226

Qar, 313
Qereri, 263

Reherytep, 147
Remenuka, 188
Reshepses, 100
Rewer, 227
Rudjzas, 299

Sabi, 77
Sabni, 77, 96, 243, 244
Sabu Ibebi, 228
Sabu Tjeti, 229
Sankhuptah, 230
Sebekhotep, 103
Sedjefaptah, 127
Sehetepu, 171
Sekhemankhptah, 231, 314
Sekhemka, 128

Sekhemkare, 5, 315
Sekhentyu, 167
Sekhentyuka, 148
Senedjemib Inti, 232
Senedjemib Mehi, 232
Sennuankh, 114
Senu, 74
Seshemnefer, 234
Seshemu, 233
Shedy, 172
Shemai, 30, 31, 32, 33, 34, 35, 37, 38, 66, 249
Shepset, 300
Sneferunefer II, 129

Tepemankh, 130
Tepemankh II, 173
Tetiseneb, 189
Tjau, 103
Tjautyiqer, 67
Tjenti, 115, 174
Tjetji, 68, 175
Tjetu, 149
Tjezi, 176
Tjy, 150, 316, 319
Ty, 177

Washptah, 235
Weni, 256
Wepemnefret, 116
Weta, 323

Yotefnen, 117

Zauib, 76
Zeftjwa, 190

Sites of Origin

Numbers refer to texts.

Abu Gurob, 11
Abusir, 10, 15, 18, 83, 85, 86, 90, 91, 92, 210, 278, 320, 331
Abydos, 17, 19, 22, 151, 255, 256, 257, 258, 295
Akhmim, 293
Ayn Asil, 15, 28, 99

Balat, 273, 274
Bir Mueilha, 75
Busiris, 272, 289, 305

Dahshur, 8, 20, 80, 162
Deir el-Gebrawi, 266, 267, 268, 269, 303
Dendera, 250, 251
Deshasha, 271

Edfu, 246, 247
Elephantine, 2, 48, 49, 50, 52, 53, 96, 97, 98, 103
el-Kab, 88
el-Qasr wa es-Sayed, 105, 252, 253, 254
el-Qusiya, 269
Gebelein, 102, 329
Giza, 4, 5, 6, 16, 23, 81, 84, 86, 106, 111, 112, 113, 115, 116, 117, 121, 125, 127, 132, 144, 148, 149, 152, 154, 155, 156, 157, 163, 164, 165, 168, 174, 175, 176, 179, 180, 181, 182, 183, 184, 185, 186, 187, 188, 191, 196, 198, 200, 206, 215, 219, 221, 227, 231, 232, 233, 234, 239, 240, 275, 276, 277, 278, 284, 287, 291, 292, 294, 297, 299, 300, 307, 313, 315, 317, 320, 321, 323, 324, 326, 327, 332

Hagarsa, 264, 265, 308
Hatnub, 69, 70, 71, 72, 73
Hawawish, 160, 170, 177, 260, 261, 262, 263
Heliopolis, 7
Hindallab, 89

Khor el-Aquiba, 76
Kom el-Koffar, 249
Koptos, 21, 24, 25, 26, 27, 30, 31, 32, 33, 34, 35, 36, 37, 38, 39, 40

Lisht, 9, 12, 120
Meidum, 79

Meir, 270, 310, 311
Moalla, 248

Philae, 51

Qau, 101
Qubbet el-Hawa, 241, 242, 243, 244, 245, 325

Saqqara, 3, 7, 12, 15, 29, 41, 78, 86, 87, 93, 94, 95, 100, 101, 104, 107, 108, 109, 114, 118, 119, 122, 123, 124, 126, 128, 129, 130, 131, 133, 134, 135, 136, 137, 138, 139, 140, 141, 142, 143, 145, 146, 147, 150, 153, 158, 159, 161, 167, 169, 171, 172, 173, 189, 192, 194, 195, 197, 199, 201, 202, 204, 205, 207, 208, 209, 211, 212, 213, 216, 217, 218, 220, 222, 223, 224, 225, 226, 228, 229, 230, 235, 236, 237, 238, 279, 280, 281, 282, 283, 285, 286, 290, 296, 298, 301, 302, 304, 306, 309, 312, 314, 316, 317, 319, 322, 328, 330, 333
Sheikh Farag, 259

Tehna, 110
Tell Basta, 13
Tomas, 77

Wadi Dungash, 74
Wadi Hammamat, 63, 64, 65, 66, 67, 68
Wadi Kharig, 57
Wadi Maghara, 54, 55, 56, 57, 58, 59, 60, 61, 62

Zawiyet el-Aryan, 82

Objects in Museums

References are to texts.

Aberdeen 1558a–c, 235
Aberdeen 1560, 235

Basel, Museum für Völkerkunde III 6206, 137
Berlin 1105, 108
Berlin 1107, 307
Berlin 7715, 45
Berlin 8869, 96
Berlin 9010, 103
Berlin 11301, 92
Berlin 11665, 166
Berlin 14105, 86
Berlin 14108, 113
Berlin 15004, 312
Berlin 15126, 190
Berlin 15726, 90
Berlin 17500, 20
Berlin 17933, 15
Berlin 21001, 90
Berlin 32190, 222
Boston, MFA 03.1896, 17
Boston, MFA 04.1760, 314
Boston, MFA 04.1761, 304
Boston, MFA 07.1005, 304
Boston, MFA 13.4331, 198
Boston, MFA 21.3081, 196
Boston, MFA 21.961, 187
Boston, MFA 47.1654, 23
Brooklyn 47.218.18, 98
Brussels E.2243, 140

Cairo Temp. no. 26.2.21.18, 16
Cairo 602, 90
Cairo, CG 376, 153
Cairo, CG 1308, 86
Cairo, CG 1415, 298
Cairo, CG 1417, 173
Cairo, CG 1421, 129
Cairo, CG 1431, 257
Cairo, CG 1432, 106
Cairo, CG 1433, 237
Cairo, CG 1435, 256
Cairo, CG 1482, 225
Cairo, CG 1564, 173
Cairo, CG 1565, 228
Cairo, CG 1566, 161
Cairo, CG 1569, 235

Cairo, CG 1570, 235
Cairo, CG 1578, 295
Cairo, CG 1579, 151
Cairo, CG 1613, 293
Cairo, CG 1634, 107
Cairo, CG 1650, 258
Cairo, CG 1674, 235
Cairo, CG 1691, 290
Cairo, CG 1702, 235
Cairo, CG 1709, 229
Cairo, CG 1732, 141
Cairo, CG 1747, 14
Cairo, CG 1756, 229
Cairo, CG 1787, 323
Cairo, CG 15048, 203
Cairo, CG 57189, 152
Cairo, CG 58043, 93
Cairo, CG 58063, 90
Cairo, JE 25975, 101
Cairo, JE 37734, 4
Cairo, JE 38566, 59
Cairo, JE 38568, 55
Cairo, JE 38569, 57
Cairo, JE 38570, 58
Cairo, JE 41491, 25
Cairo, JE 41890, 21
Cairo, JE 41892, 27
Cairo, JE 41893, 24
Cairo, JE 41894, 39
Cairo, JE 41895, 34
Cairo, JE 42787, 121
Cairo, JE 43052, 26
Cairo, JE 43053, 31
Cairo, JE 43290, 40
Cairo, JE 44608, 198
Cairo, JE 47729, 158
Cairo, JE 48852, 326
Cairo, JE 49623, 94
Cairo, JE 49889, 41
Cairo, JE 50036, 78
Cairo, JE 52001A, 95
Cairo, JE 55937, 235
Cairo, JE 56370, 29
Cairo, JE 56994, 117
Cairo, JE 57139, 115
Cairo, JE 57174, 176
Cairo, JE 58062, 90
Cairo, JE 65908, 3, 281
Cairo, JE 66844, 102
Cairo, JE 97348, 18, 91
Cambridge, Fitzwilliam Museum, E.6.1909, 289
Chicago, Oriental Institute OIM 11048, 226
Chicago, Oriental Institute OIM 13652, 7

Frankfurt, Liebieghaus 1638, 148

Hildesheim 2403, 185

Kansas City, Nelson-Atkins Museum 52-7/1, 222
Kansas City, Nelson-Atkins Museum 52-7/2, 222

Leiden, Rijksmuseum F.1904/3.1, 202
Leipzig 359, 142
Leipzig 2560, 181
Leipzig 3140, 154
London, BM EA 157C, 175
London, BM EA 568, 175
London, BM EA 626, 19
London, BM EA 682, 226
London, BM EA 1186, 193
London, BM EA 1324, 162
London, BM EA 10735, 90, 92
London, BM EA 57322, 43
London, University College UC 16163, 101

Manchester, University Museum 10780, 169
Munich, Staatliches Museum Ägyptischer Kunst ÄS 1568, p. 127 n. 26.

New York, MMA 07.228.24, 42
New York, MMA 14.7.10, 26
New York, MMA 14.7.11, 37
New York, MMA 14.7.12, 38
New York, MMA 14.7.13, 32
New York, MMA 14.7.14, 30
New York, MMA 26.7.1450, 44

New York, MMA 1992.338, 45

Paris, Louvre E 5323, 43
Paris, Louvre E 5356, 45
Paris, Louvre E 10958, 194
Paris, Louvre E 11286, 162
Paris, Louvre E 12660, 49
Paris, Louvre E 14329, 246
Paris, Louvre E 15591, 7
Paris, Louvre E 23140b, 46
Paris, Louvre E 25416a, 90
Paris, Louvre E 25416c, 90
Paris, Louvre E 26904, 248
Paris, Louvre E 31859, 190
Paris, Louvre N 527, 45
Paris, Louvre N 648ab, 47
Paris, Louvre N 657, 47
Paris, Louvre N 794, 46
Philadelphia, Pennsylvania University Museum E 15729, 123

Toronto, Royal Ontario Museum 905.2.120, 22
Toronto, Royal Ontario Museum 953.116.1, 222
Turin 1853, 239
Turin 2671/20, 7
Turin 2671/21, 7
Turin CG 54002, 97

Warsaw, National Museum 139944, 246

Zürich, Museum Rietberg RAG 6, 172

Cross-reference List of Tomb Text Types

This index is to assist the reader in locating certain types of text from tombs in cases where a text fits more than one of the chapter headings (see Chapter I, §6.5). Thus, for example, a few formulae are covered in their own chapter, but the majority of examples will be found in other sections as here. In addition, the biographical texts, which are separated in the text between Memphite and Provincial ones, have been roughly divided here between the ideal biographies and the ones which may be more personal or experience based; biographical phrases in other types of text are also indexed. Numbers refer to texts.

Offering formulae (chapter XII)
133, 134, 135, 138, 141, 143, 144, 147, 149, 152, 157, 158, 159, 164, 166, 171, 172, 177, 184, 189, 192, 196, 199, 205, 206, 208, 213, 219, 220, 221, 224, 228, 233, 238, 241, 243, 246, 247, 250, 251, 254, 255, 256, 259, 265, 266, 270, 271, 272, 273, 280, 283, 284, 285, 286, 287, 288, 289, 290, 291, 292, 293, 294, 295, 296, 297, 300, 326, 333

Appeals and warnings (chapter XIII)
180, 182, 185, 186, 187, 190, 193, 197, 198, 205, 210, 213, 216, 219, 230, 238, 241, 247, 248, 249, 252, 253, 254, 255, 260, 266, 267, 270, 271, 273, 332, 333

Commemorations and dedications (chapter XIV)
232, 235, 261, 284, 288, 290, 293, 297, 298, 299, 332, 333

Payment and tomb acquisition (chapter XV)
138, 201, 202, 210, 222, 251, 271

Biographies—ideal (chapter XVI/ Chapter XVII)
131, 132, 133, 137, 138, 141, 180, 190, 195, 197, 198, 199, 201, 202, 204, 205, 206, 207, 208, 209, 210, 211, 213, 215, 216, 217, 219, 220, 221, 222, 223, 224, 228, 230, 231, 233, 234, 239, 241, 242, 243, 244, 246, 247, 248, 249, 250, 251, 252, 253, 254, 255, 256, 257, 258, 259, 260, 261, 262, 263, 264, 265, 266, 268, 269, 270, 271, 273

Biographies—experience-based (chapter XVI/chapter XVII)
194, 196, 198, 200, 203, 205, 212, 213, 214, 218, 225, 226, 227, 228, 229, 232, 234, 235, 236, 237, 238, 240, 241, 242, 243, 244, 245, 246, 247, 249, 256, 263, 265, 266, 267, 270, 274, 333

Texts of women (chapter XVIII)
196

Captions (chapter XIX)
86, 186

Titles only (chapter XX)
321, 323

Sarcophagus lid texts (chapter XX)
322

Offering lists (chapter XX)
326, 327, 328

Concordance of Texts in *Urkunden I*

Urkunden I (Urk I; Sethe 1933) is the basic reference collection of Old Kingdom texts. Numbers refer to texts.

Urk I, 1–7	108
Urk I, 7–8	55
Urk I, 8	56, 174
Urk I, 9	163, 178
Urk I, 10	161
Urk I, 11–15	106
Urk I, 15	175
Urk I, 16	165
Urk I, 16–17	111
Urk I, 18–21	200
Urk I, 22	323
Urk I, 23	182
Urk I, 24–32	110
Urk I, 32	57
Urk I, 33	173
Urk I, 33–4	159
Urk I, 34	290
Urk I, 34–5	135
Urk I, 35	113
Urk I, 36–7	114
Urk I, 37	312
Urk I, 38–40	225
Urk I, 40–5	235
Urk I, 46–8	219
Urk I, 48–9	146
Urk I, 49–51	202
Urk I, 51–3	226
Urk I, 53–4	58
Urk I, 54	59
Urk I, 55	60
Urk I, 55–6	60
Urk I, 56	60
Urk I, 57	234
Urk I, 58	86
Urk I, 59–67	232
Urk I, 69	48
Urk I, 69–71	271
Urk I, 71–2	190
Urk I, 72–3	288
Urk I, 73	153
Urk I, 75	141
Urk I, 76–9	269
Urk I, 80	268
Urk I, 81–4	228
Urk I, 84–5	229
Urk I, 91–2	61
Urk I, 93	64
Urk I, 94	64
Urk I, 94–5	64
Urk I, 95	71
Urk I, 96–7	64
Urk I, 97	45
Urk I, 98–110	256
Urk I, 110	50
Urk I, 111	51
Urk I, 112	151
Urk I, 112–13	62
Urk I, 114–5	14
Urk I, 115	47, 53
Urk I, 115–7	105
Urk I, 117–19	257
Urk I, 119	293
Urk I, 120–31	241
Urk I, 131–5	242
Urk I, 135–40	243
Urk I, 140–1	245
Urk I, 141	68
Urk I, 142–5	266
Urk I, 144–5	266
Urk I, 145–7	267
Urk I, 148	63
Urk I, 148–9	65

Urk I, 149–50	66
Urk I, 150	258
Urk I, 152	176
Urk I, 153	41
Urk I, 153–4	7
Urk I, 154	239
Urk I, 155–6	277
Urk I, 157–8	121
Urk I, 160	16
Urk I, 161–3	110
Urk I, 163–5	115
Urk I, 165	166, 168
Urk I, 166	5, 6
Urk I, 170–2	17
Urk I, 175	122
Urk I, 176	171
Urk I, 176–7	128
Urk I, 177	123
Urk I, 177–8	129
Urk I, 178	234
Urk I, 179	15
Urk I, 179–80	100
Urk I, 180–6	212
Urk I, 186	215
Urk I, 187–8	144
Urk I, 188–9	126
Urk I, 190–1	130
Urk I, 194–6	213
Urk I, 197	147
Urk I, 198–9	224
Urk I, 200–1	223
Urk I, 201–3	197
Urk I, 204–5	322
Urk I, 205	322
Urk I, 206–7	158
Urk I, 207–8	19
Urk I, 208–9	77
Urk I, 209–13	20
Urk I, 214	21
Urk I, 215–21	198
Urk I, 221–4	270
Urk I, 225	181
Urk I, 225–6	185
Urk I, 226	187, 193
Urk I, 227	157, 162, 169
Urk I, 228	127
Urk I, 229	299
Urk I, 231	203
Urk I, 232	227
Urk I, 234	221
Urk I, 235–49	1
Urk I, 249–50	238
Urk I, 250–1	214
Urk I, 251–5	247
Urk I, 255–6	140
Urk I, 256	72
Urk I, 258	67
Urk I, 259	67
Urk I, 260	142
Urk I, 263	255
Urk I, 264	261
Urk I, 266–7	265
Urk I, 267	308
Urk I, 270	250
Urk I, 271	251
Urk I, 271–2	15
Urk I, 277–8	23
Urk I, 278–80	22
Urk I, 280–3	24
Urk I, 284–8	25
Urk I, 288–93	26
Urk I, 293–5	27
Urk I, 295–6	34
Urk I, 297–9	32
Urk I, 299	37
Urk I, 299–300	38
Urk I, 300–1	35
Urk I, 301–2	36
Urk I, 302–3	33
Urk I, 303–4	30
Urk I, 304–6	39
Urk I, 307	29